DUNGEON MASTER'S GUIDE

CREDITS

D&D Lead Designers: Mike Mearls, Jeremy Crawford

Dungeon Master's Guide **Leads:** Jeremy Crawford,
Christopher Perkins, James Wyatt

Designers: Robert J. Schwalb, Rodney Thompson, Peter Lee

Editors: Scott Fitzgerald Gray, Michele Carter, Chris Sims,
Jennifer Clarke Wilkes

Producer: Greg Bilsland

Art Directors: Kate Irwin, Dan Gelon, Jon Schindehette,
Mari Kolkowsky, Melissa Rapier, Shauna Narciso

Graphic Designers: Emi Tanji, Bree Heiss, Trish Yochum,
Barry Craig

Cover Illustrator: Tyler Jacobson

Interior Illustrators: Rob Alexander, Dave Allsop, Daren Bader,
Mark Behm, Eric Belisle, Steven Belledin, Kerem Beyit,
Noah Bradley, Aleksi Briclot, Filip Burburan, Milivoj Ćeran,
Sidharth Chaturvedi, Conceptopolis, jD, Jesper Ejsing,
Wayne England, Emily Fiegenschuh, Scott M. Fischer,
Justin Gerard, E.W.Hekaton, Jon Hodgson, Ralph Horsley,
Tyler Jacobson, Jason Juta, Sam Keiser, Chad King, Vance
Kovacs, Olly Lawson, Chuck Lukacs, Howard Lyon, Victoria
Maderna, Aaron Miller, Mark Molnar, Terese Nielsen,
William O'Connor, Hector Ortiz, Adam Paquette, Claudio
Pozas, Steve Prescott, David Rapoza, Rob Rey, Aaron J. Riley,
Amir Salehi, Mike Schley, Chris Seaman, Sean Sevestre, Ilya
Shkipin, Carmen Sinek, Craig J Spearing, John Stanko, Alex
Stone, Matias Tapia, Joel Thomas, Cory Trego-Erdner, Beth
Trott, Cyril Van Der Haegen, Raoul Vitale, Tyler Walpole,
Julian Kok Joon Wen, Richard Whitters, Eva Widermann,
Mark Winters, Ben Wootten, Kieran Yanner, James Zhang

Additional Contributors: Wolfgang Baur, C.M. Cline, Bruce R.
Cordell, Jesse Decker, Bryan Fagan, James Jacobs, Robin D.
Laws, Colin McComb, David Noonan, Rich Redman, Matt
Sernett, Lester Smith, Steve Townshend, Chris Tulach, Steve
Winter, Chris Youngs

Project Management: Neil Shinkle, John Hay, Kim Graham

Production Services: Cynda Callaway, Brian Dumas,
Jefferson Dunlap, David Gershman, Anita Williams

Brand and Marketing: Nathan Stewart, Liz Schuh,
Chris Lindsay, Shelly Mazzanoble, Hilary Ross,
Laura Tommervik, Kim Lundstrom, Trevor Kidd

Based on the original D&D game created by
E. Gary Gygax and Dave Arneson,
with Brian Blume, Rob Kuntz, James Ward, and Don Kaye

Drawing from further development by
J. Eric Holmes, Tom Moldvay, Frank Mentzer, Aaron Allston,
Harold Johnson, David "Zeb" Cook, Ed Greenwood,
Keith Baker, Tracy Hickman, Margaret Weis, Douglas Niles,
Jeff Grubb, Jonathan Tweet, Monte Cook, Skip Williams,
Richard Baker, Peter Adkison, Bill Slavicsek, Andy Collins,
and Rob Heinsoo

Playtesting provided by
over 175,000 fans of D&D. Thank you!

Additional feedback provied by
Teos Abadia, Robert Alaniz, Jason Baxter, Bill Benham,
Darron Bowley, David Callander, Mik Calow, Christopher
D'Andrea, Brian Danford, Krupal Desai, Josh Dillard, Sam
E. Simpson Jr., Tim Eagon, David Ewalt, Rob Ford, Robert
Ford, Jason Fuller, Pierce Gaithe, Richard Green, Christopher
Hackler, Adam Hennebeck, Sterling Hershey, Paul Hughes,
Gregory L. Harris, Yan Lacharité, Shane Leahy, Ryan Leary,
Tom Lommel, Jonathan Longstaff, Rory Madden, Matt
Maranda, Derek McIntosh, Paul Melamed, Shawn Merwin,
Lou Michelli, Mike Mihalas, David Milman, Daren Mitchell,
Matthew Mosher, David Muller, Kevin Neff, Adam Page, John
Proudfoot, Max Reichlin, Karl Resch, Matthew Rolston, Jason
Romein, Sam Sherry, Pieter Sleijpen, Robin Stacey, David
"Oak" Stark, Adam Strong-Morse, Arthur Wright

ON THE COVER

Tyler Jacobson illustrates the archlich Acererak
as he raises an army of undead and prepares to
unleash it on an unsuspecting world.

620A9219000001 EN
ISBN: 978-0-7869-6562-5
First Printing: December 2014

9 8 7 6 5 4 3

*Disclaimer: Wizards of the Coast does not officially endorse the following tactics, which are guaranteed to maximize your enjoyment as a Dungeon Master. First, always keep a straight face and
say OK no matter how ludicrous or doomed the players' plan of action is. Second, no matter what happens, pretend that you intended all along for everything to unfold the way it did. Third, if
you're not sure what to do next, feign illness, end the session early, and plot your next move. When all else fails, roll a bunch of dice behind your screen, study them for a moment with a look of
deep concern mixed with regret, let loose a heavy sigh, and announce that Tiamat swoops from the sky and attacks.*

Printed in the USA. ©2014 Wizards of the Coast LLC, PO Box 707, Renton, WA 98057-0707, USA. Manufactured by Hasbro SA, Rue Emile-Boéchat 31, 2800 Delémont, CH.
Represented by Hasbro Europe, 4 The Square, Stockley Park, Uxbridge, Middlesex, UB11 1ET. UK.

CONTENTS

INTRODUCTION

I
T'S GOOD TO BE THE DUNGEON MASTER! NOT ONLY
do you get to tell fantastic stories about heroes,
villains, monsters, and magic, but you also get
to create the world in which these stories live.
Whether you're running a D&D game already
or you think it's something you want to try, this
book is for you.

The *Dungeon Master's Guide* assumes that you know
the basics of how to play the D&D tabletop roleplaying
game. If you haven't played before, the *DUNGEONS &
DRAGONS Starter Set* is a great starting point for new
players and DMs.

This book has two important companions: the *Player's
Handbook*, which contains the rules your players need
to create characters and the rules you need to run the
game, and the *Monster Manual*, which contains ready-to-
use monsters to populate your D&D world.

THE DUNGEON MASTER

The Dungeon Master (DM) is the creative force
behind a D&D game. The DM creates a world for the
other players to explore, and also creates and runs
adventures that drive the story. An adventure typically
hinges on the successful completion of a quest, and
can be as short as a single game session. Longer
adventures might embroil players in great conflicts that
require multiple game sessions to resolve. When strung
together, these adventures form an ongoing **campaign**.
A D&D campaign can include dozens of adventures and
last for months or years.

A Dungeon Master gets to wear many hats. As the
architect of a campaign, the DM creates adventures
by placing monsters, traps, and treasures for the other
players' characters (the **adventurers**) to discover. As
a storyteller, the DM helps the other players visualize
what's happening around them, improvising when the
adventurers do something or go somewhere unexpected.
As an actor, the DM plays the roles of the monsters and
supporting characters, breathing life into them. And as
a referee, the DM interprets the rules and decides when to
abide by them and when to change them.

Inventing, writing, storytelling, improvising, acting,
refereeing—every DM handles these roles differently,
and you'll probably enjoy some more than others. It
helps to remember that DUNGEONS & DRAGONS is a
hobby, and being the DM should be fun. Focus on the
aspects you enjoy and downplay the rest. For example, if
you don't like creating your own adventures, you can use
published ones. You can also lean on the other players
to help you with rules mastery and world-building.

The D&D rules help you and the other players have
a good time, but the rules aren't in charge. You're the
DM, and *you* are in charge of the game. That said, your
goal isn't to slaughter the adventurers but to create a
campaign world that revolves around their actions and
decisions, and to keep your players coming back for
more! If you're lucky, the events of your campaign will
echo in the memories of your players long after the final
game session is concluded.

HOW TO USE THIS BOOK

This book is organized in three parts. The first part
helps you decide what kind of campaign you'd like to
run. The second part helps you create the adventures—
the stories—that will compose the campaign and
keep the players entertained from one game session
to the next. The last part helps you adjudicate the
rules of the game and modify them to suit the style of
your campaign.

PART 1: MASTER OF WORLDS

Every DM is the creator of his or her own campaign
world. Whether you invent a world, adapt a world from
a favorite movie or novel, or use a published setting for
the D&D game, you make that world your own over the
course of a campaign.

The world where you set your campaign is one of
countless worlds that make up the D&D **multiverse**,
a vast array of planes and worlds where adventures
happen. Even if you're using an established world such
as the Forgotten Realms, your campaign takes place
in a sort of mirror universe of the official setting where
Forgotten Realms novels, game products, and digital
games are assumed to take place. The world is yours to
change as you see fit and yours to modify as you explore
the consequences of the players' actions.

Your world is more than just a backdrop for
adventures. Like Middle Earth, Westeros, and countless
other fantasy worlds out there, it's a place to which you
can escape and witness fantastic stories unfold. A well-
designed and well-run world seems to flow around the
adventurers, so that they feel part of something, instead
of apart from it.

Consistency is a key to a believable fictional
world. When the adventurers go back into town for
supplies, they should encounter the same **nonplayer
characters** (NPCs) they met before. Soon, they'll learn
the barkeep's name, and he or she will remember
theirs as well. Once you have achieved this degree of
consistency, you can provide an occasional change. If
the adventurers come back to buy more horses at the
stables, they might discover that the man who ran the
place went back home to the large city over the hills,
and now his niece runs the family business. That sort of
change—one that has nothing to do with the adventurers
directly, but one that they'll notice—makes the players
feel as though their characters are part of a living world
that changes and grows along with them.

Part 1 of this book is all about inventing your world.
Chapter 1 asks what type of game you want to run, and
helps you nail down a few important details about your
world and its overarching conflicts. Chapter 2 helps you
put your world in the greater context of the multiverse,
expanding on the information presented in the *Player's
Handbook* to discuss the planes of existence and the
gods and how you can put them together to serve the
needs of your campaign.

PART 2: MASTER OF ADVENTURES

Whether you write your own adventures or use published ones, expect to invest preparation time beyond the hours you spend at the gaming table. You'll need to carve out some free time to exercise your creativity as you invent compelling plots, create new NPCs, craft encounters, and think of clever ways to foreshadow story events yet to come.

Part 2 of this book is devoted to helping you create and run great adventures. Chapter 3 covers the basic elements of a D&D adventure, and chapter 4 helps you create memorable NPCs. Chapter 5 presents guidelines and advice for running adventures set in dungeons, the wilderness, and other locales, and chapter 6 covers the time between adventures. Chapter 7 is all about treasure, magic items, and special rewards that help keep the players invested in your campaign.

PART 3: MASTER OF RULES

DUNGEONS & DRAGONS isn't a head-to-head competition, but it needs someone who is impartial yet involved in the game to guarantee that everyone at the table plays by the rules. As the player who creates the game world and the adventures that take place within it, the DM is a natural fit to take on the referee role.

As a referee, the DM acts as a mediator between the rules and the players. A player tells the DM what he or she wants to do, and the DM determines whether it is successful or not, in some cases asking the player to make a die roll to determine success. For example, if a player wants his or her character to take a swing at an orc, you say, "Make an attack roll" while looking up the orc's Armor Class.

The rules don't account for every possible situation that might arise during a typical D&D session. For example, a player might want his or her character to hurl a brazier full of hot coals into a monster's face. How you determine the outcome of this action is up to you. You might tell the player to make a Strength check, while mentally setting the **Difficulty Class** (DC) at 15. If the Strength check is successful, you then determine how a face full of hot coals affects the monster. You might decide that it deals 1d4 fire damage and imposes disadvantage on the monster's attack rolls until the end of its next turn. You roll the damage die (or let the player do it), and the game continues.

Sometimes mediating the rules means setting limits. If a player tells you, "I want to run up and attack the orc," but the character doesn't have enough movement to reach the orc, you say, "It's too far away to move up and still attack. What would you like to do instead?" The player takes the information and comes up with a different plan.

To referee the rules, you need to know them. You don't have to memorize this book or the *Player's Handbook*, but you should have a clear idea of their contents so that, when a situation requires a ruling, you know where to find the proper reference.

The *Player's Handbook* contains the main rules you need to play the game. Part 3 of this book offers a wealth of information to help you adjudicate the rules in a wide variety of situations. Chapter 8 presents advice for using attack rolls, ability checks, and saving throws. It also includes options appropriate for certain play styles and campaigns, including guidelines for using miniatures, a system for handling chase scenes, and rules for madness. If you like to create your own stuff, such as new monsters, races, and character backgrounds, chapter 9 shows you how. That chapter also contains optional rules for unusual situations or play styles, such as the use of firearms in a fantasy setting.

KNOW YOUR PLAYERS

The success of a D&D game hinges on your ability to entertain the other players at the game table. Whereas their role is to create characters (the protagonists of the campaign), breathe life into them, and help steer the campaign through their characters' actions, your role is to keep the players (and yourself) interested and immersed in the world you've created, and to let their characters do awesome things.

Knowing what your players enjoy most about the D&D game helps you create and run adventures that they will enjoy and remember. Once you know which of the following activities each player in your group enjoys the most, you can tailor adventures that satisfy your players' preferences as much as possible, thus keeping them engaged.

ACTING

Players who enjoy acting like getting into character and speaking in their characters' voices. Roleplayers at heart, they enjoy social interactions with NPCs, monsters, and their fellow party members.

Engage players who like acting by …
- giving them opportunities to develop their characters' personalities and backgrounds.
- allowing them to interact regularly with NPCs.
- adding roleplaying elements to combat encounters.
- incorporating elements from their characters' backgrounds into your adventures.

EXPLORING

Players who desire exploration want to experience the wonders that a fantasy world has to offer. They want to know what's around the next corner or hill. They also like to find hidden clues and treasure.

Engage players who like exploration by …
- dropping clues that hint at things yet to come.
- letting them find things when they take the time to explore.
- providing rich descriptions of exciting environments, and using interesting maps and props.
- giving monsters secrets to uncover or cultural details to learn.

INSTIGATING

Player's who like to instigate action are eager to make things happen, even if that means taking perilous risks. They would rather rush headlong into danger and face the consequences than face boredom.

Engage players who like to instigate by …
- allowing them to affect their surroundings.
- including things in your adventures to tempt them.
- letting their actions put the characters in a tight spot.
- including encounters with NPCs who are as feisty and unpredictable as they are.

FIGHTING

Players who enjoy fantasy combat like kicking the tar out of villains and monsters. They look for any excuse to start a fight, favoring bold action over careful deliberation.

Engage players who like fighting by …
- springing unexpected combat encounters on them.
- vividly describing the havoc their characters wreak with their attacks and spells.
- including combat encounters with large numbers of weak monsters.
- interrupting social interaction and exploration with combat.

OPTIMIZING

Players who enjoy optimizing their characters' capabilities like to fine-tune their characters for peak combat performance by gaining levels, new features, and magic items. They welcome any opportunity to demonstrate their characters' superiority.

Engage players who like optimization by …
- ensuring steady access to new abilities and spells.
- using desired magic items as adventure hooks.
- including encounters that let their characters shine.
- providing quantifiable rewards, like experience points, for noncombat encounters.

PROBLEM SOLVING

Players who want to solve problems like to scrutinize NPC motivations, untangle a villain's machinations, solve puzzles, and come up with plans.

Engage players who like to solve problems by …
- including encounters that emphasize problem-solving.
- rewarding planning and tactics with in-game benefits.
- occasionally allowing a smart plan to grant an easy win for the players.
- creating NPCs with complex motives.

STORYTELLING

Players who love storytelling want to contribute to a narrative. They like it when their characters are heavily invested in an unfolding story, and they enjoy encounters that are tied to and expand an overarching plot.

Engage players who like storytelling by …
- using their characters' backgrounds to help shape the stories of the campaign.
- making sure an encounter advances the story in some way.
- making their characters' actions help steer future events.
- giving NPCs ideals, bonds, and flaws that the adventurers can exploit.

PART 1

Master of Worlds

CHAPTER 1: A WORLD OF YOUR OWN

YOUR WORLD IS THE SETTING FOR YOUR CAMPAIGN, the place where adventures happen. Even if you use an existing setting, such as the Forgotten Realms, it becomes yours as you set your adventures there, create characters to inhabit it, and make changes to it over the course of your campaign. This chapter is all about building your world and then creating a campaign to take place in it.

THE BIG PICTURE

This book, the *Player's Handbook,* and the *Monster Manual* present the default assumptions for how the worlds of D&D work. Among the established settings of D&D, the Forgotten Realms, Greyhawk, Dragonlance, and Mystara don't stray very far from those assumptions. Settings such as Dark Sun, Eberron, Ravenloft, Spelljammer, and Planescape venture further away from that baseline. As you create your own world, it's up to you to decide where on the spectrum you want your world to fall.

CORE ASSUMPTIONS

The rules of the game are based on the following core assumptions about the game world.

Gods Oversee the World. The gods are real and embody a variety of beliefs, with each god claiming dominion over an aspect of the world, such as war, forests, or the sea. Gods exert influence over the world by granting divine magic to their followers and sending signs and portents to guide them. The follower of a god serves as an agent of that god in the world. The agent seeks to further the ideals of that god and defeat its rivals. While some folk might refuse to honor the gods, none can deny their existence.

Much of the World Is Untamed. Wild regions abound. City-states, confederacies, and kingdoms of various sizes dot the landscape, but beyond their borders the wilds crowd in. People know the area they live in well. They've heard stories of other places from merchants and travelers, but few know what lies beyond the mountains or in the depths of the great forest unless they've been there themselves.

The World Is Ancient. Empires rise and fall, leaving few places that have not been touched by imperial grandeur or decay. War, time, and natural forces eventually claim the mortal world, leaving it rich with places of adventure and mystery. Ancient civilizations and their knowledge survive in legends, magic items, and their ruins. Chaos and evil often follow an empire's collapse.

Conflict Shapes the World's History. Powerful individuals strive to make their mark on the world, and factions of like-minded individuals can alter the course of history. Factions include religions led by charismatic prophets, kingdoms ruled by lasting dynasties, and shadowy societies that seek to master long-lost magic. The influence of such factions waxes and wanes as they compete with each other for power. Some seek to preserve the world and usher in a golden age. Others strive toward evil ends, seeking to rule the world with an iron fist. Still others seek goals that range from the practical to the esoteric, such as the accumulation of material wealth or the resurrection of a dead god. Whatever their goals, these factions inevitably collide, creating conflict that can steer the world's fate.

The World Is Magical. Practitioners of magic are relatively few in number, but they leave evidence of their craft everywhere. The magic can be as innocuous and commonplace as a potion that heals wounds to something much more rare and impressive, such as a levitating tower or a stone golem guarding the gates of a city. Beyond the realms of civilization are caches of magic items guarded by magic traps, as well as magically constructed dungeons inhabited by monsters created by magic, cursed by magic, or endowed with magical abilities.

IT'S YOUR WORLD

In creating your campaign world, it helps to start with the core assumptions and consider how your setting might change them. The subsequent sections of this chapter address each element and give details on how to flesh out your world with gods, factions, and so forth.

The assumptions sketched out above aren't carved in stone. They inspire exciting D&D worlds full of adventure, but they're not the only set of assumptions that can do so. You can build an interesting campaign concept by altering one or more of those core assumptions, just as well-established D&D worlds have done. Ask yourself, "What if the standard assumptions weren't true in my world?"

The World Is a Mundane Place. What if magic is rare and dangerous, and even adventurers have limited or no access to it? What if your campaign is set in a version of our own world's history?

The World Is New. What if your world is new, and the characters are the first of a long line of heroes? The adventurers might be champions of the first great empires, such as the empires of Netheril and Cormanthor in the Forgotten Realms setting.

The World Is Known. What if the world is completely charted and mapped, right down to the "Here there be dragons" notations? What if great empires cover huge stretches of countryside, with clearly defined borders between them? The Five Nations of the Eberron setting were once part of a great empire, and magically aided travel between its cities is commonplace.

Monsters Are Uncommon. What if monsters are rare and terrifying? In the Ravenloft setting, horrific domains are governed by monstrous rulers. The populace lives in perpetual terror of these darklords and their evil minions, but other monsters rarely trouble people's daily lives.

Magic Is Everywhere. What if every town is ruled by a powerful wizard? What if magic item shops are common? The Eberron setting makes the use of magic an everyday occurrence, as magical flying ships and trains carry travelers from one great city to another.

Gods Inhabit the Land, or Are Entirely Absent. What if the gods regularly walk the earth? What if the characters can challenge them and seize their power? Or what if the gods are remote, and even angels never make contact with mortals? In the Dark Sun setting, the gods are extremely distant—perhaps nonexistent—and clerics rely instead on elemental power for their magic.

Gods of Your World

Appendix B of the *Player's Handbook* presents a number of pantheons (loose groupings of deities not united by a single doctrine or philosophy) for use in your game, including the gods of established D&D worlds and fantasy-historical pantheons. You can adopt one of these pantheons for your campaign, or pick and choose deities and ideas from them as you please. See "A Sample Pantheon" in this section for an example.

As far as the game's rules are concerned, it doesn't matter if your world has hundreds of deities or a church devoted to a single god. In rules terms, clerics choose domains, not deities, so your world can associate domains with deities in any way you choose.

Loose Pantheons

Most D&D worlds have a loose pantheon of gods. A multitude of deities rule the various aspects of existence, variously cooperating with and competing against one another to administer the affairs of the universe. People gather in public shrines to worship gods of life and wisdom, or meet in hidden places to venerate gods of deception or destruction.

Each deity in a pantheon has a portfolio and is responsible for advancing that portfolio. In the Greyhawk setting, Heironeous is a god of valor who calls clerics and paladins to his service and encourages them to spread the ideals of honorable warfare, chivalry, and justice in society. Even in the midst of his everlasting war with his brother Hextor, god of war and tyranny, Heironeous promotes his own portfolio: war fought nobly and in the cause of justice.

People in most D&D worlds are polytheistic, honoring deities of their own and acknowledging pantheons of other cultures. Individuals pay homage to various gods, regardless of alignment. In the Forgotten Realms, a person might propitiate Umberlee before setting out to sea, join a communal feast to celebrate Chauntea at harvest time, and pray to Malar before going hunting.

Some individuals feel a calling to a particular deity's service and claim that god as a patron. Particularly devoted individuals become priests by setting up a shrine or helping to staff a holy site. Much more rarely, those who feel such a calling become clerics or paladins invested with the responsibility of true divine power.

Shrines and temples serve as community gathering points for religious rites and festivals. Priests at such sites relate stories of the gods, teach the ethics of their patron deities, offer advice and blessings, perform religious rites, and provide training in activities their deities favor. Cities and large towns can host several temples dedicated to individual gods important to the community, while smaller settlements might have a single shrine devoted to any gods the locals revere.

To quickly build a pantheon for your world, create a single god for each of the eight domains available to clerics: Death, Knowledge, Life, Light, Nature, Tempest, Trickery, and War. You can invent names and personalities for these deities, or borrow deities from other pantheons. This approach gives you a small pantheon that covers the most significant aspects of existence, and it's easy enough to extrapolate other areas of life each deity controls. The god of Knowledge,

Dawn War Deities

Deity	Alignment	Suggested Domains	Symbol
Asmodeus, god of tyranny	LE	Trickery	Three triangles in tight formation
Avandra, goddess of change and luck	CG	Trickery	Three stacked wavy lines
Bahamut, god of justice and nobility	LG	Life, War	Dragon's head, in profile, facing left
Bane, god of war and conquest	LE	War	Claw with three talons pointing down
Corellon, god of magic and the arts	CG	Light	Eight-pointed star
Erathis, goddess of civilization and invention	LN	Knowledge	Upper half of a clockwork gear
Gruumsh, god of destruction	CE	Tempest, War	Triangular eye with bony protrusions
Ioun, goddess of knowledge	N	Knowledge	Crook shaped like a stylized eye
Kord, god of strength and storms	CN	Tempest	Sword with a lightning bolt cross guard
Lolth, goddess of spiders and lies	CE	Trickery	Eight-pointed star with a web motif
Melora, goddess of wilderness and the sea	N	Nature, Tempest	Wavelike swirl
Moradin, god of creation	LG	Knowledge, War	Flaming anvil
Pelor, god of the sun and agriculture	NG	Life, Light	Circle with six outwardly radiating points
Raven Queen, goddess of death	LN	Life, Death	Raven's head, in profile, facing left
Sehanine, goddess of the moon	CG	Trickery	Crescent moon
Tharizdun, god of madness	CE	Trickery	Jagged counter-clockwise spiral
Tiamat, goddess of wealth, greed, and vengeance	LE	Trickery, War	Five-pointed star with curved points
Torog, god of the Underdark	NE	Death	*T* attached to a circular shackle
Vecna, god of evil secrets	NE	Death, Knowledge	Partially shattered one-eyed skull
Zehir, god of darkness and poison	CE	Trickery, Death	Snake in the shape of a dagger

for example, might also be patron of magic and prophecy, while the god of Light could be the sun god and the god of time.

A SAMPLE PANTHEON

The pantheon of the Dawn War is an example of a pantheon assembled from mostly preexisting elements to suit the needs of a particular campaign. This is the default pantheon in the fourth edition *Player's Handbook* (2008). The pantheon is summarized in the Dawn War Deities table.

This pantheon draws in several nonhuman deities and establishes them as universal gods. These gods include Bahamut, Corellon, Gruumsh, Lolth, Moradin, Sehanine, and Tiamat. Humans worship Moradin and Corellon as gods of their respective portfolios, rather than as racial deities. The pantheon also includes the archdevil Asmodeus as god of domination and tyranny.

Several of the gods are drawn from other pantheons, sometimes with new names for the gods. Bane comes from the Forgotten Realms. From Greyhawk come Kord, Pelor, Tharizdun, and Vecna. From the Greek pantheon come Athena (renamed Erathis) and Tyche (renamed Avandra), though both are altered. Set (renamed Zehir) comes from the Egyptian pantheon. The Raven Queen is akin to the Norse pantheon's Hel and Greyhawk's Wee Jas. That leaves three gods created from scratch: Ioun, Melora, and Torog.

OTHER RELIGIOUS SYSTEMS

In your campaign, you can create pantheons of gods who are closely linked in a single religion, monotheistic religions (worship of a single deity), dualistic systems (centered on two opposing deities or forces), mystery cults (involving personal devotion to a single deity, usually as part of a pantheon system), animistic religions (revering the spirits inherent in nature), or even forces and philosophies that don't center on deities.

TIGHT PANTHEONS

In contrast to a loose pantheon, a tight pantheon focuses on a single religion whose teachings and edicts embrace a small group of deities. Followers of a tight pantheon might favor one of its member deities over another, but they respect all the deities and honor them with sacrifices and prayer as appropriate.

The key trait to a tight pantheon is that its worshipers embrace a single ethos or dogma that includes all the deities. The gods of the tight pantheon work as one to protect and guide their followers. You can think of a tight pantheon as similar to a family. One or two deities who lead the pantheon serve as parent figures, with the rest serving as patrons of important aspects of the culture that worships the pantheon. A single temple honors all members of the pantheon.

Most tight pantheons have one or more aberrant gods—deities whose worship isn't sanctioned by the priests of the pantheon as a whole. These are usually evil deities and enemies of the pantheon, such as the Greek Titans. These deities have cults of their own, attracting social outcasts and villains to their worship. These cults resemble mystery cults, their members

strictly devoted to their single god, though even members of aberrant cults pay lip service in the temples of the tight pantheon.

The Norse deities serve as an example of a tight pantheon. Odin is the pantheon's leader and father figure. Deities such as Thor, Tyr, and Freya embody important aspects of Norse culture. Meanwhile, Loki and his devotees lurk in the shadows, sometimes aiding the other deities, and sometimes working against them with the pantheon's enemies.

MYSTERY CULTS

A mystery cult is a secretive religious organization based on a ritual of initiation, in which the initiate is mystically identified with a god, or a handful of related gods. Mystery cults are intensely personal, concerned with the initiate's relationship with the divine.

Sometimes a mystery cult is a type of worship within a pantheon. It acknowledges the myths and rituals of the pantheon, but presents its own myths and rites as primary. For instance, a secretive order of monks might immerse themselves in a mystical relationship to a god who is part of a broadly worshiped pantheon.

A mystery cult emphasizes the history of its god, which is symbolically reenacted in its initiation ritual. The foundation myth of a mystery cult is usually simple and often involves a god's death and rising, or a journey to the underworld and a return. Mystery cults often revere sun and moon deities and agricultural deities— gods whose portfolios reflect the cycles of nature.

DIVINE RANK

The divine beings of the multiverse are often categorized according to their cosmic power. Some gods are worshiped on multiple worlds and have a different rank on each world, depending on their influence there.

Greater deities are beyond mortal understanding. They can't be summoned, and they are almost always removed from direct involvement in mortal affairs. On very rare occasions they manifest avatars similar to lesser deities, but slaying a greater god's avatar has no effect on the god itself.

Lesser deities are embodied somewhere in the planes. Some lesser deities live in the Material Plane, as does the unicorn-goddess Lurue of the Forgotten Realms and the titanic shark-god Sekolah revered by the sahuagin. Others live on the Outer Planes, as Lolth does in the Abyss. Such deities can be encountered by mortals.

Quasi-deities have a divine origin, but they don't hear or answer prayers, grant spells to clerics, or control aspects of mortal life. They are still immensely powerful beings, and in theory they could ascend to godhood if they amassed enough worshipers. Quasi-deities fall into three subcategories: demigods, titans, and vestiges.

Demigods are born from the union of a deity and a mortal being. They have some divine attributes, but their mortal parentage makes them the weakest quasi-deities.

Titans are the divine creations of deities. They might be birthed from the union of two deities, manufactured on a divine forge, born from the blood spilled by a god, or otherwise brought about through divine will or substance.

Vestiges are deities who have lost nearly all their worshipers and are considered dead, from a mortal perspective. Esoteric rituals can sometimes contact these beings and draw on their latent power.

The cult's ritual of initiation follows the pattern of its foundation myth. Neophytes retrace the god's footsteps in order to share the god's ultimate fate. In the case of dying and rising gods, the symbolic death of the initiate represents the idea of death to the old life and rebirth into a transformed existence. Initiates are born into a new life, remaining in the world of mortal affairs but feeling elevated to a higher sphere. The initiate is promised a place in the god's realm after death, but also experiences new meaning in life.

MONOTHEISM

Monotheistic religions revere only one deity, and in some cases, deny the existence of any other deity. If you introduce a monotheistic religion into your campaign, you need to decide whether other gods exist. Even if they don't, other religions can exist side by side with the monotheistic religion. If these religions have clerics with spellcasting ability, their spells might be powered by the one true deity, by lesser spirits who aren't deities (possibly including powerful aberrations, celestials, fey, fiends, or elementals), or simply by their faith.

The deity of a monotheistic religion has an extensive portfolio and is portrayed as the creator of everything, in control of everything, and concerned with every aspect of existence. Thus, a worshiper of this god offers prayers and sacrifices to the same god regardless of what aspect of life is in need of divine assistance. Whether marching into war, setting off on a journey, or hoping to win someone's affections, the worshiper prays to the same god.

Some monotheistic religions describe different aspects of their deity. A single god appears in different aspects as the Creator and the Destroyer, and the clerics of that god focus on one aspect or the other, determining their domain access and possibly even their alignment on that basis. A cleric who venerates the Destroyer aspect chooses the Tempest or War domain, while one who worships a Creator aspect chooses the Life or Nature domains. In some monotheistic religions, clerics group themselves into distinct religious orders to differentiate clerics who choose different domains.

DUALISM

A dualistic religion views the world as the stage for a conflict between two diametrically opposed deities or divine forces. Most often, the opposed forces are good and evil, or opposed deities representing those forces. In some pantheons, the forces or deities of law and chaos are the fundamental opposites in a dualistic system. Life and death, light and darkness, matter and spirit, body and mind, health and illness, purity and defilement, positive energy and negative energy—the D&D universe is full of polar opposites that could serve as the foundation for a dualistic religion. Whatever the terms in which the dualism is expressed, half of the pair is usually believed to be good—beneficial, desirable, or holy—while the other half is considered bad, if not explicitly evil. If the fundamental conflict in a religion is expressed as the opposition between matter and spirit, the followers of that religion believe that one of the two (usually matter) is evil and the other (spirit) is good, and

so seek to liberate their spirits from this material world and its evils through asceticism and contemplation.

Rare dualistic systems believe that the two opposing forces must remain in balance, always pulling away from each other but remaining bound together in creative tension.

In a cosmology defined by an eternal conflict between good and evil, mortals are expected to take sides. The majority of those who follow a dualistic religion worship the deity or force identified as good. Worshipers of the good deity trust themselves to that god's power to protect them from the evil deity's minions. Because the evil deity in such a religion is usually the source of everything that is detrimental to existence, only the perverse and depraved worship this god. Monsters and fiends serve it, as do certain secretive cults. The myths of a dualistic religion usually predict that the good deity will triumph in an apocalyptic battle, but the forces of evil believe that the outcome of that battle isn't predetermined and work to promote their deity's victory.

Deities in a dualistic system maintain large portfolios. All aspects of existence reflect the dualistic struggle, and therefore all things can fall on one side or the other of the conflict. Agriculture, mercy, the sky, medicine, and poetry reside in the portfolio of the good deity, and famine, hatred, disease, and war belong to the evil deity.

ANIMISM

Animism is the belief that spirits inhabit every part of the natural world. In an animistic worldview, everything has a spirit, from the grandest mountain to the lowliest rock, from the great ocean to a babbling brook, from the sun and moon to a fighter's ancestral sword. All these objects, and the spirits that inhabit them, are sentient, though some are more aware, alert, and intelligent than others. The most powerful spirits might even be considered deities. All are worthy of respect if not veneration.

Animists don't typically pay allegiance to one spirit over the others. Instead, they offer prayers and sacrifices to different spirits at different times, as appropriate to the situation. A pious character might make daily prayers and offerings to ancestor spirits and the spirits of the house, regular petitions to important spirits such as the Seven Fortunes of Good Luck, occasional sacrifices of incense to location spirits such as the spirit of a forest, and sporadic prayers to a host of other spirits as well.

An animistic religion very tolerant. Most spirits don't care to whom a character also offers sacrifices, as long as they receive the sacrifices and respect they are due. As new religions spread through animist lands, those religions typically win adherents but not converts. People incorporate new spirits and deities into their prayers without displacing the old ones. Contemplatives and scholars adopt complex philosophical systems and practices without changing their belief in and respect for the spirits they already venerate.

Animism functions as a large tight pantheon. Animist clerics serve the pantheon as a whole, and so can choose any domain, representing a favorite spirit for that cleric.

FORCES AND PHILOSOPHIES

Not all divine powers need to be derived from deities. In some campaigns, believers hold enough conviction in their ideas about the universe that they gain magical power from that conviction. In other campaigns, impersonal forces of nature or magic replace the gods by granting power to mortals attuned to them. Just as druids and rangers can gain their spell ability from the force of nature rather than from a specific nature deity, some clerics devote themselves to ideals rather than to a god. Paladins might serve a philosophy of justice and chivalry rather than a specific deity.

Forces and philosophies aren't worshiped; they aren't beings that can hear and respond to prayers or accept sacrifices. Devotion to a philosophy or a force isn't necessarily exclusive of service to a deity. A person can be devoted to the philosophy of good and offer worship to various good deities, or revere the force of nature and also pay homage to the gods of nature, who might be seen as personal manifestations of an impersonal force. In a world that includes deities with demonstrable power (through their clerics), it's unusual for a philosophy to deny the existence of deities, although a common philosophical belief states that the deities are more like mortals than they would have mortals believe. According to such philosophies, the gods aren't truly immortal (just very long-lived), and mortals can attain divinity. In fact, ascending to godhood is the ultimate goal of some philosophies.

The power of a philosophy stems from the belief that mortals invest in it. A philosophy that only one person believes in isn't strong enough to bestow magical power on that person.

HUMANOIDS AND THE GODS

When it comes to the gods, humans exhibit a far wider range of beliefs and institutions than other races do. In many D&D settings, orcs, elves, dwarves, goblins, and other humanoids have tight pantheons. It is expected that an orc will worship Gruumsh or one of a handful of subordinate deities. In comparison, humanity embraces a staggering variety of deities. Each human culture might have its own array of gods.

In most D&D settings, there is no single god that can claim to have created humanity. Thus, the human proclivity for building institutions extends to religion. A single charismatic prophet can convert an entire kingdom to the worship of a new god. With that prophet's death, the religion might wax or wane, or the prophet's followers might turn against one another and found several competing religions.

In comparison, religion in dwarven society is set in stone. The dwarves of the Forgotten Realms identify Moradin as their creator. While individual dwarves might follow other gods, as a culture the dwarves are pledged to Moradin and the pantheon he leads. His teachings and magic are so thoroughly ingrained in dwarven culture that it would take a cataclysmic shift to replace him.

With that in mind, consider the role of the gods in your world and their ties to different humanoid races. Does each race have a creator god? How does that god shape that race's culture? Are other folk free of such divine ties and free to worship as they wish? Has a race turned against the god that created it? Has a new race appeared, created by a god within the past few years?

A deity might also have ties to a kingdom, noble line, or other cultural institution. With the death of the emperor, a new ruler might be selected by divine portents sent by the deity who protected the empire in its earliest days. In such a land, the worship of other gods might be outlawed or tightly controlled.

Finally, consider the difference between gods who are tied to specific humanoid races and gods with more diverse followers. Do the races with their own pantheons enjoy a place of privilege in your world, with their gods taking an active role in their affairs? Are the other races ignored by the gods, or are those races the deciding factor that can tilt the balance of power in favor of one god or another?

MAPPING YOUR CAMPAIGN

When creating the world where your campaign takes place, you'll want a map. You can take one of two approaches with it: top-down or bottom-up. Some DMs like to start at the top, creating the big picture of the world at the start of the campaign by having a map that shows whole continents, and then zooming in on smaller areas. Other DMs prefer to go the opposite direction, starting with a small campaign area that is mapped at a province or kingdom scale, then zooming out as adventures take the characters into new territory.

Whichever approach you take, hexes work well for mapping outdoor environments where travel can go in any direction and calculating distance might be important. A single sheet of hex paper with 5 hexes to the inch is ideal for most maps. Use a scale for your map that's best suited to the level of detail you want. Chapter 7 offers more information about creating and mapping wilderness areas.

PROVINCE SCALE

For the most detailed areas of your world, use a province scale where each hex represents 1 mile. A full-page map at this scale represents an area that can be covered in one day's travel in any direction from the center of the map, assuming clear terrain. As such, province scale is a useful scale for mapping a campaign's starting area (see "Creating a Campaign," later in this chapter) or any location where you expect to track the adventurers' movement in hours rather than days.

The ground cover of an area this size will include broad stretches of one predominant terrain type, broken up by other isolated terrain types.

A settled region mapped at this scale might have one town and eight to twelve villages or farming hamlets. A wilder region might have only a single keep, or no settlements at all. You can also indicate the extent of the cleared farmland that surrounds each city or town. On a province-scale map, this will show as a belt a few hexes wide surrounding each town or village. Even small villages farm most of the arable land within a mile or two.

KINGDOM SCALE

On a kingdom-scale map, each hex represents 6 miles. A map at this scale covers a large region, about the size of Great Britain or half the size of the state of California. That's plenty of room for adventuring.

The first step of mapping a region at this scale is to sketch out the coastlines and any major bodies of water in the area. Is the region landlocked or on a coast? A coastal region might include islands offshore, and a landlocked area might include an inland sea or major lakes. Alternatively, the region could consist of a single large island, or an isthmus or peninsula with multiple coastlines.

Next, sketch in any major mountain ranges. Foothills form a transition between the mountains and lowlands, and broad patches of gentle hills might dot the region.

That leaves the rest of your map for relatively flat terrain: grasslands, forests, swamps, and the like. Place these elements as you see fit.

Map out the courses of any rivers that flow through the area. Rivers are born in mountains or inland areas that see a lot of rainfall, winding down to the nearest major body of water that doesn't require the river to cross over higher elevation. Tributaries join rivers as they grow larger and move toward a lake or the sea.

Finally, place the major towns and cities of the region. At this scale, you don't need to worry about small towns and villages, or about mapping every belt of farmland. Even so, a settled region this size might easily have eight to twelve cities or towns to put on the map.

CONTINENT SCALE

For mapping a whole continent, use a scale where 1 hex represents 60 miles. At this scale, you can't see more than the shape of coastlines, the biggest mountain ranges, major rivers, huge lakes, and political boundaries. A map at this scale is best for showing how multiple kingdom-scale maps fit together, rather than tracking the movement of adventurers day by day.

The same process you use for mapping a region at kingdom scale works for mapping a whole continent. A continent might have eight to twelve large cities that deserve a place on the map, most likely major trade centers and the capitals of kingdoms.

COMBINING SCALES

Whichever scale you start with, it's easy to zoom in or out on your maps. At continent scale, 1 hex represents the same area as 10 kingdom-scale hexes. Two cities that are 3 hexes (180 miles) apart on your continent map would be 30 hexes apart on your kingdom map, and might define the opposite ends of the region you're detailing. At kingdom scale, 1 hex equals 6 province-scale hexes, so it's easy to put the region covered by your province-scale map into the center of a kingdom-scale map and create interesting areas around it.

Settlements

The places where people live—bustling cities, prosperous towns, and tiny villages nestled among miles of farmland—help define the nature of civilization in your world. A single settlement—a home base for your adventurers—is a great place to start a campaign and begin your world building. Consider the following questions as you create any settlement in your world:

- What purpose does it serve in your game?
- How big is it? Who lives there?
- What does it look, smell, and sound like?
- Who governs it? Who else holds power? Is it part of a larger state?
- What are its defenses?
- Where do characters go to find the goods and services they need?
- What temples and other organizations feature prominently?
- What fantastic elements distinguish it from an ordinary town?
- Why should the characters care about the settlement?

The guidelines in this section are here to help you build the settlement you want for whatever purpose you have in mind. Disregard any advice here that runs counter to your vision for a settlement.

Purpose

A settlement exists primarily to facilitate the story and fun of your campaign. Other than that point, the settlement's purpose determines the amount of detail you put into it. Create only the features of a settlement that you know you'll need, along with notes on general features. Then allow the place to grow organically as the adventurers interact with more and more of it, keeping notes on new places you invent.

Local Color

A settlement might serve as a place where the characters stop to rest and to buy supplies. A settlement of this sort needs no more than a brief description. Include the settlement's name, decide how big it is, add a dash of flavor ("The smell of the local tanneries never lifts from this town"), and let the adventurers get on with their business. The history of the inn where the characters spend the night, the mannerisms of the shopkeeper they buy supplies from—you can add this level of detail, but you don't have to. If the characters return to the same settlement, start adding these local features so that it begins to feel a little more like a home base, albeit a temporary one. Let the settlement develop as the need arises.

Home Base

A settlement gives the adventurers a place to live, train, and recuperate between adventures. An entire campaign can center on a particular town or city. Such a settlement is the launching pad from which the characters go out into the wider world.

Designed well, a home base can hold a special place in the adventurers' hearts, particularly if they care about one or more NPCs who live there.

To make a home base come alive, you'll need to invest some time fleshing out details, but the players can help you with that work. Ask them to tell you a bit about mentors, family members, and other important people in their characters' lives. Feel free to add to and modify what they give you, but you'll start with a solid foundation of the nonplayer characters (NPCs) who are important to the characters. Let the players describe where and how their characters spend their time—a favorite tavern, library, or temple, perhaps.

Using these NPCs and locations as a starting point, flesh out the settlement's cast of characters. Detail its leadership, including law enforcement (discussed later in the chapter). Include characters who can provide information, such as sages, soothsayers, librarians, and observant vagabonds. Priests can provide spellcasting as well as information. Make note of merchants who might regularly interact with the adventurers and perhaps compete with one another for the party's business. Think about the people who run the adventurers' favorite tavern. And then add a handful of wild cards: a shady dealer, a mad prophet, a retired mercenary, a drunken rake, or anyone else who adds a dash of adventure and intrigue to your campaign.

Adventure Site

A village harboring a secret cult of devil worshipers. A town controlled by a guild of wererats. A city conquered by a hobgoblin army. These settlements aren't merely rest stops but locations where adventures unfold. In a settlement that doubles as an adventure location, detail the intended adventure areas, such as towers and warehouses. For an event-based adventure, note the NPCs who play a part in the adventure. This work is adventure preparation as much as it is world building, and the cast of characters you develop for your adventure—including allies, patrons, enemies, and extras—can become recurring figures in your campaign.

Size

Most settlements in a D&D world are villages clustered around a larger town or city. Farming villages supply the town or city population with food in exchange for goods the farmers can't produce themselves. Towns and cities are the seats of the nobles who govern the surrounding area, and who carry the responsibility for defending the villages from attack. Occasionally, a local lord or lady lives in a keep or fortress with no nearby town or city.

Village

Population: Up to about 1,000

Government: A noble (usually not a resident) rules the village, with an appointed agent (a reeve) in residence to adjudicate disputes and collect taxes.

Defense: The reeve might have a small force of soldiers. Otherwise, the village relies on a citizen militia.

Commerce: Basic supplies are readily available, possibly from an inn or a trading post. Other goods are available from traveling merchants.

Organizations: A village might contain one or two temples or shrines, but few or no other organizations.

Most settlements are agricultural villages, supporting themselves and nearby towns or cities with crops and meat. Villagers produce food in one way or another—if not by tending the crops, then supporting those who do by shoeing horses, weaving clothes, milling grain, and the like. The goods they produce feed their families and supply trade with nearby settlements.

A village's population is dispersed around a large area of land. Farmers live on their land, which spreads them widely around the village center. At the heart of the village, a handful of structures cluster together: a well, a marketplace, a small temple or two, a gathering place, and perhaps an inn for travelers.

Town

Population: Up to about 6,000

Government: A resident noble rules and appoints a lord mayor to oversee administration. An elected town council represents the interests of the middle class.

Defense: The noble commands a sizable army of professional soldiers, as well as personal bodyguards.

Commerce: Basic supplies are readily available, though exotic goods and services are harder to find. Inns and taverns support travelers.

Organizations: The town contains several temples, as well as various merchant guilds and other organizations.

Towns are major trade centers, situated where important industries and reliable trade routes enabled the population to grow. These settlements rely on commerce: the import of raw materials and food from surrounding villages, and the export of crafted items to those villages, as well as to other towns and cities. A town's population is more diverse than that of most villages.

Towns arise where roads intersect waterways, at the meeting of major land trade routes, around strategic defensive locations, or near significant mines or similar natural resources.

City

Population: Up to about 25,000

Government: A resident noble presides, with several other nobles sharing responsibility for surrounding areas and government functions. One such noble is the lord mayor, who oversees the city administration. An elected city council represents the middle class and might hold more actual power than the lord mayor. Other groups serve as important power centers as well.

Defense: The city supports an army of professional soldiers, guards, and town watch. Each noble in residence maintains a small force of personal bodyguards.

Commerce: Almost any goods or services are readily available. Many inns and taverns support travelers.

Organizations: A multitude of temples, guilds, and other organizations, some of which hold significant power in city affairs, can be found within the city's walls.

Cities are cradles of civilization. Their larger populations require considerable support from both surrounding villages and trade routes, so they're rare.

Cities typically thrive in areas where large expanses of fertile, arable land surround a location accessible to trade, almost always on a navigable waterway.

Cities almost always have walls, and the stages of a city's growth are easily identified by the expansion of the walls beyond the central core. These internal walls naturally divide the city into wards (neighborhoods defined by specific features), which have their own representatives on the city council and their own noble administrators.

Cities that hold more than twenty-five thousand people are extremely rare. Metropolises such as Waterdeep in the Forgotten Realms, Sharn in Eberron, and the Free City of Greyhawk stand as vital beacons of civilization in the D&D worlds.

Atmosphere

What do the adventurers first notice as they approach or enter a settlement? The towering wall bristling with soldiers? The beggars with hands outstretched, pleading for aid outside the gate? The noisy hubbub of merchants and buyers thronging the market square? The overpowering stench of manure?

Sensory details help bring a settlement to life and vividly communicate its personality to your players. Settle on a single defining factor that sums up a settlement's personality and extrapolate from there. Maybe a city is built around canals, like real-world Venice. That key element suggests a wealth of sensory details: the sight of colorful boats floating on muddy waters, the sound of lapping waves and perhaps singing gondoliers, the smells of fish and waste polluting the water, the feel of humidity. Or perhaps the city is shrouded in fog much of the time, and you describe the tendrils of cold mist reaching through every crack and cranny, the muffled sounds of hooves on cobblestones, the cold air with the smell of rain, and a sense of mystery and lurking danger.

The climate and terrain of a settlement's environment, its origin and inhabitants, its government and political position, and its commercial importance all have a bearing on its overall atmosphere. A city nestled against the edge of a jungle has a very different feel than one on the edge of a desert. Elf and dwarf cities present a distinct aesthetic, clearly identifiable in contrast to human-built ones. Soldiers patrol the streets to quell any hint of dissent in a city ruled by a tyrant, while a city fostering an early system of democracy might boast an open-air market where philosophical ideas are traded as freely as produce. All the possible combinations of these factors can inspire endless variety in the settlements of your campaign world.

Government

In the feudal society common in most D&D worlds, power and authority are concentrated in towns and cities. Nobles hold authority over the settlements where they live and the surrounding lands. They collect taxes from the populace, which they use for public building projects, to pay the soldiery, and to support a comfortable lifestyle for themselves (although nobles often have considerable hereditary wealth). In exchange, they promise to protect their citizens from threats such as orc marauders, hobgoblin armies, and roving human bandits.

Nobles appoint officers as their agents in villages, to supervise the collection of taxes and serve as judges in disputes and criminal trials. These reeves, sheriffs, or bailiffs are commoners native to the villages they govern, chosen for their positions because they already hold the respect of their fellow citizens.

Within towns and cities, lords share authority and administrative responsibility with lesser nobles (usually their own relatives), and also with representatives of the middle class, such as traders and artisans. A lord mayor of noble birth is appointed to head the town or city council and to perform the same administrative functions that reeves carry out in villages. The council consists of representatives elected by the middle class. Only foolish nobles ignore the wishes of their councils, since the economic power of the middle class is often more important to the prosperity of a town or city than the hereditary authority of the nobility.

The larger a settlement, the more likely that other individuals or organizations hold significant power there as well. Even in a village, a popular individual—a wise elder or a well-liked farmer—can wield more influence than the appointed reeve, and a wise reeve avoids making an enemy of such a person. In towns and cities, the same power might lie in the hands of a prominent temple, a guild independent of the council, or an individual with magical power.

FORMS OF GOVERNMENT

A settlement rarely stands alone. A given town or city might be a theocratic city-state or a prosperous free city governed by a merchant council. More likely, it's part of a feudal kingdom, a bureaucratic empire, or a remote realm ruled by an iron-fisted tyrant. Consider how your settlement fits into the bigger picture of your world or region—who rules its ruler, and what other settlements might also lie under its control.

FORMS OF GOVERNMENT

d100	Government	d100	Government
01–08	Autocracy	59–64	Militocracy
09–13	Bureaucracy	65–74	Monarchy
14–19	Confederacy	75–78	Oligarchy
20–22	Democracy	79–80	Patriarchy
23–27	Dictatorship	81–83	Meritocracy
28–42	Feudalism	84–85	Plutocracy
43–44	Gerontocracy	86–92	Republic
45–53	Hierarchy	93–94	Satrapy
54–56	Magocracy	95	Kleptocracy
57–58	Matriarchy	96–00	Theocracy

Typical and fantastical forms of government are described below. Choose one or randomly determine a form of government for a nation or city from the Forms of Government table.

Autocracy. One hereditary ruler wields absolute power. The autocrat either is supported by a well-developed bureaucracy or military or stands as the only authority in an otherwise anarchic society. The dynastic ruler could be immortal or undead. Aundair and Karrnath, two kingdoms in the Eberron campaign setting, have autocrats with royal blood in their veins. Whereas Queen Aurala of Aundair relies on wizards and spies to enforce her will, Kaius, the vampire king of Karrnath, has a formidable army of living and undead soldiers under his command.

Bureaucracy. Various departments compose the government, each responsible for an aspect of rule. The department heads, ministers, or secretaries answer to a figurehead autocrat or council.

Confederacy. Each individual city or town within the confederacy governs itself, but all contribute to a league or federation that promotes (at least in theory) the common good of all member states. Conditions and attitudes toward the central government vary from place to place within the confederacy. The Lords' Alliance in the Forgotten Realms setting is a loose confederacy of cities, while the Mror Holds in the Eberron campaign setting is a confederacy of allied dwarf clans.

Democracy. Citizens or their elected representatives determine the laws in a democracy. A bureaucracy or military carries out the day-to-day work of government, with positions filled through open elections.

Dictatorship. One supreme ruler holds absolute authority, but his or her rule isn't necessarily dynastic. In other respects this resembles an autocracy. In the Greyhawk campaign setting, a half-demon named Iuz is the dictator of a conquered land that bears his name.

Feudalism. The typical government of Europe in the Middle Ages, a feudalistic society consists of layers of lords and vassals. The vassals provide soldiers or scutage (payment in lieu of military service) to the lords, who in turn promise protection to their vassals.

Gerontocracy. Elders preside over this society. In some cases, long-lived races such as elves or dragons are entrusted with the leadership of the land.

Hierarchy. A feudal or bureaucratic government where every member, except one, is subordinate to another member. In the Dragonlance campaign setting, the dragonarmies of Krynn form a military hierarchy, with the Dragon Highlords as leaders under the dragon queen Takhisis.

Kleptocracy. This government is composed of groups or individuals primarily seeking wealth for themselves, often at the expense of their subjects. The grasping Bandit Kingdoms in the Greyhawk campaign setting are prime examples. A kingdom run by thieves' guilds would also fall into this category.

Magocracy. The governing body is composed of spellcasters who rule directly as oligarchs or feudal lords, or participate in a democracy or bureaucracy. Examples include the Red Wizards of Thay in the Forgotten Realms campaign setting and the sorcerer-kings of Athas in the Dark Sun campaign setting.

Matriarchy or Patriarchy. This society is governed by the eldest or most important members of one gender. Drow cities are examples of theocratic matriarchies, for each is ruled by a council of drow high priestesses who answer to Lolth, the Demon Queen of Spiders.

Meritocracy. The most intelligent and educated people oversee the society, often with a bureaucracy to handle the day-to-day work of government. In the Forgotten Realms, scholarly monks preside over the fortress-library of Candlekeep, overseen by a master of lore called the Keeper.

Militocracy. Military leaders run the nation under martial law, using the army and other armed forces. A militocracy might be based on an elite group of soldiers, an order of dragon riders, or a league of sea princes. Solamnia, a nation ruled by knights in the Dragonlance campaign setting, falls into this category.

Monarchy. A single hereditary sovereign wears the crown. Unlike the autocrat, the monarch's powers are limited by law, and the ruler serves as the head of a democracy, feudal state, or militocracy. The kingdom of Breland, in the Eberron campaign setting, has both a parliament that makes laws and a monarch who enforces them.

Oligarchy. A small number of absolute rulers share power, possibly dividing the land into districts or provinces under their control, or jointly ruling together. A group of adventurers who take control of a nation together might form an oligarchy. The Free City of Greyhawk is an oligarchy composed of various faction leaders, with a Lord Mayor as its figurehead.

Plutocracy. Society is governed by the wealthy. The elite form a ruling council, purchase representation at the court of a figurehead monarch, or rule by default because money is the true power in the realm. Many cities in the Forgotten Realms campaign setting, including Waterdeep and Baldur's Gate, are plutocracies.

Republic. Government is entrusted to representatives of an established electorate who rule on behalf of the electors. Any democracy in which only landowners or certain classes can vote could be considered a republic.

Satrapy. Conquerors and representatives of another government wield power, ruling the settlement or region as part of a larger empire. The satraps are bureaucrats and military officers, or unusual characters or monsters. The cities of Highport and Suderham in the Greyhawk campaign setting are satrapies controlled by agents of a vicious gang of marauders known as the Slave Lords.

Theocracy. Rulership falls to a direct representative or a collection of agents of a deity. The centers of power in a theocracy are usually located on sacred sites. In the Eberron campaign setting, the nation of Thrane is a theocracy devoted to the Silver Flame, a divine spirit that resides in Thrane's capital of Flamekeep.

SAMPLE HIERARCHY OF NOBLE TITLES

Rank	Title	Rank	Title
1st	Emperor/Empress	7th	Viscount/
2nd	King/Queen		Viscountess
3rd	Duke/Duchess	8th	Baron/Baroness
4th	Prince/Princess	9th	Baronet
5th	Marquess/Marquise	10th	Knight
6th	Earl or Count/		
	Countess		

COMMERCE

Even small villages can provide characters access to the gear they need to pursue their adventures. Provisions, tents, backpacks, and simple weapons are commonly available. Traveling merchants carry armor, martial weapons, and more specialized gear. Most villages have inns that cater to travelers, where adventurers can find a hot meal and a bed, even if the quality leaves much to be desired.

Villages rely heavily on trade with other settlements, including larger towns and cities. Merchants pass through regularly, selling necessities and luxuries to the villagers, and any successful merchant has far-reaching contacts across the region. Traveling merchants pass on gossip and adventure hooks to the characters as they conduct their business. Since merchants make their living traversing roads that might be menaced by bandits or wandering monsters, they hire guards to keep their goods safe. They also carry news from town to town, including reports of situations that cry out for the attention of adventurers.

These merchants can't provide the services normally found in a city. For instance, when the characters are in need of a library or a dedicated sage, a trainer who can handle the griffon eggs they've found, or an architect to design their castle, they're better off going to a large city than looking in a village.

CURRENCY

The straightforward terms "gold piece" (gp), "silver piece" (sp), "copper piece" (cp), "electrum piece" (ep), and "platinum piece" (pp) are used throughout the game rules for clarity. You can imbue these denominations with more interesting descriptions in your game world. People give coins specific names, whether as plain as "dime" or lively as "gold double-eagle." A country typically mints its own currency, which might correspond to the basic rules terms. In most worlds, few currencies achieve widespread distribution, but nearly all coins are accepted worldwide—except by those looking to pick a fight with a foreigner.

EXAMPLE: THE FORGOTTEN REALMS

The world of the Forgotten Realms provides an extensive example of currencies. Although barter, blood notes, and similar letters of trade are common enough in Faerûn, metal coins and trade bars are the everyday currency.

Common Coinage. Coins appear in a bewildering variety of shapes, sizes, names, and materials. Thanks to the ambitious traders of Sembia, that nation's oddly shaped coins can be found throughout Faerûn. In Sembia, square iron steelpence replace copper coins. Triangular silver pieces are ravens, diamond-shaped electrum pieces are harmarks (commonly called "blue eyes"), and five-sided gold pieces are nobles. Sembia doesn't mint platinum coins. All coinage is accepted in Sembia, including copper and platinum pieces from abroad.

In Waterdeep, the bustling cosmopolitan center of trade, coppers are called nibs, silvers are shards, electrum pieces are moons, gold pieces are dragons, and platinum coins are suns. The city's two local coins are the toal and the harbor moon. The toal is a square brass trading-coin pierced with a central hole to permit it to be easily strung on a ring or string, worth 2 gp in the city and nothing outside Waterdeep. The harbor moon is a flat crescent of platinum with a central hole and an electrum inlay, named for its traditional use in the docks for buying large amounts of cargo at once. The coin is worth 50 gp in Waterdeep and 30 gp elsewhere.

The northern city of Silverymoon mints a crescent-shaped, shining blue coin called an electrum moon, worth 1 gp in that city and 1 ep elsewhere. The city also issues a larger coin called an eclipsed moon, which looks like an electrum moon combined a darker silver wedge to form a round coin worth 5 ep within the city and 2 ep outside it.

The favored form of currency in the kingdom of Cormyr is the royal coinage of the court, stamped with a dragon on one side and a treasury date mark on the other. There, coppers are called thumbs, silvers are silver falcons, electrum pieces are blue eyes, gold pieces are golden lions, and platinum coins are tricrowns.

Even city-states mint their own copper, silver, and gold pieces. Electrum and platinum pieces are rarer in these lands. Smaller states use coinage borrowed from other nations and looted from ancient sources. Travelers from certain lands (notably the wizard-dominated realms of Thay and Halruaa) use the currencies of other realms when trading abroad because their own coins and tokens are feared to be magically cursed, and so are shunned by others.

Conversely, the coins of long-lost, legendary lands and centers of great magic are honored, though those who find them are wise to sell them to collectors rather than merely spending them in markets. The coins of the old elven court of Cormanthyr are particularly famous: thalvers (coppers), bedoars (silvers), thammarchs (electrum), shilmaers (golds), and ruendils (platinum). These coins are fine, numerous, and sometimes still used in trade among elves.

COPPER COIN

GOLD COIN

SILVER COIN

ELECTRUM COIN

PLATINUM COIN

Trade Bars. Large numbers of coins can be difficult to transport and account for. Many merchants prefer to use trade bars—ingots of precious metals and alloys (usually silver) likely to be accepted by virtually anyone. Trade bars are stamped or graven with the symbol of the trading company or government that originally crafted them. These bars are valued by weight, as follows:

- A 2-pound silver bar is worth 10 gp and is about 5 inches long, 2 inches wide, and 1/2 inch thick.
- A 5-pound silver bar is worth 25 gp and is about 6 inches long, 2 inches wide, and 1 inch thick.
- A 5-pound gold bar is worth 250 gp and is about the size of a 2-pound silver bar.

The city of Baldur's Gate mints large numbers of silver trade bars and sets the standard for this form of currency. The city of Mirabar issues black iron spindle-shaped trade bars with squared ends weighing about 2 pounds each, worth 10 gp in that city, markedly less in nearby trade centers, and as iron is normally valued elsewhere (1 sp per pound).

Odd Currency. Coins and bars aren't the only forms of hard currency. Gond bells are small brass bells worth 10 gp in trade, or 20 gp to a temple of Gond. Shaar rings, pierced and polished slices of ivory threaded onto strings by the nomads of the Shaar, are worth 3 gp per slice.

CREATING YOUR OWN

As shown in the previous examples, currency doesn't need to obey a universal standard in your world. Each country and era can have its own coins with its own values. Your adventurers might travel through many different lands and find long-lost treasures. Finding six hundred ancient bedoars from the rule of Coronal Eltargrim twelve centuries before offers a deeper sense of immersion in your world than finding 60 sp.

Varying names and descriptions of coins for the major contemporary and historical realms of your world adds an additional layer of texture. The golden lions of Cormyr convey the noble nature of that kingdom. If a nation mints gold coins stamped with leering demonic faces and called torments, that currency expresses a distinct flavor.

Creating new coins connected to specific locations, like the toals of Waterdeep or the eclipsed moons of Silverymoon, provides another level of detail. As long as you keep the value of these new coins simple (in other words, don't invent a coin worth 1.62 gp), you add local flavor to key locations in your world without adding undue complexity.

LANGUAGES AND DIALECTS

When fleshing out your world, you can create new languages and dialects to reflect its unique geography and history. You can replace the default languages presented in the *Player's Handbook* with new ones, or split languages up into several different dialects.

In some worlds, regional differences might be much more important than racial ones. Perhaps all the dwarves, elves, and humans who live in one kingdom speak a common language, which is completely different

HARPERS   ORDER OF THE GAUNTLET   EMERALD ENCLAVE   LORDS' ALLIANCE   ZHENTARIM

from that spoken in the neighboring kingdom. This might make communication (and diplomacy) between two kingdoms significantly more difficult.

Widely used languages might have ancient versions, or there might be completely different ancient tongues that adventurers find written in tombs and ruins. Such languages can add an element of mystery to inscriptions and tomes that characters encounter.

You might invent additional secret languages, besides Druidic and thieves' cant, that allow members of certain organizations or political affiliations to communicate. You could even decide that each alignment has its own language, which might be more of an argot used primarily to discuss philosophical concepts.

In a region where one race has subjugated another, the language of the conquerors can become a mark of social status. Similarly, reading and writing might be restricted by law to the upper classes of a society.

FACTIONS AND ORGANIZATIONS

Temples, guilds, orders, secret societies, and colleges are important forces in the social order of any civilization. Their influence might stretch across multiple towns and cities, with or without a similarly wide-ranging political authority. Organizations can play an important part in the lives of player characters, becoming their patrons, allies, or enemies just like individual nonplayer characters. When characters join these organizations, they become part of something larger than themselves, which can give their adventures a context in the wider world.

ADVENTURERS AND ORGANIZATIONS

At the start of a campaign, backgrounds are a great way to connect adventurers to your world. As the game progresses, though, background ties often become less important.

Factions and organizations aimed at player characters are a way to keep higher-level adventurers connected to your world, providing ties to key NPCs and a clear agenda beyond individual gain. In the same way, villainous organizations create an ongoing sense of menace above and beyond the threat of solitary foes.

Having different characters tied to different factions can create interesting situations at the gaming table, as long as those factions have similar goals and don't work in opposition to one another all the time. Adventurers

representing different factions might have competing interests or priorities while they pursue the same goals.

Adventurer organizations are also a great source of special rewards beyond experience points and treasure. Increased standing in an organization has value in and of itself, and might also come with concrete benefits such as access to an organization's information, equipment, magic, and other resources.

CREATING FACTIONS

Factions and organizations that you create for your campaign should grow out of the stories that are important to the world. Create organizations that your players will want to interact with, whether as allies, members, or enemies.

As a starting point, decide what role you want an organization to play in the world. What is it all about? What are its goals? Who founded it and why? What do its members do? Answering these questions should

---

SAMPLE FACTION: THE HARPERS

The Harpers is a scattered network of spellcasters and spies who advocate equality and covertly oppose the abuse of power, magical or otherwise.

The organization has risen, been shattered, and risen again several times. Its longevity and resilience are largely due to its decentralized, grassroots, secretive nature, and the autonomy of its various members. The Harpers have small cells and lone operatives throughout the Forgotten Realms, although they interact and share information with one another from time to time as needs warrant. The Harpers' ideology is noble, and its members pride themselves on their ingenuity and incorruptibility. Harpers don't seek power or glory, only fair and equal treatment for all.

Motto. "Down with tyranny. Fairness and equality for all."

Beliefs. The Harpers' beliefs can be summarized as follows:

- One can never have too much information or arcane knowledge.
- Too much power leads to corruption, and the abuse of magic in particular must be closely monitored.
- No one should be powerless.

Goals. Gather information throughout Faerûn, discern the political dynamics within each region, and promote fairness and equality by covert means. Act openly as a last resort. Thwart tyrants and any leader, government, or group that grows too powerful. Aid the weak, the poor, and the oppressed.

Typical Quests. Typical Harper quests include securing an artifact that would upset the balance of power in a region, gathering information on a powerful individual or organization, and determining the true intentions of an ambitious political figure or evil spellcaster.

give you a good sense of the organization's personality. From there, think about typical members. How might people describe them? What are the typical members' classes and alignments? What personality traits do they tend to share?

Choosing a symbol and a motto for the organization is a way of summing up the work you've done so far. A faction that uses a stag as a symbol probably has a very different personality from one that uses a winged viper. For a motto, choose not just a message but also a tone and style of speech that fits the organization as you've defined it. Consider the motto of the Harpers: "Down with tyranny. Fairness and equality for all." The Harpers have a straightforward message of freedom and prosperity. Contrast that with the motto of a group of politically allied cities in the North calling themselves the Lords' Alliance: "Threats to home must be terminated without prejudice. Superiority is our security." These are sophisticated people involved in a delicate political alliance, with more emphasis on stability than on fairness and equality.

Finally, think about the ways that player characters might come into contact with the organization. Who are the important members—not just the leaders, but the agents in the field that the adventurers might encounter? Where are they active, and where do they have headquarters or strongholds? If adventurers do join, what kind of missions might they be sent on? What rewards can they gain?

RENOWN

Renown is an optional rule you can use to track an adventurer's standing within a particular faction or organization. Renown is a numerical value that starts at 0, then increases as a character earns favor and reputation within a particular organization. You can tie benefits to a character's renown, including ranks and titles within the organization and access to resources.

A player tracks renown separately for each organization his or her character is a member of. For example, an adventurer might have 5 renown within one faction and 20 renown within another, based on the character's interaction with each organization over the course of the campaign.

GAINING RENOWN

A character earns renown by completing missions or quests that serve an organization's interests or involve the organization directly. You award renown at your discretion as characters complete these missions or quests, typically at the same time you award experience points.

Advancing an organization's interests increases a character's renown within that organization by 1. Completing a mission specifically assigned by that organization, or which directly benefits the organization, increases the character's renown by 2 instead.

For example, characters with connections to the noble Order of the Gauntlet complete a mission in which they free a town from the tyranny of a blue dragon. Because the order likes to punish evildoers, you might increase each character's renown within the order by 1. Conversely, if killing the dragon was a mission given to the adventurers by a senior member of the order, completing the task might instead increase each character's renown by 2, showing the adventurers as effective allies.

Meanwhile, the party's rogue might have looted a box of rare poisons from the dragon's hoard and sold it to a fence who is secretly a Zhentarim agent. You might increase the rogue's renown within the Zhentarim by 2 since this action directly increased that group's power and wealth, even though the task was not assigned by an agent of the Zhentarim.

BENEFITS OF RENOWN

The benefits of increasing renown within an organization can include rank and authority, friendly attitudes from members of the organization, and other perks.

Rank. Characters can earn promotions as their renown increases. You can establish certain thresholds of renown that serve as prerequisites (though not necessarily the only prerequisites) for advancing in rank, as shown in the Examples of Faction Ranks table. For example, a character might join the Lords' Alliance after earning 1 renown within that organization, gaining the title of cloak. As the character's renown within the organization increases, he or she might be eligible for further increases in rank.

You can add rank prerequisites. For example, a character affiliated with the Lords' Alliance might have to be at least 5th level before becoming a stingblade, at least 10th level to be a warduke, and at least 15th level to be a lioncrown.

You can set these thresholds of renown to any numbers that work for your game, creating appropriate ranks and titles for the organizations in your campaign.

Attitudes of Organization Members. As a character's renown within an organization grows, members of that organization are increasingly likely to have heard of the character. You can set thresholds at which the default attitude of an organization's members toward the character becomes indifferent or friendly. For example, members of the Emerald Enclave—a faction

EXAMPLES OF FACTION RANKS

Renown	Harpers	Order of the Gauntlet	Emerald Enclave	Lord's Alliance	Zhentarim
1	Watcher	Chevall	Springwarden	Cloak	Fang
3	Harpshadow	Marcheon	Summerstrider	Redknife	Wolf
10	Brightcandle	Whitehawk	Autumnreaver	Stingblade	Viper
25	Wise Owl	Vindicator	Winterstalker	Warduke	Ardragon
50	High Harper	Righteous Hand	Master of the Wild	Lioncrown	Dread Lord

dedicated to preserving the natural order—might be less friendly toward characters who have not cultivated at least 3 renown within that organization, becoming friendly by default only when a character has gained 10 renown within the Emerald Enclave. These thresholds apply only to the default attitude of most members of an organization, and such attitudes aren't automatic. NPC faction members might dislike an adventurer despite that character's renown—or perhaps because of it.

Perks. Earning a rank within an organization comes with certain benefits, as defined by you. A character of low rank might gain access to a reliable contact and adventure leads, a safe house, or a trader willing to offer a discount on adventuring gear. A middle-ranked character might gain a follower (see chapter 4, "Creating Nonplayer Characters"), access to potions and scrolls, the ability to call in a favor, or backup on dangerous missions. A high-ranking character might be able to call on a small army, take custody of a rare magic item, gain access to a helpful spellcaster, or assign special missions to members of lower rank.

Downtime Activities. You might allow characters to spend downtime between adventures building relationships and gaining renown within an organization. For more information on downtime activities, see chapter 6, "Between Adventures."

Losing Renown

Disagreements with members of an organization aren't enough to cause a loss of renown within that organization. However, serious offenses committed against the organization or its members can result in a loss of renown and rank within the organization. The extent of the loss depends on the infraction and is left to your discretion. A character's renown within an organization can never drop below 0.

Piety

With a few alterations, the renown system can also serve as a measure of a character's link to the gods. It's a great option for campaigns where the gods take active roles in the world.

Using this approach, you track renown based on specific divine figures in your campaign. Each character has the option to select a patron deity or pantheon with goals, doctrine, and taboos that you have created. Any renown he or she earns is called piety. A character gains piety for honoring his or her gods, fulfilling their commands, and respecting their taboos. A character loses piety for working against those gods, dishonoring them, defiling their temples, and foiling their aims.

The gods bestow favors on those who prove their devotion. With each rank of piety gained, a character can pray for divine favor once per day. This favor usually comes in the form of a cleric spell like *bless*. The favor often comes with a sign of the divine benefactor; for example, a character dedicated to Thor might receive a spell accompanied by the boom of thunder.

A high level of piety can also lead to a character gaining a more persistent benefit, in the form of a blessing or charm (see chapter 7, "Treasure," for such supernatural gifts).

Magic in Your World

In most D&D worlds, magic is natural but still wondrous and sometimes frightening. People everywhere know about magic, and most people see evidence of it at some point in their lives. It permeates the cosmos and moves through the ancient possessions of legendary heroes, the mysterious ruins of fallen empires, those touched by the gods, creatures born with supernatural power, and individuals who study the secrets of the multiverse. Histories and fireside tales are filled with the exploits of those who wield it.

What normal folk know of magic depends on where they live and whether they know characters who practice magic. Citizens of an isolated hamlet might not have seen true magic used for generations and speak in whispers of the strange powers of the old hermit living in the nearby woods. In the city of Waterdeep in the Forgotten Realms setting, the Watchful Order of Magists and Protectors is a guild of wizards. These arcanists wish to make wizardry more accessible so the order's members can profit from selling their services.

Some D&D settings have more magic in them than others. On Athas, the harsh world of the Dark Sun setting, arcane magic is a hated practice that can drain life from the world. Much of Athas's magic lies in the hands of evildoers. Conversely, in the world of Eberron, magic is as commonplace as any other commodity. Mercantile houses sell magic items and services to

> ### Sample Faction: The Zhentarim
>
> The Zhentarim (also known as the Black Network) is an unscrupulous shadow network that seeks to expand its influence and power throughout the Forgotten Realms.
>
> The public face of the Black Network appears relatively benign. It offers the best and cheapest goods and services, both legal and illicit, thus destroying its competitors and making everyone dependent on it.
>
> A member of the Zhentarim thinks of himself or herself as a member of a very large family and relies on the Black Network for resources and security. However, members are granted the autonomy to pursue their own interests and gain some measure of personal wealth and influence. As a whole, the Zhentarim promises "the best of the best," although in truth the organization is more interested in spreading its own propaganda and influence than investing in the improvement of its individual members.
>
> *Motto.* "Join us and prosper. Oppose us and suffer."
>
> *Beliefs.* The Zhentarim's beliefs can be summarized as follows:
>
> - The Zhentarim is your family. You watch out for it, and it watches out for you.
> - You are the master of your own destiny. Never be less than what you deserve to be.
> - Everything and everyone has a price.
>
> *Goals.* Amass wealth, power, and influence, and thereby dominate Faerûn.
>
> *Typical Quests.* Typical Zhentarim quests include plundering or stealing a treasure hoard, powerful magic item, or artifact; securing a lucrative business contract or enforcing a preexisting one; and establishing a foothold in a place where the Zhentarim holds little sway.

anyone who can afford them. People purchase tickets to ride airships and trains propelled by elemental magic.

Consider these questions when fitting magic into your world:

- Is some magic common? Is some socially unacceptable? Which magic is rare?
- How unusual are members of each spellcasting class? How common are those who can cast high-level spells?
- How rare are magic items, magical locations, and creatures that have supernatural powers? At what power level do these things go from everyday to exotic?
- How do authorities regulate and use magic? How do normal folks use magic and protect themselves from it?

The answers to some questions suggest the answers to others. For example, if spellcasters of low-level spells are common, as in Eberron, then authorities and common folk are more likely to have access to and use the results of such spells. Buying commonplace magic isn't only possible, but also less expensive. People are more likely to keep well-known magic in mind, and to protect against it, especially in risky situations.

RESTRICTIONS ON MAGIC

Some civilized areas might restrict or prohibit the use of magic. Spellcasting might be forbidden without a license or official permission. In such a place, magic items and continual magical effects are rare, with protections against magic being the exception.

Some localities might prohibit specific spells. It could be a crime to cast any spells used to steal or swindle, such as those that bestow invisibility or produce illusions. Enchantments that charm or dominate others are readily outlawed, since they rob their subjects of free will. Destructive spells are likewise prohibited, for obvious reasons. A local ruler could have a phobia about a specific effect or spell (such as shapeshifting effects if he or she were afraid of being impersonated) and enact a law restricting that type of magic.

SCHOOLS OF MAGIC

The rules of the game refer to the schools of magic (abjuration, illusion, necromancy, and so on), but it's up to you to determine what those schools signify in your world. Similarly, a few class options suggest the existence of magic-using organizations in the world— bardic colleges and druid circles—which are up to you to flesh out.

You could decide that no formal structures like these exist in your world. Wizards (and bards and druids) might be so rare that a player character learns from a single mentor and never meets another character of the same class, in which case wizards would learn their school specialization without any formal training.

However, if magic is more common, academies can be the embodiments of the schools of magic. These institutions have their own hierarchies, traditions, regulations, and procedures. For example, Materros the necromancer could be a brother of the necromantic

Cabal of Thar-Zad. As a sign of his high standing within its hierarchy, he is allowed to wear the red and green robes of a master. Of course, when he wears these robes, his occupation is easily identified by those who know of the cabal. This recognition could be a boon or a nuisance, since the Cabal of Thar-Zad has a fearsome reputation.

If you go this route, you can treat schools of magic, bardic colleges, and druid circles as organizations, using the guidelines for organizations presented earlier in this chapter. A player character necromancer might cultivate renown within the Cabal of Thar-Zad, while a bard seeks increasing renown within the College of Mac-Fuirmidh.

TELEPORTATION CIRCLES

The presence of permanent teleportation circles in major cities helps cement their important place in the economy of a fantasy world. Spells such as *plane shift*, *teleport*, and *teleportation circle* connect with these circles, which are found in temples, academies, the headquarters of arcane organizations, and prominent civic locations. However, since every teleportation circle is a possible means of entry into a city, they're guarded by military and magical protection.

As you design a fantasy city, think about the teleportation circles it might contain and which ones adventurers are likely to know about. If the adventurers commonly return to their home base by means of a teleportation circle, use that circle as a hook for plot developments in your campaign. What do the adventurers do if they arrive in a teleportation circle and find all the familiar wards disabled and guards lying in pools of blood? What if their arrival interrupts an argument between two feuding priests at the temple? Adventure ensues!

BRINGING BACK THE DEAD

When a creature dies, its soul departs its body, leaves the Material Plane, travels through the Astral Plane, and goes to abide on the plane where the creature's deity resides. If the creature didn't worship a deity, its soul departs to the plane corresponding to its alignment. Bringing someone back from the dead means retrieving the soul from that plane and returning it to its body.

Enemies can take steps to make it more difficult for a character to be returned from the dead. Keeping the body prevents others from using *raise dead* or *resurrection* to restore the slain character to life.

A soul can't be returned to life if it doesn't wish to be. A soul knows the name, alignment, and patron deity (if any) of the character attempting to revive it and might refuse to return on that basis. For example, if the honorable knight Sturm Brightblade is slain and a high priestess of Takhisis (god of evil dragons) grabs his body, Sturm might not wish to be raised from the dead by her. Any attempts she makes to revive him automatically fail. If the evil cleric wants to revive Sturm to interrogate him, she needs to find some way to trick his soul, such as duping a good cleric into raising him and then capturing him once he is alive again.

CREATING A CAMPAIGN

The world you create is the stage for the adventures you set in it. You don't have to give more thought to it than that. You can run adventures in an episodic format, with the characters as the only common element, and also weave themes throughout those adventures to build a greater saga of the characters' achievements in the world.

Planning an entire campaign might seem like a daunting task, but you don't have to plot out every detail right from the start. You can start with the basics, running a few adventures, and think about larger plotlines you want to explore as the campaign progresses. You're free to add as much or as little detail as you wish.

The start of a campaign resembles the start of an adventure. You want to jump quickly into the action, show the players that adventure awaits, and grab their attention right away. Give the players enough information to make them want to come back week after week to see how the story plays out.

START SMALL

When you first start building your campaign, start small. The characters need to know only about the city, town, or village where they start the game, and perhaps the nearby dungeon. You might decide that the barony is at war with a nearby duchy, or that a distant forest is crawling with ettercaps and giant spiders, and you should note these things. But at the start of the game, the local area is enough to get the campaign off the ground. Follow these steps to create that local area:

1. CREATE A HOME BASE
See the "Settlements" section earlier in this chapter for guidance on building this settlement. A small town or village at the edge of the wilderness serves as a fine home base in most D&D campaigns. Use a larger town or city if you want a campaign with urban adventuring.

2. CREATE A LOCAL REGION
See "Mapping the Campaign" earlier in this chapter for guidance. Draw a map at province scale (1 hex = 1 mile) with the home base near the center. Fill in the area within a day's travel—about 25 to 30 miles—of the home base. Pepper it with two to four dungeons or similar adventure locales. An area that size is likely to have one to three additional settlements as well as the home base, so give thought to them as well.

3. CRAFT A STARTING ADVENTURE
A single dungeon makes a good first adventure for most campaigns. See chapter 3, "Creating Adventures," for guidance.

A home base provides a common starting location for the characters. This starting point might be the village where they grew up or a city that attracted them from points beyond.

Or perhaps they begin the campaign in the dungeons of an evil baron's castle where they've been locked up for various reasons (legitimate or otherwise), throwing them into the midst of the adventure.

For each of these steps, give the locations only as much detail as they need. You don't need to identify every building in a village or label every street in a large city. If the characters start in the baron's dungeon, you'll need the details of this first adventure site, but you don't have to name all the baron's knights. Sketch out a simple map, think about the surrounding area, and consider whom the characters are most likely to interact with early in the campaign. Most important, visualize how this area fits into the theme and story you have in mind for your campaign. Then start working on your first adventure!

SET THE STAGE

As you start to develop your campaign, you'll need to fill in the players on the basics. For easy distribution, compile essential information into a campaign handout. Such a handout typically includes the following material:

- Any restrictions or new options for character creation, such as new or prohibited races.
- Any information in the backstory of your campaign that the characters would know about. If you have a theme or direction in mind for the campaign, this information could include seeds hinting at that focus.
- Basic information about the area where the characters are starting, such as the name of the town, important locations in and around it, prominent NPCs they'd know about, and perhaps rumors that point to trouble that's brewing.

Keep this handout short and to the point. Two pages is a reasonable maximum. Even if you have a burst of creative energy that produces twenty pages of great background material, save it for your adventures. Let the players uncover the details gradually in play.

INVOLVING THE CHARACTERS

Once you've identified what your campaign is about, let the players help tell the story by deciding how their characters are involved. This is their opportunity to tie their characters' history and background to the campaign, and a chance for you to determine how the various elements of each character's background tie into the campaign's story. For example, what secret has the hermit character learned? What is the status of the noble character's family? What is the folk hero's destiny?

Some players might have trouble coming up with ideas—not everyone is equally inventive. You can help spur their creativity with a few questions about their characters:

- Are you a native, born and raised in the area? If so, who's your family? What's your current occupation?
- Are you a recent arrival? Where did you come from? Why did you come to this area?

- Are you tied to any of the organizations or people involved in the events that kick off the campaign? Are they friends or enemies?

Listen to the players' ideas, and say yes if you can. Even if you want all the characters to have grown up in the starting town, consider allowing a recent arrival or a transplant if the player's story is convincing enough. Suggest alterations to a character's story so it better fits your world, or weave the first threads of your campaign into that story.

CREATING A BACKGROUND

Backgrounds are designed to root player characters in the world, and creating new backgrounds is a great way to introduce players to the special features of your world. Backgrounds that have ties to particular cultures, organizations, and historical events from your campaign are particularly strong. Perhaps the priests of a certain religion live as beggars supported by a pious populace, singing the tales of their deity's exploits to entertain and enlighten the faithful. You could create a mendicant priest background (or modify the acolyte background) to reflect these qualities. It could include musical instrument proficiency, and its feature probably involves receiving hospitality from the faithful.

Guidelines for creating a new background are provided in chapter 9, "Dungeon Master's Workshop."

CAMPAIGN EVENTS

Significant events in the history of a fantasy world tend toward immense upheavals: wars that pit the forces of good against evil in an epic confrontation, natural disasters that lay waste to entire civilizations, invasions of vast armies or extraplanar hordes, assassinations of world leaders. These world-shaking events title the chapters of history.

In a D&D game, such events provide the sparks that can ignite and sustain a campaign. The most common pitfall of serial stories without a set beginning, middle, and end is inertia. Like many television shows and comic-book series, a D&D campaign runs the risk of retreading the same ground long after the enjoyment's gone. Just as actors or writers drift away from those other mediums, so can players—the actors and writers of a D&D game. Games stagnate when the story meanders too long without a change in tone, when the same villains and similar adventures grow tiresome and predictable, and when the world doesn't change around the characters and in response to their actions.

World-shaking events force conflict. They set new events and power groups in motion. Their outcomes change the world by altering the tone of the setting in a meaningful way. They chronicle the story of your world in big, bold print. Change—especially change that occurs as a result of the characters' actions—keeps the story moving. If change is imperceptible, the actions of the characters lack significance. When the world becomes reliable, it's time to shake things up.

PUTTING EVENTS IN MOTION

World-shaking events can happen at any time in a campaign or story arc, but the biggest incidents naturally fall at the beginning, middle, and end of a story.

That placement reflects the structure of dramatic stories. At the beginning of a story, something happens to shake the protagonists' world and spur them into action. The characters take action to resolve their problems, but other forces oppose them. As they reach a significant milestone toward their goal, a major conflict disrupts the characters' plans, shaking their world again; failure seems imminent. At the end of the story, they succeed or fail, and the world is shaken again by the way the characters changed it for good or ill.

At the beginning of a D&D campaign, world-shaking events create instant adventure hooks and affect the characters' lives directly. In the middle, they make great turning points as the characters' fortunes reverse—rising after a defeat or falling after a victory. Near the end of a campaign, such events serve as excellent climactic episodes with far-reaching effects. They might even occur after the story has ended, as a result of the characters' actions.

WHEN NOT TO SHAKE IT UP

In constructing a narrative, beware of "false action," or action for its own sake. False action doesn't move a story forward, engage characters, or cause them to change. Many action movies suffer from false action, in which car chases, gunfights, and explosions abound but do little more than inconvenience the characters and eventually bore the audience with their repetition and dearth of meaningful stakes. Some D&D campaigns fall into the same trap, stringing world-spanning disasters together one after another with little impact on the characters or the world. Thus, it's probably not in the DM's best interest to reorder the world every single time there's a lull in the action, lest world-shaking events become ordinary.

As a general rule, a campaign can sustain up to three large-scale, world-shaking events: one near the beginning, one near the middle, and one near the end. Use as many small-scale events that disturb the bounded microcosms of towns, villages, tribes, fiefs, duchies, provinces, and so forth as you like. Every significant event shakes someone's world, after all, no matter how small that world might be. Let unexpected and terrible events regularly afflict the world's smaller territories, but unless your story demands it, save the large-scale map-spanning events for the biggest, most important moments of your campaign.

WORLD-SHAKING EVENTS

You can use this section for ideas and inspiration to expand on world-shaking events already occurring (or soon to occur) within your world. Alternatively, you can roll on the tables below to randomly generate an event to inspire your imagination. The attempt to justify a random result can reveal unforeseen possibilities.

To get started, select a world-shaking event category or roll on the World-Shaking Events table.

WORLD-SHAKING EVENTS

d10	Event
1	Rise of a leader or an era
2	Fall of a leader or an era
3	Cataclysmic disaster
4	Assault or invasion
5	Rebellion, revolution, overthrow
6	Extinction or depletion
7	New organization
8	Discovery, expansion, invention
9	Prediction, omen, prophecy
10	Myth and legend

1-2. RISE OR FALL OF A LEADER OR AN ERA

Eras are often defined by the prominent leaders, innovators, and tyrants of the day. These people change the world and etch their signatures indelibly on the pages of history. When they rise to power, they shape the time and place where they live in monumental ways. When they fall from power or pass away, the ghost of their presence lingers.

Determine the kind of leader that influences the new or passing era. You can choose the type of leader or determine one randomly using the Leader Types table.

LEADER TYPES

d6	Leader Type
1	Political
2	Religious
3	Military
4	Crime/underworld
5	Art/culture
6	Philosophy/learning/magic

Political leaders are monarchs, nobles, and chiefs. Religious leaders include deities' avatars, high priests, and messiahs, as well as those in charge of monasteries and leaders of influential religious sects. Major military leaders control the armed forces of countries. They include military dictators, warlords, and the heads of a ruler's war council. Minor military leaders include the heads of local militias, gangs, and other martial organizations. At the broadest scale, a criminal or underworld leader wields power through a network of spies, bribes, and black-market trade. On the smallest scale, these are local gang bosses, pirate captains, and brigands. A leader in art or culture is a virtuoso whose work reflects the spirit of the age and changes the way people think: a prominent playwright, bard, or court fool in whose words, art, or performance the people perceive universal truth. On a smaller scale, this might be an influential local poet, minstrel, satirist, or sculptor. A major leader in philosophy, learning, or magic is a genius philosopher, a counselor to emperors, an enlightened thinker, the head of the highest institution of learning in the world, or an archmage. A minor leader might be a local sage, seer, hedge wizard, wise elder, or teacher.

Rise of a Leader, Beginning of an Era. In dramatic stories, a new leader's rise often comes at the end of a period of struggle or turmoil. Sometimes it's a war or uprising; other times it's an election, the death of a tyrant, a prophecy fulfilled, or the appointment of a hero. Conversely, the new leader might be a tyrant, a fiend, or black-hearted villain, and the era that just ended could have been one of peace, tranquility, and justice.

A new leader shakes the foundations of your campaign world and begins a new era in the selected region. How does this person or this era begin to affect the world? Here are several things to consider when determining the leader's impact on the world:

- Name one thing that has been consistently true about the world, which is now no longer true due to this leader's rise or influence. This is the biggest change that occurs when the new leader takes power and becomes the prevailing trait that defines the era, the characteristic for which it is remembered.
- Name the person (or people) whose death, defeat, or loss opened the door for this leader to take power. This might be a military defeat, the overthrow of old ideas, a cultural rebirth, or something else. Who died, lost, or was defeated? What weren't they willing to compromise? Was the new leader complicit in the death, defeat, or loss, or was the opportunity serendipitous?
- Despite the leader's virtues, one flaw in particular outrages a certain segment of the populace. What is that flaw? What person or group of persons will do their utmost to foil this leader because of it? Conversely, what is this leader's greatest virtue, and who rises to the leader's defense because of it?
- Who believes in this leader now, but still retains doubts? This is someone close to the leader, who has the leader's trust and knows his or her secret fears, doubts, or vices.

Fall of a Leader, End of an Era. All that begins must end. With the fall of kings and queens, the maps of the world are redrawn. Laws change, new customs become all the rage, and old ones fall out of favor. The attitude of the citizens toward their fallen leader shifts subtly at first and then changes dramatically as they look back or reminisce about the time before.

The fallen leader might have been a benevolent ruler, an influential citizen, or even an adversary to the characters. How does the death of this person affect those formerly under his or her influence? Here are several things to consider when determining the effects of a leader's passing:

- Name one positive change that the leader brought to his or her domain or sphere of influence. Does that change persist after the leader's death?
- State the general mood or attitude of the people under this person's power. What important fact didn't they realize about this person or his or her reign, which will later come to light?
- Name one person or group that tries to fill the leader's shoes in the resulting power vacuum.

- Name one person or group that plotted against this leader.
- Name three things for which this leader will be remembered.

3. Cataclysmic Disaster

Earthquake, famine, fire, plague, flood—disasters on a grand scale can eradicate whole civilizations without warning. Natural (or magical) catastrophes redraw maps, destroy economies, and alter worlds. Sometimes the survivors rebuild from the ruins. The Great Chicago Fire, for instance, provided an opportunity to rebuild the city according to a modern plan. Most of the time the disaster leaves only ruins—buried under ash like Pompeii, or sunk beneath the waves like Atlantis.

You can choose the cataclysm or determine one randomly using the Cataclysmic Disasters table.

Cataclysmic Disasters

d10	Cataclysmic Disaster
1	Earthquake
2	Famine/drought
3	Fire
4	Flood
5	Plague/disease
6	Rain of fire (meteoric impact)
7	Storm (hurricane, tornado, tsunami)
8	Volcanic eruption
9	Magic gone awry or a planar warp
10	Divine judgment

Some of the disasters on the table might not make immediate sense in the context of your campaign world. A flood in the desert? A volcanic eruption on grassy plains? If you randomly determine a disaster that conflicts with your setting, you can reroll, but the challenge of justifying the catastrophe can produce interesting results.

With two exceptions, the disasters on the table resemble those that affect our own world. Think of planar warps and magic gone awry like nuclear incidents; they're big events that unnaturally alter the land and its people. For example, in the Eberron campaign setting, a magical catastrophe lays waste to an entire country, transforming it into a hostile wasteland and ending the Last War.

Divine judgment is something else entirely. This disaster takes whatever form you want, but it's always a big, bold, unsubtle sign of a deity's displeasure.

You might decide to wipe a town, region, or nation off the map of your world. A disaster ravages the land and effectively eliminates a place the characters once knew. Leave one or two survivors to tell the characters what happened, and ensure that the characters feel the depth of the catastrophe. What are the ongoing effects of this cataclysm? The following points can help you define the nature and consequences of the disaster:

- Decide what caused this cataclysm and where it originated.
- An omen presaged this event, or a series of signs and omens. Describe the omen in detail.

- Describe or name the creature that warned the populace about the oncoming disaster. Who listened?
- Who were the lucky (or unlucky) ones who survived?
- Describe what the area looks like after the disaster, in contrast to how it looked before.

4. Assault or Invasion

One of the most common world-shaking events, an invasion occurs when one group forcibly takes over another, usually by military strength, but also by infiltration and occupation.

An assault differs from an invasion in that the attacking force isn't necessarily interested in occupation or taking power. On the other hand, an assault might be the first step of an invasion.

Regardless of the scale, a world-shaking assault or invasion stands out because its repercussions change the characters' world, and its effects echo long after the initial attack or takeover.

Imagine that part of your campaign world is attacked or invaded. Depending on the current scale of your campaign, the area might be as small as a section of a city or as large as a continent, world, or plane of existence.

Define the aggressor and whether it represents a known enemy or a previously unknown adversary. Select a threat that already poses a danger to the area you've chosen, or use the Invading Forces table to determine the aggressor.

Invading Forces

d8	Invading Force
1	A criminal enterprise
2	Monsters or a unique monster
3	A planar threat
4	A past adversary reawakened, reborn, or resurgent
5	A splinter faction
6	A savage tribe
7	A secret society
8	A traitorous ally

Now consider these other aspects of the conflict:

- Name one element of the invasion or assault that the defenders didn't expect or couldn't repel.
- Something happened to the first defenders who stood against the invasion or assault—something no one wants to talk about. What was it?
- The attackers or invaders had a motive for their action that wasn't obvious or understood at first. What was it?
- Who turned traitor, and at what point did they turn? Why did they do it? Did an attacker try to stop the incursion, or did a prominent defender throw in with the invaders?

5. Rebellion, Revolution, Overthrow

Dissatisfied with the current order, a person or group of people overturns the dominant regime and takes over—or fails to take over. Regardless of the result, a revolution (even an attempted one) can shape the destiny of nations.

The scale of a revolution need not involve the common masses against the nobility. A revolution can be as small as a merchants' guild revolting against its leadership or a temple overthrowing its priesthood in favor of a new creed. The spirits of the forest might attempt to overthrow the forces of civilization in a nearby city that cut down trees for timber. Alternatively, the scale can be as dramatic as humanity rising to overthrow the gods.

Imagine that part of your campaign world erupts in revolution. Pick a power group in your current campaign and name (or invent) a group that opposes it, fomenting revolution. Then let the following points help you flesh out the conflict:

- Name three things the rebels want or hope to achieve.
- The rebels achieve a victory against those they wish to overthrow, even if it's a pyrrhic victory. Which of their three goals do they achieve? How long is this achievement likely to last?
- State the cost exacted upon the old order after its fall from power. Does anyone from the former power group remain in power during the next regime? If the old order remains in power, describe one way that its leaders punish the revolutionaries.
- One of the rebellion's prominent leaders—in some respects the face of the revolution—was driven by a personal reason for his or her part in events. Describe this person and state the true reason he or she led the rebellion.
- What problem existed before the revolution that persists in spite of it?

6. Extinction or Depletion

Something that once existed in the campaign world is gone. The lost resource might be a precious metal, a species of plant or animal that held an important place in the local ecology, or an entire race or culture of people. Its absence causes a chain reaction that affects every creature that uses or relies on it.

You can eliminate a people, place, or thing that previously existed in a certain location or area in your campaign world. On a small scale, the last of a family dynasty passes away or a once-thriving mining town in the region dries up and becomes a ghost town. On a grand scale, magic dies, the last dragon is slain, or the final fey noble departs the world.

What is gone from the world—or the region of the world you've chosen—that once existed there? If the answer isn't immediately evident, consult the Extinction or Depletion table for ideas.

Extinction or Depletion

d8	Lost Resource
1	A kind of animal (insect, bird, fish, livestock)
2	Habitable land
3	Magic or magic-users (all magic, or specific kinds or schools of magic)
4	A mineral resource (gems, metals, ores)
5	A type of monster (unicorn, manticore, dragon)
6	A people (family line, clan, culture, race)
7	A kind of plant (crop, tree, herb, forest)
8	A waterway (river, lake, ocean)

Then consider these additional questions:

- Name a territory, race, or type of creature that relied on the thing that was lost. How do they compensate? How do they attempt to substitute for what was lost?

- Who or what is to blame for the loss?
- Describe an immediate consequence of the loss. Forecast one way that the loss impacts or changes the world in the long term. Who or what suffers the most as a result of the loss? Who or what benefits the most from it?

7. NEW ORGANIZATION

The foundation of a new order, kingdom, religion, society, cabal, or cult can shake the world with its actions, doctrine, dogma, and policies. On a local scale, a new organization contends with existing power groups, influencing, subverting, dominating, or allying with them to create a stronger base of power. Large and powerful organizations can exert enough influence to rule the world. Some new organizations benefit the populace, while others grow to threaten the civilization they once protected.

Perhaps an important new organization arises in one part of your world. It could have humble or auspicious beginnings, but one thing is certain: it is destined to change the world as long as it progresses along its present course. Sometimes an organization's alignment is apparent from inception, but its morality can remain ambiguous until its doctrines, policies, and traditions are revealed over time. Choose the type of organization, or use the New Organizations table to generate ideas.

NEW ORGANIZATIONS

d10	New Organization
1	Crime syndicate/bandit confederacy
2	Guild (masons, apothecaries, goldsmiths)
3	Magical circle/society
4	Military/knightly order
5	New family dynasty/tribe/clan
6	Philosophy/discipline dedicated to a principle or ideal
7	Realm (village, town, duchy, kingdom)
8	Religion/sect/denomination
9	School/university
10	Secret society/cult/cabal

Then consider some or all of the following options:

- The new order supplants a current power group in the world, gaining territory, converts, or defectors and reducing the previous power group's numbers. Who or what does the foundation of this new order supplant?
- The new order appeals to a specific audience. Decide whether this order attracts a certain race, social class, or character class.
- The leader of this new order is known for a particular quality valued by his or her followers. Elaborate on why they respect him or her for this quality, and what actions this leader has taken to retain the followers' support.
- A rival group opposes the foundation of this new organization. Choose an existing power group from your campaign to oppose the new organization, or create one from the categories on the table. Decide why they oppose the new group, who leads them, and what they plan to do to stop their rival.

8. DISCOVERY, EXPANSION, INVENTION

Discoveries of new lands expand the map and change the boundaries of empires. Discoveries of new magic or technology expand the boundaries of what was once thought possible. New resources or archaeological finds create opportunity and wealth and set prospectors and power groups in motion to vie for their control.

A new discovery—or rediscovery—can impact your campaign world in a meaningful way, shaping the course of history and the events of the age. Think of this discovery as a big adventure hook or series of hooks. This is also an opportunity to create a unique monster, item, god, plane, or race for your world. As long as the discovery matters, it doesn't have to be wholly original, just flavored for your campaign.

A discovery is particularly impressive when the adventurers in your campaign are the ones who make it. If they discover a new mineral with magical properties, map a new land that's eminently suitable for colonization, or uncover an ancient weapon with the power to wreak devastation on your world, they are likely to set major events in motion. This gives the players the opportunity to see exactly how much influence their actions have on your world.

Decide on the type of discovery that is made or use the Discoveries table to generate ideas.

DISCOVERIES

d10	Discovery
1	Ancient ruin/lost city of a legendary race
2	Animal/monster/magical mutation
3	Invention/technology/magic (helpful, destructive)
4	New (or forgotten) god or planar entity
5	New (or rediscovered) artifact or religious relic
6	New land (island, continent, lost world, demiplane)
7	Otherworldly object (planar portal, alien spacecraft)
8	People (race, tribe, lost civilization, colony)
9	Plant (miracle herb, fungal parasite, sentient plant)
10	Resource or wealth (gold, gems, mithral)

Once you have determined the type of discovery, flesh it out by deciding exactly what it is, who discovered it, and what potential effect it could have on the world. Ideally, previous adventures in your campaign will help you fill in the blanks, but also keep the following in mind:

- This discovery benefits a particular person, group, or faction more than others. Who benefits most? Name three benefits they stand to gain from this discovery.
- This discovery directly harms another person, group, or faction. Who is harmed the most?
- This discovery has consequences. Name three repercussions or side effects. Who ignores the repercussions?
- Name two or three individuals or factions struggling to possess or control this discovery. Who is likely to win? What do they stand to gain, and what are they willing to do to control the discovery?

9. Prediction, Omen, Prophecy

Sometimes the foretelling of a world-shaking event becomes a world-shaking event: an omen that predicts the fall of empires, the doom of races, and the end of the world. Sometimes an omen points to change for the good, such as the arrival of a legendary hero or savior. But the most dramatic prophecies warn of future tragedies and predict dark ages. Unlike other world-shaking events, the outcome doesn't happen immediately. Instead, individuals or factions strive to fulfill or avert the prophecy—or shape the exact way it will be fulfilled—according to how it will affect them. The prophecy's helpers or hinderers create adventure hooks in the campaign by the actions they take. A prophecy should foretell a big event on a grand scale, since it will take time to come true (or be averted).

Imagine that a world-shaking prophecy comes to light. If events continue on their present course, the prophecy will come true and the world will change dramatically as a result. Don't shy away from making this prophecy both significant and alarming, keeping in mind the following points:

- Create a prophecy that foretells a major change to the campaign world. You can build one from scratch using ideas from the current campaign or randomly determine a world-shaking event and flesh out the details.
- Write a list of three or more omens that will occur before the prophecy comes to pass. You can use events that have already occurred in the campaign so that the prophecy is closer to being fulfilled. The rest are events that might or might not happen, depending on the actions of the characters.
- Describe the person or creature that discovered the prophecy and how it was found. What did this creature gain by revealing it? What did this person lose or sacrifice?
- Describe the individual or faction that supports the prophecy and works to ensure its fulfillment, and the one that will do all in its power to avert the prophecy. What is the first step each takes? Who suffers for their efforts?
- One part of the prophecy is wrong. Choose one of the omens you listed or one of the details you created for the world-shaking event that the omen predicts. The chosen omen is false, and if applicable, its opposite is true instead.

10. Myth and Legend

If wars, plagues, discoveries, and the like can be called regular world-shaking events, mythic events exceed and surpass them. A mythic event might occur as the fulfillment of an ancient or long-forgotten prophecy, or it might be an act of divine intervention.

Once again, your current campaign probably provides a few ideas for the shape of this event. If you need inspiration, roll a d8 on the World-Shaking Events table, instead of the normal d10. Address the bullet-point notes for that disaster, but magnify the result to the grandest scale you can imagine.

The rise or fall of a leader or era is the death or birth of a god, or the end of an age or the world. A cataclysmic disaster is a world-drowning deluge, an ice age, or a zombie apocalypse. An assault or invasion is a world war, a world-spanning demonic incursion, the awakening of a world-threatening monster, or the final clash between good and evil. A rebellion dethrones a god or gods, or raises a new force (such as a demon lord) to divinity. A new organization is a world-spanning empire or a pantheon of new gods. A discovery is a doomsday device or a portal to eldritch dimensions where world-shattering cosmic horrors dwell.

Tracking Time

A calendar lets you record the passage of time in the campaign. More importantly, it lets you plan ahead for the critical events that shake up the world. For simple time tracking, use a calendar for the current year in the real world. Pick a date to indicate the start of the campaign, and make note of the days that adventurers spend on their travels and various activities. The calendar tells you when the seasons change and the lunar cycle. More importantly, you can use your calendar to track important festivals and holidays, as well as key events that shape your campaign.

This method is a good starting point, but the calendar of your world need not follow a modern calendar. If you want to customize your calendar with details unique to your world, consider these types of features.

The Basics

A fantasy world's calendar doesn't have to mirror the modern one, but it can (see "The Calendar of Harptos" sidebar for an example). Do the weeks of a month have names? What about specific days of each month, like the ides, nones, and calends of the Roman calendar?

Physical Cycles

Determine when the seasons fall, marked by the solstices and equinoxes. Do the months correspond to the phases of the moon (or moons)? Do strange and magical effects occur at the same time as these phenomena?

Religious Observances

Sprinkle holy days throughout your calendar. Each significant deity in your world should have at least one holy day during the year, and some gods' holy days correspond to celestial phenomena such as new moons or equinoxes. Holy days reflect the portfolio of a deity (a god of agriculture is honored in the harvest season) or significant events in the history of the deity's worship, such as the birth or death of a holy person, the date of a god's manifestation, the accession of the current high priest, and so on.

Certain holy days are civic events, observed by every citizen of a town where a god's temple can be found. Harvest festivals are often celebrations on a grand scale. Other holy days are important only to people particularly devoted to a single deity. Still others are observed by priests, who perform private rites and sacrifices inside their temples on certain days or specific times of day. And some holy days are local, observed by the faithful of a specific temple.

Give some thought to how priests and common folk celebrate holy days. Going into a temple, sitting in a pew, and listening to a sermon is a mode of worship foreign to most fantasy religions. More commonly, celebrants offer sacrifices to their gods. The faithful bring animals to the temple to be slaughtered or burn incense as an offering. The wealthiest citizens bring the largest animals, to flaunt their wealth and demonstrate their piety. People pour out libations at the graves of their ancestors. They spend all-night vigils in darkened shrines or enjoy splendid feasts celebrating a god's bounty.

CIVIC OBSERVANCES

Holy days provide the majority of the special celebrations in most calendars, but local or national festivals account for many others. The birthday of a monarch, the anniversary of a great victory in a war, craft festivals, market days, and similar events all provide excuses for local celebrations.

FANTASTIC EVENTS

Since your setting is a fantasy world and not a mundane medieval society, add in a few events of an obviously magical nature. For example, perhaps a ghostly castle appears on a certain hill on the winter solstice every year, or every third full moon fills lycanthropes with a particularly strong bloodlust. Also, the thirteenth night of every month could mark the ghostly wanderings of a long-forgotten nomadic tribe.

Extraordinary events, such as the approach of a comet or a lunar eclipse, make good adventure elements, and you can drop them in your calendar wherever you want. Your calendar can tell you when there's a full moon for a lunar eclipse, but you can always fudge the date for a particular effect.

ENDING A CAMPAIGN

A campaign's ending should tie up all the threads of its beginning and middle, but you don't have to take a campaign all the way to 20th level for it to be satisfying. Wrap up the campaign whenever your story reaches its natural conclusion.

Make sure you allow space and time near the end of your campaign for the characters to finish up any personal goals. Their own stories need to end in a satisfying way, just as the campaign story does. Ideally, some of the characters' individual goals will be fulfilled by the ultimate goal of the final adventure. Give characters with unfinished goals a chance to finish them before the very end.

Once the campaign has ended, a new one can begin. If you intend to run a new campaign for the same group of players, using their previous characters' actions as the basis of legends gives them immediate investment in the new setting. Let the new characters experience how the world has changed because of their old characters. In the end, though, the new campaign is a new story with new protagonists. They shouldn't have to share the spotlight with the heroes of days gone by.

THE CALENDAR OF HARPTOS

The world of the Forgotten Realms uses the Calendar of Harptos, named after the long-dead wizard who invented it. Each year of 365 days is divided into twelve months of thirty days each, which roughly correspond to months in the real-world Gregorian calendar. Each month is divided into three tendays. Five special holidays fall between the months and mark the seasons. Another special holiday, Shieldmeet, is inserted into the calendar after Midwinter every four years, much like leap years in the modern Gregorian calendar.

Month	Name	Common Name
1	Hammer	Deepwinter
Annual holiday: Midwinter		
Quadrennial holiday: Shieldmeet		
2	Alturiak	The Claw of Winter
3	Ches	The Claw of the Sunsets
4	Tarsakh	The Claw of the Storms
Annual holiday: Greengrass		
5	Mirtul	The Melting
6	Kythorn	The Time of Flowers
7	Flamerule	Summertide
Annual holiday: Midsummer		
8	Eleasias	Highsun
9	Eleint	The Fading
Annual holiday: Highharvesttide		
10	Marpenoth	Leaffall
11	Uktar	The Rotting
Annual holiday: The Feast of the Moon		
12	Nightal	The Drawing Down

PLAY STYLE

By building a new world (or adopting an existing one) and creating the key events that launch your campaign, you determined what your campaign is about. Next, you have to decide how you want to run your campaign.

What's the right way to run a campaign? That depends on your play style and the motivations of your players. Consider your players' tastes, your strengths as a DM, table rules (discussed in part 3), and the type of game you want to run. Describe to the players how you envision the game experience and let them give you input. The game is theirs, too. Lay that groundwork early, so your players can make informed choices and help you maintain the type of game you want to run.

Consider the following two exaggerated examples of play style.

HACK AND SLASH

The adventurers kick in the dungeon door, fight the monsters, and grab the treasure. This style of play is straightforward, fun, exciting, and action-oriented. The players spend relatively little time developing personas for their characters, roleplaying noncombat situations, or discussing anything other than the immediate dangers of the dungeon.

In such a game, the adventurers face clearly evil monsters and opponents and occasionally meet clearly good and helpful NPCs. Don't expect the adventurers to anguish over what to do with prisoners, or to debate whether it's right or wrong to invade and wipe out a bugbear lair. Don't track money or time spent in town. Once they've completed a task, send the adventurers back into the action as quickly as possible. Character motivation need be no more developed than a desire to kill monsters and acquire treasure.

IMMERSIVE STORYTELLING

Waterdeep is threatened by political turmoil. The adventurers must convince the Masked Lords, the city's secret rulers, to resolve their differences, but can do so only after both the characters and the lords have come to terms with their differing outlooks and agendas. This style of gaming is deep, complex, and challenging. The focus isn't on combat but on negotiations, political maneuverings, and character interaction. A whole game session might pass without a single attack roll.

In this style of game, the NPCs are as complex and richly detailed as the adventurers, although the focus lies on motivation and personality, not game statistics. Expect long digressions from each player about what his or her character does, and why. Going to a temple to ask a priest for advice can be as important an encounter as fighting orcs. (And don't expect the adventurers to fight the orcs at all unless they are motivated to do so.) A character will sometimes take actions against the player's better judgment, because "that's what the character would do."

Since combat isn't the focus, game rules take a back seat to character development. Ability check modifiers and skill proficiencies take precedence over combat bonuses. Feel free to change or ignore rules to fit the players' roleplaying needs, using the advice presented in part 3 of this book.

SOMETHING IN BETWEEN

The style of play in most campaigns falls between these two extremes. There's plenty of action, but the campaign offers an ongoing storyline and interaction between characters as well. Players develop their characters' motivations and relish the chance to prove their skills in combat. To maintain the balance, provide a mixture of roleplaying encounters and combat encounters. Even in a dungeon setting, you can present NPCs that aren't meant to be fought but rather helped out, negotiated with, or just talked to.

Think about your preferred style of play by considering these questions:

- Are you a fan of realism and gritty consequences, or are you more focused on making the game seem like an action movie?
- Do you want the game to maintain a sense of medieval fantasy, or do you want to explore alternate time lines or modern thinking?
- Do you want to maintain a serious tone, or is humor your goal?
- Even if you are serious, is the action lighthearted or intense?
- Is bold action key, or do the players need to be thoughtful and cautious?
- Do you like to plan thoroughly in advance, or do you prefer improvising on the spot?
- Is the game full of varied D&D elements, or does it center on a theme such as horror?
- Is the game for all ages, or does it involve mature themes?
- Are you comfortable with moral ambiguity, such as allowing the characters to explore whether the end justifies the means? Or are you happier with straightforward heroic principles, such as justice, sacrifice, and helping the downtrodden?

A WORLD TO EXPLORE

Much of a campaign involves the adventurers traveling from place to place, exploring the environment, and learning about the fantasy world. This exploration can take place in any environment, including a vast wilderness, a labyrinthine dungeon, the shadowy passages of the Underdark, the crowded streets of a city, and the undulating waters of the sea. Determining a way around an obstacle, finding a hidden object, investigating a strange feature of a dungeon, deciphering clues, solving puzzles, and bypassing or disabling traps can all be part of exploration.

Sometimes exploration is an incidental part of the game. For instance, you might gloss over an unimportant journey by telling the players that they spend three uneventful days on the road before moving along to the next point of interest. Other times exploration is the focus, a chance to describe a wondrous part of the world or story that increases the players' feeling of immersion. Similarly, you should consider playing up exploration if your players enjoy solving puzzles, finding their way around obstacles, and searching dungeon corridors for secret doors.

Character Names

Part of your campaign style has to do with naming characters. It's a good idea to establish some ground rules with your players at the start of a new campaign. In a group consisting of Sithis, Travok, Anastrianna, and Kairon, the human fighter named Bob II sticks out, especially when he's identical to Bob I, who was killed by kobolds. If everyone takes a lighthearted approach to names, that's fine. If the group would rather take the characters and their names a little more seriously, urge Bob's player to come up with a more appropriate name.

Player character names should match each other in flavor or concept, and they should also match the flavor of your campaign world—so should the nonplayer characters' names and place names you create. Travok and Kairon don't want to undertake a quest for Lord Cupcake, visit Gumdrop Island, or take down a crazy wizard named Ray.

Continuing or Episodic Campaigns

The backbone of a campaign is a connected series of adventures, but you can connect them in two different ways.

In a continuing campaign, the connected adventures share a sense of a larger purpose or a recurring theme (or themes). The adventures might feature returning villains, grand conspiracies, or a single mastermind who's ultimately behind every adventure of the campaign.

A continuing campaign designed with a theme and a story arc in mind can feel like a great fantasy epic. The players derive the satisfaction of knowing the actions they take during one adventure matter in the next. Plotting and running that kind of campaign can be demanding on the DM, but the payoff is a great and memorable story.

An episodic campaign, in contrast, is like a television show where each week's episode is a self-contained story that doesn't play into any overarching plot. It might be built on a premise that explains its nature: the player characters are adventurers-for-hire, or explorers venturing into the unknown and facing a string of unrelated dangers. They might even be archaeologists, venturing into one ancient ruin after another in search of artifacts. An episodic game like this lets you create adventures—or buy published ones—and drop them into your campaign without worrying about how they fit with the adventures that came before and follow after.

Campaign Theme

A theme in a campaign, as in a work of literature, expresses the deeper meaning of a story and the fundamental elements of human experience that the story explores. Your campaign doesn't have to be a work of literature, but it can still draw on common themes that lend a distinctive flavor to its stories. Consider these examples:

- A campaign about confronting the inevitability of mortality, whether embodied in undead monsters or expressed through the death of loved ones.
- A campaign revolving around an insidious evil, whether dark gods, monstrous races such as the yuan-ti, or creatures of unknown realms far removed from mortal concerns. As heroes confront this evil, they must face the selfish, cold tendencies of their own kind as well.
- A campaign featuring troubled heroes who confront not only the savagery of the bestial creatures of the world, but also the beast within—the rage and fury that lies in their own hearts.
- A campaign exploring the insatiable thirst for power and domination, whether embodied by the hosts of the Nine Hells or by humanoid rulers bent on conquering the world.

With a theme such as "confrontation with mortality," you can craft a broad range of adventures that aren't necessarily connected by a common villain. One adventure might feature the dead bursting from their graves and threatening to overwhelm a whole town. In the next adventure, a mad wizard creates a flesh golem in an effort to revive his lost love. A villain could go to extreme lengths to achieve immortality to avoid confronting its own demise. The adventurers might help a ghost accept death and move on, or one of the adventurers might even become a ghost!

Variations on a Theme

Mixing things up once in a while allows your players to enjoy a variety of adventures. Even a tightly themed campaign can stray now and then. If your campaign heavily involves intrigue, mystery, and roleplaying, your players might enjoy the occasional dungeon crawl—especially if the tangent is revealed to relate to a larger plot in the campaign. If most of your adventures are dungeon expeditions, shift gears with a tense urban mystery that eventually leads the party into a dungeon crawl in an abandoned building or tower. If you run horror adventures week after week, try using a villain who turns out to be ordinary, perhaps even silly. Comic relief is a great variation on almost any D&D campaign, though players usually provide it themselves.

Tiers of Play

As characters grow in power, their ability to change the world around them grows with them. It helps to think ahead when creating your campaign to account for this change. As the characters make a greater impact on the world, they face greater danger whether they want to or not. Powerful factions see them as a threat and plot against them, while friendly ones court their favor in hopes of striking a useful alliance.

The tiers of play represent the ideal milestones for introducing new world-shaking events to the campaign. As the characters resolve one event, a new danger arises or the prior trouble transforms into a new threat in response to the characters' actions. Events need to grow in magnitude and scope, increasing the stakes and drama as the characters become increasingly powerful.

This approach also allows you to break your design work down into smaller pieces. Create material such as adventures, NPCs, maps, and so on for one tier at a time. You only need to worry about the details of the next tier as the characters approach it. Even better, as the campaign takes unexpected turns in response to the players' choices, you don't have to worry about redoing much work.

LEVELS 1–4: LOCAL HEROES

Characters in this tier are still learning the range of class features that define them, including their choice of specialization. But even 1st-level characters are heroes, set apart from the common people by natural characteristics, learned skills, and the hint of a greater destiny that lies before them.

At the start of their careers, characters use 1st- and 2nd-level spells and wield mundane gear. The magic items they find include common consumable items (potions and scrolls) and a very few uncommon permanent items. Their magic can have a big impact in a single encounter, but it doesn't change the course of an adventure.

The fate of a village might hang on the success or failure of low-level adventurers, who trust their lives to their fledgling abilities. These characters navigate dangerous terrain and explore haunted crypts, where they can expect to fight savage orcs, ferocious wolves, giant spiders, evil cultists, bloodthirsty ghouls, and hired thugs. If they face even a young dragon, they're better off avoiding a fight.

LEVELS 5–10: HEROES OF THE REALM

By the time they reach this tier, adventurers have mastered the basics of their class features, though they continue to improve throughout these levels. They have found their place in the world and have begun to involve themselves in the dangers that surround them.

Dedicated spellcasters learn 3rd-level spells at the start of this tier. Suddenly characters can fly, damage large numbers of foes with *fireball* and *lightning bolt* spells, and even breathe underwater. They master 5th-level spells by the end of the tier, and spells such as *teleportation circle*, *scrying*, *flame strike*, *legend lore*, and *raise dead* can have a significant impact on their adventures. They start acquiring more permanent magic items (uncommon and rare ones) as well, which will serve them for the rest of their careers.

The fate of a region might depend on the adventures that characters of levels 5 to 10 undertake. These adventurers venture into fearsome wilds and ancient ruins, where they confront savage giants, ferocious hydras, fearless golems, evil yuan-ti, scheming devils, bloodthirsty demons, crafty mind flayers, and drow assassins. They might have a chance of defeating a young dragon that has established a lair but not yet extended its reach far into the surrounding territory.

LEVELS 11–16: MASTERS OF THE REALM

By 11th level, characters are shining examples of courage and determination—true paragons in the world, set well apart from the masses. At this tier, adventurers are far more versatile than they were at lower levels, and they can usually find the right tool for a given challenge.

Dedicated spellcasters gain access to 6th-level spells at 11th level, including spells that completely change the way adventurers interact with the world. Their big, flashy spells are significant in combat—*disintegrate*, *blade barrier*, and *heal*, for example—but behind-the-scenes spells such as *word of recall*, *find the path*, *contingency*, *teleport*, and *true seeing* alter the way players approach their adventures. Each spell level after that point introduces new effects with an equally large impact. The adventurers find rare magic items (and very rare ones) that bestow similarly powerful abilities.

The fate of a nation or even the world depends on momentous quests that such characters undertake. Adventurers explore uncharted regions and delve into long-forgotten dungeons, where they confront terrible masterminds of the lower planes, cunning rakshasas and beholders, and hungry purple worms. They might encounter and even defeat a powerful adult dragon that has established a lair and a significant presence in the world.

At this tier, adventurers make their mark on the world in a variety of ways, from the consequences of their adventures to the manner in which they spend their hard-won treasure and exploit their well-deserved reputations. Characters of this level construct fortresses on land deeded them by local rulers. They found guilds, temples, or martial orders. They take on apprentices or students of their own. They broker peace between nations or lead them into war. And their formidable reputations attract the attention of very powerful foes.

LEVELS 17–20: MASTERS OF THE WORLD

By 17th level, characters have superheroic capabilities, and their deeds and adventures are the stuff of legend. Ordinary people can hardly dream of such heights of power—or such terrible dangers.

Dedicated spellcasters at this tier wield earthshaking 9th-level spells such as *wish*, *gate*, *storm of vengeance*, and *astral projection*. Characters have several rare and very rare magic items at their disposal, and begin discovering legendary items such as a *vorpal sword* or a *staff of the magi*.

Adventures at these levels have far-reaching consequences, possibly determining the fate of millions in the Material Plane and even places beyond. Characters traverse otherworldly realms and explore demiplanes and other extraplanar locales, where they fight savage balor demons, titans, archdevils, lich archmages, and even avatars of the gods themselves. The dragons they encounter are wyrms of tremendous power, whose sleep troubles kingdoms and whose waking threatens existence itself.

Characters who reach 20th level have attained the pinnacle of mortal achievement. Their deeds are recorded in the annals of history and recounted by bards for centuries. Their ultimate destinies come to pass. A cleric might be taken up into the heavens to serve as a god's right hand. A warlock could become a patron to other warlocks. Perhaps a wizard unlocks the secret to immortality (or undeath) and spends eons exploring the farthest reaches of the multiverse. A druid might become one with the land, transforming into a nature spirit of a particular place or an aspect of the wild. Other characters could found clans or dynasties that revere the memory of their honored ancestors from generation to generation, create masterpieces of epic literature that are sung and retold for thousands of years, or establish guilds or orders that keep the adventurers' principles and dreams alive.

Reaching this point doesn't necessarily dictate the end of the campaign. These powerful characters might be called on to undertake grand adventures on the cosmic stage. And as a result of these adventures, their capabilities can continue to evolve. Characters gain no more levels at this point, but they can still advance in meaningful ways and continue performing epic deeds that resound throughout the multiverse. Chapter 7 details epic boons you can use as rewards for these characters to maintain a sense of progress.

STARTING AT HIGHER LEVEL

Experienced players familiar with the capabilities of the character classes and impatient for more significant adventures might welcome the idea of starting a campaign with characters above 1st level. Creating a higher-level character uses the same character creation steps outlined in the *Player's Handbook*. Such a character has more hit points, class features, and spells, and probably starts with better equipment.

Starting equipment for characters above 1st level is entirely at your discretion, since you give out treasure at your own pace. That said, you can use the Starting Equipment table as a guide.

FLAVORS OF FANTASY

DUNGEONS & DRAGONS is a fantasy game, but that broad category encompasses a lot of variety. Many different flavors of fantasy exist in fiction and film. Do you want a horrific campaign inspired by the works of H. P. Lovecraft or Clark Ashton Smith? Or do you envision a world of muscled barbarians and nimble thieves, along the lines of the classic sword-and-sorcery books by Robert E. Howard and Fritz Leiber? Your choice can have a impact on the flavor of your campaign.

HEROIC FANTASY

Heroic fantasy is the baseline assumed by the D&D rules. The *Player's Handbook* describes this baseline: a multitude of humanoid races coexist with humans in fantastic worlds. Adventurers bring magical powers to bear against the monstrous threats they face. These characters typically come from ordinary backgrounds, but something impels them into an adventuring life. The adventurers are the "heroes" of the campaign, but they might not be truly heroic, instead pursuing this life for selfish reasons. Technology and society are based on medieval norms, though the culture isn't necessarily European. Campaigns often revolve around delving into ancient dungeons in search of treasure or in an effort to destroy monsters or villains.

This genre is also common in fantasy fiction. Most novels set in the Forgotten Realms are best described as heroic fantasy, following in the footsteps of many of the authors listed in appendix E of the *Player's Handbook*.

SWORD AND SORCERY

A grim, hulking fighter disembowels the high priest of the serpent god on his own altar. A laughing rogue spends ill-gotten gains on cheap wine in filthy taverns. Hardy adventurers venture into the unexplored jungle in search of the fabled City of Golden Masks.

A sword-and-sorcery campaign emulates some of the classic works of fantasy fiction, a tradition that goes back to the roots of the game. Here you'll find a dark, gritty world of evil sorcerers and decadent cities, where

---

STARTING EQUIPMENT

Character Level	Low Magic Campaign	Standard Campaign	High Magic Campaign
1st–4th	Normal starting equipment	Normal starting equipment	Normal starting equipment
5th–10th	500 gp plus 1d10 × 25 gp, normal starting equipment	500 gp plus 1d10 × 25 gp, normal starting equipment	500 gp plus 1d10 × 25 gp, one uncommon magic item, normal starting equipment
11th–16th	5,000 gp plus 1d10 × 250 gp, one uncommon magic item, normal starting equipment	5,000 gp plus 1d10 × 250 gp, two uncommon magic items, normal starting equipment	5,000 gp plus 1d10 × 250 gp, three uncommon magic items, one rare item, normal starting equipment
17th–20th	20,000 gp plus 1d10 × 250 gp, two uncommon magic items, normal starting equipment	20,000 gp plus 1d10 × 250 gp, two uncommon magic items, one rare item, normal starting equipment	20,000 gp plus 1d10 × 250 gp, three uncommon magic items, two rare items, one very rare item, normal starting equipment

the protagonists are motivated more by greed and self-interest than by altruistic virtue. Fighter, rogue, and barbarian characters tend to be far more common than wizards, clerics, or paladins. In such a pulp fantasy setting, those who wield magic often symbolize the decadence and corruption of civilization, and wizards are the classic villains of these settings. Magic items are therefore rare and often dangerous.

Certain DUNGEONS & DRAGONS novels follow in the footsteps of classic sword-and-sorcery novels. The world of Athas (as featured in numerous Dark Sun novels and game products), with its heroic gladiators and tyrannical sorcerer-kings, belongs squarely in this genre.

EPIC FANTASY

A devout paladin in gleaming plate armor braces her lance as she charges a dragon. Bidding farewell to his dear love, a noble wizard sets forth on a quest to close the gate to the Nine Hells that has opened in the remote wilderness. A close-knit band of loyal friends strives to overcome the forces of a tyrannical overlord.

An epic-fantasy campaign emphasizes the conflict between good and evil as a prominent element of the game, with the adventurers more or less squarely on the side of good. These characters are heroes in the best sense, driven by a higher purpose than selfish gain or ambition, and facing incredible dangers without blinking. Characters might struggle with moral quandaries, fighting the evil tendencies within themselves as well as the evil that threatens the world. And the stories of these campaigns often include an element of romance: tragic affairs between star-crossed lovers, passion that transcends even death, and chaste adoration between devout knights and the monarchs and nobles they serve.

The novels of the Dragonlance saga exemplify the tradition of epic fantasy in D&D.

MYTHIC FANTASY

While an angry god tries time and again to destroy him, a clever rogue makes the long journey home from war. Braving the terrifying guardians of the underworld, a noble warrior ventures into the darkness to retrieve the soul of her lost love. Calling on their divine parentage, a group of demigods undertake twelve labors to win the gods' blessings for other mortals.

A mythic-fantasy campaign draws on the themes and stories of ancient myth and legend, from Gilgamesh to Cú Chulainn. Adventurers attempt mighty feats of legend, aided or hindered by the gods or their agents—and they might have divine blood themselves. The monsters and villains they face probably have a similar origin. The minotaur in the dungeon isn't just another bull-headed humanoid, but *the* Minotaur—misbegotten offspring of a philandering god. Adventures might lead the heroes through a series of trials to the realms of the gods in search of a gift or favor.

Such a campaign can draw on the myths and legends of any culture, not just the familiar Greek tales.

DARK FANTASY

Vampires brood on the battlements of their accursed castles. Necromancers toil in dark dungeons to create horrid servants made of dead flesh. Devils corrupt the innocent, and werewolves prowl the night. All of these elements evoke horrific aspects of the fantasy genre.

If you want to put a horror spin on your campaign, you have plenty of material to work with. The *Monster Manual* is full of creatures that perfectly suit a storyline of supernatural horror. The most important element of such a campaign, though, isn't covered by the rules. A dark-fantasy setting requires an atmosphere of building dread, created through careful pacing and evocative description. Your players contribute too; they have to be willing to embrace the mood you're trying to evoke. Whether you want to run a full-fledged dark-fantasy campaign or a single creepy adventure, you should discuss your plans with the players ahead of time to make sure they're on board. Horror can be intense and personal, and not everyone is comfortable with such a game.

Novels and game products set in Ravenloft, the Demiplane of Dread, explore dark-fantasy elements in a D&D context.

INTRIGUE

The corrupt vizier schemes with the baron's oldest daughter to assassinate the baron. A hobgoblin army sends doppelganger spies to infiltrate the city before the invasion. At the embassy ball, the spy in the royal court makes contact with his employer.

Political intrigue, espionage, sabotage, and similar cloak-and-dagger activities can provide the basis for an exciting D&D campaign. In this kind of game, the characters might care more about skill training and making contacts than about attack spells and magic weapons. Roleplaying and social interaction take on greater importance than combat, and the party might go for several sessions without seeing a monster.

Again, make sure your players know ahead of time that you want to run this kind of campaign. Otherwise, a player might create a defense-focused dwarf paladin, only to find he is out of place among half-elf diplomats and tiefling spies.

The Brimstone Angels novels by Erin M. Evans focus on intrigue in the Forgotten Realms setting, from the backstabbing politics of the Nine Hells to the contested succession of Cormyrean royalty.

MYSTERY

Who stole three legendary magic weapons and hid them away in a remote dungeon, leaving a cryptic clue to their location? Who placed the duke into a magical slumber, and what can be done to awaken him? Who murdered the guildmaster, and how did the killer get into the guild's locked vault?

A mystery-themed campaign puts the characters in the role of investigators, perhaps traveling from town to town to crack tough cases the local authorities can't handle. Such a campaign emphasizes puzzles and problem-solving in addition to combat prowess.

A larger mystery might even set the stage for the whole campaign. Why did someone kill the characters' mentor, setting them on the path of adventure? Who really controls the Cult of the Red Hand? In this case, the characters might uncover clues to the greater mystery only once in a while; individual adventures might be at best tangentially related to that theme. A diet of nothing but puzzles can become frustrating, so be sure to mix up the kinds of encounters you present.

Novels in various D&D settings have explored the mystery genre with a fantasy twist. In particular, *Murder in Cormyr* (by Chet Williamson), *Murder in Halruaa* (by Richard S. Meyers), and *Spellstorm* (by Ed Greenwood) are mysteries set in the Forgotten Realms. *Murder in Tarsis* (by John Maddox Roberts) takes the same approach in the Dragonlance setting.

SWASHBUCKLING

Rapier-wielding sailors fight off boarding sahuagin. Ghouls lurk in derelict ships, waiting to devour treasure hunters. Dashing rogues and charming paladins weave their way through palace intrigues and leap from balconies onto waiting horses below.

The swashbuckling adventures of pirates and musketeers suggest opportunities for a dynamic campaign. The characters typically spend more time in cities, royal courts, and seafaring vessels than in dungeon delves, making interaction skills important (though not to the extent of a pure intrigue campaign). Nevertheless, the heroes might end up in classic dungeon situations, such as searching storm sewers beneath the palace to find the evil duke's hidden chambers.

A good example of a swashbuckling rogue in the Forgotten Realms is Jack Ravenwild, who appears in novels by Richard Baker (*City of Ravens* and *Prince of Ravens*).

WAR

A hobgoblin army marches toward the city, leading elephants and giants to batter down the stronghold's walls and ramparts. Dragons wheel above a barbarian horde, scattering enemies as the raging warriors cut a swath through field and forest. Salamanders muster at an efreeti's command, poised to assault an astral fortress.

Warfare in a fantasy world is rife with opportunities for adventure. A war campaign isn't generally concerned with the specifics of troop movements, but instead focuses on the heroes whose actions turn the tide of battle. The characters carry out specific missions: capture a magical standard that empowers undead armies, gather reinforcements to break a siege, or cut through the enemy's flank to reach a demonic commander. In other situations, the party supports the larger army by holding a strategic location until reinforcements arrive, killing enemy scouts before they can report, or cutting off supply lines. Information gathering and diplomatic missions can supplement the more combat-oriented adventures.

The War of the Lance in the Dragonlance Chronicles novels and the War of the Spider Queen in the novel series of the same name are prominent examples of wars in D&D novels.

WUXIA

When a sensei disappears mysteriously, her young students must take her place and hunt down the oni terrorizing their village. Accomplished heroes, masters of their respective martial arts, return home to free their village from an evil hobgoblin warlord. The rakshasa master of a nearby monastery performs rituals to raise troubled ghosts from their rest.

A campaign that draws on elements of Asian martial-arts movies is a perfect match for D&D. Players can define the appearance of their characters and gear however they like for the campaign, and spells need only minor flavor changes so that they better reflect such a setting. For example, when the characters use spells or special abilities that teleport them short distances, they actually make high-flying acrobatic leaps. Ability checks to climb don't involve careful searching for holds but let characters bounce up walls or from tree to tree. Warriors stun their opponents by striking pressure points. Flavorful descriptions of actions in the game don't change the nuts and bolts of the rules, but they make all the difference in the feel of a campaign.

Similarly, a class doesn't need new rules to reflect a cultural influence; a new name can do the trick. A traditional Chinese wuxia hero might be a paladin who has a sword called the Oath of Vengeance, while a Japanese samurai might be a paladin with a particular Oath of Devotion (*bushido*) that includes fealty to a lord (*daimyo*) among its tenets. A ninja is a monk who pursues the Way of Shadow. Whether called a wu jen, a tsukai, or a swami, a wizard, sorcerer, or warlock character works just fine in a game inspired by medieval Asian cultures.

WUXIA WEAPON NAMES

Having players refer to a *tetsubo* or a *katana* rather than a greatclub or a longsword can enhance the flavor of a wuxia campaign. The Wuxia Weapon Names table lists alternative names for common weapons from the *Player's Handbook* and identifies their real-world cultural origins. An alternative name changes none of the weapon's properties as they are described in the *Player's Handbook*.

CROSSING THE STREAMS

The renowned paladin Murlynd, from the world of Oerth (as featured in Greyhawk novels and game products), dresses in the traditional garb of Earth's Old West and wears a pair of six-shooters strapped to his waist. The Mace of St. Cuthbert, a holy weapon belonging to Greyhawk's god of justice, found its way to the Victoria and Albert Museum in London in 1985. Somewhere in the Barrier Peaks of Oerth, the wreckage of a spacefaring vessel is said to lie, with bizarre alien lifeforms and strange items of technology on board. And the famous wizard Elminster of the Forgotten Realms has been said to make occasional appearances in the kitchen of Canadian writer Ed Greenwood—where he is sometimes joined by wizards from the worlds of Oerth and Krynn (homeworld of the Dragonlance saga).

Deep in D&D's roots are elements of science fiction and science fantasy, and your campaign might draw on those sources as well. It's okay to send your characters hurtling through a magic mirror to Lewis Carroll's Wonderland, put them aboard a ship traveling between the stars, or set your campaign in a far-future world where laser blasters and *magic missiles* exist side by side. The possibilities are limitless. Chapter 9, "Dungeon Master's Workshop," provides tools for exploring those possibilities.

WUXIA WEAPON NAMES

Weapon	Other Names (Culture)
Battleaxe	*fu* (China); *masakari* (Japan)
Club	*bian* (China); *tonfa* (Japan)
Dagger	*bishou, tamo* (China); *kozuka, tanto* (Japan)
Dart	*shuriken* (Japan)
Flail	*nunchaku* (Japan)
Glaive	*guandao* (China); *bisento, naginata* (Japan)
Greatclub	*tetsubo* (Japan)
Greatsword	*changdao* (China); *nodachi* (Japan)
Halberd	*ji* (China); *kamayari* (Japan)
Handaxe	*ono* (Japan)
Javelin	*mau* (China); *uchi-ne* (Japan)
Lance	*umayari* (Japan)
Longbow	*daikyu* (Japan)
Longsword	*jian* (China); *katana* (Japan)
Mace	*chui* (China); *kanabo* (Japan)
Pike	*mao* (China); *nagaeyari* (Japan)
Quarterstaff	*gun* (China); *bo* (Japan)
Scimitar	*liuyedao* (China); *wakizashi* (Japan)
Shortbow	*hankyu* (Japan)
Shortsword	*shuangdao* (China)
Sickle	*kama* (Japan)
Spear	*qiang* (China); *yari* (Japan)
Trident	*cha* (China); *magariyari* (Japan)
War pick	*fang* (China); *kuwa* (Japan)

Chapter 2: Creating a Multiverse

HEN ADVENTURERS REACH HIGHER LEVELS, their path extends to other dimensions of reality: the planes of existence that form the multiverse. The characters might be called on to rescue a friend from the horrific depths of the Abyss or to sail the shining waters of the River Oceanus. They can hoist a tankard with the friendly giants of Ysgard or face the chaos of Limbo to contact a wizened githzerai sage.

Planes of existence define the extremes of strange and often dangerous environments. The most bizarre locations present settings undreamed of in the natural world. Planar adventures offer unprecedented dangers and wonders. Adventurers walk on streets made of solid fire, or test their mettle on a battlefield where the fallen are resurrected with each dawn.

The Planes

The various planes of existence are realms of myth and mystery. They're not simply other worlds, but dimensions formed and governed by spiritual and elemental principles.

The Outer Planes are realms of spirituality and thought. They are the spheres where celestials, fiends, and deities exist. The plane of Elysium, for example, isn't merely a place where good creatures dwell, and not even simply the place where spirits of good creatures go when they die. It is the plane of goodness, a spiritual realm where evil can't flourish. It is as much a state of being and of mind as it is a physical location.

The Inner Planes exemplify the physical essence and elemental nature of air, earth, fire, and water. The Elemental Plane of Fire, for example, embodies the essence of fire. The plane's entire substance is suffused with the fundamental nature of fire: energy, passion, transformation, and destruction. Even objects of solid brass or basalt seem to dance with flame, in a visible and palpable manifestation of the vibrancy of fire's dominion.

In this context, the Material Plane is the nexus where all these philosophical and elemental forces collide in the jumbled existence of mortal life and matter. The worlds of D&D exist within the Material Plane, making it the starting point for most campaigns and adventures. The rest of the multiverse is defined in relation to the Material Plane.

Planar Categories

The planes of the default D&D cosmology are grouped in the following categories:

The Material Plane and Its Echoes. The Feywild and the Shadowfell are reflections of the Material Plane.

The Transitive Planes. The Ethereal Plane and the Astral Plane are mostly featureless planes that serve primarily as pathways to travel from one plane to another.

The Inner Planes. The four Elemental Planes (Air, Earth, Fire, and Water), plus the Elemental Chaos that surrounds them, are the Inner Planes.

The Outer Planes. Sixteen Outer Planes correspond to the eight non-neutral alignments and shades of philosophical difference between them.

The Positive and Negative Planes. These two planes enfold the rest of the cosmology, providing the raw forces of life and death that underlie the rest of existence in the multiverse.

Putting the Planes Together

As described in the *Player's Handbook*, the assumed D&D cosmology includes more than two dozen planes. For your campaign, you decide what planes to include, inspired by the standard planes, drawn from Earth's myths, or created by your own imagination.

At minimum, most D&D campaigns require these elements:

- A plane of origin for fiends
- A plane of origin for celestials
- A plane of origin for elementals
- A place for deities, which might include any or all of the previous three
- The place where mortal spirits go after death, which might include any or all of the first three
- A way of getting from one plane to another
- A way for spells and monsters that use the Astral Plane and the Ethereal Plane to function

Once you've decided on the planes you want to use in your campaign, putting them into a coherent cosmology is an optional step. Since the primary way of traveling from plane to plane, even using the Transitive Planes, is through magical portals that link planes together, the exact relationship of different planes to one another is largely a theoretical concern. No being in the multiverse can look down and see the planes in their arrangement the same way as we look at a diagram in a book. No mortal can verify whether Mount Celestia is sandwiched between Bytopia and Arcadia, but it's a convenient theoretical construct based on the philosophical shading among the three planes and the relative importance they give to law and good.

Sages have constructed a few such theoretical models to make sense of the jumble of planes, particularly the Outer Planes. The three most common are the Great

> ### Inventing Your Own Planes
>
> Each of the planes described in this chapter has at least one significant effect on travelers who venture there. When you design your own planes, it's a good idea to stick to that model. Create one simple trait that players notice, that doesn't create too much complication at the gaming table, and that's easy to remember. Try to reflect the philosophy and mood of the place, not merely its physical characteristics.

Wheel, the World Tree, and the World Axis, but you can create or adapt whatever model works best for the planes you want to use in your game.

THE GREAT WHEEL

The default cosmological arrangement presented in the *Player's Handbook* visualizes the planes as a group of concentric wheels, with the Material Plane and its echoes at the center. The Inner Planes form a wheel around the Material Plane, enveloped in the Ethereal Plane. Then the Outer Planes form another wheel around and behind (or above or below) that one, arranged according to alignment, with the Outlands linking them all.

This arrangement makes sense of the way the River Styx flows among the Lower Planes, connecting Acheron, the Nine Hells, Gehenna, Hades, Carceri, the Abyss, and Pandemonium like beads on a string. But it's not the only possible explanation of the river's course.

THE WORLD TREE

A different arrangement of planes envisions them situated among the roots and branches of a great cosmic tree, literally or figuratively.

For example, the Norse cosmology centers on the World Tree Yggdrasil. The three roots of the World Tree touch the three realms: Asgard (an Outer Plane that includes Valhalla, Vanaheim, Alfheim, and other regions), Midgard (the Material Plane), and Niflheim (the underworld). The Bifrost, the rainbow bridge, is a unique transitive plane that connects Asgard and Midgard.

Similarly, one vision of the planes where the deities of the Forgotten Realms reside situates a number of celestial planes in the branches of a World Tree, while the fiendish planes are linked by a River of Blood. Neutral planes stand apart from them. Each of these planes is primarily the domain of one or more deities, though they are also the homes of celestial and fiendish creatures.

THE WORLD AXIS

In this view of the cosmos, the Material Plane and its echoes stand between two opposing realms. The Astral Plane (or Astral Sea) floats above them, holding any number of divine domains (the Outer Planes). Below the Material Plane is the Elemental Chaos, a single, undifferentiated elemental plane where all the elements clash together. At the bottom of the Elemental Chaos is the Abyss, like a hole torn in the fabric of the cosmos.

OTHER VISIONS

As you build your own cosmology, consider the following alternatives.

The Omniverse. This simple cosmology covers the bare minimum: a Material Plane; the Transitive Planes; a single Elemental Chaos; an Overheaven, where good-aligned deities and celestials live; and the Underworld, where evil deities and fiends live.

Myriad Planes. In this cosmology, countless planes clump together like soap bubbles, intersecting with each other more or less at random.

The Orrery. All the Inner and Outer Planes orbit the Material Plane, exerting greater or lesser influence on the world as they come nearer and farther. The world of Eberron uses this cosmological model.

The Winding Road. In this cosmology, every plane is a stop along an infinite road. Each plane is adjacent to two others, but there's no necessary cohesion between adjacent planes; a traveler can walk from the slopes of Mount Celestia onto the slopes of Gehenna.

Mount Olympus. In the Greek cosmology, Mount Olympus stands at the center of the world (the Material Plane), with its peak so high that it's actually another plane of existence: Olympus, the home of the gods. All the Greek gods except Hades have their own domains within Olympus. In Hades, named for its ruler, mortal souls linger as insubstantial shades until they eventually fade into nothing. Tartarus, where the titans are imprisoned in endless darkness, lies below Hades. And far to the west of the known world in the Material Plane are the blessed Elysian Fields. The souls of great heroes reside there.

Solar Barge. The Egyptian cosmology is defined by the daily path of the sun—across the sky of the Material Plane, down to the fair Offering Fields in the west, where the souls of the righteous live in eternal reward, and then beneath the world through the nightmarish Twelve Hours of Night. The Solar Barge is a tiny Outer Plane in its own right, though it exists within the Astral Plane and the other Outer Planes in the different stages of its journey.

One World. In this model, there are no other planes of existence, but the Material Plane includes places like the bottomless Abyss, the shining Mount Celestia, the strange city of Mechanus, the fortress of Acheron, and so on. All the planes are locations in the world, reachable by ordinary means of travel—though extraordinary effort is required, for example, to sail across the sea to the blessed isles of Elysium.

The Otherworld. In this model, the Material Plane has a twin realm that fills the role of all the other planes. Much like the Feywild, it overlays the Material Plane and can be reached through "thin places" where the worlds are particularly close: through caves, by sailing far across the sea, or in fairy rings in remote forests. It has dark, evil regions (homes of fiends and evil gods), sacred isles (homes of celestials and the spirits of the blessed death), and realms of elemental fury. This otherworld is sometimes overseen by an eternal city, or by four cities that each represent a different aspect of reality. The Celtic cosmology has an otherworld, called Tír na nÓg, and the cosmologies of some religions inspired by Asian myth have a similar Spirit World.

PLANAR TRAVEL

When adventurers travel to other planes of existence, they undertake a legendary journey that might force them to face supernatural guardians and undergo various ordeals. The nature of that journey and the trials along the way depend in part on the means of travel, and whether the adventurers find a magic portal or use a spell to carry them.

PLANAR PORTALS

[Raistlin's] eyes studied the Portal, studied every detail intently—although it was not really necessary. He had seen it myriad times in dreams both sleeping and waking. The spells to open it were simple, nothing elaborate or complex. Each of the five dragon heads surrounding and guarding the Portal must be propitiated with the correct phrase. Each must be spoken to in the proper order. But, once that was done and the White-Robed Cleric had exhorted Paladine to intercede and hold the Portal open, they would enter. It would close behind them.

And he would face his greatest challenge.

—Margaret Weis & Tracy Hickman, *War of the Twins*

"Portal" is a general term for a stationary interplanar connection that links a specific location on one plane to a specific location on another. Some portals function like doorways, appearing as a clear window or a fog-shrouded passage, and interplanar travel is as simple as stepping through the doorway. Other portals are locations—circles of standing stones, soaring towers, sailing ships, or even whole towns—that exist in multiple planes at once or flicker from one plane to another. Some are vortices, joining an Elemental Plane with a very similar location on the Material Plane, such as the heart of a volcano (leading to the Plane of Fire) or the depths of the ocean (to the Plane of Water).

Passing through a planar portal can be the simplest way to travel from the Material Plane to a desired location on another plane. Most of the time, though, a portal presents an adventure in itself.

First, the adventurers must find a portal that leads where they want to go. Most portals exist in distant locations, and a portal's location often has thematic similarities to the plane it leads to. For example, a portal to the heavenly mountain of Celestia might be located on a mountain peak.

Second, portals often have guardians charged with ensuring that undesirable people don't pass through. Depending on the portal's destination, "undesirable people" might include evil characters, good characters, cowards, thieves, anyone wearing a robe, or any mortal creature. A portal's guardian is typically a powerful magical creature, such as a genie, sphinx, titan, or native of the portal's destination plane.

Finally, most portals don't stand open all the time, but open only in particular situations or when a certain requirement is met. A portal can have any conceivable requirement, but the following are the most common:

Time. The portal functions only at particular times: during a full moon on the Material Plane, or every ten days, or when the stars are in a particular position. Once it opens, such a portal remains open for a limited time, such as for three days following the full moon, or for an hour, or for 1d4 + 1 rounds.

Situation. The portal functions only if a particular condition is met. A situation-keyed portal opens on a clear night, or when it rains, or when a certain spell is cast in its vicinity.

Random. A random portal functions for a random period, then shuts down for a similarly random duration. Typically, such a portal allows 1d6 + 6 travelers to pass through, then shuts down for 1d6 days.

Command Word. The portal functions only if a particular command word is spoken. Sometimes the word must be spoken as a character passes through the portal (which is otherwise a mundane doorway, window, or similar opening). Other portals open when the command word is spoken and remain open for a short time.

Key. The portal functions if the traveler is holding a particular object; the item acts much like a key to a door. This key item can be a common object or a particular key created for that portal. The city of Sigil above the Outlands is known as the City of Doors because it features an overwhelming number of such item-keyed portals.

Learning and meeting a portal's requirements can draw characters into further adventures as they chase down a key item, scour old libraries for command words, or consult sages to find the right time to visit the portal.

SPELLS

Sarya raised her hands and began to declaim the words of a very powerful spell, one of the most dangerous she knew, a spell designed to breach the barriers between the planes and create a magical bridge into another realm of existence. The mythal thrummed in response, the intangible pulse of the old device taking on a new and different note. Sarya ignored the mythal stone's change and pressed on, finishing her gate spell with skill and confidence.

"The gate is open!" she cried. "Malkizid, come forth!"

Before Sarya a great ring or hoop of golden magic coalesced from the air. Through it she glimpsed the realm of Malkizid, an infernal wasteland of parched desert, windswept rifts, and black, angry skies torn by crimson lightning. Then, through the gate, the archdevil Malkizid appeared. With one smooth step he crossed from his infernal plane into the mythal chamber.

—Richard Baker, Farthest Reach

A number of spells allow direct or indirect access to other planes of existence. *Plane shift* and *gate* can directly transport adventurers to any other plane, with different degrees of precision. *Etherealness* allows adventurers to enter the Ethereal Plane. And the *astral projection* spell lets adventurers project themselves into the Astral Plane and from there travel to the Outer Planes.

Plane Shift. The *plane shift* spell has two important limitations. The first is the material component: a small, forked, metal rod (like a tuning fork) attuned to the desired planar destination. The spell requires the proper resonating frequency to home in on the correct location, and the fork must be made of the right material (sometimes a complex alloy) to focus the spell's magic properly. Crafting the fork is expensive (at least 250 gp), but even the act of researching the correct specifications can lead to adventure. After all, not many people voluntarily travel into the depths of Carceri, so very few know what kind of tuning fork is required to get there.

Second, the spell doesn't send the caster to a specific location unless he or she has specialized information. The sigil sequence of a teleportation circle located on another plane allows the caster to travel directly to that circle, but such knowledge is even harder to come by than the specifications of the required tuning fork. Otherwise, the spell transports the caster to a location in the general vicinity of the desired spot. Wherever the adventurers arrive, they'll most likely still need to undertake a journey to reach the object of a planar quest.

Gate. The *gate* spell opens a portal linked to a specific point on another plane of existence. The spell provides a shortcut to a planar destination, bypassing many of the guardians and trials that would normally fill such a journey. But this 9th-level spell is out of reach for all but the most powerful characters, and it does nothing to negate any obstacles that wait at the destination.

The *gate* spell is powerful, but not infallible. A deity, demon lord, or other powerful entity can prevent such a portal from opening within its dominion.

ASTRAL PLANE

Halisstra opened her eyes and found herself drifting in an endless silver sea. Soft gray clouds moved slowly in the distance, while strange dark streaks twisted violently through the sky, anchored in ends so distant she couldn't perceive them, their middle parts revolving angrily like pieces of string rolled between a child's fingertips. She glanced down, wondering what supported her, and saw nothing but more of the strange pearly sky beneath her feet and all around her.

She drew in a sudden breath, surprised by the sight, and felt her lungs fill with something sweeter and perhaps a little more solid than air, but instead of gagging or drowning on the stuff she seemed perfectly acclimated to it. An electric thrill raced through her limbs as she found herself mesmerized by the simple act of respiration.

—Richard Baker, Condemnation

The Astral Plane is the realm of thought and dream, where visitors travel as disembodied souls to reach the Outer Planes. It is a great silvery sea, the same above and below, with swirling wisps of white and gray streaking among motes of light like distant stars. Most of the Astral Sea is a vast, empty expanse. Visitors occasionally stumble upon the petrified corpse of a

dead god or other chunks of rock drifting forever in the silvery void. Much more commonplace are color pools—magical pools of colored light that flicker like radiant, spinning coins.

Creatures on the Astral Plane don't age or suffer from hunger or thirst. For this reason, humanoids that live on the Astral Plane (such as the githyanki) establish outposts on other planes, often the Material Plane, so their children can grow to maturity.

A traveler in the Astral Plane can move by simply thinking about moving, but distance has little meaning. In combat, though, a creature's walking speed (in feet) is equal to 3 × its Intelligence score. The smarter a creature is, the easier it can control its movement by act of will.

ASTRAL PROJECTION

Traveling through the Astral Plane by means of the *astral projection* spell involves projecting one's consciousness there, usually in search of a gateway to an Outer Plane to visit. Since the Outer Planes are as much spiritual states of being as they are physical places, this allows a character to manifest in an Outer Plane as if he or she had physically traveled there, but as in a dream. A character's death—either in the Astral Plane or on the destination plane—causes no actual harm. Only the severing of a character's silver cord while on the Astral Plane (or the death of his or her helpless physical body on the Material Plane) can result in the character's true death. Thus, high-level characters sometimes travel to the Outer Planes by way of *astral projection* rather than seek out a portal or use a more direct spell.

Only a few things can sever a traveler's silver cord, the most common being a psychic wind (described below). The legendary silver swords of the githyanki also have this ability. A character who travels bodily to the Astral Plane (by means of the *plane shift* spell or one of the rare portals that leads directly there) has no silver cord.

COLOR POOLS

Gateways leading from the Astral Plane to other planes appear as two-dimensional pools of rippling colors, 1d6 × 10 feet in diameter. Traveling to another plane requires locating a color pool that leads to the desired plane. These gateways to other planes can be identified by color, as shown on the Astral Color Pools table. Finding the right color pool is a matter of chance: locating the correct one takes 1d4 × 10 hours of travel.

ASTRAL COLOR POOLS

d20	Plane	Pool Color
1	Ysgard	Indigo
2	Limbo	Jet black
3	Pandemonium	Magenta
4	The Abyss	Amethyst
5	Carceri	Olive
6	Hades	Rust
7	Gehenna	Russet
8	The Nine Hells	Ruby
9	Acheron	Flame red
10	Mechanus	Diamond blue
11	Arcadia	Saffron
12	Mount Celestia	Gold
13	Bytopia	Amber
14	Elysium	Orange
15	The Beastlands	Emerald green
16	Arborea	Sapphire blue
17	The Outlands	Leather brown
18	Ethereal Plane	Spiraling white
19–20	Material Plane	Silver

PSYCHIC WIND

A psychic wind isn't a physical wind like that found on the Material Plane, but a storm of thought that batters travelers' minds rather than their bodies. A psychic wind is made up of lost memories, forgotten ideas, minor musings, and subconscious fears that went astray in the Astral Plane and conglomerated into this powerful force.

A psychic wind is first sensed as a rapid darkening of the silver-gray sky. After a few rounds, the area becomes as dark as a moonless night. As the sky darkens, the traveler feels buffeting and shaking, as if the plane itself was rebelling against the storm. As quickly as it comes, the psychic wind passes, and the sky returns to normal in a few rounds.

The psychic wind has two kinds of effects: a location effect and a mental effect. A group of travelers journeying together suffers the same location effect. Each traveler affected by the wind must also make a DC 15 Intelligence saving throw. On a failed save, the traveler suffers the mental effect as well. Roll a d20 twice and consult the Psychic Wind Effects table to determine the location and mental effects.

d20	Location Effect
1–8	Diverted; add 1d6 hours to travel time
9–12	Blown off course; add 3d10 hours to travel time
13–16	Lost; at the end of the travel time, characters arrive at a location other than the intended destination
17–20	Sent through color pool to a random plane (roll on the Astral Color Pools table)

d20	Mental Effect
1–8	Stunned for 1 minute; you can repeat the saving throw at the end of each of your turns to end the effect on yourself
9–10	Short-term madness (see chapter 8)
11–12	11 (2d10) psychic damage
13–16	22 (4d10) psychic damage
17–18	Long-term madness (see chapter 8)
19–20	Unconscious for 5 (1d10) minutes; the effect on you ends if you take damage or if another creature uses an action to shake you awake

ASTRAL PLANE ENCOUNTERS

Planar travelers and refugees from other planes wander the expanses of the Astral Plane. The most prominent denizens of the Astral Plane are the githyanki, an outcast race of reavers that sail sleek astral ships, slaughter astral travelers, and raid planes touched by the Astral. Their city, Tu'narath, floats through the Astral Plane on a chunk of rock that is actually the body of a dead god.

Celestials, fiends, and mortal explorers often scour the Astral Plane for color pools leading to desired destinations. Characters who linger for too long in the Astral might have an encounter with one or more wandering angels, demons, devils, night hags, yugoloths, or other planar travelers.

ETHEREAL PLANE

Tamlin felt a hand on him, felt his body shimmer into mist. The screams and shouts sounded far off. The walls around him appeared to be only gray shadows. Rivalen and Brennus stood beside him.

"The ethereal plane," Rivalen said. "The dragon's breath cannot affect us here."

—Paul S. Kemp, *Shadowstorm*

The Ethereal Plane is a misty, fog-bound dimension. Its "shores," called the Border Ethereal, overlap the Material Plane and the Inner Planes, so that every location on those planes has a corresponding location on the Ethereal Plane. Visibility in the Border Ethereal is limited to 60 feet. The plane's depths comprise a region of swirling mist and fog called the Deep Ethereal, where visibility is limited to 30 feet.

Characters can use the *etherealness* spell to enter the Border Ethereal. The *plane shift* spell allows transport to the Border Ethereal or the Deep Ethereal, but unless the intended destination is a specific location or a teleportation circle, the point of arrival could be anywhere on the plane.

BORDER ETHEREAL

From the Border Ethereal, a traveler can see into whatever plane it overlaps, but that plane appears muted and indistinct, its colors blurring into each other and its edges turning fuzzy. Ethereal denizens watch the plane as though peering through distorted and frosted glass, and can't see anything beyond 30 feet into the other plane. Conversely, the Ethereal Plane is usually invisible to those on the overlapped planes, except with the aid of magic.

Normally, creatures in the Border Ethereal can't attack creatures on the overlapped plane, and vice versa. A traveler on the Ethereal Plane is invisible and utterly silent to someone on the overlapped plane, and solid objects on the overlapped plane don't hamper the movement of a creature in the Border Ethereal. The exceptions are certain magical effects (including anything made of magical force) and living beings. This makes the Ethereal Plane ideal for reconnaissance, spying on opponents, and moving around without being detected. The Ethereal Plane also disobeys the laws of gravity; a creature there can move up and down as easily as walking.

DEEP ETHEREAL

To reach the Deep Ethereal, one needs a *plane shift* spell or arrive by means of a *gate* spell or magical portal. Visitors to the Deep Ethereal are engulfed by roiling mist. Scattered throughout the plane are curtains of vaporous color, and passing through a curtain leads a traveler to a region of the Border Ethereal connected to a specific Inner Plane, the Material Plane, the Feywild, or the Shadowfell. The color of the curtain indicates the plane whose Border Ethereal the curtain conceals; see the Ethereal Curtains table.

ETHEREAL CURTAINS

d8	Plane	Color of Curtain
1	Material Plane	Bright turquoise
2	Shadowfell	Dusky gray
3	Feywild	Opalescent white
4	Plane of Air	Pale blue
5	Plane of Earth	Reddish-brown
6	Plane of Fire	Orange
7	Plane of Water	Green
8	Elemental Chaos	Swirling mix of colors

Traveling through the Deep Ethereal to journey from one plane to another is unlike physical travel. Distance is meaningless, so although travelers feel as if they can move by a simple act of will, it's impossible to measure speed and hard to track the passage of time. A trip between planes through the Deep Ethereal takes 1d10 × 10 hours, regardless of the origin and destination. In combat, however, creatures are considered to move at their normal speeds.

ETHER CYCLONES

An ether cyclone is a serpentine column that spins through the plane. The cyclone appears abruptly, distorting and uprooting ethereal forms in its path and carrying the debris for leagues. Travelers with a passive Wisdom (Perception) score of 15 or more receive 1d4 rounds of warning: a deep hum in the ethereal matter. Travelers who can't reach a curtain or portal leading elsewhere suffer the cyclone's effect. Roll a d20 and consult the Ether Cyclone table to determine the effect on all creatures in the vicinity.

ETHER CYCLONE

d20	Effect
1–12	Extended journey
13–19	Blown to the Border Ethereal of a random plane (roll on the Ethereal Curtains table)
20	Hurled into the Astral Plane

The most common effect of an ether cyclone is to extend the duration of a journey. Each character in a group traveling together must make a DC 15 Charisma saving throw. If at least half the group succeeds, travel is delayed by 1d10 hours. Otherwise, the journey's travel time is doubled. Less often, a group is blown into the Border Ethereal of a random plane. Rarely, the cyclone tears a hole in the fabric of the plane and hurls the party into the Astral Plane.

ETHEREAL PLANE ENCOUNTERS

Most encounters in the Border Ethereal are with creatures on the Material Plane whose senses or abilities extend into the Ethereal Plane (phase spiders, for example). Ghosts also move freely between the Ethereal and Material Planes.

In the Deep Ethereal, most encounters are with other travelers, particularly ones from the Inner Planes (such as elementals, genies, and salamanders), as well as the occasional celestial, fiend, or fey.

FEYWILD

Stepping into the portal was like settling into a warm bath, though the chill didn't fade from the air. At first everything muted—the roar of the river around the rocks below, the chirping of frogs and crickets on shore, the evening bustle of the town behind him. . . . A moment later, the world erupted into vibrant life. Frogs and night birds sang a chorus; the air was awash with autumn scents; the moonlight painted the flowers in iridescent blue, silver, and violet; and the rushing of the river became a complex symphony.

—James Wyatt, *Oath of Vigilance*

The Feywild, also called the Plane of Faerie, is a land of soft lights and wonder, a place of music and death. It is a realm of everlasting twilight, with glittering faerie lights bobbing in the gentle breeze and fat fireflies buzzing through groves and fields. The sky is alight with the faded colors of an ever-setting sun, which never truly sets (or rises for that matter); it remains stationary, dusky and low in the sky. Away from the settled areas ruled by the seelie fey that compose the Summer Court, the land is a tangle of sharp-toothed brambles and syrupy fens—perfect territory for the unseelie fey to hunt their prey.

The Feywild exists in parallel to the Material Plane, an alternate dimension that occupies the same cosmological space. The landscape of the Feywild mirrors the natural world but turns its features into spectacular forms. Where a volcano stands on the Material Plane, a mountain topped with skyscraper-sized crystals that glow with internal fire towers in the Feywild. A wide and muddy river on the Material Plane might be echoed as a clear and winding brook of great beauty. A marsh could be reflected as a vast black bog of sinister character. And moving to the Feywild from old ruins on the Material Plane might put a traveler at the door of an archfey's castle.

The Feywild is inhabited by sylvan creatures, such as elves, dryads, satyrs, pixies, and sprites, as well as centaurs and magical creatures such as blink dogs, faerie dragons, treants, and unicorns. The darker regions of the plane are home to such malevolent creatures as hags, blights, goblins, ogres, and giants.

SEELIE AND UNSEELIE FEY

Two queens hold court in the Feywild, and most fey owe allegiance to one or the other. Queen Titania and her Summer Court lead the seelie fey, and the Queen of Air and Darkness, ruler of the Gloaming Court, leads the unseelie fey.

Seelie and unseelie do not directly correlate with good and evil, though many mortals make that equation. Many seelie fey are good, and many unseelie are evil, but their opposition to each other stems from their queens' jealous rivalry, not abstract moral concerns. Ugly denizens of the Feywild, such as fomorians and hags, are almost never members of either court, and fey of independent spirit reject the courts entirely. The courts have warred at times, but they also compete in more-or-less friendly contests and even ally with one another in small and secret ways.

FEY CROSSINGS

Fey crossings are places of mystery and beauty on the Material Plane that have a near-perfect mirror in the Feywild, creating a portal where the two planes touch. A traveler passes through a fey crossing by entering a clearing, wading into a pool, stepping into a circle of mushrooms, or crawling under the trunk of a tree. To the traveler, it seems like he or she has simply walked into the Feywild with a step. To an observer, the traveler is there one moment and gone the next.

Like other portals between planes, most fey crossings open infrequently. A crossing might open only during a full moon, on the dawn of a particular day, or for someone carrying a certain type of item. A fey crossing can be closed permanently if the land on either side is dramatically altered—for example, if a castle is built over the clearing on the Material Plane.

OPTIONAL RULES: FEYWILD MAGIC

Tales speak of children kidnapped by fey creatures and spirited away to the Feywild, only to return to their parents years later without having aged a day, and with no memories of their captors or the realm they came from. Likewise, adventurers who return from an excursion to the Feywild are often alarmed to discover upon their return that time flows differently on the Plane of Faerie, and that the memories of their visit are hazy. You can use these optional rules to reflect the strange magic that suffuses the plane.

MEMORY LOSS

A creature that leaves the Feywild must make a DC 10 Wisdom saving throw. Fey creatures automatically succeed on the saving throw, as do any creatures, like elves, that have the Fey Ancestry trait. A creature that fails the saving throw remembers nothing from its time spent in the Feywild. On a successful save, the creature's memories remain intact but are a little hazy. Any spell that can end a curse can restore the creature's lost memories.

TIME WARP

While time seems to pass normally in the Feywild, characters might spend a day there and realize, upon leaving the plane, that less or more time has elapsed everywhere else in the multiverse.

Whenever a creature or group of creatures leaves the Feywild after spending at least 1 day on that plane, you can choose a time change that works best for your campaign, if any, or roll on the Feywild Time Warp table. A *wish* spell can be used to remove the effect on up to ten creatures. Some powerful fey have the ability to grant such wishes and might do so if the beneficiaries agree to subject themselves to a *geas* spell and complete a quest after the *wish* spell is cast.

FEYWILD TIME WARP

d20	Result	d20	Result
1–2	Days become minutes	14–17	Days become weeks
3–6	Days become hours	18–19	Days become months
7–13	No change	20	Days become years

SHADOWFELL

Riven stood in the uppermost room of the central tower of his citadel—a fortress of shadows and dark stone carved in relief into the sheer face of a jagged peak. . . . The starless black vault of the plane's sky hung over a landscape of gray and black, where lived the dark simulacra of actual things. Shadows and wraiths and specters and ghosts and other undead hung in the air around the citadel, or prowled the foothills and plains near it, so numerous their glowing eyes looked like swarms of fireflies. He felt the darkness in everything he could see, felt it as an extension of himself, and the feeling made him too big by half.

         —Paul S. Kemp, *The Godborn*

The Shadowfell, also called the Plane of Shadow, is a dimension of black, gray, and white where most other color has been leached from everything. It is a place of darkness that hates the light, where the sky is a black vault with neither sun nor stars.

 The Shadowfell overlaps the Material Plane in much the same way as the Feywild. Aside from the colorless landscape, it appears similar to the Material Plane. Landmarks from the Material Plane are recognizable on the Shadowfell, but they are twisted and warped— distorted reflections of what exists on the Material Plane. Where a mountain stands on the Material Plane, the corresponding feature on the Shadowfell is a jagged rock outcropping with a resemblance to a skull, a heap of rubble, or perhaps the crumbling ruin of a once-great castle. A forest on the Shadowfell is dark and twisted, its branches reaching out to snare travelers' cloaks, and its roots coiling and buckling to trip those who pass by.

 Shadow dragons and undead creatures haunt this bleak plane, as do other creatures that thrive in the gloom, including cloakers and darkmantles.

SHADOW CROSSINGS

Similar to fey crossings, shadow crossings are locations where the veil between the Material Plane and the Shadowfell is so thin that creatures can walk from one plane to the other. A blot of shadow in the corner of a dusty crypt might be a shadow crossing, as might an open grave. Shadow crossings form in gloomy places where spirits or the stench of death lingers, such as battlefields, graveyards, and tombs. They manifest only in darkness, closing as soon as they feel light's kiss.

DOMAINS OF DREAD

In remote corners of the Shadowfell, it is easy to reach horrific demiplanes ruled over by accursed beings of terrible evil. The best known of these is the valley of Barovia, overlooked by the towering spires of Castle Ravenloft and ruled by Count Strahd von Zarovich, the first vampire. Beings of the Shadowfell called the Dark Powers created these domains as prisons for

these "darklords," and through cruelty or carelessness trapped innocent mortals in these domains as well.

OPTIONAL RULE: SHADOWFELL DESPAIR

A melancholic atmosphere pervades the Shadowfell. Extended forays to this plane can afflict characters with despair, as reflected in this optional rule.

When you deem it appropriate, though usually not more than once per day, you can require a character not native to the Shadowfell to make a DC 10 Wisdom saving throw. On a failure, the character is affected by despair. Roll a d6 to determine the effects, using the Shadowfell Despair table. You can substitute different despair effects of your own creation.

SHADOWFELL DESPAIR

d6	Effect
1–3	**Apathy.** The character has disadvantage on death saving throws and on Dexterity checks for initiative, and gains the following flaw: "I don't believe I can make a difference to anyone or anything."
4–5	**Dread.** The character has disadvantage on all saving throws and gains the following flaw: "I am convinced that this place is going to kill me."
6	**Madness.** The character has disadvantage on ability checks and saving throws that use Intelligence, Wisdom, or Charisma, and gains the following flaw: "I can't tell what's real anymore."

If a character is already suffering a despair effect and fails the saving throw, the new despair effect replaces the old one. After finishing a long rest, a character can attempt to overcome the despair with a DC 15 Wisdom saving throw. (The DC is higher because it's harder to shake off despair once it has taken hold.) On a successful save, the despair effect ends for that character.

A *calm emotions* spell removes despair, as does any spell or other magical effect that removes a curse.

EVERNIGHT

The city of Neverwinter in the world of the Forgotten Realms has a dark reflection on the Shadowfell: the city of Evernight. Evernight is a city of cracked stone edifices and homes of rotten wood. Its roads are made mostly of trampled grave dust, and its few cobbled streets are missing enough stones that they appear pockmarked. The sky is corpse gray, and the breeze blows cold and humid, bringing a chill to the skin.

The city's living residents include mad necromancers, corrupt purveyors of human flesh, worshipers of evil deities, and others who are able to make themselves useful and crazy enough to want to live here. But the living are a minority in Evernight, for the bulk of the population consists of the shambling dead. Zombies, wights, vampires, and other undead make the city their home, all under the watchful eyes of the ruling caste: intelligent, flesh-eating ghouls.

Rumors abound that this foul place mirrors one city on every world.

INNER PLANES

He was lying on his back upon baked and smoldering stone, staring up at a smoky gray sky lit from distant and unseen fires. Around him, a sea of lava burped gouts of gas and jets of flame. The Elemental Plane of Fire.

Thank the fell ones, Vhok thought. I never thought I'd be so happy to be here.

—Thomas M. Reid, *The Gossamer Plain*

The Inner Planes surround and enfold the Material Plane and its echoes, providing the raw elemental substance from which all worlds were made. The four Elemental Planes—Air, Earth, Fire, and Water—form a ring around the Material Plane, suspended within a churning realm known as the Elemental Chaos. These planes are all connected, and the border regions between them are sometimes described as distinct planes in their own right.

At their innermost edges, where they are closest to the Material Plane (in a conceptual if not a literal geographical sense), the four Elemental Planes resemble places in the Material Plane. The four elements mingle together as they do in the Material Plane, forming land, sea, and sky. But the dominant element exerts a strong influence on the environment, reflecting its fundamental qualities.

The inhabitants of this inner ring include aarakocra, azers, dragon turtles, gargoyles, genies, mephits, salamanders, and xorn. Some originated on the Material Plane, and all can travel to the Material Plane (if they have access to the magic required) and survive there.

As they extend farther from the Material Plane, the Elemental Planes become increasingly alien and hostile. Here, in the outermost regions, the elements exist in their purest form: great expanses of solid earth, blazing fire, crystal-clear water, and unsullied air. Any foreign substance is extremely rare; little air can be found in the outermost reaches of the Plane of Earth, and earth is all but impossible to find in the outermost reaches of the Plane of Fire. These areas are much less hospitable to travelers from the Material Plane than the border regions are. Such regions are little known, so when discussing the Plane of Fire, for example, a speaker usually means the border region.

The outermost regions are largely the domains of elemental spirits barely recognizable as creatures. The creatures usually called elementals dwell here, including the Elemental Princes of Evil (primordial beings of pure elemental fury) and elemental spirits that spellcasters can bind into galeb duhrs, golems, invisible stalkers, magmin, and water weirds. These elemental creatures don't need food or other sustenance on their home planes, because they are sustained by the elemental energies that saturate those planes.

ELEMENTAL CHAOS

At the farthest extents of the Elemental Planes, the pure elements dissolve and bleed together into an unending tumult of clashing energies and colliding substance called the Elemental Chaos. Elementals can be found here as well, but they usually don't stay long, preferring the comfort of their native planes. Reports indicate the existence of weird hybrid elementals native to the Elemental Chaos, but such creatures are seldom seen on other planes.

PLANE OF AIR

The essential nature of air is movement, animation, and inspiration. Air is the breath of life, the winds of change, the fresh breeze that clears away the fog of ignorance and the stuffiness of old ideas.

The Plane of Air is an open expanse with constant winds of varying strength. Here and there, chunks of earth drift in the openness—the remnants of failed invasions by denizens of the Plane of Earth. These earth motes serve as homes for the creatures of elemental air, and many motes are covered with lush vegetation. Other creatures live on cloud banks infused with enough magic to become solid surfaces, strong enough to support towns and castles.

Drifting cloud banks can obscure visibility in any direction in the plane. Storms are frequent, mostly on par with a strong thunderstorm but occasionally more like fierce tornadoes or mighty hurricanes. The air is mild, except near the Plane of Water (where it is biting cold) and the Plane of Fire (where it is searing hot). Rain and snow fall only in the part of the plane nearest to the Plane of Water.

Most of the Plane of Air is a complex web of air streams, currents, and winds called the **Labyrinth Winds**. These range from stiff breezes to howling gales that can rip a creature apart. Even the most skilled flying creatures must navigate these currents carefully, flying with the winds, not against them.

Here and there among the Labyrinth Winds are hidden realms reachable only by following a particular sequence of flowing winds, and thus largely protected against attackers. One such realm is fabled **Aaqa**, a shining domain of silver spires and verdant gardens atop a fertile earth mote. The Wind Dukes of Aaqa are dedicated to law and good, and they maintain a vigilant watch against the depredations of elemental evil and the encroachment of the Elemental Chaos. They are served by aarakocra and a little-known race called the vaati.

The region of the Plane of Air nearest the Great Conflagration is called the **Sirocco Straits**. Hot, dry winds scour the earth motes in this area to dry and barren chunks of rock. Gargoyles and their allies from the Plane of Earth gather here to launch raids into the realm of Aaqa.

Between the Sea of Fire (on the Plane of Fire) and the Sirocco Straits is a towering firestorm called the **Great Conflagration**, sometimes called the Plane of Ash. Howling winds from the Plane of Air mix with the cinder storms and lava of the Plane of Fire to create an endless storm front—a wall of flames, smoke, and ash. The thick ash obscures sight beyond a few dozen feet, and the battering winds make travel difficult. Here and there, ash clusters into floating realms where outlaws and fugitives take shelter.

At the other end of the plane, near the Frostfell (the plane of ice that borders the Plane of Water), is a region of frigid winds called the **Mistral Reach**. These gales drive snowstorms into the Frostfell and away from it, toward the heart of the plane. Earth motes in the reach are covered with snow and ice.

PLANE OF EARTH

Earth symbolizes stability, rigidity, stern resolve, and tradition. The plane's position opposite the Plane of Air in the ring of the Elemental Planes reflects its opposition to almost everything air represents.

The Plane of Earth is a chain of mountains rising higher than any mountain range in the Material Plane. It has no sun of its own, and no air surrounds the peaks of its highest mountains. Most visitors to the plane arrive by way of caves and caverns that honeycomb the mountains.

The largest cavern beneath the mountains, called the Great Dismal Delve or the Sevenfold Mazework, is home to the capital city of the dao, the **City of Jewels**. The dao take great pride in their wealth and send teams of slaves across the plane in search of new veins of ore and gemstones to exploit. Thanks to their efforts, every building and significant object in the city is made from precious stones and metals, including the slender gemstone-inlaid spires that top most buildings. The city is protected by a powerful spell that alerts the entire dao population if a visitor steals even a single stone. Theft is punishable by death, with punishment extending to the thief's relatives.

The mountains nearest the Fountains of Creation (on the Plane of Fire) are called the **Furnaces**. Lava seeps through their caverns, and the air reeks of sulfur. The dao have great forges and smelting furnaces here to process their ores and shape their precious metals.

The border region between the planes of Water and Earth is a horrid swamp where twisted, gnarled trees and thick, stinging vines grow from the dense muck and slime. Here and there within the **Swamp of Oblivion** (also called the Plane of Ooze), stagnant lakes and pools play host to thickets of weeds and monstrous swarms of mosquitoes. The few settlements here consist of wooden structures suspended above the muck. Most are built on platforms between trees, but a few stand on stilts driven deep into the muck. No solid earth underlies the mud of the swamp, so houses built on poles eventually sink down into it.

It is said that any object cast into the Swamp of Oblivion can't be found again for at least a century. Now and then, a desperate soul casts an artifact of power into this place, removing it from the multiverse for a time. The promise of powerful magic lures adventurers to brave the monstrous insects and hags of the swamp in search of these treasures.

The region of the plane nearest the Swamp of Oblivion is called the **Mud Hills**. Landslides constantly wear away the slopes of the hills, sending cascades of earth and stone into the bottomless swamp. The Plane of Earth seems to constantly regenerate the land, pushing new hills up as the old ones erode to nothing.

PLANE OF FIRE

Fire represents vibrancy, passion, and change. At its worst, it is cruel and wantonly destructive, as the efreet often are, but at its best, fire reflects the light of inspiration, the warmth of compassion, and the flame of desire.

A blazing sun hangs at the zenith of a golden sky above the Plane of Fire, waxing and waning on a 24-hour cycle. It ranges from white hot at noon to deep red at midnight, so the darkest hours of the plane display a deep red twilight. At noon, the light is nearly blinding. Most business in the City of Brass (see below) takes place during the darker hours.

The weather on the plane is marked by fierce winds and thick ash. Although the air is breathable, creatures not native to the plane must cover their mouths and eyes to avoid stinging cinders. The efreet use magic to keep the cinder storms away from the City of Brass, but elsewhere in the plane, the wind is always at least blustery and rises to hurricane force during the worst storms.

The heat in the Plane of Fire is comparable to a hot desert on the Material Plane, and poses a similar threat to travelers (see "Extreme Heat" in chapter 5, "Adventure Environments"). The deeper one goes into the plane, the rarer water becomes. Beyond a point, the plane holds no sources of water, so travelers must carry their own supplies or produce water by magic.

The Plane of Fire is dominated by the vast **Cinder Wastes**, a great expanse of black cinders and embers crossed by rivers of lava. Roving bands of salamanders battle each other, raid azer outposts, and avoid the efreet. Ancient ruins dot the desert—remnants of forgotten civilizations.

A great range of volcanic mountains called the **Fountains of Creation** is home to azers. These rocky peaks curl from the edge of the Plane of Earth around the Cinder Wastes toward the fiery heart of the plane. At the edge of the plane, the mountains are also called the Plane of Magma. Fire giants and red dragons make their homes here, as well as creatures from the neighboring planes.

Lava flows through the volcanoes toward the Plane of Air and pools into a great lava sea, called the **Sea of Fire**, sailed by efreet and azers in great brass ships. Islands of obsidian and basalt jut up from the sea, dotted with ancient ruins and the lairs of powerful red dragons. On the shore of the Sea of Fire stands the **City of Brass**.

THE CITY OF BRASS

Perhaps the best-known location in the Inner Planes is the City of Brass, on the shores of the Sea of Fire. This is the fabled city of the efreet, and its ornate spires and metal walls reflect their grandiose and cruel nature. True to the nature of the Plane of Fire, everything in the city seems alive with dancing flames, reflecting the vibrant energy of the place.

Adventurers frequently come here on quests for legendary magic. If it's possible to buy magic items at all, the City of Brass is the most likely place to find any

item for sale, though the price might well be more than gold. The efreet are fond of trading in favors, especially when they have the upper hand in negotiations. Perhaps a magical disease or poison can be cured only with something that must be purchased in the bazaars of the city.

The heart of the city is the towering Charcoal Palace, where the tyrannical sultan of the efreet reigns supreme, surrounded by efreet nobles and a host of slaves, guardians, and sycophants.

PLANE OF WATER

The nature of water is to flow, not like the gusting wind or the leaping flame, but smoothly and steadily. It is the rhythm of the tide, the nectar of life, the bitter tears of mourning, and the balm of sympathy and healing. Given time, it can erode all in its path.

A warm sun arcs across the sky of the Plane of Water, seeming to rise and set from within the water at the visible edge of the horizon. Several times a day, however, the sky clouds over and releases a deluge of rain, often accompanied by spectacular shows of lightning, before clearing up again. At night, a glittering array of stars and auroras bedecks the sky.

The Plane of Water is an endless sea, called the **Sea of Worlds**, dotted here and there with atolls and islands that rise up from enormous coral reefs that seem to stretch forever into the depths. The storms that move across the sea sometimes create temporary portals to the Material Plane and draw ships into the Plane of Water. Surviving vessels from countless worlds and navies ply these waters with little hope of ever returning home.

The weather on the plane is a lesson in extremes. If the sea isn't calm, it is battered by storms. On rare occasions, a tremor in the planar firmament sends a rogue wave sweeping across the plane, swamping entire islands and driving ships down to the reefs.

Life flourishes in the upper reaches of the Sea of Worlds, called the **Sea of Light** because of the sunlight filtering down into the water. Aquatic humanoids craft castles and fortresses in the coral reefs. The marids are the distant stewards of this region, content to allow the lesser folk to compete for territory. The nominal emperor of the marids dwells in the **Citadel of Ten Thousand Pearls**, an opulent palace made of coral and studded with pearls.

The deeper extents of the plane, where no sunlight reaches, are called the **Darkened Depths**. Horrid creatures dwell here, and the absolute cold and crushing pressure mean a swift end to creatures accustomed to the surface or the Sea of Light. Krakens and other mighty leviathans claim this realm.

Any land that rises above the surface of the sea is hotly contested by the few air-breathers that live on the plane. Fleets of rafts and ships lashed together serve as solid ground where nothing else is available. Most natives of the plane never break the surface of the sea and thus ignore these habitations.

One of the few actual islands on the plane is the **Isle of Dread**. The island is connected to the Material Plane by means of a regular storm that sweeps over the island.

THE ELEMENTAL PLANES

Travelers who know the strange tides and currents of the plane can travel between worlds freely, but the storms also wreck ships from the Material Plane on the island's shore.

The region of the Plane of Water nearest the Swamp of Oblivion (on the Plane of Earth) is called the **Silt Flats**. The water is thick with soil and sludge, and turns into muddy ground before giving way to the great swamp between the planes.

At the other extreme of the plane is the **Sea of Ice**, bordering the Frostfell. The frigid water is choked with icebergs and sheet ice, inhabited by the cold-loving creatures that inhabit the Frostfell. Drifting icebergs can carry these creatures farther into the Plane of Water to threaten ships and islands in warmer seas.

The **Frostfell**, also called the Plane of Ice, forms the border between the planes of Air and Water and is a seemingly endless glacier swept by constant, raging blizzards. Frozen caverns twist through the Plane of Ice, home to yetis, remorhazes, white dragons, and other creatures of cold. The inhabitants of the plane engage in a never-ending battle to prove their strength and ensure their survival.

Its dangerous monsters and bitter cold make the Frostfell a dangerous place to travel. Most planar voyagers keep to the air, braving the powerful winds and driving snow to avoid setting foot on the great glacier.

OUTER PLANES

Streamers of noxious gas streaked that crimson dome like dirty clouds. They whirled to form what looked like giant eyes staring down, eyes that were swept away before they could focus, only to form anew, again and again. Beneath the ruby glow lay a dark nightmare land of bare rock and flumes of sparks and gouting flame, where things slithered and scrambled half-seen in the shadows. Mountains clawed the ruby sky. The Land of Teeth, Azuth had once aptly called it, surveying the endless jagged rocks. This was the Greeting Ground, the realm of horror that had claimed the lives of countless mortals. He was whirling along above Avernus, uppermost of the Nine Hells.

—Ed Greenwood, *Elminster in Hell*

If the Inner Planes are the raw matter and energy that makes up the multiverse, the Outer Planes provide the direction, thought, and purpose for its construction. Accordingly, many sages refer to the Outer Planes as divine planes, spiritual planes, or godly planes, for the Outer Planes are best known as the homes of deities.

When discussing anything to do with deities, the language used must be highly metaphorical. Their actual homes aren't literally places at all, but exemplify the idea that the Outer Planes are realms of thought and spirit. As with the Elemental Planes, one can imagine the perceptible part of the Outer Planes as a border region, while extensive spiritual regions lie beyond ordinary sensory experience.

Even in perceptible regions, appearances can be deceptive. Initially, many of the Outer Planes appear hospitable and familiar to natives of the Material Plane. But the landscape can change at a whim of the powerful forces that dwell on these planes, which can remake them completely, effectively erasing and rebuilding existence to better fulfill their divine needs.

Distance is a virtually meaningless concept on the Outer Planes. The perceptible regions of the planes can seem quite small, but they can also stretch on to what seems like infinity. Adventurers could take a guided tour of the Nine Hells, from the first layer to the ninth, in a single day—if the powers of the Hells desire it. Or it could take weeks for travelers to make a grueling trek across a single layer.

The default Outer Planes are a group of sixteen planes that correspond to the eight alignments (excluding neutrality, which is represented by the Outlands, described in the section on "Other Planes") and the shades of distinction between them.

The Outer Planes

Outer Plane	Alignment
Mount Celestia, the Seven Heavens of	LG
Bytopia, the Twin Paradises of	NG, LG
Elysium, the Blessed Fields of	NG
The Beastlands, the Wilderness of	NG, CG
Arborea, the Olympian Glades of	CG
Ysgard, the Heroic Domains of	CN, CG
Limbo, the Ever-Changing Chaos of	CN
Pandemonium, the Windswept Depths of	CN, CE
The Abyss, the Infinite Layers of	CE
Carceri, the Tarterian Depths of	NE, CE
Hades, the Gray Waste of	NE
Gehenna, the Bleak Eternity of	NE, LE
The Nine Hells of Baator	LE
Acheron, the Infinite Battlefield of	LN, LE
Mechanus, the Clockwork Nirvana of	LN
Arcadia, the Peaceable Kingdoms of	LN, LG

The planes with an element of good in their nature are called the **Upper Planes**, while those with an element of evil are the **Lower Planes**. A plane's alignment is its essence, and a character whose alignment doesn't match the plane's alignment experiences a sense of dissonance there. When a good creature visits Elysium, for example, it feels in tune with the plane, but an evil creature feels out of tune and more than a little uncomfortable.

The Upper Planes are the home of celestial creatures, including angels, couatls, and pegasi. The Lower Planes are the home of fiends: demons, devils, yugoloths, and their ilk. The planes in between host their own unique denizens: the construct race of modrons

inhabit Mechanus, and the aberrations called slaadi thrive in Limbo.

Layers of the Outer Planes

Most of the Outer Planes include a number of distinct environments or realms. These realms are often imagined and depicted as a stack of related parts of the same plane, so travelers refer to them as layers. For example, Mount Celestia resembles a seven-tiered layer cake, the Nine Hells has nine layers, and the Abyss has a seemingly endless number of layers.

Most portals from elsewhere reach the first layer of a multilayered plane. This layer is variously depicted as the top or bottom layer, depending on the plane. As the arrival point for most visitors, the first layer functions like a city gate for that plane.

Traveling the Outer Planes

Traveling between the Outer Planes isn't dissimilar from reaching the Outer Planes in the first place. Characters traveling by means of the *astral projection* spell can go from one plane into the Astral Plane, and there search out a color pool leading to the desired destination. Characters can also use *plane shift* to reach a different plane more directly. Most often, though, characters use portals—either a portal that links the two planes directly or a portal leading to Sigil, City of Doors, which holds portals to all the planes.

Two planar features connect multiple Outer Planes together: the River Styx and the Infinite Staircase. Other planar crossings might exist in your campaign, such as a World Tree whose roots touch the Lower Planes and whose branches reach to the Upper Planes, or it might be possible to walk from one plane to another in your cosmology.

The River Styx

This river bubbles with grease, foul flotsam, and the putrid remains of battles along its banks. Any creature other than a fiend that tastes or touches the water is affected by a *feeblemind* spell. The DC of the Intelligence saving throw to resist the effect is 15.

The Styx churns through the top layers of Acheron, the Nine Hells, Gehenna, Hades, Carceri, the Abyss, and Pandemonium. Tributaries of the Styx snake onto lower layers of these planes. For example, a tendril of the Styx winds through every layer of the Nine Hells, allowing passage from one layer of that plane to the next.

Sinister ferries float on the waters of the Styx, crewed by pilots skilled in negotiating the unpredictable currents and eddies of the river. For a price, these pilots are willing to carry passengers from plane to plane. Some of them are fiends, while others are the souls of dead creatures from the Material Plane.

The Infinite Staircase

The Infinite Staircase is an extradimensional spiral staircase that connects the planes. An entrance to the Infinite Staircase usually appears as a nondescript door. Beyond the portal lies a small landing with an equally nondescript stairway leading up and down. The Infinite Staircase changes appearance as it climbs and

descends, going from simple stairs of wood or stone to a chaotic jumble of stairs hanging in radiant space, where no two steps share the same gravitational orientation. It is said that one can find one's heart's desire on the Infinite Staircase through diligent searching of each landing.

Doors to the Infinite Staircase are often tucked away in dusty, half-forgotten places that no one frequents or pays any attention to. On any given plane, there can be multiple doors to the Infinite Staircase, though entrances aren't common knowledge and are occasionally guarded by devas, sphinxes, yugoloths, and other powerful monsters.

Optional Rules

Each of the Outer Planes has peculiar characteristics that make traveling through it a unique experience. A plane's influence can affect visitors in various ways, such as causing them to take on personality traits or flaws that reflect the disposition of the plane, or even shift alignment to more closely match the native inhabitants of the plane. Each plane's description includes one or more optional rules that you can use to help make the adventurers' experiences on that plane memorable.

Optional Rule: Psychic Dissonance
Each of the Outer Planes emanates a psychic dissonance that affects visitors of an incompatible alignment—good creatures on the Lower Planes, evil ones on the Upper Planes—if they spend too much time on the plane. You can reflect this dissonance with this optional rule. At the end of a long rest spent on an incompatible plane, a visitor must make a DC 10 Constitution saving throw. On a failed save, the creature gains one level of exhaustion. Incompatibility between lawful and chaotic alignments doesn't have the same effect, so Mechanus and Limbo lack this quality.

Mount Celestia

The single sacred mountain of Mount Celestia rises from a shining Silver Sea to heights barely visible and utterly incomprehensible, with seven plateaus marking its seven heavenly layers. The plane is the model of justice and order, of celestial grace and endless mercy, where angels and champions of good guard against incursions of evil. It is one of the few places on the planes where travelers can let down their guard. Its inhabitants strive constantly to be as righteous as possible. Countless creatures aim to reach the highest and most sublime peak of the mountain, but only the purest souls can. Gazing toward that peak fills even the most jaded of travelers with awe.

Optional Rule: Blessed Beneficence
In contrast to the dissonance experienced by evil creatures here, good creatures are literally blessed by the pervasive beneficence of the plane. Creatures of good alignment gain the benefit of the *bless* spell as long as they remain on the plane. In addition, finishing a long rest on the plane grants a good creature the benefit of a *lesser restoration* spell.

Bytopia

The two layers of the Twin Paradises of Bytopia are similar yet opposite: one is a tamed, pastoral landscape and the other an untamed wilderness, yet both reflect the plane's goodness and its acceptance of law and order when necessary. Bytopia is the heaven of productive work, the satisfaction of a job well done. The goodness flowing through the plane creates feelings of goodwill and happiness in creatures dwelling there.

Optional Rule: Pervasive Goodwill
At the end of each long rest taken on this plane, a visitor that is neither lawful good nor neutral good

must make a DC 10 Wisdom saving throw. On a failed save, the creature's alignment changes to lawful good or neutral good (whichever is closer to the creature's current alignment). The change becomes permanent if the creature doesn't leave the plane within 1d4 days. Otherwise, the creature's alignment reverts to normal after one day spent on a plane other than Bytopia. Casting the *dispel evil and good* spell on the creature also restores its original alignment.

ELYSIUM

Elysium is home to creatures of unfettered kindness and compassion, and a welcome refuge for planar travelers seeking a safe haven. The plane's bucolic landscapes glimmer with life and beauty in their prime. Tranquility seeps into the bones and souls of those who enter the plane. It is the heaven of well-earned rest, a place where tears of joy glisten on many a cheek.

OPTIONAL RULE: OVERWHELMING JOY

Visitors spending any time on this plane risk becoming trapped by overwhelming sensations of contentment and happiness. At the end of each long rest taken on this plane, a visitor must make a DC 10 Wisdom saving throw. On a failed save, the creature is unwilling to leave the plane before taking another long rest. After three failed saving throws, the creature never willingly leaves the plane and, if forcibly removed, does everything in its power to return to the plane. A *dispel evil and good* spell removes this effect from the creature.

THE BEASTLANDS

The Beastlands is a plane of nature unbound, of forests ranging from moss-hung mangroves to snow-laden pines, of thick jungles where the branches are woven so tight that no light penetrates, of vast plains where grains and wildflowers wave in the wind with vibrant life. The plane embodies nature's wildness and beauty, but it also speaks to the animal within all living things.

OPTIONAL RULE: HUNTER'S PARADISE

Visitors to the Beastlands find their hunting and stalking capabilities improved, and characters have advantage on Wisdom (Animal Handling), Wisdom (Perception), and Wisdom (Survival) checks while there.

OPTIONAL RULE: BEAST TRANSFORMATION

Whenever a visitor slays a beast native to the plane, the slayer must succeed on a DC 10 Charisma saving throw or become transformed (as the *polymorph* spell) into the type of beast that was slain. In this form, the creature retains its intelligence and ability to speak. At the end of each long rest, the polymorphed creature can repeat the saving throw. On a successful saving throw, the creature returns to its true form. After three failed saving throws, the transformation can be undone only by a *remove curse* spell or similar magic.

ARBOREA

Larger than life, Arborea is a place of violent moods and deep affections, of whim backed by steel, and of passions that blaze brightly until they burn out. Its good-natured inhabitants are dedicated to fighting evil, but their reckless emotions sometimes break free with devastating consequences. Rage is as common and as honored as joy in Arborea. There the mountains and forests are extravagantly massive and beautiful, and every glade and stream is inhabited by nature spirits that brook no infringement. Travelers must tread lightly.

Arborea is home to many elves and elven deities. Elves born on this plane have the celestial type and are wild at heart, ready to battle evil in a heartbeat. Otherwise, they look and behave like normal elves.

OPTIONAL RULE: INTENSE YEARNING

Keep track of how many days a visitor spends on Arborea. When the visitor leaves, it must make a Charisma saving throw against a DC of 5, plus 1 for each day spent on the plane. On a failed save, the creature becomes afflicted with a yearning to return to Arborea. As long as the effect persists, the creature has disadvantage on ability checks. At the end of each long rest, the creature can repeat the saving throw, ending the effect on a success. A *dispel evil and good* spell removes this effect from the creature.

YSGARD

Ysgard is a rugged realm of soaring mountains, deep fjords, and windswept battlefields, with summers that are long and hot, and winters that are wickedly cold and unforgiving. Its continents float above oceans of volcanic rock, below which are icy caverns so enormous as to hold entire kingdoms of giants, humans, dwarves, gnomes, and other beings. Heroes come to Ysgard to test their mettle not only against the plane itself, but also against giants, dragons, and other terrible creatures that thunder across Ysgard's vast terrain.

OPTIONAL RULE: IMMORTAL WRATH

Ysgard is the home of slain heroes who wage eternal battle on fields of glory. Any creature, other than a construct or undead, that is killed by an attack or a spell while on Ysgard is restored to life at dawn the next day. The creature has all its hit points restored, and all conditions and afflictions it suffered before its death are removed.

LIMBO

Limbo is a plane of pure chaos, a roiling soup of impermanent matter and energy. Stone melts into water that freezes into metal, then turns into diamond that burns up into smoke that becomes snow, and on and on in an endless, unpredictable process of change. Fragments of more ordinary landscapes—bits of forest, meadow, ruined castles, and even burbling streams—drift through the disorder. The whole plane is a nightmarish riot.

Limbo has no gravity, so creatures visiting the plane float in place. A creature can move up to its walking speed in any direction by merely thinking of the desired direction of travel.

Limbo conforms to the will of the creatures inhabiting it. Very disciplined and powerful minds can create whole islands of their own invention within the plane, sometimes maintaining those places for years. A simpleminded creature such as a fish, though, might have less than a minute before the pocket of water surrounding it freezes, vanishes, or turns to glass. The slaadi live here and swim amid this chaos, creating nothing, whereas githzerai monks build entire monasteries with their minds.

OPTIONAL RULE: POWER OF THE MIND

As an action, a creature on Limbo can make an Intelligence check to mentally move an object on the plane that it can see within 30 feet of it. The DC depends on the object's size: DC 5 for Tiny, DC 10 for Small, DC 15 for Medium, DC 20 for Large, and DC 25 for Huge or larger. On a successful check, the creature moves the object 5 feet plus 1 foot for every point by which it beat the DC.

A creature can also use an action to make an Intelligence check to alter a nonmagical object that isn't being worn or carried. The same rules for distance apply, and the DC is based on the object's size: DC 10 for Tiny, DC 15 for Small, DC 20 for Medium, and DC 25 for Large or larger. On a success, the creature changes the object into another nonliving form of the same size, such as turning a boulder into a ball of fire.

Finally, a creature can use an action to make an Intelligence check to stabilize a spherical area centered on the creature. The DC depends on the radius of the sphere. The base DC is 5 for a 10-foot-radius sphere; each additional 10 feet added to the radius increases the DC by 5. On a successful check, the creature prevents the area from being altered by the plane for 24 hours, or until the creature uses this ability again.

PANDEMONIUM

Pandemonium is a plane of madness, a great mass of rock riddled with tunnels carved by howling winds. It is cold, noisy, and dark, with no natural light. Wind quickly extinguishes nonmagical open flames such as torches and campfires. It also makes conversation possible only by yelling, and even then only to a maximum distance of 10 feet. Creatures have disadvantage on any ability check that relies on hearing.

Most of the plane's inhabitants are creatures that were banished to the plane with no hope of escape, and many of them have been driven mad by the incessant winds or forced to take shelter in places where the winds die down until they sound like distant cries of torment.

OPTIONAL RULE: MAD WINDS

A visitor must make a DC 10 Wisdom saving throw after each hour spent among the howling winds. On a failed save, the creature gains one level of exhaustion. A creature that reaches six levels of exhaustion while on this plane doesn't die. Instead, the creature gains a random form of indefinite madness, as described in chapter 8, "Running the Game." Finishing a long rest doesn't reduce a creature's exhaustion level unless the creature can somehow escape the maddening winds.

THE ABYSS

The Abyss embodies all that is perverse, gruesome, and chaotic. Its virtually endless layers spiral downward into ever more appalling forms.

Each layer of the Abyss boasts its own horrific environment. Although no two layers are alike, they are all harsh and inhospitable. Each layer also reflects the entropic nature of the Abyss. In fact, much of what one sees or touches on the plane seems to be in a decaying, crumbling, or corroded state.

OPTIONAL RULE: ABYSSAL CORRUPTION

A non-evil visitor that finishes a long rest in the Abyss must make a DC 10 Charisma saving throw. On a failure, the creature becomes corrupted. Refer to the Abyssal Corruption table to determine the effects of this corruption. You can substitute different corruption effects of your own creation.

After finishing a long rest, a corrupted creature can make a DC 15 Charisma saving throw. On a successful save, the corruption effect ends. A *dispel evil and good* spell or any magic that removes a curse also ends the effect.

If a corrupted creature doesn't leave the plane within 1d4 + 2 days, its alignment changes to chaotic evil. Casting the *dispel evil and good* spell on the creature restores its original alignment.

ABYSSAL CORRUPTION

d10	Result
1–4	**Treachery.** The character gains the following flaw: "I can only achieve my goals by making sure that my companions don't achieve theirs."
5–7	**Bloodlust.** The character gains the following flaw: "I enjoy killing for its own sake, and once I start, it's hard to stop."
8–9	**Mad Ambition.** The character gains the following flaw: "I am destined to rule the Abyss, and my companions are tools to that end."
10	**Demonic Possession.** The character is possessed by a demonic entity until freed by *dispel evil and good* or similar magic. Whenever the possessed character rolls a 1 on an attack roll, ability check, or saving throw, the demon takes control of the character and determines the character's behavior. At the end of each of the possessed character's turns, he or she can make a DC 15 Charisma saving throw. On a success, the character regains control until he or she rolls another 1.

IMPORTANT LAYERS

The layers of the Abyss are defined by the demon lords who rule them, as the following examples illustrate. More information about the demon lords can be found in the *Monster Manual*.

The Gaping Maw. Demogorgon's layer in the Abyss is a vast wilderness of savagery and madness known as the Gaping Maw, where even powerful demons go insane with fear. Reflecting Demogorgon's dual nature, the Gaping Maw consists of a massive primeval continent covered in dense jungle, surrounded by a seemingly endless expanse of ocean and brine flats. The Prince of Demons rules his layer from two serpentine towers, which emerge from a turbid sea. Each tower is topped with an enormous fanged skull. The spires constitute the fortress of Abysm, where few creatures can venture without descending into madness.

Thanatos. If Orcus had his way, all planes would resemble his dead realm of Thanatos, and all creatures would become undead under his control. Under its black sky, Thanatos is a land of bleak mountains, barren moors, ruined cities, and forests of twisted black trees. Tombs, mausoleums, gravestones, and sarcophagi litter the landscape. Undead swarm across the plane, bursting from their tombs and graves to tear apart any creatures foolish enough to journey here. Orcus rules Thanatos from a vast palace known as Everlost, crafted of obsidian and bone. Set within a howling wasteland called Oblivion's End, the palace is surrounded by tombs and burial sites dug into the sheer slopes of narrow valleys, creating a tiered necropolis.

The Demonweb. Lolth's layer is an immense network of thick, magical webbing that forms passageways and cocoon-like chambers. Throughout the web, buildings, structures, ships, and other objects hang as if caught in a spider's snare. The nature of Lolth's web creates random portals throughout the plane, drawing such objects in from demiplanes and Material Plane worlds that figure into the schemes of the Spider Queen. Lolth's servants also build dungeons amid the webbing, trapping and hunting Lolth's hated enemies within crisscrossing corridors of web-mortared stone.

Far beneath these dungeons lie the bottomless Demonweb Pits where the Spider Queen dwells. There, Lolth is surrounded by her handmaidens—yochlol demons created to serve her and which outrank mightier demons while in the Spider Queen's realm.

The Endless Maze. Baphomet's layer of the Abyss is a never-ending dungeon, the center of which holds the Horned King's enormous ziggurat palace. A confusing jumble of crooked hallways and myriad chambers, the palace is surrounded by a mile-wide moat concealing a maddening series of submerged stairs and tunnels leading deeper into the fortress.

The Triple Realm. The Dark Prince Graz'zt rules over the realm of Azzagrat, which encompasses three layers of the Abyss. His seat of power is the fantastic Argent Palace in the city of Zelatar, whose bustling markets and pleasure palaces draw visitors from across the multiverse in search of obscure magical lore and perverse delights. By Graz'zt's command, the demons of Azzagrat present a veneer of civility and courtly comity. However, the so-called Triple Realm holds as much danger as any other part of the Abyss, and planar visitors can vanish without a trace in its mazelike cities and in forests whose trees have serpents for branches.

Death Dells. Yeenoghu rules a layer of ravines known as Death Dells. Here, creatures must hunt to survive. Even the plants, which must bathe their roots in blood, snare the unwary. Yeenoghu's servants, helping to sate their master's hunger as he prowls his kingdom seeking prey, capture creatures from the Material Plane for release in the Gnoll Lord's realm.

CARCERI

The model for all other prisons in existence, Carceri is a plane of desolation and despair. Its six layers hold vast bogs, fetid jungles, windswept deserts, jagged mountains, frigid oceans, and black ice. All form a miserable home for the traitors and backstabbers that are trapped on this prison plane.

OPTIONAL RULE: PRISON PLANE

No one can leave Carceri easily. Magical efforts to leave the plane by any spell other than a *wish* simply fail. Portals and gates that open onto the plane become one-way only. Secret ways out of the plane exist, but they are hidden and well guarded by traps and deadly monsters.

HADES

The layers of Hades are called the Three Glooms—places without joy, hope, or passion. A gray land with an ashen sky, Hades is the destination of many souls that are unclaimed by the gods of the Upper Planes or the fiendish rulers of the Lower Planes. These souls become larvae and spend eternity in this place that lacks a sun, a moon, stars, or seasons. Leaching away color and emotion, this gloom is more than most visitors can stand. The "Shadowfell Despair" rule earlier in the chapter can be used to represent a visitor's despair.

OPTIONAL RULE: VILE TRANSFORMATION

At the end of each long rest taken on the plane, a visitor must make a DC 10 Wisdom saving throw. On a failed save, the creature gains one level of exhaustion, which can't be removed while the creature remains in Hades. If the creature reaches six levels of exhaustion, it doesn't die. Instead, the creature permanently transforms into a larva, whereupon all levels of exhaustion afflicting the creature are removed.

A larva is a miserable fiend that retains the facial features of its previous form but has the body of a fat worm. A larva has only a few faint memories of its previous life and the statistics in the larva stat block.

Hades is crawling with larvae. Night hags, liches, and rakshasas harvest them for use in vile rituals. Other fiends like to feed on them.

LARVA

Medium fiend, neutral evil

Armor Class 9
Hit Points 9 (2d8)
Speed 20 ft.

STR	DEX	CON	INT	WIS	CHA
9 (−1)	9 (−1)	10 (+0)	6 (−2)	10 (+0)	2 (−4)

Senses passive Perception 10
Languages understands the languages it knew in life but can't speak
Challenge 0 (10 XP)

ACTIONS

Bite. *Melee Weapon Attack:* +1 to hit, reach 5 ft., one target. *Hit:* 1 (1d4 − 1) piercing damage.

GEHENNA

Gehenna is the plane of suspicion and greed. It is the birthplace of the yugoloths, which dwell here in great numbers. A volcanic mountain dominates each of the four layers of Gehenna, and lesser volcanic earthbergs drift in the air and smash into the greater mountains.

The rocky slopes of the plane make movement here difficult and dangerous. The ground inclines at least 45 degrees almost everywhere. In places, steep cliffs and deep canyons present more challenging obstacles. Hazards include volcanic fissures that vent noxious fumes or searing flames.

Gehenna has no room for mercy or compassion. The fiends living here are among the greediest and most selfish in all the multiverse.

OPTIONAL RULE: CRUEL HINDRANCE

The plane's cruel nature makes it difficult for visitors to help one another. Whenever a visitor casts a spell with a beneficial effect, including a spell that restores hit points or removes a condition, the caster must first make a DC 10 Charisma saving throw. On a failed save, the spell fails, the spell slot is expended, and the action is wasted.

THE NINE HELLS

The Nine Hells of Baator inflame the imaginations of travelers, the greed of treasure seekers, and the battle fury of all moral creatures. It is the ultimate plane of law and evil and the epitome of premeditated cruelty. The devils of the Nine Hells are bound to obey the laws of their superiors, but they rebel within their individual castes. Most undertake any plot, no matter how foul, to advance themselves. At the very top of the hierarchy is Asmodeus, who has yet to be bested. If he were to be vanquished, the victor would rule the plane in turn. Such is the law of the Nine Hells.

OPTIONAL RULE: PERVASIVE EVIL

Evil pervades the Nine Hells, and visitors to this plane feel its influence. At the end of each long rest taken on this plane, a visitor that isn't evil must make a DC 10 Wisdom saving throw. On a failed save, the creature's alignment changes to lawful evil. The change becomes permanent if the creature doesn't leave the plane within 1d4 days. Otherwise, the creature's alignment reverts to normal after one day spent on a plane other than the Nine Hells. Casting the *dispel evil and good* spell on the creature also restores its original alignment.

THE NINE LAYERS

The Nine Hells has nine layers. The first eight are each ruled by archdevils that answer to Asmodeus, the Archduke of Nessus, the ninth layer. To reach the deepest layer of the Nine Hells, one must descend through all eight of the layers above it, in order. The most expeditious means of doing so is the River Styx, which plunges ever deeper as it flows from one layer to the next. Only the most courageous adventurers can withstand the torment and horror of that journey.

Avernus. No planar portals connect directly to the lower layers of the Nine Hells, by Asmodeus's orders. As such, the first layer of Avernus is the arrival point for visitors to the plane. Avernus is a rocky wasteland with rivers of blood and clouds of biting flies. Fiery comets occasionally fall from the darkened sky and leave fuming impact craters behind. Empty battlefields are littered with weapons and bones, showing where the legions of the Nine Hells met enemies on their native soil and prevailed.

The archduchess Zariel rules Avernus, supplanting her rival, Bel, who has fallen out of Asmodeus's favor and is forced to serve as Zariel's advisor. Tiamat, the Queen of Evil Dragons, is a prisoner on this layer, ruling her own domain but confined to the Nine Hells by Asmodeus in accordance with some ancient contract (the terms of which are known only to Tiamat and the Lords of the Nine).

Zariel's seat of power is a soaring basalt citadel festooned with the partially incinerated corpses of guests who failed to earn the archduchess's favor. Zariel appears as an angel whose once-beautiful skin and wings have been ruined by fire. Her eyes burn with a furious white light that can cause creatures looking upon her to burst into flame.

Dis. Dis, the second layer of the Nine Hells, is a labyrinth of canyons wedged between sheer mountains rich with iron ore. Iron roads span and wend through the canyons, watched over by the garrisons of iron fortresses perched atop jagged pinnacles.

The second layer takes its name from its current lord, Dispater. A manipulator and deceiver, the archduke is devilishly handsome, bearing only small horns, a tail, and a cloven left hoof to distinguish him from a human. His crimson throne stands in the heart of the Iron City of Dis, a hideous metropolis that is the largest in the Nine Hells. Planar travelers come here to conspire with devils and to close deals with night hags, rakshasas, incubi, succubi, and other fiends. Dispater collects a piece of every deal through special provisions that are added to contracts signed on his layer of the Nine Hells.

Dispater is one of Asmodeus's most loyal and resourceful vassals, and few beings in the multiverse can outwit him. He is more obsessed than most devils with striking deals with mortals in exchange for their souls, and his emissaries work tirelessly to foster evil schemes in the Material Plane.

Minauros. The third layer of the Nine Hells is a stench-ridden bog. Acidic rain spills from the layer's brown skies, thick layers of scum cover its putrid surface, and yawning pits lie in wait beneath the murk to engulf careless wanderers. Cyclopean cities of ornately carved stone rise up from the bog, including the great city of Minauros for which the layer is named.

The slimy walls of the city rise hundreds of feet into the air, protecting the flooded halls of Mammon. The Archduke of Minauros resembles a massive serpent with the upper torso and head of a hairless, horned humanoid. Mammon's greed is legendary, and he is one of the few archdevils who will trade favors for gold instead of souls. His lair is piled high with treasures left behind by those who tried—and failed—to best him in a deal.

Phlegethos. Phlegethos, the fourth layer, is a fiery landscape whose seas of molten magma brew hurricanes of hot wind, choking smoke, and pyroclastic ash. Within the fire-filled caldera of Phlegethos's largest volcano rises Abriymoch, a fortress city cast of obsidian and dark glass. With rivers of molten lava pouring down its outer walls, the city resembles the sculpted centerpiece of a gigantic, hellish fountain.

Abriymoch is the seat of power for the two archdevils who rule Phlegethos in tandem: Archduke Belial and Archduchess Fierna, Belial's daughter. Belial is a handsome, powerfully built devil who exudes civility, even as his words carry an undercurrent of threat. His daughter is a statuesque devil whose beauty encases the blackest heart in the Nine Hells. The alliance of Belial and Fierna is unbreakable, for both are aware that their mutual survival hinges on it.

Stygia. The fifth layer of the Nine Hells is a freezing realm of ice within which cold flames burn. A frozen sea surrounds the layer, and its gloomy sky crackles with lightning.

Archduke Levistus once betrayed Asmodeus and is now encased deep in the ice of Stygia as punishment. He rules this layer all the same, communicating telepathically with his followers and servants, both in the Nine Hells and on the Material Plane.

Stygia is also home to its previous ruler, the serpentine archdevil Geryon, who was dismissed by Asmodeus to allow the imprisoned Levistus to regain his rule. Geryon's fall from grace has spurred much debate within the infernal courts. No one is certain whether Asmodeus had some secret cause to dismiss the archdevil or whether he is testing Geryon's allegiance for some greater purpose.

Malbolge. Malbolge, the sixth layer, has outlasted many rulers, among them Malagard the Hag Countess and the archdevil Moloch. Malagard fell out of favor and was struck down by Asmodeus in a fit of pique, while her predecessor, Moloch, still lingers somewhere on the sixth layer as an imp, plotting to regain Asmodeus's favor. Malbolge is a seemingly endless slope, like the sides of an impossibly huge mountain. Parts of the layer break off from time to time, creating deadly and deafening avalanches of stone. The inhabitants of Malbolge live in crumbling fortresses and great caves carved into the mountainside.

Malbolge's current archduchess is Asmodeus's daughter, Glasya. She resembles a succubus with her small horns, leathery wings, and forked tail. She inherited her cruelty and love of dark schemes from her father. The citadel that serves as her domicile on the slopes of Malbolge is supported by cracked pillars and buttresses that are sturdy yet seem on the verge of collapse. Beneath the palace is a labyrinth lined with cells and torture chambers, where Glasya confines and torments those who displease her.

Maladomini. The seventh layer, Maladomini, is ruin-covered wasteland. Dead cities form a desolate urban landscape, and between them lie empty quarries, crumbling roads, slag heaps, the hollow shells of empty fortresses, and swarms of hungry flies.

The Archduke of Maladomini is Baalzebul, the Lord of Flies. A bloated fiend with the lower body of an enormous slug, Baalzebul's form was inflicted on him by Asmodeus as punishment for wavering loyalty. Baalzebul is a miserable and degenerate monstrosity who has long conspired to usurp Asmodeus, yet has failed at every turn. He carries a curse that causes any deal made with him to lead to calamity. Asmodeus occasionally shows Baalzebul favor for reasons no other archduke can fathom, though some suspect that the Archduke of Nessus still respects the worthiness of this fallen adversary.

Cania. Cania, the eighth layer of the Nine Hells, is an icy hellscape, whose ice storms can tear flesh from bone. Cities embedded in the ice provide shelter for guests and prisoners of Cania's ruler, the brilliant and conniving archdevil Mephistopheles.

Mephistopheles dwells in the ice citadel of Mephistar, where he plots to seize the Throne of Baator and conquer the planes. He is Asmodeus's greatest enemy and ally, and the Archduke of Nessus appears to trust Mephistopheles's counsel when it is offered. Mephistopheles knows he can't depose Asmodeus until his adversary makes a grave miscalculation, and so both wait to see what circumstances might turn them against each other. Mephistopheles is also a godfather of sorts to Glasya, further complicating the relationship.

Mephistopheles is a tall, striking devil with impressive horns and a cool demeanor. He trades in souls, as do other archdevils, but he rarely gives his time to any creatures not worthy of his personal attention. His instincts are as razor sharp as Cania's frigid winds, and it is said that only Asmodeus has ever deceived or thwarted him.

Nessus. The lowest layer of the Nine Hells, Nessus is a realm of dark pits whose walls are set with fortresses. There, pit fiend generals loyal to Asmodeus garrison their diabolical legions and plot the conquest of the multiverse. At the center of the layer stands a vast rift of unknown depth, out of which rises the great citadel-spire of Malsheem, home to Asmodeus and his infernal court.

Malsheem resembles a gigantic hollowed-out stalagmite. The citadel is also a prison for souls that Asmodeus has locked away for safekeeping. Convincing him to release even one of those souls comes at a steep price, and it is rumored that the Archduke of Nessus has claimed whole kingdoms in the past for such favors.

Asmodeus most often appears as a handsome, bearded humanoid with small horns protruding from his forehead, piercing red eyes, and flowing robes. He can also assume other forms and is seldom seen without his ruby-tipped scepter in hand. Asmodeus is the most cunning and well-mannered of archdevils. The ultimate evil he represents can be seen only when he wills it so, or if he forgets himself and flies into a rage.

ACHERON

Acheron has four layers, each made of enormous iron cubes floating in an airy void. Sometimes the cubes collide. Echoes of past collisions linger throughout the plane, mingling with the sounds of armies colliding. That's the nature of Acheron: strife and war, as the spirits of fallen soldiers join in endless battle against orcs devoted to Gruumsh, goblinoids loyal to Maglubiyet, and legions assembled by other warmongering gods.

OPTIONAL RULE: BLOODLUST

Acheron rewards a creature for harming other creatures by imbuing that creature with the strength to keep fighting. While on Acheron, a creature gains temporary hit points equal to half its hit point maximum whenever it reduces a hostile creature to 0 hit points.

MECHANUS

On Mechanus, law is reflected in a realm of clockwork gears, all interlocked and turning according to their measure. The cogs seem to be engaged in a calculation so vast that no deity can fathom its purpose. Mechanus embodies absolute order, and its influence can be felt on those who spend time here.

Modrons are the primary inhabitants of Mechanus. The plane is also home to the creator of the modrons: a godlike being called Primus.

OPTIONAL RULE: LAW OF AVERAGES

While on Mechanus, creatures always use the average damage result for attacks and spells. For example, an attack that normally deals 1d10 + 5 damage always deals 10 damage on Mechanus.

OPTIONAL RULE: IMPOSING ORDER

At the end of each long rest taken on this plane, a visitor that isn't lawful neutral must make a DC 10 Wisdom saving throw. On a failed save, the creature's alignment changes to lawful neutral. The creature's alignment reverts to normal after one day spent on a plane other than Mechanus. Casting the *dispel evil and good* spell on the creature also restores its original alignment.

ARCADIA

Arcadia thrives with orchards of perfectly lined trees, ruler-straight streams, orderly fields, perfect roads, and cities laid out in geometrically pleasing shapes. The mountains are unblemished by erosion. Everything on Arcadia works toward the common good and a flawless form of existence. Here, purity is eternal, and nothing intrudes on harmony.

Night and day are determined by an orb that floats above Arcadia's highest peak. Half of the orb radiates sunlight and brings about the day; the other half sheds moonlight and brings on the starry night. The orb rotates evenly without fail, spreading day and night across the entire plane.

The weather in Arcadia is governed by four allied demigods called the Storm Kings: the Cloud King, the Wind Queen, the Lightning King, and the Rain Queen. Each one lives in a castle surrounded by the type of weather that king or queen controls.

Hidden below Arcadia's beautiful mountains are numerous dwarven kingdoms that have withstood the passage of millennia. Dwarves born on this plane

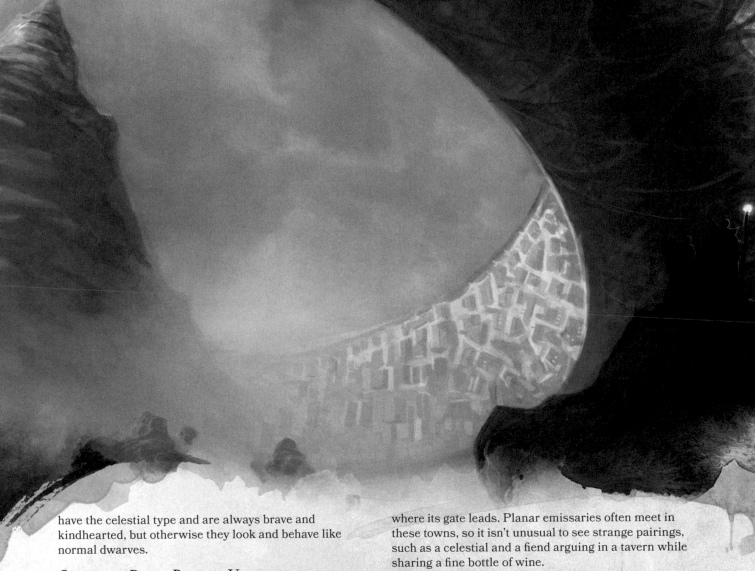

have the celestial type and are always brave and kindhearted, but otherwise they look and behave like normal dwarves.

OPTIONAL RULE: PLANAR VITALITY

While on this plane, creatures can't be frightened or poisoned, and they are immune to disease and poison.

OTHER PLANES

A variety of realms exist between or beyond the other planes.

THE OUTLANDS AND SIGIL

The Outlands is the plane between the Outer Planes. It is the plane of neutrality, incorporating a little of everything and keeping all aspects in a paradoxical balance—simultaneously concordant and in opposition. The plane has varied terrain, with prairies, mountains, and shallow rivers.

The Outlands is circular, like a great disk. In fact, those who envision the Outer Planes as a wheel point to the Outlands as proof, calling it a microcosm of the planes. That argument might be circular, since the arrangement of the Outlands inspired the idea of the Great Wheel in the first place.

Around the outside edge of the circle, evenly spaced, are the gate-towns: sixteen settlements, each built around a portal leading to one of the Outer Planes. Each town shares many of the characteristics of the plane

where its gate leads. Planar emissaries often meet in these towns, so it isn't unusual to see strange pairings, such as a celestial and a fiend arguing in a tavern while sharing a fine bottle of wine.

Given the fact that you can ride a horse in the Outlands from a heaven to a hell, a planar-themed campaign can be set there without the need for planar travel. The Outlands is the closest the Outer Planes come to being like a world on the Material Plane.

GATE-TOWNS OF THE OUTLANDS

Town	Gate Destination
Excelsior	The Seven Heavens of Mount Celestia
Tradegate	The Twin Paradises of Bytopia
Ecstasy	The Blessed Fields of Elysium
Faunel	The Wilderness of the Beastlands
Sylvania	The Olympian Glades of Arborea
Glorium	The Heroic Domains of Ysgard
Xaos	The Ever-Changing Chaos of Limbo
Bedlam	The Windswept Depths of Pandemonium
Plague-Mort	The Infinite Layers of the Abyss
Curst	The Tarterian Depths of Carceri
Hopeless	The Gray Waste of Hades
Torch	The Bleak Eternity of Gehenna
Ribcage	The Nine Hells of Baator
Rigus	The Infinite Battlefield of Acheron
Automata	The Clockwork Nirvana of Mechanus
Fortitude	The Peaceable Kingdoms of Arcadia

SIGIL, CITY OF DOORS

At the center of the Outlands, like the axle of a great wheel, is the Spire—a needle-shaped mountain that rises high into the sky. Above this mountain's narrow peak floats the ring-shaped city of Sigil, its myriad structures built on the ring's inner rim. Creatures standing on one of Sigil's streets can see the city curve up over their heads and—most disconcerting of all—the far side of the city directly overhead. Called the City of Doors, this bustling planar metropolis holds countless portals to other planes and worlds.

Sigil is a trader's paradise. Goods, merchandise, and information come here from across the planes. The city sustains a brisk trade in information about the planes, particularly the command words or items required for the operation of particular portals. Portal keys of all kinds are bought and sold here.

The city is the domain of the inscrutable Lady of Pain, a being as old as gods and with purposes unknown to even the sages of her city. Is Sigil her prison? Is she the fallen creator of the multiverse? No one knows. Or if they do, they aren't telling.

DEMIPLANES

Demiplanes are extradimensional spaces that come into being by a variety of means and boast their own physical laws. Some are created by spells. Others exist naturally, as folds of reality pinched off from the rest of the multiverse. Theoretically, a *plane shift* spell can carry travelers to a demiplane, but the proper frequency required for the tuning fork would be extremely hard to acquire. The *gate* spell is more reliable, assuming the caster knows of the demiplane.

A demiplane can be as small as a single chamber or large enough to contain an entire realm. For example, a *Mordenkainen's magnificent mansion* spell creates a demiplane consisting of a foyer with multiple adjoining rooms, while the land of Barovia (in the Ravenloft setting) exists entirely within a demiplane under the sway of its vampire lord, Strahd von Zarovich. When a demiplane is connected to the Material Plane or some other plane, entering it can be as simple as stepping through a portal or passing through a wall of mist.

THE FAR REALM

The Far Realm is outside the known multiverse. In fact, it might be an entirely separate universe with its own physical and magical laws. Where stray energies from the Far Realm leak onto another plane, matter is warped into alien shapes that defy understandable geometry and biology. Aberrations such as mind flayers and beholders are either from this plane or shaped by its strange influence.

The entities that abide in the Far Realm itself are too alien for a normal mind to accept without strain. Titanic creatures swim through nothingness there, and unspeakable things whisper awful truths to those who dare listen. For mortals, knowledge of the Far Realm is a struggle of the mind to overcome the boundaries of matter, space, and sanity. Some warlocks embrace this struggle by forming pacts with entities there. Anyone who has seen the Far Realm mutters about eyes, tentacles, and horror.

The Far Realm has no well-known portals, or at least none that are still viable. Ancient elves once opened a vast portal to the Far Realm within a mountain called Firestorm Peak, but their civilization imploded in bloody terror and the portal's location—even its home world—is long forgotten. Lost portals might still exist, marked by an alien magic that mutates the area around them.

KNOWN WORLDS OF THE MATERIAL PLANE

Worlds of the Material Plane are infinitely diverse. The most widely known worlds are the ones that have been published as official campaign settings for the D&D game over the years. If your campaign takes place on one of these worlds, that world belongs to you in your campaign. Your version of the world can diverge wildly from what's in print.

On **Toril** (the heroic-fantasy world of the Forgotten Realms setting), fantastic cities and kingdoms stand amid the remains of ancient empires and realms long forgotten. The world is vast, its dungeons rich with history. Beyond the central continent of Faerûn, Toril includes the regions of Al-Qadim, Kara-Tur, and Maztica.

On **Oerth** (the sword-and-sorcery world of the Greyhawk setting), heroes such as Bigby and Mordenkainen are driven by greed or ambition. The hub of the region called the Flanaess is the Free City of Greyhawk, a city of scoundrels and archmagi, rife with adventure. An evil demigod, Iuz, rules a nightmarish realm in the north, threatening all civilization.

On **Krynn** (the epic-fantasy world of the Dragonlance setting), the return of the gods is overshadowed by the rise of the evil dragon queen Takhisis and her dragons and dragonarmies, which plunge the continent of Ansalon into war.

On **Athas** (the sword-and-sorcery world of the Dark Sun setting), a drop of water can be worth more than a human life. The gods have abandoned this desert world, where powerful sorcerer-kings rule as tyrants, and metal is a scarce and precious commodity.

On **Eberron** (the heroic-fantasy world of the Eberron setting), a terrible war has ended, giving rise to a cold war fueled by political intrigue. On the continent of Khorvaire, magic is commonplace, dragonmarked houses rival kingdoms in power, and elemental vehicles make travel to the far corners of the world possible.

On **Aebrynis** (the heroic-fantasy world of the Birthright setting), scions born from divine bloodlines carve up the continent of Cerilia. Monarchs, prelates, guildmasters, and great wizards balance the demands of rulership against the threat of horrible abominations born from the blood of an evil god.

On **Mystara** (a heroic-fantasy world born out of the earliest editions of the D&D game), diverse cultures, savage monsters, and warring empires collide. The world is further shaped by the meddling of the Immortals—former adventurers raised to nearly divine status.

PART 2

Master of Adventures

Chapter 3: Creating Adventures

REATING ADVENTURES IS ONE OF THE GREATEST rewards of being a Dungeon Master. It's a way to express yourself, designing fantastic locations and encounters with monsters, traps, puzzles, and conflicts. When you design an adventure, you call the shots. You do things exactly the way you want to.

Fundamentally, adventures are stories. An adventure shares many of the features of a novel, a movie, an issue of a comic, or an episode of a TV show. Comic series and serialized TV dramas are particularly good comparisons, because of the way individual adventures are limited in scope but blend together to create a larger narrative. If an adventure is a single issue or episode, a campaign is the series as a whole.

Whether you're creating your own adventures or using published adventures, you'll find advice in this chapter to help you create a fun and memorable experience for your players.

Creating an adventure involves blending scenes of exploration, social interaction, and combat into a unified whole that meets the needs of your players and your campaign. But it's more than that. The basic elements of good storytelling should guide you throughout this process, so your players experience the adventure as a story and not a disjointed series of encounters.

Elements of a Great Adventure

The best adventures have several things in common.

A Credible Threat

An adventure needs a threat worthy of the heroes' attention. The threat might be a single villain or monster, a villain with lackeys, an assortment of monsters, or an evil organization. Whatever their nature, the antagonists should have goals that the heroes can uncover and thwart.

Familiar Tropes with Clever Twists

It might seem stereotypical to build an adventure around dragons, orcs, and insane wizards in towers, but these are staples of fantasy storytelling. It might also seem trite to begin an adventure in a tavern, but that's an idea that remains true to D&D. Familiar story elements are fine, as long as you and the players occasionally put a spin on them. For example, the mysterious figure who presents adventurers with a quest on behalf of the king might be the king in disguise. The crazy wizard in the tower might be a projected illusion created by a band of greedy gnome thieves to guard their loot.

A Clear Focus on the Present

An adventure is about the here and now. A little bit of history might be needed to set the story in motion, and the adventurers might discover interesting lore of the past in the course of the adventure. In general, let the world's history be evident in the present situation. Instead of dealing with what happened in the past, an adventure should focus on describing the present situation, what the bad guys are up to, and how the adventurers become involved in the story.

Heroes Who Matter

An adventure should allow the adventurers' actions and decisions to matter. Though it might resemble a novel or a TV episode, an adventure needs to allow for more than one outcome. Otherwise, players can feel as if they've been railroaded—set onto a course that has only one destination, no matter how hard they try to change it. For example, if a major villain shows up before the end of the adventure, the adventure should allow for the possibility that the heroes might defeat that villain.

Something for All Player Types

As outlined in the book's introduction, players come to the gaming table with different expectations. An adventure needs to account for the different players and characters in your group, drawing them into the story as effectively as possible.

As a starting point, think about your adventure in terms of the three basic types of activity in the game: exploration, social interaction, and combat. If your adventure includes a balance of all three, it's likely to appeal to all types of players.

An adventure you create for your home campaign doesn't have to appeal to every abstract player type—only to the players sitting down at your own table. If you don't have any players who like fighting above all else, then don't feel you have to provide a maximum amount of combat to keep the adventure moving.

Surprises

Look for opportunities to surprise and delight your players. For example, the exploration of a ruined castle on a hill might lead to the discovery of a dragon's tomb hidden underneath. A trek through the wilderness might lead to the discovery of a tower that appears only on nights of the full moon. Players remember such locations.

Too many surprises can be off-putting to players, but adding the occasional twist gets players to adjust their tactics and think creatively. For example, you could spruce up a goblin lair by including goblin sappers with kegs of oil strapped to their backs. An attack on a villain's estate might be complicated by the unexpected arrival of a special guest.

When preparing for possible combat encounters, think about odd pairings of monsters, such as a hobgoblin warlord and his pet manticore, or will-o'-wisps in league with a young black dragon. Have surprise reinforcements show up, or give the monsters unusual tactics. Throw in the occasional red herring, deception, and plot twist to keep players on their toes, but try not to go overboard. Sometimes a simple, straightforward encounter with an orc guard is just as fun for your players.

USEFUL MAPS

A good adventure needs thoughtfully constructed maps. Wilderness areas sprinkled with interesting landmarks and other features are better than vast expanses of unchanging terrain. Dungeons that have branching corridors and similar decision points give players the opportunity to choose which direction their characters should go. Presenting the characters with options allows the players to make choices that keep the adventure unpredictable.

If drawing maps isn't your strong suit, the Internet is a great place to look for adventure maps that have been made freely available for use, as well as floor plans of real-world buildings and images that can inspire your mapmaking. You can also use software to help put your maps together.

PUBLISHED ADVENTURES

Published adventures are available for purchase if you have neither the time nor the inclination to write an adventure of your own, or if you want a change of pace. A published adventure includes a pregenerated scenario with the maps, NPCs, monsters, and treasures you need to run it. An example of a published adventure appears in the D&D *Starter Set*.

You can make adjustments to a published adventure so that it better suits your campaign and appeals to your players. For example, you can replace the villain of an adventure with one the players have already encountered in your campaign, or add something to the background of the adventure so that it involves your players' characters in ways that the adventure's designer never could have imagined.

A published adventure can't account for every action the characters might take. The nice thing about published adventures is that they allow you to focus your game preparation time on highlighting plot developments in your campaign that the adventure can't address.

Published adventures also provide inspiration. You might not use an adventure as written, but it might spur ideas, or you can pull out one part of it and repurpose that part for your needs. For example, you might use a map of a temple but repopulate it with monsters of your choice, or you might use a chase sequence as a model for a pursuit scene in your campaign.

ADVENTURE STRUCTURE

Like every story, a typical adventure has a beginning, a middle, and an end.

BEGINNING

An adventure starts with a hook to get the players interested. A good adventure hook piques the interest of the players and provides a compelling reason for their characters to become involved in the adventure. Maybe the adventurers stumble onto something they're not meant to see, monsters attack them on the road, an assassin makes an attempt on their lives, or a dragon shows up at the city gates. Adventure hooks such as these can instantly draw players into your story.

The beginning of a good adventure should be exciting and focused. You want the players to go home looking forward to the next session, so give them a clear sense of where the story is headed, as well as something to look forward to.

MIDDLE

The middle of an adventure is where the bulk of the story unfolds. With each new challenge, the adventurers make important choices that have a clear effect on the conclusion of the adventure.

Over the course of the adventure, the characters might discover secrets that reveal new goals or change their original goal. Their understanding of what's going on around them might change. Maybe rumors of treasure were a trick to lure them into a death trap. Perhaps the so-called spy in the queen's court is actually a scheme concocted by the monarch herself to seize even more power.

At the same time the adventurers are working to thwart their adversaries, those adversaries are trying to carry out their nefarious plans. Such enemies might also work to hide their deeds, mislead potential adversaries, or confront problems directly, perhaps by trying to kill meddlers.

Remember that the characters are the heroes of the story. Never let them become mere spectators, watching as events unfold around them that they can't influence.

ENDING

The ending encompasses the climax—the scene or encounter in which the tension building throughout the adventure reaches its peak. A strong climax should have the players on edge, with the fate of the characters and much more hanging in the balance. The outcome, which hinges on the characters' actions and decisions, should never be a forgone conclusion.

An ending needn't tie everything up in a neat bow. Story threads can be left hanging, waiting to be resolved in a later adventure. A little bit of unfinished business is an easy way to transition from one adventure to the next.

ADVENTURE TYPES

An adventure can be location-based or event-based, as discussed in the sections that follow.

LOCATION-BASED ADVENTURES

Adventures set in crumbling dungeons and remote wilderness locations are the cornerstone of countless campaigns. Many of the greatest D&D adventures of all time are location-based.

Creating a location-based adventure can be broken down into a number of steps. Each step provides tables from which you can select the basic elements of your adventure. Alternatively, roll on the tables and see how the random results inspire you. You can mix up the order of the steps.

1. IDENTIFY THE PARTY'S GOALS

The Dungeon Goals table provides common goals that drive or lure adventurers into dungeons. The

Wilderness Goals table provides similar inspiration for an adventure focused on outdoor exploration. The Other Goals table suggests location-based adventures that don't fit neatly into the first two categories.

DUNGEON GOALS

d20	Goal
1	Stop the dungeon's monstrous inhabitants from raiding the surface world.
2	Foil a villain's evil scheme.
3	Destroy a magical threat inside the dungeon.
4	Acquire treasure.
5	Find a particular item for a specific purpose.
6	Retrieve a stolen item hidden in the dungeon.
7	Find information needed for a special purpose.
8	Rescue a captive.
9	Discover the fate of a previous adventuring party.
10	Find an NPC who disappeared in the area.
11	Slay a dragon or some other challenging monster.
12	Discover the nature and origin of a strange location or phenomenon.
13	Pursue fleeing foes taking refuge in the dungeon.
14	Escape from captivity in the dungeon.
15	Clear a ruin so it can be rebuilt and reoccupied.
16	Discover why a villain is interested in the dungeon.
17	Win a bet or complete a rite of passage by surviving in the dungeon for a certain amount of time.
18	Parley with a villain in the dungeon.
19	Hide from a threat outside the dungeon.
20	Roll twice, ignoring results of 20.

WILDERNESS GOALS

d20	Goal
1	Locate a dungeon or other site of interest (roll on the Dungeon Goals table to find out why).
2	Assess the scope of a natural or unnatural disaster.
3	Escort an NPC to a destination.
4	Arrive at a destination without being seen by the villain's forces.
5	Stop monsters from raiding caravans and farms.
6	Establish trade with a distant town.
7	Protect a caravan traveling to a distant town.
8	Map a new land.
9	Find a place to establish a colony.
10	Find a natural resource.
11	Hunt a specific monster.
12	Return home from a distant place.
13	Obtain information from a reclusive hermit.
14	Find an object that was lost in the wilds.
15	Discover the fate of a missing group of explorers.
16	Pursue fleeing foes.
17	Assess the size of an approaching army.
18	Escape the reign of a tyrant.
19	Protect a wilderness site from attackers.
20	Roll twice, ignoring results of 20.

Other Goals

d12	Goal
1	Seize control of a fortified location such as a fortress, town, or ship.
2	Defend a location from attackers.
3	Retrieve an object from inside a secure location in a settlement.
4	Retrieve an object from a caravan.
5	Salvage an object or goods from a lost vessel or caravan.
6	Break a prisoner out of a jail or prison camp.
7	Escape from a jail or prison camp.
8	Successfully travel through an obstacle course to gain recognition or reward.
9	Infiltrate a fortified location.
10	Find the source of strange occurrences in a haunted house or other location.
11	Interfere with the operation of a business.
12	Rescue a character, monster, or object from a natural or unnatural disaster.

2. Identify Important NPCs

Use the Adventure Villains, Adventure Allies, and Adventure Patrons tables to help you identify these NPCs. Chapter 4 can help you bring these NPCs to life.

Adventure Villains

d20	Villain
1	Beast or monstrosity with no particular agenda
2	Aberration bent on corruption or domination
3	Fiend bent on corruption or destruction
4	Dragon bent on domination and plunder
5	Giant bent on plunder
6–7	Undead with any agenda
8	Fey with a mysterious goal
9–10	Humanoid cultist
11–12	Humanoid conqueror
13	Humanoid seeking revenge
14–15	Humanoid schemer seeking to rule
16	Humanoid criminal mastermind
17–18	Humanoid raider or ravager
19	Humanoid under a curse
20	Misguided humanoid zealot

Adventure Allies

d12	Ally	d12	Ally
1	Skilled adventurer	7	Revenge seeker
2	Inexperienced adventurer	8	Raving lunatic
3	Enthusiastic commoner	9	Celestial ally
4	Soldier	10	Fey ally
5	Priest	11	Disguised monster
6	Sage	12	Villain posing as an ally

Adventure Patrons

d20	Patron	d20	Patron
1–2	Retired adventurer	15	Old friend
3–4	Local ruler	16	Former teacher
5–6	Military officer	17	Parent or other family member
7–8	Temple official	18	Desperate commoner
9–10	Sage	19	Embattled merchant
11–12	Respected elder	20	Villain posing as a patron
13	Deity or celestial		
14	Mysterious fey		

3. Flesh Out the Location Details

Chapter 5 offers suggestions for creating and fleshing out an adventure location, including tables that can help you establish the important elements of a dungeon, wilderness area, or urban setting.

4. Find the Ideal Introduction

An adventure can begin with a social interaction encounter in which the adventurers find out what they must do and why. It can start with a surprise attack, or with the adventurers coming across information by accident. The best introductions arise naturally from the goals and setting of the adventure. Let the entries in the Adventure Introduction table inspire you.

Adventure Introduction

d12	Introduction
1	While traveling in the wilderness, the characters fall into a sinkhole that opens beneath their feet, dropping them into the adventure location.
2	While traveling in the wilderness, the characters notice the entrance to the adventure location.
3	While traveling on a road, the characters are attacked by monsters that flee into the nearby adventure location.
4	The adventurers find a map on a dead body. In addition to the map setting up the adventure, the adventure's villain wants the map.
5	A mysterious magic item or a cruel villain teleports the characters to the adventure location.
6	A stranger approaches the characters in a tavern and urges them toward the adventure location.
7	A town or village needs volunteers to go to the adventure location.
8	An NPC the characters care about needs them to go to the adventure location.
9	An NPC the characters must obey orders them to go to the adventure location.
10	An NPC the characters respect asks them to go to the adventure location.
11	One night, the characters all dream about entering the adventure location.
12	A ghost appears and terrorizes a village. Research reveals that it can be put to rest only by entering the adventure location.

5. CONSIDER THE IDEAL CLIMAX

The climactic ending of an adventure fulfills the promise of all that came before. Although the climax must hinge on the successes and failures of the characters up to that moment, the Adventure Climax table can provide suggestions to help you shape the end of your adventure.

ADVENTURE CLIMAX

d12	Climax
1	The adventurers confront the main villain and a group of minions in a bloody battle to the finish.
2	The adventurers chase the villain while dodging obstacles designed to thwart them, leading to a final confrontation in or outside the villain's refuge.
3	The actions of the adventurers or the villain result in a cataclysmic event that the adventurers must escape.
4	The adventurers race to the site where the villain is bringing a master plan to its conclusion, arriving just as that plan is about to be completed.
5	The villain and two or three lieutenants perform separate rites in a large room. The adventurers must disrupt all the rites at the same time.
6	An ally betrays the adventurers as they're about to achieve their goal. (Use this climax carefully, and don't overuse it.)
7	A portal opens to another plane of existence. Creatures on the other side spill out, forcing the adventurers to close the portal and deal with the villain at the same time.
8	Traps, hazards, or animated objects turn against the adventurers while the main villain attacks.
9	The dungeon begins to collapse while the adventurers face the main villain, who attempts to escape in the chaos.
10	A threat more powerful than the adventurers appears, destroys the main villain, and then turns its attention on the characters.
11	The adventurers must choose whether to pursue the fleeing main villain or save an NPC they care about or a group of innocents.
12	The adventurers must discover the main villain's secret weakness before they can hope to defeat that villain.

6. PLAN ENCOUNTERS

After you've created the location and the overall story of the adventure, it's time to plan out the encounters that make up that adventure. In a location-based adventure, most encounters are keyed to specific locations on a map. For each room or wilderness area on the adventure map, your key describes what's in that area: its physical features, as well as any encounter that plays out there. The adventure key turns a simple sketch of numbered areas on graph paper into encounters designed to entertain and intrigue your players.

See "Creating Encounters" later in this chapter for guidance on crafting individual encounters.

EVENT-BASED ADVENTURES

In an event-based adventure, the focus is on what the characters and villains do and what happens as a result. The question of where those things happen is of secondary importance.

Building an event-based adventure is more work than building a location based one, but the process can be simplified by following a number of straightforward steps. Several steps include tables from which you can choose adventure elements or roll randomly for inspiration. As with location-based adventures, you don't necessarily have to follow these steps in order.

1. START WITH A VILLAIN

Putting care into creating your villain will pay off later, since the villain plays such a pivotal role in advancing the story. Use the Adventure Villains table in the previous section to get started, and use the information in chapter 4 to help flesh out the villain.

For example, your villain might be an undead creature seeking to avenge a past imprisonment or injury. An interesting aspect of an undead villain is that this past injury might have occurred centuries ago, inspiring revenge against the descendants of those that harmed it. Imagine a vampire imprisoned by the members of a religious order of knights, and who now seeks revenge against the current members of that order.

2. DETERMINE THE VILLAIN'S ACTIONS

Once you have a villain, it's time to determine what steps the villain takes to achieve its goals. Create a timeline showing what the villain does and when, assuming no interference from the adventurers.

Building on the previous example, you might decide that your vampire villain murders several knights. By slipping past locked doors in gaseous form, the vampire is able to make the deaths appear natural at first, but it soon becomes clear that a depraved killer is behind the murders.

If you need additional inspiration, consider a few different options for how the villain's actions unfold over the course of the adventure.

EVENT-BASED VILLAIN ACTIONS

d6	Type of Actions	d6	Type of Actions
1	Big event	4	One and done
2	Crime spree	5	Serial crimes
3	Growing corruption	6	Step by step

Big Event. The villain's plans come to fruition during a festival, an astrological event, a holy (or unholy) rite, a royal wedding, the birth of a child, or some similar fixed time. The villain's activities up to that point are geared toward preparation for this event.

Crime Spree. The villain commits acts that become bolder and more heinous over time. A killer might start out by targeting the destitute in the city slums before moving up to a massacre in the marketplace, increasing the horror and the body count each time.

Vampire Villain

ongoing plan to commit more crimes, the villain's goal is to lie low or flee the scene.

Serial Crimes. The villain commits crimes one after the other, but these acts are repetitive in nature, rather than escalating to greater heights of depravity. The trick to catching such a villain lies in determining the pattern underlying the crimes. Though serial killers are a common example of this type of villain, your villain could be a serial arsonist favoring a certain type of building, a magical sickness that affects spellcasters who cast a specific spell, a thief that targets a certain kind of merchant, or a doppelganger kidnapping and impersonating one noble after another.

Step by Step. In pursuit of its goal, the villain carries out a specific set of actions in a particular sequence. A wizard might steal the items needed to create a phylactery and become a lich, or a cultist might kidnap the priests of seven good-aligned gods as a sacrifice. Alternatively, the villain could be following a trail to find the object of its revenge, killing one victim after another while moving ever closer to the real target.

3. Determine the Party's Goals

You can use the Event-Based Goals table to set the party's goal. A goal can also suggest ways in which the adventurers become caught up in the villain's plans, and what exactly they must do to foil those plans.

Event-Based Goals

d20	Goal
1	Bring the villain to justice.
2	Clear the name of an innocent NPC.
3	Protect or hide an NPC.
4	Protect an object.
5	Discover the nature and origin of a strange phenomenon that might be the villain's doing.
6	Find a wanted fugitive.
7	Overthrow a tyrant.
8	Uncover a conspiracy to overthrow a ruler.
9	Negotiate peace between enemy nations or feuding families.
10	Secure aid from a ruler or council.
11	Help a villain find redemption.
12	Parley with a villain.
13	Smuggle weapons to rebel forces.
14	Stop a band of smugglers.
15	Gather intelligence on an enemy force.
16	Win a tournament.
17	Determine the villain's identity.
18	Locate a stolen item.
19	Make sure a wedding goes off without a hitch.
20	Roll twice, ignoring results of 20.

For example, you roll a 10 on the table, indicating that the party's goal is to secure aid from a ruler or council. You decide to connect that to the leadership of the order targeted by your vampire villain. Maybe the order's leaders have a chest of jewels stolen from the vampire centuries ago, and the characters can use the chest as bait to trap the villain.

Growing Corruption. As time passes, the villain's power and influence grow, affecting more victims across a larger area. This might take the form of armies conquering new territory, an evil cult recruiting new members, or a spreading plague. A pretender to the throne might attempt to secure the support of the kingdom's nobility in the days or weeks leading up to a coup, or a guild leader could corrupt the members of a town council or bribe officers of the watch.

One and Done. The villain commits a single crime and then tries to avoid the consequences. Instead of an

4. IDENTIFY IMPORTANT NPCS

Many event-based adventures require a well-detailed cast of NPCs. Some of these NPCs fall neatly into the categories of allies and patrons, but most are likely to be characters or creatures whose attitudes toward the adventurers remain undecided until the adventurers interact with them. (See chapter 4 for more information on creating NPCs.)

The elements of the adventure you've determined so far should provide a clear idea of what supporting characters you need to create, as well as how much detail you need to generate for each one. NPCs unlikely to become involved in combat don't need full combat statistics, for example, just as characters heavily involved in negotiation could have ideals, bonds, and flaws. If it's helpful, roll on the Adventure Allies or Adventure Patrons tables (in the "Location-Based Adventures" section, earlier in this chapter).

5. ANTICIPATE THE VILLAIN'S REACTIONS

As the adventurers pursue their goals and foil the villain's plans, how does the villain respond? Does it lash out in violence or send dire warnings? Does it look for simple solutions to its problems or create more complicated schemes to route around interference?

Look over the villain's actions that you outlined in step 2. For each event arising from those actions, think about how the adventurers are likely to react. If they can prevent an action or hamper its success, what effect does that have on the villain's overall plan? What can the villain do to compensate?

One way to track a villain's reactions is by using a flowchart. This might grow out of the timeline that describes the villain's plans, outlining how the villain gets back on track after the adventurers thwart its plans. Or the flowchart could be separate from the timeline, showing the various actions the adventurers might take and the villain's response to those actions.

6. DETAIL KEY LOCATIONS

Since locations aren't the focus of the adventure, they can be simpler and smaller than a dungeon complex or an expanse of wilderness. They might be specific locations in a city, or even individual rooms in locations where combat is likely to break out or significant exploration is needed, such as a throne room, a guild headquarters, a vampire's crumbling manor, or a knights' chapter house.

7. CHOOSE AN INTRODUCTION AND A CLIMAX

The Adventure Introduction table in the "Location-Based Adventures" section offers fun possibilities for hooking the characters into the events of your adventure, including dreams, hauntings, and a simple plea for help. The Adventure Climax table in that same section includes adventure endings that work just as well for event-based adventures.

For example, the Adventure Introduction table helps you decide that an ally the adventurers care about needs their help. Perhaps the NPC is a knight who believes that a vampire is trying to kill him, or a friend or relative hoping to find the knight's murderer. This NPC brings the vampire's crimes to the characters' attention.

Looking over the Adventure Climax table, you might decide to have the adventurers bait the vampire with a chest of jewels stolen from its lair. As an added twist, you decide that the vampire's true goal is to retrieve a necklace among the jewels. The necklace is set with nine gems, and with these gems the vampire can open a gate to the Nine Hells. Should the vampire succeed, the adventurers will have a more pressing threat to deal with, as a powerful devil steps through the gate and honors some ancient pact it made with the vampire.

8. PLAN ENCOUNTERS

After you've created the overall story of the adventure, it's time to plan out the encounters on which the events of that adventure will hang. In an event-based adventure, encounters occur when the villain's agenda intersects the path of the characters. You can't always anticipate exactly when or where that will happen, but you can create a list of possible encounters that the adventurers might experience. This can take the form of general descriptions of the villain's forces, details of its lieutenants and minions, as well as encounters tied to the key locations of the adventure.

See "Creating Encounters" later in this chapter for guidance on crafting individual encounters.

MYSTERIES

A mystery is a form of event-based adventure that usually focuses on the adventurers' efforts to solve a crime, usually a robbery or murder. Unlike the writer of a mystery novel, a Dungeon Master can't always predict what the characters will do in a mystery adventure.

A villain whose actions are "crime spree," "one and done," or "serial crimes" might inspire you to craft a mystery adventure around that villain's crimes. Similarly, if the adventurers' goals include determining the villain's identity, that might be part of a mystery.

To build a mystery adventure, follow the steps for creating any event-based adventure. Then consider three additional elements for the adventure: the victim, the suspects, and the clues.

VICTIM

Think about the victim's relationship to the villain. Though you can create a strong scenario with no such relationship, part of what makes a mystery exciting is the discovery of the twisted connections between NPCs and how those connections led to the crime. A random killing might be just as mysterious, but it lacks that emotional connection.

Also look for a connection between the victim and one or more of the adventurers. One surefire way to draw adventurers into a mystery—including making them suspects—is to make the victim someone with whom the characters are acquainted.

SUSPECTS

Your cast of characters should include an assortment of other NPCs who didn't commit the crime, but who had the motive, the means, or the opportunity to do so.

Suspects might be obvious or could come to light during the investigation. One technique often used in detective fiction is to create a closed circle of suspects—a finite number of individuals whose circumstances make them the only possible suspects.

One tip for keeping the players and the adventurers guessing as to the identity of the villain is to ensure that more than one suspect has a secret. When questioned by the adventurers, a suspect might appear nervous or attempt to lie, despite being innocent of the crime. A secret business deal, an illicit affair, a dark past, or an uncontrolled vice are flaws that make suspects more interesting than NPCs with nothing to hide.

CLUES

Clues point to the identity of the villain. Some clues are verbal, including the statements of the suspects and witnesses that help the adventurers develop a picture of what happened. Other clues are physical, such as an unfinished message written in the victim's blood, a piece of jewelry left behind by the villain, or a weapon found hidden in a suspect's room.

A clue should connect a suspect to the crime, typically by shedding light on the suspect's motive, means, or opportunity. Some clues connect the wrong suspect to the crime, leading the adventurers in the wrong direction. Eventually, they must find other clues pointing in a different direction, or come across evidence that absolves the suspect.

It's better to populate your adventure with too many clues than too few. If the adventurers solve the mystery too quickly, you might feel some disappointment but the players will feel a sense of accomplishment. If the mystery is too hard, though, the players will become frustrated. Since you have to account for the possibility that the adventurers will overlook some clues, use redundant clues to ensure that the players have the knowledge needed to catch the villain.

INTRIGUE

Intrigue adventures are event-based adventures that revolve around power struggles. Intrigues are common in the courts of the nobility, but power struggles can play out just as easily in merchants' guilds, crime syndicates, and temple hierarchies.

Rather than dark events and villainous plots, an intrigue adventure typically revolves around the exchange of favors, the rise and fall of individuals in power and influence, and the honeyed words of diplomacy. A prince's efforts to be named heir to the throne, a courtier's ambition to sit at the queen's right hand, and a merchant's desire to open a trade route through enemy lands are the stuff of intrigue.

Like all adventures, an intrigue adventure works only if the players and their characters are invested in the outcome. If no one cares who the king's chamberlain is or who has logging rights in the elven woods, throwing the characters into an adventure centered on those issues will fall flat. However, if having the ear of the king's chamberlain means the characters can use royal soldiers to help them defend their own stronghold on the borderlands, players will be invested in the scenario.

Adventurers usually become embroiled in intrigue when they need a favor from a powerful creature and have to perform a favor in exchange, or when the plots of powerful NPCs get in the way of the characters achieving their goals. Some of the event-based goals discussed earlier in this section lend themselves to intrigue adventures. For example, if the adventurers must uncover a conspiracy, negotiate a peace treaty, or secure aid from a ruler or council, you might be looking at an intrigue adventure.

The process of creating an intrigue adventure is similar to creating any other event-based adventure, with two main differences: how villains are handled and how the characters can gain influence.

VILLAINS

Some intrigue adventures are driven by the actions of a single villain, such as a noble plotting the assassination of a monarch. However, an intrigue adventure can have multiple villains or no villain at all.

No Villain. Some intrigue adventures revolve around the exchange of favors in the absence of a villain. For this type of adventure, skip steps 1 and 2 of the event-based adventure creation process (the villain and the villain's actions) and move straight to the adventurers' goals in step 3. Figure out why the adventurers become involved in the intrigue, then spend the bulk of your time creating the NPCs they interact with.

Many Villains. Some intrigue adventures feature a whole cast of villains, each with its own goals, motivations, and methods. The adventurers might be drawn into the struggle of a court full of nobles vying for the throne in the wake of the king's sudden death, or could find themselves negotiating the end to a deadly turf war among thieves' guilds. In this scenario, you'll spend a lot of time on steps 1 and 2, developing each of the major NPCs as a distinct villain with an agenda.

In step 5, you'll need to develop each villain's reactions to the potential setbacks they face during the adventure. However, you don't need to put equal effort into detailing the reactions of every villain, since many will likely echo each other or cancel each other out. Whenever the adventurers foil one villain's plans, it might let another villain's schemes move forward, advancing the adventure whether the foiled villain reacts or not.

INFLUENCE

Depending on the scenario, you might want to track the party's influence with different NPCs or factions, or even track influence separately for each character.

One way to handle influence is to treat it like inspiration. A character gains influence in a certain situation only if you grant it, and bringing influence into play requires spending it. Characters can gain influence by doing favors for NPCs, advancing the cause of an organization, or demonstrating their power and heroism, at your discretion. As with inspiration, a character can choose to spend influence to gain advantage on a roll relevant to that influence.

Another way to handle influence is to treat it like renown (see chapter 1), allowing characters to gain renown at court and within various key factions.

FRAMING EVENTS

You can base an entire adventure on a framing event or use such an event to grab the players' interest. The Framing Events table presents several ideas, or you can use it to inspire your own framing event.

FRAMING EVENTS

d100	Event
01–02	Anniversary of a monarch's reign
03–04	Anniversary of an important event
05–06	Arena event
07–08	Arrival of a caravan or ship
09–10	Arrival of a circus
11–12	Arrival of an important NPC
13–14	Arrival of marching modrons
15–16	Artistic performance
17–18	Athletic event
19–20	Birth of a child
21–22	Birthday of an important NPC
23–24	Civic festival
25–26	Comet appearance
27–28	Commemoration of a past tragedy
29–30	Consecration of a new temple
31–32	Coronation
33–34	Council meeting
35–36	Equinox or solstice
37–38	Execution
39–40	Fertility festival
41–42	Full moon
43–44	Funeral
45–46	Graduation of cadets or wizards
47–48	Harvest festival
49–50	Holy day
51–52	Investiture of a knight or other noble
53–54	Lunar eclipse
55–58	Midsummer festival
59–60	Midwinter festival
61–62	Migration of monsters
63–64	Monarch's ball
65–66	New moon
67–68	New year
69–70	Pardoning of a prisoner
71–72	Planar conjunction
73–74	Planetary alignment
75–76	Priestly investiture
77–78	Procession of ghosts
79–80	Remembrance for soldiers lost in war
81–82	Royal address or proclamation
83–84	Royal audience day
85–86	Signing of a treaty
87–88	Solar eclipse
89–91	Tournament
92–94	Trial
95–96	Violent uprising
97–98	Wedding or wedding anniversary
99–00	Concurrence of two events (roll twice, ignoring results of 99 or 100)

COMPLICATIONS

Sometimes an adventure isn't as straightforward as it might seem.

MORAL QUANDARIES

If you want to give the characters a crisis that no amount of spellcasting or swordplay can resolve, add a moral quandary to the adventure. A moral quandary is a problem of conscience for which the adventurers must make a single choice—but never a simple one.

MORAL QUANDARIES

d20	Quandary	d20	Quandary
1–3	Ally quandary	13–16	Rescue quandary
4–6	Friend quandary	17–20	Respect quandary
7–12	Honor quandary		

on the characters. A love interest might demand that a character turn away from a dangerous quest. A dear friend might plead with the characters to spare the villain's life, to prove that they are better than the villain. A weak NPC might beg for a chance to win favor from the characters by undertaking a dangerous but essential mission.

Honor Quandary. A character is forced to choose between victory and a personal oath or code of honor. A paladin who has sworn the Oath of Virtue might realize that the clearest path to success lies in deceit and subterfuge. A loyal cleric might be tempted to disobey the orders of his or her faith. If you present this quandary, be sure to provide an opportunity for a character to atone for violating his or her oath.

Rescue Quandary. The adventurers must choose between catching or hurting the villain and saving innocent lives. For example, the adventurers might learn that the villain is camped nearby, but they also learn that another part of the villain's forces is about to march into a village and burn it to the ground. The characters must choose between taking out the villain or protecting innocent villagers, some of whom might be friends or family members.

Respect Quandary. Two important allies give conflicting directions or advice to the adventurers. Perhaps the high priest counsels the characters to negotiate peace with militaristic elves in the nearby forest, while a veteran warrior urges them to prove their strength with a decisive first strike. The adventurers can't follow both courses, and whichever ally they choose, the other loses respect for them and might no longer aid them.

TWISTS

A twist can complicate a story and make it harder for the characters to complete their goals.

TWISTS

d10	Twist
1	The adventurers are racing against other creatures with the same or opposite goal.
2	The adventurers become responsible for the safety of a noncombatant NPC.
3	The adventurers are prohibited from killing the villain, but the villain has no compunctions about killing them.
4	The adventurers have a time limit.
5	The adventurers have received false or extraneous information.
6	Completing an adventure goal fulfills a prophecy or prevents the fulfillment of a prophecy.
7	The adventurers have two different goals, but they can complete only one.
8	Completing the goal secretly helps the villain.
9	The adventurers must cooperate with a known enemy to achieve the goal.
10	The adventurers are under magical compulsion (such as a *geas* spell) to complete their goal.

Ally Quandary. The adventurers have a better chance of achieving their goal with the help of two individuals whose expertise is all but essential. However, these two NPCs hate each other and refuse to work together even if the fate of the world hangs in the balance. The adventurers must choose the NPC that is most likely to help them accomplish their goal.

Friend Quandary. An NPC that one or more of the characters cares about makes an impossible demand

SIDE QUESTS

You can also add one or more side quests to your adventure, taking the characters off the main story path defined by location or events. Side quests are peripheral to the characters' primary goal, but successfully completing a side quest might provide a benefit toward completing the primary goal.

SIDE QUESTS

d8	Side Quest
1	Find a specific item rumored to be in the area.
2	Retrieve a stolen item in the villain's possession.
3	Receive information from an NPC in the area.
4	Rescue a captive.
5	Discover the fate of a missing NPC.
6	Slay a specific monster.
7	Discover the nature and origin of a strange phenomenon in the area.
8	Secure the aid of a character or creature in the area.

CREATING ENCOUNTERS

Encounters are the individual scenes in the larger story of your adventure.

First and foremost, an encounter should be fun for the players. Second, it shouldn't be burden for you to run. Beyond that, a well-crafted encounter usually has a straightforward objective as well as some connection to the overarching story of your campaign, building on the encounters that precede it while foreshadowing encounters yet to come.

An encounter has one of three possible outcomes: the characters succeed, the characters partly succeed, or the characters fail. The encounter needs to account for all three possibilities, and the outcome needs to have consequences so that the players feel like their successes and failures matter.

CHARACTER OBJECTIVES

When players don't know what they're supposed to do in a given encounter, anticipation and excitement can quickly turn to boredom and frustration. A transparent objective alleviates the risk of players losing interest.

For example, if the overall story of your adventure involves a quest to deliver a priceless relic to a remote monastery, each encounter along the way is an opportunity to introduce a smaller objective that moves the quest forward. Encounters during the trip might see the adventurers accosted by enemies determined to steal the relic, or by monsters that are constantly threatening the monastery.

Some players create their own objectives, which is to be expected and encouraged. It is, after all, as much the players' campaign as yours. For example, a character might try to bribe enemies rather than fight them, or chase after a fleeing enemy to see where it goes. Players who ignore objectives will have to deal with the consequences, which is another important facet of encounter design.

SAMPLE OBJECTIVES

The following objectives can be used as foundations for encounters. Although these objectives focus on a single encounter during an adventure, using the same objective in multiple encounters allows you to combine those encounters into a larger obstacle or problem the adventurers must overcome.

Make Peace. The characters must convince two opposing groups (or their leaders) to end the conflict that embroils them. As a complication, the characters might have enemies on one or both of the opposing sides, or some other group or individual might be instigating the conflict to further its own ends.

Protect an NPC or Object. The characters must act as bodyguards or protect some object in their custody. As a complication, the NPC under the party's protection might be cursed, diseased, prone to panic attacks, too young or too old to fight, or apt to risk the lives of the adventurers through dubious decisions. The object the adventurers have sworn to protect might be sentient, cursed, or difficult to transport.

Retrieve an Object. The adventurers must gain possession of a specific object in the area of the encounter, preferably before combat finishes. As a complication, enemies might desire the object as much as the adventurers do, forcing both parties to fight for it.

Run a Gauntlet. The adventurers must pass through a dangerous area. This objective is similar to retrieving an object insofar as reaching the exit is a higher priority than killing opponents in the area. A time limit adds a complication, as does a decision point that might lead characters astray. Other complications include traps, hazards, and monsters.

Sneak In. The adventurers need to move through the encounter area without making their enemies aware of their presence. Complications might ensue if they are detected.

Stop a Ritual. The plots of evil cult leaders, malevolent warlocks, and powerful fiends often involve rituals that must be foiled. Characters engaged in stopping a ritual must typically fight their way through evil minions before attempting to disrupt the ritual's powerful magic. As a complication, the ritual might be close to completion when the characters arrive, imposing a time limit. Depending on the ritual, its completion might have immediate consequences as well.

Take Out a Single Target. The villain is surrounded by minions powerful enough to kill the adventurers. The characters can flee and hope to confront the villain another day, or they can try to fight their way through the minions to take out their target. As a complication, the minions might be innocent creatures under the villain's control. Killing the villain means breaking that control, but the adventurers must endure the minions' attacks until they do.

CREATING A COMBAT ENCOUNTER

When creating a combat encounter, let your imagination run wild and build something your players will enjoy. Once you have the details figured out, use this section to adjust the difficulty of the encounter.

COMBAT ENCOUNTER DIFFICULTY

There are four categories of encounter difficulty.

Easy. An easy encounter doesn't tax the characters' resources or put them in serious peril. They might lose a few hit points, but victory is pretty much guaranteed.

Medium. A medium encounter usually has one or two scary moments for the players, but the characters should emerge victorious with no casualties. One or more of them might need to use healing resources.

Hard. A hard encounter could go badly for the adventurers. Weaker characters might get taken out of the fight, and there's a slim chance that one or more characters might die.

Deadly. A deadly encounter could be lethal for one or more player characters. Survival often requires good tactics and quick thinking, and the party risks defeat.

XP THRESHOLDS BY CHARACTER LEVEL

Character Level	Encounter Difficulty			
	Easy	Medium	Hard	Deadly
1st	25	50	75	100
2nd	50	100	150	200
3rd	75	150	225	400
4th	125	250	375	500
5th	250	500	750	1,100
6th	300	600	900	1,400
7th	350	750	1,100	1,700
8th	450	900	1,400	2,100
9th	550	1,100	1,600	2,400
10th	600	1,200	1,900	2,800
11th	800	1,600	2,400	3,600
12th	1,000	2,000	3,000	4,500
13th	1,100	2,200	3,400	5,100
14th	1,250	2,500	3,800	5,700
15th	1,400	2,800	4,300	6,400
16th	1,600	3,200	4,800	7,200
17th	2,000	3,900	5,900	8,800
18th	2,100	4,200	6,300	9,500
19th	2,400	4,900	7,300	10,900
20th	2,800	5,700	8,500	12,700

CHALLENGE RATING

When putting together an encounter or adventure, especially at lower levels, exercise caution when using monsters whose challenge rating is higher than the party's average level. Such a creature might deal enough damage with a single action to take out adventurers of a lower level. For example, an ogre has a challenge rating of 2, but it can kill a 1st-level wizard with a single blow.

In addition, some monsters have features that might be difficult or impossible for lower-level characters to overcome. For example, a rakshasa has a challenge rating of 13 and is immune to spells of 6th level and lower. Spellcasters of 12th level or lower have no spells higher than 6th level, meaning that they won't be able to affect the rakshasa with their magic, putting the adventurers at a serious disadvantage. Such an encounter would be significantly tougher for the party than the monster's challenge rating might suggest.

EVALUATING ENCOUNTER DIFFICULTY

Use the following method to gauge the difficulty of any combat encounter.

1. Determine XP Thresholds. First, determine the experience point (XP) thresholds for each character in the party. The XP Thresholds by Character Level table below has four XP thresholds for each character level, one for each category of encounter difficulty. Use a character's level to determine his or her XP thresholds. Repeat this process for every character in the party.

2. Determine the Party's XP Threshold. For each category of encounter difficulty, add up the characters' XP thresholds. This determines the party's XP threshold. You'll end up with four totals, one for each category of encounter difficulty.

For example, if your party includes three 3rd-level characters and one 2nd-level character, the party's totaled XP thresholds would be as follows:

Easy: 275 XP (75 + 75 + 75 + 50)

Medium: 550 XP (150 + 150 + 150 + 100)

Hard: 825 XP (225 + 225 + 225 + 150)

Deadly: 1,400 XP (400 + 400 + 400 + 200)

Record the totals, because you can use them for every encounter in your adventure.

3. Total the Monsters' XP. Add up the XP for all of the monsters in the encounter. Every monster has an XP value in its stat block.

4. Modify Total XP for Multiple Monsters. If the encounter includes more than one monster, apply a multiplier to the monsters' total XP. The more monsters there are, the more attack rolls you're making against the characters in a given round, and the more dangerous the encounter becomes. To correctly gauge an encounter's difficulty, multiply the total XP of all the monsters in the encounter by the value given in the Encounter Multipliers table.

For example, if an encounter includes four monsters worth a total of 500 XP, you would multiply the total XP of the monsters by 2, for an adjusted value of 1,000 XP. This adjusted value is *not* what the monsters are worth in terms of XP; the adjusted value's only purpose is to help you accurately assess the encounter's difficulty.

When making this calculation, don't count any monsters whose challenge rating is significantly below the average challenge rating of the other monsters in the group unless you think the weak monsters significantly contribute to the difficulty of the encounter.

ENCOUNTER MULTIPLIERS

Number of Monsters	Multiplier	Number of Monsters	Multiplier
1	× 1	7–10	× 2.5
2	× 1.5	11–14	× 3
3–6	× 2	15 or more	× 4

5. Compare XP. Compare the monsters' adjusted XP value to the party's XP thresholds. The closest threshold that is lower than the adjusted XP value of the monsters determines the encounter's difficulty.

For example, an encounter with one bugbear and three hobgoblins has an adjusted XP value of 1,000, making it a hard encounter for a party of three 3rd-level characters and one 2nd-level character (which has a hard encounter threshold of 825 XP and a deadly encounter threshold of 1,400 XP).

PARTY SIZE

The preceding guidelines assume that you have a party consisting of three to five adventurers.

If the party contains fewer than three characters, apply the next highest multiplier on the Encounter Multipliers table. For example, apply a multiplier of 1.5 when the characters fight a single monster, and a multiplier of 5 for groups of fifteen or more monsters.

If the party contains six or more characters, use the next lowest multiplier on the table. Use a multiplier of 0.5 for a single monster.

MULTIPART ENCOUNTERS

Sometimes an encounter features multiple enemies that the party doesn't face all at once. For example, monsters might come at the party in waves.

For such encounters, treat each discrete part or wave as a separate encounter for the purpose of determining its difficulty.

A party can't benefit from a short rest between parts of a multipart encounter, so they won't be able to spend Hit Dice to regain hit points or recover any abilities that require a short rest to regain. As a rule, if the adjusted XP value for the monsters in a multipart encounter is higher than one-third of the party's expected XP total for the adventuring day (see "The Adventuring Day," below), the encounter is going to be tougher than the sum of its parts.

BUILDING ENCOUNTERS ON A BUDGET

You can build an encounter if you know its desired difficulty. The party's XP thresholds give you an XP budget that you can spend on monsters to build easy,

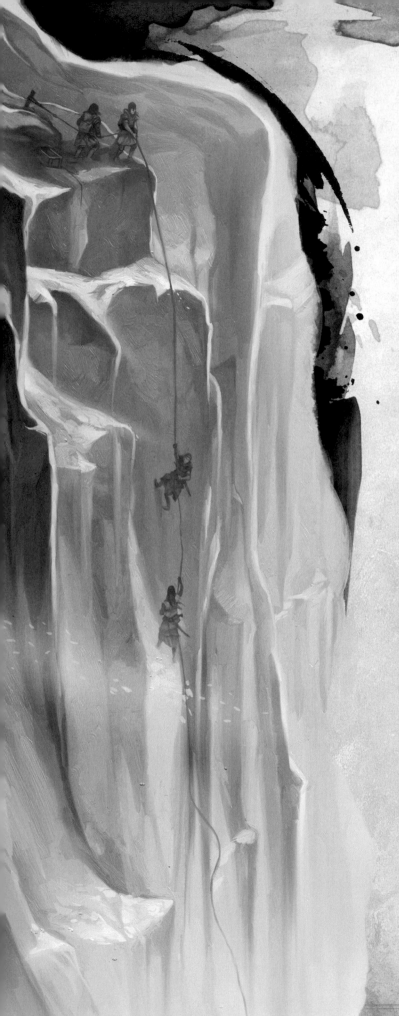

medium, hard, and deadly encounters. Just remember that groups of monsters eat up more of that budget than their base XP values would indicate (see step 4).

For example, using the party from step 2, you can build a medium encounter by making sure that the adjusted XP value of the monsters is at least 550 XP (the party's threshold for a medium encounter) and no more than 825 XP (the party's threshold for a hard encounter). A single monster of challenge rating 3 (such as a manticore or owlbear) is worth 700 XP, so that's one possibility. If you want a pair of monsters, each one will count for 1.5 times its base XP value. A pair of dire wolves (worth 200 XP each) have an adjusted XP value of 600, making them a medium encounter for the party as well.

To assist with this approach, appendix B presents a list of all monsters in the *Monster Manual* organized by challenge rating.

The Adventuring Day

Assuming typical adventuring conditions and average luck, most adventuring parties can handle about six to eight medium or hard encounters in a day. If the adventure has more easy encounters, the adventurers can get through more. If it has more deadly encounters, they can handle fewer.

In the same way you figure out the difficulty of an encounter, you can use the XP values of monsters and other opponents in an adventure as a guideline for how far the party is likely to progress.

For each character in the party, use the Adventuring Day XP table to estimate how much XP that character is expected to earn in a day. Add together the values of all party members to get a total for the party's adventuring day. This provides a rough estimate of the adjusted XP value for encounters the party can handle before the characters will need to take a long rest.

Adventuring Day XP

Level	Adjusted XP per Day per Character	Level	Adjusted XP per Day per Character
1st	300	11th	10,500
2nd	600	12th	11,500
3rd	1,200	13th	13,500
4th	1,700	14th	15,000
5th	3,500	15th	18,000
6th	4,000	16th	20,000
7th	5,000	17th	25,000
8th	6,000	18th	27,000
9th	7,500	19th	30,000
10th	9,000	20th	40,000

Short Rests

In general, over the course of a full adventuring day, the party will likely need to take two short rests, about one-third and two-thirds of the way through the day.

Modifying Encounter Difficulty

An encounter can be made easier or harder based on the choice of location and the situation.

Increase the difficulty of the encounter by one step (from easy to medium, for example) if the characters have a drawback that their enemies don't. Reduce the difficulty by one step if the characters have a benefit that their enemies don't. Any additional benefit or drawback pushes the encounter one step in the appropriate direction. If the characters have both a benefit and a drawback, the two cancel each other out.

Situational drawbacks include the following:

- The whole party is surprised, and the enemy isn't.
- The enemy has cover, and the party doesn't.
- The characters are unable to see the enemy.
- The characters are taking damage every round from some environmental effect or magical source, and the enemy isn't.
- The characters are hanging from a rope, in the midst of scaling a sheer wall or cliff, stuck to the floor, or otherwise in a situation that greatly hinders their mobility or makes them sitting ducks.

Situational benefits are similar to drawbacks except that they benefit the characters instead of the enemy.

FUN COMBAT ENCOUNTERS

The following features can add more fun and suspense to a combat encounter:

- Terrain features that pose inherent risks to both the characters and their enemies, such as a frayed rope bridge and pools of green slime
- Terrain features that provide a change of elevation, such as pits, stacks of empty crates, ledges, and balconies
- Features that either inspire or force characters and their enemies to move around, such as chandeliers, kegs of gunpowder or oil, and whirling blade traps
- Enemies in hard-to-reach locations or defensive positions, so that characters who normally attack at range are forced to move around the battlefield
- Different types of monsters working together

RANDOM ENCOUNTERS

As characters explore a wilderness area or dungeon complex, they are bound to encounter the unexpected. Random encounters are a way to deliver the unexpected. They are usually presented in the form of a table. When a random encounter occurs, you roll a die and consult the table to determine what the party encounters.

Some players and DMs view random encounters in an adventure as time-wasters, yet well-designed random encounters can serve a variety of useful purposes:

- **Create urgency.** Adventurers don't tend to dawdle if the threat of random encounters is hanging over their heads. Wanting to avoid wandering monsters creates a strong incentive to look for a safe place to rest. (Rolling dice behind the DM screen can often accomplish this even without an actual encounter.)
- **Establish atmosphere.** The appearance of thematically linked creatures as random encounters helps to create a consistent tone and atmosphere for an adventure. For example, an encounter table filled with bats, wraiths, giant spiders, and zombies creates a sense of horror, and tells the adventurers to prepare for battle with even more powerful creatures of the night.
- **Drain character resources.** Random encounters can drain the party's hit points and spell slots, leaving the adventurers feeling underpowered and vulnerable. This creates tension, as players are forced to make decisions based on the fact that their characters aren't at full strength.
- **Provide assistance.** Some random encounters can benefit the characters instead of hindering or harming them. Helpful creatures or NPCs might provide the adventurers with useful information or assistance when they need it most.
- **Add interest.** Random encounters can reveal details about your world. They can foreshadow danger or provide hints that will help the adventurers prepare for the encounters to come.
- **Reinforce campaign themes.** Random encounters can remind the players of the major themes of the campaign. For example, if your campaign features an ongoing war between two nations, you might design random encounter tables to reinforce the ever-present nature of the conflict. In friendly territory, your tables might include bedraggled troops returning from battle, refugees fleeing invading forces, heavily guarded caravans full of weapons, and lone messengers on horseback riding for the front lines. While characters are in hostile territory, the tables might include battlefields littered with the recently slain, armies of evil humanoids on the march, and improvised gibbets holding the bodies of deserters who tried to flee the conflict.

Random encounters should never be tiresome to you or your players. You don't want the players to feel as if they aren't making progress because another random encounter brings their progress to a halt whenever they try to move forward. Likewise, you don't want to spend time distracted by random encounters that add nothing to the adventure narrative or that interfere with the overall pace you're trying to set.

Not every DM likes to use random encounters. You might find that they distract from your game or are otherwise causing more trouble than you want. If random encounters don't work for you, don't use them.

TRIGGERING RANDOM ENCOUNTERS

Because you want random encounters to build on the intended narrative of a game session, not compete with it, you should choose the placement of those encounters carefully. Think about a random encounter under any of the following circumstances:

- The players are getting off track and slowing down the game.
- The characters stop for a short or long rest.
- The characters are undertaking a long, uneventful journey.
- The characters draw attention to themselves when they should be keeping a low profile.

CREATING RANDOM ENCOUNTER TABLES

Creating your own random encounter tables is straightforward. Determine what sort of encounters might occur in a given dungeon area, figure out the likelihood of a particular encounter occurring, then arrange the results. An "encounter" in this case could be a single monster or NPC, a group of monsters or NPCs, a random event (such as an earth tremor or a parade), or a random discovery (such as a charred corpse or a message scrawled on a wall).

Assemble Your Encounters. Once you've established a location through which the adventurers are likely to pass, be it a wilderness area or dungeon complex, make a list of creatures that might be found wandering there. If you're not sure which creatures to include, appendix B has lists of monsters organized by terrain type.

For a sylvan woodland, you might create a table that includes centaurs, faerie dragons, pixies, sprites, dryads, satyrs, blink dogs, elks, owlbears, treants, giant owls, and a unicorn. If elves inhabit the forest, the table might also include elf druids and elf scouts. Perhaps gnolls are threatening the woods, so adding gnolls and hyenas to the table would be a fun surprise for players. Another fun surprise would be a wandering predator, such as a displacer beast that likes to hunt blink dogs. The table could also use a few random encounters of a less monstrous nature, such as a grove of burned trees (the handiwork of the gnolls), an ivy-covered elven statue, and a plant with glowing berries that turn creatures invisible when ingested.

When choosing monsters for a random encounter table, try to imagine why the monsters would be encountered outside their lairs. What is each monster up to? Is it on patrol? Hunting for food? Searching for something? Also consider whether a creature is moving stealthily as it travels through the area.

As with planned encounters, random encounters are more interesting when they happen in memorable locations. Outdoors the adventurers might be crossing a forest clearing when they encounter a unicorn or be pushing through a dense section of forest when they come across a nest of spiders. Crossing a desert, characters might discover an oasis haunted by wights or a rocky outcropping on which a blue dragon perches.

Probabilities. A random encounter table can be created in a number of ways, ranging from simple (roll 1d6 for one of six possible encounters) to complicated (roll percentile dice, modify for time of day, and cross-index the modified number with the dungeon level). The sample encounter table presented here uses a range of 2 to 20 (nineteen entries total), generated using 1d12 + 1d8. The probability curve ensures that encounters appearing in the middle of the table are more likely to occur than encounters placed at the beginning or end of the table. A roll of 2 or 20 is rare (about a 1 percent chance of either), while each of the rolls from 9 to 13 occurs a little over 8 percent of the time.

The Sylvan Forest Encounters table is an example of a random encounter table that implements the ideas mentioned above. Creature names in **bold** refer to stat blocks that appear in the *Monster Manual*.

CHECKING FOR RANDOM ENCOUNTERS

You decide when a random encounter happens, or you roll. Consider checking for a random encounter once every hour, once every 4 to 8 hours, or once during the day and once during a long rest—whatever makes the most sense based on how active the area is.

If you roll, do so with a d20. If the result is 18 or higher, a random encounter occurs. You then roll on an appropriate random encounter table to determine what the adventurers meet, rerolling if the die result doesn't make sense given the circumstances.

Random encounter tables might be provided as part of the adventure you're running, or you can use the information in this chapter to build your own. Creating your own tables is the best way to reinforce the themes and flavor of your home campaign.

Not every run-in with another creature counts as a random encounter. Encounter tables don't usually include rabbits hopping through the undergrowth, harmless rats scurrying through dungeon halls, or average citizens walking through the streets of a city. Random encounter tables present obstacles and events that advance the plot, foreshadow important elements or themes of the adventure, and provide fun distractions.

RANDOM ENCOUNTER CHALLENGE

Random encounters need not be level-appropriate challenges for the adventurers, but it's considered bad form to slaughter a party using a random encounter, since most players consider this ending to be an unsatisfying one.

Not all random encounters with monsters need to be resolved through combat. A 1st-level party of adventurers could have a random encounter with a young dragon circling above a forest canopy in search of a quick meal, but the characters should have the option to hide or bargain for their lives if the dragon spots them. Similarly, the party might encounter a stone giant roaming the hills, but it might have no intention of harming anyone. In fact, it might shy away from the party because of its reclusive nature. The giant might attack only characters who annoy it.

That said, a random encounter table usually includes hostile (though not necessarily evil) monsters that are meant to be fought. The following monsters are considered appropriate combat challenges:

- A single monster with a challenge rating equal to or lower than the party's level.
- A group of monsters whose adjusted XP value constitutes an easy, medium, or hard challenge for the party, as determined using the encounter-building guidelines earlier in this chapter.

SYLVAN FOREST ENCOUNTERS

d12 + d8	Encounter
2	1 **displacer beast**
3	1 **gnoll pack lord** and 2d4 **gnolls**
4	1d4 **gnolls** and 2d4 **hyenas**
5	A grove of burned trees. Characters searching the area and succeeding on a DC 10 Wisdom (Survival) check find gnoll tracks. Following the tracks for 1d4 hours leads to an encounter with gnolls, or the discovery of dead gnolls with elven arrows sticking out of their flea-ridden corpses.
6	1 **giant owl**
7	An ivy-covered statue of an elven deity or hero.
8	1 **dryad** (50%) or 1d4 **satyrs** (50%)
9	1d4 **centaurs**
10	2d4 **scouts** (elves). One scout carries a horn and can use its action to blow it. If the horn is blown within the forest, roll on this table again. If the result indicates a monster encounter, the indicated monster or monsters arrive in 1d4 minutes. New arrivals other than gnolls, hyenas, owlbears, and displacer beasts are friendly toward the scouts.
11	2d4 **pixies** (50%) or 2d4 **sprites** (50%)

d12 + d8	Encounter
12	1 **owlbear**
13	1d4 **elks** (75%) or 1 **giant elk** (25%)
14	1d4 **blink dogs**
15	A magical plant with 2d4 glowing berries. A creature that ingests a berry becomes invisible for 1 hour, or until it attacks or casts a spell. Once picked, a berry loses its magic after 12 hours. Berries regrow at midnight, but if all its berries are picked, the plant becomes nonmagical and grows no more berries.
16	An elven tune carried on a gentle breeze
17	1d4 orange (75%) or blue (25%) **faerie dragons**
18	1 **druid** (elf). The druid is initially indifferent toward the party but becomes friendly if the characters agree to rid the forest of its gnoll infestation.
19	1 **treant**. The treant is friendly if the party includes one or more elves or is accompanied by a visible fey creature. The treant is hostile if the characters are carrying open flames. Otherwise, it is indifferent and doesn't announce its presence as the characters pass by.
20	1 **unicorn**

CHAPTER 4: CREATING NONPLAYER CHARACTERS

NONPLAYER CHARACTER IS ANY CHARACTER controlled by the Dungeon Master. NPCs can be enemies or allies, regular folk or named monsters. They include the local innkeeper, the old wizard who lives in the tower on the outskirts of town, the death knight out to destroy the kingdom, and the dragon counting gold in its cavernous lair.

This chapter shows you how to flesh out nonplayer characters for your game. For guidelines on generating monster-like stat blocks for an NPC, see chapter 9, "Dungeon Master's Workshop."

DESIGNING NPCs

Nothing brings your adventures and campaigns to life better than a cast of well-developed NPCs. That said, NPCs in your game rarely need as much complexity as a well-crafted character in a novel or movie. Most NPCs are bit players in the campaign, whereas the adventurers are the stars.

QUICK NPCs

An NPC doesn't need combat statistics unless it poses a threat. Moreover, most NPCs need only one or two qualities to make them memorable. For example, your players will have no trouble remembering the no-nonsense blacksmith with the tattoo of the black rose on his right shoulder or the badly dressed bard with the broken nose.

DETAILED NPCs

For NPCs who play larger roles in your adventures, allow more time to flesh out their histories and personalities. As you'll see, ten sentences can sum up the main elements of a memorable NPC, one sentence for each of the following:

- Occupation and history
- Appearance
- Abilities
- Talent
- Mannerism
- Interactions with others
- Useful knowledge
- Ideal
- Bond
- Flaw or secret

Although the material here focuses on humanoid NPCs, you can adjust details to create monstrous NPCs as well.

OCCUPATION AND HISTORY

In one sentence, describe the NPC's occupation and provide a brief historical note that hints at the character's past. For example, the NPC might have served in an army, been imprisoned for a crime, or adventured years ago.

APPEARANCE

In one sentence, describe the NPC's most distinctive physical features. You can roll on the NPC Appearance table or choose a feature that suits the character.

NPC APPEARANCE

d20	Feature
1	Distinctive jewelry: earrings, necklace, circlet, bracelets
2	Piercings
3	Flamboyant or outlandish clothes
4	Formal, clean clothes
5	Ragged, dirty clothes
6	Pronounced scar
7	Missing teeth
8	Missing fingers
9	Unusual eye color (or two different colors)
10	Tattoos
11	Birthmark
12	Unusual skin color
13	Bald
14	Braided beard or hair
15	Unusual hair color
16	Nervous eye twitch
17	Distinctive nose
18	Distinctive posture (crooked or rigid)
19	Exceptionally beautiful
20	Exceptionally ugly

ABILITIES

You don't need to roll ability scores for the NPC, but note abilities that are above or below average—great strength or monumental stupidity, for example—and use them to inform the NPC's qualities.

NPC ABILITIES

d6	High Ability
1	Strength—powerful, brawny, strong as an ox
2	Dexterity—lithe, agile, graceful
3	Constitution—hardy, hale, healthy
4	Intelligence—studious, learned, inquisitive
5	Wisdom—perceptive, spiritual, insightful
6	Charisma—persuasive, forceful, born leader

d6	Low Ability
1	Strength—feeble, scrawny
2	Dexterity—clumsy, fumbling
3	Constitution—sickly, pale
4	Intelligence—dim-witted, slow
5	Wisdom—oblivious, absentminded
6	Charisma—dull, boring

Talent

In one sentence, describe something that your NPC can do that is special, if anything. Roll on the NPC Talents table or use it to spur your own ideas.

NPC Talents

d20	Talent
1	Plays a musical instrument
2	Speaks several languages fluently
3	Unbelievably lucky
4	Perfect memory
5	Great with animals
6	Great with children
7	Great at solving puzzles
8	Great at one game
9	Great at impersonations
10	Draws beautifully
11	Paints beautifully
12	Sings beautifully
13	Drinks everyone under the table
14	Expert carpenter
15	Expert cook
16	Expert dart thrower and rock skipper
17	Expert juggler
18	Skilled actor and master of disguise
19	Skilled dancer
20	Knows thieves' cant

Mannerism

In one sentence, describe one mannerism that will help players remember the NPC. Roll on the NPC Mannerisms and Quirks table or use it to generate your own ideas.

NPC Mannerisms

d20	Mannerism
1	Prone to singing, whistling, or humming quietly
2	Speaks in rhyme or some other peculiar way
3	Particularly low or high voice
4	Slurs words, lisps, or stutters
5	Enunciates overly clearly
6	Speaks loudly
7	Whispers
8	Uses flowery speech or long words
9	Frequently uses the wrong word
10	Uses colorful oaths and exclamations
11	Makes constant jokes or puns
12	Prone to predictions of doom
13	Fidgets
14	Squints
15	Stares into the distance
16	Chews something
17	Paces
18	Taps fingers
19	Bites fingernails
20	Twirls hair or tugs beard

Interactions with Others

In one sentence, describe how the NPC interacts with others, using the NPC Interaction Traits table if necessary. An NPC's behavior can change depending on who he or she is interacting with. For example, an innkeeper might be friendly toward guests and rude to her staff.

NPC Interaction Traits

d12	Trait	d12	Trait
1	Argumentative	7	Honest
2	Arrogant	8	Hot tempered
3	Blustering	9	Irritable
4	Rude	10	Ponderous
5	Curious	11	Quiet
6	Friendly	12	Suspicious

Useful Knowledge

In a sentence, describe one bit of knowledge the NPC possesses that might be of use to the player characters. The NPC might know something as banal as the best inn in town or as important as a clue needed to solve a murder.

Ideal

In a sentence, describe one ideal that the NPC holds dear and which governs his or her greater actions. Player characters who uncover an NPC's ideal can use what they've learned to influence the NPC in a social interaction (as discussed in chapter 8, "Running the Game").

Ideals can connect to alignment, as shown on the NPC Ideals table. The alignment connections here are suggestions only; an evil character could have beauty as an ideal, for instance.

NPC Ideals

d6	Good Ideal	Evil Ideal
1	Beauty	Domination
2	Charity	Greed
3	Greater good	Might
4	Life	Pain
5	Respect	Retribution
6	Self-sacrifice	Slaughter

d6	Lawful Ideal	Chaotic Ideal
1	Community	Change
2	Fairness	Creativity
3	Honor	Freedom
4	Logic	Independence
5	Responsibility	No limits
6	Tradition	Whimsy

d6	Neutral Ideal	Other Ideals
1	Balance	Aspiration
2	Knowledge	Discovery
3	Live and let live	Glory
4	Moderation	Nation
5	Neutrality	Redemption
6	People	Self-knowledge

BOND

In a sentence, summarize the people, places, or things that are especially important to the NPC. The NPC Bonds table offers suggestions in broad categories.

The character backgrounds in the *Player's Handbook* explore bonds in more detail, and player characters who uncover an NPC's bond can use what they've learned to influence the NPC in a social interaction (as discussed in chapter 8).

NPC BONDS

d10	Bond
1	Dedicated to fulfilling a personal life goal
2	Protective of close family members
3	Protective of colleagues or compatriots
4	Loyal to a benefactor, patron, or employer
5	Captivated by a romantic interest
6	Drawn to a special place
7	Protective of a sentimental keepsake
8	Protective of a valuable possession
9	Out for revenge
10	Roll twice, ignoring results of 10

FLAW OR SECRET

In one sentence, describe the NPC's flaw—some element of the character's personality or history that could potentially undermine the character—or a secret that the NPC is trying to hide.

The NPC Flaws and Secrets table provides several ideas. The backgrounds in the *Player's Handbook* can be used to create more detailed flaws. Player characters who uncover an NPC's flaw or secret can use what they've learned to influence the NPC in a social interaction (as discussed in chapter 8).

NPC FLAWS AND SECRETS

d12	Flaw or Secret
1	Forbidden love or susceptibility to romance
2	Enjoys decadent pleasures
3	Arrogance
4	Envies another creature's possessions or station
5	Overpowering greed
6	Prone to rage
7	Has a powerful enemy
8	Specific phobia
9	Shameful or scandalous history
10	Secret crime or misdeed
11	Possession of forbidden lore
12	Foolhardy bravery

MONSTERS AS NPCS

Named monsters that play a significant role in an adventure deserve the same attention you would give to a humanoid NPC, with mannerisms as well as ideals, bonds, flaws, and secrets. If a beholder mastermind is behind the criminal activities in a city, don't rely solely on the entry in the *Monster Manual* to describe the creature's appearance and personality. Take the

time to give it a bit of background, a distinctive quirk of appearance, and especially an ideal, a bond, and a flaw.

As an example, consider the Xanathar, a beholder that runs extensive criminal operations in the city of Waterdeep. The Xanathar's spherical body is covered in leathery flesh with a texture similar to cobblestones. Its eyestalks are jointed like the legs of an insect, and some of the stalks have magic rings on them. The Xanathar's speech is slow and deliberate, and it prefers to turn its central eye away from creatures it speaks to. Like all beholders, it sees other creatures as inferiors, though it understands the usefulness of its humanoid minions. The Xanathar uses the sewers beneath Waterdeep to access virtually any location within or under the city.

The Xanathar's ideal is greed. It craves powerful magic items and surrounds itself with gold, platinum, and precious gems. Its bond is to its lair—an elaborate cavern complex carved out between the twisting sewers of Waterdeep, which it inherited from its predecessors and cherishes above all else. Its flaw is a weakness for exotic pleasures: finely prepared foods, scented oils, and rare spices and herbs.

Establishing this information allows you to play the Xanathar as more than an ordinary beholder. The complexities of the creature's characterization create more memorable interaction and interesting story possibilities.

NPC Statistics

When you give an NPC game statistics, you have three main options: giving the NPC only the few statistics it needs, give the NPC a monster stat block, or give the NPC a class and levels. The latter two options require a bit of explanation.

Using a Monster Stat Block

Appendix B of the *Monster Manual* contains statistics for many generic NPCs that you can customize as you see fit, and chapter 9 of this book offers guidelines on adjusting their statistics and creating a new stat block.

Using Classes and Levels

You can create an NPC just as you would a player character, using the rules in the *Player's Handbook*. You can even use a character sheet to keep track of the NPC's vital information.

Class Options. In addition to the class options in the *Player's Handbook*, two additional class options are available for evil player characters and NPCs: the Death domain for clerics and the oathbreaker for paladins. Both options are detailed at the end of this chapter.

Equipment. Most NPCs don't need an exhaustive list of equipment. An enemy meant to be faced in combat requires weapons and armor, plus any treasure the NPC carries (including magic items that might be used against the adventurers).

Challenge Rating. An NPC built for combat needs a challenge rating. Use the rules in chapter 9 to determine the NPC's challenge rating, just as you would for a monster you designed.

NPC Party Members

NPCs might join the adventuring party because they want a share of the loot and are willing to accept an equal share of the risk, or they might follow the adventurers because of a bond of loyalty, gratitude, or love. Such NPCs are controlled by you, or you can transfer control to the players. Even if a player controls an NPC, it's up to you to make sure the NPC is portrayed as a character in his or her own right, not just as a servant that the players can manipulate for their own benefit.

Any NPC that accompanies the adventurers acts as a party member and earns a full share of experience points. When determining the difficulty of a combat encounter (see chapter 3), make sure to include all NPC party members.

Low-Level Followers

Your campaign might allow player characters to take on lower-level NPCs as followers. For example, a paladin might have a 1st-level paladin as a squire, a wizard might accept a 2nd-level wizard as an apprentice, a cleric might choose (or be assigned) a 3rd-level cleric as an acolyte, and a bard might take on a 4th-level bard as an understudy.

One advantage of allowing lower-level characters to join the party is that players have backup characters if their main characters take time off, retire, or die. One disadvantage is that you and your players have more party members to account for.

Since lower-level NPC party members receive equal party shares of XP, they will gain levels more quickly than the adventurers (the benefit of studying under such experienced masters), and might eventually catch up to them. It also means the adventurers' advancement is slowed somewhat, as they must share their XP with an NPC shouldering only part of the adventuring burden.

Powerful monsters that are an appropriate challenge for higher-level characters can deal enough damage to instantly kill or incapacitate a low-level follower. The adventurers should expect to spend effort and resources protecting lower-level NPC party members and to provide healing when this protection fails.

ADVENTURER NPCs

If you don't have enough players to form a full party, you can use NPCs to fill out the ranks. These NPCs should be the same level as the lowest-level adventurer in the party and built (either by you or your players) using the character creation and advancement rules in the *Player's Handbook*. It's easiest on you if you let the players create and run these supporting characters.

Encourage players to roleplay supporting characters as true to the NPCs' personality traits, ideals, bonds, and flaws as possible, so that they don't come across as automatons. If you don't feel that an NPC is being portrayed well, you can take control of the NPC, give it to another player, or simply have the NPC leave the party.

NPC supporting characters are easier to play if you limit their class options. Good candidates for supporting characters include a cleric with the Life domain, a fighter with the Champion archetype, a rogue with the Thief archetype, and a wizard specializing in Evocation.

OPTIONAL RULE: LOYALTY

Loyalty is an optional rule you can use to determine how far an NPC party member will go to protect or assist the other members of the party (even those he or she doesn't particularly like). An NPC party member who is abused or ignored is likely to abandon or betray the party, whereas an NPC who owes a life debt to the characters or shares their goals might fight to the death for them. Loyalty can be roleplayed or represented by this rule.

LOYALTY SCORE

An NPC's loyalty is measured on a numerical scale from 0 to 20. The NPC's maximum loyalty score is equal to the highest Charisma score among all adventurers in the party, and its starting loyalty score is half that number. If the highest Charisma score changes—perhaps a character dies or leaves the group—adjust the NPC's loyalty score accordingly.

TRACKING LOYALTY

Keep track of an NPC's loyalty score in secret so that the players won't know for sure whether an NPC party member is loyal or disloyal (even if the NPC is currently under a player's control).

An NPC's loyalty score increases by 1d4 if other party members help the NPC achieve a goal tied to its bond. Likewise, an NPC's loyalty score increases by 1d4 if the NPC is treated particularly well (for example, given a magic weapon as a gift) or rescued by another party member. An NPC's loyalty score can never be raised above its maximum.

When other party members act in a manner that runs counter to the NPC's alignment or bond, reduce the NPC's loyalty score by 1d4. Reduce the NPC's loyalty score by 2d4 if the character is abused, misled, or endangered by other party members for purely selfish reasons.

An NPC whose loyalty score drops to 0 is no longer loyal to the party and might part ways with them. A loyalty score can never drop below 0.

An NPC with a loyalty score of 10 or higher risks life and limb to help fellow party members. If the NPC's loyalty score is between 1 and 10, its loyalty is tenuous. An NPC whose loyalty drops to 0 no longer acts in the party's best interests. The disloyal NPC either leaves the party (attacking characters who attempt to intervene) or works in secret to bring about the party's downfall.

CONTACTS

Contacts are NPCs with close ties to one or more of the player characters. They don't go on adventures, but they can provide information, rumors, supplies, or professional advice, either for free or at a cost. Some of the backgrounds in the *Player's Handbook* suggest

contacts for beginning adventurers, and characters are likely to secure more helpful contacts over the course of their adventuring careers.

A name and a few choice details are all you need for casual contacts, but take the time to flesh out a recurring contact, especially one who might become an ally or enemy at some point. At the very least, give some thought to a contact's goals and how those goals are likely to come into play.

PATRONS

A patron is a contact who employs the adventurers, providing help or rewards as well as quests and adventure hooks. Most of the time, a patron has a vested interest in the adventurers' success and doesn't need to be persuaded to help them.

A patron might be a retired adventurer who seeks younger heroes to deal with rising threats, or a mayor who knows that the town guard can't handle a dragon demanding tribute. A sheriff becomes a patron by offering a bounty for kobold raiders terrorizing the local countryside, as does a noble who wants an abandoned estate cleared of monsters.

HIRELINGS

Adventurers can pay NPCs to provide services in a variety of circumstances. Information on hirelings appears in chapter 5, "Equipment," of the *Player's Handbook*.

Hireling NPCs rarely become important in an adventure, and most require little development. When adventurers hire a coach to carry them across town or need a letter delivered, the driver or messenger is a hireling, and the adventurers might never even converse with that NPC or learn his or her name. A ship captain carrying the adventurers across the sea is also a hireling, but such a character has the potential to turn into an ally, a patron, or even an enemy as the adventure unfolds.

When the adventurers hire an NPC for long-term work, add the cost of that NPC's services to the characters' lifestyle expenses. See the "Additional Expenses" section of chapter 6, "Between Adventures," for more information.

EXTRAS

Extras are the characters and creatures in the background that the main characters rarely, if ever, interact with.

Extras might be elevated to more important roles by virtue of adventurers singling them out. For instance, a player might be hooked by a passing reference you make to a street urchin and try to strike up a conversation with the youngster. Suddenly, an extra on whom you placed no importance becomes a central figure in an improvised roleplaying scene.

Whenever extras are present, be prepared to come up with names and mannerisms on the fly. In a pinch, you can plunder the race-specific character names found in chapter 2, "Races," of the *Player's Handbook*.

VILLAINS

By their actions, villains provide job security for heroes. Chapter 3 helps you determine suitable villains for your adventures, while this section helps you flesh out their evil schemes, methods, and weaknesses. Let the tables that follow inspire you.

VILLAIN'S SCHEME

d8	Objective and Scheme
1	*Immortality (d4)*
	1 Acquire a legendary item to prolong life
	2 Ascend to godhood
	3 Become undead or obtain a younger body
	4 Steal a planar creature's essence
2	*Influence (d4)*
	1 Seize a position of power or title
	2 Win a contest or tournament
	3 Win favor with a powerful individual
	4 Place a pawn in a position of power
3	*Magic (d6)*
	1 Obtain an ancient artifact
	2 Build a construct or magical device
	3 Carry out a deity's wishes
	4 Offer sacrifices to a deity
	5 Contact a lost deity or power
	6 Open a gate to another world
4	*Mayhem (d6)*
	1 Fulfill an apocalyptic prophecy
	2 Enact the vengeful will of a god or patron
	3 Spread a vile contagion
	4 Overthrow a government
	5 Trigger a natural disaster
	6 Utterly destroy a bloodline or clan
5	*Passion (d4)*
	1 Prolong the life of a loved one
	2 Prove worthy of another person's love
	3 Raise or restore a dead loved one
	4 Destroy rivals for another person's affection
6	*Power (d4)*
	1 Conquer a region or incite a rebellion
	2 Seize control of an army
	3 Become the power behind the throne
	4 Gain the favor of a ruler
7	*Revenge (d4)*
	1 Avenge a past humiliation or insult
	2 Avenge a past imprisonment or injury
	3 Avenge the death of a loved one
	4 Retrieve stolen property and punish the thief
8	*Wealth (d4)*
	1 Control natural resources or trade
	2 Marry into wealth
	3 Plunder ancient ruins
	4 Steal land, goods, or money

VILLAIN'S METHODS

d20	Methods
1	*Agricultural devastation (d4)*
	1 Blight
	2 Crop failure
	3 Drought
	4 Famine
2	Assault or beatings
3	Bounty hunting or assassination
4	*Captivity or coercion (d10)*
	1 Bribery
	2 Enticement
	3 Eviction
	4 Imprisonment
	5 Kidnapping
	6 Legal intimidation
	7 Press gangs
	8 Shackling
	9 Slavery
	10 Threats or harassment
5	*Confidence scams (d6)*
	1 Breach of contract
	2 Cheating
	3 Fast talking
	4 Fine print
	5 Fraud or swindling
	6 Quackery or tricks
6	*Defamation (d4)*
	1 Framing
	2 Gossiping or slander
	3 Humiliation
	4 Libel or insults
7	Dueling
8	*Execution (d8)*
	1 Beheading
	2 Burning at the stake
	3 Burying alive
	4 Crucifixion
	5 Drawing and quartering
	6 Hanging
	7 Impalement
	8 Sacrifice (living)
9	Impersonation or disguise
10	Lying or perjury
11	*Magical mayhem (d8)*
	1 Hauntings
	2 Illusions
	3 Infernal bargains
	4 Mind control
	5 Petrification
	6 Raising or animating the dead
	7 Summoning monsters
	8 Weather control

d20	Methods
12	*Murder (d10)*
	1 Assassination
	2 Cannibalism
	3 Dismemberment
	4 Drowning
	5 Electrocution
	6 Euthanasia (involuntary)
	7 Disease
	8 Poisoning
	9 Stabbing
	10 Strangulation or suffocation
13	Neglect
14	*Politics (d6)*
	1 Betrayal or treason
	2 Conspiracy
	3 Espionage or spying
	4 Genocide
	5 Oppression
	6 Raising taxes
15	*Religion (d4)*
	1 Curses
	2 Desecration
	3 False gods
	4 Heresy or cults
16	Stalking
17	*Theft or Property Crime (d10)*
	1 Arson
	2 Blackmail or extortion
	3 Burglary
	4 Counterfeiting
	5 Highway robbery
	6 Looting
	7 Mugging
	8 Poaching
	9 Seizing property
	10 Smuggling
18	*Torture (d6)*
	1 Acid
	2 Blinding
	3 Branding
	4 Racking
	5 Thumbscrews
	6 Whipping
19	*Vice (d4)*
	1 Adultery
	2 Drugs or alcohol
	3 Gambling
	4 Seduction
20	*Warfare (d6)*
	1 Ambush
	2 Invasion
	3 Massacre
	4 Mercenaries
	5 Rebellion
	6 Terrorism

VILLAIN'S WEAKNESS

d8	Weakness
1	A hidden object holds the villain's soul.
2	The villain's power is broken if the death of its true love is avenged.
3	The villain is weakened in the presence of a particular artifact.
4	A special weapon deals extra damage when used against the villain.
5	The villain is destroyed if it speaks its true name.
6	An ancient prophecy or riddle reveals how the villain can be overthrown.
7	The villain falls when an ancient enemy forgives its past actions.
8	The villain loses its power if a mystic bargain it struck long ago is completed.

VILLAINOUS CLASS OPTIONS

You can use the rules in the *Player's Handbook* to create NPCs with classes and levels, the same way you create player characters. The class options below let you create two specific villainous archetypes: the evil high priest and the evil knight or antipaladin.

The Death Domain is an additional domain choice for evil clerics, and the Oathbreaker offers an alternative path for paladins who fall from grace. A player can choose one of these options with the your approval.

CLERIC: DEATH DOMAIN

The Death domain is concerned with the forces that cause death, as well as the negative energy that gives rise to undead creatures. Deities such as Chemosh, Myrkul, and Wee Jas are patrons of necromancers, death knights, liches, mummy lords, and vampires. Gods of the Death domain also embody murder (Anubis, Bhaal, and Pyremius), pain (Iuz or Loviatar), disease or poison (Incabulos, Talona, or Morgion), and the underworld (Hades and Hel).

DEATH DOMAIN SPELLS

Cleric Level	Spells
1st	*false life, ray of sickness*
3rd	*blindness/deafness, ray of enfeeblement*
5th	*animate dead, vampiric touch*
7th	*blight, death ward*
9th	*antilife shell, cloudkill*

BONUS PROFICIENCY

When the cleric chooses this domain at 1st level, he or she gains proficiency with martial weapons.

REAPER

At 1st level, the cleric learns one necromancy cantrip of his or her choice from any spell list. When the cleric casts a necromancy cantrip that normally targets only one creature, the spell can instead target two creatures within range and within 5 feet of each other.

VILLAIN'S SECRET WEAKNESS

Finding and exploiting a villain's weakness can be very gratifying for players, although a smart villain tries to conceal its weakness. A lich, for example, has a phylactery—a magical receptacle for its soul—that it keeps well hidden. Only by destroying the phylactery can the characters ensure the lich's destruction.

Channel Divinity: Touch of Death

Starting at 2nd level, the cleric can use Channel Divinity to destroy another creature's life force by touch.

When the cleric hits a creature with a melee attack, the cleric can use Channel Divinity to deal extra necrotic damage to the target. The damage equals 5 + twice his or her cleric level.

Inescapable Destruction

Starting at 6th level, the cleric's ability to channel negative energy becomes more potent. Necrotic damage dealt by the character's cleric spells and Channel Divinity options ignores resistance to necrotic damage.

Divine Strike

At 8th level, the cleric gains the ability to infuse his or her weapon strikes with necrotic energy. Once on each of the cleric's turns when he or she hits a creature with a weapon attack, the cleric can cause the attack to deal an extra 1d8 necrotic damage to the target. When the cleric reaches 14th level, the extra damage increases to 2d8.

Improved Reaper

Starting at 17th level, when the cleric casts a necromancy spell of 1st through 5th level that targets only one creature, the spell can instead target two creatures within range and within 5 feet of each other. If the spell consumes its material components, the cleric must provide them for each target.

Paladin: Oathbreaker

An Oathbreaker is a paladin who breaks his or her sacred oaths to pursue some dark ambition or serve an evil power. Whatever light burned in the paladin's heart has been extinguished. Only darkness remains.

A paladin must be evil and at least 3rd level to become an Oathbreaker. The paladin replaces the features specific to his or her Sacred Oath with Oathbreaker features.

Oathbreaker Spells

An Oathbreaker paladin loses previously gained oath spells and instead gains the following Oathbreaker spells at the paladin levels listed.

Oathbreaker Spells

Paladin Level	Spells
3rd	hellish rebuke, inflict wounds
5th	crown of madness, darkness
9th	animate dead, bestow curse
13th	blight, confusion
17th	contagion, dominate person

Channel Divinity

An Oathbreaker paladin of 3rd level or higher gains the following two Channel Divinity options.

Control Undead. As an action, the paladin targets one undead creature he or she can see within 30 feet of him or her. The target must make a Wisdom saving throw. On a failed save, the target must obey the paladin's commands for the next 24 hours, or until the paladin uses this Channel Divinity option again. An undead whose challenge rating is equal to or greater than the paladin's level is immune to this effect.

Dreadful Aspect. As an action, the paladin channels the darkest emotions and focuses them into a burst of magical menace. Each creature of the paladin's choice within 30 feet of the paladin must make a Wisdom saving throw if it can see the paladin. On a failed save, the target is frightened of the paladin for 1 minute. If a creature frightened by this effect ends its turn more than 30 feet away from the paladin, it can attempt another Wisdom saving throw to end the effect on it.

Aura of Hate

Starting at 7th level, the paladin, as well any fiends and undead within 10 feet of the paladin, gains a bonus to melee weapon damage rolls equal to the paladin's Charisma modifier (minimum of +1). A creature can benefit from this feature from only one paladin at a time.

At 18th level, the range of this aura increases to 30 feet.

Supernatural Resistance

At 15th level, the paladin gains resistance to bludgeoning, piercing, and slashing damage from nonmagical weapons.

Dread Lord

At 20th-level, the paladin can, as an action, surround himself or herself with an aura of gloom that lasts for 1 minute. The aura reduces any bright light in a 30-foot radius around the paladin to dim light. Whenever an enemy that is frightened by the paladin starts its turn in the aura, it takes 4d10 psychic damage. Additionally, the paladin and creatures he or she chooses in the aura are draped in deeper shadow. Creatures that rely on sight have disadvantage on attack rolls against creatures draped in this shadow.

While the aura lasts, the paladin can use a bonus action on his or her turn to cause the shadows in the aura to attack one creature. The paladin makes a melee spell attack against the target. If the attack hits, the target takes necrotic damage equal to 3d10 + the paladin's Charisma modifier.

After activating the aura, the paladin can't do so again until he or she finishes a long rest.

> ### Oathbreaker Atonement
>
> If you allow a player to choose the Oathbreaker option, you can later allow the paladin to atone and become a true paladin once more.
>
> The paladin who wishes to atone must first shed his or her evil alignment and demonstrate this alignment change through words and deeds. Having done so, the paladin loses all Oathbreaker features and must choose a deity and a sacred oath. (With your permission, the player can select a different deity or sacred oath than the character had previously.) However, the paladin doesn't gain the class features specific to that sacred oath until he or she completes some kind of dangerous quest or trial, as determined by the DM.
>
> A paladin who breaks his or her sacred oath a second time can become an oathbreaker once more, but can't atone.

CHAPTER 5: ADVENTURE ENVIRONMENTS

ANY D&D ADVENTURES REVOLVE around a dungeon setting. Dungeons in D&D include great halls and tombs, subterranean monster lairs, labyrinths riddled with death traps, natural caverns extending for miles beneath the surface of the world, and ruined castles.

Not every adventure takes place in a dungeon. A wilderness trek across the Desert of Desolation or a harrowing journey into the jungles of the Isle of Dread can be an exciting adventure in its own right. In the great outdoors, dragons wheel across the sky in search of prey, tribes of hobgoblins pour forth from their grim fortresses to wage war against their neighbors, ogres plunder farmsteads for food, and monstrous spiders drop from the web-shrouded canopies of trees.

Within a dungeon, adventurers are constrained by walls and doors around them, but in the wilderness, adventurers can travel in almost any direction they please. Therein lies the key difference between dungeon and wilderness: it's much easier to predict where the adventuring party might go in the dungeon because the options are limited—less so in the wilderness.

Villages, towns, and cities are cradles of civilization in a dangerous world, but they too offer opportunities for adventure. Encounters with monsters might seem unlikely within a city's walls, but urban settings have their own villains and perils. Evil, after all, takes many forms, and urban settings aren't always the safe havens they seem to be.

This chapter provides an overview of these three environments plus a few unusual environments, taking you through the process of creating an adventure location, with plenty of random tables to inspire you.

DUNGEONS

Some dungeons are old strongholds abandoned by the folk who built them. Others are natural caves or weird lairs carved out by foul monsters. They attract evil cults, monster tribes, and reclusive creatures. Dungeons are also home to ancient treasures: coins, gems, magic items, and other valuables hidden away in the darkness, often guarded by traps or jealously kept by the monsters that have collected them.

BUILDING A DUNGEON

When you set out to create a dungeon, think about its distinctive qualities. For example, a dungeon that serves as a hobgoblin stronghold has a different quality from an ancient temple inhabited by yuan-ti. This section lays out a process for creating a dungeon and bringing it to life.

DUNGEON LOCATION

You can use the Dungeon Location table to determine the locale of your dungeon. You can roll on the table or choose an entry that inspires you.

DUNGEON LOCATION

d100	Location
01–04	A building in a city
05–08	Catacombs or sewers beneath a city
09–12	Beneath a farmhouse
13–16	Beneath a graveyard
17–22	Beneath a ruined castle
23–26	Beneath a ruined city
27–30	Beneath a temple
31–34	In a chasm
35–38	In a cliff face
39–42	In a desert
43–46	In a forest
47–50	In a glacier
51–54	In a gorge
55–58	In a jungle
59–62	In a mountain pass
63–66	In a swamp
67–70	Beneath or on top of a mesa
71–74	In sea caves
75–78	In several connected mesas
79–82	On a mountain peak
83–86	On a promontory
87–90	On an island
91–95	Underwater
96–00	Roll on the Exotic Location table

EXOTIC LOCATION

d20	Location
1	Among the branches of a tree
2	Around a geyser
3	Behind a waterfall
4	Buried in an avalanche
5	Buried in a sandstorm
6	Buried in volcanic ash
7	Castle or structure sunken in a swamp
8	Castle or structure at the bottom of a sinkhole
9	Floating on the sea
10	In a meteorite
11	On a demiplane or in a pocket dimension
12	In an area devastated by a magical catastrophe
13	On a cloud
14	In the Feywild
15	In the Shadowfell
16	On an island in an underground sea
17	In a volcano
18	On the back of a Gargantuan living creature
19	Sealed inside a magical dome of force
20	Inside a *Mordenkainen's magnificent mansion*

DUNGEON CREATOR

A dungeon reflects its creators. A lost temple of the yuan-ti, choked by overgrown jungle plants, might feature ramps instead of stairs. Caverns carved by a

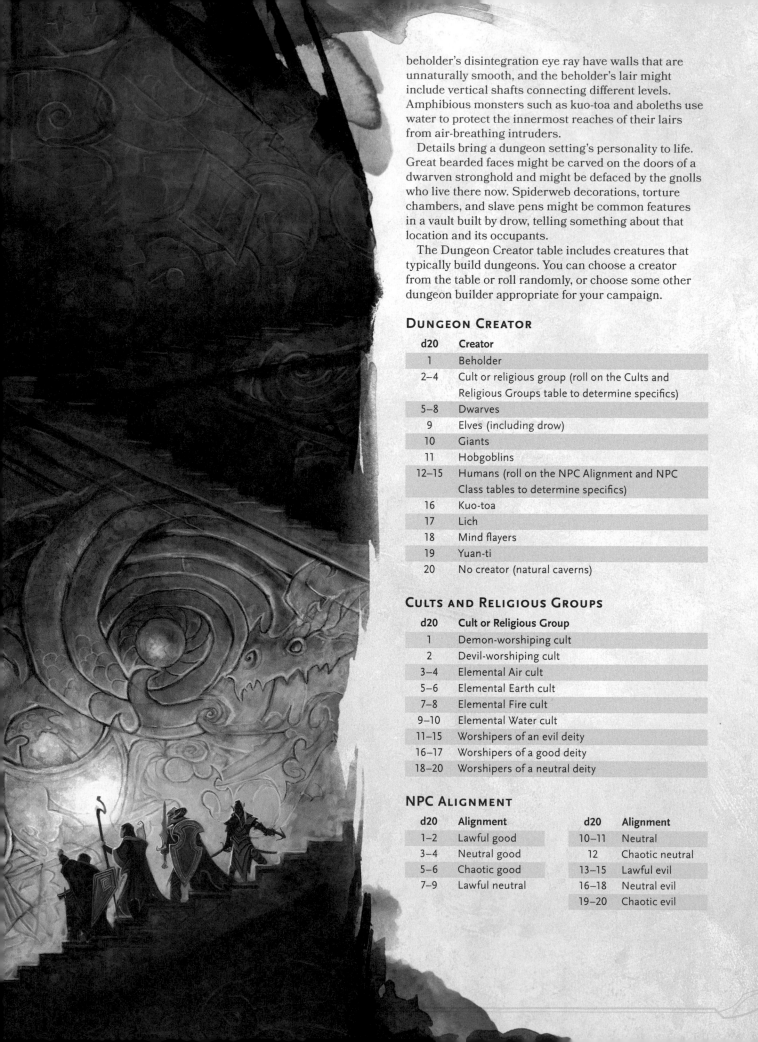

beholder's disintegration eye ray have walls that are unnaturally smooth, and the beholder's lair might include vertical shafts connecting different levels. Amphibious monsters such as kuo-toa and aboleths use water to protect the innermost reaches of their lairs from air-breathing intruders.

Details bring a dungeon setting's personality to life. Great bearded faces might be carved on the doors of a dwarven stronghold and might be defaced by the gnolls who live there now. Spiderweb decorations, torture chambers, and slave pens might be common features in a vault built by drow, telling something about that location and its occupants.

The Dungeon Creator table includes creatures that typically build dungeons. You can choose a creator from the table or roll randomly, or choose some other dungeon builder appropriate for your campaign.

DUNGEON CREATOR

d20	Creator
1	Beholder
2–4	Cult or religious group (roll on the Cults and Religious Groups table to determine specifics)
5–8	Dwarves
9	Elves (including drow)
10	Giants
11	Hobgoblins
12–15	Humans (roll on the NPC Alignment and NPC Class tables to determine specifics)
16	Kuo-toa
17	Lich
18	Mind flayers
19	Yuan-ti
20	No creator (natural caverns)

CULTS AND RELIGIOUS GROUPS

d20	Cult or Religious Group
1	Demon-worshiping cult
2	Devil-worshiping cult
3–4	Elemental Air cult
5–6	Elemental Earth cult
7–8	Elemental Fire cult
9–10	Elemental Water cult
11–15	Worshipers of an evil deity
16–17	Worshipers of a good deity
18–20	Worshipers of a neutral deity

NPC ALIGNMENT

d20	Alignment	d20	Alignment
1–2	Lawful good	10–11	Neutral
3–4	Neutral good	12	Chaotic neutral
5–6	Chaotic good	13–15	Lawful evil
7–9	Lawful neutral	16–18	Neutral evil
		19–20	Chaotic evil

NPC Class

d20	Class	d20	Class
1	Barbarian	9	Paladin
2	Bard	10	Ranger
3–4	Cleric	11–14	Rogue
5	Druid	15	Sorcerer
6–7	Fighter	16	Warlock
8	Monk	17–20	Wizard

Dungeon Purpose

Except in the case of a natural cavern, a dungeon is crafted and inhabited for a specific purpose that influences its design and features. You can choose a purpose from the Dungeon Purpose table, roll one at random, or use your own ideas.

Dungeon Purpose

d20	Purpose	d20	Purpose
1	Death trap	11–14	Stronghold
2–5	Lair	15–17	Temple or shrine
6	Maze	18–19	Tomb
7–9	Mine	20	Treasure vault
10	Planar gate		

Death Trap. This dungeon is built to eliminate any creature that dares to enter it. A death trap might guard the treasure of an insane wizard, or it might be designed to lure adventurers to their demise for some nefarious purpose, such as to feed souls to a lich's phylactery.

Lair. A lair is a place where monsters live. Typical lairs include ruins and caves.

Maze. A maze is intended to deceive or confuse those who enter it. Some mazes are elaborate obstacles that protect treasure, while others are gauntlets for prisoners banished there to be hunted and devoured by the monsters within.

Mine. An abandoned mine can quickly become infested with monsters, while miners who delve too deep can break through into the Underdark.

Planar Gate. Dungeons built around planar portals are often transformed by the planar energy seeping out through those portals.

Stronghold. A stronghold dungeon provides a secure base of operations for villains and monsters. It is usually ruled by a powerful individual, such as a wizard, vampire, or dragon, and it is larger and more complex than a simple lair.

Temple or Shrine. This dungeon is consecrated to a deity or other planar entity. The entity's worshipers control the dungeon and conduct their rites there.

Tomb. Tombs are magnets for treasure hunters, as well as monsters that hunger for the bones of the dead.

Treasure Vault. Built to protect powerful magic items and great material wealth, treasure vault dungeons are heavily guarded by monsters and traps.

History

In most cases, the original architects of a dungeon are long gone, and the question of what happened to them can help shape the dungeon's current state.

The Dungeon History table notes key events that can transform a site from its original purpose into a dungeon for adventurers to explore. Particularly old dungeons can have a history that consists of multiple events, each of which transformed the site in some way.

Dungeon History

d20	Key Event
1–3	Abandoned by creators
4	Abandoned due to plague
5–8	Conquered by invaders
9–10	Creators destroyed by attacking raiders
11	Creators destroyed by discovery made within the site
12	Creators destroyed by internal conflict
13	Creators destroyed by magical catastrophe
14–15	Creators destroyed by natural disaster
16	Location cursed by the gods and shunned
17–18	Original creator still in control
19	Overrun by planar creatures
20	Site of a great miracle

Dungeon Inhabitants

After a dungeon's creators depart, anyone or anything might move in. Intelligent monsters, mindless dungeon scavengers, predators and prey alike can be drawn to dungeons.

The monsters in a dungeon are more than a collection of random creatures that happen to live near one another. Fungi, vermin, scavengers, and predators can coexist in a complex ecology, alongside intelligent creatures who share living space through elaborate combinations of domination, negotiation, and bloodshed.

Characters might be able to sneak into a dungeon, ally with one faction, or play factions against each other to reduce the threat of the more powerful monsters. For example, in a dungeon inhabited by mind flayers and their goblinoid thralls, the adventurers might try to incite the goblins, hobgoblins, and bugbears to revolt against their illithid masters.

Dungeon Factions

A dungeon is sometimes dominated by a single group of intelligent humanoids, whether a tribe of orcs that have taken over a cavern complex or a gang of trolls inhabiting an aboveground ruin. Other times, particularly in larger dungeons, multiple groups of creatures share space and compete for resources.

For example, orcs that dwell in the mines of a ruined dwarf citadel might skirmish constantly against the hobgoblins that hold the citadel's upper tiers. Mind flayers that have established a colony in the lowest levels of the mines could manipulate and dominate key hobgoblins in an attempt to wipe out the orcs. And all the while, a hidden cell of drow scouts watches and plots to slay the mind flayers, then enslave whatever creatures are left.

It's easy to think of a dungeon as a collection of encounters, with the adventurers kicking down door after door and killing whatever lies beyond. But the ebb and flow of power between groups in a dungeon provides plenty of opportunities for more subtle interaction. Dungeon denizens are used to striking unlikely alliances, and adventurers are a wild card that canny monsters seek to exploit.

Intelligent creatures in a dungeon have goals, whether as simple as short-term survival or as ambitious as claiming the entire dungeon as the first step in founding an empire. Such creatures might approach adventurers with an offer of alliance, hoping to prevent the characters from laying waste to their lair and to secure aid against their enemies. Bring the NPC leaders of such groups to life as described in chapter 4, fleshing out their personalities, goals, and ideals. Then use those elements to shape a response to the arrival of adventurers in their territory.

Dungeon Ecology

An inhabited dungeon has its own ecosystem. The creatures that live there need to eat, drink, breathe, and sleep, just as creatures in the wilderness do. Predators need to be able to seek prey, and intelligent creatures search for lairs offering the best combination of air, food, water, and security. Keep these factors in mind when designing a dungeon you want the players to believe in. If a dungeon doesn't have some internal logic to it, adventurers will find it difficult to make reasonable decisions within that environment.

For example, characters who find a pool of fresh water in a dungeon might make the logical assumption that many of the creatures inhabiting the dungeon come to that spot to drink. The adventurers might set an ambush at the pool. Likewise, locked doors—or even doors that require hands to open—can restrict the movement of some creatures. If all the doors in a dungeon are closed, the players might wonder how the carrion crawlers or stirges they repeatedly encounter manage to survive.

Encounter Difficulty

You might be inclined to increase the encounter difficulty as the adventurers descend deeper into the dungeon, as a way to keep the dungeon challenging as the characters gain levels or to ratchet up the tension. However, this approach can turn the dungeon into a grind. A better approach is to include encounters of varying difficulty throughout. The contrast between easy and hard encounters, as well as simple and complex encounters, encourages characters to vary their tactics and keeps the encounters from seeming too similar.

Mapping a Dungeon

Every dungeon needs a map showing its layout. The dungeon's location, creator, purpose, history, and inhabitants should give you a starting point for designing your dungeon map. If you need further inspiration, you can find maps that have been made freely available for use on the Internet, or even use a map of a real-world location. Alternatively, you can borrow a map from a published adventure or randomly generate a dungeon complex using the tables presented in appendix A.

A dungeon can range in size from a few chambers in a ruined temple to a huge complex of rooms and passages extending hundreds of feet in all directions. The adventurers' goal often lies as far from the dungeon entrance as possible, forcing characters to delve deeper underground or push farther into the heart of the complex.

A dungeon is most easily mapped on graph paper, with each square on the paper representing an area of 10 feet by 10 feet. (If you play with miniatures on a grid, you might prefer a scale where each square represents 5 feet, or you can subdivide your 10-foot grid into a 5-foot grid when you draw your maps for combat.) When you draw your map, keep the following points in mind:

- Asymmetrical rooms and map layouts make a dungeon less predictable.
- Think in three dimensions. Stairs, ramps, platforms, ledges, balconies, pits, and other changes of elevation make a dungeon more interesting and make combat encounters in those areas more challenging.
- Give the dungeon some wear and tear. Unless you want to stress that the dungeon's builders were extraordinarily skillful, collapsed passages can be commonplace, cutting off formerly connected sections of the dungeon from each other. Past earthquakes might have opened chasms within a dungeon, splitting rooms and corridors to make interesting obstacles.
- Incorporate natural features into even a constructed dungeon. An underground stream might run through the middle of a dwarven stronghold, causing variation in the shapes and sizes of rooms and necessitating features such as bridges and drains.
- Add multiple entrances and exits. Nothing gives the players a stronger sense of making real decisions than having multiple ways to enter a dungeon.
- Add secret doors and secret rooms to reward players who take the time to search for them.

If you need help creating a dungeon map from scratch, see appendix A.

Dungeon Features

The atmosphere and physical characteristics of dungeons vary as widely as their origins. An old crypt might have stone walls and loose wooden doors, an odor of decay, and no light other than what adventurers bring with them. A volcanic lair might have smooth stone walls hollowed out by past eruptions, doors of magically reinforced brass, a smell of sulfur, and light provided by jets of flame in every hall and room.

Walls

Some dungeons have walls of masonry. Others have walls of solid rock, hewn with tools to give them a rough, chiseled look, or worn smooth by the passage of water or lava. An aboveground dungeon might be made of wood or composite materials.

Walls are sometimes adorned with murals, frescoes, bas-reliefs, and lighting fixtures such as sconces or torch brackets. A few even have secret doors built into them.

CATACOMBS

N

SAMPLE DUNGEON MAP

DOORS

Dungeon doorways might be set within plain arches and lintels. They might be festooned with carvings of gargoyles or leering faces or engraved with sigils that reveal clues as to what lies beyond.

Stuck Doors. Dungeon doors often become stuck when not used frequently. Opening a stuck door requires a successful Strength check. Chapter 8, "Running the Game," provides guidelines for setting the DC.

Locked Doors. Characters who don't have the key to a locked door can pick the lock with a successful Dexterity check (doing so requires thieves' tools and proficiency in their use). They can also force the door with a successful Strength check, smash the door to pieces by dealing enough damage to it, or use a *knock* spell or similar magic. Chapter 8 provides guidelines

for setting the DCs and assigning statistics to doors and other objects.

Barred Doors. A barred door is similar to a locked door, except that there's no lock to pick, and the door can be opened normally from the barred side by using an action to lift the bar from its braces.

SECRET DOORS

A secret door is crafted to blend into the wall that surrounds it. Sometimes faint cracks in the wall or scuff marks on the floor betray the secret door's presence.

Detecting a Secret Door. Use the characters' passive Wisdom (Perception) scores to determine whether anyone in the party notices a secret door without actively searching for it. Characters can also find a secret door by actively searching the location where the door is hidden and succeeding on a Wisdom

(Perception) check. To set an appropriate DC for the check, see chapter 8.

    Opening a Secret Door. Once a secret door is detected, a successful Intelligence (Investigation) check might be required to determine how to open it if the opening mechanism isn't obvious. Set the DC according to the difficulty guidelines in chapter 8.

    If adventurers can't determine how to open a secret door, breaking it down is always an option. Treat it as a locked door made of the same material as the surrounding wall, and use the guidelines in chapter 8 to determine appropriate DCs or statistics.

Concealed Doors

A concealed door is a normal door that is hidden from view. A secret door is carefully crafted to blend into its surrounding surface, whereas a concealed door is most often hidden by mundane means. It might be covered by a tapestry, covered with plaster, or (in the case of a concealed trapdoor) hidden under a rug. Normally, no ability check is required to find a concealed door. A character need only look in the right place or take the right steps to reveal the door. However, you can use the characters' passive Wisdom (Perception) scores to

determine whether any of them notices tracks or signs of a tapestry or rug having been recently disturbed.

Portcullises

A portcullis is a set of vertical bars made of wood or iron, reinforced with one or more horizontal bands. It blocks a passage or archway until it is raised up into the ceiling by a winch and chain. The main benefit of a portcullis is that it blocks a passage while still allowing guards to watch the area beyond and make ranged attacks or cast spells through it.

    Winching a portcullis up or down requires an action. If a character can't reach the winch (usually because it is on the other side of the portcullis), lifting the portcullis or bending its bars far enough apart to pass through them requires a successful Strength check. The DC of the check depends on the size and weight of the portcullis or the thickness of its bars. To determine an appropriate DC, see chapter 8.

Darkness and Light

Darkness is the default condition inside an underground complex or in the interior of aboveground ruins, but an inhabited dungeon might have light sources.

In subterranean settlements, even races that have darkvision use fire for warmth, cooking, and defense. But many creatures have no need of warmth or light. Adventurers must bring their own sources of light into dusty tombs where only undead stand guard, abandoned ruins teeming with predatory monsters and oozes, and natural caverns where sightless creatures hunt.

The light of a torch or lantern helps a character see over a short distance, but other creatures can see that light source from far away. Bright light in an environment of total darkness can be visible for miles, though a clear line of sight over such a distance is rare underground. Even so, adventurers using light sources in a dungeon often attract monsters, just as dungeon features that shed light (from phosphorescent fungi to the glow of magical portals) can draw adventurers' attention.

AIR QUALITY

Subterranean tunnels and aboveground ruins are often enclosed spaces with little airflow. Though it's rare for a dungeon to be sealed so tightly that adventurers have trouble breathing, the atmosphere is often stifling and oppressive. What's more, odors linger in a dungeon and can be magnified by the stillness of the atmosphere.

SOUNDS

A dungeon's enclosed geography helps channel sound. The groaning creak of an opening door can echo down hundreds of feet of passageway. Louder noises such as the clanging hammers of a forge or the din of battle can reverberate through an entire dungeon. Many creatures that live underground use such sounds as a way of locating prey, or go on alert at any sound of an adventuring party's intrusion.

DUNGEON HAZARDS

The hazards described here are but a few examples of the environmental dangers found underground and in other dark places. Dungeon hazards are functionally similar to traps, which are described at the end of this chapter.

Detecting a Hazard. No ability check is required to spot a hazard unless it is hidden. A hazard that resembles something benign, such as a patch of slime or mold, can be correctly identified with a successful Intelligence (Nature) check. Use the guidelines in chapter 8 to set an appropriate DC for any check made to spot or recognize a hazard.

Hazard Severity. To determine a hazard's deadliness relative to the characters, think of the hazard as a trap and compare the damage it deals with the party's level using the Damage Severity by Level table later in the chapter (the table also appears in chapter 8).

BROWN MOLD

Brown mold feeds on warmth, drawing heat from anything around it. A patch of brown mold typically covers a 10-foot square, and the temperature within 30 feet of it is always frigid.

When a creature moves to within 5 feet of the mold for the first time on a turn or starts its turn there, it must make a DC 12 Constitution saving throw, taking 22 (4d10) cold damage on a failed save, or half as much damage on a successful one.

Brown mold is immune to fire, and any source of fire brought within 5 feet of a patch causes it to instantly expand outward in the direction of the fire, covering a 10-foot-square area (with the source of the fire at the center of that area). A patch of brown mold exposed to an effect that deals cold damage is instantly destroyed.

GREEN SLIME

This acidic slime devours flesh, organic material, and metal on contact. Bright green, wet, and sticky, it clings to walls, floors, and ceilings in patches.

A patch of green slime covers a 5-foot square, has blindsight out to a range of 30 feet, and drops from walls and ceilings when it detects movement below it. Beyond that, it has no ability to move. A creature aware of the slime's presence can avoid being struck by it with a successful DC 10 Dexterity saving throw. Otherwise, the slime can't be avoided as it drops.

A creature that comes into contact with green slime takes 5 (1d10) acid damage. The creature takes the damage again at the start of each of its turns until the slime is scraped off or destroyed. Against wood or metal, green slime deals 11 (2d10) acid damage each round, and any nonmagical wood or metal weapon or tool used to scrape off the slime is effectively destroyed.

Sunlight, any effect that cures disease, and any effect that deals cold, fire, or radiant damage destroys a patch of green slime.

WEBS

Giant spiders weave thick, sticky webs across passages and at the bottom of pits to snare prey. These web-filled areas are difficult terrain. Moreover, a creature entering a webbed area for the first time on a turn or starting its turn there must succeed on a DC 12 Dexterity saving throw or become restrained by the webs. A restrained creature can use its action to try to escape, doing so with a successful DC 12 Strength (Athletics) or Dexterity (Acrobatics) check.

Each 10-foot cube of giant webs has AC 10, 15 hit points, vulnerability to fire, and immunity to bludgeoning, piercing, and psychic damage.

YELLOW MOLD

Yellow mold grows in dark places, and one patch covers a 5-foot square. If touched, the mold ejects a cloud of spores that fills a 10-foot cube originating from the mold. Any creature in the area must succeed on a DC 15 Constitution saving throw or take 11 (2d10) poison damage and become poisoned for 1 minute. While poisoned in this way, the creature takes 5 (1d10) poison damage at the start of each of its turns. The creature can repeat the saving throw at the end of each of its turns, ending the effect on itself on a successful save.

Sunlight or any amount of fire damage instantly destroys one patch of yellow mold.

WILDERNESS

Between the dungeons and settlements of your campaign world lie meadows, forests, deserts, mountain ranges, oceans, and other tracts of wilderness waiting to be traversed. Bringing wilderness areas to life can be a fun part of your game, both for you and your players. The following two approaches work particularly well.

TRAVEL-MONTAGE APPROACH

Sometimes the destination is more important than the journey. If the purpose of a wilderness trek is to get the characters to where the real adventure happens, gloss over the wilderness trek without checking for encounters along the way. Just as movies use travel montages to convey long and arduous journeys in a matter of seconds, you can use a few sentences of descriptive text to paint a picture of a wilderness trek in your players' minds before moving on.

Describe the journey as vividly as you like, but keep the forward momentum. "You walk for several miles and encounter nothing of interest" is okay, but far less evocative and memorable than, "A light rain dampens the rolling plains as you travel north. Around midday, you break for lunch under a lonely tree. There, the rogue finds a small rock that looks like a grinning face, but otherwise you encounter nothing out of the ordinary." The trick is to focus on a few details that reinforce the desired mood rather than describe everything down to the last blade of grass.

Call attention to unusual terrain features: a waterfall, a rocky outcropping that offers a breathtaking view over the tops of the surrounding trees, an area where the forest has burned or been cut down, and so on. Also describe notable smells and sounds, such as the roar of a faraway monster, the stench of burned wood, or the sweet aroma of flowers in an elven forest.

In addition to evocative language, visual aids can help set the scene for the characters' travels. Image searches on the Internet can lead you to breathtaking landscapes (in fact, that's a good phrase to search for) both real and fantastical. As striking as real-world scenery can be, wilderness travel can be used to remind the players that their characters are in a fantasy world. Once in a while, spice up your descriptions with some truly magical element. A forest might be home to tiny dragonets instead of birds, or its trees might be festooned with giant webs or have eerie, green-glowing sap. Use these elements sparingly; landscapes that are too alien can break your players' sense of immersion in the world. A single fantastic element within an otherwise realistic and memorable landscape is enough.

Use the landscape to set the mood and tone for your adventure. In one forest, close-set trees shroud all light and seem to watch the adventurers as they pass. In another, sunlight streams through the leaves above and flower-laden vines twine up every trunk. Signs of corruption—rotting wood, foul-smelling water, and rocks covered with slimy brown moss—can be a signal that the adventurers are drawing close to the site of evil power that is their destination or can provide clues to the nature of the threats to be found there.

Specific wilderness locations might have their own special features. For example, the Spirit Forest and the Spiderhaunt Woods might feature different kinds of trees, different kinds of flora and fauna, different weather, and different random encounter tables.

Finally, a wilderness trek can be enhanced by calling attention to the weather. "You spend the next three days crossing the swamp" sounds less harrowing than, "You spend the next three days trudging through knee-deep mud—the first two days and nights in the pouring rain, and then another day under the beating sun, with swarms of hungry insects feasting on your blood."

HOUR-BY-HOUR APPROACH

Sometimes the journey deserves as much time and attention as the destination. If wilderness travel features prominently in your adventure and isn't something you want to gloss over, you will need more than a descriptive overview to bring a long and harrowing journey to life; you'll need to know the party's marching order and have encounters at the ready.

Let your players determine the party's marching order (see the *Player's Handbook* for more information). Characters in the front rank are likely to be the first to notice landmarks and terrain features, as well as the ones responsible for navigating. Characters in the back rank are usually responsible for making sure that the party isn't being followed. Encourage characters in the middle ranks to do something other than blindly trudge along behind the front-rank characters. The *Player's Handbook* suggests activities such as mapmaking and foraging for food.

Wilderness journeys typically feature a combination of planned encounters (encounters that you prepare ahead of time) and random encounters (encounters determined by rolling on a table). A planned encounter might need a map of the location where the encounter is set to occur, such as a ruin, a bridge spanning a gorge, or some other memorable location. Random encounters tend to be less location-specific. The fewer planned encounters you have, the more you'll need to rely on random encounters to keep the journey interesting. See chapter 3 for guidelines on creating your own random encounter tables and when to check for random encounters.

A good way to keep wilderness encounters from becoming stale is to make sure they don't all start and end the same way. In other words, if the wilderness is your stage and your adventure is the play or movie, think of each wilderness encounter as its own scene, and try to stage each one in a slightly different way to keep your players' interest. If one encounter comes at the adventurers from the front, the next one might come at them from above or behind. If an encounter features stealthy monsters, a character tending to the party's pack animals might get the first indication that monsters are near when a pony whickers nervously. If an encounter features loud monsters, the party might have the option to hide or set an ambush. One group of monsters might attack the party on sight, and another might allow safe passage for food.

Reward characters for searching while they travel by providing things for them to find. Broken statues, tracks,

abandoned campsites, and other finds can add flavor to your world, foreshadow future encounters or events, or provide hooks for further adventures.

A wilderness journey might take multiple sessions to play out. That said, if the wilderness journey includes long periods with no encounters, use the travel-montage approach to bridge gaps between encounters.

MAPPING A WILDERNESS

In contrast to a dungeon, an outdoor setting presents seemingly limitless options. The adventurers can move in any direction over a trackless desert or an open grassland, so how do you as the DM deal with all the possible locations and events that might make up a wilderness campaign? What if you design an encounter in a desert oasis, but the characters miss the oasis because they wander off course? How do you avoid creating a boring play session of uninterrupted slogging across a rocky wasteland?

One solution is to think of an outdoor setting in the same way you think about a dungeon. Even the most wide-open terrain presents clear pathways. Roads seldom run straight because they follow the contours of the land, finding the most level or otherwise easiest routes across uneven ground. Valleys and ridges channel travel in certain directions. Mountain ranges present forbidding barriers traversed only by remote passes. Even the most trackless desert reveals favored routes, where explorers and caravan drivers have discovered areas of wind-blasted rock that are easier to traverse than shifting sand.

If the party veers off track, you might be able to relocate one or more of your planned encounters elsewhere on the map to ensure that the time spent preparing those encounters doesn't go to waste.

Chapter 1 discusses the basics of creating a wilderness map at three different scales to help you design your world and the starting area of your campaign. Especially when you get down to province scale (1 hex = 1 mile), think about paths of travel—roads, passes, ridges and valleys, and so on—that can guide character movement across your map.

MOVEMENT ON THE MAP

Narrate wilderness travel at a level of detail appropriate to the map you're using. If you're tracking hour-by-hour movement on a province-scale map (1 hex = 1 mile), you can describe each hamlet the adventurers pass. At this scale, you can assume that the characters find a noteworthy location when they enter its hex unless the site is specifically hidden. The characters might not walk directly up to the front door of a ruined castle when they enter a hex, but they can find old paths, outlying ruins, and other signs of its presence in the area.

If you're tracking a journey of several days on a kingdom-scale map (1 hex = 6 miles), don't bother with details too small to appear on your map. It's enough for the players to know that on the third day of their journey, they cross a river and the land starts rising before them, and that they reach the mountain pass two days later.

WILDERNESS FEATURES

No wilderness map is complete without a few settlements, strongholds, ruins, and other sites worthy of discovery. A dozen such locations scattered over an area roughly 50 miles across is a good start.

MONSTER LAIRS

A wilderness area approximately 50 miles across can support roughly a half-dozen monster lairs, but probably no more than one apex predator such as a dragon.

If you expect the characters to explore a monster's lair, you'll need to find or create an appropriate map for the lair and stock the lair as you would a dungeon.

MONUMENTS

In places where civilization rules or once ruled, adventurers might find monuments built to honor great leaders, gods, and cultures. Use the Monuments table for inspiration, or randomly roll to determine what monument the adventurers stumble upon.

MONUMENTS

d20	Monument
1	Sealed burial mound or pyramid
2	Plundered burial mound or pyramid
3	Faces carved into a mountainside or cliff
4	Giant statues carved out of a mountainside or cliff
5–6	Intact obelisk etched with a warning, historical lore, dedication, or religious iconography
7–8	Ruined or toppled obelisk
9–10	Intact statue of a person or deity
11–13	Ruined or toppled statue of a person or deity
14	Great stone wall, intact, with tower fortifications spaced at one-mile intervals
15	Great stone wall in ruins
16	Great stone arch
17	Fountain
18	Intact circle of standing stones
19	Ruined or toppled circle of standing stones
20	Totem pole

RUINS

Crumbling towers, ancient temples, and razed cities are perfect sites for adventures. Additionally, noting the existence of an old, crumbling wall that runs alongside a road, a sagging stone windmill on a hilltop, or a jumble of standing stones can add texture to your wilderness.

SETTLEMENTS

Settlements exist in places where food, water, farmland, and building materials are abundant. A civilized province roughly 50 miles across might have one city, a few rural towns, and a scattering of villages and trading posts. An uncivilized area might have a single trading post that stands at the edge of a wild frontier, but no larger settlements.

In addition to settlements, a province might contain ruined villages and towns that are either abandoned or serve as lairs for marauding bandits and monsters.

Strongholds

Strongholds provide the local population with protection in times of trouble. The number of strongholds in an area depends on the dominant society, the population, the strategic importance or vulnerability of the region, and the wealth of the land.

Weird Locales

Weird locales make the fantastic and the supernatural an intrinsic part of your wilderness adventures.

Weird Locales

d20	Locale
1–2	Dead magic zone (similar to an *antimagic field*)
3	Wild magic zone (roll on the Wild Magic Surge table in the *Player's Handbook* whenever a spell is cast within the zone)
4	Boulder carved with talking faces
5	Crystal cave that mystically answers questions
6	Ancient tree containing a trapped spirit
7–8	Battlefield where lingering fog occasionally assumes humanoid forms
9–10	Permanent portal to another plane of existence
11	Wishing well
12	Giant crystal shard protruding from the ground
13	Wrecked ship, which might be nowhere near water
14–15	Haunted hill or barrow mound
16	River ferry guided by a skeletal captain
17	Field of petrified soldiers or other creatures
18	Forest of petrified or awakened trees
19	Canyon containing a dragons' graveyard
20	Floating earth mote with a tower on it

Wilderness Survival

Adventuring in the wilderness presents a host of perils beyond the threats of monstrous predators and savage raiders.

Weather

You can pick weather to fit your campaign or roll on the Weather table to determine the weather for a given day, adjusting for the terrain and season as appropriate.

Weather

d20	Temperature
1–14	Normal for the season
15–17	1d4 × 10 degrees Fahrenheit colder than normal
18–20	1d4 × 10 degrees Fahrenheit hotter than normal

d20	Wind
1–12	None
13–17	Light
18–20	Strong

d20	Precipitation
1–12	None
13–17	Light rain or light snowfall
18–20	Heavy rain or heavy snowfall

Extreme Cold

Whenever the temperature is at or below 0 degrees Fahrenheit, a creature exposed to the cold must succeed on a DC 10 Constitution saving throw at the end of each hour or gain one level of exhaustion. Creatures with resistance or immunity to cold damage automatically succeed on the saving throw, as do creatures wearing cold weather gear (thick coats, gloves, and the like) and creatures naturally adapted to cold climates.

Extreme Heat

When the temperature is at or above 100 degrees Fahrenheit, a creature exposed to the heat and without access to drinkable water must succeed on a Constitution saving throw at the end of each hour or gain one level of exhaustion. The DC is 5 for the first hour and increases by 1 for each additional hour. Creatures wearing medium or heavy armor, or who are clad in heavy clothing, have disadvantage on the saving throw. Creatures with resistance or immunity to fire damage automatically succeed on the saving throw, as do creatures naturally adapted to hot climates.

Strong Wind

A strong wind imposes disadvantage on ranged weapon attack rolls and Wisdom (Perception) checks that rely on hearing. A strong wind also extinguishes open flames, disperses fog, and makes flying by nonmagical means nearly impossible. A flying creature in a strong wind must land at the end of its turn or fall.

A strong wind in a desert can create a sandstorm that imposes disadvantage on Wisdom (Perception) checks that rely on sight.

Heavy Precipitation

Everything within an area of heavy rain or heavy snowfall is lightly obscured, and creatures in the area have disadvantage on Wisdom (Perception) checks that rely on sight. Heavy rain also extinguishes open flames and imposes disadvantage on Wisdom (Perception) checks that rely on hearing.

High Altitude

Traveling at altitudes of 10,000 feet or higher above sea level is taxing for a creature that needs to breathe, because of the reduced amount of oxygen in the air. Each hour such a creature spends traveling at high altitude counts as 2 hours for the purpose of determining how long that creature can travel.

Breathing creatures can become acclimated to a high altitude by spending 30 days or more at this elevation. Breathing creatures can't become acclimated to elevations above 20,000 feet unless they are native to such environments.

Wilderness Hazards

This section describes a few examples of hazards that adventurers might encounter in the wilderness.

Some hazards, such as slippery ice and razorvine, require no ability check to spot. Others, such as defiled ground, are undetectable by normal senses.

The other hazards presented here can be identified with a successful Intelligence (Nature) check. Use the guidelines in chapter 8 to set an appropriate DC for any check made to spot or recognize a hazard.

Desecrated Ground

Some cemeteries and catacombs are imbued with the unseen traces of ancient evil. An area of desecrated ground can be any size, and a *detect evil and good* spell cast within range reveals its presence.

Undead standing on desecrated ground have advantage on all saving throws.

A vial of holy water purifies a 10-foot-square area of desecrated ground when sprinkled on it, and a *hallow* spell purifies desecrated ground within its area.

Frigid Water

A creature can be immersed in frigid water for a number of minutes equal to its Constitution score before suffering any ill effects. Each additional minute spent in frigid water requires the creature to succeed on a DC 10 Constitution saving throw or gain one level of exhaustion. Creatures with resistance or immunity to cold damage automatically succeed on the saving throw, as do creatures that are naturally adapted to living in ice-cold water.

Quicksand

A quicksand pit covers the ground in roughly a 10-foot-square area and is usually 10 feet deep. When a creature enters the area, it sinks 1d4 + 1 feet into the quicksand and becomes restrained. At the start of each of the creature's turns, it sinks another 1d4 feet. As long as the creature isn't completely submerged in quicksand, it can escape by using its action and succeeding on a Strength check. The DC is 10 plus the number of feet the creature has sunk into the quicksand. A creature that is completely submerged in quicksand can't breathe (see the suffocation rules in the *Player's Handbook*).

A creature can pull another creature within its reach out of a quicksand pit by using its action and succeeding on a Strength check. The DC is 5 plus the number of feet the target creature has sunk into the quicksand.

Razorvine

Razorvine is a plant that grows in wild tangles and hedges. It also clings to the sides of buildings and other surfaces as ivy does. A 10-foot-high, 10-foot-wide, 5-foot-thick wall or hedge of razorvine has AC 11, 25 hit points, and immunity to bludgeoning, piercing, and psychic damage.

When a creature comes into direct contact with razorvine for the first time on a turn, the creature must succeed on a DC 10 Dexterity saving throw or take 5 (1d10) slashing damage from the razorvine's bladelike thorns.

Slippery Ice

Slippery ice is difficult terrain. When a creature moves onto slippery ice for the first time on a turn, it must succeed on a DC 10 Dexterity (Acrobatics) check or fall prone.

Thin Ice

Thin ice has a weight tolerance of 3d10 × 10 pounds per 10-foot-square area. Whenever the total weight on an area of thin ice exceeds its tolerance, the ice in that area breaks. All creatures on broken ice fall through.

Foraging

Characters can gather food and water as the party travels at a normal or slow pace. A foraging character makes a Wisdom (Survival) check whenever you call for it, with the DC determined by the abundance of food and water in the region.

Foraging DCs

Food and Water Availability	DC
Abundant food and water sources	10
Limited food and water sources	15
Very little, if any, food and water sources	20

If multiple characters forage, each character makes a separate check. A foraging character finds nothing on a failed check. On a successful check, roll 1d6 + the character's Wisdom modifier to determine how much food (in pounds) the character finds, then repeat the roll for water (in gallons).

Food and Water

The food and water requirements noted in the *Player's Handbook* are for characters. Horses and other creatures require different quantities of food and water per day based on their size. Water needs are doubled if the weather is hot.

Food and Water Needs

Creature Size	Food per Day	Water per Day
Tiny	1/4 pound	1/4 gallon
Small	1 pound	1 gallon
Medium	1 pound	1 gallon
Large	4 pounds	4 gallons
Huge	16 pounds	16 gallons
Gargantuan	64 pounds	64 gallons

Becoming Lost

Unless they are following a path, or something like it, adventurers traveling in the wilderness run the risk of becoming lost. The party's navigator makes a Wisdom (Survival) check when you decide it's appropriate, against a DC determined by the prevailing terrain, as shown on the Wilderness Navigation table. If the party is moving at a slow pace, the navigator gains a +5 bonus to the check, and a fast pace imposes a −5 penalty. If the party has an accurate map of the region or can see the sun or stars, the navigator has advantage on the check.

If the Wisdom (Survival) check succeeds, the party travels in the desired direction without becoming lost. If the check fails, the party inadvertently travels in the wrong direction and becomes lost. The party's navigator can repeat the check after the party spends 1d6 hours trying to get back on course.

Wilderness Navigation

Terrain	DC
Forest, jungle, swamp, mountains, or open sea with overcast skies and no land in sight	15
Arctic, desert, hills, or open sea with clear skies and no land in sight	10
Grassland, meadow, farmland	5

Settlements

A village, town, or city makes an excellent backdrop for an adventure. The adventurers might be called on to track down a criminal who's gone into hiding, solve a murder, take out a gang of wererats or doppelgangers, or protect a settlement under siege.

When creating a settlement for your campaign, focus on the locations that are most relevant to the adventure. Don't worry about naming every street and identifying the inhabitants of every building; that way lies madness.

Random Settlements

The following tables allow you to quickly create a settlement. They assume that you've already determined its size and its basic form of government.

Race Relations

d20	Result
1–10	Harmony
11–14	Tension or rivalry
15–16	Racial majority are conquerors
17	Racial minority are rulers
18	Racial minority are refugees
19	Racial majority oppresses minority
20	Racial minority oppresses majority

Ruler's Status

d20	Ruler
1–5	Respected, fair, and just
6–8	Feared tyrant
9	Weakling manipulated by others
10	Illegitimate ruler, simmering civil war
11	Ruled or controlled by a powerful monster
12	Mysterious, anonymous cabal
13	Contested leadership, open fighting
14	Cabal seized power openly
15	Doltish lout
16	On deathbed, claimants compete for power
17–18	Iron-willed but respected
19–20	Religious leader

Notable Traits

d20	Trait
1	Canals in place of streets
2	Massive statue or monument
3	Grand temple
4	Large fortress
5	Verdant parks and orchards
6	River divides town
7	Major trade center
8	Headquarters of a powerful family or guild
9	Population mostly wealthy
10	Destitute, rundown
11	Awful smell (tanneries, open sewers)
12	Center of trade for one specific good
13	Site of many battles
14	Site of a mythic or magical event
15	Important library or archive
16	Worship of all gods banned
17	Sinister reputation
18	Notable library or academy
19	Site of important tomb or graveyard
20	Built atop ancient ruins

Known For Its ...

d20	Feature	d20	Feature
1	Delicious cuisine	11	Piety
2	Rude people	12	Gambling
3	Greedy merchants	13	Godlessness
4	Artists and writers	14	Education
5	Great hero/savior	15	Wines
6	Flowers	16	High fashion
7	Hordes of beggars	17	Political intrigue
8	Tough warriors	18	Powerful guilds
9	Dark magic	19	Strong drink
10	Decadence	20	Patriotism

Current Calamity

d20	Calamity
1	Suspected vampire infestation
2	New cult seeks converts
3	Important figure died (murder suspected)
4	War between rival thieves' guilds
5–6	Plague or famine (sparks riots)
7	Corrupt officials
8–9	Marauding monsters
10	Powerful wizard has moved into town
11	Economic depression (trade disrupted)
12	Flooding
13	Undead stirring in cemeteries
14	Prophecy of doom
15	Brink of war
16	Internal strife (leads to anarchy)
17	Besieged by enemies
18	Scandal threatens powerful families
19	Dungeon discovered (adventurers flock to town)
20	Religious sects struggle for power

RANDOM BUILDINGS

Pulse-pounding chases and harrowing escapes within the confines of a town or city can sometimes force characters to dash into buildings. When you need to flesh out a building quickly, roll on the Building Type table. Then roll on the table corresponding to that building to add further detail.

If a roll makes no sense considering where the characters are (such as a lavish mansion in a rundown part of town), you can always roll again or simply choose another result. However, such unexpected results can prompt creativity and memorable locations that help make your urban encounters distinct.

BUILDING TYPE

d20	Type
1–10	Residence (roll once on the Residence table)
11–12	Religious (roll once on the Religious Building table)
13–15	Tavern (roll once on the Tavern table and twice on the Tavern Name Generator table)
16–17	Warehouse (roll once on the Warehouse table)
18–20	Shop (roll once on the Shop table)

RESIDENCE

d20	Type
1–2	Abandoned squat
3–8	Middle-class home
9–10	Upper-class home
11–15	Crowded tenement
16–17	Orphanage
18	Hidden slavers' den
19	Front for a secret cult
20	Lavish, guarded mansion

RELIGIOUS BUILDING

d20	Type
1–10	Temple to a good or neutral deity
11–12	Temple to a false deity (run by charlatan priests)
13	Home of ascetics
14–15	Abandoned shrine
16–17	Library dedicated to religious study
18–20	Hidden shrine to a fiend or an evil deity

TAVERN

d20	Type
1–5	Quiet, low-key bar
6–9	Raucous dive
10	Thieves' guild hangout
11	Gathering place for a secret society
12–13	Upper-class dining club
14–15	Gambling den
16–17	Caters to specific race or guild
18	Members-only club
19–20	Brothel

TAVERN NAME GENERATOR

d20	First Part	Second Part
1	The Silver	Eel
2	The Golden	Dolphin
3	The Staggering	Dwarf
4	The Laughing	Pegasus
5	The Prancing	Pony
6	The Gilded	Rose
7	The Running	Stag
8	The Howling	Wolf
9	The Slaughtered	Lamb
10	The Leering	Demon
11	The Drunken	Goat
12	The Leaping	Spirit
13	The Roaring	Horde
14	The Frowning	Jester
15	The Lonely	Mountain
16	The Wandering	Eagle
17	The Mysterious	Satyr
18	The Barking	Dog
19	The Black	Spider
20	The Gleaming	Star

WAREHOUSE

d20	Type
1–4	Empty or abandoned
5–6	Heavily guarded, expensive goods
7–10	Cheap goods
11–14	Bulk goods
15	Live animals
16–17	Weapons/armor
18–19	Goods from a distant land
20	Secret smuggler's den

Shop

d20	Type	d20	Type
1	Pawnshop	11	Smithy
2	Herbs/incense	12	Carpenter
3	Fruits/vegetables	13	Weaver
4	Dried meats	14	Jeweler
5	Pottery	15	Baker
6	Undertaker	16	Mapmaker
7	Books	17	Tailor
8	Moneylender	18	Ropemaker
9	Weapons/armor	19	Mason
10	Chandler	20	Scribe

MAPPING A SETTLEMENT

When you draw a map for a settlement in your game, don't worry about the placement of every building, and concentrate instead on the major features.

For a village, sketch out the roads, including trade routes leading beyond the village and roads that connect outlying farms to the village center. Note the location of the village center. If the adventurers visit specific places in the village, mark those spots on your map.

For towns and cities, note major roads and waterways as well as surrounding terrain. Outline the walls and mark the locations of features you know will be important: the lord's keep, significant temples, and the like. For cities, add internal walls and think about the personality of each ward. Give the wards names reflecting their personalities, which also identify the kinds of trades that dominate the neighborhood (Tannery Square, Temple Row), a geographical characteristic (Hilltop, Riverside), or a dominant site (the Lords' Quarter).

URBAN ENCOUNTERS

Although they hold the promise of safety, cities and towns can be just as dangerous as the darkest dungeon. Evil hides in plain sight or in dark corners. Sewers, shadowy alleys, slums, smoke-filled taverns, dilapidated tenements, and crowded marketplaces can quickly turn into battlegrounds. On top of that, adventurers must learn to behave themselves, lest they attract unwanted attention from local authorities.

That said, characters who don't go looking for trouble can take advantage of all the benefits that a settlement has to offer.

LAW AND ORDER

Whether a settlement has a police force depends on its size and nature. A lawful, orderly city might have a city watch to maintain order and a trained militia to defend its walls, and a frontier town might rely on adventurers or its citizenry to apprehend criminals and fend off attackers.

TRIALS

In most settlements, trials are overseen by magistrates or local lords. Some trials are argued, with the conflicting parties or their advocates presenting precedent and evidence until the judge makes a decision, with or without the aid of spells or interrogation. Others are decided with a trial by ordeal or trial by combat. If the evidence against the accused is overwhelming, a magistrate or local lord can forgo a trial and skip right to the sentencing.

SENTENCES

A settlement might have a jail to hold accused criminals awaiting trial, but few settlements have prisons to incarcerate convicted criminals. A person found guilty of a crime is usually fined, condemned to forced labor for a period of several months or years, exiled, or executed, depending on the magnitude of the crime.

RANDOM URBAN ENCOUNTERS

The Random Urban Encounters table is useful for city- and town-based adventures. Check for a random encounter at least once per day, and once at night if the characters are out and about. Reroll the result if it doesn't make sense given the time of day.

RANDOM URBAN ENCOUNTERS

d12 + d8	Encounter
2	Animals on the loose
3	Announcement
4	Brawl
5	Bullies
6	Companion
7	Contest
8	Corpse
9	Draft
10	Drunk
11	Fire
12	Found trinket
13	Guard harassment
14	Pickpocket
15	Procession
16	Protest
17	Runaway cart
18	Shady transaction
19	Spectacle
20	Urchin

Animals on the Loose. The characters see one or more unexpected animals loose in the street. This challenge could be anything from a pack of baboons to an escaped circus bear, tiger, or elephant.

Announcement. A herald, town crier, mad person, or other individual makes an announcement on a street corner for all to hear. The announcement might foreshadow some upcoming event (such as a public execution), communicate important information to the general masses (such as a new royal decree), or convey a dire omen or warning.

Brawl. A brawl erupts near the adventurers. It could be a tavern brawl; a battle between rival factions, families, or gangs in the city; or a struggle between city guards and criminals. The characters could be

witnesses, hit by stray arrow fire, or mistaken for members of one group and attacked by the other.

Bullies. The characters witness 1d4 + 2 bullies harassing an out-of-towner (use the commoner statistics in the *Monster Manual* for all of them). A bully flees as soon as he or she takes any amount of damage.

Companion. One or more characters are approached by a local who takes a friendly interest in the party's activities. As a twist, the would-be companion might be a spy sent to gather information on the adventurers.

Contest. The adventurers are drawn into an impromptu contest—anything from an intellectual test to a drinking competition—or witness a duel.

Corpse. The adventurers find a humanoid corpse.

Draft. The characters are drafted by a member of the city or town watch, who needs their help to deal with an immediate problem. As a twist, the member of the watch might be a disguised criminal trying to lure the party into an ambush (use the thug statistics in the *Monster Manual* for the criminal and his or her cohorts).

Drunk. A tipsy drunk staggers toward a random party member, mistaking him or her for someone else.

Fire. A fire breaks out, and the characters have a chance to help put out the flames before it spreads.

Found Trinket. The characters find a random trinket. You can determine the trinket by rolling on the Trinkets table in the *Player's Handbook*.

Guard Harassment. The adventurers are cornered by 1d4 + 1 guards eager to throw their weight around. If threatened, the guards call out for help and might attract the attention of other guards or citizens nearby.

Pickpocket. A thief (use the spy statistics in the *Monster Manual*) tries to steal from a random character. Characters whose passive Wisdom (Perception) scores are equal to or greater than the thief's Dexterity (Sleight of Hand) check total catch the theft in progress.

Procession. The adventurers encounter a group of citizens either parading in celebration or forming a funeral procession.

Protest. The adventurers see a group of citizens peacefully protesting a new law or decree. A handful of guards maintain order.

Runaway Cart. A team of horses pulling a wagon races through the city streets. The adventurers must avoid the horses. If they stop the wagon, the owner (who is running behind the cart) is grateful.

Shady Transaction. The characters witness a shady transaction between two cloaked figures.

Spectacle. The characters witness a form of public entertainment, such as a talented bard's impersonation of a royal personage, a street circus, a puppet show, a flashy magic act, a royal visit, or a public execution.

Urchin. A street urchin gloms onto the adventurers and follows them around until frightened off.

UNUSUAL ENVIRONMENTS

Traveling through the wilderness doesn't always mean an overland trek. Adventurers might ply the open sea in a caravel or an elemental-powered galleon, soar through the air on hippogriffs or a *carpet of flying*, or ride giant sea horses to coral palaces deep beneath the sea.

UNDERWATER

See chapter 9 of the *Player's Handbook* for rules on underwater combat.

RANDOM UNDERSEA ENCOUNTERS

You can check for random undersea encounters as often as you would check for them on land (see chapter 3). The Random Undersea Encounters table presents several intriguing options. You can either roll on the table for a random result or choose whichever one works best.

RANDOM UNDERSEA ENCOUNTERS

d12 + d8	Encounter
2	Sunken ship covered in barnacles (25 percent chance that the ship contains treasure; roll randomly on the treasure tables in chapter 7)
3	Sunken ship with **reef sharks** (shallow waters) or **hunter sharks** (deep waters) circling around it (50 percent chance that the ship contains treasure; roll randomly on the treasure tables in chapter 7)
4	Bed of giant oysters (each oyster has a 1 percent chance of having a giant 5,000 gp pearl inside)
5	Underwater steam vent (25 percent chance that the vent is a portal to the Elemental Plane of Fire)
6	Sunken ruin (uninhabited)
7	Sunken ruin (inhabited or haunted)
8	Sunken statue or monolith
9	Friendly and curious **giant sea horse**
10	Patrol of friendly **merfolk**
11	Patrol of hostile **merrow** (coastal waters) or **sahuagin** (deep waters)
12	Enormous kelp bed (roll again on the table to determine what's hidden in the kelp bed)
13	Undersea cave (empty)
14	Undersea cave (**sea hag** lair)
15	Undersea cave (**merfolk** lair)
16	Undersea cave (**giant octopus** lair)
17	Undersea cave (**dragon turtle** lair)
18	**Bronze dragon** searching for treasure
19	**Storm giant** walking on the ocean floor
20	Sunken treasure chest (25 percent chance that it contains something of value; roll treasure randomly using the tables in chapter 7)

SWIMMING

Unless aided by magic, a character can't swim for a full 8 hours per day. After each hour of swimming, a character must succeed on a DC 10 Constitution saving throw or gain one level of exhaustion.

A creature that has a swimming speed—including a character with a *ring of swimming* or similar magic—can swim all day without penalty and uses the normal forced march rules in the *Player's Handbook*.

Swimming through deep water is similar to traveling at high altitudes, because of the water's pressure and cold temperature. For a creature without a swimming speed, each hour spent swimming at a depth greater than 100 feet counts as 2 hours for the purpose of determining exhaustion. Swimming for an hour at a depth greater than 200 feet counts as 4 hours.

UNDERWATER VISIBILITY

Visibility underwater depends on water clarity and the available light. Unless the characters have light sources, use the Underwater Encounter Distance table to determine the distance at which characters underwater become aware of a possible encounter.

UNDERWATER ENCOUNTER DISTANCE

Creature Size	Encounter Distance
Clear water, bright light	60 ft.
Clear water, dim light	30 ft.
Murky water or no light	10 ft.

THE SEA

Characters can row a boat for 8 hours per day, or can row longer at the risk of exhaustion (as per the rules for a forced march in chapter 8 of the *Player's Handbook*). A fully crewed sailing vessel can sail all day, assuming its sailors work in shifts.

NAVIGATION

Seagoing vessels stay close to shore when they can, because navigation is easier when landmarks are visible. As long as a ship is within sight of land, there is no chance of the vessel becoming lost. Otherwise, a ship's navigator must rely on dead reckoning (tracking

the direction and distance of the ship's travel) or the sun and the stars.

Use the Wilderness Navigation table earlier in this chapter to determine whether a ship veers off course.

RANDOM ENCOUNTERS AT SEA

You can check for random encounters at sea as often as you would check for them on land (see chapter 3 for more information). The Random Encounters at Sea table presents a number of options and ideas.

> ### SHIPWRECKS
>
> A shipwreck is a plot device that can be used sparingly to great effect, particularly if you want the characters to be washed ashore on some monster-infested island or (in the case of an airship) dropped in the middle of some exotic land. There aren't rules for determining when a shipwreck happens; it happens when you want or need it to happen.
>
> Even the strongest seafaring ship can founder in a storm, run aground on rocks or reefs, sink during a pirate attack, or be dragged underwater by a sea monster. A storm or hungry dragon can lay waste to an airship just as easily. A shipwreck has the potential to change the direction of a campaign. It isn't, however, a particularly good way to kill off characters or end a campaign.
>
> If you and your campaign conspire to wreck a ship on which the characters are traveling, it is assumed that the characters survive with the equipment they were wearing or carrying still in their possession. The fate of any NPCs and cargo aboard the wrecked ship is entirely up to you.

RANDOM ENCOUNTERS AT SEA

d12 + d8	Encounter
2	Ghost ship
3	Friendly and curious **bronze dragon**
4	Whirlpool (25 percent chance that the whirlpool is a portal to the Elemental Plane of Water)
5	**Merfolk** traders
6	Passing warship (friendly or hostile)
7–8	Pirate ship (hostile)
9–10	Passing merchant ship (galley or sailing ship)
11–12	**Killer whale** sighting
13–14	Floating debris
15	Longship crewed by hostile **berserkers**
16	Hostile **griffons** or **harpies**
17	Iceberg (easily avoided if seen from a distance)
18	**Sahuagin** boarding party
19	NPC in the water (clinging to floating debris)
20	Sea monster (such as a **dragon turtle** or **kraken**)

WEATHER AT SEA

Use the Weather table earlier in this chapter when checking for weather at sea.

If weather conditions indicate both a strong wind and heavy rain, they combine to create a storm with high waves. A crew caught in a storm loses sight of all landmarks (unless there's a lighthouse or other bright feature), and ability checks made to navigate during the storm have disadvantage.

Airborne and Waterborne Vehicles

Ship	Cost	Speed	Crew	Passengers	Cargo (tons)	AC	HP	Damage Threshold
Airship	20,000 gp	8 mph	10	20	1	13	300	—
Galley	30,000 gp	4 mph	80	—	150	15	500	20
Keelboat	3,000 gp	1 mph	1	6	1/2	15	100	10
Longship	10,000 gp	3 mph	40	150	10	15	300	15
Rowboat	50 gp	1½ mph	1	3	—	11	50	—
Sailing ship	10,000 gp	2 mph	20	20	100	15	300	15
Warship	25,000 gp	2½ mph	60	60	200	15	500	20

In a dead calm (no wind), ships can't move under sail and must be rowed. A ship sailing against a strong wind moves at half speed.

Visibility

A relatively calm sea offers great visibility. From a crow's nest, a lookout can spot another ship or a coastline up to 10 miles away, assuming clear skies. Overcast skies reduce that distance by half. Rain and fog reduce visibility just as they do on land.

Owning a Ship

At some point in your campaign, the adventurers might gain custody of a ship. They might purchase or capture one or receive one to carry out a mission. It's up to you whether a ship is available for purchase, and you have the power to deprive the adventurers of a ship at any time should it become a nuisance (see the "Shipwrecks" sidebar).

Crew. A ship needs a crew of skilled hirelings to function. As per the *Player's Handbook*, one skilled hireling costs at least 2 gp per day. The minimum number of skilled hirelings needed to crew a ship depends on the type of vessel, as shown in the Airborne and Waterborne Vehicles table.

You can track the loyalty of individual crew members or the crew as a whole using the optional loyalty rules in chapter 4. If at least half the crew becomes disloyal during a voyage, the crew turns hostile and stages a mutiny. If the ship is berthed, disloyal crew members leave the ship and never return.

Passengers. The table indicates the number of Small and Medium passengers the ship can accommodate. Accommodations consist of shared hammocks in tight quarters. A ship outfitted with private accommodations can carry one-fifth as many passengers.

A passenger is usually expected to pay 5 sp per day for a hammock, but prices can vary from ship to ship. A small private cabin usually costs 2 gp per day.

Cargo. The table indicates the maximum tonnage each kind of ship can carry.

Damage Threshold. A ship has immunity to all damage unless it takes an amount of damage equal to or greater than its damage threshold, in which case it takes damage as normal. Any damage that fails to meet or exceed the damage threshold is considered superficial and doesn't reduce the ship's hit points.

Ship Repair. Repairs to a damaged ship can be made while the vessel is berthed. Repairing 1 hit point of damage requires 1 day and costs 20 gp for materials and labor.

The Sky

Flying characters can move from one place to another in a relatively straight line, ignoring terrain and monsters that can't fly or that lack ranged attacks.

Flying by spell or magic item works the same as travel on foot, as described in the *Player's Handbook*. A creature that serves as a flying mount must rest 1 hour for every 3 hours it flies, and it can't fly for more than 9 hours per day. Thus, characters mounted on griffons (which have a flying speed of 80 feet) can travel at 8 miles per hour, covering 72 miles over 9 hours with two 1-hour-long rests over the course of the day. Mounts that don't tire (such as a flying construct) aren't subject to this limitation.

As adventurers travel through the air, check for random encounters as you normally would. Ignore any result that indicates a non-flying monster, unless the characters are flying close enough to the ground to be targeted by non-flying creatures making ranged attacks. Characters have normal chances to spot creatures on the ground and can decide whether to engage them.

TRAPS

Traps can be found almost anywhere. One wrong step in an ancient tomb might trigger a series of scything blades, which cleave through armor and bone. The seemingly innocuous vines that hang over a cave entrance might grasp and choke anyone who pushes through them. A net hidden among the trees might drop on travelers who pass underneath. In the D&D game, unwary adventurers can fall to their deaths, be burned alive, or fall under a fusillade of poisoned darts.

A trap can be either mechanical or magical in nature. **Mechanical traps** include pits, arrow traps, falling blocks, water-filled rooms, whirling blades, and anything else that depends on a mechanism to operate. **Magic traps** are either magical device traps or spell traps. Magical device traps initiate spell effects when activated. Spell traps are spells such as *glyph of warding* and *symbol* that function as traps.

TRAPS IN PLAY

When adventurers come across a trap, you need to know how the trap is triggered and what it does, as well as the possibility for the characters to detect the trap and to disable or avoid it.

TRIGGERING A TRAP

Most traps are triggered when a creature goes somewhere or touches something that the trap's creator wanted to protect. Common triggers include stepping on a pressure plate or a false section of floor, pulling a trip wire, turning a doorknob, and using the wrong key in a lock. Magic traps are often set to go off when a creature enters an area or touches an object. Some magic traps (such as the *glyph of warding* spell) have more complicated trigger conditions, including a password that prevents the trap from activating.

DETECTING AND DISABLING A TRAP

Usually, some element of a trap is visible to careful inspection. Characters might notice an uneven flagstone that conceals a pressure plate, spot the gleam of light off a trip wire, notice small holes in the walls from which jets of flame will erupt, or otherwise detect something that points to a trap's presence.

A trap's description specifies the checks and DCs needed to detect it, disable it, or both. A character actively looking for a trap can attempt a Wisdom (Perception) check against the trap's DC. You can also compare the DC to detect the trap with each character's passive Wisdom (Perception) score to determine whether anyone in the party notices the trap in passing. If the adventurers detect a trap before triggering it, they might be able to disarm it, either permanently or long enough to move past it. You might call for an Intelligence (Investigation) check for a character to deduce what needs to be done, followed by a Dexterity check using thieves' tools to perform the necessary sabotage.

Any character can attempt an Intelligence (Arcana) check to detect or disarm a magic trap, in addition to any other checks noted in the trap's description. The DCs are the same regardless of the check used. In addition, *dispel magic* has a chance of disabling most magic traps. A magic trap's description provides the DC for the ability check made when you use *dispel magic*.

In most cases, a trap's description is clear enough that you can adjudicate whether a character's actions locate or foil the trap. As with many situations, you shouldn't allow die rolling to override clever play and good planning. Use your common sense, drawing on the trap's description to determine what happens. No trap's design can anticipate every possible action that the characters might attempt.

You should allow a character to discover a trap without making an ability check if an action would clearly reveal the trap's presence. For example, if a character lifts a rug that conceals a pressure plate, the character has found the trigger and no check is required.

Foiling traps can be a little more complicated. Consider a trapped treasure chest. If the chest is opened without first pulling on the two handles set in its sides, a mechanism inside fires a hail of poison needles toward anyone in front of it. After inspecting the chest and making a few checks, the characters are still unsure if it's trapped. Rather than simply open the chest, they prop a shield in front of it and push the chest open at a distance with an iron rod. In this case, the trap still triggers, but the hail of needles fires harmlessly into the shield.

Traps are often designed with mechanisms that allow them to be disarmed or bypassed. Intelligent monsters that place traps in or around their lairs need ways to get past those traps without harming themselves. Such traps might have hidden levers that disable their triggers, or a secret door might conceal a passage that goes around the trap.

TRAP EFFECTS

The effects of traps can range from inconvenient to deadly, making use of elements such as arrows, spikes, blades, poison, toxic gas, blasts of fire,

and deep pits. The deadliest traps combine multiple elements to kill, injure, contain, or drive off any creature unfortunate enough to trigger them. A trap's description specifies what happens when it is triggered.

The attack bonus of a trap, the save DC to resist its effects, and the damage it deals can vary depending on the trap's severity. Use the Trap Save DCs and Attack Bonuses table and the Damage Severity by Level table for suggestions based on three levels of trap severity.

A trap intended to be a **setback** is unlikely to kill or seriously harm characters of the indicated levels, whereas a **dangerous** trap is likely to seriously injure (and potentially kill) characters of the indicated levels. A **deadly** trap is likely to kill characters of the indicated levels.

TRAP SAVE DCs AND ATTACK BONUSES

Trap Danger	Save DC	Attack Bonus
Setback	10–11	+3 to +5
Dangerous	12–15	+6 to +8
Deadly	16–20	+9 to +12

DAMAGE SEVERITY BY LEVEL

Character Level	Setback	Dangerous	Deadly
1st–4th	1d10	2d10	4d10
5th–10th	2d10	4d10	10d10
11th–16th	4d10	10d10	18d10
17th–20th	10d10	18d10	24d10

COMPLEX TRAPS

Complex traps work like standard traps, except once activated they execute a series of actions each round. A complex trap turns the process of dealing with a trap into something more like a combat encounter.

When a complex trap activates, it rolls initiative. The trap's description includes an initiative bonus. On its turn, the trap activates again, often taking an action. It might make successive attacks against intruders, create

an effect that changes over time, or otherwise produce a dynamic challenge. Otherwise, the complex trap can be detected and disabled or bypassed in the usual ways.

For example, a trap that causes a room to slowly flood works best as a complex trap. On the trap's turn, the water level rises. After several rounds, the room is completely flooded.

SAMPLE TRAPS

The magical and mechanical traps presented here vary in deadliness and are presented in alphabetical order.

COLLAPSING ROOF
Mechanical trap

This trap uses a trip wire to collapse the supports keeping an unstable section of a ceiling in place.

The trip wire is 3 inches off the ground and stretches between two support beams. The DC to spot the trip wire is 10. A successful DC 15 Dexterity check using thieves' tools disables the trip wire harmlessly. A character without thieves' tools can attempt this check with disadvantage using any edged weapon or edged tool. On a failed check, the trap triggers.

Anyone who inspects the beams can easily determine that they are merely wedged in place. As an action, a character can knock over a beam, causing the trap to trigger.

The ceiling above the trip wire is in bad repair, and anyone who can see it can tell that it's in danger of collapse.

When the trap is triggered, the unstable ceiling collapses. Any creature in the area beneath the unstable section must succeed on a DC 15 Dexterity saving throw, taking 22 (4d10) bludgeoning damage on a failed save, or half as much damage on a successful one. Once the trap is triggered, the floor of the area is filled with rubble and becomes difficult terrain.

FALLING NET
Mechanical trap

This trap uses a trip wire to release a net suspended from the ceiling.

The trip wire is 3 inches off the ground and stretches between two columns or trees. The net is hidden by cobwebs or foliage. The DC to spot the trip wire and net is 10. A successful DC 15 Dexterity check using thieves' tools breaks the trip wire harmlessly. A character without thieves' tools can attempt this check with disadvantage using any edged weapon or edged tool. On a failed check, the trap triggers.

When the trap is triggered, the net is released, covering a 10-foot-square area. Those in the area are trapped under the net and restrained, and those that fail a DC 10 Strength saving throw are also knocked prone. A creature can use its action to make a DC 10 Strength check, freeing itself or another creature within its reach on a success. The net has AC 10 and 20 hit points. Dealing 5 slashing damage to the net (AC 10) destroys a 5-foot-square section of it, freeing any creature trapped in that section.

FIRE-BREATHING STATUE
Magic trap

This trap is activated when an intruder steps on a hidden pressure plate, releasing a magical gout of flame from a nearby statue. The statue can be of anything, including a dragon or a wizard casting a spell.

The DC is 15 to spot the pressure plate, as well as faint scorch marks on the floor and walls. A spell or other effect that can sense the presence of magic, such as *detect magic*, reveals an aura of evocation magic around the statue.

The trap activates when more than 20 pounds of weight is placed on the pressure plate, causing the statue to release a 30-foot cone of fire. Each creature in the fire must make a DC 13 Dexterity saving throw, taking 22 (4d10) fire damage on a failed save, or half as much damage on a successful one.

Wedging an iron spike or other object under the pressure plate prevents the trap from activating. A successful *dispel magic* (DC 13) cast on the statue destroys the trap.

PITS
Mechanical trap

Four basic pit traps are presented here.

Simple Pit. A simple pit trap is a hole dug in the ground. The hole is covered by a large cloth anchored on the pit's edge and camouflaged with dirt and debris.

The DC to spot the pit is 10. Anyone stepping on the cloth falls through and pulls the cloth down into the pit, taking damage based on the pit's depth (usually 10 feet, but some pits are deeper).

Hidden Pit. This pit has a cover constructed from material identical to the floor around it.

A successful DC 15 Wisdom (Perception) check discerns an absence of foot traffic over the section of floor that forms the pit's cover. A successful DC 15 Intelligence (Investigation) check is necessary to confirm that the trapped section of floor is actually the cover of a pit.

When a creature steps on the cover, it swings open like a trapdoor, causing the intruder to spill into the pit below. The pit is usually 10 or 20 feet deep but can be deeper.

Once the pit trap is detected, an iron spike or similar object can be wedged between the pit's cover and the surrounding floor in such a way as to prevent the cover from opening, thereby making it safe to cross. The cover can also be magically held shut using the *arcane lock* spell or similar magic.

Locking Pit. This pit trap is identical to a hidden pit trap, with one key exception: the trap door that covers the pit is spring-loaded. After a creature falls into the pit, the cover snaps shut to trap its victim inside.

A successful DC 20 Strength check is necessary to pry the cover open. The cover can also be smashed open (determine the cover's statistics using the guidelines in chapter 8). A character in the pit can also attempt to disable the spring mechanism from the inside with a DC

15 Dexterity check using thieves' tools, provided that the mechanism can be reached and the character can see. In some cases, a mechanism (usually hidden behind a secret door nearby) opens the pit.

Spiked Pit. This pit trap is a simple, hidden, or locking pit trap with sharpened wooden or iron spikes at the bottom. A creature falling into the pit takes 11 (2d10) piercing damage from the spikes, in addition to any falling damage. Even nastier versions have poison smeared on the spikes. In that case, anyone taking piercing damage from the spikes must also make a DC 13 Constitution saving throw, taking an 22 (4d10) poison damage on a failed save, or half as much damage on a successful one.

POISON DARTS
Mechanical trap

When a creature steps on a hidden pressure plate, poison-tipped darts shoot from spring-loaded or pressurized tubes cleverly embedded in the surrounding walls. An area might include multiple pressure plates, each one rigged to its own set of darts.

The tiny holes in the walls are obscured by dust and cobwebs, or cleverly hidden amid bas-reliefs, murals, or frescoes that adorn the walls. The DC to spot them is 15. With a successful DC 15 Intelligence (Investigation) check, a character can deduce the presence of the pressure plate from variations in the mortar and stone used to create it, compared to the surrounding floor. Wedging an iron spike or other object under the pressure plate prevents the trap from activating. Stuffing the holes with cloth or wax prevents the darts contained within from launching.

The trap activates when more than 20 pounds of weight is placed on the pressure plate, releasing four darts. Each dart makes a ranged attack with a +8 bonus against a random target within 10 feet of the pressure plate (vision is irrelevant to this attack roll). (If there are no targets in the area, the darts don't hit anything.) A target that is hit takes 2 (1d4) piercing damage and must succeed on a DC 15 Constitution saving throw, taking 11 (2d10) poison damage on a failed save, or half as much damage on a successful one.

POISON NEEDLE
Mechanical trap

A poisoned needle is hidden within a treasure chest's lock, or in something else that a creature might open. Opening the chest without the proper key causes the needle to spring out, delivering a dose of poison.

When the trap is triggered, the needle extends 3 inches straight out from the lock. A creature within range takes 1 piercing damage and 11 (2d10) poison damage, and must succeed on a DC 15 Constitution saving throw or be poisoned for 1 hour.

A successful DC 20 Intelligence (Investigation) check allows a character to deduce the trap's presence from alterations made to the lock to accommodate the needle. A successful DC 15 Dexterity check using thieves'

tools disarms the trap, removing the needle from the lock. Unsuccessfully attempting to pick the lock triggers the trap.

ROLLING SPHERE
Mechanical trap

When 20 or more pounds of pressure are placed on this trap's pressure plate, a hidden trapdoor in the ceiling opens, releasing a 10-foot-diameter rolling sphere of solid stone.

With a successful DC 15 Wisdom (Perception) check, a character can spot the trapdoor and pressure plate. A search of the floor accompanied by a successful DC 15 Intelligence (Investigation) check reveals variations in the mortar and stone that betray the pressure plate's presence. The same check made while inspecting the ceiling notes variations in the stonework that reveal the trapdoor. Wedging an iron spike or other object under the pressure plate prevents the trap from activating.

Activation of the sphere requires all creatures present to roll initiative. The sphere rolls initiative with a +8 bonus. On its turn, it moves 60 feet in a straight line. The sphere can move through creatures' spaces, and creatures can move through its space, treating it as difficult terrain. Whenever the sphere enters a creature's space or a creature enters its space while it's rolling, that creature must succeed on a DC 15 Dexterity saving throw or take 55 (10d10) bludgeoning damage and be knocked prone.

The sphere stops when it hits a wall or similar barrier. It can't go around corners, but smart dungeon builders incorporate gentle, curving turns into nearby passages that allow the sphere to keep moving.

As an action, a creature within 5 feet of the sphere can attempt to slow it down with a DC 20 Strength check. On a successful check, the sphere's speed is reduced by 15 feet. If the sphere's speed drops to 0, it stops moving and is no longer a threat.

SPHERE OF ANNIHILATION
Magic trap

Magical, impenetrable darkness fills the gaping mouth of a stone face carved into a wall. The mouth is 2 feet in diameter and roughly circular. No sound issues from it, no light can illuminate the inside of it, and any matter that enters it is instantly obliterated.

A successful DC 20 Intelligence (Arcana) check reveals that the mouth contains a *sphere of annihilation* that can't be controlled or moved. It is otherwise identical to a normal *sphere of annihilation*, as described in chapter 7, "Treasure."

Some versions of the trap include an enchantment placed on the stone face, such that specified creatures feel an overwhelming urge to approach it and crawl inside its mouth. This effect is otherwise like the *sympathy* aspect of the *antipathy/sympathy* spell. A successful *dispel magic* (DC 18) removes this enchantment.

Chapter 6: Between Adventures

CAMPAIGN IS MUCH MORE THAN A SERIES OF adventures. It also includes the moments between them—the various distractions and side pursuits that engage the characters when they're not exploring the wilderness, plundering dungeons, and gallivanting around the multiverse on some epic quest.

The natural pace of a campaign offers lulls between adventures, time for the characters to spend their treasure and pursue their goals. This downtime gives the characters an opportunity to sink their roots a little deeper into the world, building a personal investment in what happens to the people and places around them, which can, in turn, draw them into further adventures.

Chapter 5, "Equipment," of the *Player's Handbook* details the expenses that a character incurs for basic necessities, depending on the lifestyle the character chooses, from poverty to luxury. Chapter 8, "Adventuring," of that book describes some of the downtime activities they can pursue between adventures. This chapter fills in the gaps, describing the expenses of owning property and hiring NPCs, and a variety of additional downtime activities characters can pursue. The beginning of the chapter also offers suggestions for linking adventures together and keeping track of events in your campaign.

Linking Adventures

A campaign in the style of an episodic television show rarely needs story links between its adventures. Each adventure features its own villains, and once the characters complete the adventure, there are typically no loose plot threads. The next adventure presents an altogether different challenge having nothing to do with the adventure that preceded it. As the characters gain experience points, they become more powerful, as do the threats they must overcome. This kind of campaign is easy to run, since it requires little effort beyond finding or creating adventures appropriate for the party's level.

A campaign with a narrative lets the players feel as though their actions have far-reaching consequences. They're not just racking up experience points. A few simple modifications can help you overlay overarching elements to create a serialized campaign in which early adventures help set up later ones.

Using an Overarching Story

This section presents a couple of examples of overarching stories which have, over the years, fueled many classic D&D campaigns.

The adventurers' goal in the first example is to amass the power they need to defeat a powerful enemy that threatens the world. Their goal in the second example is to defend something they care about by destroying whatever threatens it. The two examples are, in effect, the same story (variations of the battle between good and evil) told in different ways.

Example 1: The Quest of Many Parts

You can tie adventures together using an overarching goal that can be fulfilled only by first completing a series of related quests. For example, you could create a villain who can't be defeated until the characters explore nine dungeons in which the Nine Dread Princes reside, with each of these dungeons stocked with enough monsters and hazards to advance the adventurers two or three levels. The adventurers spend their whole careers fighting the Nine Dread Princes before finally pursuing an epic quest to destroy the princes' monstrous progenitor. As long as every dungeon is unique and interesting, your players will appreciate the tight focus of the campaign.

In a similar type of quest campaign, the adventurers might need to collect fragments of an artifact that are scattered in ruins across the multiverse, before reassembling the artifact and using it to defeat a cosmic threat.

Example 2: Agents of X

You can also build a campaign around the idea that the adventurers are agents of something larger than themselves—a kingdom or secret organization, for example. Wherever their allegiance lies, the adventurers are motivated by loyalty and the goal of protecting whatever it is they serve.

The characters' overarching mission might be to explore and map an uncharted region, forging alliances where they can and overcoming threats they encounter along the way. Their goal might be to find the ancient capital of a fallen empire, which lies beyond the realm of a known enemy and forces them to navigate hostile territory. The characters could be pilgrims in search of a holy site or members of a secret order dedicated to defending the last bastions of civilization in an ever-declining world. Or they might be spies and assassins, striving to weaken an enemy country by targeting its evil leaders and plundering its treasures.

Planting Adventure Seeds

You can make a campaign feel like one story with many chapters by planting the seeds of the next adventure before the current one is finished. This technique can naturally moves the characters along to their next goal.

If you've planted a seed well, the characters have something else to do when they finish an adventure. Perhaps a character drinks from a magic fountain in a dungeon and receives a mystifying vision that leads to the next quest. The party might find a cryptic map or relic that, once its meaning or purpose is determined, points to a new destination. Perhaps an NPC warns the characters of impending danger or implores them for help.

The trick is to not distract the characters from the adventure at hand. Designing an effective hook for a future adventure requires finesse. The lure should be compelling, but not so irresistible that the players stop caring about what their characters are doing right now.

To keep players from straying, save your best ideas for the very end of your adventures, or insert them during periods of downtime.

Here are a few examples of ways in which an adventure seed can be revealed:

- On a villain's corpse, the characters find evidence that the villain was working for someone else.
- A captured NPC reveals the location of someone or something that might interest the characters.
- The characters are heading to a local tavern when they spot a wanted poster or a missing person poster (complete with the promise of a sizable reward).
- Members of the local militia or city watch put out the word that a crime has been committed, and they're looking for potential witnesses and suspects.
- The characters receive an anonymous letter that sheds light on a plot or impending event of which they were previously unaware.

Foreshadowing

Foreshadowing is an exercise in subtlety, involving the delicate planting of seeds for future adventures. Not all foreshadowing bears fruit, particularly if the clues are too subtle or if events conspire to take your campaign in a new direction. The goal of foreshadowing is to hint at upcoming events and new threats in your campaign without making it obvious to players that you're telling them what the future holds. Here are a few examples:

- An object worn or carried by an enemy has the symbol of a previously unknown organization engraved or written on it.
- A mad woman standing on a street corner spouts fragments of an ancient prophecy, while pointing a crooked finger at the characters.
- The king and queen announce the marriage of their son to the daughter of a neighboring monarch, but various factions oppose the union. Trouble is brewing.
- Bugbear scouts are making incursions into civilized lands and spying on settlements, as a prelude to a hobgoblin warlord's invasion.
- A puppet show in a market square predicts a tragic outcome if two noble houses on the cusp of declaring war on each other refuse to reconcile.
- NPC adventurers in a city are being murdered in a similar yet unusual manner, hinting at a future threat to the player characters.

Campaign Tracking

Consistent details bring your campaign to life, and continuity helps players imagine that their characters are living in a real world. If the adventurers frequent a particular tavern, the staff, layout of the building, and decor shouldn't change much from one visit to the next. That said, changes can occur as a result of the characters' actions or of actions they learn about. When the adventurers kill a monster, it stays dead, unless someone raises it. When they remove treasure from a room, it doesn't reappear the next time they enter—assuming it hasn't been stolen from them! If they leave a door open, it should stay open until someone closes it.

No one's memory is infallible, so it pays to keep records. Jot notes directly on an adventure map to keep track of open doors, disarmed traps, and the like. Events beyond the scope of a single adventure are best recorded in a notebook dedicated to your campaign. Whether it's a physical book or an electronic file, such a record is a great way to keep your notes organized.

Your notebook might include any of the following elements.

Campaign Planner. Write down the main story arc of your campaign, and keep track of things that you hope appear in future adventures. Update it as the campaign develops, adding ideas as they come to you.

Character Notes. Write down the characters' backgrounds and goals, since these notes can help you design adventure content that provides opportunities for character development.

Keep a running tally of the adventurers' classes and levels, as well as any quests and downtime activities they're engaged in.

If the characters have a ship or stronghold, record its name and whereabouts, as well as any hirelings in the characters' employ.

Player Handouts. Keep a copy of all handouts you make for your players so that you don't have to remember their contents later.

Adventure Log. Think of this log as an episode guide for your campaign. Summarize each game session or adventure to help you keep track of the unfolding campaign story. You can give your players access to this log as well, or to an edited version stripped of your notes and secrets. (The players might also keep their own record of adventures, which you can refer to if your own log is incomplete.)

NPC Notes. Record statistics and roleplaying notes for any NPC the characters interact with more than once. For example, your notes might differentiate important people in a town by their different voices, as well as their names, the places where they live and work, the names of their family members and associates, and maybe even a secret that each one of them has.

Campaign Calendar. Your world feels more real to your players when the characters notice the passage of time. Note details such as the change of seasons and major holidays, and keep track of any important events that affect the larger story.

Toolbox. Keep notes whenever you create or significantly alter a monster, magic item, or trap. Keep any maps, random dungeons, or encounters you create. This information ensures you won't repeat your work, and you'll be able to draw on this material later.

Recurring Expenses

Besides the expenses associated with maintaining a particular lifestyle, adventurers might have additional drains on their adventuring income. Player characters who come into possession of property, own businesses, and employ hirelings must cover the expenses that accompany these ventures.

Maintenance Costs

Property	Total Cost per Day	Skilled Hirelings	Untrained Hirelings
Abbey	20 gp	5	25
Farm	5 sp	1	2
Guildhall, town or city	5 gp	5	3
Inn, rural roadside	10 gp	5	10
Inn, town or city	5 gp	1	5
Keep or small castle	100 gp	50	50
Lodge, hunting	5 sp	1	—
Noble estate	10 gp	3	15
Outpost or fort	50 gp	20	40
Palace or large castle	400 gp	200	100
Shop	2 gp	1	—
Temple, large	25 gp	10	10
Temple, small	1 gp	2	—
Tower, fortified	25 gp	10	—
Trading post	10 gp	4	2

It's not unusual for adventurers—especially after 10th level—to gain possession of a castle, a tavern, or another piece of property. They might buy it with their hard-won loot, take it by force, obtain it in a lucky draw from a *deck of many things*, or acquire it by other means.

The Maintenance Costs table shows the per-day upkeep cost for any such property. (The cost of a normal residence isn't included here because it falls under lifestyle expenses, as discussed in the *Player's Handbook*.) Maintenance expenses need to be paid every 30 days. Given that adventurers spend much of their time adventuring, staff includes a steward who can make payments in the party's absence.

Total Cost per Day. The cost includes everything it takes to maintain the property and keep things running smoothly, including the salaries of hirelings. If the property earns money that can offset maintenance costs (by charging fees, collecting tithes or donations, or selling goods), that is taken into account in the table.

Skilled and Untrained Hirelings. The *Player's Handbook* explains the difference between a skilled hireling and an untrained one.

Businesses

An adventurer-owned business can earn enough money to cover its own maintenance costs. However, the owner needs to periodically ensure that everything is running smoothly by tending to the business between adventures. See the information on running a business in the "Downtime Activities" section of this chapter.

Garrisons

Castles and keeps employ soldiers (use the veteran and guard statistics in the *Monster Manual*) to defend them. Roadside inns, outposts and forts, palaces, and temples rely on less-experienced defenders (use the guard statistics in the *Monster Manual*). These armed warriors make up the bulk of a property's skilled hirelings.

Downtime Activities

The campaign benefits when characters have time between adventures to engage in other activities. Allowing days, weeks, or months to pass between adventures stretches the campaign over a longer period of time and helps to manage the characters' level progression, preventing them from gaining too much power too quickly.

Allowing characters to pursue side interests between adventures also encourages players to become more invested in the campaign world. When a character owns a tavern in a village or spends time carousing with the locals, that character's player is more likely to respond to threats to the village and its inhabitants.

As your campaign progresses, your players' characters will not only become more powerful but also more influential and invested in the world. They might be inclined to undertake projects that require more time between adventures, such as building and maintaining a stronghold. As the party gains levels, you can add more downtime between adventures to give characters the time they need to pursue such interests. Whereas days or weeks might pass between low-level adventures, the amount of downtime between higher-level adventures might be measured in months or years.

MORE DOWNTIME ACTIVITIES

Chapter 8, "Adventuring," of the *Player's Handbook* describes a few downtime activities to fill the void between adventures. Depending on the style of your campaign and the particular backgrounds and interests of the adventurers, you can make some or all of the following additional activities available as options.

BUILDING A STRONGHOLD

A character can spend time between adventures building a stronghold. Before work can begin, the character must acquire a plot of land. If the estate lies within a kingdom or similar domain, the character will need a royal charter (a legal document granting permission to oversee the estate in the name of the crown), a land grant (a legal document bequeathing custody of the land to the character for as long as he or she remains loyal to the crown), or a deed (a legal document that serves as proof of ownership). Land can also be acquired by inheritance or other means.

Royal charters and land grants are usually given by the crown as a reward for faithful service, although they can also be bought. Deeds can be bought or inherited. A small estate might sell for as little as 100 gp or as much as 1,000 gp. A large estate might cost 5,000 gp or more, if it can be bought at all.

Once the estate is secured, a character needs access to building materials and laborers. The Building a Stronghold table shows the cost of building the stronghold (including materials and labor) and the amount of time it takes, provided that the character is using downtime to oversee construction. Work can continue while the character is away, but each day the character is away adds 3 days to the construction time.

BUILDING A STRONGHOLD

Stronghold	Construction Cost	Construction Time
Abbey	50,000 gp	400 days
Guildhall, town or city	5,000 gp	60 days
Keep or small castle	50,000 gp	400 days
Noble estate with manor	25,000 gp	150 days
Outpost or fort	15,000 gp	100 days
Palace or large castle	500,000 gp	1,200 days
Temple	50,000 gp	400 days
Tower, fortified	15,000 gp	100 days
Trading post	5,000 gp	60 days

CAROUSING

Characters can spend their downtime engaged in a variety of hedonistic activities such as attending parties, binge drinking, gambling, or anything else that helps them cope with the perils they face on their adventures.

A carousing character spends money as though maintaining a wealthy lifestyle (see chapter 5, "Equipment," of the *Player's Handbook*). At the end of the period spent carousing, the player rolls percentile dice and adds the character's level, then compares the total to the Carousing table to determine what happens to the character, or you choose.

CAROUSING

d100 + Level	Result
01–10	You are jailed for 1d4 days at the end of the downtime period on charges of disorderly conduct and disturbing the peace. You can pay a fine of 10 gp to avoid jail time, or you can try to resist arrest.
11–20	You regain consciousness in a strange place with no memory of how you got there, and you have been robbed of 3d6 × 5 gp.
21–30	You make an enemy. This person, business, or organization is now hostile to you. The DM determines the offended party. You decide how you offended them.
31–40	You are caught up in a whirlwind romance. Roll a d20. On a 1–5, the romance ends badly. On a 6–10, the romance ends amicably. On an 11–20, the romance is ongoing. You determine the identity of the love interest, subject to your DM's approval. If the romance ends badly, you might gain a new flaw. If it ends well or is ongoing, your new love interest might represent a new bond.
41–80	You earn modest winnings from gambling and recuperate your lifestyle expenses for the time spent carousing.
81–90	You earn modest winnings from gambling. You recuperate your lifestyle expenses for the time spent carousing and gain 1d20 × 4 gp.
91 or higher	You make a small fortune gambling. You recuperate your lifestyle expenses for the time spent carousing and gain 4d6 × 10 gp. Your carousing becomes the stuff of local legend.

CRAFTING A MAGIC ITEM

Magic items are the DM's purview, so you decide how they fall into the party's possession. As an option, you can allow player characters to craft magic items.

The creation of a magic item is a lengthy, expensive task. To start, a character must have a formula that describes the construction of the item. The character must also be a spellcaster with spell slots and must be able to cast any spells that the item can produce. Moreover, the character must meet a level minimum determined by the item's rarity, as shown in the Crafting Magic Items table. For example, a 3rd-level character could create a *wand of magic missiles* (an uncommon item), as long as the character has spell slots and can

cast *magic missile*. That same character could make a *+1 weapon* (another uncommon item), no particular spell required.

You can decide that certain items also require special materials or locations to be created. For example, a character might need alchemist's supplies to brew a particular potion, or the formula for a *flame tongue* might require that the weapon be forged with lava.

CRAFTING MAGIC ITEMS

Item Rarity	Creation Cost	Minimum Level
Common	100 gp	3rd
Uncommon	500 gp	3rd
Rare	5,000 gp	6th
Very rare	50,000 gp	11th
Legendary	500,000 gp	17th

An item has a creation cost specified in the Crafting Magic Items table. A character engaged in the crafting of a magic item makes progress in 25 gp increments, spending that amount for each day of work until the total cost is paid. The character is assumed to work for 8 hours each of those days. Thus, creating an uncommon magic item takes 20 days and 500 gp. You are free to adjust the costs to better suit your campaign.

If a spell will be produced by the item being created, the creator must expend one spell slot of the spell's level for each day of the creation process. The spell's material components must also be at hand throughout the process. If the spell normally consumes those components, they are consumed by the creation process. If the item will be able to produce the spell only once, as with a *spell scroll*, the components are consumed only once by the process. Otherwise, the components are consumed once each day of the item's creation.

Multiple characters can combine their efforts to create a magic item if each of them meets the level prerequisite. Each character can contribute spells, spell slots, and components, as long as everyone participates during the entire crafting process. Each character can contribute 25 gp worth of effort for each day spent helping to craft the item.

Normally, a character who undertakes this activity creates a magic item described in chapter 7, "Treasure." At your discretion, you can allow players to design their own magic items, using the guidelines in chapter 9, "Dungeon Master's Workshop."

While crafting a magic item, a character can maintain a modest lifestyle without having to pay the 1 gp per day, or a comfortable lifestyle at half the normal cost (see chapter 5, "Equipment," of the *Player's Handbook*).

GAINING RENOWN

A character can spend downtime improving his or her renown within a particular organization (see "Renown" in chapter 1). Between adventures, a character undertakes minor tasks for the organization and socializes with its members. After pursuing these activities for a combined number of days equal to his or her current renown multiplied by 10, the character's renown increases by 1.

PERFORMING SACRED RITES

A pious character can spend time between adventures performing sacred rites in a temple affiliated with a god he or she reveres. Between rites, the character spends time in meditation and prayer.

A character who is a priest in the temple can lead these rites, which might include weddings, funerals, and ordinations. A layperson can offer sacrifices in a temple or assist a priest with a rite.

A character who spends at least 10 days performing sacred rites gains inspiration (described in chapter 4 of the *Player's Handbook*) at the start of each day for the next 2d6 days.

RUNNING A BUSINESS

Adventurers can end up owning businesses that have nothing to do with delving into dungeons or saving the world. A character might inherit a smithy, or the party might be given a parcel of farmland or a tavern as a reward. If they hold on to the business, they might feel obliged to spend time between adventures maintaining the venture and making sure it runs smoothly.

A character rolls percentile dice and adds the number of days spent on this downtime activity (maximum 30), then compares the total to the Running a Business table to determine what happens.

If the character is required to pay a cost as a result of rolling on this table but fails to do so, the business begins to fail. For each unpaid debt incurred in this manner, the character takes a −10 penalty to subsequent rolls made on this table.

RUNNING A BUSINESS

d100 + Days	Result
01–20	You must pay one and a half times the business's maintenance cost for each of the days.
21–30	You must pay the business's full maintenance cost for each of the days.
31–40	You must pay half the business's maintenance cost for each of the days. Profits cover the other half.
41–60	The business covers its own maintenance cost for each of the days.
61–80	The business covers its own maintenance cost for each of the days. It earns a profit of 1d6 × 5 gp.
81–90	The business covers its own maintenance cost for each of the days. It earns a profit of 2d8 × 5 gp.
91 or higher	The business covers its own maintenance cost for each of the days. It earns a profit of 3d10 × 5 gp.

SELLING MAGIC ITEMS

Few people can afford to buy a magic item, and fewer still know how to find one. Adventurers are exceptional in this regard due to the nature of their profession.

A character who comes into possession of a common, uncommon, rare, or very rare magic item that he or she wants to sell can spend downtime searching for a buyer. This downtime activity can be performed only in a city or another location where one can find wealthy

individuals interested in buying magic items. Legendary magic items and priceless artifacts can't be sold during downtime. Finding someone to buy such an item can be the substance of an adventure or quest.

For each salable item, the character makes a DC 20 Intelligence (Investigation) check to find buyers. Another character can use his or her downtime to assist with the search, granting advantage on the checks. On a failed check, no buyer for the item is found after a search that lasts 10 days. On a successful check, a buyer for the item is found after a number of days based on the item's rarity, as shown in the Salable Magic Item table.

A character can attempt to find buyers for multiple magic items at once. Although this requires multiple Intelligence (Investigation) checks, the searches are occurring simultaneously, and the results of multiple failures or successes aren't added together. For example, if the character finds a buyer for a common magic item in 2 days and a buyer for an uncommon item in 5 days, but fails to find a buyer for a rare item up for grabs, the entire search takes 10 days.

For each item a character wishes to sell, the player rolls percentile dice and consults the Selling a Magic Item table, applying a modifier based on the item's rarity, as shown in the Salable Magic Items table. The character also makes a Charisma (Persuasion) check and adds that check's total to the roll. The subsequent total determines what a buyer offers to pay for the item.

You determine a buyer's identity. Buyers sometimes procure rare and very rare items through proxies to ensure that their identities remain unknown. If the buyer is shady, it's up to you whether the sale creates legal complications for the party later.

Salable Magic Items

Rarity	Base Price	Days to Find Buyer	d100 Roll Modifier*
Common	100 gp	1d4	+10
Uncommon	500 gp	1d6	+0
Rare	5,000 gp	1d8	–10
Very rare	50,000 gp	1d10	–20

* Apply this modifier to rolls on the Selling a Magic Item table.

Selling a Magic Item

d100 + Mod.	You Find ...
20 or lower	A buyer offering a tenth of the base price
21–40	A buyer offering a quarter of the base price, and a shady buyer offering half the base price
41–80	A buyer offering half the base price, and a shady buyer offering the full base price
81–90	A buyer offering the full base price
91 or higher	A shady buyer offering one and a half times the base price, no questions asked

SOWING RUMORS

Swaying public opinion can be an effective way to bring down a villain or elevate a friend. Spreading rumors is an efficient, if underhanded, way to accomplish that goal. Well-placed rumors can increase the subject's standing in a community or embroil someone in scandal. A rumor needs to be simple, concrete, and hard to disprove. An effective rumor also has to be believable, playing off what people want to believe about the person in question.

Sowing a rumor about an individual or organization requires a number of days depending on the size of the community, as shown in the Sowing Rumors table. In a town or city, the time spent must be continuous. If the character spreads a rumor for ten days, disappears on an adventure for another few days and then returns, the rumor fades away without the benefit of constant repetition.

SOWING RUMORS

Settlement Size	Time Required
Village	2d6 days
Town	4d6 days
City	6d6 days

The character must spend 1 gp per day to cover the cost of drinks, social appearances, and the like. At the end of the time spent sowing the rumor, the character must make a DC 15 Charisma (Deception or Persuasion) check. If the check succeeds, the community's prevailing attitude toward the subject shifts one step toward friendly or hostile, as the character wishes. If the check fails, the rumor gains no traction, and further attempts to propagate it fail.

Shifting a community's general attitude toward a person or organization doesn't affect everyone in the community. Individuals might hold to their own opinions, particularly if they have personal experience in dealing with the subject of the rumors.

TRAINING TO GAIN LEVELS

As a variant rule, you can require characters to spend downtime training or studying before they gain the benefits of a new level. If you choose this option, once a character has earned enough experience points to attain a new level, he or she must train for a number of days before gaining any class features associated with the new level.

The training time required depends on the level to be gained, as shown on the Training to Gain Levels table. The training cost is for the total training time.

TRAINING TO GAIN LEVELS

Level Attained	Training Time	Training Cost
2nd–4th	10 days	20 gp
5th–10th	20 days	40 gp
11th–16th	30 days	60 gp
17th–20th	40 days	80 gp

CREATING DOWNTIME ACTIVITIES

Your players might be interested in pursuing downtime activities that aren't covered in this chapter or in the *Player's Handbook*. If you invent new downtime activities, remember the following:

- An activity should never negate the need or desire for characters to go on adventures.
- Activities that have a monetary cost associated with them provide opportunities for player characters to spend their hard-won treasure.
- Activities that reveal new adventure hooks and previously unknown facts about your campaign can help you foreshadow future events and conflicts.
- For an activity you expect a character to repeat with variable degrees of success, consider creating a random outcome table, modeled on the ones in this chapter.
- If a character belongs to a class or has a proficiency or background that would make him or her well suited to a particular activity, consider granting a bonus to ability checks made by the character to complete that activity successfully.

CHAPTER 7: TREASURE

DVENTURERS STRIVE FOR MANY THINGS, including glory, knowledge, and justice. Many adventurers also seek something more tangible: fortune. Strands of golden chains, stacks of platinum coins, bejeweled crowns, enameled scepters, bolts of silk cloth, and powerful magic items all wait to be seized or unearthed by intrepid, treasure-seeking adventurers.

This chapter details magic items and the placement of treasure in an adventure, as well as special rewards that can be granted instead of or in addition to magic items and mundane treasure.

TYPES OF TREASURE

Treasure comes in many forms.

Coins. The most basic type of treasure is money, including copper pieces (cp), silver pieces (sp), electrum pieces (ep), gold pieces (gp), and platinum pieces (pp). Fifty coins of any type weigh 1 pound.

Gemstones. Gemstones are small, lightweight, and easily secured compared to their same value in coins. See the "Gemstones" section for types of stones, gems, and jewels that can be found as treasure.

Art Objects. Idols cast of solid gold, necklaces studded with precious stones, paintings of ancient kings, bejeweled dishes—art objects include all these and more. See the "Art Objects" section for types of decorative and valuable artworks that can be found as treasure.

Magic Items. Types of magic items include armor, potions, scrolls, rings, rods, staffs, wands, weapons, and wondrous items. Magic items also have rarities: common, uncommon, rare, very rare, and legendary.

Intelligent monsters often use magic items in their possession, while others might hide them away to ensure they don't get lost or stolen. For example, if a hobgoblin tribe has a *+1 longsword* and an *alchemy jug* in its treasure hoard, the tribe's warlord might wield the sword, while the jug is kept somewhere safe.

RANDOM TREASURE

The following pages contain tables that you can use to randomly generate treasures carried by monsters, stashed in their lairs, or otherwise hidden away. The placement of treasure is left to your discretion. The key is to make sure the players feel rewarded for playing, and that their characters are rewarded for overcoming dangerous challenges.

TREASURE TABLES

Treasure can be randomly allocated based on a monster's challenge rating. There are tables for challenge rating 0–4, challenge rating 5–10, challenge rating 11–16, and challenge rating 17 and higher. Use these tables to randomly determine how much money an individual monster carries (the D&D equivalent of pocket change) or the amount of wealth found in a larger treasure hoard.

USING THE INDIVIDUAL TREASURE TABLES

An Individual Treasure table helps you randomly determine how much treasure one creature carries on its person. If a monster has no interest in amassing treasure, you can use this table to determine the incidental treasure left behind by the monster's victims.

Use the Individual Treasure table that corresponds to the monster's challenge rating. Roll a d100, and read the result across to determine how many coins of each type the monster carries. The table also includes the average result in parentheses, should you wish to forgo another roll and save time. To determine the total amount of individual treasure for a group of similar creatures, you can save time by rolling once and multiplying the result by the number of creatures in the group.

If it doesn't make sense for a monster to carry a large pile of coins, you can convert the coins into gemstones or art objects of equal value.

USING THE TREASURE HOARD TABLES

A Treasure Hoard table helps you randomly determine the contents of a large cache of treasure, the accumulated wealth of a large group of creatures (such as an orc tribe or a hobgoblin army), the belongings of a single powerful creature that likes to hoard treasure (such as a dragon), or the reward bestowed upon a party after completing a quest for a benefactor. You can also split up a treasure hoard so that the adventurers don't find or receive it all at once.

When determining the contents of a hoard belonging to one monster, use the table that corresponds to that monster's challenge rating. When rolling to determine a treasure hoard belonging to a large group of monsters, use the challenge rating of the monster that leads the group. If the hoard belongs to no one, use the challenge rating of the monster that presides over the dungeon or lair you are stocking. If the hoard is a gift from a benefactor, use the challenge rating equal to the party's average level.

Every treasure hoard contains a random number of coins, as shown at the top of each table. Roll a d100 and consult the table to determine how many gemstones or art objects the hoard contains, if any. Use the same roll to determine whether the hoard contains magic items.

As with the individual treasure tables, average values are given in parentheses. You can use an average value instead of rolling dice to save time.

If a treasure hoard seems too small, you can roll multiple times on the table. Use this approach for monsters that are particularly fond of amassing treasure. Legendary creatures that accumulate treasure are wealthier than normal. Always roll at least twice on the appropriate table and add the results together.

You can hand out as much or as little treasure as you want. Over the course of a typical campaign, a party finds treasure hoards amounting to seven rolls on the Challenge 0–4 table, eighteen rolls on the Challenge 5–10 table, twelve rolls on the Challenge 11–16 table, and eight rolls on the Challenge 17+ table.

Gemstones

If a treasure hoard includes gemstones, you can use the following tables to randomly determine the kind of gemstones found, based on their value. You can roll once and assume all the gems are the same, or roll multiple times to create mixed collections of gemstones.

10 gp Gemstones

d12	Stone Description
1	Azurite (opaque mottled deep blue)
2	Banded agate (translucent striped brown, blue, white, or red)
3	Blue quartz (transparent pale blue)
4	Eye agate (translucent circles of gray, white, brown, blue, or green)
5	Hematite (opaque gray-black)
6	Lapis lazuli (opaque light and dark blue with yellow flecks)
7	Malachite (opaque striated light and dark green)
8	Moss agate (translucent pink or yellow-white with mossy gray or green markings)
9	Obsidian (opaque black)
10	Rhodochrosite (opaque light pink)
11	Tiger eye (translucent brown with golden center)
12	Turquoise (opaque light blue-green)

50 gp Gemstones

d12	Stone Description
1	Bloodstone (opaque dark gray with red flecks)
2	Carnelian (opaque orange to red-brown)
3	Chalcedony (opaque white)
4	Chrysoprase (translucent green)
5	Citrine (transparent pale yellow-brown)
6	Jasper (opaque blue, black, or brown)
7	Moonstone (translucent white with pale blue glow)
8	Onyx (opaque bands of black and white, or pure black or white)
9	Quartz (transparent white, smoky gray, or yellow)
10	Sardonyx (opaque bands of red and white)
11	Star rose quartz (translucent rosy stone with white star-shaped center)
12	Zircon (transparent pale blue-green)

100 gp Gemstones

d10	Stone Description
1	Amber (transparent watery gold to rich gold)
2	Amethyst (transparent deep purple)
3	Chrysoberyl (transparent yellow-green to pale green)
4	Coral (opaque crimson)
5	Garnet (transparent red, brown-green, or violet)
6	Jade (translucent light green, deep green, or white)
7	Jet (opaque deep black)
8	Pearl (opaque lustrous white, yellow, or pink)
9	Spinel (transparent red, red-brown, or deep green)
10	Tourmaline (transparent pale green, blue, brown, or red)

500 gp Gemstones

d6	Stone Description
1	Alexandrite (transparent dark green)
2	Aquamarine (transparent pale blue-green)
3	Black pearl (opaque pure black)
4	Blue spinel (transparent deep blue)
5	Peridot (transparent rich olive green)
6	Topaz (transparent golden yellow)

1,000 gp Gemstones

d8	Stone Description
1	Black opal (translucent dark green with black mottling and golden flecks)
2	Blue sapphire (transparent blue-white to medium blue)
3	Emerald (transparent deep bright green)
4	Fire opal (translucent fiery red)
5	Opal (translucent pale blue with green and golden mottling)
6	Star ruby (translucent ruby with white star-shaped center)
7	Star sapphire (translucent blue sapphire with white star-shaped center)
8	Yellow sapphire (transparent fiery yellow or yellow-green)

5,000 gp Gemstones

d4	Stone Description
1	Black sapphire (translucent lustrous black with glowing highlights)
2	Diamond (transparent blue-white, canary, pink, brown, or blue)
3	Jacinth (transparent fiery orange)
4	Ruby (transparent clear red to deep crimson)

Art Objects

If a treasure hoard includes art objects, you can use the following tables to randomly determine what art objects are found, based on their value. Roll on a table as many times as there are art objects in the treasure hoard. There can be more than one of a given art object.

25 gp Art Objects

d10	Object
1	Silver ewer
2	Carved bone statuette
3	Small gold bracelet
4	Cloth-of-gold vestments
5	Black velvet mask stitched with silver thread
6	Copper chalice with silver filigree
7	Pair of engraved bone dice
8	Small mirror set in a painted wooden frame
9	Embroidered silk handkerchief
10	Gold locket with a painted portrait inside

250 GP ART OBJECTS

d10	Object
1	Gold ring set with bloodstones
2	Carved ivory statuette
3	Large gold bracelet
4	Silver necklace with a gemstone pendant
5	Bronze crown
6	Silk robe with gold embroidery
7	Large well-made tapestry
8	Brass mug with jade inlay
9	Box of turquoise animal figurines
10	Gold bird cage with electrum filigree

750 GP ART OBJECTS

d10	Object
1	Silver chalice set with moonstones
2	Silver-plated steel longsword with jet set in hilt
3	Carved harp of exotic wood with ivory inlay and zircon gems
4	Small gold idol
5	Gold dragon comb set with red garnets as eyes
6	Bottle stopper cork embossed with gold leaf and set with amethysts
7	Ceremonial electrum dagger with a black pearl in the pommel
8	Silver and gold brooch
9	Obsidian statuette with gold fittings and inlay
10	Painted gold war mask

2,500 GP ART OBJECTS

d10	Object
1	Fine gold chain set with a fire opal
2	Old masterpiece painting
3	Embroidered silk and velvet mantle set with numerous moonstones
4	Platinum bracelet set with a sapphire
5	Embroidered glove set with jewel chips
6	Jeweled anklet
7	Gold music box
8	Gold circlet set with four aquamarines
9	Eye patch with a mock eye set in blue sapphire and moonstone
10	A necklace string of small pink pearls

7,500 GP ART OBJECTS

d8	Object
1	Jeweled gold crown
2	Jeweled platinum ring
3	Small gold statuette set with rubies
4	Gold cup set with emeralds
5	Gold jewelry box with platinum filigree
6	Painted gold child's sarcophagus
7	Jade game board with solid gold playing pieces
8	Bejeweled ivory drinking horn with gold filigree

MAGIC ITEMS

Magic items are gleaned from the hoards of conquered monsters or discovered in long-lost vaults. Such items grant capabilities a character could rarely have otherwise, or they complement their owner's capabilities in wondrous ways.

RARITY

Each magic item has a rarity: common, uncommon, rare, very rare, or legendary. Common magic items, such as a *potion of healing*, are the most plentiful. Some legendary items, such as the *apparatus of Kwalish*, are unique. The game assumes that the secrets of creating the most powerful items arose centuries ago and were then gradually lost as a result of wars, cataclysms, and mishaps. Even uncommon items can't be easily created. Thus, many magic items are well-preserved antiquities.

Rarity provides a rough measure of an item's power relative to other magic items. Each rarity corresponds to character level, as shown in the Magic Item Rarity table. A character doesn't typically find a rare magic item, for example, until around 5th level. That said, rarity shouldn't get in the way of your campaign's story. If you want a *ring of invisibility* to fall into the hands of a 1st-level character, so be it. No doubt a great story will arise from that event.

If your campaign allows for trade in magic items, rarity can also help you set prices for them. As the DM, you determine the value of an individual magic item based on its rarity. Suggested values are provided in the Magic Item Rarity table. The value of a consumable item, such as a potion or scroll, is typically half the value of a permanent item of the same rarity.

MAGIC ITEM RARITY

Rarity	Character Level	Value
Common	1st or higher	50–100 gp
Uncommon	1st or higher	101–500 gp
Rare	5th or higher	501–5,000 gp
Very rare	11th or higher	5,001–50,000 gp
Legendary	17th or higher	50,001+ gp

BUYING AND SELLING

Unless you decide your campaign works otherwise, most magic items are so rare that they aren't available for purchase. Common items, such as a *potion of healing*, can be procured from an alchemist, herbalist, or spellcaster. Doing so is rarely as simple as walking into a shop and selecting an item from a shelf. The seller might ask for a service, rather than coin.

In a large city with an academy of magic or a major temple, buying and selling magic items might be possible, at your discretion. If your world includes a large number of adventurers engaged in retrieving ancient magic items, trade in these items might be more common. Even so, it's likely to remain similar to the market for fine art in the real world, with invitation-only auctions and a tendency to attract thieves.

Selling magic items is difficult in most D&D worlds primarily because of the challenge of finding a buyer.

Plenty of people might like to have a magic sword, but few of them can afford it. Those who can afford such an item usually have more practical things to spend on. See chapter 6, "Between Adventures," for one way to handle selling magic items.

In your campaign, magic items might be prevalent enough that adventurers can buy and sell them with some effort. Magic items might be for sale in bazaars or auction houses in fantastical locations, such as the City of Brass, the planar metropolis of Sigil, or even in more ordinary cities. Sale of magic items might be highly regulated, accompanied by a thriving black market. Artificers might craft items for use by military forces or adventurers, as they do in the world of Eberron. You might also allow characters to craft their own magic items, as discussed in chapters 6.

IDENTIFYING A MAGIC ITEM

Some magic items are indistinguishable from their nonmagical counterparts, whereas other magic items display their magical nature conspicuously. Whatever a magic item's appearance, handling the item is enough to give a character a sense that something is extraordinary about it. Discovering a magic item's properties isn't automatic, however.

The *identify* spell is the fastest way to reveal an item's properties. Alternatively, a character can focus on one magic item during a short rest, while being in physical contact with the item. At the end of the rest, the character learns the item's properties, as well as how to use them. Potions are an exception; a little taste is enough to tell the taster what the potion does.

Sometimes a magic item carries a clue to its properties. The command word to activate a ring might be etched in tiny letters inside it, or a feathered design might suggest that it's a *ring of feather falling*.

Wearing or experimenting with an item can also offer hints about its properties. For example, if a character puts on a *ring of jumping*, you could say, "Your steps feel strangely springy." Perhaps the character then jumps up and down to see what happens. You then say the character jumps unexpectedly high.

VARIANT: MORE DIFFICULT IDENTIFICATION

If you prefer magic items to have a greater mystique, consider removing the ability to identify the properties of a magic item during a short rest, and require the *identify* spell, experimentation, or both to reveal what a magic item does.

ATTUNEMENT

Some magic items require a creature to form a bond with them before their magical properties can be used. This bond is called attunement, and certain items have a prerequisite for it. If the prerequisite is a class, a creature must be a member of that class to attune to the item. (If the class is a spellcasting class, a monster

INDIVIDUAL TREASURE: CHALLENGE 0–4

d100	CP	SP	EP	GP	PP
01–30	5d6 (17)	—	—	—	—
31–60	—	4d6 (14)	—	—	—
61–70	—	—	3d6 (10)	—	—
71–95	—	—	—	3d6 (10)	—
96–00	—	—	—	—	1d6 (3)

INDIVIDUAL TREASURE: CHALLENGE 5–10

d100	CP	SP	EP	GP	PP
01–30	4d6 × 100 (1,400)	—	1d6 × 10 (35)	—	—
31–60	—	6d6 × 10 (210)	—	2d6 × 10 (70)	—
61–70	—	—	3d6 × 10 (105)	2d6 × 10 (70)	—
71–95	—	—	—	4d6 × 10 (140)	—
96–00	—	—	—	2d6 × 10 (70)	3d6 (10)

INDIVIDUAL TREASURE: CHALLENGE 11–16

d100	CP	SP	EP	GP	PP
01–20	—	4d6 × 100 (1,400)	—	1d6 × 100 (350)	—
21–35	—	—	1d6 × 100 (350)	1d6 × 100 (350)	—
36–75	—	—	—	2d6 × 100 (700)	1d6 × 10 (35)
76–00	—	—	—	2d6 × 100 (700)	2d6 × 10 (70)

INDIVIDUAL TREASURE: CHALLENGE 17+

d100	CP	SP	EP	GP	PP
01–15	—	—	2d6 × 1,000 (7,000)	8d6 × 100 (2,800)	—
16–55	—	—	—	1d6 × 1,000 (3,500)	1d6 × 100 (350)
56–00	—	—	—	1d6 × 1,000 (3,500)	2d6 × 100 (700)

Treasure Hoard: Challenge 0–4

	CP	SP	EP	GP	PP
Coins	6d6 × 100 (2,100)	3d6 × 100 (1,050)	—	2d6 × 10 (70)	—

d100	Gems or Art Objects	Magic Items
01–06	—	—
07–16	2d6 (7) 10 gp gems	—
17–26	2d4 (5) 25 gp art objects	—
27–36	2d6 (7) 50 gp gems	—
37–44	2d6 (7) 10 gp gems	Roll 1d6 times on Magic Item Table A.
45–52	2d4 (5) 25 gp art objects	Roll 1d6 times on Magic Item Table A.
53–60	2d6 (7) 50 gp gems	Roll 1d6 times on Magic Item Table A.
61–65	2d6 (7) 10 gp gems	Roll 1d4 times on Magic Item Table B.
66–70	2d4 (5) 25 gp art objects	Roll 1d4 times on Magic Item Table B.
71–75	2d6 (7) 50 gp gems	Roll 1d4 times on Magic Item Table B.
76–78	2d6 (7) 10 gp gems	Roll 1d4 times on Magic Item Table C.
79–80	2d4 (5) 25 gp art objects	Roll 1d4 times on Magic Item Table C.
81–85	2d6 (7) 50 gp gems	Roll 1d4 times on Magic Item Table C.
86–92	2d4 (5) 25 gp art objects	Roll 1d4 times on Magic Item Table F.
93–97	2d6 (7) 50 gp gems	Roll 1d4 times on Magic Item Table F.
98–99	2d4 (5) 25 gp art objects	Roll once on Magic Item Table G.
00	2d6 (7) 50 gp gems	Roll once on Magic Item Table G.

Treasure Hoard: Challenge 5–10

	CP	SP	EP	GP	PP
Coins	2d6 × 100 (700)	2d6 × 1,000 (7,000)	—	6d6 × 100 (2,100)	3d6 × 10 (105)

d100	Gems or Art Objects	Magic Items
01–04	—	—
05–10	2d4 (5) 25 gp art objects	—
11–16	3d6 (10) 50 gp gems	—
17–22	3d6 (10) 100 gp gems	—
23–28	2d4 (5) 250 gp art objects	—
29–32	2d4 (5) 25 gp art objects	Roll 1d6 times on Magic Item Table A.
33–36	3d6 (10) 50 gp gems	Roll 1d6 times on Magic Item Table A.
37–40	3d6 (10) 100 gp gems	Roll 1d6 times on Magic Item Table A.
41–44	2d4 (5) 250 gp art objects	Roll 1d6 times on Magic Item Table A.
45–49	2d4 (5) 25 gp art objects	Roll 1d4 times on Magic Item Table B.
50–54	3d6 (10) 50 gp gems	Roll 1d4 times on Magic Item Table B.
55–59	3d6 (10) 100 gp gems	Roll 1d4 times on Magic Item Table B.
60–63	2d4 (5) 250 gp art objects	Roll 1d4 times on Magic Item Table B.
64–66	2d4 (5) 25 gp art objects	Roll 1d4 times on Magic Item Table C.
67–69	3d6 (10) 50 gp gems	Roll 1d4 times on Magic Item Table C.
70–72	3d6 (10) 100 gp gems	Roll 1d4 times on Magic Item Table C.
73–74	2d4 (5) 250 gp art objects	Roll 1d4 times on Magic Item Table C.
75–76	2d4 (5) 25 gp art objects	Roll once on Magic Item Table D.
77–78	3d6 (10) 50 gp gems	Roll once on Magic Item Table D.
79	3d6 (10) 100 gp gems	Roll once on Magic Item Table D.
80	2d4 (5) 250 gp art objects	Roll once on Magic Item Table D.
81–84	2d4 (5) 25 gp art objects	Roll 1d4 times on Magic Item Table F.
85–88	3d6 (10) 50 gp gems	Roll 1d4 times on Magic Item Table F.
89–91	3d6 (10) 100 gp gems	Roll 1d4 times on Magic Item Table F.
92–94	2d4 (5) 250 gp art objects	Roll 1d4 times on Magic Item Table F.
95–96	3d6 (10) 100 gp gems	Roll 1d4 times on Magic Item Table G.
97–98	2d4 (5) 250 gp art objects	Roll 1d4 times on Magic Item Table G.
99	3d6 (10) 100 gp gems	Roll once on Magic Item Table H.
00	2d4 (5) 250 gp art objects	Roll once on Magic Item Table H.

qualifies if that monster has spell slots and uses that class's spell list.)

Without becoming attuned to an item that requires attunement, a creature gains only its nonmagical benefits, unless its description states otherwise. For example, a magic shield that requires attunement provides the benefits of a normal shield to a creature not attuned to it, but none of its magical properties.

Attuning to an item requires a creature to spend a short rest focused on only that item while being in physical contact with it (this can't be the same short rest used to learn the item's properties). This focus can take the form of weapon practice (for a weapon), meditation (for a wondrous item), or some other appropriate activity. If the short rest is interrupted, the attunement attempt fails. Otherwise, at the end of the short rest, the creature gains an intuitive understanding of how to activate any magical properties of the item, including any necessary command words.

An item can be attuned to only one creature at a time, and a creature can be attuned to no more than three magic items at a time. Any attempt to attune to a fourth item fails; the creature must end its attunement to an item first. Additionally, a creature can't attune to more than one copy of an item. For example, a creature can't attune to more than one *ring of protection* at a time.

A creature's attunement to an item ends if the creature no longer satisfies the prerequisites for attunement, if the item has been more than 100 feet away for at least 24 hours, if the creature dies, or if another creature attunes to the item. A creature can also voluntarily end attunement by spending another short rest focused on the item, unless the item is cursed.

CURSED ITEMS

Some magic items bear curses that bedevil their users, sometimes long after a user has stopped using an item. A magic item's description specifies whether the item

TREASURE HOARD: CHALLENGE 11–16

	CP	SP	EP	GP	PP
Coins	—	—	—	4d6 × 1,000 (14,000)	5d6 × 100 (1,750) pp

d100	Gems or Art Objects	Magic Items
01–03	—	—
04–06	2d4 (5) 250 gp art objects	—
07–09	2d4 (5) 750 gp art objects	—
11–12	3d6 (10) 500 gp gems	—
13–15	3d6 (10) 1,000 gp gems	—
16–19	2d4 (5) 250 gp art objects	Roll 1d4 times on Magic Item Table A and 1d6 times on Magic Item Table B.
20–23	2d4 (5) 750 gp art objects	Roll 1d4 times on Magic Item Table A and 1d6 times on Magic Item Table B.
24–26	3d6 (10) 500 gp gems	Roll 1d4 times on Magic Item Table A and 1d6 times on Magic Item Table B.
27–29	3d6 (10) 1,000 gp gems	Roll 1d4 times on Magic Item Table A and 1d6 times on Magic Item Table B.
30–35	2d4 (5) 250 gp art objects	Roll 1d6 times on Magic Item Table C.
36–40	2d4 (5) 750 gp art objects	Roll 1d6 times on Magic Item Table C.
41–45	3d6 (10) 500 gp gems	Roll 1d6 times on Magic Item Table C.
46–50	3d6 (10) 1,000 gp gems	Roll 1d6 times on Magic Item Table C.
51–54	2d4 (5) 250 gp art objects	Roll 1d4 times on Magic Item Table D.
55–58	2d4 (5) 750 gp art objects	Roll 1d4 times on Magic Item Table D.
59–62	3d6 (10) 500 gp gems	Roll 1d4 times on Magic Item Table D.
63–66	3d6 (10) 1,000 gp gems	Roll 1d4 times on Magic Item Table D.
67–68	2d4 (5) 250 gp art objects	Roll once on Magic Item Table E.
69–70	2d4 (5) 750 gp art objects	Roll once on Magic Item Table E.
71–72	3d6 (10) 500 gp gems	Roll once on Magic Item Table E.
73–74	3d6 (10) 1,000 gp gems	Roll once on Magic Item Table E.
75–76	2d4 (5) 250 gp art objects	Roll once on Magic Item Table F and 1d4 times on Magic Item Table G.
77–78	2d4 (5) 750 gp art objects	Roll once on Magic Item Table F and 1d4 times on Magic Item Table G.
79–80	3d6 (10) 500 gp gems	Roll once on Magic Item Table F and 1d4 times on Magic Item Table G.
81–82	3d6 (10) 1,000 gp gems	Roll once on Magic Item Table F and 1d4 times on Magic Item Table G.
83–85	2d4 (5) 250 gp art objects	Roll 1d4 times on Magic Item Table H.
86–88	2d4 (5) 750 gp art objects	Roll 1d4 times on Magic Item Table H.
89–90	3d6 (10) 500 gp gems	Roll 1d4 times on Magic Item Table H.
91–92	3d6 (10) 1,000 gp gems	Roll 1d4 times on Magic Item Table H.
93–94	2d4 (5) 250 gp art objects	Roll once on Magic Item Table I.
95–96	2d4 (5) 750 gp art objects	Roll once on Magic Item Table I.
97–98	3d6 (10) 500 gp gems	Roll once on Magic Item Table I.
99–00	3d6 (10) 1,000 gp gems	Roll once on Magic Item Table I.

is cursed. Most methods of identifying items, including the *identify* spell, fail to reveal such a curse, although lore might hint at it. A curse should be a surprise to the item's user when the curse's effects are revealed.

Attunement to a cursed item can't be ended voluntarily unless the curse is broken first, such as with the *remove curse* spell.

MAGIC ITEM CATEGORIES

Each magic item belongs to a category: armor, potions, rings, rods, scrolls, staffs, wands, weapons, or wondrous items.

ARMOR

Unless an armor's description says otherwise, armor must be worn for its magic to function.

Some suits of magic armor specify the type of armor they are, such as chain mail or plate. If a magic armor doesn't specify its armor type, you may choose the type or determine it randomly.

POTIONS

Different kinds of magical liquids are grouped in the category of potions: brews made from enchanted herbs, water from magical fountains or sacred springs, and oils that are applied to a creature or object. Most potions consist of one ounce of liquid.

Potions are consumable magic items. Drinking a potion or administering a potion to another character requires an action. Applying an oil might take longer, as specified in its description. Once used, a potion takes effect immediately, and it is used up.

RINGS

Magic rings offer an amazing array of powers to those lucky enough to find them. Unless a ring's description says otherwise, a ring must be worn on a finger, or a similar digit, for the ring's magic to function.

RODS

A scepter or just a heavy cylinder, a magic rod is typically made of metal, wood, or bone. It's about 2 or 3 feet long, 1 inch thick, and 2 to 5 pounds.

SCROLLS

Most scrolls are spells stored in written form, while a few bear unique incantations that produce potent wards. Whatever its contents, a scroll is a roll of paper, sometimes attached to wooden rods, and typically kept safe in a tube of ivory, jade, leather, metal, or wood.

A scroll is a consumable magic item. Whatever the nature of the magic contained in a scroll, unleashing that magic requires using an action to read the scroll. When its magic has been invoked, the scroll can't be used again. Its words fade, or it crumbles into dust.

Any creature that can understand a written language can read the arcane script on a scroll and attempt to activate it.

TREASURE HOARD: CHALLENGE 17+

	CP	SP	EP	GP	PP
Coins	—	—	—	12d6 × 1,000 (42,000)	8d6 × 1,000 (28,000)

d100	Gems or Art Objects	Magic Items
01–02	—	—
03–05	3d6 (10) 1,000 gp gems	Roll 1d8 times on Magic Item Table C.
06–08	1d10 (5) 2,500 gp art objects	Roll 1d8 times on Magic Item Table C.
09–11	1d4 (2) 7,500 gp art objects	Roll 1d8 times on Magic Item Table C.
12–14	1d8 (4) 5,000 gp gems	Roll 1d8 times on Magic Item Table C.
15–22	3d6 (10) 1,000 gp gems	Roll 1d6 times on Magic Item Table D.
23–30	1d10 (5) 2,500 gp art objects	Roll 1d6 times on Magic Item Table D.
31–38	1d4 (2) 7,500 gp art objects	Roll 1d6 times on Magic Item Table D.
39–46	1d8 (4) 5,000 gp gems	Roll 1d6 times on Magic Item Table D.
47–52	3d6 (10) 1,000 gp gems	Roll 1d6 times on Magic Item Table E.
53–58	1d10 (5) 2,500 gp art objects	Roll 1d6 times on Magic Item Table E.
59–63	1d4 (2) 7,500 gp art objects	Roll 1d6 times on Magic Item Table E.
64–68	1d8 (4) 5,000 gp gems	Roll 1d6 times on Magic Item Table E.
69	3d6 (10) 1,000 gp gems	Roll 1d4 times on Magic Item Table G.
70	1d10 (5) 2,500 gp art objects	Roll 1d4 times on Magic Item Table G.
71	1d4 (2) 7,500 gp art objects	Roll 1d4 times on Magic Item Table G.
72	1d8 (4) 5,000 gp gems	Roll 1d4 times on Magic Item Table G.
73–74	3d6 (10) 1,000 gp gems	Roll 1d4 times on Magic Item Table H.
75–76	1d10 (5) 2,500 gp art objects	Roll 1d4 times on Magic Item Table H.
77–78	1d4 (2) 7,500 gp art objects	Roll 1d4 times on Magic Item Table H.
79–80	1d8 (4) 5,000 gp gems	Roll 1d4 times on Magic Item Table H.
81–85	3d6 (10) 1,000 gp gems	Roll 1d4 times on Magic Item Table I.
86–90	1d10 (5) 2,500 gp art objects	Roll 1d4 times on Magic Item Table I.
91–95	1d4 (2) 7,500 gp art objects	Roll 1d4 times on Magic Item Table I.
96–00	1d8 (4) 5,000 gp gems	Roll 1d4 times on Magic Item Table I.

STAFFS

A magic staff is about 5 or 6 feet long. Staffs vary widely in appearance: some are of nearly equal diameter throughout and smooth, others are gnarled and twisted, some are made of wood, and others are composed of polished metal or crystal. Depending on the material, a staff weighs between 2 and 7 pounds.

Unless a staff's description says otherwise, a staff can be used as a quarterstaff.

WANDS

A magic wand is about 15 inches long and crafted of metal, bone, or wood. It is tipped with metal, crystal, stone, or some other material.

WEAPONS

Whether crafted for some fell purpose or forged to serve the highest ideals of chivalry, magic weapons are coveted by many adventurers.

Some magic weapons specify the type of weapon they are in their descriptions, such as a longsword or longbow. If a magic weapon doesn't specify its weapon type, you may choose the type or determine it randomly.

WONDROUS ITEMS

Wondrous items include worn items such as boots, belts, capes, gloves, and various pieces of jewelry and decoration, such as amulets, brooches, and circlets. Bags, carpets, crystal balls, figurines, horns, musical instruments, and other objects also fall into this catch-all category.

WEARING AND WIELDING ITEMS

Using a magic item's properties might mean wearing or wielding it. A magic item meant to be worn must be donned in the intended fashion: boots go on the feet, gloves on the hands, hats and helmets on the head, and rings on the finger. Magic armor must be donned, a shield strapped to the arm, a cloak fastened about the shoulders. A weapon must be held in hand.

In most cases, a magic item that's meant to be worn can fit a creature regardless of size or build. Many magic garments are made to be easily adjustable, or they magically adjust themselves to the wearer.

Rare exceptions exist. If the story suggests a good reason for an item to fit only creatures of a certain size or shape, you can rule that it doesn't adjust. For example, armor made by the drow might fit elves only.

VARIANT: MIXING POTIONS

A character might drink one potion while still under the effects of another, or pour several potions into a single container. The strange ingredients used in creating potions can result in unpredictable interactions.

When a character mixes two potions together, you can roll on the Potion Miscibility table. If more than two are combined, roll again for each subsequent potion, combining the results. Unless the effects are immediately obvious, reveal them only when they become evident.

POTION MISCIBILITY

d100	Result
01	The mixture creates a magical explosion, dealing 6d10 force damage to the mixer and 1d10 force damage to each creature within 5 feet of the mixer.
02–08	The mixture becomes an ingested poison of the DM's choice.
09–15	Both potions lose their effects.
16–25	One potion loses its effect.
26–35	Both potions work, but with their numerical effects and durations halved. A potion has no effect if it can't be halved in this way.
36–90	Both potions work normally.
91–99	The numerical effects and duration of one potion are doubled. If neither potion has anything to double in this way, they work normally.
00	Only one potion works, but its effect is permanent. Choose the simplest effect to make permanent, or the one that seems the most fun. For example, a *potion of healing* might increase the drinker's hit point maximum by 4, or *oil of etherealness* might permanently trap the user in the Ethereal Plane. At your discretion, an appropriate spell, such as *dispel magic* or *remove curse*, might end this lasting effect.

VARIANT: SCROLL MISHAPS

A creature who tries and fails to cast a spell from a *spell scroll* must make a DC 10 Intelligence saving throw. If the saving throw fails, roll on the Scroll Mishap table.

SCROLL MISHAP

d6	Result
1	A surge of magical energy deals the caster 1d6 force damage per level of the spell.
2	The spell affects the caster or an ally (determined randomly) instead of the intended target, or it affects a random target nearby if the caster was the intended target.
3	The spell affects a random location within the spell's range.
4	The spell's effect is contrary to its normal one, but neither harmful nor beneficial. For instance, a *fireball* might produce an area of harmless cold.
5	The caster suffers a minor but bizarre effect related to the spell. Such effects last only as long as the original spell's duration, or 1d10 minutes for spells that take effect instantaneously. For example, a *fireball* might cause smoke to billow from the caster's ears for 1d10 minutes.
6	The spell activates after 1d12 hours. If the caster was the intended target, the spell takes effect normally. If the caster was not the intended target, the spell goes off in the general direction of the intended target, up to the spell's maximum range, if the target has moved away.

Dwarves might make items usable only by dwarf-sized and dwarf-shaped characters.

When a nonhumanoid tries to wear an item, use your discretion as to whether the item functions as intended. A ring placed on a tentacle might work, but a yuan-ti with a snakelike tail instead of legs can't wear boots.

MULTIPLE ITEMS OF THE SAME KIND

Use common sense to determine whether more than one of a given kind of magic item can be worn. A character can't normally wear more than one pair of footwear, one pair of gloves or gauntlets, one pair of bracers, one suit of armor, one item of headwear, and one cloak. You can make exceptions; a character might be able to wear a circlet under a helmet, for example, or be able to layer two cloaks.

PAIRED ITEMS

Items that come in pairs—such as boots, bracers, gauntlets, and gloves—impart their benefits only if both items of the pair are worn. For example, a character wearing a *boot of striding and springing* on one foot and a *boot of elvenkind* on the other foot gains no benefit from either item.

ACTIVATING AN ITEM

Activating some magic items requires a user to do something special, such as holding the item and uttering a command word. The description of each item category or individual item details how an item is activated. Certain items use one or more of the following rules for their activation.

If an item requires an action to activate, that action isn't a function of the Use an Item action, so a feature such as the rogue's Fast Hands can't be used to activate the item.

COMMAND WORD

A command word is a word or phrase that must be spoken for an item to work. A magic item that requires a command word can't be activated in an area where sound is prevented, as in the area of the *silence* spell.

CONSUMABLES

Some items are used up when they are activated. A potion or an elixir must be swallowed, or an oil applied to the body. The writing vanishes from a scroll when it is read. Once used, a consumable item loses its magic.

MAGIC ITEM FORMULAS

A magic item formula explains how to make a particular magic item. Such a formula can be an excellent reward if you allow player characters to craft magic items, as explained in chapter 6, "Between Adventures."

You can award a formula in place of a magic item. Usually written in a book or on a scroll, a formula is one step rarer than the item it allows a character to create. For example, the formula for a common magic item is uncommon. No formulas exist for legendary items.

If the creation of magic items is commonplace in your campaign, a formula can have a rarity that matches the rarity of the item it allows a character to create. Formulas for common and uncommon items might even be for sale, each with a cost double that of its magic item.

SPELLS

Some magic items allow the user to cast a spell from the item. The spell is cast at the lowest possible spell level, doesn't expend any of the user's spell slots, and requires no components, unless the item's description says otherwise. The spell uses its normal casting time, range, and duration, and the user of the item must concentrate if the spell requires concentration. Many items, such as potions, bypass the casting of a spell and confer the spell's effects, with their usual duration. Certain items make exceptions to these rules, changing the casting time, duration, or other parts of a spell.

A magic item, such as certain staffs, may require you to use your own spellcasting ability when you cast a spell from the item. If you have more than one spellcasting ability, you choose which one to use with the item. If you don't have a spellcasting ability—perhaps you're a rogue with the Use Magic Device feature—your spellcasting ability modifier is +0 for the item, and your proficiency bonus does apply.

CHARGES

Some magic items have charges that must be expended to activate their properties. The number of charges an item has remaining is revealed when an *identify* spell is cast on it, as well as when a creature attunes to it. Additionally, when an item regains charges, the creature attuned to it learns how many charges it regained.

MAGIC ITEM RESILIENCE

Most magic items are objects of extraordinary artisanship. Thanks to a combination of careful crafting and magical reinforcement, a magic item is at least as durable as a nonmagical item of its kind. Most magic items, other than potions and scrolls, have resistance to all damage. Artifacts are practically indestructible, requiring extraordinary measures to destroy.

SPECIAL FEATURES

You can add distinctiveness to a magic item by thinking about its backstory. Who made the item? Is anything unusual about its construction? Why was it made, and how was it originally used? What minor magical quirks set it apart from other items of its kind? Answering these questions can help turn a generic magic item, such as a *+1 longsword*, into a more flavorful discovery.

The tables that follow can help you come up with answers. Roll on as many of these tables as you like. Some of the table entries make more sense for certain items than for others. Some magic items are made only by certain kinds of creatures, for instance; a *cloak of elvenkind* is made by elves, rather than dwarves. If you roll something that doesn't make sense, roll again, choose a more appropriate entry, or use the rolled detail as inspiration to make up your own.

VARIANT: WANDS THAT DON'T RECHARGE

A typical wand has expendable charges. If you'd like wands to be a limited resource, you can make some of them incapable of regaining charges. Consider increasing the base number of charges in such a wand, to a maximum of 25 charges. These charges are never regained once they're expended.

Who Created It or Was Intended to Use It?

d20	Creator or Intended User
1	**Aberration.** The item was created by aberrations in ancient times, possibly for the use of favored humanoid thralls. When seen from the corner of the eye, the item seems to be moving.
2–4	**Human.** The item was created during the heyday of a fallen human kingdom, or it is tied to a human of legend. It might hold writing in a forgotten tongue or symbols whose significance is lost to the ages.
5	**Celestial.** The weapon is half the normal weight and inscribed with feathered wings, suns, and other symbols of good. Fiends find the item's presence repulsive.
6	**Dragon.** This item is made from scales and talons shed by a dragon. Perhaps it incorporates precious metals and gems from the dragon's hoard. It grows slightly warm when within 120 feet of a dragon.
7	**Drow.** The item is half the normal weight. It is black and inscribed with spiders and webs in honor of Lolth. It might function poorly, or disintegrate, if exposed to sunlight for 1 minute or more.
8–9	**Dwarf.** The item is durable and has Dwarven runes worked into its design. It might be associated with a clan that would like to see it returned to their ancestral halls.
10	**Elemental Air.** The item is half the normal weight and feels hollow. If it's made of fabric, it is diaphanous.
11	**Elemental Earth.** This item might be crafted from stone. Any cloth or leather elements are studded with finely polished rock.

d20	Creator or Intended User
12	**Elemental Fire.** This item is warm to the touch, and any metal parts are crafted from black iron. Sigils of flames cover its surface. Shades of red and orange are the prominent colors.
13	**Elemental Water.** Lustrous fish scales replace leather or cloth on this item, and metal portions are instead crafted from seashells and worked coral as hard as any metal.
14–15	**Elf.** The item is half the normal weight. It is adorned with symbols of nature: leaves, vines, stars, and the like.
16	**Fey.** The item is exquisitely crafted from the finest materials and glows with a pale radiance in moonlight, shedding dim light in a 5-foot radius. Any metal in the item is silver or mithral, rather than iron or steel.
17	**Fiend.** The item is made of black iron or horn inscribed with runes, and any cloth or leather components are crafted from the hide of fiends. It is warm to the touch and features leering faces or vile runes engraved on its surface. Celestials find the item's presence repulsive.
18	**Giant.** The item is larger than normal and was crafted by giants for use by their smaller allies.
19	**Gnome.** The item is crafted to appear ordinary, and it might look worn. It could also incorporate gears and mechanical components, even if these aren't essential to the item's function.
20	**Undead.** The item incorporates imagery of death, such as bones and skulls, and it might be crafted from parts of corpses. It feels cold to the touch.

What Is a Detail from Its History?

d8	History
1	**Arcane.** This item was created for an ancient order of spellcasters and bears the order's symbol.
2	**Bane.** This item was created by the foes of a particular culture or kind of creature. If the culture or creatures are still around, they might recognize the item and single out the bearer as an enemy.
3	**Heroic.** A great hero once wielded this item. Anyone who's familiar with the item's history expects great deeds from the new owner.
4	**Ornament.** The item was created to honor a special occasion. Inset gemstones, gold or platinum inlays, and gold or silver filigree adorn its surface.
5	**Prophecy.** The item features in a prophecy: its bearer is destined to play a key role in future events. Someone else who wants to play that role might try to steal the item, or someone who wants to prevent the prophecy from being fulfilled might try to kill the item's bearer.

d8	History
6	**Religious.** This item was used in religious ceremonies dedicated to a particular deity. It has holy symbols worked into it. The god's followers might try to persuade its owner to donate it to a temple, steal the item for themselves, or celebrate its use by a cleric or paladin of the same deity.
7	**Sinister.** This item is linked to a deed of great evil, such as a massacre or an assassination. It might have a name or be closely associated with a villain who used it. Anyone familiar with the item's history is likely to treat it and its owner with suspicion.
8	**Symbol of Power.** This item was once used as part of royal regalia or as a badge of high office. Its former owner or that person's descendants might desire it, or someone might mistakenly assume its new owner is the item's legitimate inheritor.

What Minor Property Does It Have?

d20	Minor Property
1	**Beacon.** The bearer can use a bonus action to cause the item to shed bright light in a 10-foot radius and dim light for an additional 10 feet, or to extinguish the light.
2	**Compass.** The wielder can use an action to learn which way is north.
3	**Conscientious.** When the bearer of this item contemplates or undertakes a malevolent act, the item enhances pangs of conscience.
4	**Delver.** While underground, the bearer of this item always knows the item's depth below the surface and the direction to the nearest staircase, ramp, or other path leading upward.
5	**Gleaming.** This item never gets dirty.
6	**Guardian.** The item whispers warnings to its bearer, granting a +2 bonus to initiative if the bearer isn't incapacitated.
7	**Harmonious.** Attuning to this item takes only 1 minute.
8	**Hidden Message.** A message is hidden somewhere on the item. It might be visible only at a certain time of the year, under the light of one phase of the moon, or in a specific location.
9	**Key.** The item is used to unlock a container, chamber, vault, or other entryway.
10	**Language.** The bearer can speak and understand a language of the DM's choice while the item is on the bearer's person.
11	**Sentinel.** Choose a kind of creature that is an enemy of the item's creator. This item glows faintly when such creatures are within 120 feet of it.

d20	Minor Property
12	**Song Craft.** Whenever this item is struck or is used to strike a foe, its bearer hears a fragment of an ancient song.
13	**Strange Material.** The item was created from a material that is bizarre given its purpose. Its durability is unaffected.
14	**Temperate.** The bearer suffers no harm in temperatures as cold as –20 degrees Fahrenheit or as warm as 120 degrees Fahrenheit.
15	**Unbreakable.** The item can't be broken. Special means must be used to destroy it.
16	**War Leader.** The bearer can use an action to cause his or her voice to carry clearly for up to 300 feet until the end of the bearer's next turn.
17	**Waterborne.** This item floats on water and other liquids. Its bearer has advantage on Strength (Athletics) checks to swim.
18	**Wicked.** When the bearer is presented with an opportunity to act in a selfish or malevolent way, the item heightens the bearer's urge to do so.
19	**Illusion.** The item is imbued with illusion magic, allowing its bearer to alter the item's appearance in minor ways. Such alterations don't change how the item is worn, carried, or wielded, and they have no effect on its other magical properties. For example, the wearer could make a red robe appear blue, or make a gold ring look like it's made of ivory. The item reverts to its true appearance when no one is carrying or wearing it.
20	Roll twice, rerolling any additional 20s.

What Quirk Does It Have?

d12	Quirk
1	**Blissful.** While in possession of the item, the bearer feels fortunate and optimistic about what the future holds. Butterflies and other harmless creatures might frolic in the item's presence.
2	**Confident.** The item helps its bearer feel self-assured.
3	**Covetous.** The item's bearer becomes obsessed with material wealth.
4	**Frail.** The item crumbles, frays, chips, or cracks slightly when wielded, worn, or activated. This quirk has no effect on its properties, but if the item has seen much use, it looks decrepit.
5	**Hungry.** This item's magical properties function only if fresh blood from a humanoid has been applied to it within the past 24 hours. It needs only a drop to activate.
6	**Loud.** The item makes a loud noise—such as a clang, a shout, or a resonating gong—when used.

d12	Quirk
7	**Metamorphic.** The item periodically and randomly alters its appearance in slight ways. The bearer has no control over these minor alterations, which have no effect on the item's use.
8	**Muttering.** The item grumbles and mutters. A creature who listens carefully to the item might learn something useful.
9	**Painful.** The bearer experiences a harmless flash of pain when using the item.
10	**Possessive.** The item demands attunement when first wielded or worn, and it doesn't allow its bearer to attune to other items. (Other items already attuned to the bearer remain so until their attunement ends.)
11	**Repulsive.** The bearer feels a sense of distaste when in contact with the item, and continues to sense discomfort while bearing it.
12	**Slothful.** The bearer of this item feels slothful and lethargic. While attuned to the item, the bearer requires 10 hours to finish a long rest.

RANDOM MAGIC ITEMS

When you use a Treasure Hoard table to randomly determine the contents of a treasure hoard and your roll indicates the presence of one or more magic items, you can determine the specific magic items by rolling on the appropriate table(s) here.

MAGIC ITEM TABLE A

d100	Magic Item
01–50	Potion of healing
51–60	Spell scroll (cantrip)
61–70	Potion of climbing
71–90	Spell scroll (1st level)
91–94	Spell scroll (2nd level)
95–98	Potion of greater healing
99	Bag of holding
00	Driftglobe

MAGIC ITEM TABLE B

d100	Magic Item
01–15	Potion of greater healing
16–22	Potion of fire breath
23–29	Potion of resistance
30–34	Ammunition, +1
35–39	Potion of animal friendship
40–44	Potion of hill giant strength
45–49	Potion of growth
50–54	Potion of water breathing
55–59	Spell scroll (2nd level)
60–64	Spell scroll (3rd level)
65–67	Bag of holding
68–70	Keoghtom's ointment
71–73	Oil of slipperiness
74–75	Dust of disappearance
76–77	Dust of dryness
78–79	Dust of sneezing and choking
80–81	Elemental gem
82–83	Philter of love
84	Alchemy jug
85	Cap of water breathing
86	Cloak of the manta ray
87	Driftglobe
88	Goggles of night
89	Helm of comprehending languages
90	Immovable rod
91	Lantern of revealing
92	Mariner's armor
93	Mithral armor
94	Potion of poison
95	Ring of swimming
96	Robe of useful items
97	Rope of climbing
98	Saddle of the cavalier
99	Wand of magic detection
00	Wand of secrets

Magic Item Table C

d100	Magic Item
01–15	Potion of superior healing
16–22	Spell scroll (4th level)
23–27	Ammunition, +2
28–32	Potion of clairvoyance
33–37	Potion of diminution
38–42	Potion of gaseous form
43–47	Potion of frost giant strength
48–52	Potion of stone giant strength
53–57	Potion of heroism
58–62	Potion of invulnerability
63–67	Potion of mind reading
68–72	Spell scroll (5th level)
73–75	Elixir of health
76–78	Oil of etherealness
79–81	Potion of fire giant strength
82–84	Quaal's feather token
85–87	Scroll of protection
88–89	Bag of beans
90–91	Bead of force
92	Chime of opening
93	Decanter of endless water
94	Eyes of minute seeing
95	Folding boat
96	Heward's handy haversack
97	Horseshoes of speed
98	Necklace of fireballs
99	Periapt of health
00	Sending stones

Magic Item Table D

d100	Magic Item
01–20	Potion of supreme healing
21–30	Potion of invisibility
31–40	Potion of speed
41–50	Spell scroll (6th level)
51–57	Spell scroll (7th level)
58–62	Ammunition, +3
63–67	Oil of sharpness
68–72	Potion of flying
73–77	Potion of cloud giant strength
78–82	Potion of longevity
83–87	Potion of vitality
88–92	Spell scroll (8th level)
93–95	Horseshoes of a zephyr
96–98	Nolzur's marvelous pigments
99	Bag of devouring
00	Portable hole

Magic Item Table E

d100	Magic Item
01–30	Spell scroll (8th level)
31–55	Potion of storm giant strength
56–70	Potion of supreme healing
71–85	Spell scroll (9th level)
86–93	Universal solvent
94–98	Arrow of slaying
99–00	Sovereign glue

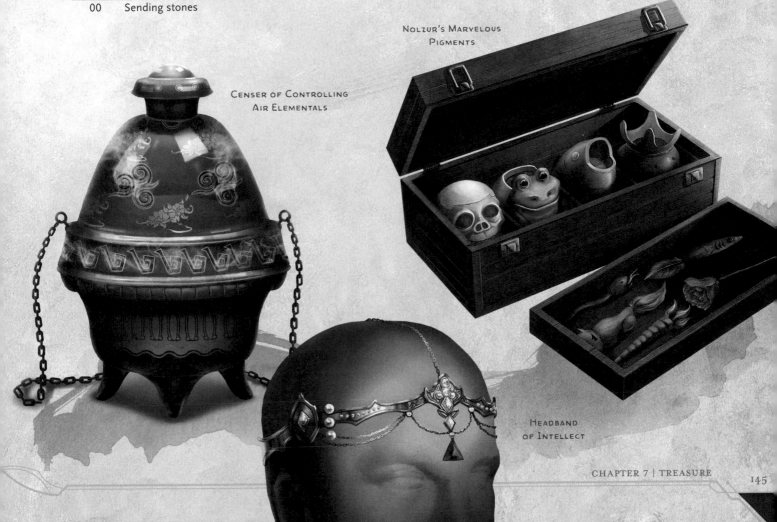

NOLZUR'S MARVELOUS
PIGMENTS

CENSER OF CONTROLLING
AIR ELEMENTALS

HEADBAND
OF INTELLECT

Magic Item Table F

d100	Magic Item
01–15	Weapon, +1
16–18	Shield, +1
19–21	Sentinel shield
22–23	Amulet of proof against detection and location
24–25	Boots of elvenkind
26–27	Boots of striding and springing
28–29	Bracers of archery
30–31	Brooch of shielding
32–33	Broom of flying
34–35	Cloak of elvenkind
36–37	Cloak of protection
38–39	Gauntlets of ogre power
40–41	Hat of disguise
42–43	Javelin of lightning
44–45	Pearl of power
46–47	Rod of the pact keeper, +1
48–49	Slippers of spider climbing
50–51	Staff of the adder
52–53	Staff of the python
54–55	Sword of vengeance
56–57	Trident of fish command
58–59	Wand of magic missiles
60–61	Wand of the war mage, +1
62–63	Wand of web
64–65	Weapon of warning
66	Adamantine armor (chain mail)
67	Adamantine armor (chain shirt)
68	Adamantine armor (scale mail)
69	Bag of tricks (gray)
70	Bag of tricks (rust)
71	Bag of tricks (tan)
72	Boots of the winterlands
73	Circlet of blasting
74	Deck of illusions
75	Eversmoking bottle
76	Eyes of charming
77	Eyes of the eagle
78	Figurine of wondrous power (silver raven)
79	Gem of brightness
80	Gloves of missile snaring
81	Gloves of swimming and climbing
82	Gloves of thievery
83	Headband of intellect
84	Helm of telepathy
85	Instrument of the bards (Doss lute)
86	Instrument of the bards (Fochlucan bandore)
87	Instrument of the bards (Mac-Fuimidh cittern)
88	Medallion of thoughts
89	Necklace of adaptation
90	Periapt of wound closure
91	Pipes of haunting
92	Pipes of the sewers
93	Ring of jumping
94	Ring of mind shielding
95	Ring of warmth
96	Ring of water walking
97	Quiver of Ehlonna
98	Stone of good luck
99	Wind fan
00	Winged boots

Fochlucan Bandore

Elven Chain

Bracers of Archery

Boots of Speed

Arrow of Slaying

MAGIC ITEM TABLE G

d100	Magic Item		d100	Magic Item
01–11	Weapon, +2		54	Ioun stone (sustenance)
12–14	Figurine of wondrous power (roll d8)		55	Iron bands of Bilarro
	1 Bronze griffon		56	Armor, +1 leather
	2 Ebony fly		57	Armor of resistance (leather)
	3 Golden lions		58	Mace of disruption
	4 Ivory goats		59	Mace of smiting
	5 Marble elephant		60	Mace of terror
	6–7 Onyx dog		61	Mantle of spell resistance
	8 Serpentine owl		62	Necklace of prayer beads
15	Adamantine armor (breastplate)		63	Periapt of proof against poison
16	Adamantine armor (splint)		64	Ring of animal influence
17	Amulet of health		65	Ring of evasion
18	Armor of vulnerability		66	Ring of feather falling
19	Arrow-catching shield		67	Ring of free action
20	Belt of dwarvenkind		68	Ring of protection
21	Belt of hill giant strength		69	Ring of resistance
22	Berserker axe		70	Ring of spell storing
23	Boots of levitation		71	Ring of the ram
24	Boots of speed		72	Ring of X-ray vision
25	Bowl of commanding water elementals		73	Robe of eyes
26	Bracers of defense		74	Rod of rulership
27	Brazier of commanding fire elementals		75	Rod of the pact keeper, +2
28	Cape of the mountebank		76	Rope of entanglement
29	Censer of controlling air elementals		77	Armor, +1 scale mail
30	Armor, +1 chain mail		78	Armor of resistance (scale mail)
31	Armor of resistance (chain mail)		79	Shield, +2
32	Armor, +1 chain shirt		80	Shield of missile attraction
33	Armor of resistance (chain shirt)		81	Staff of charming
34	Cloak of displacement		82	Staff of healing
35	Cloak of the bat		83	Staff of swarming insects
36	Cube of force		84	Staff of the woodlands
37	Daern's instant fortress		85	Staff of withering
38	Dagger of venom		86	Stone of controlling earth elementals
39	Dimensional shackles		87	Sun blade
40	Dragon slayer		88	Sword of life stealing
41	Elven chain		89	Sword of wounding
42	Flame tongue		90	Tentacle rod
43	Gem of seeing		91	Vicious weapon
44	Giant slayer		92	Wand of binding
45	Glamoured studded leather		93	Wand of enemy detection
46	Helm of teleportation		94	Wand of fear
47	Horn of blasting		95	Wand of fireballs
48	Horn of Valhalla (silver or brass)		96	Wand of lightning bolts
49	Instrument of the bards (Canaith mandolin)		97	Wand of paralysis
50	Instrument of the bards (Cli lyre)		98	Wand of the war mage, +2
51	Ioun stone (awareness)		99	Wand of wonder
52	Ioun stone (protection)		00	Wings of flying
53	Ioun stone (reserve)			

BROOM OF FLYING

Magic Item Table H

d100	Magic Item
01–10	Weapon, +3
11–12	Amulet of the planes
13–14	Carpet of flying
15–16	Crystal ball (very rare version)
17–18	Ring of regeneration
19–20	Ring of shooting stars
21–22	Ring of telekinesis
23–24	Robe of scintillating colors
25–26	Robe of stars
27–28	Rod of absorption
29–30	Rod of alertness
31–32	Rod of security
33–34	Rod of the pact keeper, +3
35–36	Scimitar of speed
37–38	Shield, +3
39–40	Staff of fire
41–42	Staff of frost
43–44	Staff of power
45–46	Staff of striking
47–48	Staff of thunder and lightning
49–50	Sword of sharpness
51–52	Wand of polymorph
53–54	Wand of the war mage, +3
55	Adamantine armor (half plate)
56	Adamantine armor (plate)
57	Animated shield
58	Belt of fire giant strength
59	Belt of frost (or stone) giant strength
60	Armor, +1 breastplate
61	Armor of resistance (breastplate)
62	Candle of invocation
63	Armor, +2 chain mail
64	Armor, +2 chain shirt
65	Cloak of arachnida

d100	Magic Item
66	Dancing sword
67	Demon armor
68	Dragon scale mail
69	Dwarven plate
70	Dwarven thrower
71	Efreeti bottle
72	Figurine of wondrous power (obsidian steed)
73	Frost brand
74	Helm of brilliance
75	Horn of Valhalla (bronze)
76	Instrument of the bards (Anstruth harp)
77	Ioun stone (absorption)
78	Ioun stone (agility)
79	Ioun stone (fortitude)
80	Ioun stone (insight)
81	Ioun stone (intellect)
82	Ioun stone (leadership)
83	Ioun stone (strength)
84	Armor, +2 leather
85	Manual of bodily health
86	Manual of gainful exercise
87	Manual of golems
88	Manual of quickness of action
89	Mirror of life trapping
90	Nine lives stealer
91	Oathbow
92	Armor, +2 scale mail
93	Spellguard shield
94	Armor, +1 splint
95	Armor of resistance (splint)
96	Armor, +1 studded leather
97	Armor of resistance (studded leather)
98	Tome of clear thought
99	Tome of leadership and influence
00	Tome of understanding

Manual of
Iron Golems

Dragon Scale Mail

Magic Item Table I

d100	Magic Item		d100	Magic Item
01–05	Defender		77	Apparatus of Kwalish
06–10	Hammer of thunderbolts		78	Armor of invulnerability
11–15	Luck blade		79	Belt of storm giant strength
16–20	Sword of answering		80	Cubic gate
21–23	Holy avenger		81	Deck of many things
24–26	Ring of djinni summoning		82	Efreeti chain
27–29	Ring of invisibility		83	Armor of resistance (half plate)
30–32	Ring of spell turning		84	Horn of Valhalla (iron)
33–35	Rod of lordly might		85	Instrument of the bards (Ollamh harp)
36–38	Staff of the magi		86	Ioun stone (greater absorption)
39–41	Vorpal sword		87	Ioun stone (mastery)
42–43	Belt of cloud giant strength		88	Ioun stone (regeneration)
44–45	Armor, +2 breastplate		89	Plate armor of etherealness
46–47	Armor, +3 chain mail		90	Plate armor of resistance
48–49	Armor, +3 chain shirt		91	Ring of air elemental command
50–51	Cloak of invisibility		92	Ring of earth elemental command
52–53	Crystal ball (legendary version)		93	Ring of fire elemental command
54–55	Armor, +1 half plate		94	Ring of three wishes
56–57	Iron flask		95	Ring of water elemental command
58–59	Armor, +3 leather		96	Sphere of annihilation
60–61	Armor, +1 plate		97	Talisman of pure good
62–63	Robe of the archmagi		98	Talisman of the sphere
64–65	Rod of resurrection		99	Talisman of ultimate evil
66–67	Armor, +1 scale mail		00	Tome of the stilled tongue
68–69	Scarab of protection			
70–71	Armor, +2 splint			
72–73	Armor, +2 studded leather			
74–75	Well of many worlds			
76	Magic armor (roll d12)			

1–2	Armor, +2 half plate
3–4	Armor, +2 plate
5–6	Armor, +3 studded leather
7–8	Armor, +3 breastplate
9–10	Armor, +3 splint
11	Armor, +3 half plate
12	Armor, +3 plate

PLATE ARMOR OF RESISTANCE

CANDLE OF INVOCATION

BELT OF STORM GIANT STRENGTH

ALCHEMY JUG

AMULET OF PROOF AGAINST
DETECTION AND LOCATION

MAGIC ITEMS A–Z

Magic items are presented in alphabetical order. A magic item's description gives the item's name, its category, its rarity, and its magical properties.

ADAMANTINE ARMOR

Armor (medium or heavy, but not hide), uncommon

This suit of armor is reinforced with adamantine, one of the hardest substances in existence. While you're wearing it, any critical hit against you becomes a normal hit.

ALCHEMY JUG

Wondrous item, uncommon

This ceramic jug appears to be able to hold a gallon of liquid and weighs 12 pounds whether full or empty. Sloshing sounds can be heard from within the jug when it is shaken, even if the jug is empty.

You can use an action and name one liquid from the table below to cause the jug to produce the chosen liquid. Afterward, you can uncork the jug as an action and pour that liquid out, up to 2 gallons per minute. The maximum amount of liquid the jug can produce depends on the liquid you named.

Once the jug starts producing a liquid, it can't produce a different one, or more of one that has reached its maximum, until the next dawn.

Liquid	Max Amount	Liquid	Max Amount
Acid	8 ounces	Oil	1 quart
Basic poison	1/2 ounce	Vinegar	2 gallons
Beer	4 gallons	Water, fresh	8 gallons
Honey	1 gallon	Water, salt	12 gallons
Mayonnaise	2 gallons	Wine	1 gallon

AMMUNITION, +1, +2, OR +3

Weapon (any ammunition), uncommon (+1), rare (+2), or very rare (+3)

You have a bonus to attack and damage rolls made with this piece of magic ammunition. The bonus is determined by the rarity of the ammunition. Once it hits a target, the ammunition is no longer magical.

AMULET OF HEALTH

Wondrous item, rare (requires attunement)

Your Constitution score is 19 while you wear this amulet. It has no effect on you if your Constitution is already 19 or higher.

AMULET OF PROOF AGAINST DETECTION AND LOCATION

Wondrous item, uncommon (requires attunement)

While wearing this amulet, you are hidden from divination magic. You can't be targeted by such magic or perceived through magical scrying sensors.

AMULET OF THE PLANES

Wondrous item, very rare (requires attunement)

While wearing this amulet, you can use an action to name a location that you are familiar with on another plane of existence. Then make a DC 15 Intelligence check. On a successful check, you cast the *plane shift* spell. On a failure, you and each creature and object within 15 feet of you travel to a random destination. Roll a d100. On a 1–60, you travel to a random location on the plane you named. On a 61–100, you travel to a randomly determined plane of existence.

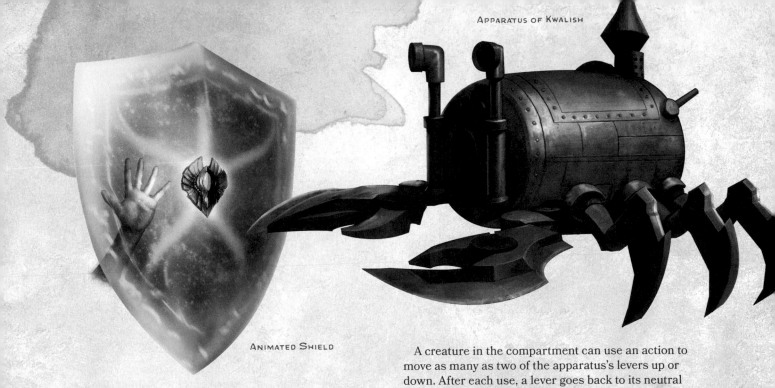

ANIMATED SHIELD

A creature in the compartment can use an action to move as many as two of the apparatus's levers up or down. After each use, a lever goes back to its neutral position. Each lever, from left to right, functions as shown in the Apparatus of Kwalish Levers table.

ANIMATED SHIELD

Armor (shield), very rare (requires attunement)

While holding this shield, you can speak its command word as a bonus action to cause it to animate. The shield leaps into the air and hovers in your space to protect you as if you were wielding it, leaving your hands free. The shield remains animated for 1 minute, until you use a bonus action to end this effect, or until you are incapacitated or die, at which point the shield falls to the ground or into your hand if you have one free.

APPARATUS OF KWALISH

Wondrous item, legendary

This item first appears to be a Large sealed iron barrel weighing 500 pounds. The barrel has a hidden catch, which can be found with a successful DC 20 Intelligence (Investigation) check. Releasing the catch unlocks a hatch at one end of the barrel, allowing two Medium or smaller creatures to crawl inside. Ten levers are set in a row at the far end, each in a neutral position, able to move either up or down. When certain levers are used, the apparatus transforms to resemble a giant lobster.

The apparatus of Kwalish is a Large object with the following statistics:

Armor Class: 20
Hit Points: 200
Speed: 30 ft., swim 30 ft. (or 0 ft. for both if the legs and tail aren't extended)
Damage Immunities: poison, psychic

To be used as a vehicle, the apparatus requires one pilot. While the apparatus's hatch is closed, the compartment is airtight and watertight. The compartment holds enough air for 10 hours of breathing, divided by the number of breathing creatures inside.

The apparatus floats on water. It can also go underwater to a depth of 900 feet. Below that, the vehicle takes 2d6 bludgeoning damage per minute from pressure.

APPARATUS OF KWALISH LEVERS

Lever	Up	Down
1	Legs and tail extend, allowing the apparatus to walk and swim.	Legs and tail retract, reducing the apparatus's speed to 0 and making it unable to benefit from bonuses to speed.
2	Forward window shutter opens.	Forward window shutter closes.
3	Side window shutters open (two per side).	Side window shutters close (two per side).
4	Two claws extend from the front sides of the apparatus.	The claws retract.
5	Each extended claw makes the following melee weapon attack: +8 to hit, reach 5 ft., one target. *Hit:* 7 (2d6) bludgeoning damage.	Each extended claw makes the following melee weapon attack: +8 to hit, reach 5 ft., one target. *Hit:* The target is grappled (escape DC 15).
6	The apparatus walks or swims forward.	The apparatus walks or swims backward.
7	The apparatus turns 90 degrees left.	The apparatus turns 90 degrees right.
8	Eyelike fixtures emit bright light in a 30-foot radius and dim light for an additional 30 feet.	The light turns off.
9	The apparatus sinks as much as 20 feet in liquid.	The apparatus rises up to 20 feet in liquid.
10	The rear hatch unseals and opens.	The rear hatch closes and seals.

ANIMATED SHIELD

ARMOR OF
COLD RESISTANCE

ARMOR OF
INVULNERABILITY

ARMOR, +1, +2, OR +3

Armor (light, medium, or heavy), rare (+1), very rare (+2), or legendary (+3)

You have a bonus to AC while wearing this armor. The bonus is determined by its rarity.

ARMOR OF INVULNERABILITY

Armor (plate), legendary (requires attunement)

You have resistance to nonmagical damage while you wear this armor. Additionally, you can use an action to make yourself immune to nonmagical damage for 10 minutes or until you are no longer wearing the armor. Once this special action is used, it can't be used again until the next dawn.

ARMOR OF RESISTANCE

Armor (light, medium, or heavy), rare (requires attunement)

You have resistance to one type of damage while you wear this armor. The DM chooses the type or determines it randomly from the options below.

d10	Damage Type	d10	Damage Type
1	Acid	6	Necrotic
2	Cold	7	Poison
3	Fire	8	Psychic
4	Force	9	Radiant
5	Lightning	10	Thunder

ARMOR OF VULNERABILITY

Armor (plate), rare (requires attunement)

While wearing this armor, you have resistance to one of the following damage types: bludgeoning, piercing, or slashing. The DM chooses the type or determines it randomly.

Curse. This armor is cursed, a fact that is revealed only when an *identify* spell is cast on the armor or you attune to it. Attuning to the armor curses you until you are targeted by the *remove curse* spell or similar magic; removing the armor fails to end the curse. While cursed, you have vulnerability to two of the three damage types associated with the armor (not the one to which it grants resistance).

ARROW-CATCHING SHIELD

Armor (shield), rare (requires attunement)

You gain a +2 bonus to AC against ranged attacks while you wield this shield. This bonus is in addition to the shield's normal bonus to AC. In addition, whenever an attacker makes a ranged attack against a target within 5 feet of you, you can use your reaction to become the target of the attack instead.

ARROW OF SLAYING

Weapon (arrow), very rare

An *arrow of slaying* is a magic weapon meant to slay a particular kind of creature. Some are more focused than others; for example, there are both *arrows of dragon slaying* and *arrows of blue dragon slaying*. If a creature belonging to the type, race, or group associated with an *arrow of slaying* takes damage from the arrow, the creature must make a DC 17 Constitution saving throw, taking an extra 6d10 piercing damage on a failed save, or half as much extra damage on a successful one.

Once an *arrow of slaying* deals its extra damage to a creature, it becomes a nonmagical arrow.

Other types of magic ammunition of this kind exist, such as *bolts of slaying* meant for a crossbow, though arrows are most common.

BAG OF BEANS

Wondrous item, rare

Inside this heavy cloth bag are 3d4 dry beans. The bag weighs 1/2 pound plus 1/4 pound for each bean it contains.

If you dump the bag's contents out on the ground, they explode in a 10-foot radius, extending from the beans. Each creature in the area, including you, must make a DC 15 Dexterity saving throw, taking 5d4 fire damage on a failed save, or half as much damage on a successful one. The fire ignites flammable objects in the area that aren't being worn or carried.

If you remove a bean from the bag, plant it in dirt or sand, and then water it, the bean produces an effect 1 minute later from the ground where it was planted. The DM can choose an effect from the following table, determine it randomly, or create an effect.

BAG OF
DEVOURING

d100	Effect
01	5d4 toadstools sprout. If a creature eats a toadstool, roll any die. On an odd roll, the eater must succeed on a DC 15 Constitution saving throw or take 5d6 poison damage and become poisoned for 1 hour. On an even roll, the eater gains 5d6 temporary hit points for 1 hour.
02–10	A geyser erupts and spouts water, beer, berry juice, tea, vinegar, wine, or oil (DM's choice) 30 feet into the air for 1d12 rounds.
11–20	A **treant** sprouts (see the *Monster Manual* for statistics). There's a 50 percent chance that the treant is chaotic evil and attacks.
21–30	An animate, immobile stone statue in your likeness rises. It makes verbal threats against you. If you leave it and others come near, it describes you as the most heinous of villains and directs the newcomers to find and attack you. If you are on the same plane of existence as the statue, it knows where you are. The statue becomes inanimate after 24 hours.
31–40	A campfire with blue flames springs forth and burns for 24 hours (or until it is extinguished).
41–50	1d6 + 6 **shriekers** sprout (see the *Monster Manual* for statistics).
51–60	1d4 + 8 bright pink toads crawl forth. Whenever a toad is touched, it transforms into a Large or smaller monster of the DM's choice. The monster remains for 1 minute, then disappears in a puff of bright pink smoke.
61–70	A hungry **bulette** (see the *Monster Manual* for statistics) burrows up and attacks.
71–80	A fruit tree grows. It has 1d10 + 20 fruit, 1d8 of which act as randomly determined magic potions, while one acts as an ingested poison of the DM's choice. The tree vanishes after 1 hour. Picked fruit remains, retaining any magic for 30 days.
81–90	A nest of 1d4 + 3 eggs springs up. Any creature that eats an egg must make a DC 20 Constitution saving throw. On a successful save, a creature permanently increases its lowest ability score by 1, randomly choosing among equally low scores. On a failed save, the creature takes 10d6 force damage from an internal magical explosion.
91–99	A pyramid with a 60-foot-square base bursts upward. Inside is a sarcophagus containing a **mummy lord** (see the *Monster Manual* for statistics). The pyramid is treated as the mummy lord's lair, and its sarcophagus contains treasure of the DM's choice.
00	A giant beanstalk sprouts, growing to a height of the DM's choice. The top leads where the DM chooses, such as to a great view, a cloud giant's castle, or a different plane of existence.

BAG OF DEVOURING

Wondrous item, very rare

This bag superficially resembles a *bag of holding* but is a feeding orifice for a gigantic extradimensional creature. Turning the bag inside out closes the orifice.

The extradimensional creature attached to the bag can sense whatever is placed inside the bag. Animal or vegetable matter placed wholly in the bag is devoured and lost forever. When part of a living creature is placed in the bag, as happens when someone reaches inside it, there is a 50 percent chance that the creature is pulled inside the bag. A creature inside the bag can use its action to try to escape with a successful DC 15 Strength check. Another creature can use its action to reach into the bag to pull a creature out, doing so with a successful DC 20 Strength check (provided it isn't pulled inside the bag first). Any creature that starts its turn inside the bag is devoured, its body destroyed.

Inanimate objects can be stored in the bag, which can hold a cubic foot of such material. However, once each day, the bag swallows any objects inside it and spits them out into another plane of existence. The DM determines the time and plane.

If the bag is pierced or torn, it is destroyed, and anything contained within it is transported to a random location on the Astral Plane.

BAG OF HOLDING

Wondrous item, uncommon

This bag has an interior space considerably larger than its outside dimensions, roughly 2 feet in diameter at the mouth and 4 feet deep. The bag can hold up to 500 pounds, not exceeding a volume of 64 cubic feet. The bag weighs 15 pounds, regardless of its contents. Retrieving an item from the bag requires an action.

If the bag is overloaded, pierced, or torn, it ruptures and is destroyed, and its contents are scattered in the

Berserker Axe

Bag of Tricks

Belt of Stone Giant Strength

Belt of Dwarvenkind

Astral Plane. If the bag is turned inside out, its contents spill forth, unharmed, but the bag must be put right before it can be used again. Breathing creatures inside the bag can survive up to a number of minutes equal to 10 divided by the number of creatures (minimum 1 minute), after which time they begin to suffocate.

Placing a *bag of holding* inside an extradimensional space created by a *Heward's handy haversack*, *portable hole*, or similar item instantly destroys both items and opens a gate to the Astral Plane. The gate originates where the one item was placed inside the other. Any creature within 10 feet of the gate is sucked through it to a random location on the Astral Plane. The gate then closes. The gate is one-way only and can't be reopened.

Bag of Tricks
Wondrous item, uncommon

This ordinary bag, made from gray, rust, or tan cloth, appears empty. Reaching inside the bag, however, reveals the presence of a small, fuzzy object. The bag weighs 1/2 pound.

You can use an action to pull the fuzzy object from the bag and throw it up to 20 feet. When the object lands, it transforms into a creature you determine by rolling a d8 and consulting the table that corresponds to the bag's color. See the *Monster Manual* for the creature's statistics.

The creature is friendly to you and your companions, and it acts on your turn. You can use a bonus action to command how the creature moves and what action it takes on its next turn, or to give it general orders, such as to attack your enemies. In the absence of such orders, the creature acts in a fashion appropriate to its nature.

Once three fuzzy objects have been pulled from the bag, the bag can't be used again until the next dawn.

Gray Bag of Tricks

d8	Creature		d8	Creature
1	Weasel		5	Panther
2	Giant rat		6	Giant badger
3	Badger		7	Dire wolf
4	Boar		8	Giant elk

Rust Bag of Tricks

d8	Creature		d8	Creature
1	Rat		5	Giant goat
2	Owl		6	Giant boar
3	Mastiff		7	Lion
4	Goat		8	Brown bear

Tan Bag of Tricks

d8	Creature		d8	Creature
1	Jackal		5	Black bear
2	Ape		6	Giant weasel
3	Baboon		7	Giant hyena
4	Axe beak		8	Tiger

Bead of Force
Wondrous item, rare

This small black sphere measures 3/4 of an inch in diameter and weighs an ounce. Typically, 1d4 + 4 *beads of force* are found together.

You can use an action to throw the bead up to 60 feet. The bead explodes on impact and is destroyed. Each creature within a 10-foot radius of where the bead landed must succeed on a DC 15 Dexterity saving throw or take 5d4 force damage. A sphere of transparent force then encloses the area for 1 minute. Any creature that failed the save and is completely within the area is trapped inside this sphere. Creatures that succeeded on the save, or are partially within the area, are pushed

BOOTS OF ELVENKIND

away from the center of the sphere until they are no longer inside it. Only breathable air can pass through the sphere's wall. No attack or other effect can.

An enclosed creature can use its action to push against the sphere's wall, moving the sphere up to half the creature's walking speed. The sphere can be picked up, and its magic causes it to weigh only 1 pound, regardless of the weight of creatures inside.

BELT OF DWARVENKIND
Wondrous item, rare (requires attunement)

While wearing this belt, you gain the following benefits:

- Your Constitution score increases by 2, to a maximum of 20.
- You have advantage on Charisma (Persuasion) checks made to interact with dwarves.

In addition, while attuned to the belt, you have a 50 percent chance each day at dawn of growing a full beard if you're capable of growing one, or a visibly thicker beard if you already have one.

If you aren't a dwarf, you gain the following additional benefits while wearing the belt:

- You have advantage on saving throws against poison, and you have resistance against poison damage.
- You have darkvision out to a range of 60 feet.
- You can speak, read, and write Dwarvish.

BELT OF GIANT STRENGTH
Wondrous item, rarity varies (requires attunement)

While wearing this belt, your Strength score changes to a score granted by the belt. If your Strength is already equal to or greater than the belt's score, the item has no effect on you.

Six varieties of this belt exist, corresponding with and having rarity according to the six kinds of true giants.

The *belt of stone giant strength* and the *belt of frost giant strength* look different, but they have the same effect.

Type	Strength	Rarity
Hill giant	21	Rare
Stone/frost giant	23	Very rare
Fire giant	25	Very rare
Cloud giant	27	Legendary
Storm giant	29	Legendary

BERSERKER AXE
Weapon (any axe), rare (requires attunement)

You gain a +1 bonus to attack and damage rolls made with this magic weapon. In addition, while you are attuned to this weapon, your hit point maximum increases by 1 for each level you have attained.

Curse. This axe is cursed, and becoming attuned to it extends the curse to you. As long as you remain cursed, you are unwilling to part with the axe, keeping it within reach at all times. You also have disadvantage on attack rolls with weapons other than this one, unless no foe is within 60 feet of you that you can see or hear.

Whenever a hostile creature damages you while the axe is in your possession, you must succeed on a DC 15 Wisdom saving throw or go berserk. While berserk, you must use your action each round to attack the creature nearest to you with the axe. If you can make extra attacks as part of the Attack action, you use those extra attacks, moving to attack the next nearest creature after you fell your current target. If you have multiple possible targets, you attack one at random. You are berserk until you start your turn with no creatures within 60 feet of you that you can see or hear.

BOOTS OF ELVENKIND
Wondrous item, uncommon

While you wear these boots, your steps make no sound, regardless of the surface you are moving across. You also have advantage on Dexterity (Stealth) checks that rely on moving silently.

BOOTS OF LEVITATION
Wondrous item, rare (requires attunement)

While you wear these boots, you can use an action to cast the *levitate* spell on yourself at will.

BOOTS OF SPEED
Wondrous item, rare (requires attunement)

While you wear these boots, you can use a bonus action and click the boots' heels together. If you do, the boots double your walking speed, and any creature that makes an opportunity attack against you has disadvantage on the attack roll. If you click your heels together again, you end the effect.

When the boots' property has been used for a total of 10 minutes, the magic ceases to function until you finish a long rest.

BRAZIER OF COMMANDING
FIRE ELEMENTALS

BOOTS OF THE
WINTERLANDS

BOWL OF COMMANDING
WATER ELEMENTALS

BOOTS OF STRIDING AND SPRINGING

Wondrous item, uncommon (requires attunement)

While you wear these boots, your walking speed becomes 30 feet, unless your walking speed is higher, and your speed isn't reduced if you are encumbered or wearing heavy armor. In addition, you can jump three times the normal distance, though you can't jump farther than your remaining movement would allow.

BOOTS OF THE WINTERLANDS

Wondrous item, uncommon (requires attunement)

These furred boots are snug and feel quite warm. While you wear them, you gain the following benefits:

- You have resistance to cold damage.
- You ignore difficult terrain created by ice or snow.
- You can tolerate temperatures as low as −50 degrees Fahrenheit without any additional protection. If you wear heavy clothes, you can tolerate temperatures as low as −100 degrees Fahrenheit.

BOWL OF COMMANDING WATER ELEMENTALS

Wondrous item, rare

While this bowl is filled with water, you can use an action to speak the bowl's command word and summon a water elemental, as if you had cast the *conjure elemental* spell. The bowl can't be used this way again until the next dawn.

The bowl is about 1 foot in diameter and half as deep. It weighs 3 pounds and holds about 3 gallons.

BRACERS OF ARCHERY

Wondrous item, uncommon (requires attunement)

While wearing these bracers, you have proficiency with the longbow and shortbow, and you gain a +2 bonus to damage rolls on ranged attacks made with such weapons.

BRACERS OF DEFENSE

Wondrous item, rare (requires attunement)

While wearing these bracers, you gain a +2 bonus to AC if you are wearing no armor and using no shield.

BRAZIER OF COMMANDING FIRE ELEMENTALS

Wondrous item, rare

While a fire burns in this brass brazier, you can use an action to speak the brazier's command word and summon a fire elemental, as if you had cast the *conjure elemental* spell. The brazier can't be used this way again until the next dawn.

The brazier weighs 5 pounds.

BROOCH OF SHIELDING

Wondrous item, uncommon (requires attunement)

While wearing this brooch, you have resistance to force damage, and you have immunity to damage from the *magic missile* spell.

BROOM OF FLYING

Wondrous item, uncommon

This wooden broom, which weighs 3 pounds, functions like a mundane broom until you stand astride it and speak its command word. It then hovers beneath you and can be ridden in the air. It has a flying speed of 50 feet. It can carry up to 400 pounds, but its flying speed becomes 30 feet while carrying over 200 pounds. The broom stops hovering when you land.

You can send the broom to travel alone to a destination within 1 mile of you if you speak the command word, name the location, and are familiar with that place. The broom comes back to you when you speak another command word, provided that the broom is still within 1 mile of you.

BOOTS OF STRIDING
AND SPRINGING

BRACERS OF DEFENSE

CAPE OF THE
MOUNTEBANK

BROOCH
OF SHIELDING

CANDLE OF INVOCATION

Wondrous item, very rare (requires attunement)

This slender taper is dedicated to a deity and shares that deity's alignment. The candle's alignment can be detected with the *detect evil and good* spell. The DM chooses the god and associated alignment or determines the alignment randomly.

d20	Alignment	d20	Alignment
1–2	Chaotic evil	10–11	Neutral
3–4	Chaotic neutral	12–13	Neutral good
5–7	Chaotic good	14–15	Lawful evil
8–9	Neutral evil	16–17	Lawful neutral
		18–20	Lawful good

The candle's magic is activated when the candle is lit, which requires an action. After burning for 4 hours, the candle is destroyed. You can snuff it out early for use at a later time. Deduct the time it burned in increments of 1 minute from the candle's total burn time.

While lit, the candle sheds dim light in a 30-foot radius. Any creature within that light whose alignment matches that of the candle makes attack rolls, saving throws, and ability checks with advantage. In addition, a cleric or druid in the light whose alignment matches the candle's can cast 1st-level spells he or she has prepared without expending spell slots, though the spell's effect is as if cast with a 1st-level slot.

Alternatively, when you light the candle for the first time, you can cast the *gate* spell with it. Doing so destroys the candle.

CAP OF WATER BREATHING

Wondrous item, uncommon

While wearing this cap underwater, you can speak its command word as an action to create a bubble of air around your head. It allows you to breathe normally underwater. This bubble stays with you until you speak the command word again, the cap is removed, or you are no longer underwater.

CAPE OF THE MOUNTEBANK

Wondrous item, rare

This cape smells faintly of brimstone. While wearing it, you can use it to cast the *dimension door* spell as an action. This property of the cape can't be used again until the next dawn.

When you disappear, you leave behind a cloud of smoke, and you appear in a similar cloud of smoke at your destination. The smoke lightly obscures the space you left and the space you appear in, and it dissipates at the end of your next turn. A light or stronger wind disperses the smoke.

CARPET OF FLYING

Wondrous item, very rare

You can speak the carpet's command word as an action to make the carpet hover and fly. It moves according to your spoken directions, provided that you are within 30 feet of it.

Four sizes of *carpet of flying* exist. The DM chooses the size of a given carpet or determines it randomly.

d100	Size	Capacity	Flying Speed
01–20	3 ft. × 5 ft.	200 lb.	80 feet
21–55	4 ft. × 6 ft.	400 lb.	60 feet
56–80	5 ft. × 7 ft.	600 lb.	40 feet
81–100	6 ft. × 9 ft.	800 lb.	30 feet

A carpet can carry up to twice the weight shown on the table, but it flies at half speed if it carries more than its normal capacity.

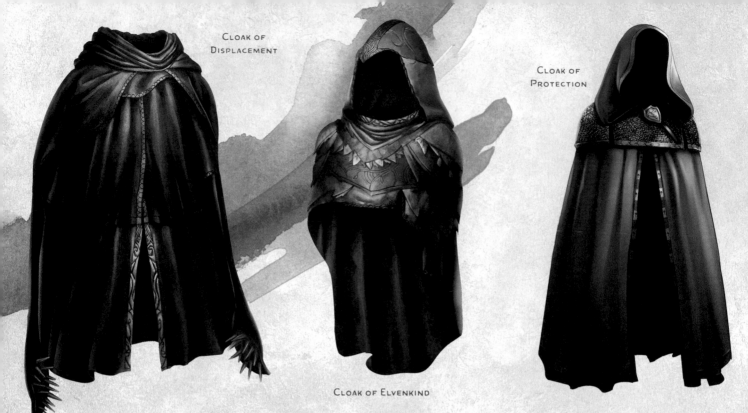

CLOAK OF
DISPLACEMENT

CLOAK OF
PROTECTION

CLOAK OF ELVENKIND

CENSER OF CONTROLLING AIR ELEMENTALS
Wondrous item, rare

While incense is burning in this censer, you can use an action to speak the censer's command word and summon an air elemental, as if you had cast the *conjure elemental* spell. The censer can't be used this way again until the next dawn.

This 6-inch-wide, 1-foot-high vessel resembles a chalice with a decorated lid. It weighs 1 pound.

CHIME OF OPENING
Wondrous item, rare

This hollow metal tube measures about 1 foot long and weighs 1 pound. You can strike it as an action, pointing it at an object within 120 feet of you that can be opened, such as a door, lid, or lock. The chime issues a clear tone, and one lock or latch on the object opens unless the sound can't reach the object. If no locks or latches remain, the object itself opens.

The chime can be used ten times. After the tenth time, it cracks and becomes useless.

CIRCLET OF BLASTING
Wondrous item, uncommon

While wearing this circlet, you can use an action to cast the *scorching ray* spell with it. When you make the spell's attacks, you do so with an attack bonus of +5. The circlet can't be used this way again until the next dawn.

CLOAK OF ARACHNIDA
Wondrous item, very rare (requires attunement)

This fine garment is made of black silk interwoven with faint silvery threads. While wearing it, you gain the following benefits:

- You have resistance to poison damage.
- You have a climbing speed equal to your walking speed.

- You can move up, down, and across vertical surfaces and upside down along ceilings, while leaving your hands free.
- You can't be caught in webs of any sort and can move through webs as if they were difficult terrain.
- You can use an action to cast the *web* spell (save DC 13). The web created by the spell fills twice its normal area. Once used, this property of the cloak can't be used again until the next dawn.

CLOAK OF DISPLACEMENT
Wondrous item, rare (requires attunement)

While you wear this cloak, it projects an illusion that makes you appear to be standing in a place near your actual location, causing any creature to have disadvantage on attack rolls against you. If you take damage, the property ceases to function until the start of your next turn. This property is suppressed while you are incapacitated, restrained, or otherwise unable to move.

CLOAK OF ELVENKIND
Wondrous item, uncommon (requires attunement)

While you wear this cloak with its hood up, Wisdom (Perception) checks made to see you have disadvantage, and you have advantage on Dexterity (Stealth) checks made to hide, as the cloak's color shifts to camouflage you. Pulling the hood up or down requires an action.

CLOAK OF INVISIBILITY
Wondrous item, legendary (requires attunement)

While wearing this cloak, you can pull its hood over your head to cause yourself to become invisible. While you are invisible, anything you are carrying or wearing is invisible with you. You become visible when you cease wearing the hood. Pulling the hood up or down requires an action.

CIRCLET
OF BLASTING

CLOAK OF THE
MANTA RAY

CUBE OF FORCE

CHIME OF
OPENING

Deduct the time you are invisible, in increments of 1 minute, from the cloak's maximum duration of 2 hours. After 2 hours of use, the cloak ceases to function. For every uninterrupted period of 12 hours the cloak goes unused, it regains 1 hour of duration.

CLOAK OF PROTECTION

Wondrous item, uncommon (requires attunement)

You gain a +1 bonus to AC and saving throws while you wear this cloak.

CLOAK OF THE BAT

Wondrous item, rare (requires attunement)

While wearing this cloak, you have advantage on Dexterity (Stealth) checks. In an area of dim light or darkness, you can grip the edges of the cloak with both hands and use it to fly at a speed of 40 feet. If you ever fail to grip the cloak's edges while flying in this way, or if you are no longer in dim light or darkness, you lose this flying speed. .

While wearing the cloak in an area of dim light or darkness, you can use your action to cast *polymorph* on yourself, transforming into a bat. While you are in the form of the bat, you retain your Intelligence, Wisdom, and Charisma scores. The cloak can't be used this way again until the next dawn.

CLOAK OF THE MANTA RAY

Wondrous item, uncommon

While wearing this cloak with its hood up, you can breathe underwater, and you have a swimming speed of 60 feet. Pulling the hood up or down requires an action.

CRYSTAL BALL

Wondrous item, very rare or legendary (requires attunement)

The typical *crystal ball*, a very rare item, is about 6 inches in diameter. While touching it, you can cast the *scrying* spell (save DC 17) with it.

The following *crystal ball* variants are legendary items and have additional properties.

Crystal Ball of Mind Reading. You can use an action to cast the *detect thoughts* spell (save DC 17) while you are scrying with the *crystal ball*, targeting creatures you can see within 30 feet of the spell's sensor. You don't need to concentrate on this *detect thoughts* to maintain it during its duration, but it ends if *scrying* ends.

Crystal Ball of Telepathy. While scrying with the crystal ball, you can communicate telepathically with creatures you can see within 30 feet of the spell's sensor. You can also use an action to cast the *suggestion* spell (save DC 17) through the sensor on one of those creatures. You don't need to concentrate on this *suggestion* to maintain it during its duration, but it ends if *scrying* ends. Once used, the *suggestion* power of the *crystal ball* can't be used again until the next dawn.

Crystal Ball of True Seeing. While scrying with the crystal ball, you have truesight with a radius of 120 feet centered on the spell's sensor.

CUBE OF FORCE

Wondrous item, rare (requires attunement)

This cube is about an inch across. Each face has a distinct marking on it that can be pressed. The cube starts with 36 charges, and it regains 1d20 expended charges daily at dawn.

You can use an action to press one of the cube's faces, expending a number of charges based on the chosen face, as shown in the Cube of Force Faces table. Each face has a different effect. If the cube has insufficient charges remaining, nothing happens. Otherwise, a barrier of invisible force springs into existence, forming a cube 15 feet on a side. The barrier is centered on you, moves with you, and lasts for 1 minute, until you use an action to press the cube's sixth face, or the cube runs out of charges. You can change the barrier's effect by pressing a different face of the cube and expending the requisite number of charges, resetting the duration.

If your movement causes the barrier to come into contact with a solid object that can't pass through the cube, you can't move any closer to that object as long as the barrier remains.

CUBE OF FORCE FACES

Face	Charges	Effect
1	1	Gases, wind, and fog can't pass through the barrier.
2	2	Nonliving matter can't pass through the barrier. Walls, floors, and ceilings can pass through at your discretion.
3	3	Living matter can't pass through the barrier.
4	4	Spell effects can't pass through the barrier.
5	5	Nothing can pass through the barrier. Walls, floors, and ceilings can pass through at your discretion.
6	0	The barrier deactivates.

The cube loses charges when the barrier is targeted by certain spells or comes into contact with certain spell or magic item effects, as shown in the table below.

Spell or Item	Charges Lost
Disintegrate	1d12
Horn of blasting	1d10
Passwall	1d6
Prismatic spray	1d20
Wall of fire	1d4

CUBIC GATE
Wondrous item, legendary

This cube is 3 inches across and radiates palpable magical energy. The six sides of the cube are each keyed to a different plane of existence, one of which is the Material Plane. The other sides are linked to planes determined by the DM.

You can use an action to press one side of the cube to cast the *gate* spell with it, opening a portal to the plane keyed to that side. Alternatively, if you use an action to press one side twice, you can cast the *plane shift* spell (save DC 17) with the cube and transport the targets to the plane keyed to that side.

The cube has 3 charges. Each use of the cube expends 1 charge. The cube regains 1d3 expended charges daily at dawn.

DAERN'S INSTANT FORTRESS
Wondrous item, rare

You can use an action to place this 1-inch metal cube on the ground and speak its command word. The cube rapidly grows into a fortress that remains until you use an action to speak the command word that dismisses it, which works only if the fortress is empty.

The fortress is a square tower, 20 feet on a side and 30 feet high, with arrow slits on all sides and a battlement atop it. Its interior is divided into two floors, with a ladder running along one wall to connect them. The ladder ends at a trapdoor leading to the roof. When activated, the tower has a small door on the side facing you. The door opens only at your command, which you can speak as a bonus action. It is immune to the *knock* spell and similar magic, such as that of a *chime of opening*.

Each creature in the area where the fortress appears must make a DC 15 Dexterity saving throw, taking 10d10 bludgeoning damage on a failed save, or half as much damage on a successful one. In either case, the creature is pushed to an unoccupied space outside but next to the fortress. Objects in the area that aren't being worn or carried take this damage and are pushed automatically.

DAGGER OF VENOM

DECANTER OF ENDLESS WATER

CUBIC GATE

The tower is made of adamantine, and its magic prevents it from being tipped over. The roof, the door, and the walls each have 100 hit points, immunity to damage from nonmagical weapons excluding siege weapons, and resistance to all other damage. Only a *wish* spell can repair the fortress (this use of the spell counts as replicating a spell of 8th level or lower). Each casting of *wish* causes the roof, the door, or one wall to regain 50 hit points.

DAGGER OF VENOM
Weapon (dagger), rare

You gain a +1 bonus to attack and damage rolls made with this magic weapon.

You can use an action to cause thick, black poison to coat the blade. The poison remains for 1 minute or until an attack using this weapon hits a creature. That creature must succeed on a DC 15 Constitution saving throw or take 2d10 poison damage and become poisoned for 1 minute. The dagger can't be used this way again until the next dawn.

DANCING SWORD
Weapon (any sword), very rare (requires attunement)

You can use a bonus action to toss this magic sword into the air and speak the command word. When you do so, the sword begins to hover, flies up to 30 feet, and attacks one creature of your choice within 5 feet of it. The sword uses your attack roll and ability score modifier to damage rolls.

While the sword hovers, you can use a bonus action to cause it to fly up to 30 feet to another spot within 30 feet of you. As part of the same bonus action, you can cause the sword to attack one creature within 5 feet of it.

After the hovering sword attacks for the fourth time, it flies up to 30 feet and tries to return to your hand. If you have no hand free, it falls to the ground at your feet. If the sword has no unobstructed path to you, it moves as close to you as it can and then falls to the ground. It also ceases to hover if you grasp it or move more than 30 feet away from it.

DECANTER OF ENDLESS WATER
Wondrous item, uncommon

This stoppered flask sloshes when shaken, as if it contains water. The decanter weighs 2 pounds.

You can use an action to remove the stopper and speak one of three command words, whereupon an amount of fresh water or salt water (your choice) pours out of the flask. The water stops pouring out at the start of your next turn. Choose from the following options:

- "Stream" produces 1 gallon of water.
- "Fountain" produces 5 gallons of water.
- "Geyser" produces 30 gallons of water that gushes forth in a geyser 30 feet long and 1 foot wide. As a bonus action while holding the decanter, you can aim the geyser at a creature you can see within 30 feet of you. The target must succeed on a DC 13 Strength saving throw or take 1d4 bludgeoning damage and fall prone. Instead of a creature, you can target an object that isn't being worn or carried and that weighs no more than 200 pounds. The object is either knocked over or pushed up to 15 feet away from you.

DECK OF ILLUSIONS
Wondrous item, uncommon

This box contains a set of parchment cards. A full deck has 34 cards. A deck found as treasure is usually missing 1d20 − 1 cards.

The magic of the deck functions only if cards are drawn at random (you can use an altered deck of playing cards to simulate the deck). You can use an action to draw a card at random from the deck and throw it to the ground at a point within 30 feet of you.

An illusion of one or more creatures forms over the thrown card and remains until dispelled. An illusory creature appears real, of the appropriate size, and behaves as if it were a real creature (as presented in the *Monster Manual*), except that it can do no harm. While you are within 120 feet of the illusory creature and can see it, you can use an action to move it magically anywhere within 30 feet of its card. Any physical interaction with the illusory creature reveals it to be an illusion, because objects pass through it. Someone who

DANCING SWORD

DAERN'S INSTANT
FORTRESS

uses an action to visually inspect the creature identifies it as illusory with a successful DC 15 Intelligence (Investigation) check. The creature then appears translucent.

The illusion lasts until its card is moved or the illusion is dispelled. When the illusion ends, the image on its card disappears, and that card can't be used again.

Playing Card	Illusion
Ace of hearts	Red dragon
King of hearts	Knight and four guards
Queen of hearts	Succubus or incubus
Jack of hearts	Druid
Ten of hearts	Cloud giant
Nine of hearts	Ettin
Eight of hearts	Bugbear
Two of hearts	Goblin
Ace of diamonds	Beholder
King of diamonds	Archmage and mage apprentice
Queen of diamonds	Night hag
Jack of diamonds	Assassin
Ten of diamonds	Fire giant
Nine of diamonds	Ogre mage
Eight of diamonds	Gnoll
Two of diamonds	Kobold
Ace of spades	Lich
King of spades	Priest and two acolytes
Queen of spades	Medusa
Jack of spades	Veteran
Ten of spades	Frost giant
Nine of spades	Troll
Eight of spades	Hobgoblin
Two of spades	Goblin
Ace of clubs	Iron golem
King of clubs	Bandit captain and three bandits
Queen of clubs	Erinyes
Jack of clubs	Berserker
Ten of clubs	Hill giant
Nine of clubs	Ogre
Eight of clubs	Orc
Two of clubs	Kobold
Jokers (2)	You (the deck's owner)

DECK OF MANY THINGS
Wondrous item, legendary

Usually found in a box or pouch, this deck contains a number of cards made of ivory or vellum. Most (75 percent) of these decks have only thirteen cards, but the rest have twenty-two.

Before you draw a card, you must declare how many cards you intend to draw and then draw them randomly (you can use an altered deck of playing cards to simulate the deck). Any cards drawn in excess of this number have no effect. Otherwise, as soon as you draw a card from the deck, its magic takes effect. You must draw each card no more than 1 hour after the previous draw. If you fail to draw the chosen number, the remaining

number of cards fly from the deck on their own and take effect all at once.

Once a card is drawn, it fades from existence. Unless the card is the Fool or the Jester, the card reappears in the deck, making it possible to draw the same card twice.

Playing Card	Card
Ace of diamonds	Vizier*
King of diamonds	Sun
Queen of diamonds	Moon
Jack of diamonds	Star
Two of diamonds	Comet*
Ace of hearts	The Fates*
King of hearts	Throne
Queen of hearts	Key
Jack of hearts	Knight
Two of hearts	Gem*
Ace of clubs	Talons*
King of clubs	The Void
Queen of clubs	Flames
Jack of clubs	Skull
Two of clubs	Idiot*
Ace of spades	Donjon*
King of spades	Ruin
Queen of spades	Euryale
Jack of spades	Rogue
Two of spades	Balance*
Joker (with TM)	Fool*
Joker (without TM)	Jester

*Found only in a deck with twenty-two cards

Balance. Your mind suffers a wrenching alteration, causing your alignment to change. Lawful becomes chaotic, good becomes evil, and vice versa. If you are true neutral or unaligned, this card has no effect on you.

Comet. If you single-handedly defeat the next hostile monster or group of monsters you encounter, you gain experience points enough to gain one level. Otherwise, this card has no effect.

Donjon. You disappear and become entombed in a state of suspended animation in an extradimensional sphere. Everything you were wearing and carrying stays behind in the space you occupied when you disappeared. You remain imprisoned until you are found and removed from the sphere. You can't be located by

---

A QUESTION OF ENMITY

Two of the cards in a *deck of many things* can earn a character the enmity of another being. With the Flames card, the enmity is overt. The character should experience the devil's malevolent efforts on multiple occasions. Seeking out the fiend shouldn't be a simple task, and the adventurer should clash with the devil's allies and followers a few times before being able to confront the devil itself.

In the case of the Rogue card, the enmity is secret and should come from someone thought to be a friend or an ally. As Dungeon Master, you should wait for a dramatically appropriate moment to reveal this enmity, leaving the adventurer guessing who is likely to become a betrayer.

SUN

DONJON

JESTER

BALANCE

EURYALE

RUIN

SKULL

KNIGHT

KEY

any divination magic, but a *wish* spell can reveal the location of your prison. You draw no more cards.

Euryale. The card's medusa-like visage curses you. You take a −2 penalty on saving throws while cursed in this way. Only a god or the magic of The Fates card can end this curse.

The Fates. Reality's fabric unravels and spins anew, allowing you to avoid or erase one event as if it never happened. You can use the card's magic as soon as you draw the card or at any other time before you die.

Flames. A powerful devil becomes your enemy. The devil seeks your ruin and plagues your life, savoring your suffering before attempting to slay you. This enmity lasts until either you or the devil dies.

Fool. You lose 10,000 XP, discard this card, and draw from the deck again, counting both draws as one of your declared draws. If losing that much XP would cause you to lose a level, you instead lose an amount that leaves you with just enough XP to keep your level.

Gem. Twenty-five pieces of jewelry worth 2,000 gp each or fifty gems worth 1,000 gp each appear at your feet.

Idiot. Permanently reduce your Intelligence by 1d4 + 1 (to a minimum score of 1). You can draw one additional card beyond your declared draws.

Jester. You gain 10,000 XP, or you can draw two additional cards beyond your declared draws.

Key. A rare or rarer magic weapon with which you are proficient appears in your hands. The DM chooses the weapon.

Knight. You gain the service of a 4th-level fighter who appears in a space you choose within 30 feet of you. The fighter is of the same race as you and serves you loyally until death, believing the fates have drawn him or her to you. You control this character.

Moon. You are granted the ability to cast the *wish* spell 1d3 times.

Rogue. A nonplayer character of the DM's choice becomes hostile toward you. The identity of your new enemy isn't known until the NPC or someone else reveals it. Nothing less than a *wish* spell or divine intervention can end the NPC's hostility toward you.

Ruin. All forms of wealth that you carry or own, other than magic items, are lost to you. Portable property vanishes. Businesses, buildings, and land you own are lost in a way that alters reality the least. Any documentation that proves you should own something lost to this card also disappears.

Skull. You summon an avatar of death—a ghostly humanoid skeleton clad in a tattered black robe and carrying a spectral scythe. It appears in a space of the DM's choice within 10 feet of you and attacks you, warning all others that you must win the battle alone. The avatar fights until you die or it drops to 0 hit points, whereupon it disappears. If anyone tries to help you, the helper summons its own avatar of death. A creature slain by an avatar of death can't be restored to life.

Star. Increase one of your ability scores by 2. The score can exceed 20 but can't exceed 24.

Sun. You gain 50,000 XP, and a wondrous item (which the DM determines randomly) appears in your hands.

AVATAR OF DEATH
Medium undead, neutral evil

Armor Class 20
Hit Points half the hit point maximum of its summoner
Speed 60 ft., fly 60 ft. (hover)

STR	DEX	CON	INT	WIS	CHA
16 (+3)	16 (+3)	16 (+3)	16 (+3)	16 (+3)	16 (+3)

Damage Immunities necrotic, poison
Condition Immunities charmed, frightened, paralyzed, petrified, poisoned, unconscious
Senses darkvision 60 ft., truesight 60 ft., passive Perception 13
Languages all languages known to its summoner
Challenge — (0 XP)

Incorporeal Movement. The avatar can move through other creatures and objects as if they were difficult terrain. It takes 5 (1d10) force damage if it ends its turn inside an object.

Turning Immunity. The avatar is immune to features that turn undead.

ACTIONS

Reaping Scythe. The avatar sweeps its spectral scythe through a creature within 5 feet of it, dealing 7 (1d8 + 3) slashing damage plus 4 (1d8) necrotic damage.

Talons. Every magic item you wear or carry disintegrates. Artifacts in your possession aren't destroyed but do vanish.

Throne. You gain proficiency in the Persuasion skill, and you double your proficiency bonus on checks made with that skill. In addition, you gain rightful ownership of a small keep somewhere in the world. However, the keep is currently in the hands of monsters, which you must clear out before you can claim the keep as yours.

Vizier. At any time you choose within one year of drawing this card, you can ask a question in meditation and mentally receive a truthful answer to that question. Besides information, the answer helps you solve a puzzling problem or other dilemma. In other words, the knowledge comes with wisdom on how to apply it.

The Void. This black card spells disaster. Your soul is drawn from your body and contained in an object in a place of the DM's choice. One or more powerful beings guard the place. While your soul is trapped in this way, your body is incapacitated. A *wish* spell can't restore your soul, but the spell reveals the location of the object that holds it. You draw no more cards.

DEFENDER
Weapon (any sword), legendary (requires attunement)

You gain a +3 bonus to attack and damage rolls made with this magic weapon.

The first time you attack with the sword on each of your turns, you can transfer some or all of the sword's bonus to your Armor Class, instead of using the bonus on any attacks that turn. For example, you could reduce the bonus to your attack and damage rolls to +1 and gain a +2 bonus to AC. The adjusted bonuses remain in effect until the start of your next turn, although you must hold the sword to gain a bonus to AC from it.

DEMON ARMOR

Armor (plate), very rare (requires attunement)

While wearing this armor, you gain a +1 bonus to AC, and you can understand and speak Abyssal. In addition, the armor's clawed gauntlets turn unarmed strikes with your hands into magic weapons that deal slashing damage, with a +1 bonus to attack rolls and damage rolls and a damage die of 1d8.

   Curse. Once you don this cursed armor, you can't doff it unless you are targeted by the *remove curse* spell or similar magic. While wearing the armor, you have disadvantage on attack rolls against demons and on saving throws against their spells and special abilities.

DIMENSIONAL SHACKLES

Wondrous item, rare

You can use an action to place these shackles on an incapacitated creature. The shackles adjust to fit a creature of Small to Large size. In addition to serving as mundane manacles, the shackles prevent a creature bound by them from using any method of extradimensional movement, including teleportation or travel to a different plane of existence. They don't prevent the creature from passing through an interdimensional portal.

   You and any creature you designate when you use the shackles can use an action to remove them. Once every 30 days, the bound creature can make a DC 30 Strength (Athletics) check. On a success, the creature breaks free and destroys the shackles.

DRAGON SCALE MAIL

Armor (scale mail), very rare (requires attunement)

Dragon scale mail is made of the scales of one kind of dragon. Sometimes dragons collect their cast-off scales and gift them to humanoids. Other times, hunters carefully skin and preserve the hide of a dead dragon. In either case, dragon scale mail is highly valued.

   While wearing this armor, you gain a +1 bonus to AC, you have advantage on saving throws against the Frightful Presence and breath weapons of dragons, and you have resistance to one damage type that is determined by the kind of dragon that provided the scales (see the table).

   Additionally, you can focus your senses as an action to magically discern the distance and direction to the closest dragon within 30 miles of you that is of the same type as the armor. This special action can't be used again until the next dawn.

Dragon	Resistance	Dragon	Resistance
Black	Acid	Gold	Fire
Blue	Lightning	Green	Poison
Brass	Fire	Red	Fire
Bronze	Lightning	Silver	Cold
Copper	Acid	White	Cold

DEMON ARMOR

DEFENDER

DIMENSIONAL
SHACKLES

Dwarven Thrower

Dwarven Plate

Dragon Slayer

Efreeti Bottle

DRAGON SLAYER
Weapon (any sword), rare

You gain a +1 bonus to attack and damage rolls made with this magic weapon.

When you hit a dragon with this weapon, the dragon takes an extra 3d6 damage of the weapon's type. For the purpose of this weapon, "dragon" refers to any creature with the dragon type, including dragon turtles and wyverns.

DRIFTGLOBE
Wondrous item, uncommon

This small sphere of thick glass weighs 1 pound. If you are within 60 feet of it, you can speak its command word and cause it to emanate the *light* or *daylight* spell. Once used, the *daylight* effect can't be used again until the next dawn.

You can speak another command word as an action to make the illuminated globe rise into the air and float no more than 5 feet off the ground. The globe hovers in this way until you or another creature grasps it. If you move more than 60 feet from the hovering globe, it follows you until it is within 60 feet of you. It takes the shortest route to do so. If prevented from moving, the globe sinks gently to the ground and becomes inactive, and its light winks out.

DUST OF DISAPPEARANCE
Wondrous item, uncommon

Found in a small packet, this powder resembles very fine sand. There is enough of it for one use. When you use an action to throw the dust into the air, you and each creature and object within 10 feet of you become invisible for 2d4 minutes. The duration is the same for all subjects, and the dust is consumed when its magic takes effect. If a creature affected by the dust attacks or casts a spell, the invisibility ends for that creature.

DUST OF DRYNESS
Wondrous item, uncommon

This small packet contains 1d6 + 4 pinches of dust. You can use an action to sprinkle a pinch of it over water. The dust turns a cube of water 15 feet on a side into one marble-sized pellet, which floats or rests near where the dust was sprinkled. The pellet's weight is negligible.

Someone can use an action to smash the pellet against a hard surface, causing the pellet to shatter and release the water the dust absorbed. Doing so ends that pellet's magic.

An elemental composed mostly of water that is exposed to a pinch of the dust must make a DC 13 Constitution saving throw, taking 10d6 necrotic damage on a failed save, or half as much damage on a successful one.

DUST OF SNEEZING AND CHOKING
Wondrous item, uncommon

Found in a small container, this powder resembles very fine sand. It appears to be *dust of disappearance*, and an *identify* spell reveals it to be such. There is enough of it for one use.

When you use an action to throw a handful of the dust into the air, you and each creature that needs to breathe within 30 feet of you must succeed on a DC 15 Constitution saving throw or become unable to breathe,

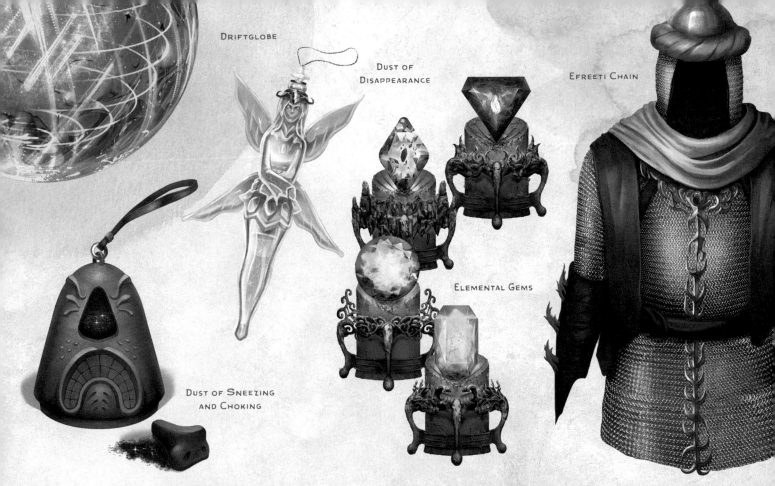

DRIFTGLOBE

DUST OF
DISAPPEARANCE

EFREETI CHAIN

ELEMENTAL GEMS

DUST OF SNEEZING
AND CHOKING

while sneezing uncontrollably. A creature affected in this way is incapacitated and suffocating. As long as it is conscious, a creature can repeat the saving throw at the end of each of its turns, ending the effect on it on a success. The *lesser restoration* spell can also end the effect on a creature.

DWARVEN PLATE
Armor (plate), very rare

While wearing this armor, you gain a +2 bonus to AC. In addition, if an effect moves you against your will along the ground, you can use your reaction to reduce the distance you are moved by up to 10 feet.

DWARVEN THROWER
Weapon (warhammer), very rare (requires attunement by a dwarf)

You gain a +3 bonus to attack and damage rolls made with this magic weapon. It has the thrown property with a normal range of 20 feet and a long range of 60 feet. When you hit with a ranged attack using this weapon, it deals an extra 1d8 damage or, if the target is a giant, 2d8 damage. Immediately after the attack, the weapon flies back to your hand.

EFREETI BOTTLE
Wondrous item, very rare

This painted brass bottle weighs 1 pound. When you use an action to remove the stopper, a cloud of thick smoke flows out of the bottle. At the end of your turn, the smoke disappears with a flash of harmless fire, and an efreeti appears in an unoccupied space within

30 feet of you. See the *Monster Manual* for the efreeti's statistics.

The first time the bottle is opened, the DM rolls to determine what happens.

d100	Effect
01–10	The efreeti attacks you. After fighting for 5 rounds, the efreeti disappears, and the bottle loses its magic.
11–90	The efreeti serves you for 1 hour, doing as you command. Then the efreeti returns to the bottle, and a new stopper contains it. The stopper can't be removed for 24 hours. The next two times the bottle is opened, the same effect occurs. If the bottle is opened a fourth time, the efreeti escapes and disappears, and the bottle loses its magic.
91–00	The efreeti can cast the *wish* spell three times for you. It disappears when it grants the final wish or after 1 hour, and the bottle loses its magic.

EFREETI CHAIN
Armor (chain mail), legendary (requires attunement)

While wearing this armor, you gain a +3 bonus to AC, you are immune to fire damage, and you can understand and speak Primordial. In addition, you can stand on and walk across molten rock as if it were solid ground.

ELEMENTAL GEM
Wondrous item, uncommon

This gem contains a mote of elemental energy. When you use an action to break the gem, an elemental is

EYES OF CHARMING

EVERSMOKING BOTTLE

GOLDEN LIONS

IVORY GOATS

summoned as if you had cast the *conjure elemental* spell, and the gem's magic is lost. The type of gem determines the elemental summoned by the spell.

Gem	Summoned Elemental
Blue sapphire	Air elemental
Yellow diamond	Earth elemental
Red corundum	Fire elemental
Emerald	Water elemental

ELIXIR OF HEALTH
Potion, rare

When you drink this potion, it cures any disease afflicting you, and it removes the blinded, deafened, paralyzed, and poisoned conditions. The clear red liquid has tiny bubbles of light in it.

ELVEN CHAIN
Armor (chain shirt), rare

You gain a +1 bonus to AC while you wear this armor. You are considered proficient with this armor even if you lack proficiency with medium armor.

EVERSMOKING BOTTLE
Wondrous item, uncommon

Smoke leaks from the lead-stoppered mouth of this brass bottle, which weighs 1 pound. When you use an action to remove the stopper, a cloud of thick smoke pours out in a 60-foot radius from the bottle. The cloud's area is heavily obscured. Each minute the bottle remains open and within the cloud, the radius increases by 10 feet until it reaches its maximum radius of 120 feet.

The cloud persists as long as the bottle is open. Closing the bottle requires you to speak its command word as an action. Once the bottle is closed, the cloud disperses after 10 minutes. A moderate wind (11 to 20 miles per hour) can also disperse the smoke after 1 minute, and a strong wind (21 or more miles per hour) can do so after 1 round.

EYES OF CHARMING
Wondrous item, uncommon (requires attunement)

These crystal lenses fit over the eyes. They have 3 charges. While wearing them, you can expend 1 charge as an action to cast the *charm person* spell (save DC 13) on a humanoid within 30 feet of you, provided that you and the target can see each other. The lenses regain all expended charges daily at dawn.

EYES OF MINUTE SEEING
Wondrous item, uncommon

These crystal lenses fit over the eyes. While wearing them, you can see much better than normal out to a range of 1 foot. You have advantage on Intelligence (Investigation) checks that rely on sight while searching an area or studying an object within that range.

EYES OF THE EAGLE
Wondrous item, uncommon (requires attunement)

These crystal lenses fit over the eyes. While wearing them, you have advantage on Wisdom (Perception) checks that rely on sight. In conditions of clear visibility, you can make out details of even extremely distant creatures and objects as small as 2 feet across.

EYES OF THE EAGLE

SERPENTINE OWL

OBSIDIAN STEED

MARBLE ELEPHANT

ONYX DOG

EBONY FLY

FIGURINE OF WONDROUS POWER
Wondrous item, rarity by figurine

A *figurine of wondrous power* is a statuette of a beast small enough to fit in a pocket. If you use an action to speak the command word and throw the figurine to a point on the ground within 60 feet of you, the figurine becomes a living creature. If the space where the creature would appear is occupied by other creatures or objects, or if there isn't enough space for the creature, the figurine doesn't become a creature.

The creature is friendly to you and your companions. It understands your languages and obeys your spoken commands. If you issue no commands, the creature defends itself but takes no other actions. See the *Monster Manual* for the creature's statistics, except for the giant fly.

The creature exists for a duration specific to each figurine. At the end of the duration, the creature reverts to its figurine form. It reverts to a figurine early if it drops to 0 hit points or if you use an action to speak the command word again while touching it. When the creature becomes a figurine again, its property can't be used again until a certain amount of time has passed, as specified in the figurine's description.

Bronze Griffon (Rare). This bronze statuette is of a griffon rampant. It can become a griffon for up to 6 hours. Once it has been used, it can't be used again until 5 days have passed.

Ebony Fly (Rare). This ebony statuette is carved in the likeness of a horsefly. It can become a giant fly for up to 12 hours and can be ridden as a mount. Once it has been used, it can't be used again until 2 days have passed.

GIANT FLY
Large beast, unaligned

Armor Class 11
Hit Points 19 (3d10 + 3)
Speed 30 ft., fly 60 ft.

STR	DEX	CON	INT	WIS	CHA
14 (+2)	13 (+1)	13 (+1)	2 (−4)	10 (+0)	3 (−4)

Senses darkvision 60 ft., passive Perception 10
Languages —

Golden Lions (Rare). These gold statuettes of lions are always created in pairs. You can use one figurine or both simultaneously. Each can become a lion for up to 1 hour. Once a lion has been used, it can't be used again until 7 days have passed.

Ivory Goats (Rare). These ivory statuettes of goats are always created in sets of three. Each goat looks unique and functions differently from the others. Their properties are as follows:

- The *goat of traveling* can become a Large goat with the same statistics as a riding horse. It has 24 charges, and each hour or portion thereof it spends in beast form costs 1 charge. While it has charges, you can use it as often as you wish. When it runs out of charges, it reverts to a figurine and can't be used again until 7 days have passed, when it regains all its charges.
- The *goat of travail* becomes a giant goat for up to 3 hours. Once it has been used, it can't be used again until 30 days have passed.

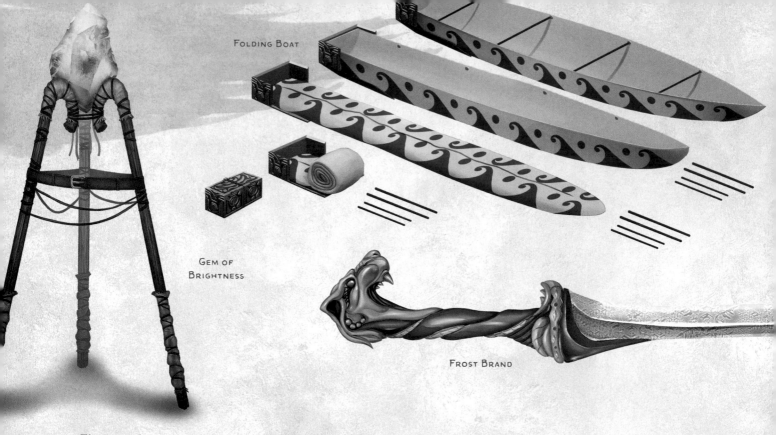

FOLDING BOAT

GEM OF
BRIGHTNESS

FROST BRAND

- The *goat of terror* becomes a giant goat for up to 3 hours. The goat can't attack, but you can remove its horns and use them as weapons. One horn becomes a *+1 lance*, and the other becomes a *+2 longsword*. Removing a horn requires an action, and the weapons disappear and the horns return when the goat reverts to figurine form. In addition, the goat radiates a 30-foot-radius aura of terror while you are riding it. Any creature hostile to you that starts its turn in the aura must succeed on a DC 15 Wisdom saving throw or be frightened of the goat for 1 minute, or until the goat reverts to figurine form. The frightened creature can repeat the saving throw at the end of each of its turns, ending the effect on itself on a success. Once it successfully saves against the effect, a creature is immune to the goat's aura for the next 24 hours. Once the figurine has been used, it can't be used again until 15 days have passed.

Marble Elephant (Rare). This marble statuette is about 4 inches high and long. It can become an elephant for up to 24 hours. Once it has been used, it can't be used again until 7 days have passed.

Obsidian Steed (Very Rare). This polished obsidian horse can become a nightmare for up to 24 hours. The nightmare fights only to defend itself. Once it has been used, it can't be used again until 5 days have passed.

If you have a good alignment, the figurine has a 10 percent chance each time you use it to ignore your orders, including a command to revert to figurine form. If you mount the nightmare while it is ignoring your orders, you and the nightmare are instantly transported to a random location on the plane of Hades, where the nightmare reverts to figurine form.

Onyx Dog (Rare). This onyx statuette of a dog can become a mastiff for up to 6 hours. The mastiff has

an Intelligence of 8 and can speak Common. It also has darkvision out to a range of 60 feet and can see invisible creatures and objects within that range. Once it has been used, it can't be used again until 7 days have passed.

Serpentine Owl (Rare). This serpentine statuette of an owl can become a giant owl for up to 8 hours. Once it has been used, it can't be used again until 2 days have passed. The owl can telepathically communicate with you at any range if you and it are on the same plane of existence.

Silver Raven (Uncommon). This silver statuette of a raven can become a raven for up to 12 hours. Once it has been used, it can't be used again until 2 days have passed. While in raven form, the figurine allows you to cast the *animal messenger* spell on it at will.

Flame Tongue

Weapon (any sword), rare (requires attunement)

You can use a bonus action to speak this magic sword's command word, causing flames to erupt from the blade. These flames shed bright light in a 40-foot radius and dim light for an additional 40 feet. While the sword is ablaze, it deals an extra 2d6 fire damage to any target it hits. The flames last until you use a bonus action to speak the command word again or until you drop or sheathe the sword.

Folding Boat

Wondrous item, rare

This object appears as a wooden box that measures 12 inches long, 6 inches wide, and 6 inches deep. It weighs 4 pounds and floats. It can be opened to store items inside. This item also has three command words, each requiring you to use an action to speak it.

FLAME TONGUE

GAUNTLETS OF
OGRE POWER

One command word causes the box to unfold into a boat 10 feet long, 4 feet wide, and 2 feet deep. The boat has one pair of oars, an anchor, a mast, and a lateen sail. The boat can hold up to four Medium creatures comfortably.

The second command word causes the box to unfold into a ship 24 feet long, 8 feet wide, and 6 feet deep. The ship has a deck, rowing seats, five sets of oars, a steering oar, an anchor, a deck cabin, and a mast with a square sail. The ship can hold fifteen Medium creatures comfortably.

When the box becomes a vessel, its weight becomes that of a normal vessel its size, and anything that was stored in the box remains in the boat.

The third command word causes the *folding boat* to fold back into a box, provided that no creatures are aboard. Any objects in the vessel that can't fit inside the box remain outside the box as it folds. Any objects in the vessel that can fit inside the box do so.

FROST BRAND
Weapon (any sword), very rare (requires attunement)

When you hit with an attack using this magic sword, the target takes an extra 1d6 cold damage. In addition, while you hold the sword, you have resistance to fire damage.

In freezing temperatures, the blade sheds bright light in a 10-foot radius and dim light for an additional 10 feet.

When you draw this weapon, you can extinguish all nonmagical flames within 30 feet of you. This property can be used no more than once per hour.

GAUNTLETS OF OGRE POWER
Wondrous item, uncommon (requires attunement)

Your Strength score is 19 while you wear these gauntlets. They have no effect on you if your Strength is already 19 or higher.

GEM OF BRIGHTNESS
Wondrous item, uncommon

This prism has 50 charges. While you are holding it, you can use an action to speak one of three command words to cause one of the following effects:

- The first command word causes the gem to shed bright light in a 30-foot radius and dim light for an additional 30 feet. This effect doesn't expend a charge. It lasts until you use a bonus action to repeat the command word or until you use another function of the gem.
- The second command word expends 1 charge and causes the gem to fire a brilliant beam of light at one creature you can see within 60 feet of you. The creature must succeed on a DC 15 Constitution saving throw or become blinded for 1 minute. The creature can repeat the saving throw at the end of each of its turns, ending the effect on itself on a success.
- The third command word expends 5 charges and causes the gem to flare with blinding light in a 30-foot cone originating from it. Each creature in the cone must make a saving throw as if struck by the beam created with the second command word.

When all of the gem's charges are expended, the gem becomes a nonmagical jewel worth 50 gp.

GEM OF SEEING

GIANT SLAYER

GLOVES OF
MISSILE SNARING

GOGGLES OF NIGHT

GEM OF SEEING

Wondrous item, rare (requires attunement)

This gem has 3 charges. As an action, you can speak the gem's command word and expend 1 charge. For the next 10 minutes, you have truesight out to 120 feet when you peer through the gem.

The gem regains 1d3 expended charges daily at dawn.

GIANT SLAYER

Weapon (any axe or sword), rare

You gain a +1 bonus to attack and damage rolls made with this magic weapon.

When you hit a giant with it, the giant takes an extra 2d6 damage of the weapon's type and must succeed on a DC 15 Strength saving throw or fall prone. For the purpose of this weapon, "giant" refers to any creature with the giant type, including ettins and trolls.

GLAMOURED STUDDED LEATHER

Armor (studded leather), rare

While wearing this armor, you gain a +1 bonus to AC. You can also use a bonus action to speak the armor's command word and cause the armor to assume the appearance of a normal set of clothing or some other kind of armor. You decide what it looks like, including color, style, and accessories, but the armor retains its normal bulk and weight. The illusory appearance lasts until you use this property again or remove the armor.

GLOVES OF MISSILE SNARING

Wondrous item, uncommon (requires attunement)

These gloves seem to almost meld into your hands when you don them. When a ranged weapon attack hits you while you're wearing them, you can use your reaction to reduce the damage by 1d10 + your Dexterity modifier, provided that you have a free hand. If you reduce the damage to 0, you can catch the missile if it is small enough for you to hold in that hand.

GLOVES OF SWIMMING AND CLIMBING

Wondrous item, uncommon (requires attunement)

While wearing these gloves, climbing and swimming don't cost you extra movement, and you gain a +5 bonus to Strength (Athletics) checks made to climb or swim.

GLOVES OF THIEVERY

Wondrous item, uncommon

These gloves are invisible while worn. While wearing them, you gain a +5 bonus to Dexterity (Sleight of Hand) checks and Dexterity checks made to pick locks.

GOGGLES OF NIGHT

Wondrous item, uncommon

While wearing these dark lenses, you have darkvision out to a range of 60 feet. If you already have darkvision, wearing the goggles increases its range by 60 feet.

HAMMER OF THUNDERBOLTS
Weapon (maul), legendary

You gain a +1 bonus to attack and damage rolls made with this magic weapon.

Giant's Bane (Requires Attunement). You must be wearing a *belt of giant strength* (any variety) and *gauntlets of ogre power* to attune to this weapon. The attunement ends if you take off either of those items. While you are attuned to this weapon and holding it, your Strength score increases by 4 and can exceed 20, but not 30. When you roll a 20 on an attack roll made with this weapon against a giant, the giant must succeed on a DC 17 Constitution saving throw or die.

The hammer also has 5 charges. While attuned to it, you can expend 1 charge and make a ranged weapon attack with the hammer, hurling it as if it had the thrown property with a normal range of 20 feet and a long range of 60 feet. If the attack hits, the hammer unleashes a thunderclap audible out to 300 feet. The target and every creature within 30 feet of it must succeed on a DC 17 Constitution saving throw or be stunned until the end of your next turn. The hammer regains 1d4 + 1 expended charges daily at dawn.

HAT OF DISGUISE
Wondrous item, uncommon (requires attunement)

While wearing this hat, you can use an action to cast the *disguise self* spell from it at will. The spell ends if the hat is removed.

HEADBAND OF INTELLECT
Wondrous item, uncommon (requires attunement)

Your Intelligence score is 19 while you wear this headband. It has no effect on you if your Intelligence is already 19 or higher.

HELM OF BRILLIANCE
Wondrous item, very rare (requires attunement)

This dazzling helm is set with 1d10 diamonds, 2d10 rubies, 3d10 fire opals, and 4d10 opals. Any gem pried from the helm crumbles to dust. When all the gems are removed or destroyed, the helm loses its magic.

You gain the following benefits while wearing it:

- You can use an action to cast one of the following spells (save DC 18), using one of the helm's gems of the specified type as a component: *daylight* (opal), *fireball* (fire opal), *prismatic spray* (diamond), or *wall of fire* (ruby). The gem is destroyed when the spell is cast and disappears from the helm.
- As long as it has at least one diamond, the helm emits dim light in a 30-foot radius when at least one undead is within that area. Any undead that starts its turn in that area takes 1d6 radiant damage.
- As long as the helm has at least one ruby, you have resistance to fire damage.
- As long as the helm has at least one fire opal, you can use an action and speak a command word to cause one weapon you are holding to burst into flames. The flames emit bright light in a 10-foot radius and dim light for an additional 10 feet. The flames are harmless to you and the weapon. When you hit with

HAMMER OF
THUNDERBOLTS

HELM OF BRILLIANCE

HELM OF
COMPREHENDING LANGUAGES

an attack using the blazing weapon, the target takes an extra 1d6 fire damage. The flames last until you use a bonus action to speak the command word again or until you drop or stow the weapon.

Roll a d20 if you are wearing the helm and take fire damage as a result of failing a saving throw against a spell. On a roll of 1, the helm emits beams of light from its remaining gems. Each creature within 60 feet of the helm other than you must succeed on a DC 17 Dexterity saving throw or be struck by a beam, taking radiant damage equal to the number of gems in the helm. The helm and its gems are then destroyed.

HELM OF COMPREHENDING LANGUAGES
Wondrous item, uncommon

While wearing this helm, you can use an action to cast the *comprehend languages* spell from it at will.

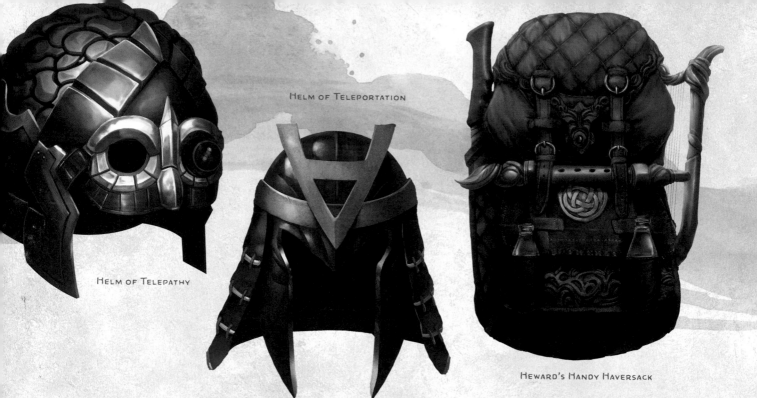

HELM OF TELEPORTATION

HELM OF TELEPATHY

HEWARD'S HANDY HAVERSACK

HELM OF TELEPATHY

Wondrous item, uncommon (requires attunement)

While wearing this helm, you can use an action to cast the *detect thoughts* spell (save DC 13) from it. As long as you maintain concentration on the spell, you can use a bonus action to send a telepathic message to a creature you are focused on. It can reply—using a bonus action to do so—while your focus on it continues.

While focusing on a creature with *detect thoughts*, you can use an action to cast the *suggestion* spell (save DC 13) from the helm on that creature. Once used, the *suggestion* property can't be used again until the next dawn.

HELM OF TELEPORTATION

Wondrous item, rare (requires attunement)

This helm has 3 charges. While wearing it, you can use an action and expend 1 charge to cast the *teleport* spell from it. The helm regains 1d3 expended charges daily at dawn.

HEWARD'S HANDY HAVERSACK

Wondrous item, rare

This backpack has a central pouch and two side pouches, each of which is an extradimensional space. Each side pouch can hold up to 20 pounds of material, not exceeding a volume of 2 cubic feet. The large central pouch can hold up to 8 cubic feet or 80 pounds of material. The backpack always weighs 5 pounds, regardless of its contents.

Placing an object in the haversack follows the normal rules for interacting with objects. Retrieving an item from the haversack requires you to use an action. When you reach into the haversack for a specific item, the item is always magically on top.

The haversack has a few limitations. If it is overloaded, or if a sharp object pierces it or tears it, the haversack ruptures and is destroyed. If the haversack is destroyed, its contents are lost forever, although an artifact always turns up again somewhere. If the haversack is turned inside out, its contents spill forth, unharmed, and the haversack must be put right before it can be used again. If a breathing creature is placed within the haversack, the creature can survive for up to 10 minutes, after which time it begins to suffocate.

Placing the haversack inside an extradimensional space created by a *bag of holding*, *portable hole*, or similar item instantly destroys both items and opens a gate to the Astral Plane. The gate originates where the one item was placed inside the other. Any creature within 10 feet of the gate is sucked through it and deposited in a random location on the Astral Plane. The gate then closes. The gate is one-way only and can't be reopened.

HOLY AVENGER

Weapon (any sword), legendary (requires attunement by a paladin)

You gain a +3 bonus to attack and damage rolls made with this magic weapon. When you hit a fiend or an undead with it, that creature takes an extra 2d10 radiant damage.

While you hold the drawn sword, it creates an aura in a 10-foot radius around you. You and all creatures friendly to you in the aura have advantage on saving throws against spells and other magical effects. If you have 17 or more levels in the paladin class, the radius of the aura increases to 30 feet.

HORN OF BLASTING

Wondrous item, rare

You can use an action to speak the horn's command word and then blow the horn, which emits a thunderous blast in a 30-foot cone that is audible 600 feet away. Each creature in the cone must make a DC 15

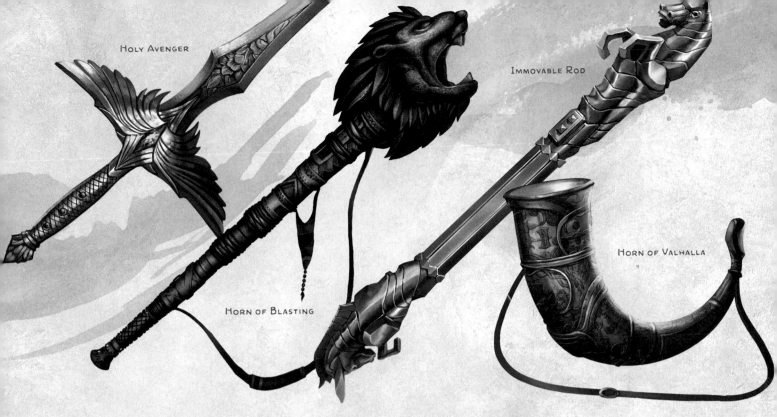

HOLY AVENGER

IMMOVABLE ROD

HORN OF BLASTING

HORN OF VALHALLA

Constitution saving throw. On a failed save, a creature takes 5d6 thunder damage and is deafened for 1 minute. On a successful save, a creature takes half as much damage and isn't deafened. Creatures and objects made of glass or crystal have disadvantage on the saving throw and take 10d6 thunder damage instead of 5d6.

Each use of the horn's magic has a 20 percent chance of causing the horn to explode. The explosion deals 10d6 fire damage to the blower and destroys the horn.

HORN OF VALHALLA
Wondrous item, rare (silver or brass), very rare (bronze), or legendary (iron)

You can use an action to blow this horn. In response, warrior spirits from the plane of Ysgard appear within 60 feet of you. These spirits use the berserker statistics from the *Monster Manual*. They return to Ysgard after 1 hour or when they drop to 0 hit points. Once you use the horn, it can't be used again until 7 days have passed.

Four types of *horn of Valhalla* are known to exist, each made of a different metal. The horn's type determines how many berserkers answer its summons, as well as the requirement for its use. The DM chooses the horn's type or determines it randomly.

d100	Horn Type	Berserkers Summoned	Requirement
01–40	Silver	2d4 + 2	None
41–75	Brass	3d4 + 3	Proficiency with all simple weapons
76–90	Bronze	4d4 + 4	Proficiency with all medium armor
91–00	Iron	5d4 + 5	Proficiency with all martial weapons

If you blow the horn without meeting its requirement, the summoned berserkers attack you. If you meet the requirement, they are friendly to you and your companions and follow your commands.

HORSESHOES OF A ZEPHYR
Wondrous item, very rare

These iron horseshoes come in a set of four. While all four shoes are affixed to the hooves of a horse or similar creature, they allow the creature to move normally while floating 4 inches above the ground. This effect means the creature can cross or stand above nonsolid or unstable surfaces, such as water or lava. The creature leaves no tracks and ignores difficult terrain. In addition, the creature can move at normal speed for up to 12 hours a day without suffering exhaustion from a forced march.

HORSESHOES OF SPEED
Wondrous item, rare

These iron horseshoes come in a set of four. While all four shoes are affixed to the hooves of a horse or similar creature, they increase the creature's walking speed by 30 feet.

IMMOVABLE ROD
Rod, uncommon

This flat iron rod has a button on one end. You can use an action to press the button, which causes the rod to become magically fixed in place. Until you or another creature uses an action to push the button again, the rod doesn't move, even if it is defying gravity. The rod can hold up to 8,000 pounds of weight. More weight causes the rod to deactivate and fall. A creature can use an action to make a DC 30 Strength check, moving the fixed rod up to 10 feet on a success.

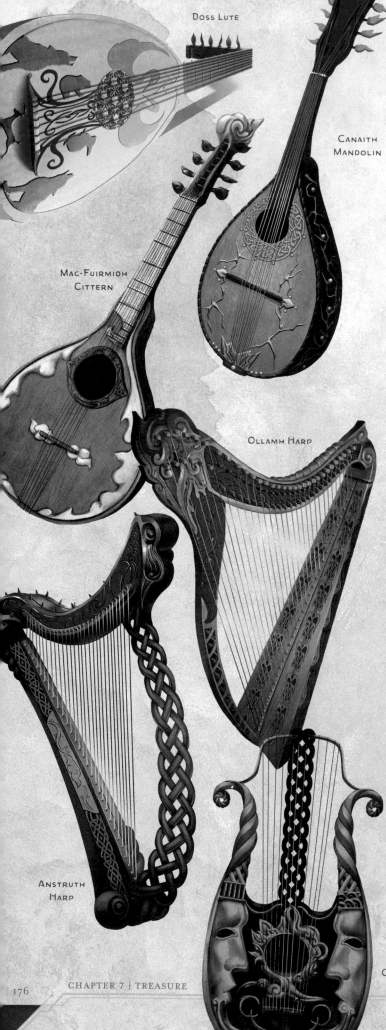

DOSS LUTE

CANAITH MANDOLIN

MAC-FUIRMIDH CITTERN

OLLAMH HARP

ANSTRUTH HARP

CLI LYRE

INSTRUMENT OF THE BARDS
Wondrous item, rarity varies (requires attunement by a bard)

An *instrument of the bards* is an exquisite example of its kind, superior to an ordinary instrument in every way. Seven types of these instruments exist, each named after a legendary bard college. The following table lists the spells common to all instruments, as well as the spells specific to each one and its rarity. A creature that attempts to play the instrument without being attuned to it must succeed on a DC 15 Wisdom saving throw or take 2d4 psychic damage.

You can use an action to play the instrument and cast one of its spells. Once the instrument has been used to cast a spell, it can't be used to cast that spell again until the next dawn. The spells use your spellcasting ability and spell save DC.

When you use the instrument to cast a spell that causes targets to become charmed on a failed save, the targets have disadvantage on the saving throw. This effect applies whether you are using the instrument as the source of the spell or as a spellcasting focus.

Instrument	Rarity	Spells
All	—	*Fly, invisibility, levitate, protection from evil and good,* plus the spells listed for the particular instrument
Anstruth harp	Very rare	*Control weather, cure wounds* (5th level), *wall of thorns*
Canaith mandolin	Rare	*Cure wounds* (3rd level), *dispel magic, protection from energy* (lightning only)
Cli lyre	Rare	*Stone shape, wall of fire, wind wall*
Doss lute	Uncommon	*Animal friendship, protection from energy* (fire only), *protection from poison*
Fochlucan bandore	Uncommon	*Entangle, faerie fire, shillelagh, speak with animals*
Mac-Fuirmidh cittern	Uncommon	*Barkskin, cure wounds, fog cloud*
Ollamh harp	Legendary	*Confusion, control weather, fire storm*

IOUN STONE
Wondrous item, rarity varies (requires attunement)

An *Ioun stone* is named after Ioun, a god of knowledge and prophecy revered on some worlds. Many types of *Ioun stone* exist, each type a distinct combination of shape and color.

When you use an action to toss one of these stones into the air, the stone orbits your head at a distance of 1d3 feet and confers a benefit to you. Thereafter, another creature must use an action to grasp or net the stone to separate it from you, either by making a successful attack roll against AC 24 or a successful DC 24 Dexterity (Acrobatics) check. You can use an action to seize and stow the stone, ending its effect.

A stone has AC 24, 10 hit points, and resistance to all damage. It is considered to be an object that is being worn while it orbits your head.

Absorption (Very Rare). While this pale lavender ellipsoid orbits your head, you can use your reaction to cancel a spell of 4th level or lower cast by a creature you can see and targeting only you.

Once the stone has canceled 20 levels of spells, it burns out and turns dull gray, losing its magic. If you are targeted by a spell whose level is higher than the number of spell levels the stone has left, the stone can't cancel it.

Agility (Very Rare). Your Dexterity score increases by 2, to a maximum of 20, while this deep red sphere orbits your head.

Awareness (Rare). You can't be surprised while this dark blue rhomboid orbits your head.

Fortitude (Very Rare). Your Constitution score increases by 2, to a maximum of 20, while this pink rhomboid orbits your head.

Greater Absorption (Legendary). While this marbled lavender and green ellipsoid orbits your head, you can use your reaction to cancel a spell of 8th level or lower cast by a creature you can see and targeting only you.

Once the stone has canceled 50 levels of spells, it burns out and turns dull gray, losing its magic. If you are targeted by a spell whose level is higher than the number of spell levels the stone has left, the stone can't cancel it.

Insight (Very Rare). Your Wisdom score increases by 2, to a maximum of 20, while this incandescent blue sphere orbits your head.

Intellect (Very Rare). Your Intelligence score increases by 2, to a maximum of 20, while this marbled scarlet and blue sphere orbits your head.

Leadership (Very Rare). Your Charisma score increases by 2, to a maximum of 20, while this marbled pink and green sphere orbits your head.

Mastery (Legendary). Your proficiency bonus increases by 1 while this pale green prism orbits your head.

Protection (Rare). You gain a +1 bonus to AC while this dusty rose prism orbits your head.

Regeneration (Legendary). You regain 15 hit points at the end of each hour this pearly white spindle orbits your head, provided that you have at least 1 hit point.

Reserve (Rare). This vibrant purple prism stores spells cast into it, holding them until you use them. The stone can store up to 3 levels worth of spells at a time. When found, it contains 1d4 − 1 levels of stored spells chosen by the DM.

Any creature can cast a spell of 1st through 3rd level into the stone by touching it as the spell is cast. The spell has no effect, other than to be stored in the stone. If the stone can't hold the spell, the spell is expended without effect. The level of the slot used to cast the spell determines how much space it uses.

While this stone orbits your head, you can cast any spell stored in it. The spell uses the slot level, spell save DC, spell attack bonus, and spellcasting ability of the original caster, but is otherwise treated as if you cast the

IOUN STONES

IRON BANDS OF BILARRO

spell. The spell cast from the stone is no longer stored in it, freeing up space.

Strength (Very Rare). Your Strength score increases by 2, to a maximum of 20, while this pale blue rhomboid orbits your head.

Sustenance (Rare). You don't need to eat or drink while this clear spindle orbits your head.

IRON BANDS OF BILARRO
Wondrous item, rare

This rusty iron sphere measures 3 inches in diameter and weighs 1 pound. You can use an action to speak the command word and throw the sphere at a Huge or smaller creature you can see within 60 feet of you. As the sphere moves through the air, it opens into a tangle of metal bands.

Make a ranged attack roll with an attack bonus equal to your Dexterity modifier plus your proficiency bonus. On a hit, the target is restrained until you take a bonus action to speak the command word again to release it. Doing so, or missing with the attack, causes the bands to contract and become a sphere once more.

A creature, including the one restrained, can use an action to make a DC 20 Strength check to break the iron bands. On a success, the item is destroyed, and the restrained creature is freed. If the check fails, any further attempts made by that creature automatically fail until 24 hours have elapsed.

Once the bands are used, they can't be used again until the next dawn.

IRON FLASK

Wondrous item, legendary

This iron bottle has a brass stopper. You can use an action to speak the flask's command word, targeting a creature that you can see within 60 feet of you. If the target is native to a plane of existence other than the one you're on, the target must succeed on a DC 17 Wisdom saving throw or be trapped in the flask. If the target has been trapped by the flask before, it has advantage on the saving throw. Once trapped, a creature remains in the flask until released. The flask can hold only one creature at a time. A creature trapped in the flask doesn't need to breathe, eat, or drink and doesn't age.

You can use an action to remove the flask's stopper and release the creature the flask contains. The creature is friendly to you and your companions for 1 hour and obeys your commands for that duration. If you give no commands or give it a command that is likely to result in its death, it defends itself but otherwise takes no actions. At the end of the duration, the creature acts in accordance with its normal disposition and alignment.

An *identify* spell reveals that a creature is inside the flask, but the only way to determine the type of creature is to open the flask. A newly discovered bottle might already contain a creature chosen by the DM or determined randomly.

IRON FLASK

KEOGHTOM'S OINTMENT

LANTERN OF REVEALING

d100	Contents	d100	Contents
01–50	Empty	77–78	Elemental (any)
51	Arcanaloth	79	Githyanki knight
52	Cambion	80	Githzerai zerth
53–54	Dao	81–82	Invisible stalker
55–57	Demon (type 1)	83–84	Marid
58–60	Demon (type 2)	85–86	Mezzoloth
61–62	Demon (type 3)	87–88	Night hag
63–64	Demon (type 4)	89–90	Nycaloth
65	Demon (type 5)	91	Planetar
66	Demon (type 6)	92–93	Salamander
67	Deva	94–95	Slaad (any)
68–69	Devil (greater)	96	Solar
70–72	Devil (lesser)	97–98	Succubus/incubus
73–74	Djinni	99	Ultroloth
75–76	Efreeti	00	Xorn

JAVELIN OF LIGHTNING

Weapon (javelin), uncommon

This javelin is a magic weapon. When you hurl it and speak its command word, it transforms into a bolt of lightning, forming a line 5 feet wide that extends out from you to a target within 120 feet. Each creature in the line excluding you and the target must make a DC 13 Dexterity saving throw, taking 4d6 lightning damage on a failed save, and half as much damage on a successful one. The lightning bolt turns back into a javelin when it reaches the target. Make a ranged weapon attack against the target. On a hit, the target takes damage from the javelin plus 4d6 lightning damage.

The javelin's property can't be used again until the next dawn. In the meantime, the javelin can still be used as a magic weapon.

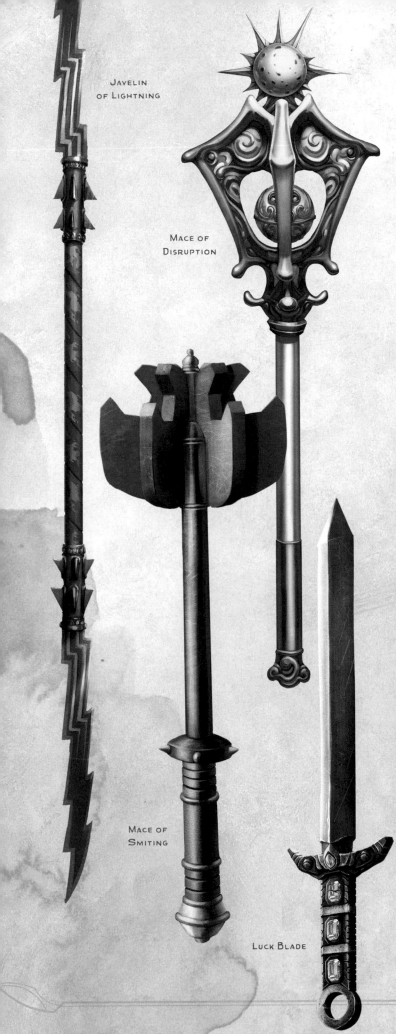

JAVELIN
OF LIGHTNING

MACE OF
DISRUPTION

MACE OF
SMITING

LUCK BLADE

KEOGHTOM'S OINTMENT
Wondrous item, uncommon

This glass jar, 3 inches in diameter, contains 1d4 + 1 doses of a thick mixture that smells faintly of aloe. The jar and its contents weigh 1/2 pound.

As an action, one dose of the ointment can be swallowed or applied to the skin. The creature that receives it regains 2d8 + 2 hit points, ceases to be poisoned, and is cured of any disease.

LANTERN OF REVEALING
Wondrous item, uncommon

While lit, this hooded lantern burns for 6 hours on 1 pint of oil, shedding bright light in a 30-foot radius and dim light for an additional 30 feet. Invisible creatures and objects are visible as long as they are in the lantern's bright light. You can use an action to lower the hood, reducing the light to dim light in a 5-foot radius.

LUCK BLADE
Weapon (any sword), legendary (requires attunement)

You gain a +1 bonus to attack and damage rolls made with this magic weapon. While the sword is on your person, you also gain a +1 bonus to saving throws.

Luck. If the sword is on your person, you can call on its luck (no action required) to reroll one attack roll, ability check, or saving throw you dislike. You must use the second roll. This property can't be used again until the next dawn.

Wish. The sword has 1d4 − 1 charges. While holding it, you can use an action to expend 1 charge and cast the *wish* spell from it. This property can't be used again until the next dawn. The sword loses this property if it has no charges.

MACE OF DISRUPTION
Weapon (mace), rare (requires attunement)

When you hit a fiend or an undead with this magic weapon, that creature takes an extra 2d6 radiant damage. If the target has 25 hit points or fewer after taking this damage, it must succeed on a DC 15 Wisdom saving throw or be destroyed. On a successful save, the creature becomes frightened of you until the end of your next turn.

While you hold this weapon, it sheds bright light in a 20-foot radius and dim light for an additional 20 feet.

MACE OF SMITING
Weapon (mace), rare

You gain a +1 bonus to attack and damage rolls made with this magic weapon. The bonus increases to +3 when you use the mace to attack a construct.

When you roll a 20 on an attack roll made with this weapon, the target takes an extra 7 bludgeoning damage, or an extra 14 bludgeoning damage if it's a construct. If a construct has 25 hit points or fewer after taking this damage, it is destroyed.

MANTLE OF
SPELL RESISTANCE

MANUAL OF
STONE GOLEMS

MANUAL OF CLAY GOLEMS

MACE OF TERROR

MACE OF TERROR
Weapon (mace), rare (requires attunement)

This magic weapon has 3 charges. While holding it, you can use an action and expend 1 charge to release a wave of terror. Each creature of your choice in a 30-foot radius extending from you must succeed on a DC 15 Wisdom saving throw or become frightened of you for 1 minute. While it is frightened in this way, a creature must spend its turns trying to move as far away from you as it can, and it can't willingly move to a space within 30 feet of you. It also can't take reactions. For its action, it can use only the Dash action or try to escape from an effect that prevents it from moving. If it has nowhere it can move, the creature can use the Dodge action. At the end of each of its turns, a creature can repeat the saving throw, ending the effect on itself on a success.

The mace regains 1d3 expended charges daily at dawn.

MANTLE OF SPELL RESISTANCE
Wondrous item, rare (requires attunement)

You have advantage on saving throws against spells while you wear this cloak.

MANUAL OF BODILY HEALTH
Wondrous item, very rare

This book contains health and diet tips, and its words are charged with magic. If you spend 48 hours over a period of 6 days or fewer studying the book's contents and practicing its guidelines, your Constitution score increases by 2, as does your maximum for that score. The manual then loses its magic, but regains it in a century.

MANUAL OF GAINFUL EXERCISE
Wondrous item, very rare

This book describes fitness exercises, and its words are charged with magic. If you spend 48 hours over a period of 6 days or fewer studying the book's contents and practicing its guidelines, your Strength score increases by 2, as does your maximum for that score. The manual then loses its magic, but regains it in a century.

MANUAL OF GOLEMS
Wondrous item, very rare

This tome contains information and incantations necessary to make a particular type of golem. The DM chooses the type or determines it randomly. To decipher and use the manual, you must be a spellcaster with at least two 5th-level spell slots. A creature that can't use a *manual of golems* and attempts to read it takes 6d6 psychic damage.

d20	Golem	Time	Cost
1–5	Clay	30 days	65,000 gp
6–17	Flesh	60 days	50,000 gp
18	Iron	120 days	100,000 gp
19–20	Stone	90 days	80,000 gp

To create a golem, you must spend the time shown on the table, working without interruption with the manual at hand and resting no more than 8 hours per day. You must also pay the specified cost to purchase supplies.

Once you finish creating the golem, the book is consumed in eldritch flames. The golem becomes animate when the ashes of the manual are sprinkled on it. It is under your control, and it understands and obeys your spoken commands. See the *Monster Manual* for its game statistics.

MANUAL OF QUICKNESS OF ACTION
Wondrous item, very rare

This book contains coordination and balance exercises, and its words are charged with magic. If you spend 48 hours over a period of 6 days or fewer studying the book's contents and practicing its guidelines, your Dexterity score increases by 2, as does your maximum for that score. The manual then loses its magic, but regains it in a century.

MARINER'S ARMOR
Armor (light, medium, or heavy), uncommon

While wearing this armor, you have a swimming speed equal to your walking speed. In addition, whenever you start your turn underwater with 0 hit points, the armor causes you to rise 60 feet toward the surface. The armor is decorated with fish and shell motifs.

MEDALLION OF THOUGHTS
Wondrous item, uncommon (requires attunement)

The medallion has 3 charges. While wearing it, you can use an action and expend 1 charge to cast the *detect thoughts* spell (save DC 13) from it. The medallion regains 1d3 expended charges daily at dawn.

MIRROR OF LIFE TRAPPING
Wondrous item, very rare

When this 4-foot-tall mirror is viewed indirectly, its surface shows faint images of creatures. The mirror weighs 50 pounds, and it has AC 11, 10 hit points, and vulnerability to bludgeoning damage. It shatters and is destroyed when reduced to 0 hit points.

If the mirror is hanging on a vertical surface and you are within 5 feet of it, you can use an action to speak its command word and activate it. It remains activated until you use an action to speak the command word again.

Any creature other than you that sees its reflection in the activated mirror while within 30 feet of it must succeed on a DC 15 Charisma saving throw or be trapped, along with anything it is wearing or carrying, in one of the mirror's twelve extradimensional cells. This saving throw is made with advantage if the creature knows the mirror's nature, and constructs succeed on the saving throw automatically.

An extradimensional cell is an infinite expanse filled with thick fog that reduces visibility to 10 feet. Creatures trapped in the mirror's cells don't age, and they don't need to eat, drink, or sleep. A creature trapped within a cell can escape using magic that permits planar travel. Otherwise, the creature is confined to the cell until freed.

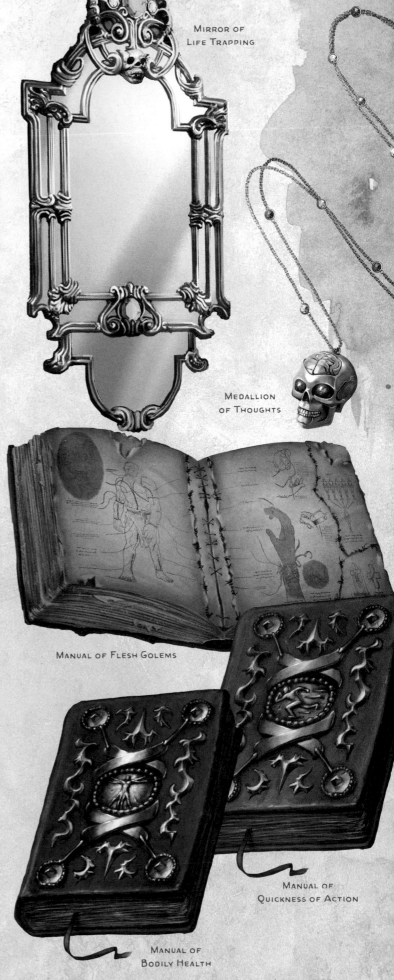

MIRROR OF
LIFE TRAPPING

MEDALLION
OF THOUGHTS

MANUAL OF FLESH GOLEMS

MANUAL OF
QUICKNESS OF ACTION

MANUAL OF
BODILY HEALTH

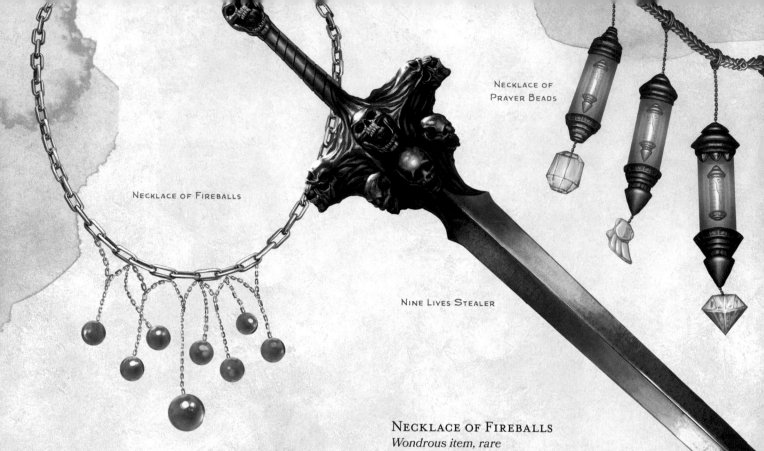

Necklace of Fireballs

Necklace of Prayer Beads

Nine Lives Stealer

If the mirror traps a creature but its twelve extradimensional cells are already occupied, the mirror frees one trapped creature at random to accommodate the new prisoner. A freed creature appears in an unoccupied space within sight of the mirror but facing away from it. If the mirror is shattered, all creatures it contains are freed and appear in unoccupied spaces near it.

While within 5 feet of the mirror, you can use an action to speak the name of one creature trapped in it or call out a particular cell by number. The creature named or contained in the named cell appears as an image on the mirror's surface. You and the creature can then communicate normally.

In a similar way, you can use an action to speak a second command word and free one creature trapped in the mirror. The freed creature appears, along with its possessions, in the unoccupied space nearest to the mirror and facing away from it.

Mithral Armor
Armor (medium or heavy, but not hide), uncommon

Mithral is a light, flexible metal. A mithral chain shirt or breastplate can be worn under normal clothes. If the armor normally imposes disadvantage on Dexterity (Stealth) checks or has a Strength requirement, the mithral version of the armor doesn't.

Necklace of Adaptation
Wondrous item, uncommon (requires attunement)

While wearing this necklace, you can breathe normally in any environment, and you have advantage on saving throws made against harmful gases and vapors (such as *cloudkill* and *stinking cloud* effects, inhaled poisons, and the breath weapons of some dragons).

Necklace of Fireballs
Wondrous item, rare

This necklace has 1d6 + 3 beads hanging from it. You can use an action to detach a bead and throw it up to 60 feet away. When it reaches the end of its trajectory, the bead detonates as a 3rd-level *fireball* spell (save DC 15).

You can hurl multiple beads, or even the whole necklace, as one action. When you do so, increase the level of the *fireball* by 1 for each bead beyond the first.

Necklace of Prayer Beads
Wondrous item, rare (requires attunement by a cleric, druid, or paladin)

This necklace has 1d4 + 2 magic beads made from aquamarine, black pearl, or topaz. It also has many nonmagical beads made from stones such as amber, bloodstone, citrine, coral, jade, pearl, or quartz. If a magic bead is removed from the necklace, that bead loses its magic.

Six types of magic beads exist. The DM decides the type of each bead on the necklace or determines it randomly. A necklace can have more than one bead of the same type. To use one, you must be wearing the necklace. Each bead contains a spell that you can cast from it as a bonus action (using your spell save DC if a save is necessary). Once a magic bead's spell is cast, that bead can't be used again until the next dawn.

d20	Bead of ...	Spell
1–6	Blessing	*Bless*
7–12	Curing	*Cure wounds* (2nd level) or *lesser restoration*
13–16	Favor	*Greater restoration*
17–18	Smiting	*Branding smite*
19	Summons	*Planar ally*
20	Wind walking	*Wind walk*

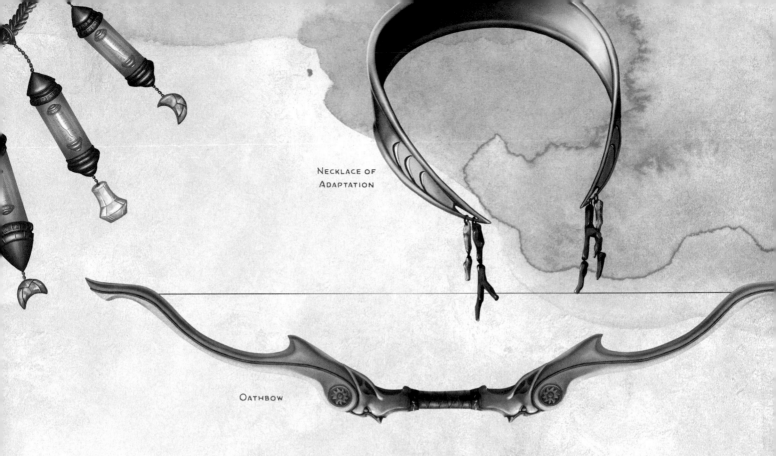

NECKLACE OF
ADAPTATION

OATHBOW

NINE LIVES STEALER

Weapon (any sword), very rare (requires attunement)

You gain a +2 bonus to attack and damage rolls made
with this magic weapon.

The sword has 1d8 + 1 charges. If you score a critical
hit against a creature that has fewer than 100 hit points,
it must succeed on a DC 15 Constitution saving throw or
be slain instantly as the sword tears its life force from its
body (a construct or an undead is immune). The sword
loses 1 charge if the creature is slain. When the sword
has no charges remaining, it loses this property.

NOLZUR'S MARVELOUS PIGMENTS

Wondrous item, very rare

Typically found in 1d4 pots inside a fine wooden box
with a brush (weighing 1 pound in total), these pigments
allow you to create three-dimensional objects by
painting them in two dimensions. The paint flows from
the brush to form the desired object as you concentrate
on its image.

Each pot of paint is sufficient to cover 1,000 square
feet of a surface, which lets you create inanimate objects
or terrain features—such as a door, a pit, flowers, trees,
cells, rooms, or weapons—that are up to 10,000 cubic
feet. It takes 10 minutes to cover 100 square feet.

When you complete the painting, the object or terrain
feature depicted becomes a real, nonmagical object.
Thus, painting a door on a wall creates an actual door
that can be opened to whatever is beyond. Painting a pit
on a floor creates a real pit, and its depth counts against
the total area of objects you create.

Nothing created by the pigments can have a value
greater than 25 gp. If you paint an object of greater value

(such as a diamond or a pile of gold), the object looks
authentic, but close inspection reveals it is made from
paste, bone, or some other worthless material.

If you paint a form of energy such as fire or lightning,
the energy appears but dissipates as soon as you
complete the painting, doing no harm to anything.

OATHBOW

Weapon (longbow), very rare (requires attunement)

When you nock an arrow on this bow, it whispers in
Elvish, "Swift defeat to my enemies." When you use
this weapon to make a ranged attack, you can, as a
command phrase, say, "Swift death to you who have
wronged me." The target of your attack becomes your
sworn enemy until it dies or until dawn seven days later.
You can have only one such sworn enemy at a time.
When your sworn enemy dies, you can choose a new
one after the next dawn.

When you make a ranged attack roll with this weapon
against your sworn enemy, you have advantage on the
roll. In addition, your target gains no benefit from cover,
other than total cover, and you suffer no disadvantage
due to long range. If the attack hits, your sworn enemy
takes an extra 3d6 piercing damage.

While your sworn enemy lives, you have disadvantage
on attack rolls with all other weapons.

OIL OF ETHEREALNESS

Potion, rare

Beads of this cloudy gray oil form on the outside of its
container and quickly evaporate. The oil can cover a
Medium or smaller creature, along with the equipment
it's wearing and carrying (one additional vial is required

PERIAPT OF
WOUND CLOSURE

PERIAPT OF HEALTH

for each size category above Medium). Applying the oil takes 10 minutes. The affected creature then gains the effect of the *etherealness* spell for 1 hour.

OIL OF SHARPNESS
Potion, very rare

This clear, gelatinous oil sparkles with tiny, ultrathin silver shards. The oil can coat one slashing or piercing weapon or up to 5 pieces of slashing or piercing ammunition. Applying the oil takes 1 minute. For 1 hour, the coated item is magical and has a +3 bonus to attack and damage rolls.

OIL OF SLIPPERINESS
Potion, uncommon

This sticky black unguent is thick and heavy in the container, but it flows quickly when poured. The oil can cover a Medium or smaller creature, along with the equipment it's wearing and carrying (one additional vial is required for each size category above Medium). Applying the oil takes 10 minutes. The affected creature then gains the effect of a *freedom of movement* spell for 8 hours.

   Alternatively, the oil can be poured on the ground as an action, where it covers a 10-foot square, duplicating the effect of the *grease* spell in that area for 8 hours.

PEARL OF POWER
Wondrous item, uncommon (requires attunement by a spellcaster)

You can use an action to speak this pearl's command word and regain one expended spell slot of up to 3rd level. Once you have used the pearl, it can't be used again until the next dawn.

PERIAPT OF HEALTH
Wondrous item, uncommon

You are immune to contracting any disease while you wear this pendant. If you are already infected with a disease, the effects of the disease are suppressed you while you wear the pendant.

PERIAPT OF PROOF AGAINST POISON
Wondrous item, rare

This delicate silver chain has a brilliant-cut black gem pendant. While you wear it, poisons have no effect on you. You are immune to the poisoned condition and have immunity to poison damage.

PERIAPT OF WOUND CLOSURE
Wondrous item, uncommon (requires attunement)

While you wear this pendant, you stabilize whenever you are dying at the start of your turn. In addition, whenever you roll a Hit Die to regain hit points, double the number of hit points it restores.

PHILTER OF LOVE
Potion, uncommon

The next time you see a creature within 10 minutes after drinking this philter, you become charmed by that creature for 1 hour. If the creature is of a species and gender you are normally attracted to, you regard it as your true love while you are charmed. This potion's rose-hued, effervescent liquid contains one easy-to-miss bubble shaped like a heart.

PIPES OF HAUNTING

PIPES OF THE SEWERS

PIPES OF HAUNTING
Wondrous item, uncommon

You must be proficient with wind instruments to use these pipes. They have 3 charges. You can use an action to play them and expend 1 charge to create an eerie, spellbinding tune. Each creature within 30 feet of you that hears you play must succeed on a DC 15 Wisdom saving throw or become frightened of you for 1 minute. If you wish, all creatures in the area that aren't hostile toward you automatically succeed on the saving throw. A creature that fails the saving throw can repeat it at the end of each of its turns, ending the effect on itself on a success. A creature that succeeds on its saving throw is immune to the effect of these pipes for 24 hours. The pipes regain 1d3 expended charges daily at dawn.

PIPES OF THE SEWERS
Wondrous item, uncommon (requires attunement)

You must be proficient with wind instruments to use these pipes. While you are attuned to the pipes, ordinary rats and giant rats are indifferent toward you and will not attack you unless you threaten or harm them.

The pipes have 3 charges. If you play the pipes as an action, you can use a bonus action to expend 1 to 3 charges, calling forth one swarm of rats (see the *Monster Manual* for statistics) with each expended charge, provided that enough rats are within half a mile of you to be called in this fashion (as determined by the DM). If there aren't enough rats to form a swarm, the charge is wasted. Called swarms move toward the music by the shortest available route but aren't under your control otherwise. The pipes regain 1d3 expended charges daily at dawn.

Whenever a swarm of rats that isn't under another creature's control comes within 30 feet of you while you are playing the pipes, you can make a Charisma check contested by the swarm's Wisdom check. If you lose the contest, the swarm behaves as it normally would and can't be swayed by the pipes' music for the next 24 hours. If you win the contest, the swarm is swayed by the pipes' music and becomes friendly to you and your companions for as long as you continue to play the pipes each round as an action. A friendly swarm obeys your commands. If you issue no commands to a friendly swarm, it defends itself but otherwise takes no actions. If a friendly swarm starts its turn and can't hear the pipes' music, your control over that swarm ends, and the swarm behaves as it normally would and can't be swayed by the pipes' music for the next 24 hours.

PLATE ARMOR OF ETHEREALNESS
Armor (plate), legendary (requires attunement)

While you're wearing this armor, you can speak its command word as an action to gain the effect of the *etherealness* spell, which last for 10 minutes or until you remove the armor or use an action to speak the command word again. This property of the armor can't be used again until the next dawn.

PORTABLE HOLE
Wondrous item, rare

This fine black cloth, soft as silk, is folded up to the dimensions of a handkerchief. It unfolds into a circular sheet 6 feet in diameter.

You can use an action to unfold a *portable hole* and place it on or against a solid surface, whereupon the *portable hole* creates an extradimensional hole 10 feet deep. The cylindrical space within the hole exists

on a different plane, so it can't be used to create open passages. Any creature inside an open *portable hole* can exit the hole by climbing out of it.

You can use an action to close a *portable hole* by taking hold of the edges of the cloth and folding it up. Folding the cloth closes the hole, and any creatures or objects within remain in the extradimensional space. No matter what's in it, the hole weighs next to nothing.

If the hole is folded up, a creature within the hole's extradimensional space can use an action to make a DC 10 Strength check. On a successful check, the creature forces its way out and appears within 5 feet of the *portable hole* or the creature carrying it. A breathing creature within a closed *portable hole* can survive for up to 10 minutes, after which time it begins to suffocate.

Placing a *portable hole* inside an extradimensional space created by a *bag of holding*, *Heward's handy haversack*, or similar item instantly destroys both items and opens a gate to the Astral Plane. The gate originates where the one item was placed inside the other. Any creature within 10 feet of the gate is sucked through it and deposited in a random location on the Astral Plane. The gate then closes. The gate is one-way only and can't be reopened.

POTION OF ANIMAL FRIENDSHIP
Potion, uncommon

When you drink this potion, you can cast the *animal friendship* spell (save DC 13) for 1 hour at will. Agitating this muddy liquid brings little bits into view: a fish scale, a hummingbird tongue, a cat claw, or a squirrel hair.

POTION OF CLAIRVOYANCE
Potion, rare

When you drink this potion, you gain the effect of the *clairvoyance* spell. An eyeball bobs in this yellowish liquid but vanishes when the potion is opened.

POTION OF CLIMBING
Potion, common

When you drink this potion, you gain a climbing speed equal to your walking speed for 1 hour. During this time, you have advantage on Strength (Athletics) checks you make to climb. The potion is separated into brown, silver, and gray layers resembling bands of stone. Shaking the bottle fails to mix the colors.

POTION OF DIMINUTION
Potion, rare

When you drink this potion, you gain the "reduce" effect of the *enlarge/reduce* spell for 1d4 hours (no concentration required). The red in the potion's liquid continuously contracts to a tiny bead and then expands to color the clear liquid around it. Shaking the bottle fails to interrupt this process.

POTION OF FIRE BREATH
Potion, uncommon

After drinking this potion, you can use a bonus action to exhale fire at a target within 30 feet of you. The target must make a DC 13 Dexterity saving throw, taking 4d6 fire damage on a failed save, or half as much damage on a successful one. The effect ends after you exhale the fire three times or when 1 hour has passed.

This potion's orange liquid flickers, and smoke fills the top of the container and wafts out whenever it is opened.

POTION OF FLYING
Potion, very rare

When you drink this potion, you gain a flying speed equal to your walking speed for 1 hour and can hover. If you're in the air when the potion wears off, you fall unless you have some other means of staying aloft. This potion's clear liquid floats at the top of its container and has cloudy white impurities drifting in it.

POTION OF GASEOUS FORM
Potion, rare

When you drink this potion, you gain the effect of the *gaseous form* spell for 1 hour (no concentration required) or until you end the effect as a bonus action. This potion's container seems to hold fog that moves and pours like water.

POTION OF GIANT STRENGTH
Potion, rarity varies

When you drink this potion, your Strength score changes for 1 hour. The type of giant determines the score (see the table below). The potion has no effect on you if your Strength is equal to or greater than that score.

This potion's transparent liquid has floating in it a sliver of fingernail from a giant of the appropriate type. The *potion of frost giant strength* and the *potion of stone giant strength* have the same effect.

Type of Giant	Strength	Rarity
Hill giant	21	Uncommon
Frost/stone giant	23	Rare
Fire giant	25	Rare
Cloud giant	27	Very rare
Storm giant	29	Legendary

POTION OF GROWTH
Potion, uncommon

When you drink this potion, you gain the "enlarge" effect of the *enlarge/reduce* spell for 1d4 hours (no concentration required). The red in the potion's liquid continuously expands from a tiny bead to color the clear liquid around it and then contracts. Shaking the bottle fails to interrupt this process.

POTION OF HEALING
Potion, rarity varies

You regain hit points when you drink this potion. The number of hit points depends on the potion's rarity, as shown in the Potions of Healing table. Whatever its potency, the potion's red liquid glimmers when agitated.

POTIONS OF HEALING

Potion of ...	Rarity	HP Regained
Healing	Common	2d4 + 2
Greater healing	Uncommon	4d4 + 4
Superior healing	Rare	8d4 + 8
Supreme healing	Very rare	10d4 + 20

POTION OF HEROISM
Potion, rare

For 1 hour after drinking it, you gain 10 temporary hit points that last for 1 hour. For the same duration, you are under the effect of the *bless* spell (no concentration required). This blue potion bubbles and steams as if boiling.

POTION OF INVISIBILITY
Potion, very rare

This potion's container looks empty but feels as though it holds liquid. When you drink it, you become invisible for 1 hour. Anything you wear or carry is invisible with you. The effect ends early if you attack or cast a spell.

POTION OF INVULNERABILITY
Potion, rare

For 1 minute after you drink this potion, you have resistance to all damage. The potion's syrupy liquid looks like liquified iron.

POTION OF LONGEVITY
Potion, very rare

When you drink this potion, your physical age is reduced by 1d6 + 6 years, to a minimum of 13 years. Each time you subsequently drink a *potion of longevity*, there is 10 percent cumulative chance that you instead age by 1d6 + 6 years. Suspended in this amber liquid are a scorpion's tail, an adder's fang, a dead spider, and a tiny heart that, against all reason, is still beating. These ingredients vanish when the potion is opened.

POTION OF MIND READING
Potion, rare

When you drink this potion, you gain the effect of the *detect thoughts* spell (save DC 13). The potion's dense, purple liquid has an ovoid cloud of pink floating in it.

POTION OF POISON
Potion, uncommon

This concoction looks, smells, and tastes like a *potion of healing* or other beneficial potion. However, it is actually poison masked by illusion magic. An *identify* spell reveals its true nature.

If you drink it, you take 3d6 poison damage, and you must succeed on a DC 13 Constitution saving throw or be poisoned. At the start of each of your turns while you are poisoned in this way, you take 3d6 poison damage. At the end of each of your turns, you can repeat the saving throw. On a successful save, the poison damage you take on your subsequent turns decreases by 1d6. The poison ends when the damage decreases to 0.

POTION OF RESISTANCE
Potion, uncommon

When you drink this potion, you gain resistance to one type of damage for 1 hour. The DM chooses the type or determines it randomly from the options below.

d10	Damage Type	d10	Damage Type
1	Acid	6	Necrotic
2	Cold	7	Poison
3	Fire	8	Psychic
4	Force	9	Radiant
5	Lightning	10	Thunder

POTION OF SPEED
Potion, very rare

When you drink this potion, you gain the effect of the *haste* spell for 1 minute (no concentration required). The potion's yellow fluid is streaked with black and swirls on its own.

POTION OF VITALITY
Potion, very rare

When you drink this potion, it removes any exhaustion you are suffering and cures any disease or poison affecting you. For the next 24 hours, you regain the maximum number of hit points for any Hit Die you spend. The potion's crimson liquid regularly pulses with dull light, calling to mind a heartbeat.

POTION OF WATER BREATHING
Potion, uncommon

You can breathe underwater for 1 hour after drinking this potion. Its cloudy green fluid smells of the sea and has a jellyfish-like bubble floating in it.

QUAAL'S FEATHER TOKEN
Wondrous item, rare

This tiny object looks like a feather. Different types of feather tokens exist, each with a different single-use effect. The DM chooses the kind of token or determines it randomly.

d100	Feather Token	d100	Feather Token
01–20	Anchor	51–65	Swan boat
21–35	Bird	66–90	Tree
36–50	Fan	91–00	Whip

Anchor. You can use an action to touch the token to a boat or ship. For the next 24 hours, the vessel can't be moved by any means. Touching the token to the vessel again ends the effect. When the effect ends, the token disappears.

Bird. You can use an action to toss the token 5 feet into the air. The token disappears and an enormous, multicolored bird takes its place. The bird has the statistics of a roc (see the *Monster Manual*), but it obeys your simple commands and can't attack. It can carry up to 500 pounds while flying at its maximum speed (16 miles an hour for a maximum of 144 miles per day, with a one-hour rest for every 3 hours of flying), or 1,000 pounds at half that speed. The bird disappears after flying its maximum distance for a day or if it drops to 0 hit points. You can dismiss the bird as an action.

Fan. If you are on a boat or ship, you can use an action to toss the token up to 10 feet in the air. The token disappears, and a giant flapping fan takes its place. The fan floats and creates a wind strong enough to fill the sails of one ship, increasing its speed by 5 miles per hour for 8 hours. You can dismiss the fan as an action.

Swan Boat. You can use an action to touch the token to a body of water at least 60 feet in diameter. The token disappears, and a 50-foot-long, 20-foot-wide boat shaped like a swan takes its place. The boat is self-propelled and moves across water at a speed of 6 miles per hour. You can use an action while on the boat to command it to move or to turn up to 90 degrees. The boat can carry up to thirty-two Medium or smaller creatures. A Large creature counts as four Medium creatures, while a Huge creature counts as nine. The boat remains for 24 hours and then disappears. You can dismiss the boat as an action.

Tree. You must be outdoors to use this token. You can use an action to touch it to an unoccupied space on the ground. The token disappears, and in its place a nonmagical oak tree springs into existence. The tree is 60 feet tall and has a 5-foot-diameter trunk, and its branches at the top spread out in a 20-foot radius.

Whip. You can use an action to throw the token to a point within 10 feet of you. The token disappears, and a floating whip takes its place. You can then use a bonus action to make a melee spell attack against a creature within 10 feet of the whip, with an attack bonus of +9. On a hit, the target takes 1d6 + 5 force damage.

As a bonus action on your turn, you can direct the whip to fly up to 20 feet and repeat the attack against a creature within 10 feet of it. The whip disappears after 1 hour, when you use an action to dismiss it, or when you are incapacitated or die.

QUIVER OF EHLONNA
Wondrous item, uncommon

Each of the quiver's three compartments connects to an extradimensional space that allows the quiver to hold numerous items while never weighing more than 2 pounds. The shortest compartment can hold up to sixty arrows, bolts, or similar objects. The midsize compartment holds up to eighteen javelins or similar objects. The longest compartment holds up to six long objects, such as bows, quarterstaffs, or spears.

You can draw any item the quiver contains as if doing so from a regular quiver or scabbard.

RING OF ANIMAL INFLUENCE
Ring, rare

This ring has 3 charges, and it regains 1d3 expended charges daily at dawn. While wearing the ring, you can use an action to expend 1 of its charges to cast one of the following spells:

- *Animal friendship* (save DC 13)
- *Fear* (save DC 13), targeting only beasts that have an Intelligence of 3 or lower
- *Speak with animals*

QUAAL'S
FEATHER TOKENS

SWAN BOAT TOKEN

FAN TOKEN

ANCHOR TOKEN

TREE TOKEN

BIRD TOKEN

WHIP TOKEN

QUIVER OF
EHLONNA

RING OF ANIMAL INFLUENCE

RING OF
DJINNI SUMMONING

RING OF
FREE ACTION

RING OF AIR
ELEMENTAL COMMAND

RING OF DJINNI SUMMONING

Ring, legendary (requires attunement)

While wearing this ring, you can speak its command word as an action to summon a particular djinni from the Elemental Plane of Air. The djinni appears in an unoccupied space you choose within 120 feet of you. It remains as long as you concentrate (as if concentrating on a spell), to a maximum of 1 hour, or until it drops to 0 hit points. It then returns to its home plane.

While summoned, the djinni is friendly to you and your companions. It obeys any commands you give it, no matter what language you use. If you fail to command it, the djinni defends itself against attackers but takes no other actions.

After the djinni departs, it can't be summoned again for 24 hours, and the ring becomes nonmagical if the djinni dies.

RING OF ELEMENTAL COMMAND

Ring, legendary (requires attunement)

This ring is linked to one of the four Elemental Planes. The DM chooses or randomly determines the linked plane.

While wearing this ring, you have advantage on attack rolls against elementals from the linked plane, and they have disadvantage on attack rolls against you. In addition, you have access to properties based on the linked plane.

The ring has 5 charges. It regains 1d4 + 1 expended charges daily at dawn. Spells cast from the ring have a save DC of 17.

Ring of Air Elemental Command. You can expend 2 of the ring's charges to cast *dominate monster* on an air elemental. In addition, when you fall, you descend 60 feet per round and take no damage from falling. You can also speak and understand Auran.

If you help slay an air elemental while attuned to the ring, you gain access to the following additional properties:

- You have resistance to lightning damage.
- You have a flying speed equal to your walking speed and can hover.
- You can cast the following spells from the ring, expending the necessary number of charges: *chain lightning* (3 charges), *gust of wind* (2 charges), or *wind wall* (1 charge).

Ring of Earth Elemental Command. You can expend 2 of the ring's charges to cast *dominate monster* on an earth elemental. In addition, you can move in difficult terrain that is composed of rubble, rocks, or dirt as if it were normal terrain. You can also speak and understand Terran.

If you help slay an earth elemental while attuned to the ring, you gain access to the following additional properties:

- You have resistance to acid damage.
- You can move through solid earth or rock as if those areas were difficult terrain. If you end your turn there, you are shunted out to the nearest unoccupied space you last occupied.
- You can cast the following spells from the ring, expending the necessary number of charges: *stone shape* (2 charges), *stoneskin* (3 charges), or *wall of stone* (3 charges).

Ring of Fire Elemental Command. You can expend 2 of the ring's charges to cast *dominate monster* on a fire elemental. In addition, you have resistance to fire damage. You can also speak and understand Ignan.

If you help slay a fire elemental while attuned to the ring, you gain access to the following additional properties:

- You are immune to fire damage.
- You can cast the following spells from the ring, expending the necessary number of charges: *burning hands* (1 charge), *fireball* (2 charges), and *wall of fire* (3 charges).

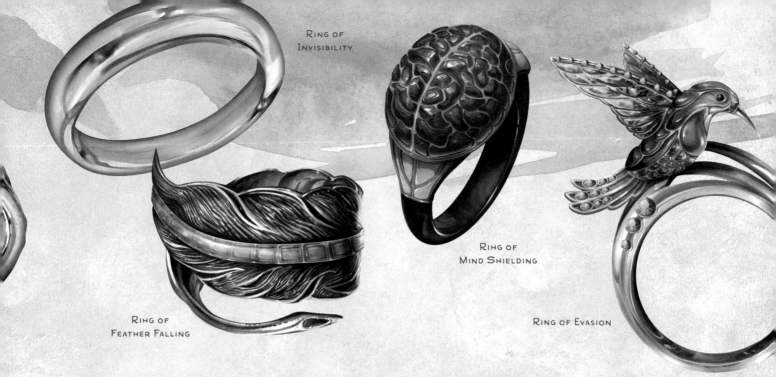

RING OF INVISIBILITY

RING OF MIND SHIELDING

RING OF FEATHER FALLING

RING OF EVASION

Ring of Water Elemental Command. You can expend 2 of the ring's charges to cast *dominate monster* on a water elemental. In addition, you can stand on and walk across liquid surfaces as if they were solid ground. You can also speak and understand Aquan.

If you help slay a water elemental while attuned to the ring, you gain access to the following additional properties:

- You can breathe underwater and have a swimming speed equal to your walking speed.
- You can cast the following spells from the ring, expending the necessary number of charges: *create or destroy water* (1 charge), *control water* (3 charges), *ice storm* (2 charges), or *wall of ice* (3 charges).

RING OF EVASION
Ring, rare (requires attunement)

This ring has 3 charges, and it regains 1d3 expended charges daily at dawn. When you fail a Dexterity saving throw while wearing it, you can use your reaction to expend 1 of its charges to succeed on that saving throw instead.

RING OF FEATHER FALLING
Ring, rare (requires attunement)

When you fall while wearing this ring, you descend 60 feet per round and take no damage from falling.

RING OF FREE ACTION
Ring, rare (requires attunement)

While you wear this ring, difficult terrain doesn't cost you extra movement. In addition, magic can neither reduce your speed nor cause you to be paralyzed or restrained.

RING OF INVISIBILITY
Ring, legendary (requires attunement)

While wearing this ring, you can turn invisible as an action. Anything you are wearing or carrying is invisible with you. You remain invisible until the ring is removed, until you attack or cast a spell, or until you use a bonus action to become visible again.

RING OF JUMPING
Ring, uncommon (requires attunement)

While wearing this ring, you can cast the *jump* spell from it as a bonus action at will, but can target only yourself when you do so.

RING OF MIND SHIELDING
Ring, uncommon (requires attunement)

While wearing this ring, you are immune to magic that allows other creatures to read your thoughts, determine whether you are lying, know your alignment, or know your creature type. Creatures can telepathically communicate with you only if you allow it.

You can use an action to cause the ring to become invisible until you use another action to make it visible, until you remove the ring, or until you die.

If you die while wearing the ring, your soul enters it, unless it already houses a soul. You can remain in the ring or depart for the afterlife. As long as your soul is in the ring, you can telepathically communicate with any creature wearing it. A wearer can't prevent this telepathic communication.

RING OF PROTECTION
Ring, rare (requires attunement)

You gain a +1 bonus to AC and saving throws while wearing this ring.

RING OF REGENERATION
Ring, very rare (requires attunement)

While wearing this ring, you regain 1d6 hit points every 10 minutes, provided that you have at least 1 hit point. If you lose a body part, the ring causes the missing part to regrow and return to full functionality after 1d6 + 1 days if you have at least 1 hit point the whole time.

RING OF PROTECTION

RING OF SPELL STORING

RING OF FIRE RESISTANCE

RING OF REGENERATION

RING OF TELEKINESIS

RING OF RESISTANCE

Ring, rare (requires attunement)

You have resistance to one damage type while wearing this ring. The gem in the ring indicates the type, which the DM chooses or determines randomly.

d10	Damage Type	Gem
1	Acid	Pearl
2	Cold	Tourmaline
3	Fire	Garnet
4	Force	Sapphire
5	Lightning	Citrine
6	Necrotic	Jet
7	Poison	Amethyst
8	Psychic	Jade
9	Radiant	Topaz
10	Thunder	Spinel

RING OF SHOOTING STARS

Ring, very rare (requires attunement outdoors at night)

While wearing this ring in dim light or darkness, you can cast *dancing lights* and *light* from the ring at will. Casting either spell from the ring requires an action.

The ring has 6 charges for the following other properties. The ring regains 1d6 expended charges daily at dawn.

Faerie Fire. You can expend 1 charge as an action to cast *faerie fire* from the ring.

Ball Lightning. You can expend 2 charges as an action to create one to four 3-foot-diameter spheres of lightning. The more spheres you create, the less powerful each sphere is individually.

Each sphere appears in an unoccupied space you can see within 120 feet of you. The spheres last as long as you concentrate (as if concentrating on a spell), up to 1 minute. Each sphere sheds dim light in a 30-foot radius.

As a bonus action, you can move each sphere up to 30 feet, but no farther than 120 feet away from you. When a creature other than you comes within 5 feet of a

sphere, the sphere discharges lightning at that creature and disappears. That creature must make a DC 15 Dexterity saving throw. On a failed save, the creature takes lightning damage based on the number of spheres you created.

Spheres	Lightning Damage
4	2d4
3	2d6
2	5d4
1	4d12

Shooting Stars. You can expend 1 to 3 charges as an action. For every charge you expend, you launch a glowing mote of light from the ring at a point you can see within 60 feet of you. Each creature within a 15-foot cube originating from that point is showered in sparks and must make a DC 15 Dexterity saving throw, taking 5d4 fire damage on a failed save, or half as much damage on a successful one.

RING OF SPELL STORING

Ring, rare (requires attunement)

This ring stores spells cast into it, holding them until the attuned wearer uses them. The ring can store up to 5 levels worth of spells at a time. When found, it contains 1d6 − 1 levels of stored spells chosen by the DM.

Any creature can cast a spell of 1st through 5th level into the ring by touching the ring as the spell is cast. The spell has no effect, other than to be stored in the ring. If the ring can't hold the spell, the spell is expended without effect. The level of the slot used to cast the spell determines how much space it uses.

While wearing this ring, you can cast any spell stored in it. The spell uses the slot level, spell save DC, spell attack bonus, and spellcasting ability of the original caster, but is otherwise treated as if you cast the spell. The spell cast from the ring is no longer stored in it, freeing up space.

RING OF
THREE WISHES

RING OF
SPELL TURNING

RING OF
SHOOTING STARS

RING OF
WATER WALKING

RING OF THE RAM

RING OF
X-RAY VISION

RING OF SPELL TURNING
Ring, legendary (requires attunement)

While wearing this ring, you have advantage on saving throws against any spell that targets only you (not in an area of effect). In addition, if you roll a 20 for the save and the spell is 7th level or lower, the spell has no effect on you and instead targets the caster, using the slot level, spell save DC, attack bonus, and spellcasting ability of the caster.

RING OF SWIMMING
Ring, uncommon

You have a swimming speed of 40 feet while wearing this ring.

RING OF TELEKINESIS
Ring, very rare (requires attunement)

While wearing this ring, you can cast the *telekinesis* spell at will, but you can target only objects that aren't being worn or carried.

RING OF THE RAM
Ring, rare (requires attunement)

This ring has 3 charges, and it regains 1d3 expended charges daily at dawn. While wearing the ring, you can use an action to expend 1 to 3 of its charges to attack one creature you can see within 60 feet of you. The ring produces a spectral ram's head and makes its attack roll with a +7 bonus. On a hit, for each charge you spend, the target takes 2d10 force damage and is pushed 5 feet away from you.

Alternatively, you can expend 1 to 3 of the ring's charges as an action to try to break an object you can see within 60 feet of you that isn't being worn or carried. The ring makes a Strength check with a +5 bonus for each charge you spend.

RING OF THREE WISHES
Ring, legendary

While wearing this ring, you can use an action to expend 1 of its 3 charges to cast the *wish* spell from

it. The ring becomes nonmagical when you use the last charge.

RING OF WARMTH
Ring, uncommon (requires attunement)

While wearing this ring, you have resistance to cold damage. In addition, you and everything you wear and carry are unharmed by temperatures as low as −50 degrees Fahrenheit.

RING OF WATER WALKING
Ring, uncommon

While wearing this ring, you can stand on and move across any liquid surface as if it were solid ground.

RING OF X-RAY VISION
Ring, rare (requires attunement)

While wearing this ring, you can use an action to speak its command word. When you do so, you can see into and through solid matter for 1 minute. This vision has a radius of 30 feet. To you, solid objects within that radius appear transparent and don't prevent light from passing through them. The vision can penetrate 1 foot of stone, 1 inch of common metal, or up to 3 feet of wood or dirt. Thicker substances block the vision, as does a thin sheet of lead.

Whenever you use the ring again before taking a long rest, you must succeed on a DC 15 Constitution saving throw or gain one level of exhaustion.

ROBE OF EYES
Wondrous item, rare (requires attunement)

This robe is adorned with eyelike patterns. While you wear the robe, you gain the following benefits:

- The robe lets you see in all directions, and you have advantage on Wisdom (Perception) checks that rely on sight.
- You have darkvision out to a range of 120 feet.
- You can see invisible creatures and objects, as well as see into the Ethereal Plane, out to a range of 120 feet.

ROBE OF EYES

ROBE OF STARS

The eyes on the robe can't be closed or averted. Although you can close or avert your own eyes, you are never considered to be doing so while wearing this robe.

A *light* spell cast on the robe or a *daylight* spell cast within 5 feet of the robe causes you to be blinded for 1 minute. At the end of each of your turns, you can make a Constitution saving throw (DC 11 for *light* or DC 15 for *daylight*), ending the blindness on a success.

ROBE OF SCINTILLATING COLORS

Wondrous item, very rare (requires attunement)

This robe has 3 charges, and it regains 1d3 expended charges daily at dawn. While you wear it, you can use an action and expend 1 charge to cause the garment to display a shifting pattern of dazzling hues until the end of your next turn. During this time, the robe sheds bright light in a 30-foot radius and dim light for an additional 30 feet. Creatures that can see you have disadvantage on attack rolls against you. In addition, any creature in the bright light that can see you when the robe's power is activated must succeed on a DC 15 Wisdom saving throw or become stunned until the effect ends.

ROBE OF STARS

Wondrous item, very rare (requires attunement)

This black or dark blue robe is embroidered with small white or silver stars. You gain a +1 bonus to saving throws while you wear it.

Six stars, located on the robe's upper front portion, are particularly large. While wearing this robe, you can use an action to pull off one of the stars and use it to cast *magic missile* as a 5th-level spell. Daily at dusk, 1d6 removed stars reappear on the robe.

While you wear the robe, you can use an action to enter the Astral Plane along with everything you are wearing and carrying. You remain there until you use an action to return to the plane you were on. You reappear in the last space you occupied, or if that space is occupied, the nearest unoccupied space.

ROBE OF THE ARCHMAGI

Wondrous item, legendary (requires attunement by a sorcerer, warlock, or wizard)

This elegant garment is made from exquisite cloth of white, gray, or black and adorned with silvery runes. The robe's color corresponds to the alignment for which the item was created. A white robe was made for good, gray for neutral, and black for evil. You can't attune to a *robe of the archmagi* that doesn't correspond to your alignment.

You gain these benefits while wearing the robe:

- If you aren't wearing armor, your base Armor Class is 15 + your Dexterity modifier.
- You have advantage on saving throws against spells and other magical effects.
- Your spell save DC and spell attack bonus each increase by 2.

ROBE OF USEFUL ITEMS
Wondrous item, uncommon

This robe has cloth patches of various shapes and colors covering it. While wearing the robe, you can use an action to detach one of the patches, causing it to become the object or creature it represents. Once the last patch is removed, the robe becomes an ordinary garment.

The robe has two of each of the following patches:

- Dagger
- Bullseye lantern (filled and lit)
- Steel mirror
- 10-foot pole
- Hempen rope (50 feet, coiled)
- Sack

In addition, the robe has 4d4 other patches. The DM chooses the patches or determines them randomly.

d100	Patch
01–08	Bag of 100 gp
09–15	Silver coffer (1 foot long, 6 inches wide and deep) worth 500 gp
16–22	Iron door (up to 10 feet wide and 10 feet high, barred on one side of your choice), which you can place in an opening you can reach; it conforms to fit the opening, attaching and hinging itself
23–30	10 gems worth 100 gp each
31–44	Wooden ladder (24 feet long)
45–51	A **riding horse** with saddle bags (see the *Monster Manual* for statistics)
52–59	Pit (a cube 10 feet on a side), which you can place on the ground within 10 feet of you
60–68	4 *potions of healing*
69–75	Rowboat (12 feet long)
76–83	*Spell scroll* containing one spell of 1st to 3rd level
84–90	2 **mastiffs** (see the *Monster Manual* for statistics)
91–96	Window (2 feet by 4 feet, up to 2 feet deep), which you can place on a vertical surface you can reach
97–00	Portable ram

ROD OF ABSORPTION
Rod, very rare (requires attunement)

While holding this rod, you can use your reaction to absorb a spell that is targeting only you and not with an area of effect. The absorbed spell's effect is canceled, and the spell's energy—not the spell itself—is stored in the rod. The energy has the same level as the spell when it was cast. The rod can absorb and store up to 50 levels of energy over the course of its existence. Once the rod absorbs 50 levels of energy, it can't absorb more. If you are targeted by a spell that the rod can't store, the rod has no effect on that spell.

When you become attuned to the rod, you know how many levels of energy the rod has absorbed over the course of its existence, and how many levels of spell energy it currently has stored.

If you are a spellcaster holding the rod, you can convert energy stored in it into spell slots to cast spells you have prepared or know. You can create spell slots only of a level equal to or lower than your own spell

ROD OF ABSORPTION

ROBE OF THE ARCHMAGI

ROBE OF USEFUL ITEMS

Rod of
Rulership

Rod of
Lordly Might

Rod of
Resurrection

slots, up to a maximum of 5th level. You use the stored levels in place of your slots, but otherwise cast the spell as normal. For example, you can use 3 levels stored in the rod as a 3rd-level spell slot.

A newly found rod has 1d10 levels of spell energy stored in it already. A rod that can no longer absorb spell energy and has no energy remaining becomes nonmagical.

ROD OF ALERTNESS
Rod, very rare (requires attunement)

This rod has a flanged head and the following properties.

Alertness. While holding the rod, you have advantage on Wisdom (Perception) checks and on rolls for initiative.

Spells. While holding the rod, you can use an action to cast one of the following spells from it: *detect evil and good*, *detect magic*, *detect poison and disease*, or *see invisibility*.

Protective Aura. As an action, you can plant the haft end of the rod in the ground, whereupon the rod's head sheds bright light in a 60-foot radius and dim light for an additional 60 feet. While in that bright light, you and any creature that is friendly to you gain a +1 bonus to AC and saving throws and can sense the location of any invisible hostile creature that is also in the bright light.

The rod's head stops glowing and the effect ends after 10 minutes, or when a creature uses an action to pull the rod from the ground. This property can't be used again until the next dawn.

ROD OF LORDLY MIGHT
Rod, legendary (requires attunement)

This rod has a flanged head, and it functions as a magic mace that grants a +3 bonus to attack and damage rolls made with it. The rod has properties associated with six different buttons that are set in a row along the haft. It has three other properties as well, detailed below.

Six Buttons. You can press one of the rod's six buttons as a bonus action. A button's effect lasts until you push a different button or until you push the same button again, which causes the rod to revert to its normal form.

If you press **button 1**, the rod becomes a *flame tongue*, as a fiery blade sprouts from the end opposite the rod's flanged head.

If you press **button 2**, the rod's flanged head folds down and two crescent-shaped blades spring out, transforming the rod into a magic battleaxe that grants a +3 bonus to attack and damage rolls made with it.

If you press **button 3**, the rod's flanged head folds down, a spear point springs from the rod's tip, and the rod's handle lengthens into a 6-foot haft, transforming the rod into a magic spear that grants a +3 bonus to attack and damage rolls made with it.

If you press **button 4**, the rod transforms into a climbing pole up to 50 feet long, as you specify. In surfaces as hard as granite, a spike at the bottom and three hooks at the top anchor the pole. Horizontal bars 3 inches long fold out from the sides, 1 foot apart, forming a ladder. The pole can bear up to 4,000 pounds.

More weight or lack of solid anchoring causes the rod to revert to its normal form.

If you press **button 5**, the rod transforms into a handheld battering ram and grants its user a +10 bonus to Strength checks made to break through doors, barricades, and other barriers.

If you press **button 6**, the rod assumes or remains in its normal form and indicates magnetic north. (Nothing happens if this function of the rod is used in a location that has no magnetic north.) The rod also gives you knowledge of your approximate depth beneath the ground or your height above it.

Drain Life. When you hit a creature with a melee attack using the rod, you can force the target to make a DC 17 Constitution saving throw. On a failure, the target takes an extra 4d6 necrotic damage, and you regain a number of hit points equal to half that necrotic damage. This property can't be used again until the next dawn.

Paralyze. When you hit a creature with a melee attack using the rod, you can force the target to make a DC 17 Strength saving throw. On a failure, the target is paralyzed for 1 minute. The target can repeat the saving throw at the end of each of its turns, ending the effect on a success. This property can't be used again until the next dawn.

Terrify. While holding the rod, you can use an action to force each creature you can see within 30 feet of you to make a DC 17 Wisdom saving throw. On a failure, a target is frightened of you for 1 minute. A frightened target can repeat the saving throw at the end of each of its turns, ending the effect on itself on a success. This property can't be used again until the next dawn.

ROD OF THE PACT KEEPER
Rod, uncommon (+1), rare (+2), or very rare (+3)
(requires attunement by a warlock)

While holding this rod, you gain a bonus to spell attack rolls and to the saving throw DCs of your warlock spells. The bonus is determined by the rod's rarity.

In addition, you can regain one warlock spell slot as an action while holding the rod. You can't use this property again until you finish a long rest.

ROD OF RESURRECTION
Rod, legendary (requires attunement by a cleric, druid, or paladin)

The rod has 5 charges. While you hold it, you can use an action to cast one of the following spells from it: *heal* (expends 1 charge) or *resurrection* (expends 5 charges).

The rod regains 1 expended charge daily at dawn. If the rod is reduced to 0 charges, roll a d20. On a 1, the rod disappears in a burst of radiance.

ROD OF RULERSHIP
Rod, rare (requires attunement)

You can use an action to present the rod and command obedience from each creature of your choice that you can see within 120 feet of you. Each target must succeed on a DC 15 Wisdom saving throw or be charmed by you for 8 hours. While charmed in this way, the creature regards you as its trusted leader. If harmed by you or your companions, or commanded to do something contrary to its nature, a target ceases to be charmed in this way. The rod can't be used again until the next dawn.

ROD OF SECURITY
Rod, very rare

While holding this rod, you can use an action to activate it. The rod then instantly transports you and up to 199 other willing creatures you can see to a paradise that exists in an extraplanar space. You choose the form that the paradise takes. It could be a tranquil garden, lovely glade, cheery tavern, immense palace, tropical island, fantastic carnival, or whatever else you can imagine. Regardless of its nature, the paradise contains enough water and food to sustain its visitors. Everything else that can be interacted with inside the extraplanar space can exist only there. For example, a flower picked from a garden in the paradise disappears if it is taken outside the extraplanar space.

For each hour spent in the paradise, a visitor regains hit points as if it had spent 1 Hit Die. Also, creatures don't age while in the paradise, although time passes normally. Visitors can remain in the paradise for up to 200 days divided by the number of creatures present (round down).

When the time runs out or you use an action to end it, all visitors reappear in the location they occupied when you activated the rod, or an unoccupied space nearest that location. The rod can't be used again until ten days have passed.

ROPE OF CLIMBING
Wondrous item, uncommon

This 60-foot length of silk rope weighs 3 pounds and can hold up to 3,000 pounds. If you hold one end of the rope and use an action to speak the command word, the rope animates. As a bonus action, you can command the other end to move toward a destination you choose. That end moves 10 feet on your turn when you first command it and 10 feet on each of your turns until reaching its destination, up to its maximum length away, or until you tell it to stop. You can also tell the rope to fasten itself securely to an object or to unfasten itself, to knot or unknot itself, or to coil itself for carrying.

If you tell the rope to knot, large knots appear at 1-foot intervals along the rope. While knotted, the rope shortens to a 50-foot length and grants advantage on checks made to climb it.

The rope has AC 20 and 20 hit points. It regains 1 hit point every 5 minutes as long as it has at least 1 hit point. If the rope drops to 0 hit points, it is destroyed.

ROPE OF ENTANGLEMENT
Wondrous item, rare

This rope is 30 feet long and weighs 3 pounds. If you hold one end of the rope and use an action to speak its command word, the other end darts forward to entangle a creature you can see within 20 feet of you. The target must succeed on a DC 15 Dexterity saving throw or become restrained.

You can release the creature by using a bonus action to speak a second command word. A target restrained

ROPE OF
ENTANGLEMENT

SENDING STONES

SCARAB OF
PROTECTION

by the rope can use an action to make a DC 15 Strength or Dexterity check (target's choice). On a success, the creature is no longer restrained by the rope.

The rope has AC 20 and 20 hit points. It regains 1 hit point every 5 minutes as long as it has at least 1 hit point. If the rope drops to 0 hit points, it is destroyed.

SADDLE OF THE CAVALIER
Wondrous item, uncommon

While in this saddle on a mount, you can't be dismounted against your will if you're conscious, and attack rolls against the mount have disadvantage.

SCARAB OF PROTECTION
Wondrous item, legendary (requires attunement)

If you hold this beetle-shaped medallion in your hand for 1 round, an inscription appears on its surface revealing its magical nature. It provides two benefits while it is on your person:

- You have advantage on saving throws against spells.
- The scarab has 12 charges. If you fail a saving throw against a necromancy spell or a harmful effect originating from an undead creature, you can use your reaction to expend 1 charge and turn the failed save into a successful one. The scarab crumbles into powder and is destroyed when its last charge is expended.

SCIMITAR OF SPEED
Weapon (scimitar), very rare (requires attunement)

You gain a +2 bonus to attack and damage rolls made with this magic weapon. In addition, you can make one attack with it as a bonus action on each of your turns.

SCROLL OF PROTECTION
Scroll, rare

Each *scroll of protection* works against a specific type of creature chosen by the DM or determined randomly by rolling on the following table.

d100	Creature Type	d100	Creature Type
01–10	Aberrations	41–50	Fey
11–20	Beasts	51–75	Fiends
21–30	Celestials	76–80	Plants
31–40	Elementals	81–00	Undead

Using an action to read the scroll encloses you in an invisible barrier that extends from you to form a 5-foot-radius, 10-foot-high cylinder. For 5 minutes, this barrier prevents creatures of the specified type from entering or affecting anything within the cylinder.

The cylinder moves with you and remains centered on you. However, if you move in such a way that a creature of the specified type would be inside the cylinder, the effect ends.

A creature can attempt to overcome the barrier by using an action to make a DC 15 Charisma check. On a success, the creature ceases to be affected by the barrier.

SENDING STONES
Wondrous item, uncommon

Sending stones come in pairs, with each smooth stone carved to match the other so the pairing is easily recognized. While you touch one stone, you can use an action to cast the *sending* spell from it. The target is the bearer of the other stone. If no creature bears the other stone, you know that fact as soon as you use the stone and don't cast the spell.

Once *sending* is cast through the stones, they can't be used again until the next dawn. If one of the stones in a pair is destroyed, the other one becomes nonmagical.

SENTINEL SHIELD
Armor (shield), uncommon

While holding this shield, you have advantage on initiative rolls and Wisdom (Perception) checks. The shield is emblazoned with a symbol of an eye.

**SLIPPERS OF
SPIDER CLIMBING**

**SHIELD OF MISSILE
ATTRACTION**

**SPELLGUARD
SHIELD**

SHIELD, +1, +2, OR +3

*Armor (shield), uncommon (+1), rare (+2), or very
rare (+3)*

While holding this shield, you have a bonus to AC
determined by the shield's rarity. This bonus is in
addition to the shield's normal bonus to AC.

SHIELD OF MISSILE ATTRACTION

Armor (shield), rare (requires attunement)

While holding this shield, you have resistance to
damage from ranged weapon attacks.

   Curse. This shield is cursed. Attuning to it curses
you until you are targeted by the *remove curse* spell
or similar magic. Removing the shield fails to end the
curse on you. Whenever a ranged weapon attack is
made against a target within 10 feet of you, the curse
causes you to become the target instead.

SLIPPERS OF SPIDER CLIMBING

Wondrous item, uncommon (requires attunement)

While you wear these light shoes, you can move up,
down, and across vertical surfaces and upside down
along ceilings, while leaving your hands free. You have
a climbing speed equal to your walking speed. However,
the slippers don't allow you to move this way on a
slippery surface, such as one covered by ice or oil.

SOVEREIGN GLUE

Wondrous item, legendary

This viscous, milky-white substance can form a
permanent adhesive bond between any two objects.
It must be stored in a jar or flask that has been coated
inside with *oil of slipperiness*. When found, a container
contains 1d6 + 1 ounces.

   One ounce of the glue can cover a 1-foot square
surface. The glue takes 1 minute to set. Once it has
done so, the bond it creates can be broken only by the
application of *universal solvent* or *oil of etherealness*, or
with a *wish* spell.

SPELL SCROLL

Scroll, varies

A *spell scroll* bears the words of a single spell, written in
a mystical cipher. If the spell is on your class's spell list,
you can use an action to read the scroll and cast its spell
without having to provide any of the spell's components.
Otherwise, the scroll is unintelligible.

   If the spell is on your class's spell list but of a higher
level than you can normally cast, you must make an
ability check using your spellcasting ability to determine
whether you cast it successfully. The DC equals 10 + the
spell's level. On a failed check, the spell disappears from
the scroll with no other effect.

   Once the spell is cast, the words on the scroll fade,
and the scroll itself crumbles to dust.

   The level of the spell on the scroll determines the
spell's saving throw DC and attack bonus, as well as the
scroll's rarity, as shown in the Spell Scroll table.

SPELL SCROLL

Spell Level	Rarity	Save DC	Attack Bonus
Cantrip	Common	13	+5
1st	Common	13	+5
2nd	Uncommon	13	+5
3rd	Uncommon	15	+7
4th	Rare	15	+7
5th	Rare	17	+9
6th	Very rare	17	+9
7th	Very rare	18	+10
8th	Very rare	18	+10
9th	Legendary	19	+11

   A wizard spell on a *spell scroll* can be copied just
as spells in spellbooks can be copied. When a spell is
copied from a *spell scroll*, the copier must succeed on
an Intelligence (Arcana) check with a DC equal to 10
+ the spell's level. If the check succeeds, the spell is

successfully copied. Whether the check succeeds or fails, the *spell scroll* is destroyed.

Spellguard Shield
Armor (shield), very rare (requires attunement)

While holding this shield, you have advantage on saving throws against spells and other magical effects, and spell attacks have disadvantage against you.

Sphere of Annihilation
Wondrous item, legendary

This 2-foot-diameter black sphere is a hole in the multiverse, hovering in space and stabilized by a magical field surrounding it.

The sphere obliterates all matter it passes through and all matter that passes through it. Artifacts are the exception. Unless an artifact is susceptible to damage from a *sphere of annihilation*, it passes through the sphere unscathed. Anything else that touches the sphere but isn't wholly engulfed and obliterated by it takes 4d10 force damage.

The sphere is stationary until someone controls it. If you are within 60 feet of an uncontrolled sphere, you can use an action to make a DC 25 Intelligence (Arcana) check. On a success, the sphere levitates in one direction of your choice, up to a number of feet equal to 5 × your Intelligence modifier (minimum 5 feet). On a failure, the sphere moves 10 feet toward you. A creature whose space the sphere enters must succeed on a DC 13 Dexterity saving throw or be touched by it, taking 4d10 force damage.

If you attempt to control a sphere that is under another creature's control, you make an Intelligence (Arcana) check contested by the other creature's Intelligence (Arcana) check. The winner of the contest gains control of the sphere and can levitate it as normal.

If the sphere comes into contact with a planar portal, such as that created by the *gate* spell, or an extradimensional space, such as that within a *portable hole*, the DM determines randomly what happens, using the following table.

d100	Result
01–50	The sphere is destroyed.
51–85	The sphere moves through the portal or into the extradimensional space.
86–00	A spatial rift sends each creature and object within 180 feet of the sphere, including the sphere, to a random plane of existence.

Staff of Charming
Staff, rare (requires attunement by a bard, cleric, druid, sorcerer, warlock, or wizard)

While holding this staff, you can use an action to expend 1 of its 10 charges to cast *charm person, command, or comprehend languages* from it using your spell save DC. The staff can also be used as a magic quarterstaff.

If you are holding the staff and fail a saving throw against an enchantment spell that targets only you, you can turn your failed save into a successful one. You can't use this property of the staff again until the next

STAFF OF FIRE

STAFF OF CHARMING

SOVEREIGN GLUE

dawn. If you succeed on a save against an enchantment spell that targets only you, with or without the staff's intervention, you can use your reaction to expend 1 charge from the staff and turn the spell back on its caster as if you had cast the spell.

The staff regains 1d8 + 2 expended charges daily at dawn. If you expend the last charge, roll a d20. On a 1, the staff becomes a nonmagical quarterstaff.

Staff of Fire
Staff, very rare (requires attunement by a druid, sorcerer, warlock, or wizard)

You have resistance to fire damage while you hold this staff.

The staff has 10 charges. While holding it, you can use an action to expend 1 or more of its charges to cast one of the following spells from it, using your spell save DC: *burning hands* (1 charge), *fireball* (3 charges), or *wall of fire* (4 charges).

The staff regains 1d6 + 4 expended charges daily at dawn. If you expend the last charge, roll a d20. On a 1, the staff blackens, crumbles into cinders, and is destroyed.

STAFF OF POWER

STAFF OF FROST

STAFF OF SWARMING INSECTS

STAFF OF HEALING

STAFF OF THE MAGI

STAFF OF FROST

Staff, very rare (requires attunement by a druid, sorcerer, warlock, or wizard)

You have resistance to cold damage while you hold this staff.

The staff has 10 charges. While holding it, you can use an action to expend 1 or more of its charges to cast one of the following spells from it, using your spell save DC: *cone of cold* (5 charges), *fog cloud* (1 charge), *ice storm* (4 charges), or *wall of ice* (4 charges).

The staff regains 1d6 + 4 expended charges daily at dawn. If you expend the last charge, roll a d20. On a 1, the staff turns to water and is destroyed.

STAFF OF HEALING

Staff, rare (requires attunement by a bard, cleric, or druid)

This staff has 10 charges. While holding it, you can use an action to expend 1 or more of its charges to cast one of the following spells from it, using your spell save DC and spellcasting ability modifier: *cure wounds* (1 charge per spell level, up to 4th), *lesser restoration* (2 charges), or *mass cure wounds* (5 charges).

The staff regains 1d6 + 4 expended charges daily at dawn. If you expend the last charge, roll a d20. On a 1, the staff vanishes in a flash of light, lost forever.

STAFF OF POWER

Staff, very rare (requires attunement by a sorcerer, warlock, or wizard)

This staff can be wielded as a magic quarterstaff that grants a +2 bonus to attack and damage rolls made with it. While holding it, you gain a +2 bonus to Armor Class, saving throws, and spell attack rolls.

The staff has 20 charges for the following properties. The staff regains 2d8 + 4 expended charges daily at dawn. If you expend the last charge, roll a d20. On a 1, the staff retains its +2 bonus to attack and damage rolls but loses all other properties. On a 20, the staff regains 1d8 + 2 charges.

Power Strike. When you hit with a melee attack using the staff, you can expend 1 charge to deal an extra 1d6 force damage to the target.

Spells. While holding this staff, you can use an action to expend 1 or more of its charges to cast one of the following spells from it, using your spell save DC and spell attack bonus: *cone of cold* (5 charges), *fireball* (5th-level version, 5 charges), *globe of invulnerability* (6 charges), *hold monster* (5 charges), *levitate* (2 charges), *lightning bolt* (5th-level version, 5 charges), *magic missile* (1 charge), *ray of enfeeblement* (1 charge), or *wall of force* (5 charges).

Retributive Strike. You can use an action to break the staff over your knee or against a solid surface, performing a retributive strike. The staff is destroyed and releases its remaining magic in an explosion that expands to fill a 30-foot-radius sphere centered on it.

You have a 50 percent chance to instantly travel to a random plane of existence, avoiding the explosion. If you fail to avoid the effect, you take force damage equal to 16 × the number of charges in the staff. Every other creature in the area must make a DC 17 Dexterity saving throw. On a failed save, a creature takes an amount of damage based on how far away it is from the point of origin, as shown in the following table. On a successful save, a creature takes half as much damage.

Distance from Origin	Damage
10 ft. away or closer	8 × the number of charges in the staff
11 to 20 ft. away	6 × the number of charges in the staff
21 to 30 ft. away	4 × the number of charges in the staff

STAFF OF STRIKING
Staff, very rare (requires attunement)

This staff can be wielded as a magic quarterstaff that grants a +3 bonus to attack and damage rolls made with it.

The staff has 10 charges. When you hit with a melee attack using it, you can expend up to 3 of its charges. For each charge you expend, the target takes an extra 1d6 force damage. The staff regains 1d6 + 4 expended charges daily at dawn. If you expend the last charge, roll a d20. On a 1, the staff becomes a nonmagical quarterstaff.

STAFF OF SWARMING INSECTS
Staff, rare (requires attunement by a bard, cleric, druid, sorcerer, warlock, or wizard)

This staff has 10 charges and regains 1d6 + 4 expended charges daily at dawn. If you expend the last charge, roll a d20. On a 1, a swarm of insects consumes and destroys the staff, then disperses.

Spells. While holding the staff, you can use an action to expend some of its charges to cast one of the following spells from it, using your spell save DC: *giant insect* (4 charges) or *insect plague* (5 charges).

Insect Cloud. While holding the staff, you can use an action and expend 1 charge to cause a swarm of harmless flying insects to spread out in a 30-foot radius from you. The insects remain for 10 minutes, making the area heavily obscured for creatures other than you. The swarm moves with you, remaining centered on you. A wind of at least 10 miles per hour disperses the swarm and ends the effect.

STAFF OF THE ADDER
Staff, uncommon (requires attunement by a cleric, druid, or warlock)

You can use a bonus action to speak this staff's command word and make the head of the staff become that of an animate poisonous snake for 1 minute. By using another bonus action to speak the command word again, you return the staff to its normal inanimate form.

You can make a melee attack using the snake head, which has a reach of 5 feet. Your proficiency bonus applies to the attack roll. On a hit, the target takes 1d6 piercing damage and must succeed on a DC 15 Constitution saving throw or take 3d6 poison damage.

The snake head can be attacked while it is animate. It has an Armor Class of 15 and 20 hit points. If the head drops to 0 hit points, the staff is destroyed. As long as it's not destroyed, the staff regains all lost hit points when it reverts to its inanimate form.

STAFF OF THE MAGI
Staff, legendary (requires attunement by a sorcerer, warlock, or wizard)

This staff can be wielded as a magic quarterstaff that grants a +2 bonus to attack and damage rolls made with it. While you hold it, you gain a +2 bonus to spell attack rolls.

The staff has 50 charges for the following properties. It regains 4d6 + 2 expended charges daily at dawn. If you expend the last charge, roll a d20. On a 20, the staff regains 1d12 + 1 charges.

Spell Absorption. While holding the staff, you have advantage on saving throws against spells. In addition, you can use your reaction when another creature casts a spell that targets only you. If you do, the staff absorbs the magic of the spell, canceling its effect and gaining a number of charges equal to the absorbed spell's level. However, if doing so brings the staff's total number of charges above 50, the staff explodes as if you activated its retributive strike (see below).

Spells. While holding the staff, you can use an action to expend some of its charges to cast one of the following spells from it, using your spell save DC and spellcasting ability: *conjure elemental* (7 charges), *dispel magic* (3 charges), *fireball* (7th-level version, 7 charges), *flaming sphere* (2 charges), *ice storm* (4 charges), *invisibility* (2 charges), *knock* (2 charges), *lightning bolt* (7th-level version, 7 charges), *passwall* (5 charges), *plane shift* (7 charges), *telekinesis* (5 charges), *wall of fire* (4 charges), or *web* (2 charges).

You can also use an action to cast one of the following spells from the staff without using any charges: *arcane lock, detect magic, enlarge/reduce, light, mage hand,* or *protection from evil and good.*

Retributive Strike. You can use an action to break the staff over your knee or against a solid surface, performing a retributive strike. The staff is destroyed and releases its remaining magic in an explosion that expands to fill a 30-foot-radius sphere centered on it.

You have a 50 percent chance to instantly travel to a random plane of existence, avoiding the explosion. If you fail to avoid the effect, you take force damage equal to 16 × the number of charges in the staff. Every other creature in the area must make a DC 17 Dexterity saving throw. On a failed save, a creature takes an amount of damage based on how far away it is from the point of origin, as shown in the following table. On a successful save, a creature takes half as much damage.

Distance from Origin	Damage
10 ft. away or closer	8 × the number of charges in the staff
11 to 20 ft. away	6 × the number of charges in the staff
21 to 30 ft. away	4 × the number of charges in the staff

STAFF OF THE PYTHON

Staff, uncommon (requires attunement by a cleric, druid, or warlock)

You can use an action to speak this staff's command word and throw the staff on the ground within 10 feet of you. The staff becomes a giant constrictor snake (see the *Monster Manual* for statistics) under your control and acts on its own initiative count. By using a bonus action to speak the command word again, you return the staff to its normal form in a space formerly occupied by the snake.

On your turn, you can mentally command the snake if it is within 60 feet of you and you aren't incapacitated. You decide what action the snake takes and where it moves during its next turn, or you can issue it a general command, such as to attack your enemies or guard a location.

If the snake is reduced to 0 hit points, it dies and reverts to its staff form. The staff then shatters and is destroyed. If the snake reverts to staff form before losing all its hit points, it regains all of them.

STAFF OF THE WOODLANDS

Staff, rare (requires attunement by a druid)

This staff can be wielded as a magic quarterstaff that grants a +2 bonus to attack and damage rolls made with it. While holding it, you have a +2 bonus to spell attack rolls.

The staff has 10 charges for the following properties. It regains 1d6 + 4 expended charges daily at dawn. If you expend the last charge, roll a d20. On a 1, the staff loses its properties and becomes a nonmagical quarterstaff.

Spells. You can use an action to expend 1 or more of the staff's charges to cast one of the following spells from it, using your spell save DC: *animal friendship* (1 charge), *awaken* (5 charges), *barkskin* (2 charges), *locate animals or plants* (2 charges), *speak with animals* (1 charge), *speak with plants* (3 charges), or *wall of thorns* (6 charges).

You can also use an action to cast the *pass without trace* spell from the staff without using any charges.

Tree Form. You can use an action to plant one end of the staff in fertile earth and expend 1 charge to transform the staff into a healthy tree. The tree is 60 feet tall and has a 5-foot-diameter trunk, and its branches at the top spread out in a 20-foot radius. The tree appears ordinary but radiates a faint aura of transmutation magic if targeted by *detect magic*. While touching the tree and using another action to speak its command word, you return the staff to its normal form. Any creature in the tree falls when it reverts to a staff.

STAFF OF THUNDER AND LIGHTNING

Staff, very rare (requires attunement)

This staff can be wielded as a magic quarterstaff that grants a +2 bonus to attack and damage rolls made with it. It also has the following additional properties. When one of these properties is used, it can't be used again until the next dawn.

STAFF OF THE PYTHON

STAFF OF THE ADDER

SUN BLADE

STONE OF GOOD LUCK

STAFF OF THE WOODLANDS

STAFF OF WITHERING

STAFF OF THUNDER
AND LIGHTNING

STONE OF CONTROLLING
EARTH ELEMENTALS

Lightning. When you hit with a melee attack using the staff, you can cause the target to take an extra 2d6 lightning damage.

Thunder. When you hit with a melee attack using the staff, you can cause the staff to emit a crack of thunder, audible out to 300 feet. The target you hit must succeed on a DC 17 Constitution saving throw or become stunned until the end of your next turn.

Lightning Strike. You can use an action to cause a bolt of lightning to leap from the staff's tip in a line that is 5 feet wide and 120 feet long. Each creature in that line must make a DC 17 Dexterity saving throw, taking 9d6 lightning damage on a failed save, or half as much damage on a successful one.

Thunderclap. You can use an action to cause the staff to issue a deafening thunderclap, audible out to 600 feet. Each creature within 60 feet of you (not including you) must make a DC 17 Constitution saving throw. On a failed save, a creature takes 2d6 thunder damage and becomes deafened for 1 minute. On a successful save, a creature takes half damage and isn't deafened.

Thunder and Lightning. You can use an action to use the Lightning Strike and Thunderclap properties at the same time. Doing so doesn't expend the daily use of those properties, only the use of this one.

STAFF OF WITHERING
Staff, rare (requires attunement by a cleric, druid, or warlock)

This staff has 3 charges and regains 1d3 expended charges daily at dawn.

The staff can be wielded as a magic quarterstaff. On a hit, it deals damage as a normal quarterstaff, and you can expend 1 charge to deal an extra 2d10 necrotic damage to the target. In addition, the target must succeed on a DC 15 Constitution saving throw or have disadvantage for 1 hour on any ability check or saving throw that uses Strength or Constitution.

STONE OF CONTROLLING EARTH ELEMENTALS
Wondrous item, rare

If the stone is touching the ground, you can use an action to speak its command word and summon an earth elemental, as if you had cast the *conjure elemental* spell. The stone can't be used this way again until the next dawn. The stone weighs 5 pounds.

STONE OF GOOD LUCK (LUCKSTONE)
Wondrous item, uncommon (requires attunement)

While this polished agate is on your person, you gain a +1 bonus to ability checks and saving throws.

SUN BLADE
Weapon (longsword), rare (requires attunement)

This item appears to be a longsword hilt. While grasping the hilt, you can use a bonus action to cause a blade of pure radiance to spring into existence, or make the blade disappear. While the blade exists, this magic longsword has the finesse property. If you are proficient with shortswords or longswords, you are proficient with the *sun blade.*

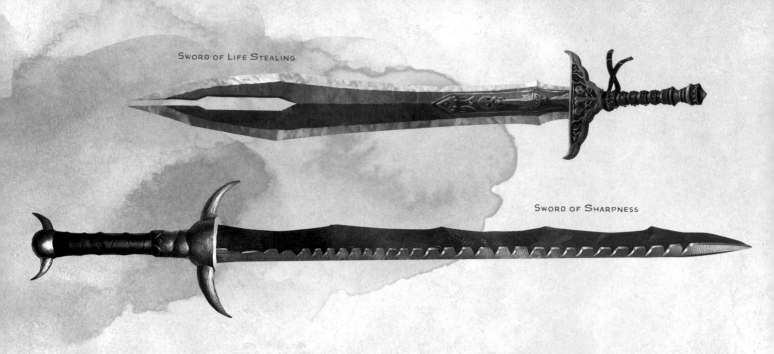

Sword of Life Stealing

Sword of Sharpness

You gain a +2 bonus to attack and damage rolls made with this weapon, which deals radiant damage instead of slashing damage. When you hit an undead with it, that target takes an extra 1d8 radiant damage.

The sword's luminous blade emits bright light in a 15-foot radius and dim light for an additional 15 feet. The light is sunlight. While the blade persists, you can use an action to expand or reduce its radius of bright and dim light by 5 feet each, to a maximum of 30 feet each or a minimum of 10 feet each.

Sword of Answering

Weapon (longsword), legendary (requires attunement by a creature with the same alignment as the sword)

In the world of Greyhawk, only nine of these blades are known to exist. Each is patterned after the legendary sword Fragarach, which is variously translated as "Final Word." Each of the nine swords has its own name and alignment, and each bears a different gem in its pommel.

Name	Alignment	Gem
Answerer	Chaotic good	Emerald
Back Talker	Chaotic evil	Jet
Concluder	Lawful neutral	Amethyst
Last Quip	Chaotic neutral	Tourmaline
Rebutter	Neutral good	Topaz
Replier	Neutral	Peridot
Retorter	Lawful good	Aquamarine
Scather	Lawful evil	Garnet
Squelcher	Neutral evil	Spinel

You gain a +3 bonus to attack and damage rolls made with this sword. In addition, while you hold the sword, you can use your reaction to make one melee attack with it against any creature in your reach that deals damage to you. You have advantage on the attack roll, and any damage dealt with this special attack ignores any damage immunity or resistance the target has.

Sword of Life Stealing

Weapon (any sword), rare (requires attunement)

When you attack a creature with this magic weapon and roll a 20 on the attack roll, that target takes an extra 10 necrotic damage if it isn't a construct or an undead. You also gain 10 temporary hit points.

Sword of Sharpness

Weapon (any sword that deals slashing damage), very rare (requires attunement)

When you attack an object with this magic sword and hit, maximize your weapon damage dice against the target.

When you attack a creature with this weapon and roll a 20 on the attack roll, that target takes an extra 14 slashing damage. Then roll another d20. If you roll a 20, you lop off one of the target's limbs, with the effect of such loss determined by the DM. If the creature has no limb to sever, you lop off a portion of its body instead.

In addition, you can speak the sword's command word to cause the blade to shed bright light in a 10-foot radius and dim light for an additional 10 feet. Speaking the command word again or sheathing the sword puts out the light.

Sword of Vengeance

Weapon (any sword), uncommon (requires attunement)

You gain a +1 bonus to attack and damage rolls made with this magic weapon.

Curse. This sword is cursed and possessed by a vengeful spirit. Becoming attuned to it extends the curse to you. As long as you remain cursed, you are unwilling to part with the sword, keeping it on your person at all times. While attuned to this weapon, you have disadvantage on attack rolls made with weapons other than this one.

In addition, while the sword is on your person, you must succeed on a DC 15 Wisdom saving throw whenever you take damage in combat. On a failed save, you must attack the creature that damaged you until you

Talisman
of the Sphere

Talisman of
Ultimate Evil

drop to 0 hit points or it does, or until you can't reach the creature to make a melee attack against it.

You can break the curse in the usual ways. Alternatively, casting *banishment* on the sword forces the vengeful spirit to leave it. The sword then becomes a +1 weapon with no other properties.

Sword of Wounding
Weapon (any sword), rare (requires attunement)

Hit points lost to this weapon's damage can be regained only through a short or long rest, rather than by regeneration, magic, or any other means.

Once per turn, when you hit a creature with an attack using this magic weapon, you can wound the target. At the start of each of the wounded creature's turns, it takes 1d4 necrotic damage for each time you've wounded it, and it can then make a DC 15 Constitution saving throw, ending the effect of all such wounds on itself on a success. Alternatively, the wounded creature, or a creature within 5 feet of it, can use an action to make a DC 15 Wisdom (Medicine) check, ending the effect of such wounds on it on a success.

Talisman of Pure Good
Wondrous item, legendary (requires attunement by a creature of good alignment)

This talisman is a mighty symbol of goodness. A creature that is neither good nor evil in alignment takes 6d6 radiant damage upon touching the talisman. An evil creature takes 8d6 radiant damage upon touching the talisman. Either sort of creature takes the damage again each time it ends its turn holding or carrying the talisman.

If you are a good cleric or paladin, you can use the talisman as a holy symbol, and you gain a +2 bonus to spell attack rolls while you wear or hold it.

The talisman has 7 charges. If you are wearing or holding it, you can use an action to expend 1 charge from it and choose one creature you can see on the ground within 120 feet of you. If the target is of evil alignment, a flaming fissure opens under it. The target must succeed on a DC 20 Dexterity saving throw or fall into the fissure and be destroyed, leaving no remains. The fissure then closes, leaving no trace of its existence. When you expend the last charge, the talisman disperses into motes of golden light and is destroyed.

Talisman of the Sphere
Wondrous item, legendary (requires attunement)

When you make an Intelligence (Arcana) check to control a *sphere of annihilation* while you are holding this talisman, you double your proficiency bonus on the check. In addition, when you start your turn with control over a *sphere of annihilation*, you can use an action to levitate it 10 feet plus a number of additional feet equal to 10 × your Intelligence modifier.

Talisman of Ultimate Evil
Wondrous item, legendary (requires attunement by a creature of evil alignment)

This item symbolizes unrepentant evil. A creature that is neither good nor evil in alignment takes 6d6 necrotic damage upon touching the talisman. A good creature takes 8d6 necrotic damage upon touching the talisman. Either sort of creature takes the damage again each time it ends its turn holding or carrying the talisman.

If you are an evil cleric or paladin, you can use the talisman as a holy symbol, and you gain a +2 bonus to spell attack rolls while you wear or hold it.

The talisman has 6 charges. If you are wearing or holding it, you can use an action to expend 1 charge from the talisman and choose one creature you can see on the ground within 120 feet of you. If the target is of good alignment, a flaming fissure opens under it. The target must succeed on a DC 20 Dexterity saving throw or fall into the fissure and be destroyed, leaving no remains. The fissure then closes, leaving no trace of its existence. When you expend the last charge, the talisman dissolves into foul-smelling slime and is destroyed.

Vicious Weapon

Tentacle Rod

Tome of Leadership

Tome of Understanding

Tome of Clear Thought

TENTACLE ROD
Rod, rare (requires attunement)

Made by the drow, this rod is a magic weapon that ends in three rubbery tentacles. While holding the rod, you can use an action to direct each tentacle to attack a creature you can see within 15 feet of you. Each tentacle makes a melee attack roll with a +9 bonus. On a hit, the tentacle deals 1d6 bludgeoning damage. If you hit a target with all three tentacles, it must make a DC 15 Constitution saving throw. On a failure, the creature's speed is halved, it has disadvantage on Dexterity saving throws, and it can't use reactions for 1 minute. Moreover, on each of its turns, it can take either an action or a bonus action, but not both. At the end of each of its turns, it can repeat the saving throw, ending the effect on itself on a success.

TOME OF CLEAR THOUGHT
Wondrous item, very rare

This book contains memory and logic exercises, and its words are charged with magic. If you spend 48 hours over a period of 6 days or fewer studying the book's contents and practicing its guidelines, your Intelligence score increases by 2, as does your maximum for that score. The manual then loses its magic, but regains it in a century.

TOME OF LEADERSHIP AND INFLUENCE
Wondrous item, very rare

This book contains guidelines for influencing and charming others, and its words are charged with magic. If you spend 48 hours over a period of 6 days or fewer studying the book's contents and practicing its guidelines, your Charisma score increases by 2, as does your maximum for that score. The manual then loses its magic, but regains it in a century.

TOME OF THE STILLED TONGUE
Wondrous item, legendary (requires attunement by a wizard)

This thick leather-bound volume has a desiccated tongue pinned to the front cover. Five of these tomes exist, and it's unknown which one is the original. The grisly cover decoration on the first *tome of the stilled tongue* once belonged to a treacherous former servant of the lich-god Vecna, keeper of secrets. The tongues pinned to the covers of the four copies came from other spellcasters who crossed Vecna. The first few pages of each tome are filled with indecipherable scrawls. The remaining pages are blank and pristine.

If you can attune to this item, you can use it as a spellbook and an arcane focus. In addition, while holding the tome, you can use a bonus action to cast a spell you have written in this tome, without expending a spell slot or using any verbal or somatic components. Once used, this property of the tome can't be used again until the next dawn.

While attuned to the book, you can remove the tongue from the book's cover. If you do so, all spells written in the book are permanently erased.

Tome of Understanding

Vecna watches anyone using this tome. He can also write cryptic messages in the book. These messages appear at midnight and fade away after they are read.

TOME OF UNDERSTANDING
Wondrous item, very rare

This book contains intuition and insight exercises, and its words are charged with magic. If you spend 48 hours over a period of 6 days or fewer studying the book's contents and practicing its guidelines, your Wisdom score increases by 2, as does your maximum for that score. The manual then loses its magic, but regains it in a century.

TRIDENT OF FISH COMMAND
Weapon (trident), uncommon (requires attunement)

This trident is a magic weapon. It has 3 charges. While you carry it, you can use an action and expend 1 charge to cast *dominate beast* (save DC 15) from it on a beast that has an innate swimming speed. The trident regains 1d3 expended charges daily at dawn.

UNIVERSAL SOLVENT
Wondrous item, legendary

This tube holds milky liquid with a strong alcohol smell. You can use an action to pour the contents of the tube onto a surface within reach. The liquid instantly dissolves up to 1 square foot of adhesive it touches, including *sovereign glue*.

VICIOUS WEAPON
Weapon (any), rare

When you roll a 20 on your attack roll with this magic weapon, the target takes an extra 7 damage of the weapon's type.

VORPAL SWORD
Weapon (any sword that deals slashing damage), legendary (requires attunement)

You gain a +3 bonus to attack and damage rolls made with this magic weapon. In addition, the weapon ignores resistance to slashing damage.

When you attack a creature that has at least one head with this weapon and roll a 20 on the attack roll, you cut off one of the creature's heads. The creature dies if it can't survive without the lost head. A creature is immune to this effect if it is immune to slashing damage, doesn't have or need a head, has legendary actions, or the DM decides that the creature is too big for its head to be cut off with this weapon. Such a creature instead takes an extra 6d8 slashing damage from the hit.

WAND OF BINDING
Wand, rare (requires attunement by a spellcaster)

This wand has 7 charges for the following properties. It regains 1d6 + 1 expended charges daily at dawn. If you expend the wand's last charge, roll a d20. On a 1, the wand crumbles into ashes and is destroyed.

Spells. While holding the wand, you can use an action to expend some of its charges to cast one of the

VORPAL SWORD

TRIDENT OF FISH COMMAND

UNIVERSAL SOLVENT

Wand of Binding

Wand of Enemy Detection

Wand of Fear

Wand of Fireballs

Wand of Polymorph

following spells (save DC 17): *hold monster* (5 charges) or *hold person* (2 charges).

Assisted Escape. While holding the wand, you can use your reaction to expend 1 charge and gain advantage on a saving throw you make to avoid being paralyzed or restrained, or you can expend 1 charge and gain advantage on any check you make to escape a grapple.

Wand of Enemy Detection
Wand, rare (requires attunement)

This wand has 7 charges. While holding it, you can use an action and expend 1 charge to speak its command word. For the next minute, you know the direction of the nearest creature hostile to you within 60 feet, but not its distance from you. The wand can sense the presence of hostile creatures that are ethereal, invisible, disguised, or hidden, as well as those in plain sight. The effect ends if you stop holding the wand.

The wand regains 1d6 + 1 expended charges daily at dawn. If you expend the wand's last charge, roll a d20. On a 1, the wand crumbles into ashes and is destroyed.

Wand of Fear
Wand, rare (requires attunement)

This wand has 7 charges for the following properties. It regains 1d6 + 1 expended charges daily at dawn. If you expend the wand's last charge, roll a d20. On a 1, the wand crumbles into ashes and is destroyed.

Command. While holding the wand, you can use an action to expend 1 charge and command another creature to flee or grovel, as with the *command* spell (save DC 15).

Cone of Fear. While holding the wand, you can use an action to expend 2 charges, causing the wand's tip to emit a 60-foot cone of amber light. Each creature in the cone must succeed on a DC 15 Wisdom saving throw or become frightened of you for 1 minute. While it is frightened in this way, a creature must spend its turns trying to move as far away from you as it can, and it can't willingly move to a space within 30 feet of you. It also can't take reactions. For its action, it can use only the Dash action or try to escape from an effect that prevents it from moving. If it has nowhere it can move, the creature can use the Dodge action. At the end of each of its turns, a creature can repeat the saving throw, ending the effect on itself on a success.

Wand of Fireballs
Wand, rare (requires attunement by a spellcaster)

This wand has 7 charges. While holding it, you can use an action to expend 1 or more of its charges to cast the *fireball* spell (save DC 15) from it. For 1 charge, you cast the 3rd-level version of the spell. You can increase the spell slot level by one for each additional charge you expend.

The wand regains 1d6 + 1 expended charges daily at dawn. If you expend the wand's last charge, roll a d20. On a 1, the wand crumbles into ashes and is destroyed.

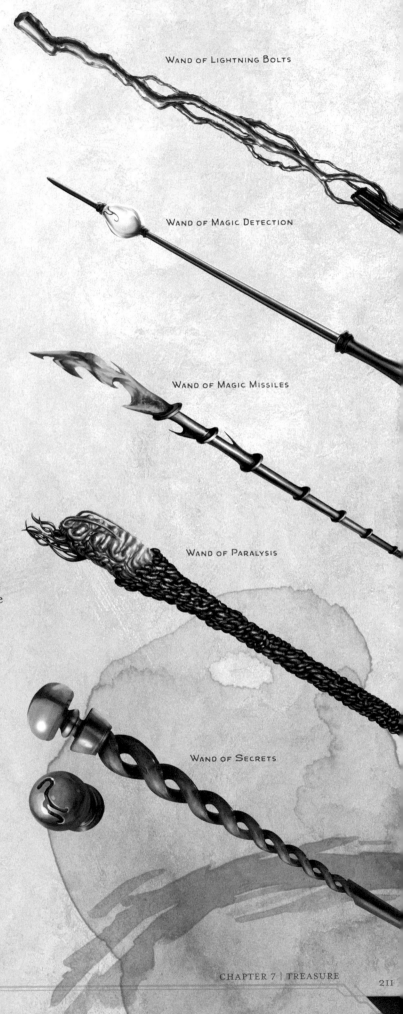

WAND OF LIGHTNING BOLTS

Wand, rare (requires attunement by a spellcaster)

This wand has 7 charges. While holding it, you can use an action to expend 1 or more of its charges to cast the *lightning bolt* spell (save DC 15) from it. For 1 charge, you cast the 3rd-level version of the spell. You can increase the spell slot level by one for each additional charge you expend.

The wand regains 1d6 + 1 expended charges daily at dawn. If you expend the wand's last charge, roll a d20. On a 1, the wand crumbles into ashes and is destroyed.

WAND OF MAGIC DETECTION

Wand, uncommon

This wand has 3 charges. While holding it, you can expend 1 charge as an action to cast the *detect magic* spell from it. The wand regains 1d3 expended charges daily at dawn.

WAND OF MAGIC MISSILES

Wand, uncommon

This wand has 7 charges. While holding it, you can use an action to expend 1 or more of its charges to cast the *magic missile* spell from it. For 1 charge, you cast the 1st-level version of the spell. You can increase the spell slot level by one for each additional charge you expend.

The wand regains 1d6 + 1 expended charges daily at dawn. If you expend the wand's last charge, roll a d20. On a 1, the wand crumbles into ashes and is destroyed.

WAND OF PARALYSIS

Wand, rare (requires attunement by a spellcaster)

This wand has 7 charges. While holding it, you can use an action to expend 1 of its charges to cause a thin blue ray to streak from the tip toward a creature you can see within 60 feet of you. Make a ranged attack roll against that creature using your spell attack bonus. On a hit, the target is paralyzed for 1 minute. At the end of each of the target's turns, it can repeat the saving throw, ending the effect on itself on a success.

The wand regains 1d6 + 1 expended charges daily at dawn. If you expend the wand's last charge, roll a d20. On a 1, the wand crumbles into ashes and is destroyed.

WAND OF POLYMORPH

Wand, very rare (requires attunement by a spellcaster)

This wand has 7 charges. While holding it, you can use an action to expend 1 of its charges to cast the *polymorph* spell (save DC 15) from it.

The wand regains 1d6 + 1 expended charges daily at dawn. If you expend the wand's last charge, roll a d20. On a 1, the wand crumbles into ashes and is destroyed.

WAND OF SECRETS

Wand, uncommon

The wand has 3 charges. While holding it, you can use an action to expend 1 of its charges, and if a secret door or trap is within 30 feet of you, the wand pulses and points at the one nearest to you. The wand regains 1d3 expended charges daily at dawn.

WAND OF LIGHTNING BOLTS

WAND OF MAGIC DETECTION

WAND OF MAGIC MISSILES

WAND OF PARALYSIS

WAND OF SECRETS

Wand of the War Mage, +1, +2, or +3

Wand, uncommon (+1), rare (+2), or very rare (+3) (requires attunement by a spellcaster)

While holding this wand, you gain a bonus to spell attack rolls determined by the wand's rarity. In addition, you ignore half cover when making a spell attack.

Wand of Web

Wand, uncommon (requires attunement by a spellcaster)

This wand has 7 charges. While holding it, you can use an action to expend 1 of its charges to cast the *web* spell (save DC 15) from it.

The wand regains 1d6 + 1 expended charges daily at dawn. If you expend the wand's last charge, roll a d20. On a 1, the wand crumbles into ashes and is destroyed.

Wand of Wonder

Wand, rare (requires attunement by a spellcaster)

This wand has 7 charges. While holding it, you can use an action to expend 1 of its charges and choose a target within 120 feet of you. The target can be a creature, an object, or a point in space. Roll d100 and consult the following table to discover what happens.

If the effect causes you to cast a spell from the wand, the spell's save DC is 15. If the spell normally has a range expressed in feet, its range becomes 120 feet if it isn't already.

If an effect covers an area, you must center the spell on and include the target. If an effect has multiple possible subjects, the DM randomly determines which ones are affected.

The wand regains 1d6 + 1 expended charges daily at dawn. If you expend the wand's last charge, roll a d20. On a 1, the wand crumbles into dust and is destroyed.

d100	Effect
01–05	You cast *slow*.
06–10	You cast *faerie fire*.
11–15	You are stunned until the start of your next turn, believing something awesome just happened.
16–20	You cast *gust of wind*.
21–25	You cast *detect thoughts* on the target you chose. If you didn't target a creature, you instead take 1d6 psychic damage.
26–30	You cast *stinking cloud*.
31–33	Heavy rain falls in a 60-foot radius centered on the target. The area becomes lightly obscured. The rain falls until the start of your next turn.
34–36	An animal appears in the unoccupied space nearest the target. The animal isn't under your control and acts as it normally would. Roll a d100 to determine which animal appears. On a 01–25, a **rhinoceros** appears; on a 26–50, an **elephant** appears; and on a 51–100, a **rat** appears. See the *Monster Manual* for the animal's statistics.
37–46	You cast *lightning bolt*.
47–49	A cloud of 600 oversized butterflies fills a 30-foot radius centered on the target. The area becomes heavily obscured. The butterflies remain for 10 minutes.
50–53	You enlarge the target as if you had cast *enlarge/ reduce*. If the target can't be affected by that spell, or if you didn't target a creature, you become the target.

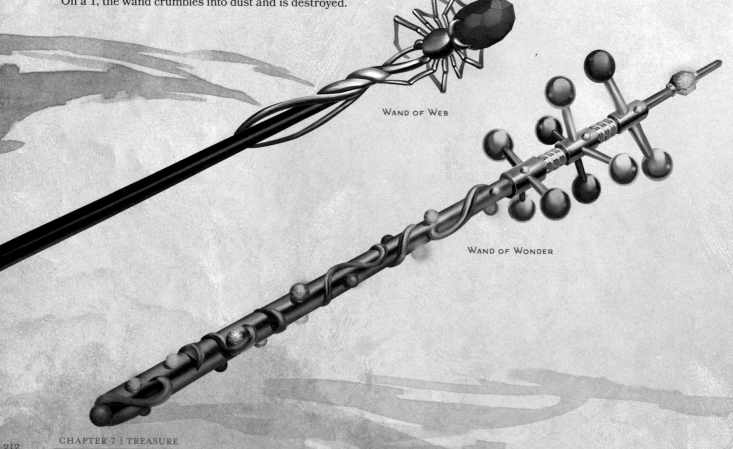

WAND OF WEB

WAND OF WONDER

d100	Effect
54–58	You cast *darkness*.
59–62	Grass grows on the ground in a 60-foot radius centered on the target. If grass is already there, it grows to ten times its normal size and remains overgrown for 1 minute.
63–65	An object of the DM's choice disappears into the Ethereal Plane. The object must be neither worn nor carried, within 120 feet of the target, and no larger than 10 feet in any dimension.
66–69	You shrink yourself as if you had cast *enlarge/reduce* on yourself.
70–79	You cast *fireball*.
80–84	You cast *invisibility* on yourself.
85–87	Leaves grow from the target. If you chose a point in space as the target, leaves sprout from the creature nearest to that point. Unless they are picked off, the leaves turn brown and fall off after 24 hours.
88–90	A stream of 1d4 × 10 gems, each worth 1 gp, shoots from the wand's tip in a line 30 feet long and 5 feet wide. Each gem deals 1 bludgeoning damage, and the total damage of the gems is divided equally among all creatures in the line.
91–95	A burst of colorful shimmering light extends from you in a 30-foot radius. You and each creature in the area that can see must succeed on a DC 15 Constitution saving throw or become blinded for 1 minute. A creature can repeat the saving throw at the end of each of its turns, ending the effect on itself on a success.
96–97	The target's skin turns bright blue for 1d10 days. If you chose a point in space, the creature nearest to that point is affected.
98–00	If you targeted a creature, it must make a DC 15 Constitution saving throw. If you didn't target a creature, you become the target and must make the saving throw. If the saving throw fails by 5 or more, the target is instantly petrified. On any other failed save, the target is restrained and begins to turn to stone. While restrained in this way, the target must repeat the saving throw at the end of its next turn, becoming petrified on a failure or ending the effect on a success. The petrification lasts until the target is freed by the *greater restoration* spell or similar magic.

Weapon, +1, +2, or +3
Weapon (any), uncommon (+1), rare (+2), or very rare (+3)

You have a bonus to attack and damage rolls made with this magic weapon. The bonus is determined by the weapon's rarity.

Weapon of Warning
Weapon (any), uncommon (requires attunement)

This magic weapon warns you of danger. While the weapon is on your person, you have advantage on initiative rolls. In addition, you and any of your companions within 30 feet of you can't be surprised, except when incapacitated by something other than nonmagical sleep. The weapon magically awakens you and your companions within range if any of you are sleeping naturally when combat begins.

Well of Many Worlds
Wondrous item, legendary

This fine black cloth, soft as silk, is folded up to the dimensions of a handkerchief. It unfolds into a circular sheet 6 feet in diameter.

You can use an action to unfold and place the *well of many worlds* on a solid surface, whereupon it creates a two-way portal to another world or plane of existence. Each time the item opens a portal, the DM decides where it leads. You can use an action to close an open portal by taking hold of the edges of the cloth and folding it up. Once *well of many worlds* has opened a portal, it can't do so again for 1d8 hours.

Wind Fan
Wondrous item, uncommon

While holding this fan, you can use an action to cast the *gust of wind* spell (save DC 13) from it. Once used, the fan shouldn't be used again until the next dawn. Each time it is used again before then, it has a cumulative 20 percent chance of not working and tearing into useless, nonmagical tatters.

Wind Fan

Trident of Warning

WINGS OF FLYING

WINGED BOOTS

SENTIENT MAGIC ITEMS

Some magic items possess sentience and personality. Such an item might be possessed, haunted by the spirit of a previous owner, or self-aware thanks to the magic used to create it. In any case, the item behaves like a character, complete with personality quirks, ideals, bonds, and sometimes flaws. A sentient item might be a cherished ally to its wielder or a continual thorn in the side.

Most sentient items are weapons. Other kinds of items can manifest sentience, but consumable items such as potions and scrolls are never sentient.

Sentient magic items function as NPCs under the DM's control. Any activated property of the item is under the item's control, not its wielder's. As long as the wielder maintains a good relationship with the item, the wielder can access those properties normally. If the relationship is strained, the item can suppress its activated properties or even turn them against the wielder.

CREATING SENTIENT MAGIC ITEMS

When you decide to make a magic item sentient, you create the item's persona in the same way you would create an NPC, with a few exceptions described here.

ABILITIES

A sentient magic item has Intelligence, Wisdom, and Charisma scores. You can choose the item's abilities or determine them randomly. To determine them randomly, roll 4d6 for each one, dropping the lowest roll and totaling the rest.

COMMUNICATION

A sentient item has some ability to communicate, either by sharing its emotions, broadcasting its thoughts telepathically, or speaking aloud. You can choose how it communicates or roll on the following table.

d100	Communication
01–60	The item communicates by transmitting emotion to the creature carrying or wielding it.
61–90	The item can speak, read, and understand one or more languages.
91–00	The item can speak, read, and understand one or more languages. In addition, the item can communicate telepathically with any character that carries or wields it.

SENSES

With sentience comes awareness. A sentient item can perceive its surroundings out to a limited range. You can choose its senses or roll on the following table.

d4	Senses
1	Hearing and normal vision out to 30 feet.
2	Hearing and normal vision out to 60 feet
3	Hearing and normal vision out to 120 feet.
4	Hearing and darkvision out to 120 feet.

WINGED BOOTS

Wondrous item, uncommon (requires attunement)

While you wear these boots, you have a flying speed equal to your walking speed. You can use the boots to fly for up to 4 hours, all at once or in several shorter flights, each one using a minimum of 1 minute from the duration. If you are flying when the duration expires, you descend at a rate of 30 feet per round until you land.

The boots regain 2 hours of flying capability for every 12 hours they aren't in use.

WINGS OF FLYING

Wondrous item, rare (requires attunement)

While wearing this cloak, you can use an action to speak its command word. Thish turns the cloak into a pair of bat wings or bird wings on your back for 1 hour or until you repeat the command word as an action. The wings give you a flying speed of 60 feet. When they disappear, you can't use them again for 1d12 hours.

ALIGNMENT

A sentient magic item has an alignment. Its creator or nature might suggest an alignment. If not, you can pick an alignment or roll on the following table.

d100	Alignment	d100	Alignment
01–15	Lawful good	74–85	Chaotic neutral
16–35	Neutral good	86–89	Lawful evil
36–50	Chaotic good	90–96	Neutral evil
51–63	Lawful neutral	97–00	Chaotic evil
64–73	Neutral		

CHARACTERISTICS

Use the information on creating NPCs in chapter 4 to develop a sentient item's mannerisms, personality traits, ideals, bonds, and flaws. You can also draw on the "Special Features" section earlier in this chapter.

If you determine these characteristics randomly, ignore or adapt any result that doesn't make sense for an inanimate object. You can reroll until you get a result you like.

SPECIAL PURPOSE

You can give a sentient item an objective it pursues, perhaps to the exclusion of all else. As long as the wielder's use of the item aligns with that special purpose, the item remains cooperative. Deviating from this course might cause conflict between the wielder and the item, and could even cause the item to prevent the use of its activated properties. You can pick a special purpose or roll on the following table.

d10	Purpose
1	*Aligned:* The item seeks to defeat or destroy those of a diametrically opposed alignment. (Such an item is never neutral.)
2	*Bane:* The item seeks to defeat or destroy creatures of a particular kind, such as fiends, shapechangers, trolls, or wizards.
3	*Protector:* The item seeks to defend a particular race or kind of creature, such as elves or druids.
4	*Crusader:* The item seeks to defeat, weaken, or destroy the servants of a particular deity.
5	*Templar:* The item seeks to defend the servants and interests of a particular deity.
6	*Destroyer:* The item craves destruction and goads its user to fight arbitrarily.
7	*Glory Seeker:* The item seeks renown as the greatest magic item in the world, by establishing its user as a famous or notorious figure.
8	*Lore Seeker:* The item craves knowledge or is determined to solve a mystery, learn a secret, or unravel a cryptic prophecy.
9	*Destiny Seeker:* The item is convinced that it and its wielder have key roles to play in future events.
10	*Creator Seeker:* The item seeks its creator and wants to understand why it was created.

CONFLICT

A sentient item has a will of its own, shaped by its personality and alignment. If its wielder acts in a manner opposed to the item's alignment or purpose, conflict can arise. When such a conflict occurs, the item makes a Charisma check contested by the wielder's Charisma check. If the item wins the contest, it makes one or more of the following demands:

- The item insists on being carried or worn at all times.
- The item demands that its wielder dispose of anything the item finds repugnant.
- The item demands that its wielder pursue the item's goals to the exclusion of all other goals.
- The item demands to be given to someone else.

If its wielder refuses to comply with the item's wishes, the item can do any or all of the following:

- Make it impossible for its wielder to attune to it.
- Suppress one or more of its activated properties.
- Attempt to take control of its wielder.

If a sentient item attempts to take control of its wielder, the wielder must make a Charisma saving throw, with a DC equal to 12 + the item's Charisma modifier. On a failed save, the wielder is charmed by the item for 1d12 hours. While charmed, the wielder must try to follow the item's commands. If the wielder takes damage, it can repeat the saving throw, ending the effect on a success. Whether the attempt to control its user succeeds or fails, the item can't use this power again until the next dawn.

SAMPLE SENTIENT ITEMS

The sentient weapons described here have storied histories.

BLACKRAZOR

Weapon (greatsword), legendary (requires attunement by a creature of non-lawful alignment)

Hidden in the dungeon of White Plume Mountain, *Blackrazor* shines like a piece of night sky filled with stars. Its black scabbard is decorated with pieces of cut obsidian.

You gain a +3 bonus to attack and damage rolls made with this magic weapon. It has the following additional properties.

Devour Soul. Whenever you use it to reduce a creature to 0 hit points, the sword slays the creature and devours its soul, unless it is a construct or an undead. A creature whose soul has been devoured by *Blackrazor* can be restored to life only by a *wish* spell.

When it devours a soul, *Blackrazor* grants you temporary hit points equal to the slain creature's hit point maximum. These hit points fade after 24 hours. As long as these temporary hit points last and you keep *Blackrazor* in hand, you have advantage on attack rolls, saving throws, and ability checks.

If you hit an undead with this weapon, you take 1d10 necrotic damage and the target regains 1d10 hit points. If this necrotic damage reduces you to 0 hit points, *Blackrazor* devours your soul.

Soul Hunter. While you hold the weapon, you are aware of the presence of Tiny or larger creatures within 60 feet of you that aren't constructs or undead. You also can't be charmed or frightened.

Blackrazor can cast the *haste* spell on you once per day. It decides when to cast the spell and maintains concentration on it so that you don't have to.

Sentience. *Blackrazor* is a sentient chaotic neutral weapon with an Intelligence of 17, a Wisdom of 10, and a Charisma of 19. It has hearing and darkvision out to a range of 120 feet.

The weapon can speak, read, and understand Common, and can communicate with its wielder telepathically. Its voice is deep and echoing. While you are attuned to it, *Blackrazor* also understands every language you know.

Personality. *Blackrazor* speaks with an imperious tone, as though accustomed to being obeyed.

The sword's purpose is to consume souls. It doesn't care whose souls it eats, including the wielder's. The sword believes that all matter and energy sprang from a void of negative energy and will one day return to it. *Blackrazor* is meant to hurry that process along.

Despite its nihilism, *Blackrazor* feels a strange kinship to *Wave* and *Whelm*, two other weapons locked away under White Plume Mountain. It wants the three weapons to be united again and wielded together in combat, even though it violently disagrees with *Whelm* and finds *Wave* tedious.

Blackrazor's hunger for souls must be regularly fed. If the sword goes three days or more without consuming a soul, a conflict between it and its wielder occurs at the next sunset.

Moonblade

Weapon (longsword), legendary (requires attunement by an elf or half-elf of neutral good alignment)

Of all the magic items created by the elves, one of the most prized and jealously guarded is a *moonblade*. In ancient times, nearly all elven noble houses claimed one such blade. Over the centuries, some blades have faded from the world, their magic lost as family lines have become extinct. Other blades have vanished with their bearers during great quests. Thus, only a few of these weapons remain.

A *moonblade* passes down from parent to child. The sword chooses its bearer and remains bonded to that person for life. If the bearer dies, another heir can claim the blade. If no worthy heir exists, the sword lies dormant. It functions like a normal longsword until a worthy soul finds it and lays claim to its power.

A *moonblade* serves only one master at a time. The attunement process requires a special ritual in the throne room of an elven regent or in a temple dedicated to the elven gods.

A *moonblade* won't serve anyone it regards as craven, erratic, corrupt, or at odds with preserving and protecting elvenkind. If the blade rejects you, you make ability checks, attack rolls, and saving throws with disadvantage for 24 hours. If the blade accepts you, you become attuned to it and a new rune appears on the blade. You remain attuned to the weapon until you die or the weapon is destroyed.

A *moonblade* has one rune on its blade for each master it has served (typically 1d6 + 1). The first rune always grants a +1 bonus to attack and damage rolls made with this magic weapon. Each rune beyond the first grants the *moonblade* an additional property. The DM chooses each property or determines it randomly on the Moon Blade Properties table.

Moonblade Properties

d100	Property
01–40	Increase the bonus to attack and damage rolls by 1, to a maximum of +3. Reroll if the *moonblade* already has a +3 bonus.
41–80	The *moonblade* gains a randomly determined minor property (see "Special Features" earlier in this chapter).
81–82	The *moonblade* gains the finesse property.
83–84	The *moonblade* gains the thrown property (range 20/60 feet).
85–86	The *moonblade* functions as a *defender*.
87–90	The *moonblade* scores a critical hit on a roll of 19 or 20.
91–92	When you hit with an attack using the *moonblade*, the attack an extra 1d6 slashing damage.
93–94	When you hit a creature of a specific type (such as dragon, fiend, or undead) with the *moonblade*, the target takes an extra 1d6 damage of one of these types: acid, cold, fire, lightning, or thunder.
95–96	You can use a bonus action to cause the *moonblade* to flash brightly. Each creature that can see you and is within 30 feet of you must succeed on a DC 15 Constitution saving throw or become blinded for 1 minute. A creature can repeat the saving throw at the end of each of its turns, ending the effect on itself on a success. This property can't be used again until you take a short rest while attuned to the weapon.
97–98	The *moonblade* functions as a *ring of spell storing*.
99	You can use an action to call forth an elfshadow, provided that you don't already have one serving you. The elfshadow appears in an unoccupied space within 120 feet of you. It uses the statistics for a **shadow** from the *Monster Manual*, except it is neutral, immune to effects that turn undead, and doesn't create new shadows. You control this creature, deciding how it acts and moves. It remains until it drops to 0 hit points or you dismiss it as an action.
00	The *moonblade* functions as a *vorpal sword*.

Sentience. A *moonblade* is a sentient neutral good weapon with an Intelligence of 12, a Wisdom of 10, and a Charisma of 12. It has hearing and darkvision out to a range of 120 feet.

The weapon communicates by transmitting emotions, sending a tingling sensation through the wielder's hand when it wants to communicate something it has sensed. It can communicate more explicitly, through visions or dreams, when the wielder is either in a trance or asleep.

Personality. Every *moonblade* seeks the advancement of elvenkind and elven ideals. Courage, loyalty, beauty, music, and life are all part of this purpose.

The weapon is bonded to the family line it is meant to serve. Once it has bonded with an owner who shares its ideals, its loyalty is absolute.

If a *moonblade* has a flaw, it is overconfidence. Once it has decided on an owner, it believes that only that person should wield it, even if the owner falls short of elven ideals.

WAVE

Weapon (trident), legendary (requires attunement by a creature that worships a god of the sea)

Held in the dungeon of White Plume Mountain, this trident is an exquisite weapon engraved with images of waves, shells, and sea creatures. Although you must worship a god of the sea to attune to this weapon, *Wave* happily accepts new converts.

You gain a +3 bonus to attack and damage rolls made with this magic weapon. If you score a critical hit with it, the target takes extra necrotic damage equal to half its hit point maximum.

The weapon also functions as a *trident of fish command* and a *weapon of warning*. It can confer the benefit of a *cap of water breathing* while you hold it, and you can use it as a *cube of force* by choosing the effect, instead of pressing cube sides to select it.

Sentience. *Wave* is a sentient weapon of neutral alignment, with an Intelligence of 14, a Wisdom of 10, and a Charisma of 18. It has hearing and darkvision out to a range of 120 feet.

The weapon communicates telepathically with its wielder and can speak, read, and understand Aquan. It can also speak with aquatic animals as if using a *speak with animals* spell, using telepathy to involve its wielder in the conversation.

Personality. When it grows restless, *Wave* has a habit of humming tunes that vary from sea chanteys to sacred hymns of the sea gods.

Wave zealously desires to convert mortals to the worship of one or more sea gods, or else to consign the faithless to death. Conflict arises if the wielder fails to further the weapon's objectives in the world.

The trident has a nostalgic attachment to the place where it was forged, a desolate island called Thunderforge. A sea god imprisoned a family of storm giants there, and the giants forged *Wave* in an act of devotion to—or rebellion against—that god.

Wave harbors a secret doubt about its own nature and purpose. For all its devotion to the sea gods, *Wave* fears that it was intended to bring about a particular sea god's demise. This destiny is something *Wave* might not be able to avert.

WHELM

Weapon (warhammer), legendary (requires attunement by a dwarf)

Whelm is a powerful warhammer forged by dwarves and lost in the dungeon of White Plume Mountain.

You gain a +3 bonus to attack and damage rolls made with this magic weapon. At dawn the day after you first make an attack roll with *Whelm*, you develop a fear of being outdoors that persists as long as you remain attuned to the weapon. This causes you to have disadvantage on attack rolls, saving throws, and ability checks while you can see the daytime sky.

Thrown Weapon. *Whelm* has the thrown property, with a normal range of 20 feet and a long range of 60 feet. When you hit with a ranged weapon attack using it, the target takes an extra 1d8 bludgeoning damage, or an extra 2d8 bludgeoning damage if the target is a giant. Each time you throw the weapon, it flies back to your hand after the attack. If you don't have a hand free, the weapon lands at your feet.

Shock Wave. You can use an action to strike the ground with *Whelm* and send a shock wave out from the point of impact. Each creature of your choice on the ground within 60 feet of that point must succeed on a DC 15 Constitution saving throw or become stunned for 1 minute. A creature can repeat the saving throw at the end of each of its turns, ending the effect on itself on a success. Once used, this property can't be used again until the next dawn.

Supernatural Awareness. While you are holding the weapon, it alerts you to the location of any secret or concealed doors within 30 feet of you. In addition, you can use an action to cast *detect evil and good* or *locate object* from the weapon. Once you cast either spell, you can't cast it from the weapon again until the next dawn.

Sentience. *Whelm* is a sentient lawful neutral weapon with an Intelligence of 15, a Wisdom of 12, and a Charisma of 15. It has hearing and darkvision out to a range of 120 feet.

The weapon communicates telepathically with its wielder and can speak, read, and understand Dwarvish, Giant, and Goblin. It shouts battle cries in Dwarvish when used in combat.

Personality. *Whelm's* purpose is to slaughter giants and goblinoids. It also seeks to protect dwarves against all enemies. Conflict arises if the wielder fails to destroy goblins and giants or to protect dwarves.

Whelm has ties to the dwarf clan that created it, variously called the Dankil or the Mightyhammer clan. It longs to be returned to that clan. It would do anything to protect those dwarves from harm.

The hammer also carries a secret shame. Centuries ago, a dwarf named Ctenmiir wielded it valiantly for a time. But Ctenmiir was turned into a vampire. His will was strong enough that he bent *Whelm* to his evil purposes, even killing members of his own clan.

ARTIFACTS

An artifact is a unique magic item of tremendous power, with its own origin and history. An artifact might have been created by gods or mortals of awesome power. It could have been created in the midst of a crisis that threatened a kingdom, a world, or the entire multiverse, and carry the weight of that pivotal moment in history.

Some artifacts appear when they are needed most. For others, the reverse is true; when discovered, the world trembles at the ramifications of the find. In either case, introducing an artifact into a campaign requires forethought. The artifact could be an item that opposing sides are hoping to claim, or it might be something the adventurers need to overcome their greatest challenge.

Characters don't typically find artifacts in the normal course of adventuring. In fact, artifacts only appear when you want them to, for they are as much plot devices as magic items. Tracking down and recovering an artifact is often the main goal of an adventure. Characters must chase down rumors, undergo significant trials, and venture into dangerous, half-forgotten places to find the artifact they seek. Alternatively, a major villain might already have the artifact. Obtaining and destroying the artifact could be the only way to ensure that its power can't be used for evil.

ARTIFACT PROPERTIES

Each artifact has its own magical properties, as other magic items do, and the properties are often exceptionally powerful. An artifact might have other properties that are either beneficial or detrimental. You can choose such properties from the tables in this section or determine them randomly. You can also invent new beneficial and detrimental properties. These properties typically change each time an artifact appears in the world.

An artifact can have as many as four minor beneficial properties and two major beneficial properties. It can have as many as four minor detrimental properties and two major detrimental properties.

MINOR BENEFICIAL PROPERTIES

d100	Property
01–20	While attuned to the artifact, you gain proficiency in one skill of the DM's choice.
21–30	While attuned to the artifact, you are immune to disease.
31–40	While attuned to the artifact, you can't be charmed or frightened.
41–50	While attuned to the artifact, you have resistance against one damage type of the DM's choice.
51–60	While attuned to the artifact, you can use an action to cast one cantrip (chosen by the DM) from it.
61–70	While attuned to the artifact, you can use an action to cast one 1st-level spell (chosen by the DM) from it. After you cast the spell, roll a d6. On a roll of 1–5, you can't cast it again until the next dawn.
71–80	As 61–70 above, except the spell is 2nd level.
81–90	As 61–70 above, except the spell is 3rd level.
91–00	While attuned to the artifact, you gain a +1 bonus to Armor Class.

MAJOR BENEFICIAL PROPERTIES

d100	Property
01–20	While attuned to the artifact, one of your ability scores (DM's choice) increases by 2, to a maximum of 24.
21–30	While attuned to the artifact, you regain 1d6 hit points at the start of your turn if you have at least 1 hit point.
31–40	When you hit with a weapon attack while attuned to the artifact, the target takes an extra 1d6 damage of the weapon's type.
41–50	While attuned to the artifact, your walking speed increases by 10 feet.
51–60	While attuned to the artifact, you can use an action to cast one 4th-level spell (chosen by the DM) from it. After you cast the spell, roll a d6. On a roll of 1–5, you can't cast it again until the next dawn.
61–70	As 51–60 above, except the spell is 5th level.
71–80	As 51–60 above, except the spell is 6th level.
81–90	As 51–60 above, except the spell is 7th level.
91–00	While attuned to the artifact, you can't be blinded, deafened, petrified, or stunned.

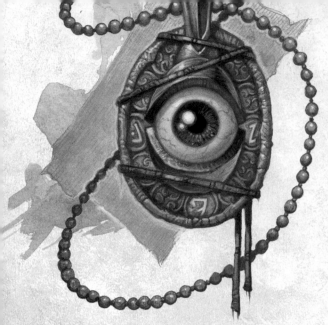

Minor Detrimental Properties

d100	Property
01–05	While attuned to the artifact, you have disadvantage on saving throws against spells.
06–10	The first time you touch a gem or piece of jewelry while attuned to this artifact, the value of the gem or jewelry is reduced by half.
11–15	While attuned to the artifact, you are blinded when you are more than 10 feet away from it.
16–20	While attuned to the artifact, you have disadvantage on saving throws against poison.
21–30	While attuned to the artifact, you emit a sour stench noticeable from up to 10 feet away.
31–35	While attuned to the artifact, all holy water within 10 feet of you is destroyed.
36–40	While attuned to the artifact, you are physically ill and have disadvantage on any ability check or saving throw that uses Strength or Constitution.
41–45	While attuned to the artifact, your weight increases by 1d4 × 10 pounds.
46–50	While attuned to the artifact, your appearance changes as the DM decides.
51–55	While attuned to the artifact, you are deafened when you are more than 10 feet away from it.
56–60	While attuned to the artifact, your weight drops by 1d4 × 5 pounds.
61–65	While attuned to the artifact, you can't smell.
66–70	While attuned to the artifact, nonmagical flames are extinguished within 30 feet of you.
71–80	While you are attuned to the artifact, other creatures can't take short or long rests while within 300 feet of you.
81–85	While attuned to the artifact, you deal 1d6 necrotic damage to any plant you touch that isn't a creature.
86–90	While you are attuned to the artifact, animals within 30 feet of you are hostile toward you.
91–95	While attuned to the artifact, you must eat and drink six times the normal amount each day.
96–00	While you are attuned to the artifact, your flaw is amplified in a way determined by the DM.

Major Detrimental Properties

d100	Property
01–05	While you are attuned to the artifact, your body rots over the course of four days, after which the rotting stops. You lose your hair by the end of day 1, finger tips and toe tips by the end of day 2, lips and nose by the end of day 3, and ears by the end of day 4. A *regenerate* spell restores lost body parts.
06–10	While you are attuned to the artifact, you determine your alignment daily at dawn by rolling a d6 twice. On the first roll, a 1–2 indicates lawful, 3–4 neutral, and 5–6 chaotic. On the second roll, a 1–2 indicates good, 3–4 neutral, and 5–6 evil.
11–15	When you first attune to the artifact, it gives you a quest determined by the DM. You must complete this quest as if affected by the *geas* spell. Once you complete the quest, you are no longer affected by this property.
16–20	The artifact houses a bodiless life force that is hostile toward you. Each time you use an action to use one of the artifact's properties, there is a 50 percent chance that the life force tries to leave the artifact and enter your body. If you fail a DC 20 Charisma saving throw, it succeeds, and you become an NPC under the DM's control until the intruding life force is banished using magic such as the *dispel evil and good* spell.
21–25	Creatures with a challenge rating of 0, as well as plants that aren't creatures, drop to 0 hit points when within 10 feet of the artifact.
26–30	The artifact imprisons a **death slaad** (see the *Monster Manual*). Each time you use one of the artifact's properties as an action, the slaad has a 10 percent chance of escaping, whereupon it appears within 15 feet of you and attacks you.
31–35	While you are attuned to the artifact, creatures of a particular type other than humanoid (as chosen by the DM) are always hostile toward you.
36–40	The artifact dilutes magic potions within 10 feet of it, rendering them nonmagical.
41–45	The artifact erases magic scrolls within 10 feet of it, rendering them nonmagical.
46–50	Before using one of the artifact's properties as an action, you must use a bonus action to draw blood, either from yourself or from a willing or incapacitated creature within your reach, using a piercing or slashing melee weapon. The subject takes 1d4 damage of the appropriate type.
51–60	When you become attuned to the artifact, you gain a form of long-term madness (see chapter 8, "Running the Game").
61–65	You take 4d10 psychic damage when you become attuned to the artifact.
66–70	You take 8d10 psychic damage when you become attuned to the artifact.
71–75	Before you can become attuned to the artifact, you must kill a creature of your alignment.

d100	Property
76–80	When you become attuned to the artifact, one of your ability scores is reduced by 2 at random. A *greater restoration* spell restores the ability to normal.
81–85	Each time you become attuned to the artifact, you age 3d10 years. You must succeed on a DC 10 Constitution saving throw or die from the shock. If you die, you are instantly transformed into a **wight** (see the *Monster Manual*) under the DM's control that is sworn to protect the artifact.
86–90	While attuned to the artifact, you lose the ability to speak.
91–95	While attuned to the artifact, you have vulnerability to all damage.
96–00	When you become attuned to the artifact, there is a 10 percent chance that you attract the attention of a god that sends an avatar to wrest the artifact from you. The avatar has the same alignment as its creator and the statistics of an **empyrean** (see the *Monster Manual*). Once it obtains the artifact, the avatar vanishes.

DESTROYING ARTIFACTS

An artifact must be destroyed in some special way. Otherwise, it is impervious to damage.

Each artifact has a weakness by which its creation can be undone. Learning this weakness might require extensive research or the successful completion of a quest. The DM decides how a particular artifact can be destroyed. Some suggestions are provided here:

- The artifact must be melted down in the volcano, forge, or crucible in which it was created.
- The artifact must be dropped into the River Styx.
- The artifact must be swallowed and digested by the tarrasque or some other ancient creature.
- The artifact must be bathed in the blood of a god or an angel.
- The artifact must be struck and shattered by a special weapon crafted for that purpose.
- The artifact must be pulverized between the titanic gears of Mechanus.
- The artifact must be returned to its creator, who can destroy it by touch.

SAMPLE ARTIFACTS

The artifacts presented here have appeared in one or more of D&D worlds. Use them as guides when creating your own artifacts, or modify them as you see fit.

AXE OF THE DWARVISH LORDS

Weapon (battleaxe), artifact (requires attunement)

Seeing the peril his people faced, a young dwarf prince came to believe that his people needed something to unite them. Thus, he set out to forge a weapon that would be such a symbol.

Venturing deep under the mountains, deeper than any dwarf had ever delved, the young prince came to the blazing heart of a great volcano. With the aid of Moradin, the dwarven god of creation, he first crafted four great tools: the *Brutal Pick*, the *Earthheart Forge*, the *Anvil of Songs*, and the *Shaping Hammer*. With them, he forged the *Axe of the Dwarvish Lords*.

Armed with the artifact, the prince returned to the dwarf clans and brought peace. His axe ended grudges and answered slights. The clans became allies, and they threw back their enemies and enjoyed an era of prosperity. This young dwarf is remembered as the First King. When he became old, he passed the weapon, which had become his badge of office, to his heir. The rightful inheritors passed the axe on for many generations.

Later, in a dark era marked by treachery and wickedness, the axe was lost in a bloody civil war fomented by greed for its power and the status it bestowed. Centuries later, the dwarves still search for the axe, and many adventurers have made careers of chasing after rumors and plundering old vaults to find it.

Magic Weapon. The *Axe of the Dwarvish Lords* is a magic weapon that grants a +3 bonus to attack and damage rolls made with it. The axe also functions as a *belt of dwarvenkind*, a *dwarven thrower*, and a *sword of sharpness*.

Random Properties. The axe has the following randomly determined properties:

- 2 minor beneficial properties
- 1 major beneficial property
- 2 minor detrimental properties

AXE OF THE
DWARVISH LORDS

Blessings of Moradin. If you are a dwarf attuned to the axe, you gain the following benefits:

- You have immunity to poison damage.
- The range of your darkvision increases by 60 feet.
- You gain proficiency with artisan's tools related to blacksmithing, brewing, and stonemasonry.

Conjure Earth Elemental. If you are holding the axe, you can use your action to cast the *conjure elemental* spell from it, summoning an earth elemental. You can't use this property again until the next dawn.

Travel the Depths. You can use an action to touch the axe to a fixed piece of dwarven stonework and cast the *teleport* spell from the axe. If your intended destination is underground, there is no chance of a mishap or arriving somewhere unexpected. You can't use this property again until 3 days have passed.

Curse. The axe bears a curse that affects any non-dwarf that becomes attuned to it. Even if the attunement ends, the curse remains. With each passing day, the creature's physical appearance and stature become more dwarflike. After seven days, the creature looks like a typical dwarf, but the creature neither loses its racial traits nor gains the racial traits of a dwarf. The physical changes wrought by the axe aren't considered magical in nature (and therefore can't be dispelled), but they can be undone by any effect that removes a curse, such as a *greater restoration* or *remove curse* spell.

Destroying the Axe. The only way to destroy the axe is to melt it down in the *Earthheart Forge*, where it was created. It must remain in the burning forge for fifty years before it finally succumbs to the fire and is consumed.

BOOK OF EXALTED DEEDS

Wondrous item, artifact (requires attunement by a creature of good alignment)

The definitive treatise on all that is good in the multiverse, the fabled *Book of Exalted Deeds* figures prominently in many religions. Rather than being a scripture devoted to a particular faith, the book's various authors filled the pages with their own vision of true virtue, providing guidance for defeating evil.

The *Book of Exalted Deeds* rarely lingers in one place. As soon as the book is read, it vanishes to some other corner of the multiverse where its moral guidance can bring light to a darkened world. Although attempts have been made to copy the work, efforts to do so fail to capture its magical nature or translate the benefits it offers to those pure of heart and firm of purpose.

A heavy clasp, wrought to look like angel wings, keeps the book's contents secure. Only a creature of good alignment that is attuned to the book can release the clasp that holds it shut. Once the book is opened, the attuned creature must spend 80 hours reading and studying the book to digest its contents and gain its benefits. Other creatures that peruse the book's open pages can read the text but glean no deeper meaning and reap no benefits. An evil creature that tries to read from the book takes 24d6 radiant damage. This damage ignores resistance and immunity, and can't be reduced or avoided by any means. A creature reduced to 0 hit points by this damage disappears in a blinding flash and is destroyed, leaving its possessions behind.

Benefits granted by the *Book of Exalted Deeds* last only as long as you strive to do good. If you fail to perform at least one act of kindness or generosity within the span of 10 days, or if you willingly perform an evil act, you lose all the benefits granted by the book.

Random Properties. The *Book of Exalted Deeds* has the following random properties:

- 2 minor beneficial properties
- 2 major beneficial properties

Increased Wisdom. After you spend the requisite amount of time reading and studying the book, your Wisdom score increases by 2, to a maximum of 24. You can't gain this benefit from the book more than once.

Enlightened Magic. Once you've read and studied the book, any spell slot you expend to cast a cleric or paladin spell counts as a spell slot of one level higher.

Halo. Once you've read and studied the book, you gain a protective halo. This halo sheds bright light in a 10-foot radius and dim light for an additional 10 feet. You can dismiss or manifest the halo as a bonus action. While present, the halo gives you advantage on Charisma (Persuasion) checks made to interact with good creatures and Charisma (Intimidation) checks made to interact with evil creatures. In addition, fiends and undead within the halo's bright light make attack rolls against you with disadvantage.

Destroying the Book. It is rumored that the *Book of Exalted Deeds* can't be destroyed as long as good exists in the multiverse. However, drowning the book in the River Styx removes all writing and imagery from its pages and renders the book powerless for 1d100 years.

BOOK OF VILE DARKNESS

Wondrous item, artifact (requires attunement)

The contents of this foul manuscript of ineffable wickedness are the meat and drink of those in evil's thrall. No mortal was meant to know the secrets it contains, knowledge so horrid that to even glimpse the scrawled pages invites madness.

Most believe the lich-god Vecna authored the *Book of Vile Darkness*. He recorded in its pages every diseased idea, every unhinged thought, and every example of blackest magic he came across or devised. Vecna covered every vile topic he could, making the book a gruesome catalog of all mortal wrongs.

Other practitioners of evil have held the book and added their own input to its catalog of vile knowledge. Their additions are clear, for the writers of later works stitched whatever they were writing into the tome or, in some cases, made notations and additions to existing text. There are places where pages are missing, torn, or covered so completely with ink, blood, and scratches that the original text can't be divined.

Nature can't abide the book's presence. Ordinary plants wither in its presence, animals are unwilling to approach it, and the book gradually destroys whatever it touches. Even stone cracks and turns to powder if the book rests on it long enough.

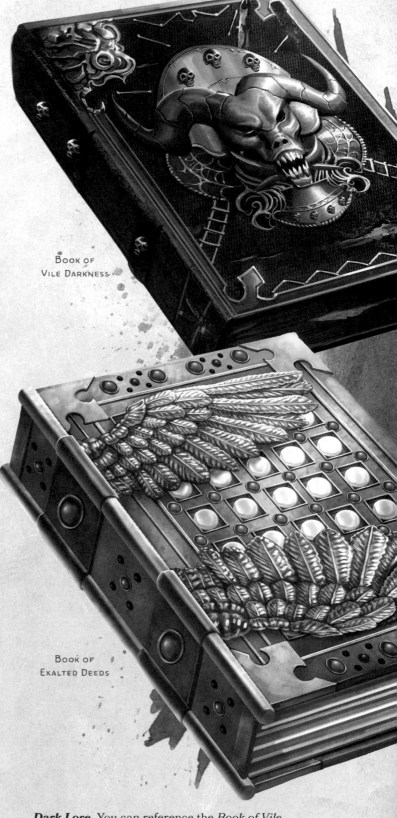

BOOK OF VILE DARKNESS

BOOK OF EXALTED DEEDS

VILE LORE

The *Book of Vile Darkness* touches on every evil in the cosmos. A character can use the lore the book contains to unearth terrible secrets no mortal should know. Among the contents a character might find are the following, plus whatever else you choose:

- **Vile Apotheosis.** The book could hold a ritual that allows a character to become a lich or death knight.
- **True Names.** The true names of any number of fiends might be in the book.
- **Dark Magic.** Several spells of horrific evil of the DM's design and choosing could be in the book. Spells could impose dreadful curses, disfigure others, require human sacrifice, afflict creatures with crippling pain, spread vile plagues, and so on.

A creature attuned to the book must spend 80 hours reading and studying it to digest its contents and reap its benefits. The creature can then freely modify the book's contents, provided that those modifications advance evil and expand the lore already contained within.

Whenever a non-evil creature attunes to the *Book of Vile Darkness*, that creature must make a DC 17 Charisma saving throw. On a failed save, the creature's alignment changes to neutral evil.

The *Book of Vile Darkness* remains with you only as long as you strive to work evil in the world. If you fail to perform at least one evil act within the span of 10 days, or if you willingly perform a good act, the book disappears. If you die while attuned to the book, an entity of great evil claims your soul. You can't be restored to life by any means while your soul remains imprisoned.

Random Properties. The *Book of Vile Darkness* has the following random properties:

- 3 minor beneficial properties
- 1 major beneficial property
- 3 minor detrimental properties
- 2 major detrimental properties

Adjusted Ability Scores. After you spend the requisite amount of time reading and studying the book, one ability score of your choice increases by 2, to a maximum of 24. Another ability score of your choice decreases by 2, to a minimum of 3. The book can't adjust your ability scores again.

Mark of Darkness. After you spend the requisite amount of time reading and studying the book, you acquire a physical disfigurement as a hideous sign of your devotion to vile darkness. An evil rune might appear on your face, your eyes might become glossy black, or horns might sprout from your forehead. Or you might become wizened and hideous, lose all facial features, gain a forked tongue, or some other feature the DM chooses. The mark of darkness grants you advantage on Charisma (Persuasion) checks made to interact with evil creatures and Charisma (Intimidation) checks made to interact with non-evil creatures.

Command Evil. While you are attuned to the book and holding it, you can use an action to cast the *dominate monster* spell on an evil target (save DC 18). You can't use this property again until the next dawn.

Dark Lore. You can reference the *Book of Vile Darkness* whenever you make an Intelligence check to recall information about some aspect of evil, such as lore about demons. When you do so, double your proficiency bonus on that check.

Dark Speech. While you carry the *Book of Vile Darkness* and are attuned to it, you can use an action to recite words from its pages in a foul language known as Dark Speech. Each time you do so, you take 1d12 psychic damage, and each non-evil creature within 15 feet of you takes 3d6 psychic damage.

Destroying the Book. The *Book of Vile Darkness* allows pages to be torn from it, but any evil lore contained on those pages finds its way back into the book eventually, usually when a new author adds pages to the tome.

If a solar tears the book in two, the book is destroyed for 1d100 years, after which it reforms in some dark corner of the multiverse.

A creature attuned to the book for one hundred years can unearth a phrase hidden in the original text that, when translated to Celestial and spoken aloud, destroys both the speaker and the book in a blinding flash of radiance. However, as long as evil exists in the multiverse, the book reforms 1d10 × 100 years later.

If all evil in the multiverse is wiped out, the book turns to dust and is forever destroyed.

EYE AND HAND OF VECNA
Wondrous item, artifact (requires attunement)

Seldom is the name of Vecna spoken except in a hushed voice. Vecna was, in his time, one of the mightiest of all wizards. Through dark magic and conquest, he forged a terrible empire. For all his power, Vecna couldn't escape his own mortality. He began to fear death and take steps to prevent his end from ever coming about.

Orcus, the demon prince of undeath, taught Vecna a ritual that would allow him to live on as a lich. Beyond death, he became the greatest of all liches. Even though his body gradually withered and decayed, Vecna continued to expand his evil dominion. So formidable and hideous was his temper that his subjects feared to speak his name. He was the Whispered One, the Master of the Spider Throne, the Undying King, and the Lord of the Rotted Tower.

Some say that Vecna's lieutenant Kas coveted the Spider Throne for himself, or that the sword his lord made for him seduced him into rebellion. Whatever the reason, Kas brought the Undying King's rule to an end in a terrible battle that left Vecna's tower a heap of ash. Of Vecna, all that remained were one hand and one eye, grisly artifacts that still seek to work the Whispered One's will in the world.

The *Eye of Vecna* and the *Hand of Vecna* might be found together or separately. The eye looks like a bloodshot organ torn free from the socket. The hand is a mummified and shriveled left extremity.

To attune to the eye, you must gouge out your own eye and press the artifact into the empty socket. The eye grafts itself to your head and remains there until you die. Once in place, the eye transforms into a golden eye with a slit for a pupil, much like that of a cat. If the eye is ever removed, you die.

To attune to the hand, you must lop off your left hand at the wrist and the press the artifact against the stump. The hand grafts itself to your arm and becomes a functioning appendage. If the hand is ever removed, you die.

Random Properties. The *Eye of Vecna* and the *Hand of Vecna* each have the following random properties:

- 1 minor beneficial property
- 1 major beneficial property
- 1 minor detrimental property

Properties of the Eye. Your alignment changes to neutral evil, and you gain the following benefits:

- You have truesight.
- You can use an action to see as if you were wearing a *ring of X-ray vision*. You can end this effect as a bonus action.
- The eye has 8 charges. You can use an action and expend 1 or more charges to cast one of the following spells (save DC 18) from it: *clairvoyance* (2 charges), *crown of madness* (1 charge), *disintegrate* (4 charges), *dominate monster* (5 charges), or *eyebite* (4 charges). The eye regains 1d4 + 4 expended charges daily at dawn. Each time you cast a spell from the eye, there is a 5 percent chance that Vecna tears your soul from your body, devours it, and then takes control of the body like a puppet. If that happens, you become an NPC under the DM's control.

Properties of the Hand. Your alignment changes to neutral evil, and you gain the following benefits:

- Your Strength score becomes 20, unless it is already 20 or higher.
- Any melee spell attack you make with the hand, and any melee weapon attack made with a weapon held by it, deals an extra 2d8 cold damage on a hit.
- The hand has 8 charges. You can use an action and expend 1 or more charges to cast one of the following spells (save DC 18) from it: *finger of death* (5 charges), *sleep* (1 charge), *slow* (2 charges), or *teleport* (3 charges). The hand regains 1d4 + 4 expended charges daily at dawn. Each time you cast a spell from the hand, it casts the *suggestion* spell on you (save DC 18), demanding that you commit an evil act. The hand might have a specific act in mind or leave it up to you.

Properties of the Eye and Hand. If you are attuned to both the hand and eye, you gain the following additional benefits:

- You are immune to disease and poison.
- Using the eye's X-ray vision never causes you to suffer exhaustion.
- You experience premonitions of danger and, unless you are incapacitated, can't be surprised.
- If you start your turn with at least 1 hit point, you regain 1d10 hit points.
- If a creature has a skeleton, you can attempt to turn its bones to jelly with a touch of the *Hand of Vecna*. You can do so by using an action to make a melee attack against a creature you can reach, using your choice of your melee attack bonus for weapons or spells. On a hit, the target must succeed on a DC 18 Constitution saving throw or drop to 0 hit points.
- You can use an action to cast *wish*. This property can't be used again until 30 days have passed.

Destroying the Eye and Hand. If the *Eye of Vecna* and the *Hand of Vecna* are both attached to the same creature, and that creature is slain by the *Sword of Kas*, both the eye and the hand burst into flame, turn

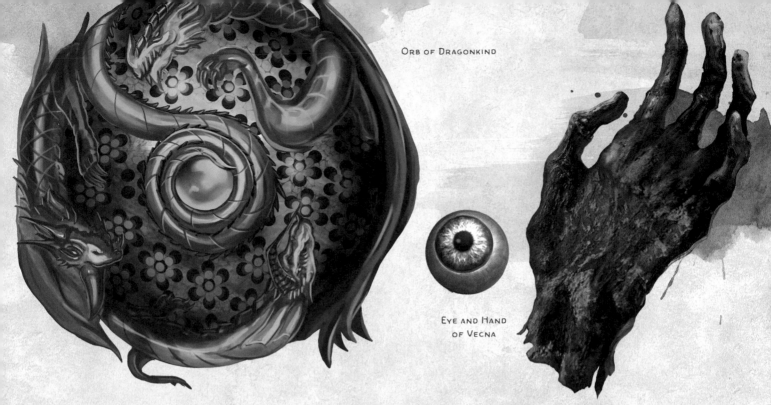

EYE AND HAND
OF VECNA

to ash, and are destroyed forever. Any other attempt to destroy the eye or hand seems to work, but the artifact reappears in one of Vecna's many hidden vaults, where it waits to be rediscovered.

ORB OF DRAGONKIND

Wondrous item, artifact (requires attunement)

Ages past, on the world of Krynn, elves and humans waged a terrible war against evil dragons. When the world seemed doomed, the wizards of the Towers of High Sorcery came together and worked their greatest magic, forging five *Orbs of Dragonkind* (or *Dragon Orbs*) to help them defeat the dragons. One orb was taken to each of the five towers, and there they were used to speed the war toward a victorious end. The wizards used the orbs to lure dragons to them, then destroyed the dragons with powerful magic.

As the Towers of High Sorcery fell in later ages, the orbs were destroyed or faded into legend, and only three are thought to survive. Their magic has been warped and twisted over the centuries, so although their primary purpose of calling dragons still functions, they also allow some measure of control over dragons.

Each orb contains the essence of an evil dragon, a presence that resents any attempt to coax magic from it. Those lacking in force of personality might find themselves enslaved to an orb.

An orb is an etched crystal globe about 10 inches in diameter. When used, it grows to about 20 inches in diameter, and mist swirls inside it.

While attuned to an orb, you can use an action to peer into the orb's depths and speak its command word. You must then make a DC 15 Charisma check. On a successful check, you control the orb for as long as you remain attuned to it. On a failed check, you become charmed by the orb for as long as you remain attuned to it.

While you are charmed by the orb, you can't voluntarily end your attunement to it, and the orb casts *suggestion* on you at will (save DC 18), urging you to work toward the evil ends it desires. The dragon essence within the orb might want many things: the annihilation of a particular people, freedom from the orb, to spread suffering in the world, to advance the worship of Takhisis (Tiamat's name on Krynn), or something else the DM decides.

Random Properties. An *Orb of Dragonkind* has the following random properties:

- 2 minor beneficial properties
- 1 minor detrimental property
- 1 major detrimental property

Spells. The orb has 7 charges and regains 1d4 + 3 expended charges daily at dawn. If you control the orb, you can use an action and expend 1 or more charges to cast one of the following spells (save DC 18) from it: *cure wounds* (5th-level version, 3 charges), *daylight* (1 charge), *death ward* (2 charges), or *scrying* (3 charges).

You can also use an action to cast the *detect magic* spell from the orb without using any charges.

Call Dragons. While you control the orb, you can use an action to cause the artifact to issue a telepathic call that extends in all directions for 40 miles. Evil dragons in range feel compelled to come to the orb as soon as possible by the most direct route. Dragon deities such as Tiamat are unaffected by this call. Dragons drawn to the orb might be hostile toward you for compelling them against their will. Once you have used this property, it can't be used again for 1 hour.

Destroying an Orb. An *Orb of Dragonkind* appears fragile but is impervious to most damage, including the attacks and breath weapons of dragons. A *disintegrate* spell or one good hit from a +3 magic weapon is sufficient to destroy an orb, however.

SWORD OF KAS

Wondrous item, artifact (requires attunement)

When Vecna grew in power, he appointed an evil and ruthless lieutenant, Kas the Bloody Handed, to act as his bodyguard and right hand. This despicable villain served as advisor, warlord, and assassin. His successes earned him Vecna's admiration and a reward: a sword with as dark a pedigree as the man who would wield it.

For a long time, Kas faithfully served the lich, but as Kas's power grew, so did his hubris. His sword urged him to supplant Vecna, so that they could rule the lich's empire in Vecna's stead. Legend says Vecna's destruction came at Kas's hand, but Vecna also wrought his rebellious lieutenant's doom, leaving only Kas's sword behind. The world was made brighter thereby.

The *Sword of Kas* is a magic, sentient longsword that grants a +3 bonus to attack and damage rolls made with it. It scores a critical hit on a roll of 19 or 20, and deals an extra 2d10 slashing damage to undead.

If the sword isn't bathed in blood within 1 minute of being drawn from its scabbard, its wielder must make a DC 15 Charisma saving throw. On a successful save, the wielder take 3d6 psychic damage. On a failed save, the wielder is dominated by the sword, as if by the *dominate monster* spell, and the sword demands that it be bathed in blood. The spell effect ends when the sword's demand is met.

Random Properties. The *Sword of Kas* has the following random properties:

- 1 minor beneficial property
- 1 major beneficial property
- 1 minor detrimental property
- 1 major detrimental property

Spirit of Kas. While the sword is on your person, you add a d10 to your initiative at the start of every combat. In addition, when you use an action to attack with the sword, you can transfer some or all of its attack bonus to your Armor Class instead. The adjusted bonuses remain in effect until the start of your next turn.

Spells. While the sword is on your person, you can use an action to cast one of the following spells (save DC 18) from it: *call lightning*, *divine word*, or *finger of death*. Once you use the sword to cast a spell, you can't cast that spell again from it until the next dawn.

Sentience. The *Sword of Kas* is a sentient chaotic evil weapon with an Intelligence of 15, a Wisdom of 13, and a Charisma of 16. It has hearing and darkvision out to a range of 120 feet.

The weapon communicates telepathically with its wielder and can speak, read, and understand Common.

Personality. The sword's purpose is to bring ruin to Vecna. Killing Vecna's worshipers, destroying the lich's works, and foiling his machinations all help to fulfill this goal.

The *Sword of Kas* also seeks to destroy anyone corrupted by the *Eye and Hand of Vecna*. The sword's obsession with those artifacts eventually becomes a fixation for its wielder.

Destroying the Sword. A creature attuned to both the *Eye of Vecna* and the *Hand of Vecna* can use the *wish* property of those combined artifacts to unmake the *Sword of Kas*. The creature must cast the *wish* spell and make a Charisma check contested by the Charisma check of the sword. The sword must be within 30 feet of the creature, or the spell fails. If the sword wins the contest, nothing happens, and the *wish* spell is wasted. If the sword loses the contest, it is destroyed.

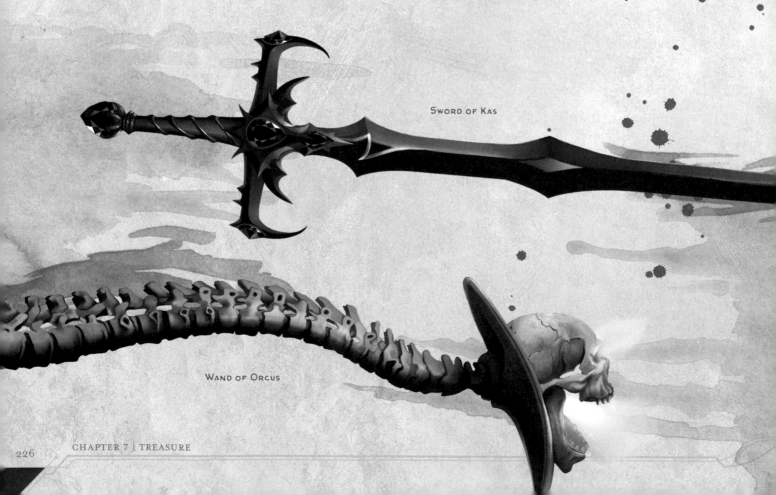

SWORD OF KAS

WAND OF ORCUS

Wand of Orcus

Wand, artifact (requires attunement)

The ghastly *Wand of Orcus* rarely leaves Orcus's side. The device, as evil as its creator, shares the demon lord's aims to snuff out the lives of all living things and bind the Material Plane in the stasis of undeath. Orcus allows the wand to slip from his grasp from time to time. When it does, it magically appears wherever its master senses an opportunity to achieve some fell goal.

Made from bones as hard as iron, the wand is topped with a magically enlarged skull that once belonged to a human hero slain by Orcus. The wand can magically change in size to better conform to the grip of its user. Plants wither, drinks spoil, flesh rots, and vermin thrive in the wand's presence.

Any creature besides Orcus that tries to attune to the wand must make a DC 17 Constitution saving throw. On a successful save, the creature takes 10d6 necrotic damage. On a failed save, the creature dies and rises as a zombie.

In the hands of one who is attuned to it, the wand can be wielded as a magic mace that grants a +3 bonus to attack and damage rolls made with it. The wand deals an extra 2d12 necrotic damage on a hit.

Random Properties. The *Wand of Orcus* has the following random properties:

- 2 minor beneficial properties
- 1 major beneficial property
- 2 minor detrimental properties
- 1 major detrimental property

The detrimental properties of the *Wand of Orcus* are suppressed while the wand is attuned to Orcus himself.

Protection. You gain a +3 bonus to Armor Class while holding the wand.

Spells. The wand has 7 charges. While holding it, you can use an action and expend 1 or more of its charges to cast one of the following spells (save DC 18) from it: *animate dead* (1 charge), *blight* (2 charges), *circle of death* (3 charges), *finger of death* (3 charges), *power word kill* (4 charges), or *speak with dead* (1 charge). The wand regains 1d4 + 3 expended charges daily at dawn.

While attuned to the wand, Orcus or a follower blessed by him can cast each of the wand's spells using 2 fewer charges (minimum of 0).

Call Undead. While you are holding the wand, you can use an action to conjure skeletons and zombies, calling forth as many of them as you can divide 500 hit points among, each undead having average hit points (see the *Monster Manual* for statistics). The undead magically rise up from the ground or otherwise form in unoccupied spaces within 300 feet of you and obey your commands until they are destroyed or until dawn of the next day, when they collapse into inanimate piles of bones and rotting corpses. Once you use this property of the wand, you can't use it again until the next dawn.

While attuned to the wand, Orcus can summon any kind of undead, not just skeletons and zombies. The undead don't perish or disappear at dawn the following day, remaining until Orcus dismisses them.

Sentience. The *Wand of Orcus* is a sentient, chaotic evil item with an Intelligence of 16, a Wisdom of 12, and a Charisma of 16. It has hearing and darkvision out to a range of 120 feet.

The wand communicates telepathically with its wielder and can speak, read, and understand Abyssal and Common.

Personality. The wand's purpose is to help satisfy Orcus's desire to slay everything in the multiverse. The wand is cold, cruel, nihilistic, and bereft of humor.

In order to further its master's goals, the wand feigns devotion to its current user and makes grandiose promises that it has no intention of fulfilling, such as vowing to help its user overthrow Orcus.

Destroying the Wand. Destroying the *Wand of Orcus* requires that it be taken to the Positive Energy Plane by the ancient hero whose skull surmounts it. For this to happen, the long-lost hero must first be restored to life—no easy task, given the fact that Orcus has imprisoned the hero's soul and keeps it hidden and well guarded.

Bathing the wand in positive energy causes it to crack and explode, but unless the above conditions are met, the wand instantly reforms on Orcus's layer of the Abyss.

Other Rewards

As much as adventurers desire treasure, they often appreciate other forms of reward. This section presents a variety of ways that gods, monarchs, and other beings of power might recognize the characters' accomplishments, including supernatural gifts that give characters new capabilities; titles, lands, and other marks of prestige; and boons that are available only to adventurers who have reached 20th level.

Supernatural Gifts

A supernatural gift is a special reward granted by a being or force of great magical power. Such supernatural gifts come in two forms: blessings and charms. A blessing is usually bestowed by a god or a godlike being. A charm is typically the work of a powerful spirit, a location of ancient magic, or a creature that has legendary actions. Unlike a magic item, a supernatural gift isn't an object and doesn't require attunement. It gives a character an extraordinary ability, which can be used one or more times.

Blessings

A character might receive a blessing from a deity for doing something truly momentous—an accomplishment that catches the attention of both gods and mortals. Killing rampaging gnolls rarely warrants such a blessing, but slaying the high priest of Tiamat as he attempts to summon the Dragon Queen might.

A blessing is an appropriate reward for one of the following accomplishments:

- Restoring the most sacred shrine of a god
- Foiling an earthshaking plot by the enemies of a god
- Helping a god's favored servant complete a holy quest

An adventurer might also receive a blessing in advance of a perilous quest. For example, a paladin could receive one before setting out on a quest to slay a terrifying lich that is responsible for a magical plague sweeping the land.

A character should receive only a blessing that is useful to him or her, and some blessings come with expectations on the part of the benefactor. A god typically gives a blessing for a particular purpose, such as recovering a holy person's remains or toppling a tyrannical empire. The god might revoke a blessing if a character fails to pursue that purpose or acts counter to it.

A character retains the benefits of a blessing forever or until it is taken away by the god who granted it. Unlike a magic item, such a blessing can't be suppressed by an *antimagic field* or similar effect.

Most adventurers go their entire lives without receiving even one of these blessings. There is no limit on the number of blessings a character can receive, but it should be rare for a character to have more than one at a time. Moreover, a character can't benefit from multiple instances of a blessing at the same time. For example, a character can't benefit from two instances of the Blessing of Health at once.

Example blessings are provided below. The text of a blessing addresses its user. If you decide to create more blessings, consider this: a typical blessing mimics the properties of a wondrous item.

Blessing of Health. Your Constitution score increases by 2, up to a maximum of 22.

Blessing of Protection. You gain a +1 bonus to AC and saving throws.

Blessing of Magic Resistance. You have advantage on saving throws against spells and other magical effects.

Blessing of Understanding. Your Wisdom score increases by 2, up to a maximum of 22.

Blessing of Valhalla. This blessing grants you the power to summon spirit warriors, as if you had blown a silver *horn of Valhalla*. Once you use this blessing, you can't use it again until 7 days have passed.

Blessing of Weapon Enhancement. One nonmagical weapon in your possession becomes a *+1 weapon* whenever you wield it.

Blessing of Wound Closure. This blessing grants you the benefits of a *periapt of wound closure*.

Charms

A charm is a minor supernatural gift, which can be received in a large variety of ways. For example, a wizard who finds an eldritch secret in a dead archmage's spellbook might be infused with the magic of a charm, as might a character who solves a sphinx's riddle or drinks from a magic fountain. Legendary creatures, such as ancient gold dragons and unicorns, sometimes grace their allies with charms, and some explorers find themselves bearing the magic of a charm after discovering a long-lost location that is drenched in primeval magic.

Some charms can be used only once, and others can be used a specific number of times before vanishing. If a charm lets you cast a spell, you are able to do so without spending a spell slot or providing any components (verbal, somatic, or material). In any case, a charm can't be used in the area created by an *antimagic field* or a similar effect, and a charm's effects are susceptible to *dispel magic* and the like. But the charm itself can't be

removed from a creature by anything short of divine intervention or the *wish* spell.

Example charms are provided below. The text of a charm addresses its user. A typical charm mimics the effects of a potion or a spell, so it is easy to create more charms of your own, if you like.

Charm of Animal Conjuring. This charm allows you to cast the *conjure animals* spell (3rd-level version) as an action. Once used three times, the charm vanishes from you.

Charm of Darkvision. This charm allows you to cast the *darkvision* spell as an action, no components required. Once used three times, the charm goes away.

Charm of Feather Falling. This charm grants you the benefits of a *ring of feather falling*. These benefits last for 10 days, after which the charm vanishes from you.

Charm of Heroism. This charm allows you to give yourself the benefit of a *potion of heroism* as an action. Once you do so, the charm vanishes from you.

Charm of Restoration. This charm has 6 charges. You can use an action to expend some of its charges to cast one of the following spells: *greater restoration* (4 charges) or *lesser restoration* (2 charges). Once all its charges have been expended, the charm vanishes from you.

Charm of the Slayer. One sword in your possession becomes a *dragon slayer* or *giant slayer* (DM's choice) for the next 9 days. The charm then vanishes from you, and the weapon returns to normal.

Charm of Vitality. This charm allows you to give yourself the benefit of a *potion of vitality* as an action. Once you do so, the charm vanishes from you.

Marks of Prestige

Sometimes the most memorable reward for adventurers is the prestige that they acquire throughout a realm. Their adventures often earn them fame and power, allies and enemies, and titles that they can pass on to their descendants. Some lords and ladies began as commoners who ventured into the dangerous places of the world and made names for themselves through their brave deeds.

This section details the most common marks of prestige that adventures might acquire during a campaign. These marks are usually gained along with treasure, but sometimes they stand on their own.

Letters of Recommendation

When gold is in short supply, the adventurers' benefactor might provide them with a letter of recommendation instead of monetary payment. Such a letter is usually enclosed in a handsome folio, case, or scroll tube for safe transport, and it usually bears the signature and seal of whoever wrote it.

A letter of recommendation from a person of impeccable reputation can grant adventurers access to NPCs that they would otherwise have trouble meeting on their own, such as a duke, viceroy, or queen. Moreover, carrying such a recommendation on one's person can help clear up "misunderstandings" with local authorities who might not otherwise take the adventurers at their word.

A letter of recommendation is worth only as much as the person who wrote it and offers no benefit in places where its writer holds no sway.

MEDALS

Although they are often fashioned from gold and other precious materials, medals have an even greater symbolic value to those who award and receive them.

Medals are typically awarded by powerful political figures for acts of heroism, and wearing a medal is usually enough to earn the respect of those who understand its significance.

Different acts of heroism can warrant different kinds of medals. The King of Breland (in the Eberron campaign setting) might award a Royal Badge of Valor (shaped like a shield and made of ruby and electrum) to adventurers for defending Brelish citizens, while the Golden Bear of Breland (a medal made of gold and shaped in a likeness of a bear's head, with gems for eyes) might be reserved for adventurers who prove their allegiance to the Brelish Crown by uncovering and defeating a plot to end the Treaty of Thronehold and reignite the Last War.

A medal doesn't offer a specific in-game benefit to one who wears it, but it can affect dealings with NPCs. For example, a character who proudly displays the Golden Bear of Breland will be regarded as a hero of the people within the kingdom of Breland. Outside Breland, the medal carries far less weight, except among allies of Breland's king.

PARCELS OF LAND

A parcel of land is just that, and usually comes with a royal letter affirming that the land has been granted as a reward for some service. Such land usually remains the property of the local ruler or ruling body, but is leased to a character with the understanding that it can be taken away, especially if his or her loyalty is ever called into question.

A parcel of land, if sufficiently large, might have one or more farms or villages on it already, in which case the recipient is pronounced lord or lady of the land and is expected to collect taxes, along with any other duties.

A character who receives a parcel of land is free to build on it and is expected to safeguard it. He or she may yield the land as part of an inheritance, but can't sell or trade it without permission from the local ruler or ruling body.

Parcels of land make fine rewards for adventurers who are looking for a place to settle or who have family or some kind of personal investment in the region where the land is located.

SPECIAL FAVORS

A reward might come in the form of a favor that the characters can call on at some future date. Special favors work best when the individual granting them is trustworthy. A lawful good or lawful neutral NPC will do whatever can be done to fulfill an obligation when the time comes, short of breaking laws. A lawful evil NPC does the same, but only because a deal is a deal. A neutral good or neutral NPC might pay off favors to protect his or her reputation. A chaotic good NPC is

MEDALS

LETTER OF RECOMMENDATON

more concerned about doing right by the adventurers, honoring any obligations without worrying too much about personal risk or adherence to the law.

SPECIAL RIGHTS

A politically powerful person can reward characters by giving them special rights, which are usually articulated in some sort of official document. For example, characters might be granted special rights to carry weapons in public places, kill enemies of the crown, or negotiate on a duke's behalf. They might earn the right to demand free room and board from any establishment within a particular community, or have the right to draft local militia to assist them as needed.

Special rights last only as long as the legal document dictates, and such rights can be revoked if the adventurers abuse them.

STRONGHOLDS

A stronghold is a reward usually given to seasoned adventurers who demonstrate unwavering fealty to a powerful political figure or ruling body, such as a king, a knighthood, or a council of wizards. A stronghold can be anything from a fortified tower in the heart of a city to a provincial keep on the borderlands. While the stronghold is for the characters to govern as they see fit, the land on which it sits remains the property of the crown or local ruler. Should the characters prove disloyal or unworthy of the gift, they can be asked or forced to relinquish custody of the stronghold.

As an additional reward, the individual bequeathing the stronghold might offer to pay its maintenance costs for a period of one or more months, after which the characters inherit that responsibility. See chapter 6 for more information on stronghold maintenance.

TITLES

A politically powerful figure has the ability to dispense titles. A title often comes with a parcel of land (see above). For example, a character might be awarded the title Earl of Stormriver or Countess of Dun Fjord, along with a parcel of land that includes a settlement or region of the same name.

A character can hold more than one title, and in a feudal society, those titles can be passed down to (or distributed among) one's children. While a character holds a title, he or she is expected to act in a manner befitting that title. By decree, titles can be stripped away if the local ruler or ruling body has reason to question the character's loyalty or competence.

ALTERNATIVES TO EPIC BOONS

You might decide to grant one of the following rewards to a 20th-level character, instead of awarding an epic boon. These two options can be awarded to a character more than once.

Ability Score Improvement. The character can increase one ability score by 2 or increase two ability scores by 1 each. The ability score can now be increased above 20, up to a maximum of 30.

New Feat. The character gains a new feat chosen by the player, but subject to your approval.

Training

A character might be offered special training in lieu of a financial reward. This kind of training isn't widely available and thus is highly desirable. It presumes the existence of a skilled trainer—perhaps a retired adventurer or champion who is willing to serve as a mentor. The trainer might be a reclusive wizard or haughty sorcerer who owes the queen a favor, the knight-commander of the King's Guard, the leader of a powerful druid circle, a quirky monk who lives in a remote mountaintop pagoda, a barbarian chieftain, a warlock living among nomads as a fortune-teller, or an absentminded bard whose plays and poetry are known throughout the land.

A character who agrees to training as a reward must spend downtime with the trainer (see chapter 6 for more information on downtime activities). In exchange, the character is guaranteed to receive a special benefit. Possible training benefits include the following:

- The character gains inspiration daily at dawn for 1d4 + 6 days.
- The character gains proficiency in a skill.
- The character gains a feat.

Epic Boons

An epic boon is a special power available only to 20th level characters. Characters at that level gain such boons only if you want them to and only when you feel it's appropriate. Epic boons are best awarded after the characters complete a major quest, or accomplish something else particularly notable. A character might gain an epic boon after destroying an evil artifact, defeating an ancient dragon, or halting an incursion from the Outer Planes.

Epic boons can also be used as a form of advancement, a way to provide greater power to characters who have no more levels to gain. With this approach, consider awarding one epic boon to each character for every 30,000 XP he or she earns above 355,000 XP.

You determine which epic boon a character gains. Ideally, the boon you pick is something the character would put to use in future adventures. You can allow a player to select a boon for his or her character, subject to your approval.

Whatever boon a character ends up with, consider its place in your story and world. Many of the boons are extraordinary and represent the gradual transformation of a character into something resembling a demigod. The acquisition of a boon might visibly transform a character. For example, the eyes of a character with the Boon of Truesight might glow when he or she feels strong emotion, and a character who has the Boon of High Magic might have faint motes of light glimmering around his or her head. Also, decide how the boon first appears. Does the boon appear spontaneously and mysteriously? Or does a being of cosmic power manifest to bestow it? The bestowal of a boon can itself be an exciting scene in an adventure.

The text of a boon addresses its user. Unless a boon says otherwise, a character can't gain it more than once.

Boon of Combat Prowess

When you miss with a melee weapon attack, you can choose to hit instead. Once you use this boon, you can't use it again until you finish a short rest.

Boon of Dimensional Travel

As an action, you can cast the *misty step* spell, without using a spell slot or any components. Once you do so, you can't use this boon again until you finish a short rest.

Boon of Fate

When another creature that you can see within 60 feet of you makes an ability check, an attack roll, or a saving throw, you can roll a d10 and apply the result as a bonus or penalty to the roll. Once you use this boon, you can't use it again until you finish a short rest.

Boon of Fortitude

Your hit point maximum increases by 40.

Boon of High Magic

You gain one 9th-level spell slot, provided that you already have one.

Boon of Immortality

You stop aging. You are immune to any effect that would age you, and you can't die from old age.

Boon of Invincibility

When you take damage from any source, you can reduce that damage to 0. Once you use this boon, you can't use it again until you finish a short rest.

Boon of Irresistible Offense

You can bypass the damage resistances of any creature.

Boon of Luck

You can add a d10 roll to any ability check, attack roll, or saving throw you make. Once you use this boon, you can't use it again until you finish a short rest.

Boon of Magic Resistance

You have advantage on saving throws against spells and other magical effects.

Boon of Peerless Aim

You can give yourself a +20 bonus to a ranged attack roll you make. Once you use this boon, you can't use it again until you finish a short rest.

Boon of Perfect Health

You are immune to all diseases and poisons, and you have advantage on Constitution saving throws.

Boon of Planar Travel

When you gain this boon, choose a plane of existence other than the Material Plane. You can now use an action to cast the *plane shift* spell (no spell slot or components required), targeting yourself only, and travel to the chosen plane, or from that plane back to the Material Plane. Once you use this boon, you can't use it again until you finish a short rest.

Boon of Quick Casting

Choose one of your spells of 1st through 3rd level that has a casting time of 1 action. That spell's casting time is now 1 bonus action for you.

Boon of Recovery

You can use a bonus action to regain a number of hit points equal to half your hit point maximum. Once you use this boon, you can't use it again until you finish a long rest.

Boon of Resilience

You have resistance to bludgeoning, piercing, and slashing damage from nonmagical weapons.

Boon of Skill Proficiency

You gain proficiency in all skills.

Boon of Speed

Your walking speed increases by 30 feet.

In addition, you can use a bonus action to take the Dash or Disengage action. Once you do so, you can't do so again until you finish a short rest.

Boon of Spell Mastery

Choose one 1st-level sorcerer, warlock, or wizard spell that you can cast. You can now cast that spell at its lowest level without expending a spell slot.

Boon of Spell Recall

You can cast any spell you know or have prepared without expending a spell slot. Once you do so, you can't use this boon again until you finish a long rest.

Boon of the Fire Soul

You have immunity to fire damage. You can also cast *burning hands* (save DC 15) at will, without using a spell slot or any components.

Boon of the Night Spirit

While completely in an area of dim light or darkness, you can become invisible as an action. You remain invisible until you take an action or a reaction.

Boon of the Stormborn

You have immunity to lightning and thunder damage. You can also cast *thunderwave* (save DC 15) at will, without using a spell slot or any components.

Boon of the Unfettered

You have advantage on ability checks made to resist being grappled. In addition, you can use an action to automatically escape a grapple or free yourself of restraints of any kind.

Boon of Truesight

You have truesight out to a range of 60 feet.

Boon of Undetectability

You gain a +10 bonus to Dexterity (Stealth) checks, and you can't be detected or targeted by divination magic, including scrying sensors.

PART 3

Master of Rules

CHAPTER 8: RUNNING THE GAME

RULES ENABLE YOU AND YOUR PLAYERS TO HAVE fun at the table. The rules serve you, not vice versa. There are the rules of the game, and there are table rules for how the game is played. For instance, players need to know what happens when one of them misses a session. They need to know whether to bring miniatures, any special rules you've decided to use, and how to treat a cocked die (a die that lands so that its face can't be clearly read). These topics and more are covered in this chapter.

TABLE RULES

Ideally, players come to the gaming table with the same goal: to have a fun time together. This section gives recommendations for table rules you can establish to help meet that goal. Here are some fundamentals:

Foster respect. Don't bring personal conflicts to the table or let disagreements escalate into bad feelings. Don't touch others' dice if they're sensitive about it.

Avoid distractions. Turn off the television and video games. If you have young children, hire a babysitter. Reducing distractions helps players stay in character and enjoy the story. It might be fine to have players wandering away from the table and back, but some players prefer planned breaks.

Have snacks. Decide before a session who will bring food and drink. This is often something the players can handle.

TABLE TALK

Set expectations about how players talk at the table:

- Make it clear who's speaking: the character or the player (out of character).
- Decide how you feel about a player sharing information that his or her character wouldn't know or that the character is incapable of sharing as a result of being unconscious, dead, or far away.
- Are you all right with players retracting what they just said their characters did?

DICE ROLLING

Establish expectations about rolling dice. Rolling in full view of everyone is a good starting point. If you see a player rolling and scooping the dice up before anyone else can see, encourage that player to be less secretive.

When a die falls on the floor, do you count it or reroll it? When it lands cocked against a book, do you pull the book away and see where it lands, or reroll it?

What about you, the DM? Do you make your rolls in the open or hide them behind a DM screen? Consider the following:

- If you roll dice where the players can see, they know you're playing impartially and not fudging rolls.
- Rolling behind a screen keeps the players guessing about the strength of their opposition. When a

monster hits all the time, is it of a much higher level than the characters, or are you rolling high numbers?

- Rolling behind a screen lets you fudge the results if you want to. If two critical hits in a row would kill a character, you could change the second critical hit into a normal hit, or even a miss. Don't distort die rolls too often, though, and don't let on that you're doing it. Otherwise, your players might think they don't face any real risks—or worse, that you're playing favorites.
- A roll behind a screen can help preserve mystery. For example, if a player thinks there might be someone invisible nearby and makes a Wisdom (Perception) check, consider rolling a die behind the screen even if no one is there, making the player think someone is, indeed, hiding. Try not to overuse this trick.
- You might choose to make a roll for a player because you don't want the player to know how good the check total is. For example, if a player suspects a baroness might be charmed and wants to make a Wisdom (Insight) check, you could make the roll in secret for the player. If the player rolled and got a high number but didn't sense anything amiss, the player would be confident that the baroness wasn't charmed. With a low roll, a negative answer wouldn't mean much. A hidden roll allows uncertainty.

ROLLING ATTACKS AND DAMAGE

Players are accustomed to rolling an attack roll first and then a damage roll. If players make attack rolls and damage rolls at the same time, the action moves a little faster around the table.

RULES DISCUSSIONS

You might need to set a policy on rules discussions at the table. Some groups don't mind putting the game on hold while they hash out different interpretations of a rule. Others prefer to let the DM make a call and continue with the action. If you gloss over a rules issue in play, make a note of it (a good task to delegate to a player) and return to the issue later.

METAGAME THINKING

Metagame thinking means thinking about the game as a *game*. It's like when a character in a movie knows it's a movie and acts accordingly. For example, a player might say, "The DM wouldn't throw such a powerful monster at us!" or you might hear, "The read-aloud text spent a lot of time describing that door—let's search it again!"

Discourage metagame thinking by giving players a gentle reminder: "What do your *characters* think?" You can curb metagame thinking by setting up situations that will be difficult for the characters and that might require negotiation or retreat to survive.

MISSING PLAYERS

How should you deal with the characters of missing players? Consider these options:

- Have another player run the missing player's character. The player running the extra character should strive to keep the character alive and use resources wisely.
- Run the character yourself. It's an extra burden for you, but it can work.
- Decide the character isn't there. Invent a good reason for the character to miss the adventure, perhaps by having him or her linger in town or continue a downtime activity. Leave a way for the character to rejoin the party when the player returns.
- Have the character fade into the background. This solution requires everyone to step out of the game world a bit and suspend disbelief, but might be the easiest solution. You act as if the character's not there, but don't try to come up with any in-game explanation for this absence. Monsters don't attack the character, who returns the favor. On returning, the player resumes playing as if he or she was never gone.

SMALL GROUPS

Most of the time, each player runs one character. The game plays best that way, without overwhelming anyone. But if your group is small, players can control more than one character. Or you can fill out the group with NPC followers, using the guidelines in chapter 4, "Creating Nonplayer Characters." You can also make the characters more resilient by using the healing surge option in chapter 9, "Dungeon Master's Workshop."

Don't force a reluctant player to take on multiple characters, and don't show favoritism by allowing only one player to do so. If one character is the mentor of the other, the player can focus on roleplaying just one character. Otherwise, players can end up awkwardly talking to themselves in character, or avoiding roleplaying altogether.

Multiple characters can be a good idea in a game that features nonstop peril and a high rate of character death. If your group agrees to the premise, have each player keep one or two additional characters on hand, ready to jump in whenever the current character dies. Each time the main character gains a level, the backup characters do as well.

NEW PLAYERS

When a new player joins the group, allow the new player to create a character of a level equal to the lowest-level member of the party. The only exception to this guideline is when the new player is completely unfamiliar with the D&D game. In that case, have that player start with a 1st-level character. If the rest of the party is significantly higher in level, consider taking a short break from the campaign and having everyone play a 1st-level character for a few sessions while the new player learns the ropes.

Integrating a new character into the group can be difficult if the party is in the middle of an adventure. The following approaches can help make it easier:

- The new character is a friend or relative of one of the adventurers who has been searching for the group.
- The new character is a prisoner of the foes the other characters are fighting. When rescued, this character joins their group.
- The new character is the sole survivor of another adventuring group.

THE ROLE OF DICE

Dice are neutral arbiters. They can determine the outcome of an action without assigning any motivation to the DM and without playing favorites. The extent to which you use them is entirely up to you.

ROLLING WITH IT

Some DMs rely on die rolls for almost everything. When a character attempts a task, the DM calls for a check and picks a DC. As a DM using this style, you can't rely on the characters succeeding or failing on any one check to move the action in a specific direction. You must be ready to improvise and react to a changing situation.

Relying on dice also gives the players the sense that anything is possible. Sure, it might seem unlikely that the party's halfling can leap on the ogre's back, pull a sack over its head, and then dive to safety, but with a lucky enough roll it just might work.

A drawback of this approach is that roleplaying can diminish if players feel that their die rolls, rather than their decisions and characterizations, always determine success.

IGNORING THE DICE

One approach is to use dice as rarely as possible. Some DMs use them only during combat, and determine success or failure as they like in other situations.

With this approach, the DM decides whether an action or a plan succeeds or fails based on how well the players make their case, how thorough or creative they are, or other factors. For example, the players might describe how they search for a secret door, detailing how they tap on a wall or twist a torch sconce to find its trigger. That could be enough to convince the DM that they find the secret door without having to make an ability check to do so.

This approach rewards creativity by encouraging players to look to the situation you've described for an answer, rather than looking to their character sheet or their character's special abilities. A downside is that no DM is completely neutral. A DM might come to favor certain players or approaches, or even work against good ideas if they send the game in a direction he or she doesn't like. This approach can also slow the game if the DM focuses on one "correct" action that the characters must describe to overcome an obstacle.

THE MIDDLE PATH

Many DMs find that using a combination of the two approaches works best. By balancing the use of dice against deciding on success, you can encourage your players to strike a balance between relying on their bonuses and abilities and paying attention to the game and immersing themselves in its world.

Remember that dice don't run your game—you do. Dice are like rules. They're tools to help keep the action moving. At any time, you can decide that a player's action is automatically successful. You can also grant the player advantage on any ability check, reducing the chance of a bad die roll foiling the character's plans. By the same token, a bad plan or unfortunate circumstances can transform the easiest task into an impossibility, or at least impose disadvantage.

USING ABILITY SCORES

When a player wants to do something, it's often appropriate to let the attempt succeed without a roll or a reference to the character's ability scores. For example, a character doesn't normally need to make a Dexterity check to walk across an empty room or a Charisma check to order a mug of ale. Only call for a roll if there is a meaningful consequence for failure.

When deciding whether to use a roll, ask yourself two questions:

- Is a task so easy and so free of conflict and stress that there should be no chance of failure?
- Is a task so inappropriate or impossible—such as hitting the moon with an arrow—that it can't work?

If the answer to both of these questions is no, some kind of roll is appropriate. The following sections provide guidance on determining whether to call for an ability check, attack roll, or saving throw; how to assign DCs; when to use advantage and disadvantage; and other related topics.

ABILITY CHECKS

An ability check is a test to see whether a character succeeds at a task that he or she has decided to attempt. The *Player's Handbook* includes examples of what each ability score is used for. The Ability Checks table summarizes that material for easy reference.

MULTIPLE ABILITY CHECKS

Sometimes a character fails an ability check and wants to try again. In some cases, a character is free to do so; the only real cost is the time it takes. With enough attempts and enough time, a character should

eventually succeed at the task. To speed things up, assume that a character spending ten times the normal amount of time needed to complete a task automatically succeeds at that task. However, no amount of repeating the check allows a character to turn an impossible task into a successful one.

In other cases, failing an ability check makes it impossible to make the same check to do the same thing again. For example, a rogue might try to trick a town guard into thinking the adventurers are undercover agents of the king. If the rogue loses a contest of Charisma (Deception) against the guard's Wisdom (Insight), the same lie told again won't work. The characters can come up with a different way to get past the guard or try the check again against another guard at a different gate. But you might decide that the initial failure makes those checks more difficult to pull off.

ABILITY CHECKS		
Ability	Used for ...	Example Uses
Strength	Physical force and athleticism	Smash down a door, move a boulder, use a spike to wedge a door shut
Dexterity	Agility, reflexes, and balance	Sneak past a guard, walk along a narrow ledge, wriggle free from chains
Constitution	Stamina and health	Endure a marathon, grasp hot metal without flinching, win a drinking contest
Intelligence	Memory and reason	Recall a bit of lore, recognize a clue's significance, decode an encrypted message
Wisdom	Perceptiveness and willpower	Spot a hidden creature, sense that someone is lying
Charisma	Social influence and confidence	Persuade a creature to do something, cow a crowd, lie to someone convincingly

CONTESTS

A contest is a kind of ability check that matches two creatures against each other. Use a contest if a character attempts something that either directly foils or is directly opposed by another creature's efforts. In a contest, the ability checks are compared to each other, rather than to a target number.

When you call for a contest, you pick the ability that each side must use, deciding whether both sides use the same ability or whether different abilities should counter each other. For example, when a creature tries to hide, it engages in a contest of Dexterity against Wisdom. But if two creatures arm wrestle, or if one creature is holding a door closed against another's attempt to push it open, both use Strength.

ATTACK ROLLS

Call for an attack roll when a character tries to hit a creature or an object with an attack, especially when the attack could be foiled by the target's armor or shield or by another object providing cover. You can also use attack rolls to resolve noncombat activities such as archery contests or a game of darts.

SAVING THROWS

A saving throw is an instant response to a harmful effect and is almost never done by choice. A save makes the most sense when something bad happens to a character and the character has a chance to avoid that effect. An ability check is something a character actively attempts to accomplish, whereas a saving throw is a split-second response to the activity of someone or something else.

Most of the time, a saving throw comes into play when an effect—such as a spell, monster ability, or trap—calls for it, telling you what kind of saving throw is involved and providing a DC for it.

Other times, a situation arises that clearly calls for a saving throw, especially when a character is subjected to a harmful effect that can't be hedged out by armor or a shield. It's up to you to decide which ability score is involved. The Saving Throws table offers suggestions.

INTELLIGENCE CHECK VS. WISDOM CHECK

If you have trouble deciding whether to call for an Intelligence or a Wisdom check to determine whether a character notices something, think of it in terms of what a very high or low score in those two abilities might mean.

A character with a high Wisdom but low Intelligence is aware of the surroundings but is bad at interpreting what things mean. The character might spot that one section of a wall is clean and dusty compared to the others, but he or she wouldn't necessarily make the deduction that a secret door is there.

In contrast, a character with high Intelligence and low Wisdom is probably oblivious but clever. The character might not spot the clean section of wall but, if asked about it, could immediately deduce why it's clean.

Wisdom checks allow characters to perceive what is around them (the wall is clean here), while Intelligence checks answer why things are that way (there's probably a secret door).

SAVING THROWS

Ability	Used For ...
Strength	Opposing a force that would physically move or bind you
Dexterity	Dodging out of harm's way
Constitution	Enduring a disease, poison, or other hazard that saps vitality
Intelligence	Disbelieving certain illusions and resisting mental assaults that can be refuted with logic, sharp memory, or both
Wisdom	Resisting effects that charm, frighten, or otherwise assault your willpower
Charisma	Withstanding effects, such as possession, that would subsume your personality or hurl you to another plane of existence

DIFFICULTY CLASS

It's your job to establish the Difficulty Class for an ability check or a saving throw when a rule or an adventure doesn't give you one. Sometimes you'll even want to change such established DCs. When you do so, think of how difficult a task is and then pick the associated DC from the Typical DCs table.

TYPICAL DCs

Task	DC	Task	DC
Very easy	5	Hard	20
Easy	10	Very hard	25
Moderate	15	Nearly impossible	30

The numbers associated with these categories of difficulty are meant to be easy to keep in your head, so that you don't have to refer to this book every time you decide on a DC. Here are some tips for using DC categories at the gaming table.

If you've decided that an ability check is called for, then most likely the task at hand isn't a **very easy** one. Most people can accomplish a DC 5 task with little chance of failure. Unless circumstances are unusual, let characters succeed at such a task without making a check.

Then ask yourself, "Is this task's difficulty easy, moderate, or hard?" If the only DCs you ever use are 10, 15, and 20, your game will run just fine. Keep in mind that a character with a 10 in the associated ability and no proficiency will succeed at an **easy** task around 50 percent of the time. A **moderate** task requires a higher score or proficiency for success, whereas a **hard** task typically requires both. A big dose of luck with the d20 also doesn't hurt.

If you find yourself thinking, "This task is especially hard," you can use a higher DC, but do so with caution and consider the level of the characters. A DC 25 task is **very hard** for low-level characters to accomplish, but it becomes more reasonable after 10th level or so. A DC 30 check is **nearly impossible** for most low-level characters. A 20th-level character with proficiency and a relevant ability score of 20 still needs a 19 or 20 on the die roll to succeed at a task of this difficulty.

VARIANT: AUTOMATIC SUCCESS

Sometimes the randomness of a d20 roll leads to ludicrous results. Let's say a door requires a successful DC 15 Strength check to be battered down. A fighter with a Strength of 20 might helplessly flail against the door because of bad die rolls. Meanwhile, the rogue with a Strength of 10 rolls a 20 and knocks the door from its hinges.

If such results bother you, consider allowing automatic success on certain checks. Under this optional rule, a character automatically succeeds on any ability check with a DC less than or equal to the relevant ability score minus 5. So in the example above, the fighter would automatically kick in the door. This rule doesn't apply to contests, saving throws, or attack rolls.

Having proficiency with a skill or tool can also grant automatic success. If a character's proficiency bonus applies to his or her ability check, the character automatically succeeds if the DC is 10 or less. If that character is 11th level or higher, the check succeeds if the DC is 15 or less.

The downside of this whole approach is its predictability. For example, once a character's ability score reaches 20, checks of DC 15 and lower using that ability become automatic successes. Smart players will then always match the character with the highest ability score against any given check. If you want some risk of failure, you need to set higher DCs. Doing this, though, can aggravate the problem you're trying to solve: higher DCs require higher die rolls, and thus rely even more on luck.

PROFICIENCY

When you ask a player to make an ability check, consider whether a skill or tool proficiency might apply to it. The player might also ask you if a particular proficiency applies.

One way to think about this question is to consider whether a character could become better at a particular task through training and practice. If the answer is no, it's fine to say that no proficiency applies. But if the answer is yes, assign an appropriate skill or tool proficiency to reflect that training and practice.

SKILLS

As described in the *Player's Handbook*, a skill proficiency represents a character's focus on one aspect of an ability. Among all the things a character's Dexterity score describes, the character might be particularly skilled at sneaking around, reflected in proficiency in the Stealth skill. When that skill is used for an ability check, it is usually used with Dexterity.

Under certain circumstances, you can decide a character's proficiency in a skill can be applied to a different ability check. For example, you might decide that a character forced to swim from an island to the mainland must succeed on a Constitution check (as opposed to a Strength check) because of the distance involved. The character is proficient in the Athletics skill, which covers swimming, so you allow the character's proficiency bonus to apply to this ability

check. In effect, you're asking for a Constitution (Athletics) check, instead of a Strength (Athletics) check.

Often, players ask whether they can apply a skill proficiency to an ability check. If a player can provide a good justification for why a character's training and aptitude in a skill should apply to the check, go ahead and allow it, rewarding the player's creative thinking.

TOOLS

Having proficiency with a tool allows you to apply your proficiency bonus to an ability check you make using that tool. For example, a character proficient with carpenter's tools can apply his or her proficiency bonus to a Dexterity check to craft a wooden flute, an Intelligence check to craft a wooden secret door, or a Strength check to build a working trebuchet. However, the proficiency bonus wouldn't apply to an ability check made to identify unsafe wooden construction or to discern the origin of a crafted item, since neither check requires tool use.

SAVING THROWS AND ATTACK ROLLS

Characters are either proficient with a saving throw or attack, or they aren't. The bonus always applies if a character is proficient.

ADVANTAGE AND DISADVANTAGE

Advantage and disadvantage are among the most useful tools in your DM's toolbox. They reflect temporary circumstances that might affect the chances of a character succeeding or failing at a task. Advantage is also a great way to reward a player who shows exceptional creativity in play.

Characters often gain advantage or disadvantage through the use of special abilities, actions, spells, or other features of their classes or backgrounds. In other cases, you decide whether a circumstance influences a roll in one direction or another, and you grant advantage or impose disadvantage as a result.

Consider granting **advantage** when ...

- Circumstances not related to a creature's inherent capabilities provide it with an edge.
- Some aspect of the environment contributes to the character's chance of success.
- A player shows exceptional creativity or cunning in attempting or describing a task.
- Previous actions (whether taken by the character making the attempt or some other creature) improve the chances of success.

Consider imposing **disadvantage** when ...

- Circumstances hinder success in some way.
- Some aspect of the environment makes success less likely (assuming that aspect doesn't already impose a penalty to the roll being made).
- An element of the plan or description of an action makes success less likely.

Because advantage and disadvantage cancel each other out, there's no need to keep track of how many circumstances weigh on both sides.

For example, imagine a wizard is running down a dungeon corridor to escape from a beholder. Around the corner ahead, two ogres lie in wait. Does the wizard hear the ogres readying their ambush? You look at the wizard's passive Wisdom (Perception) score and consider all the factors weighing on it.

The wizard is running, not paying attention to what's ahead of him. This imposes disadvantage on the wizard's ability check. However, the ogres are readying a portcullis trap and making a lot of noise with a winch, which could grant the wizard advantage on the check. As a result, the character has neither advantage nor disadvantage on the Wisdom check, and you don't need to consider any additional factors. Past encounters with an ogre ambush, the fact that the wizard's ears are still ringing from the *thunderwave* spell he cast at the beholder, the overall noise level of the dungeon—none of that matters any more. They all cancel out.

INSPIRATION

Awarding inspiration is an effective way to encourage roleplaying and risk-taking. As explained in the *Player's Handbook*, having inspiration gives a character an obvious benefit: being able to gain advantage on one ability check, attack roll, or saving throw. Remember that a character can have no more than one inspiration at a time.

AWARDING INSPIRATION

Think of inspiration as a spice that you can use to enhance your campaign. Some DMs forgo using inspiration, while others embrace it as a key part of the game. If you take away anything from this section, remember this golden rule: inspiration should make the game more enjoyable for everyone. Award inspiration when players take actions that make the game more exciting, amusing, or memorable.

As a rule of thumb, aim to award inspiration to each character about once per session of play. Over time, you might want to award inspiration more or less often, at a rate that works best for your table. You might use the same rate for your entire DMing career, or you might change it with each campaign.

Offering inspiration as a reward encourages certain types of behavior in your players. Think of your style as a DM and your group's preferences. What helps make the game more fun for your group? What type of actions fit in with your campaign's style or genre? Your answers to those questions help determine when you award inspiration.

Roleplaying. Using inspiration to reward roleplaying is a good place to start for most groups. Reward a player with inspiration when that player causes his or her character to do something that is consistent with the character's personality trait, flaw, or bond. The character's action should be notable in some way. It might drive the story forward, push the adventurers into danger, or make everyone at the table laugh. In essence, you reward the player for roleplaying in a way that makes the game more enjoyable for everyone else.

Take into account each player's roleplaying style, and try not to favor one style over another. For example, Allison might be comfortable speaking in an accent and adopting her character's mannerisms, but Paul feels self-conscious when trying to act and prefers to describe his character's attitude and actions. Neither style is better than the other. Inspiration encourages players to take part and make a good effort, and awarding it fairly makes the game better for everyone.

Heroism. You can use inspiration to encourage player characters to take risks. A fighter might not normally hurl himself over a balcony to land in the midst of a pack of hungry ghouls, but you can reward the character's daring maneuver with inspiration. Such a reward tells the players that you want them to embrace swashbuckling action.

This approach is great for campaigns that emphasize action-packed heroics. For such campaigns, consider allowing inspiration to be spent after a d20 roll, rather than before. This approach turns inspiration into a cushion against failure—and a guarantee that it comes into play only when a player is faced directly by failure. Such an assurance makes risky tactics less daunting.

A Reward for Victory. Some DMs prefer to play an impartial role in their campaigns. Inspiration normally requires a DM's judgment to award, which might run against your style if you like a campaign where you let dice determine most outcomes. If that's your style, consider using inspiration as a reward when the characters achieve an important goal or victory, representing a surge of confidence and energy.

Under this model, give everyone in the party inspiration if the characters manage to defeat a powerful foe, execute a cunning plan to achieve a goal, or otherwise overcome a daunting obstacle in the campaign.

Genre Emulation. Inspiration is a handy tool for reinforcing the conventions of a particular genre. Under this approach, think of the motifs of a genre as personality traits, flaws, and bonds that can apply to any of the adventurers. For example, in a campaign inspired by film noir, characters could have an additional flaw: "I can't resist helping a person I find alluring despite warnings that he or she is nothing but trouble." If the characters agree to help a suspicious but seductive noble and thereby become entangled in a web of intrigue and betrayal, reward them with inspiration.

Similarly, characters in a horror story typically can't help but spend a night in a haunted house to learn its secrets. They probably also go off alone when they shouldn't. If the party splits up, consider giving each character inspiration.

A sensible person would avoid the noble's intrigues and the haunted house, but in film noir or horror, we're not dealing with sensible people; we're dealing with protagonists in a particular type of story. For this approach to work, create a list of your genre's main conventions and share it with your players. Before the campaign begins, talk about the list to make sure your group is on board for embracing those conventions.

Players and Inspiration. Remember that a player with inspiration can award it to another player. Some groups even like to treat inspiration as a group resource, deciding collectively when to spend it on a roll. It's best to let players award their inspiration as they see fit, but feel free to talk to them about following certain guidelines, particularly if you're trying to reinforce conventions of a certain genre.

When Do You Award Inspiration?

Consider the timing of your inspiration rewards. Some DMs like to award inspiration in response to an action. Other DMs like to encourage specific actions by offering inspiration while a player is considering options. Both approaches have their strengths and weaknesses.

Waiting until after an action preserves the flow of play, but it also means players don't know whether their decisions will earn them inspiration. It also means the player can't spend the inspiration on the act that earned it, unless you allow a player to retroactively spend it or are quick enough to award it before any rolls. This approach works best for groups that want to focus on immersion and player agency, where the DM steps back and gives the players more freedom to do what they want.

Telling a player that an action will earn inspiration provides clarity, but it can make it feel like you are manipulating the players or making choices for them. Offering inspiration before an action works great with groups that are comfortable with an emphasis on genre emulation and group storytelling, where character freedom isn't as important as weaving a compelling tale together.

Start with awarding inspiration after an action, especially for your first campaign or when playing with a new group. That approach is the least disruptive to the flow of play and avoids making the players feel as if you are being manipulative.

Tracking Inspiration

A player typically notes on a character sheet whether he or she has inspiration, or you can use poker chips or some other token Alternatively, you can hand out special d20s to represent inspiration. When a player spends inspiration, he or she rolls the die and then hands it back to you. If the player instead gives the inspiration to someone else, the d20 can go to that other person.

Ignoring Inspiration

Inspiration might not work for your campaign. Some DMs feel it adds a layer of metagame thinking, and others feel that heroism, roleplaying, and other parts of the game are their own rewards that don't need incentives like inspiration.

If you choose to ignore inspiration, you're telling the players that your campaign is one where you let the dice fall where they may. It's a good option for gritty campaigns or ones where the DM focuses on playing an impartial role as a rules arbiter.

Variant: Only Players Award Inspiration

As a DM, you have a lot to track during the game. Sometimes you can lose track of inspiration and forget to award it. As a variant rule, you can allow the players to handle awarding inspiration entirely. During every session, each player can award inspiration to another player. A player follows whatever guidelines the group has agreed on for awarding inspiration.

This approach makes your life easier and also gives players the chance to recognize each other for good play. You still need to make sure that inspiration is being awarded fairly.

This approach works best with groups that are focused on the story. It falls flat if the players merely manipulate it to gain advantage in key situations, without earning inspiration by way of good roleplaying or whatever other criteria the group has established.

In this variant, you can allow each player to award inspiration more than once per session. If you do so, the first time that a player awards inspiration in a session is free. Whenever that player awards it later in the same session, you gain inspiration that you can spend to give advantage to any foe of the player characters. There's no limit to the number of inspirations you can gain in this way, and unspent inspiration carries over from one session to the next.

RESOLUTION AND CONSEQUENCES

You determine the consequences of attack rolls, ability checks, and saving throws. In most cases, doing so is straightforward. When an attack hits, it deals damage. When a creature fails a saving throw, the creature suffers a harmful effect. When an ability check equals or exceeds the DC, the check succeeds.

As a DM, you have a variety of flourishes and approaches you can take when adjudicating success and failure to make things a little less black-and-white.

SUCCESS AT A COST

Failure can be tough, but the agony is compounded when a character fails by the barest margin. When a character fails a roll by only 1 or 2, you can allow the character to succeed at the cost of a complication or hindrance. Such complications can run along any of the following lines:

- A character manages to get her sword past a hobgoblin's defenses and turn a near miss into a hit, but the hobgoblin twists its shield and disarms her.
- A character narrowly escapes the full brunt of a *fireball* but ends up prone.
- A character fails to intimidate a kobold prisoner, but the kobold reveals its secrets anyway while shrieking at the top of its lungs, alerting other nearby monsters.
- A character manages to finish an arduous climb to the top of a cliff despite slipping, only to realize that the rope on which his companions dangle below him is close to breaking.

When you introduce costs such as these, try to make them obstacles and setbacks that change the nature of the adventuring situation. In exchange for success, players must consider new ways of facing the challenge.

You can also use this technique when a character succeeds on a roll by hitting the DC exactly, complicating marginal success in interesting ways.

DEGREES OF FAILURE

Sometimes a failed ability check has different consequences depending on the degree of failure. For example, a character who fails to disarm a trapped chest might accidentally spring the trap if the check fails by 5 or more, whereas a lesser failure means that the trap wasn't triggered during the botched disarm attempt. Consider adding similar distinctions to other checks. Perhaps a failed Charisma (Persuasion) check means a queen won't help, whereas a failure of 5 or more means she throws you in the dungeon for your impudence.

CRITICAL SUCCESS OR FAILURE

Rolling a 20 or a 1 on an ability check or a saving throw doesn't normally have any special effect. However, you can choose to take such an exceptional roll into account when adjudicating the outcome. It's up to you to determine how this manifests in the game. An easy approach is to increase the impact of the success or failure. For example, rolling a 1 on a failed attempt to pick a lock might break the thieves' tools being used, and rolling a 20 on a successful Intelligence (Investigation) check might reveal an extra clue.

EXPLORATION

This section provides guidance for running exploration, especially travel, tracking, and visibility.

USING A MAP

Whatever environment the adventurers are exploring, you can use a map to follow their progress as you relate the details of their travels. In a dungeon, tracking movement on a map lets you describe the branching passages, doors, chambers, and other features the adventurers encounter as they go, and gives the players the opportunity to choose their own path. Similarly, a wilderness map can show roads, rivers, terrain, and other features that might guide the characters on their travels—or lead them astray.

The Map Travel Pace table helps you track travel on maps of different scales. The table shows how much distance on a map the adventurers can cover on foot in minutes, hours, or days. The table uses the travel paces—slow, normal, and fast—described in the *Player's Handbook*. Characters moving at a normal pace can walk about 24 miles in a day.

MAP TRAVEL PACE

Map Scale	Slow Pace	Normal Pace	Fast Pace
Dungeon (1 sq. = 10 ft.)	20 sq./min.	30 sq./min.	40 sq./min.
City (1 sq. = 100 ft.)	2 sq./min.	3 sq./min.	4 sq./min.
Province (1 hex = 1 mi.)	2 hexes/hr., 18 hexes/day	3 hexes/hr., 24 hexes/day	4 hexes/hr., 30 hexes/day
Kingdom (1 hex = 6 mi.)	1 hex/3 hr., 3 hexes/day	1 hex/2 hr., 4 hexes/day	1 hex/1½ hr., 5 hexes/day

SPECIAL TRAVEL PACE

The rules on travel pace in the *Player's Handbook* assume that a group of travelers adopts a pace that, over time, is unaffected by the individual members' walking speeds. The difference between walking speeds can be significant during combat, but during an overland journey, the difference vanishes as travelers pause to catch their breath, the faster ones wait for the slower ones, and one traveler's quickness is matched by another traveler's endurance.

A character bestride a phantom steed, soaring through the air on a *carpet of flying*, or riding a sailboat or a steam-powered gnomish contraption doesn't travel at a normal rate, since the magic, engine, or wind doesn't tire the way a creature does and the air doesn't contain the types of obstructions found on land. When a creature is traveling with a flying speed or with a speed granted by magic, an engine, or a natural force (such as wind or a water current), translate that speed into travel rates using the following rules:

- In 1 minute, you can move a number of feet equal to your speed times 10.
- In 1 hour, you can move a number of miles equal to your speed divided by 10.

- For daily travel, multiply your hourly rate of travel by the number of hours traveled (typically 8 hours).
- For a fast pace, increase the rate of travel by one-third.
- For a slow pace, multiply the rate by two-thirds.

For example, a character under the effect of a *wind walk* spell gains a flying speed of 300 feet. In 1 minute, the character can move 3,000 feet at a normal pace, 4,000 feet at a fast pace, or 2,000 feet at a slow pace. The character can also cover 20, 30, or 40 miles in an hour. The spell lasts for 8 hours, allowing the character to travel 160, 240, or 320 miles in a day.

Similarly, a *phantom steed* spell creates a magical mount with a speed of 100 feet that doesn't tire like a real horse. A character on a phantom steed can cover 1,000 feet in 1 minute at a normal pace, 1,333 feet at a fast pace, or 666 feet at a slow pace. In 1 hour, the character can travel 7, 10, or 13 miles.

VISIBILITY OUTDOORS

When traveling outdoors, characters can see about 2 miles in any direction on a clear day, or until the point where trees, hills, or other obstructions block their view.

Rain normally cuts maximum visibility down to 1 mile, and fog can cut it down to between 100 and 300 feet.

On a clear day, the characters can see 40 miles if they are atop a mountain or a tall hill, or are otherwise able to look down on the area around them from a height.

NOTICING OTHER CREATURES

While exploring, characters might encounter other creatures. An important question in such a situation is who notices whom.

Indoors, whether the sides can see one another usually depends on the configuration of rooms and passageways. Vision might also be limited by light sources. Outdoor visibility can be hampered by terrain, weather, and time of day. Creatures can be more likely to hear one another before they see anything.

If neither side is being stealthy, creatures automatically notice each other once they are within sight or hearing range of one another. Otherwise, compare the Dexterity (Stealth) check results of the creatures in the group that is hiding with the passive Wisdom (Perception) scores of the other group, as explained in the *Player's Handbook*.

Tracking

Adventurers sometimes choose their path by following the tracks of other creatures—or other creatures might track the adventurers! To track, one or more creatures must succeed on a Wisdom (Survival) check. You might require trackers to make a new check in any of the following circumstances:

- They stop tracking and resume after finishing a short or long rest.
- The trail crosses an obstacle, such as a river, that shows no tracks.
- The weather conditions or terrain changes in a way that makes tracking harder.

The DC for the check depends on how well the ground shows signs of a creature's passage. No roll is necessary in situations where the tracks are obvious. For example, no check is needed to track an army advancing along a muddy road. Spotting tracks on a bare stone floor is more challenging, unless the creature being tracked leaves a distinct trail. Additionally, the passage of time often makes tracks harder to follow. In a situation where there is no trail to follow, you can rule that tracking is impossible.

The Tracking DCs table offers guidelines for setting the DC or, if you prefer, you can choose a DC based on your assessment of the difficulty. You can also grant advantage on the check if there's more than one set of tracks to follow, or disadvantage if the trail being followed passes through a well-trafficked area.

On a failed check, the character loses the trail but can attempt to find it again by making a careful search of the area. It takes 10 minutes to find a trail in a confined area such as a dungeon, or 1 hour outdoors.

Tracking DCs

Ground Surface	DC
Soft surface such as snow	10
Dirt or grass	15
Bare stone	20
Each day since the creature passed	+5
Creature left a trail such as blood	−5

Social Interaction

During a social interaction, the adventurers usually have a goal. They want to extract information, secure aid, win someone's trust, escape punishment, avoid combat, negotiate a treaty, or achieve whatever other objective led to the interaction in the first place. The creatures they interact with also have agendas.

Some DMs prefer to run a social interaction as a free-form roleplaying exercise, where dice rarely come into play. Other DMs prefer to resolve the outcome of an interaction by having characters make Charisma checks. Either approach works, and most games fall somewhere in between, balancing player skill (roleplaying and persuading) with character skill (reflected by ability checks).

Resolving Interactions

The *Player's Handbook* provides guidelines for balancing roleplaying and ability checks in a social interaction (see chapter 8, "Adventuring," in that book). This section adds to that material by providing a structured way to resolve a social interaction. Much of this structure will be invisible to your players in play and isn't meant to be a substitute for roleplaying.

1. Starting Attitude

Choose the starting attitude of a creature the adventurers are interacting with: friendly, indifferent, or hostile.

A **friendly** creature wants to help the adventurers and wishes for them to succeed. For tasks or actions that require no particular risk, effort, or cost, friendly creatures usually help without question. If an element of personal risk is involved, a successful Charisma check might be required to convince a friendly creature to take that risk.

An **indifferent** creature might help or hinder the party, depending on what the creature sees as most beneficial. A creature's indifference doesn't necessarily make it standoffish or disinterested. Indifferent creatures might be polite and genial, surly and irritable, or anything in between. A successful Charisma check is necessary when the adventurers try to persuade an indifferent creature to do something.

A **hostile** creature opposes the adventurers and their goals but doesn't necessarily attack them on sight. For example, a condescending noble might wish to see a group of upstart adventurers fail so as to keep them from becoming rivals for the king's attention, thwarting them with slander and scheming rather than direct threats and violence. The adventurers need to succeed on one or more challenging Charisma checks to convince a hostile creature to do anything on their behalf. That said, a hostile creature might be so ill-disposed toward the party that no Charisma check can improve its attitude, in which case any attempt to sway it through diplomacy fails automatically.

2. Conversation

Play out the conversation. Let the adventurers make their points, trying to frame their statements in terms that are meaningful to the creature they are interacting with.

Changing Attitude. The attitude of a creature might change over the course of a conversation. If the adventurers say or do the right things during an interaction (perhaps by touching on a creature's ideal, bond, or flaw), they can make a hostile creature temporarily indifferent, or make an indifferent creature temporarily friendly. Likewise, a gaffe, insult, or harmful deed might make a friendly creature temporarily indifferent or turn an indifferent creature hostile.

Whether the adventurers can shift a creature's attitude is up to you. You decide whether the adventurers have successfully couched their statements in terms that matter to the creature. Typically, a creature's attitude can't shift more than one step during a single interaction, whether temporarily or permanently.

Determining Characteristics. The adventurers don't necessarily enter into a social interaction with a full understanding of a creature's ideal, bond, or flaw. If they want to shift a creature's attitude by playing on these characteristics, they first need to determine what the creature cares about. They can guess, but doing so runs the risk of shifting the creature's attitude in the wrong direction if they guess badly.

After interacting with a creature long enough to get a sense of its personality traits and characteristics through conversation, an adventurer can attempt a Wisdom (Insight) check to uncover one of the creature's characteristics. You set the DC. A check that fails by 10 or more might misidentify a characteristic, so you should provide a false characteristic or invert one of the creature's existing characteristics. For example, if an old sage's flaw is that he is prejudiced against the uneducated, an adventurer who badly fails the check might be told that the sage enjoys personally seeing to the education of the downtrodden.

Given time, adventurers can also learn about a creature's characteristics from other sources, including its friends and allies, personal letters, and publicly told stories. Acquiring such information might be the basis of an entirely different set of social interactions.

3. Charisma Check

When the adventurers get to the point of their request, demand, or suggestion—or if you decide the conversation has run its course—call for a Charisma check. Any character who has actively participated in the conversation can make the check. Depending on how the adventurers handled the conversation, the Persuasion, Deception, or Intimidation skill might apply to the check. The creature's current attitude determines the DC required to achieve a specific reaction, as shown in the Conversation Reaction table.

Conversation Reaction

DC	Friendly Creature's Reaction
0	The creature does as asked without taking risks or making sacrifices.
10	The creature accepts a minor risk or sacrifice to do as asked.
20	The creature accepts a significant risk or sacrifice to do as asked.

DC	Indifferent Creature's Reaction
0	The creature offers no help but does no harm.
10	The creature does as asked as long as no risks or sacrifices are involved.
20	The creature accepts a minor risk or sacrifice to do as asked.

DC	Hostile Creature's Reaction
0	The creature opposes the adventurers' actions and might take risks to do so.
10	The creature offers no help but does no harm.
20	The creature does as asked as long as no risks or sacrifices are involved.

Aiding the Check. Other characters who make substantial contributions to the conversation can help the character making the check. If a helping character says or does something that would influence the interaction in a positive way, the character making the Charisma check can do so with advantage. If the other character inadvertently says something counterproductive or offensive, the character making the Charisma check has disadvantage on that check.

Multiple Checks. Certain situations might call for more than one check, particularly if the adventurers come into the interaction with multiple goals.

4. Repeat?

Once a Charisma check has been made, further attempts to influence the target of the interaction might be fruitless or run the risk of upsetting or angering the subject creature, potentially shifting its attitude toward hostility. Use your best judgment. For example, if the party's rogue says something that pushes a noble's attitude toward the party from indifferent to hostile, another character might be able to diffuse the noble's hostility with clever roleplaying and a successful Charisma (Persuasion) check.

Roleplaying

For some DMs, roleplaying comes naturally. If it doesn't come naturally for you, don't worry. The main thing is for you to have fun portraying your NPCs and monsters and to amuse your players in the process. You don't need to be a practiced thespian or comedian to create drama or humor. The key is to pay attention to the story elements and characterizations that make your players laugh or feel emotionally engaged and to incorporate those things into your roleplaying.

Being the NPC

Imagine how a character or monster you bring to life would react to the adventurers. Consider what it cares about. Does it have any ideals, flaws, or bonds? By working such things into your portrayal, you not only make the character or monster more believable, but you also enhance the sense that the adventurers are in a living world.

Strive for responses and actions that introduce twists into the game. For example, an old woman whose family was killed at the hands of an evil wizard might regard the party's wizard with grave suspicion.

However you roleplay a character or monster, the classic advice for writers holds true: show, don't tell. For example, rather than describe an NPC as shallow and self-centered, have the individual act the way you would expect a shallow, self-centered person to behave. The NPC might have off-the-cuff answers for everything, an over-willingness to share personal anecdotes, and a desperate need to make himself or herself the subject of every conversation.

Using Your Voice

Most of what you say during a session will be at a consistent level. For dramatic effect, be ready to shout out a battle cry or speak in a conspiratorial whisper.

Also, characters and monsters with distinctive voices are memorable. If you're not a natural mimic or actor, borrowing distinctive speech patterns from real life, the movies, or television is a good place to start. Practice different voices and impersonations of famous people, then use those voices to bring your NPCs to life.

Experiment with different speech patterns. For instance, a barmaid and a city magistrate probably use their words differently. Similarly, peasants could speak in earthy dialects, while rich folk talk in haughty drawls. Let a pirate NPC say, "Arrrr, maties!" in your best Long John Silver voice. Let intelligent monsters unfamiliar with Common stumble along with awkward grammar. Let drunkards and monsters mutter with slurred speech, while lizardfolk hiss their threats.

In any interaction with multiple NPCs, make sure the adventurers remain the focus. Have the NPCs talk to them, not so much to each other. If possible, let one NPC do most of the talking, but if multiple NPCs need to talk, give them distinct voices so the players know who's who.

Using Your Face and Arms

Use your facial expressions to help show a character's emotions. Scowl, smile, grin, snarl, pout, cross your eyes—do whatever it takes to make the character or monster memorable to the players. When you combine facial expressions with an unusual voice, a character truly comes to life.

Though you don't need to stand up out of your chair, you can use your arms to bring even more life to an NPC. A noble could chop the air with one hand while speaking in a deadpan monotone, while an archmage might express her displeasure by silently rolling her eyes and massaging her temples with her fingers.

Engaging the Players

Some players enjoy roleplaying and interaction more than others. Whatever your players' tastes, your lively portrayal of NPCs and monsters can inspire players to make just as much investment in portraying their characters. This makes social interactions an opportunity for everyone to become more immersed in the game, creating a story whose protagonists have depth.

To make sure everyone has something to do during a roleplaying-heavy game session, consider one or more of the following approaches.

Appeal to Player Preferences. There are in-game activities that players enjoy more than others, as discussed in this book's introduction. Players who like acting thrive in interaction situations, and it's fine to let those players take the spotlight. They often inspire other players by their example, but make sure those other players have an opportunity to join in the fun.

Players who like exploring and storytelling are usually amenable to roleplaying, as long as it moves the campaign forward and reveals more about the world. Players who like problem-solving often enjoy figuring out the right thing to say to shift an NPC's attitude. Players who are instigators like provoking reactions from NPCs, so they're often easily engaged—though not always productively.

Players who like to optimize their characters and slay monsters also like to argue, and having conflict within an interaction can help those players embrace roleplaying. Still, creating combat connections to an extended interaction (such as a corrupt vizier sending assassins to kill the adventurers) is often the best way to keep action-focused players engaged.

Target Specific Characters. Create situations where characters who might not otherwise be engaged with a social interaction have to do at least some of the talking. Perhaps the NPC in question is a family member or a contact of a particular adventurer and talks only to that character. An NPC of a certain race or class might listen only to characters he or she feels a kinship with. Creating a sense of importance can be a great way to get specific players engaged, but don't shut out players who are already roleplaying.

If a couple of players are dominating the conversation, take a moment now and then to involve the others. You can do this in character if you like: "And what about your hulking friend? Speak, barbarian! What will you pledge in exchange for my favor?" Or just ask the player what his or her character is doing while the conversation is going on. The first approach is better for players who are already comfortable speaking in their characters' voices. The second approach works better for players who need encouragement to engage in a roleplaying scenario.

Objects

When characters need to saw through ropes, shatter a window, or smash a vampire's coffin, the only hard and fast rule is this: given enough time and the right tools, characters can destroy any destructible object. Use common sense when determining a character's success at damaging an object. Can a fighter cut through a section of a stone wall with a sword? No, the sword is likely to break before the wall does.

For the purpose of these rules, an object is a discrete, inanimate item like a window, door, sword, book, table, chair, or stone, not a building or a vehicle that is composed of many other objects.

Statistics for Objects

When time is a factor, you can assign an Armor Class and hit points to a destructible object. You can also give it immunities, resistances, and vulnerabilities to specific types of damage.

Armor Class. An object's Armor Class is a measure of how difficult it is to deal damage to the object when striking it (because the object has no chance of dodging out of the way). The Object Armor Class table provides suggested AC values for various substances.

Object Armor Class

Substance	AC	Substance	AC
Cloth, paper, rope	11	Iron, steel	19
Crystal, glass, ice	13	Mithral	21
Wood, bone	15	Adamantine	23
Stone	17		

Hit Points. An object's hit points measure how much damage it can take before losing its structural integrity. Resilient objects have more hit points than fragile ones. Large objects also tend to have more hit points than small ones, unless breaking a small part of the object is just as effective as breaking the whole thing. The Object Hit Points table provides suggested hit points for fragile and resilient objects that are Large or smaller.

OBJECT HIT POINTS

Size	Fragile	Resilient
Tiny (bottle, lock)	2 (1d4)	5 (2d4)
Small (chest, lute)	3 (1d6)	10 (3d6)
Medium (barrel, chandelier)	4 (1d8)	18 (4d8)
Large (cart, 10-ft.-by-10-ft. window)	5 (1d10)	27 (5d10)

Huge and Gargantuan Objects. Normal weapons are of little use against many Huge and Gargantuan objects, such as a colossal statue, towering column of stone, or massive boulder. That said, one torch can burn a Huge tapestry, and an *earthquake* spell can reduce a colossus to rubble. You can track a Huge or Gargantuan object's hit points if you like, or you can simply decide how long the object can withstand whatever weapon or force is acting against it. If you track hit points for the object, divide it into Large or smaller sections, and track each section's hit points separately. Destroying one of those sections could ruin the entire object. For example, a Gargantuan statue of a human might topple over when one of its Large legs is reduced to 0 hit points.

Objects and Damage Types. Objects are immune to poison and psychic damage. You might decide that some damage types are more effective against a particular object or substance than others. For example, bludgeoning damage works well for smashing things but not for cutting through rope or leather. Paper or cloth objects might be vulnerable to fire and lightning damage. A pick can chip away stone but can't effectively cut down a tree. As always, use your best judgment.

Damage Threshold. Big objects such as castle walls often have extra resilience represented by a damage threshold. An object with a damage threshold has immunity to all damage unless it takes an amount of damage from a single attack or effect equal to or greater than its damage threshold, in which case it takes damage as normal. Any damage that fails to meet or exceed the object's damage threshold is considered superficial and doesn't reduce the object's hit points.

COMBAT

This section builds on the combat rules in the *Player's Handbook* and offers tips for keeping the game running smoothly when a fight breaks out.

TRACKING INITIATIVE

You can use several different methods for keeping track of who goes when in combat.

HIDDEN LIST

Many DMs keep track of initiative on a list the players can't see: usually a piece of paper behind a DM screen

or a spreadsheet on a tablet computer. This method allows you to keep track of combatants who haven't been revealed yet, and you can use the initiative list as a place to record the current hit points of monsters, as well as other useful notes.

A downside of this approach is that you have to remind the players round after round when their turns come up.

VISIBLE LIST

You can use a whiteboard to track initiative. As the players tell you their initiative numbers, write them on the whiteboard in order from highest to lowest, leaving space between each name. Either write the monsters' initiatives on the list at the same time or add them to the list on each monster's first turn.

As a further improvement, use magnets that you can attach to a metal-based whiteboard with characters' and monsters' names written on them, or write those names on cards held in place by magnets.

A visible list lets everyone see the order of play. Players know when their turns are coming up, and they can start planning their actions in advance. A visible list also removes any uncertainty about when the monsters will act in the fight.

A variation on the visible list is to give one player responsibility for keeping track of initiative, either on a whiteboard or on a piece of paper the other players can see. This method reduces the number of things you need to keep track of yourself.

INDEX CARDS

In this approach, each character gets an index card, as does each group of identical monsters. When the players tell you their initiative numbers, write the numbers on their characters' index cards. Do the same when you roll the monsters' initiative. Then arrange the cards in order from highest to lowest. Starting at the top, you move down through the stack. When you call out the name of the character whose turn it is, also mention who's next, prompting that player to start thinking ahead. After each character or group of monsters acts, the top card is moved to the bottom of the stack.

At first, players don't know the order of play when you use combat cards, and they don't know where the monsters fall into the order until the monsters act.

TRACKING MONSTER HIT POINTS

During a combat encounter, you need to track how much damage each monster takes. Most DMs track damage in secret so that their players don't know how many hit points a monster has remaining. Whether you choose to be secretive or not is up to you. What's important is that every monster's hit points be tracked individually.

Tracking damage for one or two monsters isn't onerous, but it helps to have a system for larger groups of monsters. If you aren't using miniatures or other visual aids, the easiest way to keep track of your monsters is to assign them unique features. Descriptions such as "the ogre with the nasty scar" and "the ogre with the horned helm" help you and your players track which monster is which. For example, imagine that you're running an encounter with three ogres, each of which has 59 hit points. Once initiative is rolled, jot down each ogre's hit points and add notes (and even a name, if you like) to differentiate each one:

Krag (ogre w/ scar): 59

Thod (ogre w/ helm): 59

Mur (ogre who smells like poo): 59

If you use miniatures to represent monsters, one easy way to differentiate them is to give each one a unique miniature. If you use identical miniatures to represent multiple monsters, you can tag the miniatures with small stickers of different colors or stickers with different letters or numbers on them.

For example, in a combat encounter with three ogres, you could use three identical ogre miniatures tagged with stickers marked A, B, and C, respectively. To track the ogres' hit points, you can sort them by letter, then subtract damage from their hit points as they take it. Your records might look something like this after a few rounds of combat:

Ogre A: ~~59~~ ~~53~~ ~~45~~ ~~24~~ ~~14~~ 9 dead

Ogre B: ~~59~~ ~~51~~ 30

Ogre C: 59

Players often ask how hurt a monster looks. Don't ever feel as though you need to reveal exact hit points, but if a monster is below half its hit point maximum, it's fair to say that it has visible wounds and appears beaten down. You can describe a monster taken to half its hit points as bloodied, giving the players a sense of progress in a fight against a tough opponent, and helping them judge when to use their most powerful spells and abilities.

Using and Tracking Conditions

Various rules and features in the game are clear about when they apply a condition to a creature. You can also apply conditions on the fly. They're meant to be intuitive for you to do so. For example, if a character is in a state, such as sleep, that lacks consciousness, you can say the character is unconscious. Or did a character just stumble onto the ground? He or she is now prone.

Keeping track of conditions can become tricky. For monsters, it's often easiest to track conditions on combat cards or wherever you track initiative. Players should remember any conditions affecting their characters. Because players have incentive to forget or overlook hampering conditions, character conditions can also be marked on combat cards or a whiteboard.

You might also try keeping a supply of index cards on hand, marked with conditions and their effects. Then hand the cards to players as the conditions come up. Having a bright pink index card on top of a character sheet can help even the most absentminded player remember the effects of being charmed or frightened.

Monsters and Critical Hits

A monster follows the same rule for critical hits as a player character. That said, if you use a monster's average damage, rather than rolling, you might wonder how to handle a critical hit. When the monster scores a critical hit, roll all the damage dice associated with the hit and add them to the average damage. For example, if a goblin normally deals 5 (1d6 + 2) slashing damage on a hit and scores a critical hit, it deals 5 + 1d6 slashing damage.

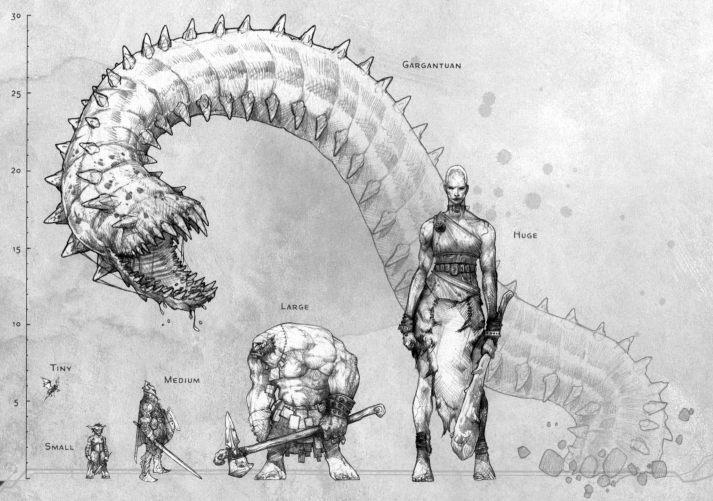

Creature Size on Squares and Hexes

| Tiny | Small or Medium | Large | Huge | Gargantuan |

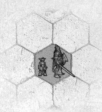

Improvising Damage

A monster or effect typically specifies the amount of damage it deals. In some cases, though, you need to determine damage on the fly. The Improvising Damage table gives you suggestions for when you do so.

Improvising Damage

Dice	Examples
1d10	Burned by coals, hit by a falling bookcase, pricked by a poison needle
2d10	Being struck by lightning, stumbling into a fire pit
4d10	Hit by falling rubble in a collapsing tunnel, stumbling into a vat of acid
10d10	Crushed by compacting walls, hit by whirling steel blades, wading through a lava stream
18d10	Being submerged in lava, being hit by a crashing flying fortress
24d10	Tumbling into a vortex of fire on the Elemental Plane of Fire, being crushed in the jaws of a godlike creature or a moon-sized monster

The Damage Severity and Level table is a guide to how deadly these damage numbers are for characters of various levels. Cross-reference a character's level with the damage being dealt to gauge the severity of the damage.

Damage Severity and Level

Character Level	Setback	Dangerous	Deadly
1st–4th	1d10	2d10	4d10
5th–10th	2d10	4d10	10d10
11th–16th	4d10	10d10	18d10
17th–20th	10d10	18d10	24d10

Damage sufficient to cause a **setback** rarely poses a risk of death to characters of the level shown, but a severely weakened character might be laid low by this damage.

In contrast, **dangerous** damage values pose a significant threat to weaker characters and could potentially kill a character of the level shown if that character is missing many hit points.

As the name suggests, **deadly** damage is enough to drop a character of the level shown to 0 hit points. This level of damage can kill even powerful characters outright if they are already wounded.

Adjudicating Areas of Effect

Many spells and other game features create areas of effect, such as the cone and the sphere. If you're not using miniatures or another visual aid, it can sometimes be difficult to determine who's in an area of effect and who isn't. The easiest way to address such uncertainty is to go with your gut and make a call.

If you would like more guidance, consider using the Targets in Areas of Effect table. To use the table, imagine which combatants are near one another, and let the table guide you in determining the number of those combatants that are caught in an area of effect. Add or subtract targets based on how bunched up the potential targets are. Consider rolling 1d3 to determine the amount to add or subtract.

Targets in Areas of Effect

Area	Number of Targets
Cone	Size ÷ 10 (round up)
Cube or square	Size ÷ 5 (round up)
Cylinder	Radius ÷ 5 (round up)
Line	Length ÷ 30 (round up)
Sphere or circle	Radius ÷ 5 (round up)

For example, if a wizard directs *burning hands* (a 15-foot cone) at a nearby group of orcs, you could use the table and say that two orcs are targeted (15 ÷ 10 = 1.5, rounded up to 2). Similarly, a sorcerer could launch a *lightning bolt* (100-foot line) at some ogres and hobgoblins, and you could use the table to say four of the monsters are targeted (100 ÷ 30 = 3.33, rounded up to 4).

This approach aims at simplicity instead of spatial precision. If you prefer more tactical nuance, consider using miniatures.

HANDLING MOBS

Keeping combat moving along at a brisk pace can be difficult when there are dozens of monsters involved in a battle. When handling a crowded battlefield, you can speed up play by forgoing attack rolls in favor of approximating the average number of hits a large group of monsters can inflict on a target.

Instead of rolling an attack roll, determine the minimum d20 roll a creature needs in order to hit a target by subtracting its attack bonus from the target's AC. You'll need to refer to the result throughout the battle, so it's best to write it down.

Look up the minimum d20 roll needed on the Mob Attacks table. The table shows you how many creatures that need that die roll or higher must attack a target in order for one of them to hit. If that many creatures attack the target, their combined efforts result in one of them hitting the target.

For example, eight orcs surround a fighter. The orcs' attack bonus is +5, and the fighter's AC is 19. The orcs need a 14 or higher to hit the fighter. According to the table, for every three orcs that attack the fighter, one of them hits. There are enough orcs for two groups of three. The remaining two orcs fail to hit the fighter.

If the attacking creatures deal different amounts of damage, assume that the creature that deals the most damage is the one that hits. If the creature that hits has multiple attacks with the same attack bonus, assume that it hits once with each of those attacks. If a creature's attacks have different attack bonuses, resolve each attack separately.

This attack resolution system ignores critical hits in favor of reducing the number of die rolls. As the number of combatants dwindles, switch back to using individual die rolls to avoid situations where one side can't possibly hit the other.

MOB ATTACKS

d20 Roll Needed	Attackers Needed for One to Hit
1–5	1
6–12	2
13–14	3
15–16	4
17–18	5
19	10
20	20

USING MINIATURES

In combat, players can often rely on your descriptions to visualize where their characters are in relation to their surroundings and their enemies. Some complex battles, however, are easier to run with visual aids, the most common of which are miniatures and a grid. If you like to construct model terrain, build three-dimensional dungeons, or draw maps on large vinyl mats, you should also consider using miniatures.

The *Player's Handbook* offers simple rules for depicting combat using miniature figures on a grid. This section expands on that material.

TACTICAL MAPS

You can draw tactical maps with colored markers on a wet-erase vinyl mat with 1-inch squares, on a large sheet of paper, or on a similar flat surface. Preprinted poster-sized maps, maps assembled from cardboard tiles, and terrain made of sculpted plaster or resin are also fun.

The most common unit for tactical maps is the 5-foot square, and maps with grids are readily available and easy to create. However, you don't have to use a grid at all. You can track distances with a tape measure, string, craft sticks, or pipe cleaners cut to specific lengths. Another option is a play surface covered by 1-inch hexagons (often called hexes), which combines the easy counting of a grid with the more flexible movement of using no grid. Dungeon corridors with straight walls and right angles don't map easily onto hexes, though.

FLANKING (SQUARES)

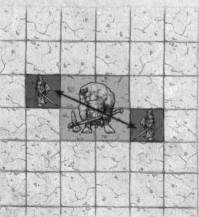

HALF COVER (SQUARES)

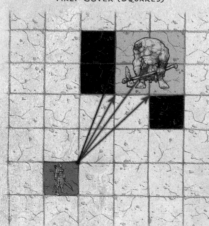

THREE-QUARTERS COVER (SQUARES)

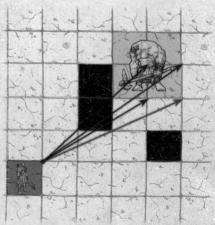

CREATURE SIZE ON SQUARES AND HEXES

A creature's size determines how much space it occupies on squares or hexes, as shown in the Creature Size and Space table. If the miniature you use for a monster takes up an amount of space different from what's on the table, that's fine, but treat the monster as its official size for all other rules. For example, you might use a miniature that has a Large base to represent a Huge giant. That giant takes up less space on the battlefield than its size suggests, but it is still Huge for the purposes of rules like grappling.

CREATURE SIZE AND SPACE

Size	Space: Squares	Space: Hexes
Tiny	4 per square	4 per hex
Small	1 square	1 hex
Medium	1 square	1 hex
Large	4 squares (2 by 2)	3 hexes
Huge	9 squares (3 by 3)	7 hexes
Gargantuan	16 squares (4 by 4) or more	12 hexes or more

AREAS OF EFFECT

The area of effect of a spell, monster ability, or other feature must be translated onto squares or hexes to determine which potential targets are in the area and which aren't.

Choose an intersection of squares or hexes as the point of origin of an area of effect, then follow its rules as normal. If an area of effect is circular and covers at least half a square, it affects that square.

LINE OF SIGHT

To precisely determine whether there is line of sight between two spaces, pick a corner of one space and trace an imaginary line from that corner to any part of another space. If at least one such line doesn't pass through or touch an object or effect that blocks vision—such as a stone wall, a thick curtain, or a dense cloud of fog—then there is line of sight.

COVER

To determine whether a target has cover against an attack or other effect on a grid, choose a corner of the attacker's space or the point of origin of an area of effect. Then trace imaginary lines from that corner to every corner of any one square the target occupies. If one or two of those lines are blocked by an obstacle (including another creature), the target has half cover. If three or four of those lines are blocked but the attack can still reach the target (such as when the target is behind an arrow slit), the target has three-quarters cover.

On hexes, use the same procedure as a grid, drawing lines between the corners of the hexagons. The target has half cover if up to three lines are blocked by an obstacle, and three-quarters cover if four or more lines are blocked but the attack can still reach the target.

OPTIONAL RULE: FLANKING

If you regularly use miniatures, flanking gives combatants a simple way to gain advantage on attack rolls against a common enemy.

A creature can't flank an enemy that it can't see. A creature also can't flank while it is incapacitated. A Large or larger creature is flanking as long as at least one square or hex of its space qualifies for flanking.

Flanking on Squares. When a creature and at least one of its allies are adjacent to an enemy and on opposite sides or corners of the enemy's space, they flank that enemy, and each of them has advantage on melee attack rolls against that enemy.

When in doubt about whether two creatures flank an enemy on a grid, trace an imaginary line between the centers of the creatures' spaces. If the line passes through opposite sides or corners of the enemy's space, the enemy is flanked.

Flanking on Hexes. When a creature and at least one of its allies are adjacent to an enemy and on opposite sides of the enemy's space, they flank that enemy, and each of them has advantage on attack rolls against that enemy. On hexes, count around the enemy from one creature to its ally. Against a Medium or smaller creature, the allies flank if there are 2 hexes between them. Against a Large creature, the allies flank if there are 4 hexes between them. Against a Huge creature, they must have 5 hexes between them. Against a Gargantuan creature, they must have at least 6 hexes between them.

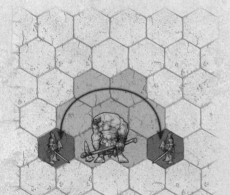

FLANKING (HEXES)

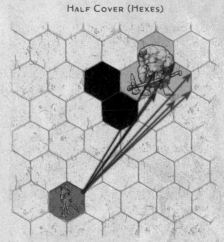

HALF COVER (HEXES)

THREE-QUARTERS COVER (HEXES)

OPTIONAL RULE: DIAGONALS

The *Player's Handbook* presents a simple method for counting movement and measuring range on a grid: count every square as 5 feet, even if you're moving diagonally. Though this is fast in play, it breaks the laws of geometry and is inaccurate over long distances. This optional rule provides more realism, but it requires more effort during combat.

When measuring range or moving diagonally on a grid, the first diagonal square counts as 5 feet, but the second diagonal square counts as 10 feet. This pattern of 5 feet and then 10 feet continues whenever you're counting diagonally, even if you move horizontally or vertically between different bits of diagonal movement. For example, a character might move one square diagonally (5 feet), then three squares straight (15 feet), and then another square diagonally (10 feet) for a total movement of 30 feet.

OPTIONAL RULE: FACING

If you want the precision of knowing which way a creature is facing, consider using this optional rule.

Whenever a creature ends its move, it can change its facing. Each creature has a front arc (the direction it faces), left and right side arcs, and a rear arc. A creature can also change its facing as a reaction when any other creature moves.

A creature can normally target only creatures in its front or side arcs. It can't see into its rear arc. This means an attacker in the creature's rear arc makes attack rolls against it with advantage.

Shields apply their bonus to AC only against attacks from the front arc or the same side arc as the shield. For example, a fighter with a shield on the left arm can use it only against attacks from the front and left arcs.

Feel free to determine that not all creatures have every type of arc. For example, an amorphous ochre jelly could treat all of its arcs as front ones, while a hydra might have three front arcs and one rear one.

On squares, you pick one side of a creature's space as the direction it is facing. Draw a diagonal line outward from each corner of this side to determine the squares in its front arc. The opposite side of the space determines its rear arc in the same way. The remaining spaces to either side of the creature form its side arcs.

On hexes, determining the front, rear, and side arcs requires more judgment. Pick one side of the creature's space and create a wedge shape expanding out from there for the front arc, and another on the opposite side of the creature for the rear arc. The remaining spaces to either side of the creature are its side arcs.

A square or hex might be in more than one arc, depending on how you draw the lines from a creature's space. If more than half of a square or hex lies in one arc, it is in that arc. If it is split exactly down the middle, use this rule: if half of it lies in the front arc, it's in that arc. If half of it is in a side arc and the rear arc, it's in the side arc.

ADJUDICATING REACTION TIMING

Typical combatants rely on the opportunity attack and the Ready action for most of their reactions in a fight. Various spells and features give a creature more reaction options, and sometimes the timing of a reaction can be difficult to adjudicate. Use this rule of thumb: follow whatever timing is specified in the reaction's description. For example, the opportunity attack and the *shield* spell are clear about the fact that they can interrupt their triggers. If a reaction has no timing specified, or the timing is unclear, the reaction occurs after its trigger finishes, as in the Ready action.

CHASES

Strict application of the movement rules can turn a potentially exciting chase into a dull, predictable affair. Faster creatures always catch up to slower ones, while creatures with the same speed never close the distance between each other. This set of rules can make chases more exciting by introducing random elements.

BEGINNING A CHASE

A chase requires a quarry and at least one pursuer. Any participants not already in initiative order must roll initiative. As in combat, each participant in the chase can take one action and move on its turn. The chase ends when one side drops out or the quarry escapes.

When a chase begins, determine the starting distance between the quarry and the pursuers. Track the distance between them, and designate the pursuer closest to the quarry as the lead. The lead pursuer might change from round to round.

RUNNING THE CHASE

Participants in the chase are strongly motivated to use the Dash action every round. Pursuers who stop to cast spells and make attacks run the risk of losing their quarry, and a quarry that does so is likely to be caught.

DASHING

During the chase, a participant can freely use the Dash action a number of times equal to 3 + its Constitution modifier. Each additional Dash action it takes during the chase requires the creature to succeed on a DC 10 Constitution check at the end of its turn or gain one level of exhaustion.

A participant drops out of the chase if its exhaustion reaches level 5, since its speed becomes 0. A creature can remove the levels of exhaustion it gained during the chase by finishing a short or long rest.

SPELLS AND ATTACKS

A chase participant can make attacks and cast spells against other creatures within range. Apply the normal rules for cover, terrain, and so on to the attacks and spells.

Chase participants can't normally make opportunity attacks against each other, since they are all assumed to be moving in the same direction at the same time.

However, participants can still be the targets of opportunity attacks from creatures not participating in the chase. For example, adventurers who chase a thief past a gang of thugs in an alley might provoke opportunity attacks from the thugs.

ENDING A CHASE

A chase ends when one side or the other stops, when the quarry escapes, or when the pursuers are close enough to their quarry to catch it.

If neither side gives up the chase, the quarry makes a Dexterity (Stealth) check at the end of each round, after every participant in the chase has taken its turn. The result is compared to the passive Wisdom (Perception) scores of the pursuers. If the quarry consists of multiple creatures, they all make the check.

If the quarry is never out of the lead pursuer's sight, the check fails automatically. Otherwise, if the result of the quarry's check is greater than the highest passive score, that quarry escapes. If not, the chase continues for another round.

The quarry gains advantage or disadvantage on its check based on prevailing circumstances, as shown in the Escape Factors table. If one or more factors give the quarry both advantage and disadvantage on its check, the quarry has neither, as usual.

ESCAPE FACTORS

Factor	Check Has ...
Quarry has many things to hide behind	Advantage
Quarry is in a very crowded or noisy area	Advantage
Quarry has few things to hide behind	Disadvantage
Quarry is in an uncrowded or quiet area	Disadvantage
The lead pursuer is a ranger or has proficiency in Survival	Disadvantage

Other factors might help or hinder the quarry's ability to escape, at your discretion. For example, a quarry with a *faerie fire* spell cast on it might have disadvantage on checks made to escape because it's much easier to spot.

Escape doesn't necessarily mean the quarry has outpaced its pursuers. For example, in an urban setting, escape might mean the quarry ducked into a crowd or slipped around a corner, leaving no clue as to where it went.

CHASE COMPLICATIONS

As with any good chase scene, complications can arise to make a chase more pulse-pounding. The Urban Chase Complications table and the Wilderness Chase Complications table provide several examples.

Complications occur randomly. Each participant in the chase rolls a d20 at the end of its turn. Consult the appropriate table to determine whether a complication occurs. If it does, it affects the next chase participant in the initiative order, not the participant who rolled the die. The participant who rolled the die or the participant affected by the complication can spend inspiration to negate the complication.

Characters can create their own complications to shake off pursuers (for example, casting the *web* spell in a narrow alleyway). Adjudicate these as you see fit.

URBAN CHASE COMPLICATIONS

d20	Complication
1	A large obstacle such as a horse or cart blocks your way. Make a DC 15 Dexterity (Acrobatics) check to get past the obstacle. On a failed check, the obstacle counts as 10 feet of difficult terrain.
2	A crowd blocks your way. Make a DC 10 Strength (Athletics) or Dexterity (Acrobatics) check (your choice) to make your way through the crowd unimpeded. On a failed check, the crowd counts as 10 feet of difficult terrain.
3	A large stained-glass window or similar barrier blocks your path. Make a DC 10 Strength saving throw to smash through the barrier and keep going. On a failed save, you bounce off the barrier and fall prone.
4	A maze of barrels, crates, or similar obstacles stands in your way. Make a DC 10 Dexterity (Acrobatics) or Intelligence check (your choice) to navigate the maze. On a failed check, the maze counts as 10 feet of difficult terrain.
5	The ground beneath your feet is slippery with rain, spilled oil, or some other liquid. Make a DC 10 Dexterity saving throw. On a failed save, you fall prone.
6	You come upon a pack of dogs fighting over food. Make a DC 10 Dexterity (Acrobatics) check to get through the pack unimpeded. On a failed check, you are bitten and take 1d4 piercing damage, and the dogs count as 5 feet of difficult terrain.
7	You run into a brawl in progress. Make a DC 15 Strength (Athletics), Dexterity (Acrobatics), or Charisma (Intimidation) check (your choice) to get past the brawlers unimpeded. On a failed check, you take 2d4 bludgeoning damage, and the brawlers count as 10 feet of difficult terrain.
8	A beggar blocks your way. Make a DC 10 Strength (Athletics), Dexterity (Acrobatics), or Charisma (Intimidation) check (your choice) to slip past the beggar. You succeed automatically if you toss the beggar a coin. On a failed check, the beggar counts as 5 feet of difficult terrain.
9	An overzealous **guard** (see the *Monster Manual* for game statistics) mistakes you for someone else. If you move 20 feet or more on your turn, the guard makes an opportunity attack against you with a spear (+3 to hit; 1d6 + 1 piercing damage on a hit).
10	You are forced to make a sharp turn to avoid colliding with something impassable. Make a DC 10 Dexterity saving throw to navigate the turn. On a failed save, you collide with something hard and take 1d4 bludgeoning damage.
11–20	No complication.

WILDERNESS CHASE COMPLICATIONS

d20	Complication
1	Your path takes you through a rough patch of brush. Make a DC 10 Strength (Athletics) or Dexterity (Acrobatics) check (your choice) to get past the brush. On a failed check, the brush counts as 5 feet of difficult terrain.
2	Uneven ground threatens to slow your progress. Make a DC 10 Dexterity (Acrobatics) check to navigate the area. On a failed check, the ground counts as 10 feet of difficult terrain.
3	You run through a **swarm of insects** (see the *Monster Manual* for game statistics, with the DM choosing whichever kind of insects makes the most sense). The swarm makes an opportunity attack against you (+3 to hit; 4d4 piercing damage on a hit).
4	A stream, ravine, or rock bed blocks your path. Make a DC 10 Strength (Athletics) or Dexterity (Acrobatics) check (your choice) to cross the impediment. On a failed check, the impediment counts as 10 feet of difficult terrain.
5	Make a DC 10 Constitution saving throw. On a failed save, you are blinded by blowing sand, dirt, ash, snow, or pollen until the end of your turn. While blinded in this way, your speed is halved.
6	A sudden drop catches you by surprise. Make a DC 10 Dexterity saving throw to navigate the impediment. On a failed save, you fall 1d4 × 5 feet, taking 1d6 bludgeoning damage per 10 feet fallen as normal, and land prone.
7	You blunder into a hunter's snare. Make a DC 15 Dexterity saving throw to avoid it. On a failed save, you are caught in a net and restrained. See chapter 5, "Equipment," of the *Player's Handbook* for rules on escaping a net.
8	You are caught in a stampede of spooked animals. Make a DC 10 Dexterity saving throw. On a failed save, you are knocked about and take 1d4 bludgeoning damage and 1d4 piercing damage.
9	Your path takes you near a patch of razorvine. Make a DC 15 Dexterity saving throw or use 10 feet of movement (your choice) to avoid the razorvine. On a failed save, you take 1d10 slashing damage.
10	A creature indigenous to the area chases after you. The DM chooses a creature appropriate for the terrain.
11–20	No complication.

DESIGNING YOUR OWN CHASE TABLES

The tables presented here don't work for all possible environments. A chase through the sewers of Baldur's Gate or through the spiderweb-filled alleys of Menzoberranzan might inspire you to create your own table.

SPLITTING UP

Creatures being chased can split up into smaller groups. This tactic forces pursuers to either divide their forces or allow some of the quarry to escape. If a pursuit splits into several smaller chases, resolve each chase separately. Run a round of one chase, then a round of the next, and so on, tracking the distances for each separate group.

Mapping the Chase

If you have the opportunity to plan out a chase, take the time to draw a rough map that shows the route. Insert obstacles at specific points, especially ones that require the characters to make ability checks or saving throws to avoid slowing or stopping, or use a random table of complications similar to the ones in this section. Otherwise, improvise as you play.

Complications can be barriers to progress or opportunities for mayhem. Characters being chased through a forest by bugbears might spot a wasp nest and slow down long enough to attack the nest or throw rocks at it, thus creating an obstacle for their pursuers.

A map of a chase can be linear or have many branches, depending on the nature of the chase. For example, a mine cart chase might have few (if any) branches, while a sewer chase might have several.

Role Reversal

During a chase, it's possible for the pursuers to become the quarry. For example, characters chasing a thief through a marketplace might draw unwanted attention from other members of the thieves' guild. As they pursue the fleeing thief, they must also evade the thieves pursuing them. Roll initiative for the new arrivals, and run both chases simultaneously. In another scenario, the fleeing thief might run into the waiting arms of his accomplices. The outnumbered characters might decide to flee with the thieves in pursuit.

Siege Equipment

Siege weapons are designed to assail castles and other walled fortifications. They see much use in campaigns that feature war. Most siege weapons don't move around a battlefield on their own; they require creatures to move them, as well as to load, aim, and fire them.

Ballista

Large object

Armor Class: 15
Hit Points: 50
Damage Immunities: poison, psychic

A ballista is a massive crossbow that fires heavy bolts. Before it can be fired, it must be loaded and aimed. It takes one action to load the weapon, one action to aim it, and one action to fire it.

Bolt. *Ranged Weapon Attack:* +6 to hit, range 120/480 ft., one target. *Hit:* 16 (3d10) piercing damage.

Cannon

Large object

Armor Class: 19
Hit Points: 75
Damage Immunities: poison, psychic

A cannon uses gunpowder to propel heavy balls of cast iron through the air at destructive speeds. In a campaign without gunpowder, a cannon might be an arcane device built by clever gnomes or wizardly engineers.

A cannon is usually supported in a wooden frame with wheels. Before it can be fired, the cannon must be loaded and aimed. It takes one action to load the weapon, one action to aim it, and one action to fire it.

Cannon Ball. *Ranged Weapon Attack:* +6 to hit, range 600/2,400 ft., one target. *Hit:* 44 (8d10) bludgeoning damage.

Cauldron, Suspended

Large object

Armor Class: 19
Hit Points: 20
Damage Immunities: poison, psychic

A cauldron is an iron pot suspended so that it can be tipped easily, spilling its contents. Once emptied, a cauldron must be refilled—and its contents must usually be reheated—before it can be used again. It takes three actions to fill a cauldron and one action to tip it.

Cauldrons can be filled with other liquids, such as acid or green slime, with different effects.

Boiling Oil. The cauldron pours boiling oil onto a 10-foot-square area directly below it. Any creature in the area must make a DC 15 Dexterity saving throw, taking 10 (3d6) fire damage on a failed save, or half as much damage on a successful one.

Mangonel

Large object

Armor Class: 15
Hit Points: 100
Damage Immunities: poison, psychic

A mangonel is a type of catapult that hurls heavy projectiles in a high arc. This payload can hit targets behind cover. Before the mangonel can be fired, it must be loaded and aimed. It takes two actions to load the weapon, two actions to aim it, and one action to fire it.

A mangonel typically hurls a heavy stone, although it can hurl other kinds of projectiles, with different effects.

Mangonel Stone. *Ranged Weapon Attack:* +5 to hit, range 200/800 ft. (can't hit targets within 60 feet of it), one target. *Hit:* 27 (5d10) bludgeoning damage.

Ram

Large object

Armor Class: 15
Hit Points: 100
Damage Immunities: poison, psychic

A ram consists of a movable gallery equipped with a heavy log suspended from two roof beams by chains. The log is shod in iron and used to batter through doors and barricades.

It takes a minimum of four Medium creatures to operate a ram. Because of the gallery roof, these operators have total cover against attacks from above.

Ram. *Melee Weapon Attack:* +8 to hit, reach 5 ft., one object. *Hit:* 16 (3d10) bludgeoning damage.

Siege Tower
Gargantuan object

Armor Class: 15
Hit Points: 200
Damage Immunities: poison, psychic

A siege tower is a mobile wooden structure with a beam frame and slats in its walls. Large wooden wheels or rollers allow the tower to be pushed or pulled by soldiers or beasts of burden. Medium or smaller creatures can use the siege tower to reach the top of walls up to 40 feet high. A creature in the tower has total cover from attacks outside the tower.

Trebuchet
Huge object

Armor Class: 15
Hit Points: 150
Damage Immunities: poison, psychic

A trebuchet is a powerful catapult that throws its payload in a high arc, so it can hit targets behind cover. Before the trebuchet can be fired, it must be loaded and aimed. It takes two actions to load the weapon, two actions to aim it, and one action to fire it.

A trebuchet typically hurls a heavy stone. However, it can launch other kinds of projectiles, such as barrels of oil or sewage, with different effects.

Trebuchet Stone. *Ranged Weapon Attack:* +5 to hit, range 300/1,200 ft. (can't hit targets within 60 feet of it), one target. *Hit:* 44 (8d10) bludgeoning damage.

Diseases

A plague ravages the kingdom, setting the adventurers on a quest to find a cure. An adventurer emerges from an ancient tomb, unopened for centuries, and soon finds herself suffering from a wasting illness. A warlock offends some dark power and contracts a strange affliction that spreads whenever he casts spells.

A simple outbreak might amount to little more than a small drain on party resources, curable by a casting of *lesser restoration*. A more complicated outbreak can form the basis of one or more adventures as characters search for a cure, stop the spread of the disease, and deal with the consequences.

A disease that does more than infect a few party members is primarily a plot device. The rules help describe the effects of the disease and how it can be cured, but the specifics of how a disease works aren't bound by a common set of rules. Diseases can affect any creature, and a given illness might or might not pass from one race or kind of creature to another. A plague might affect only constructs or undead, or sweep through a halfling neighborhood but leave other races untouched. What matters is the story you want to tell.

Sample Diseases

The diseases here illustrate the variety of ways disease can work in the game. Feel free to alter the saving throw DCs, incubation times, symptoms, and other characteristics of these diseases to suit your campaign.

CACKLE FEVER

This disease targets humanoids, although gnomes are strangely immune. While in the grips of this disease, victims frequently succumb to fits of mad laughter, giving the disease its common name and its morbid nickname: "the shrieks."

Symptoms manifest 1d4 hours after infection and include fever and disorientation. The infected creature gains one level of exhaustion that can't be removed until the disease is cured.

Any event that causes the infected creature great stress—including entering combat, taking damage, experiencing fear, or having a nightmare—forces the creature to make a DC 13 Constitution saving throw. On a failed save, the creature takes 5 (1d10) psychic damage and becomes incapacitated with mad laughter for 1 minute. The creature can repeat the saving throw at the end of each of its turns, ending the mad laughter and the incapacitated condition on a success.

Any humanoid creature that starts its turn within 10 feet of an infected creature in the throes of mad laughter must succeed on a DC 10 Constitution saving throw or also become infected with the disease. Once a creature succeeds on this save, it is immune to the mad laughter of that particular infected creature for 24 hours.

At the end of each long rest, an infected creature can make a DC 13 Constitution saving throw. On a successful save, the DC for this save and for the save to avoid an attack of mad laughter drops by 1d6. When the saving throw DC drops to 0, the creature recovers from the disease. A creature that fails three of these saving throws gains a randomly determined form of indefinite madness, as described later in this chapter.

SEWER PLAGUE

Sewer plague is a generic term for a broad category of illnesses that incubate in sewers, refuse heaps, and stagnant swamps, and which are sometimes transmitted by creatures that dwell in those areas, such as rats and otyughs.

When a humanoid creature is bitten by a creature that carries the disease, or when it comes into contact with filth or offal contaminated by the disease, the creature must succeed on a DC 11 Constitution saving throw or become infected.

It takes 1d4 days for sewer plague's symptoms to manifest in an infected creature. Symptoms include fatigue and cramps. The infected creature suffers one level of exhaustion, and it regains only half the normal number of hit points from spending Hit Dice and no hit points from finishing a long rest.

At the end of each long rest, an infected creature must make a DC 11 Constitution saving throw. On a failed save, the character gains one level of exhaustion. On a successful save, the character's exhaustion level decreases by one level. If a successful saving throw reduces the infected creature's level of exhaustion below 1, the creature recovers from the disease.

SIGHT ROT

This painful infection causes bleeding from the eyes and eventually blinds the victim.

A beast or humanoid that drinks water tainted by sight rot must succeed on a DC 15 Constitution saving throw or become infected. One day after infection, the creature's vision starts to become blurry. The creature takes a −1 penalty to attack rolls and ability checks that rely on sight. At the end of each long rest after the symptoms appear, the penalty worsens by 1. When it reaches −5, the victim is blinded until its sight is restored by magic such as *lesser restoration* or *heal*.

Sight rot can be cured using a rare flower called Eyebright, which grows in some swamps. Given an hour, a character who has proficiency with an herbalism kit can turn the flower into one dose of ointment. Applied to the eyes before a long rest, one dose of it prevents the disease from worsening after that rest. After three doses, the ointment cures the disease entirely.

POISONS

Given their insidious and deadly nature, poisons are illegal in most societies but are a favorite tool among assassins, drow, and other evil creatures.

Poisons come in the following four types.

Contact. A creature that touches contact poison with exposed skin suffers its effects.

Ingested. A creature must swallow an entire dose of ingested poison to suffer its effects. You might decide that a partial dose has a reduced effect, such as allowing advantage on the saving throw or dealing only half damage on a failed save.

Inhaled. These poisons are powders or gases that take effect when they are inhaled. A single dose fills a 5-foot cube.

Injury. A creature that takes slashing or piercing damage from a weapon or piece of ammunition coated with injury poison is exposed to its effects.

POISONS

Item	Type	Price per Dose
Assassin's blood	Ingested	150 gp
Burnt othur fumes	Inhaled	500 gp
Carrion crawler mucus	Contact	200 gp
Drow poison	Injury	200 gp
Essence of ether	Inhaled	300 gp
Malice	Inhaled	250 gp
Midnight tears	Ingested	1,500 gp
Oil of taggit	Contact	400 gp
Pale tincture	Ingested	250 gp
Purple worm poison	Injury	2,000 gp
Serpent venom	Injury	200 gp
Torpor	Ingested	600 gp
Truth serum	Ingested	150 gp
Wyvern poison	Injury	1,200 gp

SAMPLE POISONS

Each type of poison has its own debilitating effects.

Assassin's Blood (Ingested). A creature subjected to this poison must make a DC 10 Constitution saving throw. On a failed save, it takes 6 (1d12) poison damage and is poisoned for 24 hours. On a successful save, the creature takes half damage and isn't poisoned.

Burnt Othur Fumes (Inhaled). A creature subjected to this poison must succeed on a DC 13 Constitution saving throw or take 10 (3d6) poison damage, and must repeat the saving throw at the start of each of its turns. On each successive failed save, the character takes 3 (1d6) poison damage. After three successful saves, the poison ends.

Carrion Crawler Mucus (Contact). This poison must be harvested from a dead or incapacitated carrion crawler. A creature subjected to this poison must succeed on a DC 13 Constitution saving throw or be poisoned for 1 minute. The poisoned creature is paralyzed. The creature can repeat the saving throw at the end of each of its turns, ending the effect on itself on a success.

Drow Poison (Injury). This poison is typically made only by the drow, and only in a place far removed from sunlight. A creature subjected to this poison must succeed on a DC 13 Constitution saving throw or be poisoned for 1 hour. If the saving throw fails by 5 or more, the creature is also unconscious while poisoned in this way. The creature wakes up if it takes damage or if another creature takes an action to shake it awake.

Essence of Ether (Inhaled). A creature subjected to this poison must succeed on a DC 15 Constitution saving throw or become poisoned for 8 hours. The poisoned creature is unconscious. The creature wakes up if it takes damage or if another creature takes an action to shake it awake.

Malice (Inhaled). A creature subjected to this poison must succeed on a DC 15 Constitution saving throw or become poisoned for 1 hour. The poisoned creature is blinded.

Midnight Tears (Ingested). A creature that ingests this poison suffers no effect until the stroke of midnight. If the poison has not been neutralized before then, the creature must succeed on a DC 17 Constitution saving throw, taking 31 (9d6) poison damage on a failed save, or half as much damage on a successful one.

Oil of Taggit (Contact). A creature subjected to this poison must succeed on a DC 13 Constitution saving throw or become poisoned for 24 hours. The poisoned creature is unconscious. The creature wakes up if it takes damage.

Pale Tincture (Ingested). A creature subjected to this poison must succeed on a DC 16 Constitution saving throw or take 3 (1d6) poison damage and become poisoned. The poisoned creature must repeat the saving throw every 24 hours, taking 3 (1d6) poison damage on a failed save. Until this poison ends, the damage the poison deals can't be healed by any means. After seven successful saving throws, the effect ends and the creature can heal normally.

Purple Worm Poison (Injury). This poison must be harvested from a dead or incapacitated purple worm. A creature subjected to this poison must make a DC 19 Constitution saving throw, taking 42 (12d6) poison damage on a failed save, or half as much damage on a successful one.

Serpent Venom (Injury). This poison must be harvested from a dead or incapacitated giant poisonous snake. A creature subjected to this poison must succeed on a DC 11 Constitution saving throw, taking 10 (3d6) poison damage on a failed save, or half as much damage on a successful one.

Torpor (Ingested). A creature subjected to this poison must succeed on a DC 15 Constitution saving throw or become poisoned for 4d6 hours. The poisoned creature is incapacitated.

Truth Serum (Ingested). A creature subjected to this poison must succeed on a DC 11 Constitution saving throw or become poisoned for 1 hour. The poisoned creature can't knowingly speak a lie, as if under the effect of a *zone of truth* spell.

Wyvern Poison (Injury). This poison must be harvested from a dead or incapacitated wyvern. A creature subjected to this poison must make a DC 15 Constitution saving throw, taking 24 (7d6) poison damage on a failed save, or half as much damage on a successful one.

PURCHASING POISON

In some settings, strict laws prohibit the possession and use of poison, but a black-market dealer or unscrupulous apothecary might keep a hidden stash. Characters with criminal contacts might be able to acquire poison relatively easily. Other characters might have to make extensive inquiries and pay bribes before they track down the poison they seek.

The Poisons table gives suggested prices for single doses of various poisons.

CRAFTING AND HARVESTING POISON

During downtime between adventures, a character can use the crafting rules in the *Player's Handbook* to create basic poison if the character has proficiency with a poisoner's kit. At your discretion, the character can craft other kinds of poison. Not all poison ingredients are available for purchase, and tracking down certain ingredients might form the basis of an entire adventure.

A character can instead attempt to harvest poison from a poisonous creature, such as a snake, wyvern, or carrion crawler. The creature must be incapacitated or dead, and the harvesting requires 1d6 minutes followed by a DC 20 Intelligence (Nature) check. (Proficiency with the poisoner's kit applies to this check if the character doesn't have proficiency in Nature.) On a successful check, the character harvests enough poison for a single dose. On a failed check, the character is unable to extract any poison. If the character fails the check by 5 or more, the character is subjected to the creature's poison.

MADNESS

In a typical campaign, characters aren't driven mad by the horrors they face and the carnage they inflict day after day, but sometimes the stress of being an adventurer can be too much to bear. If your campaign has a strong horror theme, you might want to use madness as a way to reinforce that theme, emphasizing the extraordinarily horrific nature of the threats the adventurers face.

GOING MAD

Various magical effects can inflict madness on an otherwise stable mind. Certain spells, such as *contact other plane* and *symbol*, can cause insanity, and you can use the madness rules here instead of the spell effects in the *Player's Handbook*. Diseases, poisons, and planar effects such as psychic wind or the howling winds of Pandemonium can all inflict madness. Some artifacts can also break the psyche of a character who uses or becomes attuned to them.

Resisting a madness-inducing effect usually requires a Wisdom or Charisma saving throw. If your game includes the Sanity score (see chapter 9, "Dungeon Master's Workshop"), a creature makes a Sanity saving throw instead.

MADNESS EFFECTS

Madness can be short-term, long-term, or indefinite. Most relatively mundane effects impose short-term madness, which lasts for just a few minutes. More horrific effects or cumulative effects can result in long-term or indefinite madness.

A character afflicted with **short-term madness** is subjected to an effect from the Short-Term Madness table for 1d10 minutes.

A character afflicted with **long-term madness** is subjected to an effect from the Long-Term Madness table for 1d10 × 10 hours.

A character afflicted with **indefinite madness** gains a new character flaw from the Indefinite Madness table that lasts until cured.

SHORT-TERM MADNESS

d100	Effect (lasts 1d10 minutes)
01–20	The character retreats into his or her mind and becomes paralyzed. The effect ends if the character takes any damage.
21–30	The character becomes incapacitated and spends the duration screaming, laughing, or weeping.
31–40	The character becomes frightened and must use his or her action and movement each round to flee from the source of the fear.
41–50	The character begins babbling and is incapable of normal speech or spellcasting.
51–60	The character must use his or her action each round to attack the nearest creature.
61–70	The character experiences vivid hallucinations and has disadvantage on ability checks.
71–75	The character does whatever anyone tells him or her to do that isn't obviously self-destructive.
76–80	The character experiences an overpowering urge to eat something strange such as dirt, slime, or offal.
81–90	The character is stunned.
91–100	The character falls unconscious.

LONG-TERM MADNESS

d100	Effect (lasts 1d10 × 10 hours)
01–10	The character feels compelled to repeat a specific activity over and over, such as washing hands, touching things, praying, or counting coins.
11–20	The character experiences vivid hallucinations and has disadvantage on ability checks.
21–30	The character suffers extreme paranoia. The character has disadvantage on Wisdom and Charisma checks.
31–40	The character regards something (usually the source of madness) with intense revulsion, as if affected by the antipathy effect of the *antipathy/sympathy* spell.
41–45	The character experiences a powerful delusion. Choose a potion. The character imagines that he or she is under its effects.
46–55	The character becomes attached to a "lucky charm," such as a person or an object, and has disadvantage on attack rolls, ability checks, and saving throws while more than 30 feet from it.
56–65	The character is blinded (25%) or deafened (75%).
66–75	The character experiences uncontrollable tremors or tics, which impose disadvantage on attack rolls, ability checks, and saving throws that involve Strength or Dexterity.
76–85	The character suffers from partial amnesia. The character knows who he or she is and retains racial traits and class features, but doesn't recognize other people or remember anything that happened before the madness took effect.
86–90	Whenever the character takes damage, he or she must succeed on a DC 15 Wisdom saving throw or be affected as though he or she failed a saving throw against the *confusion* spell. The *confusion* effect lasts for 1 minute.
91–95	The character loses the ability to speak.
96–100	The character falls unconscious. No amount of jostling or damage can wake the character.

CURING MADNESS

A *calm emotions* spell can suppress the effects of madness, while a *lesser restoration* spell can rid a character of a short-term or long-term madness. Depending on the source of the madness, *remove curse* or *dispel evil* might also prove effective. A *greater restoration* spell or more powerful magic is required to rid a character of indefinite madness.

EXPERIENCE POINTS

Experience points (XP) fuel level advancement for player characters and are most often the reward for completing combat encounters.

Each monster has an XP value based on its challenge rating. When adventurers defeat one or more monsters—typically by killing, routing, or capturing

INDEFINITE MADNESS

d100	Flaw (lasts until cured)
01–15	"Being drunk keeps me sane."
16–25	"I keep whatever I find."
26–30	"I try to become more like someone else I know—adopting his or her style of dress, mannerisms, and name."
31–35	"I must bend the truth, exaggerate, or outright lie to be interesting to other people."
36–45	"Achieving my goal is the only thing of interest to me, and I'll ignore everything else to pursue it."
46–50	"I find it hard to care about anything that goes on around me."
51–55	"I don't like the way people judge me all the time."
56–70	"I am the smartest, wisest, strongest, fastest, and most beautiful person I know."
71–80	"I am convinced that powerful enemies are hunting me, and their agents are everywhere I go. I am sure they're watching me all the time."
81–85	"There's only one person I can trust. And only I can see this special friend."
86–95	"I can't take anything seriously. The more serious the situation, the funnier I find it."
96–100	"I've discovered that I really like killing people."

them—they divide the total XP value of the monsters evenly among themselves. If the party received substantial assistance from one or more NPCs, count those NPCs as party members when dividing up the XP. (Because the NPCs made the fight easier, individual characters receive fewer XP.)

Chapter 3, "Creating Adventures," provides guidelines for designing combat encounters using experience points.

ABSENT CHARACTERS

Typically, adventurers earn experience only for encounters they participate in. If a player is absent for a session, the player's character misses out on the experience points.

Over time, you might end up with a level gap between the characters of players who never miss a session and characters belonging to players who are more sporadic in their attendance. Nothing is wrong with that. A gap of two or three levels between different characters in the same party isn't going to ruin the game for anyone. Some DMs treat XP as a reward for participating in the game, and keeping up with the rest of the party is good incentive for players to attend as many sessions as possible.

As an alternative, give absent characters the same XP that the other characters earned each session, keeping the group at the same level. Few players will intentionally miss out on the fun of gaming just because they know they'll receive XP for it even if they don't show up.

Noncombat Challenges

You decide whether to award experience to characters for overcoming challenges outside combat. If the adventurers complete a tense negotiation with a baron, forge a trade agreement with a clan of surly dwarves, or successfully navigate the Chasm of Doom, you might decide that they deserve an XP reward.

As a starting point, use the rules for building combat encounters in chapter 3 to gauge the difficulty of the challenge. Then award the characters XP as if it had been a combat encounter of the same difficulty, but only if the encounter involved a meaningful risk of failure.

Milestones

You can also award XP when characters complete significant milestones. When preparing your adventure, designate certain events or challenges as milestones, as with the following examples:

- Accomplishing one in a series of goals necessary to complete the adventure.
- Discovering a hidden location or piece of information relevant to the adventure.
- Reaching an important destination.

When awarding XP, treat a major milestone as a hard encounter and a minor milestone as an easy encounter.

If you want to reward your players for their progress through an adventure with something more than XP and treasure, give them additional small rewards at milestone points. Here are some examples:

- The adventurers gain the benefit of a short rest.
- Characters can recover a Hit Die or a low-level spell slot.
- Characters can regain the use of magic items that have had their limited uses expended.

Level Advancement without XP

You can do away with experience points entirely and control the rate of character advancement. Advance characters based on how many sessions they play, or when they accomplish significant story goals in the campaign. In either case, you tell the players when their characters gain a level.

This method of level advancement can be particularly helpful if your campaign doesn't include much combat, or includes so much combat that tracking XP becomes tiresome.

Session-Based Advancement

A good rate of session-based advancement is to have characters reach 2nd level after the first session of play, 3rd level after another session, and 4th level after two more sessions. Then spend two or three sessions for each subsequent level. This rate mirrors the standard rate of advancement, assuming sessions are about four hours long.

Story-Based Advancement

When you let the story of the campaign drive advancement, you award levels when adventurers accomplish significant goals in the campaign.

Chapter 9: Dungeon Master's Workshop

S THE DUNGEON MASTER, YOU AREN'T LIMITED by the rules in the *Player's Handbook*, the guidelines in this book, or the selection of monsters in the *Monster Manual*. You can let your imagination run wild. This chapter contains optional rules that you can use to customize your campaign, as well as guidelines on creating your own material, such as monsters and magic items.

The options in this chapter relate to many different parts of the game. Some of them are variants of rules, and others are entirely new rules. Each option represents a different genre, style of play, or both. Consider trying no more than one or two of the options at a time so that you can clearly assess their effects on your campaign before adding other options.

Before you add a new rule to your campaign, ask yourself two questions:

- Will the rule improve the game?
- Will my players like it?

If you're confident that the answer to both questions is yes, then you have nothing to lose by giving it a try. Urge your players to provide feedback. If the rule or game element isn't functioning as intended or isn't adding much to your game, you can refine it or ditch it. No matter what a rule's source, a rule serves you, not the other way around.

Beware of adding anything to your game that allows a character to concentrate on more than one effect at a time, use more than one reaction or bonus action per round, or attune to more than three magic items at a time. Rules and game elements that override the rules for concentration, reactions, bonus actions, and magic item attunement can seriously unbalance or overcomplicate your game.

Ability Options

The optional rules in this section pertain to using ability scores.

Proficiency Dice

This optional rule replaces a character's proficiency bonus with a proficiency die, adding more randomness to the game and making proficiency a less reliable indicator of mastery. Instead of adding a proficiency bonus to an ability check, an attack roll, or saving throw, the character's player rolls a die. The Proficiency Die table shows which die or dice to roll, as determined by the character's level.

Whenever a feature, such as the rogue's Expertise, lets a character double his or her proficiency bonus, the player rolls the character's proficiency die twice instead of once.

This option is intended for player characters and nonplayer characters who have levels, as opposed to monsters who don't.

Proficiency Die

Level	Proficiency Bonus	Proficiency Die
1st–4th	+2	1d4
5th–8th	+3	1d6
9th–12th	+4	1d8
13th–16th	+5	1d10
17th–20th	+6	1d12

Skill Variants

A skill dictates the circumstances under which a character can add his or her proficiency bonus to an ability check. Skills define those circumstances by referring to different aspects of the six ability scores. For example, Acrobatics and Stealth are two different aspects of Dexterity, and a character can specialize in either or both.

You can dispense with skills and use one of the following variants. Choose whichever one best suits your campaign.

Ability Check Proficiency

With this variant rule, characters don't have skill proficiencies. Instead, each character has proficiency in two abilities: one tied to the character's class and one tied to the character's background. The Ability Proficiencies by Class table suggests a proficiency for each class, and you choose which ability is tied to a given background. Starting at 1st level, a character adds his or her proficiency bonus to any ability check tied to one or the other of these two abilities.

Ability Check Proficiencies by Class

Class	Ability Check
Barbarian	Strength, Dexterity, or Wisdom
Bard	Any one
Cleric	Intelligence, Wisdom, or Charisma
Druid	Intelligence or Wisdom
Fighter	Strength, Dexterity, or Wisdom
Monk	Strength, Dexterity, or Intelligence
Paladin	Strength, Wisdom, or Charisma
Ranger	Strength, Dexterity, or Wisdom
Rogue	Dexterity, Intelligence, Wisdom, or Charisma
Sorcerer	Intelligence or Charisma
Warlock	Intelligence or Charisma
Wizard	Intelligence or Wisdom

The Expertise feature works differently than normal under this rule. At 1st level, instead of choosing two skill proficiencies, a character with the Expertise class feature chooses one of the abilities in which he or she has proficiency. Selecting an ability counts as two of the character's Expertise choices. If the character would gain an additional skill proficiency, that character instead selects another ability check in which to gain proficiency.

This option removes skills from the game and doesn't allow for much distinction among characters. For example, a character can't choose to emphasize persuasion or intimidation; he or she is equally adept at both.

BACKGROUND PROFICIENCY

With this variant rule, characters don't have skill or tool proficiencies. Anything that would grant the character a skill or tool proficiency provides no benefit. Instead, a character can add his or her proficiency bonus to any ability check to which the character's prior training and experience (reflected in the character's background) reasonably applies. The DM is the ultimate judge of whether the character's background applies.

For example, the player of a character with the noble background could reasonably argue that the proficiency bonus should apply to a Charisma check the character makes to secure an audience with the king. The player should be encouraged to explain in specific terms how the character's background applies. Not simply "I'm a noble," but "I spent three years before starting my adventuring career serving as my family's ambassador to the court, and this sort of thing is second nature to me now."

This simple system relies heavily on players developing their characters' histories. Don't let it result in endless debates about whether a character's proficiency bonus applies in a given situation. Unless a player's attempt to explain the relevance of the character's background makes everyone else at the table roll their eyes at its absurdity, go ahead and reward the player for making the effort.

If a character has the Expertise feature, instead of choosing skills and tools to gain the benefit of that feature, the player defines aspects of his or her background to which the benefit applies. Continuing the noble example, the player might decide to apply Expertise to "situations where courtly manners and etiquette are paramount" and "figuring out the secret plots that court members hatch against one another."

PERSONALITY TRAIT PROFICIENCY

With this variant rule, characters don't have skill proficiencies. Instead, a character can add his or her proficiency bonus to any ability check directly related to the character's positive personality traits. For example, a character with a positive personality trait of "I never have a plan, but I'm great at making things up as I go along" might apply the bonus when engaging in some off-the-cuff deception to get out of a tight spot. A player should come up with at least four positive personality traits when creating a character.

When a character's negative personality trait directly impacts an ability check, the character has disadvantage on the check. For example, a hermit whose negative trait is "I often get lost in my own thoughts and contemplation, oblivious to my surroundings" might have disadvantage on an ability check made to notice creatures sneaking up.

If a character has the Expertise feature, the player can apply its benefit to personality traits related to ability

checks, instead of to skills or tools. If a character would gain a new skill or tool proficiency, the character instead gains a new positive personality trait.

This system relies heavily on players developing their characters' personalities. Make sure that different characters' traits—positive and negative—come into play with about the same frequency. Don't let a player get away with a positive trait that always seems to apply and a negative trait that never does.

At your discretion, you can also tie a character's ideals, bonds, and flaws to this system.

HERO POINTS

Hero points work well in epic fantasy and mythic campaigns in which the characters are meant to be more like superheroes than the average adventurer is.

With this option, a character starts with 5 hero points at 1st level. Each time the character gains a level, he or she loses any unspent hero points and gains a new total equal to 5 + half the character's level.

A player can spend a hero point whenever he or she makes an attack roll, an ability check, or a saving throw. The player can spend the hero point after the roll is made but before any of its results are applied. Spending the hero point allows the player to roll a d6 and add it to the d20, possibly turning a failure into a success. A player can spend only 1 hero point per roll.

In addition, whenever a character fails a death saving throw, the player can spend one hero point to turn the failure into a success.

NEW ABILITY SCORES: HONOR AND SANITY

If you're running a campaign shaped by a strict code of honor or the constant risk of insanity, consider adding one or both these new ability scores: Honor and Sanity. These abilities function like the standard six abilities, with exceptions specified in each ability below.

Here's how to incorporate these optional abilities at character creation:

- If your players use the standard array of ability scores, add one 11 to the array for each optional ability you add.
- If your players use the optional point-buy system, add 3 points to the number of points for each optional ability you add.
- If your players roll their ability scores, have them roll for the added ability scores.

If you ever need to make a check or saving throw for Honor or Sanity for a monster that lacks the score, you can use Charisma for Honor and Wisdom for Sanity.

HONOR SCORE

If your campaign involves cultures where a rigid code of honor is part of daily life, consider using the Honor score as a means of measuring a character's devotion to that code. This ability fits well in a setting inspired by Asian cultures, such as Kara-Tur in the Forgotten Realms. The Honor ability is also useful in any campaign that revolves around orders of knights.

Honor measures not only a character's devotion to a code but also the character's understanding of it. The Honor score can also reflect how others perceive a character's honor. A character with a high Honor usually has a reputation that others know about, especially those who have high Honor scores themselves.

Unlike other abilities, Honor can't be raised with normal ability score increases. Instead, you can award increases to Honor—or impose reductions—based on a character's actions. At the end of an adventure, if you think a character's actions in the adventure reflected well or poorly on his or her understanding of the code, you can increase or decrease the character's Honor by 1. As with other ability scores, a character's Honor can't exceed 20 or fall below 1.

Honor Checks. Honor checks can be used in social situations, much as Charisma would, when a character's understanding of a code of conduct is the most defining factor in the way a social interaction will play out.

You might also call for an Honor check when a character is in one of the following situations:

- Being unsure how to act with honor
- Surrendering while trying to save face
- Trying to determine another character's Honor score
- Trying to use the proper etiquette in a delicate social situation
- Using his or her honorable or dishonorable reputation to influence someone else

Honor Saving Throws. An Honor saving throw comes into play when you want to determine whether a character might inadvertently do something dishonorable. You might call for an Honor saving throw in the following situations:

- Avoiding an accidental breach of honor or etiquette
- Resisting the urge to respond to goading or insults from an enemy
- Recognizing when an enemy attempts to trick a character into a breach of honor

SANITY SCORE

Consider using the Sanity score if your campaign revolves around entities of an utterly alien and unspeakable nature, such as Great Cthulhu, whose powers and minions can shatter a character's mind.

A character with a high Sanity is level-headed even in the face of insane circumstances, while a character with low Sanity is unsteady, breaking easily when confronted by eldritch horrors that are beyond normal reason.

Sanity Checks. You might ask characters to make a Sanity check in place of an Intelligence check to recall lore about the alien creatures of madness featured in your campaign, to decipher the writings of raving lunatics, or to learn spells from tomes of forbidden lore. You might also call for a Sanity check when a character tries one of the following activities:

- Deciphering a piece of text written in a language so alien that it threatens to break a character's mind
- Overcoming the lingering effects of madness
- Comprehending a piece of alien magic foreign to all normal understanding of magic

Sanity Saving Throws. You might call for a Sanity saving throw when a character runs the risk of succumbing to madness, such as in the following situations:

- Seeing a creature from the Far Realm or other alien realms for the first time
- Making direct contact with the mind of an alien creature
- Being subjected to spells that affect mental stability, such as the insanity option of the *symbol* spell
- Passing through a demiplane built on alien physics
- Resisting an effect conferred by an attack or spell that deals psychic damage

A failed Sanity save might result in short-term, long-term, or indefinite madness, as described in chapter 8, "Running the Game." Any time a character suffers from long-term or indefinite madness, the character's Sanity is reduced by 1. A *greater restoration* spell can restore Sanity lost in this way, and a character can increase his or her Sanity through level advancement.

ADVENTURING OPTIONS

This section provides options for changing how rests work, as well as for adding unusual things to your campaign, such as modern weapons.

FEAR AND HORROR

The rules for fear and horror can help you sustain an atmosphere of dread in a dark fantasy campaign.

FEAR

When adventurers confront threats they have no hope of overcoming, you can call for them to make a Wisdom saving throw. Set the DC according to the circumstances. A character who fails the save becomes frightened for 1 minute. The character can repeat the saving throw at the end of each of his or her turns, ending the effect on the character on a successful save.

HORROR

Horror involves more than simple fright. It entails revulsion and anguish. Often it arises when adventurers see something completely contrary to the common understanding of what can and should occur in the world, or upon the realization of a dreadful truth.

In such a situation, you can call on characters to make a Charisma saving throw to resist the horror. Set the DC based on the magnitude of the horrific circumstances. On a failed save, a character gains a short-term or long-term form of madness that you choose or determine randomly, as detailed in chapter 8, "Running the Game."

HEALING

These optional rules make it easier or harder for adventurers to recover from injury, either increasing or reducing the amount of time your players can spend adventuring before rest is required.

HEALER'S KIT DEPENDENCY

A character can't spend any Hit Dice after finishing a short rest until someone expends one use of a healer's kit to bandage and treat the character's wounds.

HEALING SURGES

This optional rule allows characters to heal up in the thick of combat and works well for parties that feature few or no characters with healing magic, or for campaigns in which magical healing is rare.

As an action, a character can use a healing surge and spend up to half his or her Hit Dice. For each Hit Die spent in this way, the player rolls the die and adds the character's Constitution modifier. The character regains hit points equal to the total. The player can decide to spend an additional Hit Die after each roll.

A character who uses a healing surge can't do so again until he or she finishes a short or long rest.

Under this optional rule, a character regains all spent Hit Dice at the end of a long rest. With a short rest, a character regains Hit Dice equal to his or her level divided by four (minimum of one die).

For a more superheroic feel, you can let a character use a healing surge as a bonus action, rather than as an action.

SLOW NATURAL HEALING

Characters don't regain hit points at the end of a long rest. Instead, a character can spend Hit Dice to heal at the end of a long rest, just as with a short rest.

This optional rule prolongs the amount of time that characters need to recover from their wounds without the benefits of magical healing and works well for grittier, more realistic campaigns.

REST VARIANTS

The rules for short and long rests presented in chapter 8 of the *Player's Handbook* work well for a heroic-style campaign. Characters can go toe-to-toe with deadly foes, take damage to within an inch of their lives, yet still be ready to fight again the next day. If this approach doesn't fit your campaign, consider the following variants.

EPIC HEROISM

This variant uses a short rest of 5 minutes and a long rest of 1 hour. This change makes combat more routine, since characters can easily recover from every battle. You might want to make combat encounters more difficult to compensate.

Spellcasters using this system can afford to burn through spell slots quickly, especially at higher levels. Consider allowing spellcasters to restore expended spell slots equal to only half their maximum spell slots (rounded down) at the end of a long rest, and to limit spell slots restored to 5th level or lower. Only a full 8-hour rest will allow a spellcaster to restore all spell slots and to regain spell slots of 6th level or higher.

GRITTY REALISM

This variant uses a short rest of 8 hours and a long rest of 7 days. This puts the brakes on the campaign, requiring the players to carefully judge the benefits and drawbacks of combat. Characters can't afford to engage in too many battles in a row, and all adventuring requires careful planning.

This approach encourages the characters to spend time out of the dungeon. It's a good option for campaigns that emphasize intrigue, politics, and interactions among other NPCs, and in which combat is rare or something to be avoided rather than rushed into.

FIREARMS

If you want to model the swashbuckling style of *The Three Musketeers* and similar tales, you can introduce gunpowder weapons to your campaign that are associated with the Renaissance. Similarly, in a campaign where a spaceship has crashed or elements of modern-day Earth are present, futuristic or modern firearms might appear. The Firearms table provides examples of firearms from all three of those periods. The modern and futuristic items are priceless.

PROFICIENCY

It's up to you to decide whether a character has proficiency with a firearm. Characters in most D&D worlds wouldn't have such proficiency. During their downtime, characters can use the training rules in the *Player's Handbook* to acquire proficiency, assuming that they have enough ammunition to keep the weapons working while mastering their use.

PROPERTIES

Firearms use special ammunition, and some of them have the burst fire or reload property.

Ammunition. The ammunition of a firearm is destroyed upon use. Renaissance and modern firearms use bullets. Futuristic firearms are powered by a special type of ammunition called energy cells. An energy cell contains enough power for all the shots its firearm can make.

Burst Fire. A weapon that has the burst fire property can make a normal single-target attack, or it can spray a 10-foot-cube area within normal range with shots. Each creature in the area must succeed on a DC 15 Dexterity saving throw or take the weapon's normal damage. This action uses ten pieces of ammunition.

Reload. A limited number of shots can be made with a weapon that has the reload property. A character must then reload it using an action or a bonus action (the character's choice).

EXPLOSIVES

A campaign might include explosives from the Renaissance or the modern world (the latter are priceless), as presented in the Explosives table.

BOMB

As an action, a character can light this bomb and throw it at a point up to 60 feet away. Each creature within 5 feet of that point must succeed on a DC 12 Dexterity saving throw or take 3d6 fire damage.

GUNPOWDER

Gunpowder is chiefly used to propel a bullet out of the barrel of a pistol or rifle, or it is formed into a bomb. Gunpowder is sold in small wooden kegs and in water-resistant powder horns.

Setting fire to a container full of gunpowder can cause it to explode, dealing fire damage to creatures within 10 feet of it (3d6 for a powder horn, 7d6 for a keg). A successful DC 12 Dexterity saving throw halves the damage. Setting fire to an ounce of gunpowder causes it to flare for 1 round, shedding bright light in a 30-foot radius and dim light for an additional 30 feet.

DYNAMITE

As an action, a creature can light a stick of dynamite and throw it at a point up to 60 feet away. Each creature within 5 feet of that point must make a DC 12 Dexterity saving throw, taking 3d6 bludgeoning damage on a failed save, or half as much damage on a successful one.

A character can bind sticks of dynamite together so they explode at the same time. Each additional stick increases the damage by 1d6 (to a maximum of 10d6) and the burst radius by 5 feet (to a maximum of 20 feet).

Dynamite can be rigged with a longer fuse to explode after a set amount of time, usually 1 to 6 rounds. Roll initiative for the dynamite. After the set number of rounds goes by, the dynamite explodes on that initiative.

GRENADES

As an action, a character can throw a grenade at a point up to 60 feet away. With a grenade launcher, the character can propel the grenade up to 120 feet away.

Each creature within 20 feet of an exploding **fragmentation grenade** must make a DC 15 Dexterity saving throw, taking 5d6 piercing damage on a failed save, or half as much damage on a successful one.

One round after a **smoke grenade** lands, it emits a cloud of smoke that creates a heavily obscured area in a 20-foot radius. A moderate wind (at least 10 miles per hour) disperses the smoke in 4 rounds; a strong wind (20 or more miles per hour) disperses it in 1 round.

FIGURING OUT ALIEN TECHNOLOGY

Int. Check Total	Result
9 or lower	One failure; one charge or use is wasted, if applicable; character has disadvantage on next check
10–14	One failure
15–19	One success
20 or higher	One success; character has advantage on next check

FIREARMS

Renaissance Item	Cost	Damage	Weight	Properties
Martial Ranged Weapons				
Pistol	250 gp	1d10 piercing	3 lb.	Ammunition (range 30/90), loading
Musket	500 gp	1d12 piercing	10 lb.	Ammunition (range 40/120), loading, two-handed
Ammunition				
Bullets (10)	3 gp	—	2 lb.	—

Modern Item	Cost	Damage	Weight	Properties
Martial Ranged Weapons				
Pistol, automatic	—	2d6 piercing	3 lb.	Ammunition (range 50/150), reload (15 shots)
Revolver	—	2d8 piercing	3 lb.	Ammunition (range 40/120), reload (6 shots)
Rifle, hunting	—	2d10 piercing	8 lb.	Ammunition (range 80/240), reload (5 shots), two-handed
Rifle, automatic	—	2d8 piercing	8 lb.	Ammunition (range 80/240), burst fire, reload (30 shots), two-handed
Shotgun	—	2d8 piercing	7 lb.	Ammunition (range 30/90), reload (2 shots), two-handed
Ammunition				
Bullets (10)	—	—	1 lb.	—

Futuristic Item	Cost	Damage	Weight	Properties
Martial Ranged Weapons				
Laser pistol	—	3d6 radiant	2 lb.	Ammunition (range 40/120), reload (50 shots)
Antimatter rifle	—	6d8 necrotic	10 lb.	Ammunition (range 120/360), reload (2 shots), two-handed
Laser rifle	—	3d8 radiant	7 lb.	Ammunition (range 100/300), reload (30 shots), two-handed
Ammunition				
Energy cell	—	—	5 oz.	—

ALIEN TECHNOLOGY

When adventurers find a piece of technology that isn't from their world or time period, the players might understand what the object is, but the characters rarely will. To simulate a character's ignorance about the technology, have the character make a series of Intelligence checks to figure it out.

To determine how the technology works, a character must succeed on a number of Intelligence checks based on the complexity of the item: two successes for a simple item (such as a cigarette lighter, calculator, or revolver) and four successes for a complex item (such as a computer, chainsaw, or hovercraft). Then consult the Figuring Out Alien Technology table. Consider making the item break if a character fails four or more times before taking a long rest.

A character who has seen an item used or has operated a similar item has advantage on Intelligence checks made to figure out its use.

EXPLOSIVES

Renaissance Item	Cost	Weight
Bomb	150 gp	1 lb.
Gunpowder, keg	250 gp	20 lb.
Gunpowder, powder horn	35 gp	2 lb.

Modern Item	Cost	Weight
Dynamite (stick)	—	1 lb.
Grenade, fragmentation	—	1 lb.
Grenade, smoke	—	2 lb.
Grenade launcher	—	7 lb.

PLOT POINTS

Plot points allow players to change the course of the campaign, introduce plot complications, alter the world, and even assume the role of the DM. If your first reaction to reading this optional rule is to worry that your players might abuse it, it's probably not for you.

USING PLOT POINTS

Each player starts with 1 plot point. During a session, a player can spend that point for one effect. The effect depends on your group's approach to this optional rule. Three options are presented below.

A player can spend no more than 1 plot point per session. You can increase this limit if you like, especially if you want the players to drive more of the story. Once every player at the table has spent a plot point, they each gain 1 plot point.

OPTION 1: WHAT A TWIST!

A player who spends a plot point gets to add some element to the setting or situation that the group (including you) must accept as true. For example, a player can spend a plot point and state that his or her character has found a secret door, an NPC appears, or a monster turns out to be a long-lost ally polymorphed into a horrid beast.

A player who wants to spend a plot point in this way should take a minute to discuss his or her idea with everyone else at the table and get feedback before settling on a plot development.

OPTION 2: THE PLOT THICKENS

Whenever a player spends a plot point, the player to his or her right must add a complication to the scene. For example, if the player who spends the plot point decides that her character has found a secret door, the player to the right might state that opening the door triggers a magical trap that teleports the party to another part of the dungeon.

OPTION 3: THE GODS MUST BE CRAZY

With this approach, there is no permanent DM. Everyone makes a character, and one person starts as the DM and runs the game as normal. That person's character becomes an NPC who can tag along with the group or remain on the sidelines, as the group wishes.

At any time, a player can spend a plot point to become the DM. That player's character becomes an NPC, and play continues. It's probably not a good idea to swap roles in the middle of combat, but it can happen if your group allows time for the new DM to settle into his or her role and pick up where the previous DM left off.

Using plot points in this way can make for an exciting campaign as each new DM steers the game in unexpected directions. This approach is also a great way for would-be DMs to try running a game in small, controlled doses.

In a campaign that uses plot points this way, everyone should come to the table with a bit of material prepared or specific encounters in mind. A player who isn't prepared or who doesn't feel like DMing can choose to not spend a plot point that session.

For this approach to work, it's a good idea to establish some shared assumptions about the campaign so that DMs aren't duplicating efforts or trampling on each other's plans.

COMBAT OPTIONS

The options in this section provide alternative ways to handle combat. The main risk of adding some of these rules is slowing down play.

INITIATIVE VARIANTS

This section offers different ways to handle initiative.

INITIATIVE SCORE

With this optional rule, creature don't roll initiative at the start of combat. Instead, each creature has an initiative score, which is a passive Dexterity check: 10 + Dexterity modifier.

By cutting down on die rolls, math done on the fly, and the process of asking for and recording totals, you can speed your game up considerably—at the cost of an initiative order that is often predictable.

SIDE INITIATIVE

Recording initiative for each PC and monster, arranging everyone in the correct order, and remembering where you are in the list can bog the game down. If you want quicker combats, at the risk of those combats becoming unbalanced, try using the side initiative rule.

Under this variant, the players roll a d20 for their initiative as a group, or side. You also roll a d20. Neither roll receives any modifiers. Whoever rolls highest wins initiative. In case of a tie, keep rerolling until the tie is broken.

When it's a side's turn, the members of that side can act in any order they choose. Once everyone on the side has taken a turn, the other side goes. A round ends when both sides have completed their turns.

If more than two sides take part in a battle, each side rolls for initiative. Sides act from the highest roll to lowest. Combat continues in the initiative order until the battle is complete.

This variant encourages teamwork and makes your life as a DM easier, since you can more easily coordinate monsters. On the downside, the side that wins initiative can gang up on enemies and take them out before they have a chance to act.

SPEED FACTOR

Some DMs find the regular progression of initiative too predictable and prone to abuse. Players can use their knowledge of the initiative order to influence their decisions. For example, a badly wounded fighter might charge a troll because he knows that the cleric goes before the monster and can heal him.

Speed factor is an option for initiative that introduces more uncertainty into combat, at the cost of speed of play. Under this variant, the participants in a battle roll initiative each round. Before rolling, each character or monster must choose an action.

Initiative Modifiers. Modifiers might apply to a creature's initiative depending on its size and the action it takes. For example, a creature that fights with a light weapon or casts a simple spell is more likely to act before a creature armed with a heavy or slow weapon. See the Speed Factor Initiative Modifiers table for details. If an action has no modifier listed, the action has no effect on initiative. If more than one modifier applies (such as wielding a two-handed, heavy melee weapon), apply them all to the initiative roll.

SPEED FACTOR INITIATIVE MODIFIERS

Factor	Initiative Modifier
Spellcasting	Subtract the spell's level
Melee, heavy weapon	−2
Melee, light or finesse weapon	+2
Melee, two-handed weapon	−2
Ranged, loading weapon	−5

Creature Size	Initiative Modifier
Tiny	+5
Small	+2
Medium	+0
Large	−2
Huge	−5
Gargantuan	−8

Don't apply the same modifier more than once on a creature's turn. For example, a rogue fighting with two daggers gains the +2 bonus for using a light or finesse weapon only once. In the case of spellcasting, apply only the modifier from the highest-level spell.

Apply any modifiers for bonus actions to that creature's turn, remembering never to apply the same modifier twice. For instance, a paladin casts a 2nd-level spell as a bonus action and then attacks with a shortsword. The paladin takes a −2 penalty for the spell and gains a +2 bonus for using a light weapon, for a total modifier of +0.

The table is only a starting point. You can refer to it when adjudicating any actions a character takes that you think should be faster or slower. Quick, easy actions should grant a bonus, while slow, difficult ones should incur a penalty. As a rule of thumb, apply a bonus or penalty of 2 or 5 for an action.

For example, a fighter wants to turn a winch to raise a portcullis. This is a complex, difficult action. You could rule that it incurs a −5 initiative penalty.

Rolling Initiative. After deciding on an action, everyone rolls initiative and applies modifiers, keeping the result secret. You then announce an initiative number, starting with 30 and working down (it helps to call out ranges of numbers at the start). Break any ties by having the combatant with the highest Dexterity act first. Otherwise, roll to determine who goes first.

Turns. On its turn, a creature moves as normal but must take the action it selected or take no action at all.

Once everyone has acted, the process repeats. Everyone in the battle selects an action, rolls initiative, and takes turns in order.

ACTION OPTIONS

This section provides new action options for combat. They can be added as a group or individually to your game.

CLIMB ONTO A BIGGER CREATURE

If one creature wants to jump onto another creature, it can do so by grappling. A Small or Medium creature has little chance of making a successful grapple against a Huge or Gargantuan creature, however, unless magic has granted the grappler supernatural might.

As an alternative, a suitably large opponent can be treated as terrain for the purpose of jumping onto its back or clinging to a limb. After making any ability checks necessary to get into position and onto the larger creature, the smaller creature uses its action to make a Strength (Athletics) or Dexterity (Acrobatics) check contested by the target's Dexterity (Acrobatics) check. If it wins the contest, the smaller creature successfully moves into the target creature's space and clings to its body. While in the target's space, the smaller creature moves with the target and has advantage on attack rolls against it.

The smaller creature can move around within the larger creature's space, treating the space as difficult terrain. The larger creature's ability to attack the smaller creature depends on the smaller creature's location, and is left to your discretion. The larger creature can dislodge the smaller creature as an action—knocking it off, scraping it against a wall, or grabbing and throwing it—by making a Strength (Athletics) check contested by the smaller creature's Strength (Athletics) or Dexterity (Acrobatics) check. The smaller creature chooses which ability to use.

DISARM

A creature can use a weapon attack to knock a weapon or another item from a target's grasp. The attacker makes an attack roll contested by the target's Strength (Athletics) check or Dexterity (Acrobatics) check. If the attacker wins the contest, the attack causes no damage or other ill effect, but the defender drops the item.

The attacker has disadvantage on its attack roll if the target is holding the item with two or more hands. The target has advantage on its ability check if it is larger than the attacking creature, or disadvantage if it is smaller.

MARK

This option makes it easier for melee combatants to harry each other with opportunity attacks.

When a creature makes a melee attack, it can also mark its target. Until the end of the attacker's next turn, any opportunity attack it makes against the marked target has advantage. The opportunity attack doesn't expend the attacker's reaction, but the attacker can't make the attack if anything, such as the incapacitated condition or the *shocking grasp* spell, is preventing it from taking reactions. The attacker is limited to one opportunity attack per turn.

Overrun

When a creature tries to move through a hostile creature's space, the mover can try to force its way through by overrunning the hostile creature. As an action or a bonus action, the mover makes a Strength (Athletics) check contested by the hostile creature's Strength (Athletics) check. The creature attempting the overrun has advantage on this check if it is larger than the hostile creature, or disadvantage if it is smaller. If the mover wins the contest, it can move through the hostile creature's space once this turn.

Shove Aside

With this option, a creature uses the special shove attack from the *Player's Handbook* to force a target to the side, rather than away. The attacker has disadvantage on its Strength (Athletics) check when it does so. If that check is successful, the attacker moves the target 5 feet to a different space within its reach.

Tumble

A creature can try to tumble through a hostile creature's space, ducking and weaving past the opponent. As an action or a bonus action, the tumbler makes a Dexterity (Acrobatics) check contested by the hostile creature's Dexterity (Acrobatics) check. If the tumbler wins the contest, it can move through the hostile creature's space once this turn.

Hitting Cover

When a ranged attack misses a target that has cover, you can use this optional rule to determine whether the cover was struck by the attack.

First, determine whether the attack roll would have hit the protected target without the cover. If the attack roll falls within a range low enough to miss the target but high enough to strike the target if there had been no cover, the object used for cover is struck. If a creature is providing cover for the missed creature and the attack roll exceeds the AC of the covering creature, the covering creature is hit.

Cleaving through Creatures

If your player characters regularly fight hordes of lower-level monsters, consider using this optional rule to help speed up such fights.

When a melee attack reduces an undamaged creature to 0 hit points, any excess damage from that attack might carry over to another creature nearby. The attacker targets another creature within reach and, if the original attack roll can hit it, applies any remaining damage to it. If that creature was undamaged and is likewise reduced to 0 hit points, repeat this process, carrying over the remaining damage until there are no valid targets, or until the damage carried over fails to reduce an undamaged creature to 0 hit points.

Injuries

Damage normally leaves no lingering effects. This option introduces the potential for long-term injuries.

It's up to you to decide when to check for a lingering injury. A creature might sustain a lingering injury under the following circumstances:

- When it takes a critical hit
- When it drops to 0 hit points but isn't killed outright
- When it fails a death saving throw by 5 or more

To determine the nature of the injury, roll on the Lingering Injuries table. This table assumes a typical humanoid physiology, but you can adapt the results for creatures with different body types.

Lingering Injuries

d20	Injury
1	**Lose an Eye.** You have disadvantage on Wisdom (Perception) checks that rely on sight and on ranged attack rolls. Magic such as the *regenerate* spell can restore the lost eye. If you have no eyes left after sustaining this injury, you're blinded.
2	**Lose an Arm or a Hand.** You can no longer hold anything with two hands, and you can hold only a single object at a time. Magic such as the *regenerate* spell can restore the lost appendage.
3	**Lose a Foot or Leg.** Your speed on foot is halved, and you must use a cane or crutch to move unless you have a peg leg or other prosthesis. You fall prone after using the Dash action. You have disadvantage on Dexterity checks made to balance. Magic such as the *regenerate* spell can restore the lost appendage.
4	**Limp.** Your speed on foot is reduced by 5 feet. You must make a DC 10 Dexterity saving throw after using the Dash action. If you fail the save, you fall prone. Magical healing removes the limp.
5–7	**Internal Injury.** Whenever you attempt an action in combat, you must make a DC 15 Constitution saving throw. On a failed save, you lose your action and can't use reactions until the start of your next turn. The injury heals if you receive magical healing or if you spend ten days doing nothing but resting.
8–10	**Broken Ribs.** This has the same effect as Internal Injury above, except that the save DC is 10.
11–13	**Horrible Scar.** You are disfigured to the extent that the wound can't be easily concealed. You have disadvantage on Charisma (Persuasion) checks and advantage on Charisma (Intimidation) checks. Magical healing of 6th level or higher, such as *heal* and *regenerate*, removes the scar.
14–16	**Festering Wound.** Your hit point maximum is reduced by 1 every 24 hours the wound persists. If your hit point maximum drops to 0, you die. The wound heals if you receive magical healing. Alternatively, someone can tend to the wound and make a DC 15 Wisdom (Medicine) check once every 24 hours. After ten successes, the wound heals.
17–20	**Minor Scar.** The scar doesn't have any adverse effect. Magical healing of 6th level or higher, such as *heal* and *regenerate*, removes the scar.

Instead of using the effect described in the table, you can put the responsibility of representing a character's lingering injury in the hands of the player. Roll on the Lingering Injuries table as usual, but instead of suffering the effect described for that result, that character gains a new flaw with the same name. It's up to the player to express the lingering injury during play, just like any other flaw, with the potential to gain inspiration when the injury affects the character in a meaningful way.

Massive Damage

This optional rule makes it easier for a creature to be felled by massive damage.

When a creature takes damage from a single source equal to or greater than half its hit point maximum, it must succeed on a DC 15 Constitution saving throw or suffer a random effect determined by a roll on the System Shock table. For example, a creature that has a hit point maximum of 30 must make that Constitution save if it takes 15 damage or more from a single source.

System Shock

d10	Effect
1	The creature drops to 0 hit points.
2–3	The creature drops to 0 hit points but is stable.
4–5	The creature is stunned until the end of its next turn.
6–7	The creature can't take reactions and has disadvantage on attack rolls and ability checks until the end of its next turn.
8–10	The creature can't take reactions until the end of its next turn.

Morale

Some combatants might run away when a fight turns against them. You can use this optional rule to help determine when monsters and NPCs flee.

A creature might flee under any of the following circumstances:

- The creature is surprised.
- The creature is reduced to half its hit points or fewer for the first time in the battle.
- The creature has no way to harm the opposing side on its turn.

A group of creatures might flee under any of the following circumstances:

- All the creatures in the group are surprised.
- The group's leader is reduced to 0 hit points, incapacitated, taken prisoner, or removed from battle.
- The group is reduced to half its original size with no losses on the opposing side.

To determine whether a creature or group of creatures flees, make a DC 10 Wisdom saving throw for the creature or the group's leader. If the opposition is overwhelming, the saving throw is made with disadvantage, or you can decide that the save fails automatically. If a group's leader can't make the saving throw for whatever reason, have the creature in the group with the next highest Charisma score make the saving throw instead.

On a failed save, the affected creature or group flees by the most expeditious route. If escape is impossible, the creature or group surrenders. If a creature or group that surrenders is attacked by its conquerors, the battle might resume, and it's unlikely that further attempts to flee or surrender will be made.

A failed saving throw isn't always to the adventurers' benefit. For example, an ogre that flees from combat might put the rest of the dungeon on alert or run off with treasure that the characters had hoped to plunder.

Creating a Monster

The *Monster Manual* contains hundreds of ready-to-play monsters, but it doesn't include every monster that you can imagine. Part of the D&D experience is the simple joy of creating new monsters and customizing existing ones, if for no other reason than to surprise and delight your players with something they've never faced before.

The first step in the process is coming up with the concept for your monster. What makes it unique? Where does it live? What role do you want it to serve in your adventure, your campaign, or your world? What does it look like? Does it have any weird abilities? Once you have the answers to these questions, you can start figuring out how to represent your monster in the game.

Modifying a Monster

Once you have an idea for a monster, you'll need statistics to represent it. The first question you should ask yourself is: Can I use statistics that already exist?

A stat block in the *Monster Manual* might make a good starting point for your monster. Imagine, for example, that you want to create an intelligent arboreal predator that hunts elves. There is no such monster in the *Monster Manual*, but the quaggoth is a savage humanoid predator with a climbing speed. You can borrow the quaggoth stat block for your new monster, changing nothing but the creature's name. You can make minor tweaks, such as replacing the quaggoth's language, Undercommon, with one that's more appropriate, such as Elvish or Sylvan.

Need a fiery phoenix? Take the giant eagle or roc, give it immunity to fire, and allow it to deal fire damage with its attacks. Need a flying monkey? Consider a baboon with wings and a flying speed. Almost any monster you can imagine can be built using one that already exists.

Adapting a stat block is far less time-consuming than creating one from scratch, and there are changes you can make to an existing monster that have no effect on its challenge rating, such as swapping languages, changing its alignment, or adding special senses. However, once you change the creature's offensive or defensive ability, such as its hit points or damage, its challenge rating might need to change, as shown later.

Switching Weapons

If a monster wields a manufactured weapon, you can replace that weapon with a different one. For example, you could replace a hobgoblin's longsword with a halberd. Don't forget to change the damage and the attack's reach where appropriate. Also be aware of the consequences of switching from a one-handed weapon to a two-handed weapon, or vice versa. For example, a hobgoblin wielding a halberd (a two-handed weapon) loses the benefit of its shield, so its AC decreases by 2.

ADDING A SPECIAL TRAIT

Another simple way to customize a monster is to add a special trait. You can add a special trait of your own devising or pick up a special trait from one of the many creatures in the *Monster Manual*. For example, you can create a goblin-spider hybrid by giving the normal goblin the Spider Climb special trait, turn an ordinary troll into a two-headed troll by giving it the Two Heads special trait, or turn an owlbear into a flying owlbear by giving it wings and a giant owl's flying speed.

CREATING QUICK MONSTER STATS

If all you need are simple stats for a monster of a particular challenge rating, follow the steps here. If you

MONSTER STATISTICS BY CHALLENGE RATING

		— Defensive —		— Offensive —		
CR	Prof. Bonus	Armor Class	Hit Points	Attack Bonus	Damage/ Round	Save DC
0	+2	≤ 13	1–6	≤ +3	0–1	≤ 13
1/8	+2	13	7–35	+3	2–3	13
1/4	+2	13	36–49	+3	4–5	13
1/2	+2	13	50–70	+3	6–8	13
1	+2	13	71–85	+3	9–14	13
2	+2	13	86–100	+3	15–20	13
3	+2	13	101–115	+4	21–26	13
4	+2	14	116–130	+5	27–32	14
5	+3	15	131–145	+6	33–38	15
6	+3	15	146–160	+6	39–44	15
7	+3	15	161–175	+6	45–50	15
8	+3	16	176–190	+7	51–56	16
9	+4	16	191–205	+7	57–62	16
10	+4	17	206–220	+7	63–68	16
11	+4	17	221–235	+8	69–74	17
12	+4	17	236–250	+8	75–80	17
13	+5	18	251–265	+8	81–86	18
14	+5	18	266–280	+8	87–92	18
15	+5	18	281–295	+8	93–98	18
16	+5	18	296–310	+9	99–104	18
17	+6	19	311–325	+10	105–110	19
18	+6	19	326–340	+10	111–116	19
19	+6	19	341–355	+10	117–122	19
20	+6	19	356–400	+10	123–140	19
21	+7	19	401–445	+11	141–158	20
22	+7	19	446–490	+11	159–176	20
23	+7	19	491–535	+11	177–194	20
24	+7	19	536–580	+12	195–212	21
25	+8	19	581–625	+12	213–230	21
26	+8	19	626–670	+12	231–248	21
27	+8	19	671–715	+13	249–266	22
28	+8	19	716–760	+13	267–284	22
29	+9	19	761–805	+13	285–302	22
30	+9	19	806–850	+14	303–320	23

want to create something more akin to the monster stat blocks in the *Monster Manual*, skip ahead to the "Creating a Monster Stat Block" section.

STEP 1. EXPECTED CHALLENGE RATING

Pick the expected challenge rating (CR) for your monster. Knowing the monster's expected challenge rating will help you figure out the monster's proficiency bonus and other important combat statistics. Don't worry about getting the challenge rating exactly right; you can make adjustments in later steps.

A single monster with a challenge rating equal to the adventurers' level is, by itself, a fair challenge for a group of four characters. If the monster is meant to be fought in pairs or groups, its expected challenge rating should be lower than the party's level.

Don't fall into the trap of thinking that your monster must have a challenge rating equal to the level of the characters to be a worthy challenge. Keep in mind that monsters with a lower challenge rating can be a threat to higher-level characters when encountered in groups.

STEP 2. BASIC STATISTICS

Use the Monster Statistics by Challenge Rating table to determine the monster's Armor Class, hit points, attack bonus, and damage output per round based on the challenge rating you chose in step 1.

STEP 3. ADJUST STATISTICS

Raise or lower the monster's Armor Class, hit points, attack bonus, damage output per round, and save DC as you see fit, based on whatever concept you have in mind for the monster. For example, if you need a well-armored monster, increase its Armor Class.

Once you've made the desired adjustments, record the monster's statistics. If there are any other statistics you think the monster needs (such as ability scores), follow the appropriate steps under "Creating a Monster Stat Block."

STEP 4. FINAL CHALLENGE RATING

Calculate the monster's final challenge rating, accounting for the adjustments you made in step 3.

Defensive Challenge Rating. Read down the Hit Points column of the Monster Statistics by Challenge Rating table until you find your monster's hit points. Then look across and note the challenge rating suggested for a monster with those hit points.

Now look at the Armor Class suggested for a monster of that challenge rating. If your monster's AC is at least two points higher or lower than that number, adjust the challenge rating suggested by its hit points up or down by 1 for every 2 points of difference.

Offensive Challenge Rating. Read down the Damage/ Round column of the Monster Statistics by Challenge Rating table until you find your monster's damage output per round. Then look across and note the challenge rating suggested for a monster that deals that much damage.

Now look at the attack bonus suggested for a monster of that challenge rating. If your monster's attack bonus is at least two points higher or lower than that number, adjust the challenge rating suggested by its damage output up or down by 1 for every 2 points of difference.

If the monster relies more on effects with saving throws than on attacks, use the monster's save DC instead of its attack bonus.

If your monster uses different attack bonuses or save DCs, use the ones that will come up the most often.

Average Challenge Rating. The monster's final challenge rating is the average of its defensive and offensive challenge ratings. Round the average up or down to the nearest challenge rating to determine your monster's final challenge rating. For example, if the creature's defensive challenge rating is 2 and its offensive rating is 3, its final rating is 3.

With the final challenge rating, you can determine the monster's proficiency bonus using the Monster Statistics by Challenge Rating table. Use the Experience Points by Challenge Rating table to determine how much XP the monster is worth. A monster of challenge rating 0 is worth 0 XP if it poses no threat. Otherwise, it is worth 10 XP.

Creating a monster isn't just a number-crunching exercise. The guidelines in this chapter can help you create monsters, but the only way to know whether a monster is fun is to playtest it. After seeing your monster in action, you might want to adjust the challenge rating up or down based on your experiences.

EXPERIENCE POINTS BY CHALLENGE RATING

CR	XP	CR	XP
0	0 or 10	14	11,500
1/8	25	15	13,000
1/4	50	16	15,000
1/2	100	17	18,000
1	200	18	20,000
2	450	19	22,000
3	700	20	25,000
4	1,100	21	33,000
5	1,800	22	41,000
6	2,300	23	50,000
7	2,900	24	62,000
8	3,900	25	75,000
9	5,000	26	90,000
10	5,900	27	105,000
11	7,200	28	120,000
12	8,400	29	135,000
13	10,000	30	155,000

CREATING A MONSTER STAT BLOCK

If you want a full monster stat block, use the following method to create your new monster.

The introduction to the *Monster Manual* explains all the components of a monster's stat block. Familiarize yourself with that material before you begin. In the course of creating your monster, if you find yourself unable to make a decision, let the examples in the *Monster Manual* guide you.

Once you have a monster concept in mind, follow the steps below.

STEP 1. NAME

A monster's name should be given as much consideration as any other aspect of the monster, if not more.

Your monster might be based on a real-world creature or a monster from myth, in which case its name might be obvious. If you need to invent a name, keep in mind that the best names either reflect the monster's appearance or nature (such as the mimic and the owlbear) or have a nice ring to them (such as the chuul and the thri-kreen).

STEP 2. SIZE

Make your monster whatever size you want: Tiny, Small, Medium, Large, Huge, or Gargantuan.

A monster's size determines which die is used to calculate its hit points in step 8. Size also determines how much space the monster occupies, as discussed in the *Player's Handbook*.

STEP 3. TYPE

A monster's type provides insight into its origins and nature. The *Monster Manual* describes each monster type. Choose the type that best fits your concept for the monster.

STEP 4. ALIGNMENT

If your monster has no concept of morals, it is unaligned. Otherwise, it has an alignment appropriate to its nature and moral outlook, as discussed in the *Player's Handbook*.

STEP 5. ABILITY SCORES AND MODIFIERS

Monsters, like player characters, have the six ability scores. A monster can't have a score lower than 1 or higher than 30 in any ability.

A monster's score in any ability determines its ability modifier, as shown in the Ability Scores and Modifiers table in the *Player's Handbook*.

If you can't decide what a monster's ability scores should be, look for comparable monsters in the *Monster Manual* and mimic their ability scores. For example, if your monster is roughly as smart as a human commoner, give it an Intelligence of 10 (+0 modifier). If it's as strong as an ogre, give it a Strength of 19 (+4 modifier).

STEP 6. EXPECTED CHALLENGE RATING

Choose a challenge rating for your monster. See step 1 under "Creating Quick Monster Stats" for more information. You will use the proficiency bonus in later steps, so jot it down now or remember it.

STEP 7. ARMOR CLASS

A monster's Armor Class has a direct bearing on its challenge rating, and vice versa. You can determine your monster's Armor Class in one of two ways.

Use the Table. You can choose an appropriate AC based on the monster's expected challenge rating, as shown in the Monster Statistics by Challenge Rating table. The table provides the baseline AC for a monster of a specific challenge rating. Feel free to adjust the AC as you see fit. For example, the baseline AC for a

challenge rating 1 monster is 13, but if your monster is well armored, raise its AC accordingly. Don't worry if the monster's AC isn't matching up with the expected challenge rating for the monster. Other factors can affect a monster's challenge rating, as shown in later steps.

Determine an Appropriate AC. Alternatively, you can determine an appropriate AC based on the type of armor the monster wears, its natural armor, or some other Armor Class booster (such as the *mage armor* spell). Again, don't worry if the monster's AC isn't matching up with the expected challenge rating for the monster.

If your monster wears manufactured armor, its Armor Class is based on the type of armor worn (see the *Player's Handbook* for armor types). If the monster carries a shield, apply the shield bonus to its AC as normal.

A monster that doesn't wear armor might have natural armor, in which case it has an AC equal to 10 + its Dexterity modifier + its natural armor bonus. A monster with a thick hide generally has a natural armor bonus of +1 to +3. The bonus can be higher if the creature is exceptionally well armored. A gorgon, for example, is covered in steely plates and has a natural armor bonus of +9.

STEP 8. HIT POINTS

A monster's hit points have a direct bearing on its challenge rating, and vice versa. You can determine your monster's hit points in one of two ways.

Use the Table. You can start with the monster's expected challenge rating and use the Monster Statistics by Challenge Rating table to determine an appropriate number of hit points. The table presents a range of hit points for each challenge rating.

Assign Hit Dice. Alternatively, you can assign a number of Hit Dice to a monster, then calculate its average hit points. Don't worry if the hit points aren't matching up with the expected challenge rating for the monster. Other factors can affect a monster's challenge rating, as shown in later steps, and you can always adjust a monster's Hit Dice and hit points later on.

A monster can have as many Hit Dice as you want, but the size of the die used to calculate its hit points depends on the monster's size, as shown in the Hit Dice by Size table. For example, a Medium monster uses d8s for hit points, so a Medium monster with 5 Hit Dice and a Constitution of 13 (+1 modifier) has 5d8 + 5 hit points.

A monster typically has average hit points based on its Hit Dice. For example, a creature with 5d8 + 5 hit points has an average of 27 hit points ($5 \times 4.5 + 5$).

HIT DICE BY SIZE

Monster Size	Hit Die	Average HP per Die
Tiny	d4	2½
Small	d6	3½
Medium	d8	4½
Large	d10	5½
Huge	d12	6½
Gargantuan	d20	10½

Step 9. Damage Vulnerabilities, Resistances, and Immunities

Decide whether your monster has vulnerability, resistance, or immunity to one or more types of damage (see the *Player's Handbook* for descriptions of the various damage types). Assign a vulnerability, resistance, or immunity to a monster only when it's intuitive. For example, it makes sense for a monster made of molten lava to have immunity to fire damage.

Giving a monster resistances and immunities to three or more damage types (especially bludgeoning, piercing, and slashing damage) is like giving it extra hit points. However, adventurers have more resources at higher levels to counteract such defenses, making resistances and immunities less relevant at higher levels.

Effective Hit Points. If a monster has resistance or immunity to several damage types—especially bludgeoning, piercing, and slashing damage from nonmagical weapons—and not all the characters in the party possess the means to counteract that resistance or immunity, you need to take these defenses into account when comparing your monster's hit points to its expected challenge rating. Using the Effective Hit Points Based on Resistances and Immunities table, apply the appropriate multiplier to the monster's hit points to determine its effective hit points for the purpose of gauging its final challenge rating. (The monster's actual hit points shouldn't change.)

For example, a monster with an expected challenge rating of 6, 150 hit points, and resistance to bludgeoning, piercing, and slashing damage from nonmagical weapons effectively has 225 hit points (using the 1.5 multiplier for resistances) for the purpose of gauging its final challenge rating.

Monsters don't normally have vulnerability to more than one or two types of damage. Vulnerabilities don't significantly affect a monster's challenge rating, unless a monster has vulnerabilities to multiple damage types that are prevalent, especially bludgeoning, piercing, and slashing. For such a strange monster, reduce its effective hit points by half. Or even better, eliminate the vulnerabilities and give the brittle monster fewer hit points.

Effective Hit Points Based on Resistances and Immunities

Expected Challenge Rating	HP Multiplier for Resistances	HP Multiplier for Immunities
1–4	× 2	× 2
5–10	× 1.5	× 2
11–16	× 1.25	× 1.5
17 or more	× 1	× 1.25

Step 10. Attack Bonuses

A monster's attack bonuses have a direct bearing on its challenge rating, and vice versa. You can determine a monster's attack bonuses in one of two ways.

Use the Table. You can start with the monster's expected challenge rating and use the Monster Statistics by Challenge Rating table to determine an appropriate attack bonus for all the monster's attacks, regardless of its ability scores.

The table provides the baseline attack bonus for each challenge rating. Feel free to adjust the attack bonus as you see fit to match whatever concept you have in mind. For example, the baseline attack bonus for a challenge rating 1 monster is +3, but if your monster needs more accuracy, raise its bonus accordingly. Don't worry if the monster's attack bonus isn't matching up with the expected challenge rating for the monster. Other factors can affect a monster's challenge rating, as shown in later steps.

Calculate Attack Bonuses. Alternatively, you can calculate a monster's attack bonuses the same way players calculate the attack bonuses of a character.

When a monster has an action that requires an attack roll, its attack bonus is equal to its proficiency bonus + its Strength or Dexterity modifier. A monster usually applies its Strength modifier to melee attacks and its Dexterity modifier to ranged attacks, although smaller monsters sometimes use Dexterity for both.

Again, don't worry if the attack bonuses aren't matching up with the expected challenge rating for the monster. You can always adjust a monster's attack bonuses later.

Step 11. Damage

A monster's damage output—the amount of damage it deals every round—has a direct bearing on its challenge rating, and vice versa. You can determine a monster's damage output in one of two ways.

Use the Table. You can start with the monster's expected challenge rating and use the Monster Statistics by Challenge Rating table to determine how much damage the monster should deal every round. The table presents a range at each challenge rating. It doesn't matter how this damage is apportioned or distributed; for example, a monster might deal the damage every round with a single attack, or the damage could be split among multiple attacks against one or more foes.

Choose the type of damage based on how you imagine the damage being delivered. For example, if the monster is attacking with razor-sharp claws, the damage it deals is probably slashing damage. If its claws are poisonous, some portion of the damage might be poison damage instead of slashing damage.

If you want the damage output to vary slightly from round to round, you can translate the damage range into a single die expression (for a monster with one attack) or multiple die expressions (for a monster with multiple attacks). For example, a challenge rating 2 monster deals 15–20 damage per round. If you imagine the creature having a Strength of 18 (+4 modifier), you could give it one melee attack that deals 3d8 + 4 (average 17.5) damage, split the damage output into two separate attacks that deal 1d10 + 4 (average 9) damage each, or use any other combination where the average damage output falls within the desired range.

Base the Damage on the Weapon. Alternatively, you can use a die expression to represent the damage that a monster deals with each of its attacks based on whatever weapon it is using.

Don't worry if the damage output isn't matching up with the expected challenge rating for the monster. Other factors can affect a monster's challenge rating, as will be discussed in later steps, and you can always adjust a monster's damage output later on.

Some monsters use natural weapons, such as claws or tail spikes. Others wield manufactured weapons.

If a monster has natural weapons, you decide how much damage it deals with those attacks, as well as the type of damage. See the *Monster Manual* for examples.

If a monster wields a manufactured weapon, it deals damage appropriate to the weapon. For example, a greataxe in the hands of a Medium monster deals 1d12 slashing damage plus the monster's Strength modifier, as is normal for that weapon.

Big monsters typically wield oversized weapons that deal extra dice of damage on a hit. Double the weapon dice if the creature is Large, triple the weapon dice if it's Huge, and quadruple the weapon dice if it's Gargantuan. For example, a Huge giant wielding an appropriately sized greataxe deals 3d12 slashing damage (plus its Strength bonus), instead of the normal 1d12.

A creature has disadvantage on attack rolls with a weapon that is sized for a larger attacker. You can rule that a weapon sized for an attacker two or more sizes larger is too big for the creature to use at all.

Overall Damage Output. To determine a monster's overall damage output, take the average damage it deals with each of its attacks in a round and add them together. If a monster has different attack options, use the monster's most effective attacks to determine its damage output. For example, a fire giant can make two greatsword attacks or one rock attack in a round. The greatsword attacks deal more damage, so that attack routine determines the fire giant's damage output.

If a monster's damage output varies from round to round, calculate its damage output each round for the first three rounds of combat, and take the average. For example, a young white dragon has a multiattack routine (one bite attack and two claw attacks) that deals an average of 37 damage each round, as well as a breath weapon that deals 45 damage, or 90 if it hits two targets (and it probably will). In the first three rounds of combat, the dragon will probably get to use its breath weapon once and its multiattack routine twice, so its average damage output for the first three rounds would be (90 + 37 + 37) ÷ 3, or 54 damage (rounded down).

When calculating a monster's damage output, also account for special off-turn damage-dealing features, such as auras, reactions, legendary actions, or lair

actions. For example, a balor's Fire Aura deals 10 fire damage to any creature that hits the balor with a melee attack. The aura also deals 10 fire damage to all creatures within 5 feet of the balor at the start of each of the balor's turns. If you assume that one character in the party is within 5 feet of the balor at all times, hitting it with a melee weapon every round, then the balor's damage output per round increases by 20.

Step 12. Save DCs

A monster might have an attack or some other trait that requires a target to make a saving throw. The save DCs to resist such effects have a direct bearing on the monster's challenge rating, and vice versa. You can determine save DCs in one of two ways.

Use the Table. You can start with the monster's expected challenge rating and use the Monster Statistics by Challenge Rating table to determine an appropriate save DC for any effect that requires a target to make a saving throw.

Calculate the DCs. Alternatively, you can calculate a monster's save DCs as follows: 8 + the monster's proficiency bonus + the monster's relevant ability modifier. You choose the ability that best applies.

For example, if the effect is a poison, the relevant ability is probably the monster's Constitution. If the effect is similar to that of a spell, the relevant ability might be the monster's Intelligence, Wisdom, or Charisma.

Don't worry if the save DCs aren't matching up with the expected challenge rating for the monster. Other factors can affect a monster's challenge rating, as shown in later steps, and you can always adjust the save DCs later on.

Step 13. Special Traits, Actions, and Reactions

Some special traits (such as Magic Resistance), special actions (such as Superior Invisibility), and special reactions (such as Parry) can improve a monster's combat effectiveness and potentially increase its challenge rating.

The Monster Features table lists various features that you can plunder from the *Monster Manual*. The table notes which features increase a monster's effective Armor Class, hit points, attack bonus, or damage output for the purpose of determining its challenge rating. (The features don't actually change the monster's statistics.) Features that have no effect on a monster's challenge rating are noted with a dash (—).

When assigning special traits, actions, or reactions to a monster, keep in mind that not all monsters need them. The more you add, the more complex (and harder to run) the monster becomes.

Innate Spellcasting and Spellcasting. The impact that the Innate Spellcasting and Spellcasting special traits have on a monster's challenge rating depends on the spells that the monster can cast. Spells that deal more damage than the monster's normal attack routine and spells that increase the monster's AC or hit points need to be accounted for when determining the monster's final challenge rating. See the "Special Traits" section in the introduction of the *Monster Manual* for more information on these two special traits.

STEP 14. SPEED

Every monster has a walking speed. (Immobile monsters have a walking speed of 0 feet.) In addition to its walking speed, a monster might have one or more other speeds, including a burrowing, climbing, flying, or swimming speed.

Flying Monster. Increase the monster's effective Armor Class by 2 (not its actual AC) if it can fly and deal damage at range and if its expected challenge rating is 10 or lower (higher-level characters have a greater ability to deal with flying creatures).

STEP 15. SAVING THROW BONUSES

If you want a monster to be unusually resistant to certain kinds of effects, you can give it a bonus to saving throws tied to a particular ability.

A saving throw bonus is best used to counteract a low ability score. For example, an undead monster with a low Wisdom score might need a Wisdom saving throw bonus to account for the fact that it's more difficult to charm, frighten, or turn than its Wisdom would indicate.

A saving throw bonus is equal to the monster's proficiency bonus + the monster's relevant ability modifier.

A monster with three or more saving throw bonuses has a significant defensive advantage, so its effective AC (not its actual AC) should be raised when determining its challenge rating. If it has three or four bonuses, increase its effective AC by 2. If it has five or more bonuses, increase its effective AC by 4.

STEP 16. FINAL CHALLENGE RATING

At this point, you have all the statistical information you need to calculate the monster's final challenge rating. This step is identical to step 4 under "Creating Quick Monster Stats." Calculate the monster's defensive challenge rating and its offensive challenge rating, then take the average to get its final challenge rating.

STEP 17. SKILL BONUSES

If you want a monster to be proficient in a skill, you can give it a bonus equal to its proficiency bonus on ability checks related to that skill. For example, a monster with sharp senses might have a bonus on Wisdom (Perception) checks, while a duplicitous monster might have a bonus on Charisma (Deception) checks.

You can double the proficiency bonus to account for heightened mastery. For example, a doppelganger is so good at deceiving others that its bonus on Charisma (Deception) checks is equal to double its proficiency bonus + its Charisma modifier.

Skill bonuses have no bearing on a monster's challenge rating.

STEP 18. CONDITION IMMUNITIES

A monster can be immune to one or more debilitating conditions, and these immunities have no bearing on its challenge rating. For descriptions of the various conditions, see appendix A of the *Player's Handbook*.

As with damage immunities, condition immunities should be intuitive and logical. For example, it makes sense that a stone golem can't be poisoned, since it's a construct without a nervous system or internal organs.

STEP 19. SENSES

A monster might have one or more of the following special senses, which are described in the *Monster Manual*: blindsight, darkvision, tremorsense, and truesight. Whether the monster has special senses or not has no bearing on its challenge rating.

Passive Perception Score. All monsters have a passive Wisdom (Perception) score, which is most often used to determine whether a monster detects approaching or hidden enemies. A monster's passive Wisdom (Perception) score is 10 + its Wisdom modifier. If the monster has proficiency in the Perception skill, its score is 10 + its Wisdom (Perception) bonus.

STEP 20. LANGUAGES

Whether a monster can speak a language has no bearing on its challenge rating.

A monster can master as many spoken languages as you want, although few monsters know more than one or two, and many monsters (beasts in particular) have no spoken language whatsoever. A monster that lacks the ability to speak might still understand a language.

Telepathy. Whether or not a monster has telepathy has no bearing on its challenge rating. For more information on telepathy, see the *Monster Manual*.

NPC STAT BLOCKS

Appendix B of the *Monster Manual* contains stat blocks for common NPC archetypes such as bandits and guards, as well as tips for customizing them. Those tips include adding racial traits from the *Player's Handbook*, equipping NPCs with magic items, and swapping armor, weapons, and spells.

Monster Features

Name	Example Monster	Effect on Challenge Rating
Aggressive	Orc	Increase the monster's effective per-round damage output by 2.
Ambusher	Doppelganger	Increase the monster's effective attack bonus by 1.
Amorphous	Black pudding	—
Amphibious	Kuo-toa	—
Angelic Weapons	Deva	Increase the monster's effective per-round damage by the amount noted in the trait.
Antimagic Susceptibility	Flying sword	—
Avoidance	Demilich	Increase the monster's effective AC by 1.
Blind Senses	Grimlock	—
Blood Frenzy	Sahuagin	Increase the monster's effective attack bonus by 4.
Breath Weapon	Ancient black dragon	For the purpose of determining effective damage output, assume the breath weapon hits two targets, and that each target fails its saving throw.
Brute	Bugbear	Increase the monster's effective per-round damage by the amount noted in the trait.
Chameleon Skin	Troglodyte	—
Change Shape	Ancient brass dragon	—
Charge	Centaur	Increase the monster's damage on one attack by the amount noted in the trait.
Charm	Vampire	—
Constrict	Constrictor snake	Increase the monster's effective AC by 1.
Damage Absorption	Flesh golem	—
Damage Transfer	Darkmantle	Double the monster's effective hit points. Add one-third of the monster's hit points to its per-round damage.
Death Burst	Magmin	Increase the monster's effective damage output for 1 round by the amount noted in the trait, and assume it affects two creatures.
Devil Sight	Barbed devil	—
Dive	Aarakocra	Increase the monster's effective damage on one attack by the amount noted in the trait.
Echolocation	Hook horror	—
Elemental Body	Azer	Increase the monster's effective per-round damage by the amount noted in the trait.
Enlarge	Duergar	Increase the monster's effective per-round damage by the amount noted in the trait.
Etherealness	Night hag	—
False Appearance	Gargoyle	—
Fey Ancestry	Drow	—
Fiendish Blessing	Cambion	Apply the monster's Charisma modifier to its actual AC.
Flyby	Peryton	—
Frightful Presence	Ancient black dragon	Increase the monster's effective hit points by 25% if the monster is meant to face characters of 10th level or lower.
Grappler	Mimic	—
Hold Breath	Lizardfolk	—
Horrifying Visage	Banshee	See Frightful Presence.
Illumination	Flameskull	—
Illusory Appearance	Green hag	—
Immutable Form	Iron golem	—
Incorporeal Movement	Ghost	—
Innate Spellcasting	Djinni	See step 13 under "Creating a Monster Stat Block."
Inscrutable	Androsphinx	—
Invisibility	Imp	—
Keen Senses	Hell hound	—
Labyrinthine Recall	Minotaur	—
Leadership	Hobgoblin captain	—
Legendary Resistance	Ancient black dragon	Each per-day use of this trait increases the monster's effective hit points based on the expected challenge rating: 1–4, 10 hp; 5–10, 20 hp; 11 or higher, 30 hp.
Life Drain	Wight	—

Name	Example Monster	Effect on Challenge Rating
Light Sensitivity	Shadow demon	—
Magic Resistance	Balor	Increase the monster's effective AC by 2.
Magic Weapons	Balor	—
Martial Advantage	Hobgoblin	Increase the effective damage of one attack per round by the amount gained from this trait.
Mimicry	Kenku	—
Nimble Escape	Goblin	Increase the monster's effective AC and effective attack bonus by 4 (assuming the monster hides every round).
Otherworldly Perception	Kuo-toa	—
Pack Tactics	Kobold	Increase the monster's effective attack bonus by 1.
Parry	Hobgoblin warlord	Increase the monster's effective AC by 1.
Possession	Ghost	Double the monster's effective hit points.
Pounce	Tiger	Increase the monster's effective damage for 1 round by the amount it deals with the bonus action gained from this trait.
Psychic Defense	Githzerai monk	Apply the monster's Wisdom modifier to its actual AC if the monster isn't wearing armor or wielding a shield.
Rampage	Gnoll	Increase the monster's effective per-round damage by 2.
Reactive	Marilith	—
Read Thoughts	Doppelganger	—
Reckless	Minotaur	—
Redirect Attack	Goblin boss	—
Reel	Roper	—
Regeneration	Troll	Increase the monster's effective hit points by 3 × the number of hit points the monster regenerates each round.
Rejuvenation	Lich	—
Relentless	Wereboar	Increase the monster's effective hit points based on the expected challenge rating: 1–4, 7 hp; 5–10, 14 hp; 11–16, 21 hp; 17 or higher, 28 hp.
Shadow Stealth	Shadow demon	Increase the monster's effective AC by 4.
Shapechanger	Wererat	—
Siege Monster	Earth elemental	—
Slippery	Kuo-toa	—
Spellcasting	Lich	See step 13 under "Creating a Monster Stat Block."
Spider Climb	Ettercap	—
Standing Leap	Bullywug	—
Steadfast	Bearded devil	—
Stench	Troglodyte	Increase the monster's effective AC by 1.
Sunlight Sensitivity	Kobold	—
Superior Invisibility	Faerie dragon	Increase the monster's effective AC by 2.
Sure-Footed	Dao	—
Surprise Attack	Bugbear	Increase the monster's effective damage for 1 round by the amount noted in the trait.
Swallow	Behir	Assume the monster swallows one creature and deals 2 rounds of acid damage to it.
Teleport	Balor	—
Terrain Camouflage	Bullywug	—
Tunneler	Umber hulk	—
Turn Immunity	Revenant	—
Turn Resistance	Lich	—
Two Heads	Ettin	—
Undead Fortitude	Zombie	Increase the monster's effective hit points based on the expected challenge rating: 1–4, 7 hp; 5–10, 14 hp; 11–16, 21 hp; 17 or higher, 28 hp.
Web	Giant spider	Increase the monster's effective AC by 1.
Web Sense	Giant spider	—
Web Walker	Giant spider	—
Wounded Fury	Quaggoth	Increase the monster's damage for 1 round by the amount noted in the trait.

If you want to take an NPC stat block and adapt it for a specific monster race, apply the ability modifiers and add the features listed in the NPC Features table. If the NPC's AC, hit points, attack bonus, or damage changes, recalculate its challenge rating.

CREATING NPCS FROM SCRATCH

If you need completely new statistics for an NPC, you have two options:

- You can create an NPC stat block (similar to the ones in the *Monster Manual*) as you would a monster stat block, as discussed in the previous section.
- You can build the NPC as you would a player character, as discussed in the *Player's Handbook*.

If you decide to build an NPC the same way you build a player character, you can skip choosing a background and instead pick two skill proficiencies for the NPC.

NPC FEATURES

Race	Ability Modifiers	Features
Aarakocra	+2 Dex, +2 Wis	Dive Attack; talon attack action; speed 20 ft., fly 50 ft.; speaks Auran
Bullywug	−2 Int, −2 Cha	Amphibious, Speak with Frogs and Toads, Swamp Camouflage, Standing Leap; speed 20 ft., swim 40 ft.; speaks Bullywug
Dragonborn*	+2 Str, +1 Cha	Breath Weapon (use challenge rating instead of level to determine damage), Damage Resistance, Draconic Ancestry; speaks Common and Draconic
Drow*	+2 Dex, +1 Cha	Fey Ancestry, Innate Spellcasting feature of the drow, Sunlight Sensitivity; darkvision 120 ft.; speaks Elvish and Undercommon
Dwarf*	+2 Str or Wis, +2 Con	Dwarven Resilience, Stonecunning; speed 25 ft.; darkvision 60 ft.; speaks Common and Dwarvish
Elf*	+2 Dex, +1 Int or Wis	Fey Ancestry, Trance; darkvision 60 ft.; proficiency in the Perception skill; speaks Common and Elvish
Gnoll	+2 Str, −2 Int	Rampage; darkvision 60 ft.
Gnome*	+2 Int, +2 Dex or Con	Gnome Cunning; Small size; speed 25 ft.; darkvision 60 ft.; speaks Common and Gnomish
Gnome, deep	+1 Str, +2 Dex	Gnome Cunning, Innate Spellcasting, Stone Camouflage; Small size; speed 20 ft.; darkvision 120 ft.; speaks Gnomish, Terran, and Undercommon
Goblin	−2 Str, +2 Dex	Nimble Escape; Small size; darkvision 60 ft.; speaks Common and Goblin
Grimlock	+2 Str, −2 Cha	Blind Senses, Keen Hearing and Smell, Stone Camouflage; can't be blinded; blindsight 30 ft., or 10 ft. while deafened (blind beyond this radius); speaks Undercommon
Half-elf*	+1 Dex, +1 Int, +2 Cha	Fey Ancestry; darkvision 60 ft.; proficiency in two skills; speaks Common and Elvish
Half-orc*	+2 Str, +1 Con	Relentless Endurance; darkvision 60 ft.; proficiency in the Intimidation skill; speaks Common and Orc
Halfling*	+2 Dex, +1 Con or Cha	Brave, Halfling Nimbleness, Lucky; Small size; speed 25 ft.; speaks Common and Halfling
Hobgoblin	None	Martial Advantage; darkvision 60 ft.; speaks Common and Goblin
Kenku	+2 Dex	Ambusher, Mimicry; understands Auran and Common but speaks only through the use of its Mimicry trait
Kobold	−4 Str, +2 Dex	Pack Tactics, Sunlight Sensitivity; Small size; darkvision 60 ft.; speaks Common and Draconic
Kuo-toa	None	Amphibious, Otherworldly Perception, Slippery, Sunlight Sensitivity; speed 30 ft., swim 30 ft.; darkvision 120 ft.; speaks Undercommon
Lizardfolk	+2 Str, −2 Int	Hold Breath (15 min.); +3 natural armor bonus to AC; speed 30 ft., swim 30 ft.; speaks Draconic
Merfolk	None	Amphibious; speed 10 ft., swim 40 ft.; speaks Aquan and Common
Orc	+2 Str, −2 Int	Aggressive; darkvision 60 ft.; speaks Common and Orc
Skeleton	+2 Dex, −4 Int, −4 Cha	Vulnerable to bludgeoning damage; immune to poison damage and exhaustion; can't be poisoned; darkvision 60 ft.; can't speak but understands the languages it knew in life
Tiefling*	+1 Int, +2 Cha	Infernal Legacy (use challenge rating instead of level to determine spells), resistance to fire damage; darkvision 60 ft.; speaks Common and Infernal
Troglodyte	+2 Str, +2 Con, −4 Int, −4 Cha	Chameleon Skin, Stench, Sunlight Sensitivity; +1 natural armor bonus to AC; darkvision 60 ft.; speaks Troglodyte
Zombie	+1 Str, +2 Con, −6 Int, −4 Wis, −4 Cha	Undead Fortitude; immune to poison damage; can't be poisoned; darkvision 60 ft.; can't speak but understands the languages it knew in life

* See the *Player's Handbook* for descriptions of this race's features, none of which alter the NPC's challenge rating.

The NPC Features table summarizes the ability modifiers and features of various nonhuman races, as well as various creatures from the *Monster Manual* with a challenge rating lower than 1. Apply these modifiers and add these features to the NPC's stat block, then determine the NPC's challenge rating just as you would for a monster. Features that can affect a monster's challenge rating are listed in the Monster Features table. The NPC's proficiency bonus is determined by its level, just like a character, rather than by its challenge rating.

If the monster you want to use isn't listed on the table, use the process described below under "Monsters with Classes."

MONSTERS WITH CLASSES

You can use the rules in chapter 3 of the *Player's Handbook* to give class levels to a monster. For example, you can turn an ordinary werewolf into a werewolf with four levels of the barbarian class (such a monster would be expressed as "Werewolf, 4th-level barbarian").

Start with the monster's stat block. The monster gains all the class features for every class level you add, with the following exceptions:

- The monster doesn't gain the starting equipment of the added class.
- For each class level you add, the monster gains one Hit Die of its normal type (based on its size), ignoring the class's Hit Die progression.
- The monster's proficiency bonus is based on its challenge rating, not its class levels.

Once you finish adding class levels to a monster, feel free to tweak its ability scores as you see fit (for example, raising the monster's Intelligence score so that the monster is a more effective wizard), and make whatever other adjustments are needed. You'll need to recalculate its challenge rating as though you had designed the monster from scratch.

Depending on the monster and the number of class levels you add to it, its challenge rating might change very little or increase dramatically. For example, a werewolf that gains four barbarian levels is a much greater threat than it was before. In contrast, the hit points, spells, and other class features that an ancient red dragon gains from five levels of wizard don't increase its challenge rating.

CREATING A SPELL

When creating a new spell, use existing spells as guidelines. Here are some things to consider:

- If a spell is so good that a caster would want to use it all the time, it might be too powerful for its level.
- A long duration or large area can make up for a lesser effect, depending on the spell.
- Avoid spells that have very limited use, such as one that works only against good dragons. Though such a spell could exist in the world, few characters will bother to learn or prepare it unless they know in advance that doing so will be worthwhile.
- Make sure the spell fits with the identity of the class. Wizards and sorcerers don't typically have access to

healing spells, for example, and adding a healing spell to the wizard class list would step on the cleric's turf.

SPELL DAMAGE

For any spell that deals damage, use the Spell Damage table to determine approximately how much damage is appropriate given the spell's level. The table assumes the spell deals half damage on a successful saving throw or a missed attack. If your spell doesn't deal damage on a successful save, you can increase the damage by 25 percent.

You can use different damage dice than the ones in the table, provided that the average result is about the same. Doing so can add a little variety to the spell. For example, you could change a cantrip's damage from 1d10 (average 5.5) to 2d4 (average 5), reducing the maximum damage and making an average result more likely.

SPELL DAMAGE

Spell Level	One Target	Multiple Targets
Cantrip	1d10	1d6
1st	2d10	2d6
2nd	3d10	4d6
3rd	5d10	6d6
4th	6d10	7d6
5th	8d10	8d6
6th	10d10	11d6
7th	11d10	12d6
8th	12d10	13d6
9th	15d10	14d6

HEALING SPELLS

You can also use the Spell Damage table to determine how many hit points a healing spell restores. A cantrip shouldn't offer healing.

CREATING A MAGIC ITEM

The magic items in chapter 7, "Treasure," are but a few of the magic treasures that characters can discover during their adventures. If your players are seasoned veterans and you want to surprise them, you can either modify an existing item or come up with something new.

MODIFYING AN ITEM

The easiest way to invent a new item is to tweak an existing one. If a paladin uses a flail as her main weapon, you could change a *holy avenger* so that it's a flail instead of a sword. You can turn a *ring of the ram* into a wand, or a *cloak of protection* into a *circlet of protection*, all without altering the item's properties.

Other substitutions are equally easy. An item that deals damage of one type can easily deal damage of another type. A *flame tongue* sword could deal lightning damage instead of fire, for example. One capability can replace another, so a *potion of climbing* can easily become a *potion of stealth*.

You can also modify an item by fusing it with properties from another item. For example, you could combine the effects of a *helm of comprehending languages* with those of a *helm of telepathy* into a single helmet. This makes the item more powerful (and probably increases its rarity), but it won't break your game.

Finally, remember the tools that are provided for modifying items in chapter 7, "Treasure." Giving an item an interesting minor property, a quirk, or sentience can alter its flavor significantly.

CREATING A NEW ITEM

If modifying an item doesn't quite do the trick, you can create one from scratch. A magic item should either let a character do something he or she couldn't do before, or improve the character's ability to do something he or she can do already. For example, the *ring of jumping* lets its wearer jump greater distances, thus augmenting what a character can already do. A *ring of the ram*, however, gives a character the ability to deal force damage.

The simpler your approach, the easier it is for a character to use the item in play. Giving the item charges is fine, especially if it has several different abilities, but simply deciding that an item is always active or can be used a fixed number of times per day is easier to manage.

POWER LEVEL

If you make an item that lets a character kill whatever he or she hits with it, that item will likely unbalance your game. On the other hand, an item whose benefit rarely comes into play isn't much of a reward and probably not worth doling out as one.

Use the Magic Item Power by Rarity table as a guide to help you determine how powerful an item should be, based on its rarity.

MAGIC ITEM POWER BY RARITY

Rarity	Max Spell Level	Max Bonus
Common	1st	—
Uncommon	3rd	+1
Rare	6th	+2
Very rare	8th	+3
Legendary	9th	+4

Maximum Spell Level. This column of the table indicates the highest-level spell effect the item should confer, in the form of a once-per-day or similarly limited property. For example, a common item might confer the benefit of a 1st-level spell once per day (or just once, if it's consumable). A rare, very rare, or legendary item might allow its possessor to cast a lower-level spell more frequently.

Maximum Bonus. If an item delivers a static bonus to AC, attack rolls, saving throws, or ability checks, this column suggests an appropriate bonus based on the item's rarity.

ATTUNEMENT

Decide whether the item requires a character to be attuned to it to use its properties. Use these rules of thumb to help you decide:

- If having all the characters in a party pass an item around to gain its lasting benefits would be disruptive, the item should require attunement.
- If the item grants a bonus that other items also grant, it's a good idea to require attunement so that characters don't try to collect too many of those items.

CREATING NEW CHARACTER OPTIONS

If the options for player characters in the *Player's Handbook* don't meet all the needs of your campaign, consult the following sections for advice on creating new race, class, and background options.

CREATING A RACE OR SUBRACE

This section teaches you how to modify existing races, as well as create new ones. The most important step in customizing or designing races for your campaign is to start with the story behind the race or subrace you wish to create. Having a firm idea of a race's story in your campaign will help you make decisions during the creation process. Ask yourself several questions:

- Why does my campaign need the race to be playable?
- What does the race look like?
- How would I describe the race's culture?
- Where do the members of this race live?
- Are there interesting conflicts built into the race's history and culture that make the race compelling from a storytelling standpoint?
- What is the race's relationship to the other playable races?
- What classes and backgrounds are well suited to members of the race?
- What are the race's signature traits?
- In the case of a new subrace, what sets it apart from the other subraces of the parent race?

Compare the race you have in mind with the other race options available to players, to make sure that the new race doesn't pale in comparison to the existing options (which would result in the race being unpopular) or completely overshadow them (so that players don't feel as if the other options are inferior).

When the time comes to design the game elements of the race, such as its traits, take a look at the game's existing races and let them inspire you.

COSMETIC ALTERATIONS

A simple way to modify an existing race is to change its appearance. Changes to a race's appearance need not affect its game elements. For example, you could transform halflings into anthropomorphic mice without changing their racial traits at all.

CULTURAL ALTERATIONS

In your world, elves might be desert nomads instead of forest dwellers, halflings might live in cloud cities, and dwarves might be sailors instead of miners. When you change the culture of a race, you can also make minor alterations to the race's proficiencies and traits to reflect that culture.

For example, imagine that the dwarves of your world are seafarers and inventors of gunpowder. You could add the pistol and musket to the list of weapons that dwarves are proficient with, and give them proficiency with waterborne vehicles instead of artisan's tools. These two small changes tell a different story than the default assumptions about dwarves in the *Player's Handbook*, without changing the power level of the race.

CREATING A NEW SUBRACE

Creating a new subrace is more involved than making some minor tweaks to existing racial features, but it does have the advantage of increasing the diversity of options for a particular race, rather than replacing some options with other ones.

The following example walks through the creation of an elf subrace: the eladrin. This subrace has history in the D&D multiverse, so you already have some stories to draw on when building its traits.

limited use of the *misty step* spell. Since *misty step* is a 2nd-level spell, this ability is potent enough that the subrace doesn't need additional traits. This leaves us with the following features for the eladrin subrace:

Ability Score Increase. Your Intelligence score increases by 1.

Elf Weapon Training. You have proficiency with the longsword, shortsword, shortbow, and longbow.

Fey Step. You can cast the *misty step* spell once using this trait. You regain the ability to do so when you finish a short or long rest.

CREATING A NEW RACE

When creating a race from scratch, begin with the story and proceed from there. Compare your creation to the other races of your world, and borrow freely from the traits of other races. As an example, consider the aasimar, a race similar to the tiefling but with a celestial heritage.

EXAMPLE RACE: AASIMAR

Whereas tieflings have fiendish blood in their veins, aasimar are the descendants of celestial beings. These folk generally appear as glorious humans with lustrous hair, flawless skin, and piercing eyes. Aasimar often attempt to pass as humans in order to right wrongs and defend goodness on the Material Plane without drawing undue attention to their celestial heritage. They strive to fit into society, although they usually rise to the top, becoming revered leaders and honorable heroes.

You might decide to use the aasimar as a counterpoint to the tiefling race. The two races could even be at odds, reflecting some greater conflict between the forces of good and evil in your campaign.

Here are our basic goals for the aasimar:

- Aasimar should make effective clerics and paladins.
- Aasimar should be to celestials and humans what tieflings are to fiends and humans.

Given that aasimar and tieflings are like two sides of the same coin, the tiefling makes a good starting point for coming up with the new race's traits. Since we want aasimar to be effective paladins and clerics, it makes sense to improve their Wisdom and Charisma instead of Intelligence and Charisma.

Like tieflings, aasimar have darkvision. Instead of resistance to fire damage, we give them resistance to radiant damage to reflect their celestial nature. However, radiant damage isn't as common as fire damage, so we give them resistance to necrotic damage as well, making them good at facing undead.

The tiefling's Infernal Legacy trait is a good model for a similar trait to reflect a magical, celestial heritage, replacing the tiefling's spells with spells of similar levels that more closely match the aasimar's celestial ancestry. However, the aasimar's expanded resistance might require limiting this trait to basic utility spells.

Filling in the remaining details, we end up with the following racial traits for the aasimar:

Ability Score Increase. Your Wisdom score increases by 1, and your Charisma score increases by 2.

EXAMPLE SUBRACE: ELADRIN

Creatures of magic with strong ties to nature, eladrin live in the twilight realm of the Feywild. Their cities sometimes cross over to the Material Plane, appearing briefly in mountain valleys or deep forest glades before fading back into the Feywild.

The elf subraces in the *Player's Handbook* include an ability score increase, a weapon training feature, and two or three additional traits. Given the story of the eladrin and their magical nature, an increase to an eladrin character's Intelligence is appropriate. There's no need to alter the basic weapon training shared by high elves and wood elves.

An ability that sets the eladrin apart from other elves is their ability to step through the boundary between the planes, disappearing for a moment before reappearing somewhere else. In the game, this is reflected in a

Age. Aasimar mature at the same rate as humans but live a few years longer.

Alignment. Due to their celestial heritage, aasimar are often good. However, some aasimar fall into evil, rejecting their heritage.

Size. Aasimar are built like well-proportioned humans. Your size is Medium.

Speed. Your base walking speed is 30 feet.

Darkvision. Thanks to your celestial heritage, you have superior vision in dark and dim conditions. You can see in dim light within 60 feet of you as if it were bright light, and in darkness as if it were dim light. You can't discern color in darkness, only shades of gray.

Celestial Resistance. You have resistance to necrotic damage and radiant damage.

Celestial Legacy. You know the *light* cantrip. Once you reach 3rd level, you can cast the *lesser restoration* spell once with this trait, and you regain the ability to do so when you finish a long rest. Once you reach 5th level, you can cast the *daylight* spell once with this trait as a 3rd-level spell, and you regain the ability to do so when you finish a long rest. Charisma is your spellcasting ability for these spells.

Languages. You can speak, read, and write Common and Celestial.

MODIFYING A CLASS

The classes in the *Player's Handbook* capture a wide range of character archetypes, but your campaign world might have need of something more. The following section discusses ways to modify existing classes to better serve your game's needs.

CHANGING PROFICIENCIES

Changing a class's proficiencies is a safe and simple way to modify a class to better reflect your world. Swapping out one skill or tool proficiency for another doesn't make a character any stronger or weaker, but doing so can change the flavor of a class in subtle ways.

For example, a prominent guild of rogues in your world might worship a patron deity, performing secret missions in that deity's name. To reflect this cultural detail, you could add Religion to the list of skills that a rogue character can choose as a proficiency. You could even mandate that skill as one of the choices for rogues who belong to this guild.

You can also change armor and weapon proficiencies to reflect certain aspects of your world. For example, you could decide that the clerics of a particular deity belong to an order that forbids the accumulation of material goods, other than magic items useful for their divine mission. Such clerics carry a staff, but they are forbidden from wearing armor or using weapons other than that staff. To reflect this, you could remove the armor and weapon proficiencies for clerics of this faith, making them proficient with the quarterstaff and nothing else. You could give them a benefit to make up for the loss of proficiencies—something like the monk's Unarmored Defense class feature, but presented as a divine blessing.

CHANGING SPELL LISTS

Modifying a class's spell list usually has little effect on a character's power but can change the flavor of a class significantly. In your world, paladins might not swear their oaths to ideals, but instead swear fealty to powerful sorcerers. To capture this story concept, you could build a new paladin spell list with spells meant to protect their masters, drawn from the sorcerer or wizard lists. Suddenly, the paladin feels like a different class.

Be cautious when changing the warlock spell list. Since warlocks regain their spell slots after a short rest, they have the potential to use certain spells more times in a day than other classes do.

RESTRICTING CLASS ACCESS

Without changing the way a class functions, you can root it more firmly in the world by associating the class with a particular race or culture.

For example, you might decide that bards, sorcerers, warlocks, and wizards represent the magical traditions of four different races or cultures. The bardic colleges might be closed to everyone except elves, dragonborn might be the only creatures capable of becoming sorcerers, and all warlocks in your world might be human. You could break that down still further: bards of the College of Lore could be high elves, and bards of the College of War could be wood elves. Gnomes discovered the school of illusion, so all wizards who specialize in that school are gnomes. Different human cultures produce warlocks with different pacts, and so on. Similarly, different cleric domains might reflect entirely separate religions associated with different races or cultures.

You decide how flexible you want to be in allowing a player character to break these restrictions. Can a half-elf live among the elves and study their bardic traditions? Can a dwarf stumble into a warlock pact despite having no connection to a culture that normally produces warlocks? As always, it's better to say yes and use the player's desire as an opportunity to develop the character's story and that of your world, rather than shutting down possibilities.

SUBSTITUTING CLASS FEATURES

If one or more features of a given class don't exactly fit the theme or tone of your campaign, you can pull them out of the class and replace them with new ones. In doing so, you should strive to make sure that the new options are just as appealing as the ones you are removing, and that the substitute class features contribute to the class's effectiveness at social interaction, exploration, or combat just as well as those being replaced.

Ultimately, a class exists to help a player express a particular character concept, and any class feature you replace is also removing an aspect of that character. Substituting a class feature should be done only to fit a specific need for your campaign, or to appeal to a player trying to create a specific kind of character (perhaps one modeled after a character from a novel, TV series, comic book, or movie).

The first step is to figure out what class feature or group of class features you're going to replace. Then you need to evaluate what each feature provides to the class, so that the features you are adding don't make the class over- or underpowered. Ask yourself the following questions about a feature you're replacing:

- What impact does replacing the feature have on exploration, social interaction, or combat?
- Does replacing the feature affect how long the party can continue adventuring in a day?
- Does the feature consume resources provided elsewhere in the class?
- Does the feature work all the time, or is it regained after a short rest, a long rest, or some other length of time?

Armed with answers to these questions, you can start designing new features that replace the ones you are removing. It's fine if the new class features drift closer to exploration, social interaction, or combat than the ones you are replacing, but be wary of going too far. For example, if you replace an exploration-focused feature with something purely combat focused, you've just made that class more powerful in combat, and it could overshadow the other classes in a way that you didn't intend.

There's no formula that can tell you how to design new class features. The best place to start is by looking at other class features, or at spells, feats, or any other rules for inspiration. You're almost certainly going to have some missteps, as features that seem good on the surface fall apart in play. That's all right. Everything you design will need to be playtested. When introducing new class features, be sure the players using them are comfortable with the fact that you might need to go back and make some changes after seeing them in play.

CREATING NEW CLASS OPTIONS

Each class has at least one major choice point. Clerics choose a divine domain, fighters choose a martial archetype, wizards choose an arcane tradition, and so forth. Creating a new option doesn't require you to remove anything from the class, but any new option you add should be compared to existing options to make sure it's no more or less powerful, yet remains distinctive in flavor. Like anything in class design, be prepared to playtest your ideas and make changes if things aren't playing out the way you want them to.

Once you have the concept for the class option in mind, it's time to design the specifics. If you're not sure where to begin, look at the existing options and see what class features they provide. It's perfectly acceptable for two class options to have similar features, and it's also fine to look at other classes for examples of mechanics you can draw on for inspiration. As you design each class feature, ask the following questions:

- How does the class feature reinforce the story or theme of the class option?
- Is there an existing feature that can be used as a model?
- How does the new class feature compare to other features of the same level?

VARIANT: SPELL POINTS

One way to modify how a class feels is to change how it uses its spells. With this variant system, a character who has the Spellcasting feature uses spell points instead of spell slots to fuel spells. Spell points give a caster more flexibility, at the cost of greater complexity.

In this variant, each spell has a point cost based on its level. The Spell Point Cost table summarizes the cost in spell points of slots from 1st to 9th level. Cantrips don't require slots and therefore don't require spell points.

Instead of gaining a number of spell slots to cast your spells from the Spellcasting feature, you gain a pool of spell points instead. You expend a number of spell points to create a spell slot of a given level, and then use that slot to cast a spell. You can't reduce your spell point total to less than 0, and you regain all spent spell points when you finish a long rest.

Spells of 6th level and higher are particularly taxing to cast. You can use spell points to create one slot of each level of 6th or higher. You can't create another slot of the same level until you finish a long rest.

The number of spell points you have to spend is based on your level as a spellcaster, as shown in the Spell Points by Level table. Your level also determines the maximum-level spell slot you can create. Even though you might have enough points to create a slot above this maximum, you can't do so.

The Spell Points by Level table applies to bards, clerics, druids, sorcerers, and wizards. For a paladin or ranger, halve the character's level in that class and then consult the table. For a fighter (Eldritch Knight) or rogue (Arcane Trickster), divide the character's level in that class by three.

This system can be applied to monsters that cast spells using spell slots, but it isn't recommended that you do so. Tracking spell point expenditures for a monster can be a hassle.

SPELL POINT COST

Spell Level	Point Cost	Spell Level	Point Cost
1st	2	5th	7
2nd	3	6th	9
3rd	5	7th	10
4th	6	8th	11
		9th	13

SPELL POINTS BY LEVEL

Class Level	Spell Points	Max Spell Level
1st	4	1st
2nd	6	1st
3rd	14	2nd
4th	17	2nd
5th	27	3rd
6th	32	3rd
7th	38	4th
8th	44	4th
9th	57	5th
10th	64	5th
11th	73	6th
12th	73	6th
13th	83	7th
14th	83	7th
15th	94	8th
16th	94	8th
17th	107	9th
18th	114	9th
19th	123	9th
20th	133	9th

CREATING A BACKGROUND

A well-crafted background can help a player create a character that feels like an exciting addition to your campaign. It helps define the character's place in the world, rather than what a character is in terms of game mechanics.

Instead of focusing on a generic character background, such as merchant or wanderer, think about the factions, organizations, and cultures of your campaign and how they might be leveraged to create flavorful backgrounds for player characters. For example, you could create an acolyte of Candlekeep background that is functionally similar to a sage background, but which ties a character more closely to a place and organization in your world.

A character with the acolyte of Candlekeep background probably has friends among the Avowed—the monks who maintain the great library at Candlekeep. The character can enter the library and consult its lore freely, while others must donate a rare or valuable tome of knowledge before they are allowed entry. Candlekeep's enemies are the character's enemies, and its allies, the character's friends. Acolytes of Candlekeep are generally regarded as learned sages and protectors of knowledge. It's possible to envision many interesting interactions as NPCs discover the character's background and approach the character in search of assistance.

To create your own background, follow these steps.

STEP 1. ROOT IT IN YOUR WORLD

To ground a new background in your campaign's setting, determine what element of your campaign the background is tied to: a faction, an organization, a trade, a person, an event, or a location.

STEP 2. SUGGEST PERSONAL CHARACTERISTICS

Create tables of suggested characteristics—personality traits, ideals, bonds, and flaws—that fit the background, or plunder entries from the tables presented in the *Player's Handbook*. Even if your players don't use the tables, this step helps you paint a picture of the background's place in your world. The tables need not be extensive; two or three entries per table are enough.

STEP 3. ASSIGN PROFICIENCIES OR LANGUAGES

Choose two skill proficiencies and two tool proficiencies for the background. You can replace tool proficiencies with languages on a one-for-one basis.

STEP 4. INCLUDE STARTING EQUIPMENT

Make sure your background offers a package of starting equipment. In addition to a small amount of money that a character can use to buy adventuring gear, the starting equipment should include items that a character would have acquired prior to becoming an adventurer, as well as one or two items unique to the background.

For example, starting equipment for a character with the acolyte of Candlekeep background might include a set of traveler's clothes, a scholar's robe, five candles, a tinderbox, an empty scroll case engraved with the symbol of Candlekeep, and a belt pouch containing 10 gp. The scroll case might be a gift given to an acolyte of Candlekeep who embarks on a life of adventure. At your discretion, it might also contain a useful map.

STEP 5. SETTLE ON A BACKGROUND FEATURE

Choose an existing background feature or create a new one, as you prefer. If you choose an existing feature, add or tweak a few details to make it unique.

For example, the acolyte of Candlekeep background might have the Researcher feature of the sage (as presented in the *Player's Handbook*), with the additional benefit that the character is allowed to enter Candlekeep without paying the normal cost.

A background feature should avoid strict game benefits, such as a bonus to an ability check or an attack roll. Instead, the feature should open up new options for roleplaying, exploring, and otherwise interacting with the world.

For example, the sage's Researcher feature is designed to send the character on adventures. It doesn't provide information or an automatic success for a check. Instead, if a character with the sage background fails to recall information, he or she instead knows where to learn it. This might be a pointer to another sage or to a library long lost within an ancient tomb.

The best background features give characters a reason to strike out on quests, to make contact with NPCs, and to develop bonds to the setting you've devised.

APPENDIX A: RANDOM DUNGEONS

HIS APPENDIX HELPS YOU QUICKLY GENERATE
a dungeon. The tables work in an iterative
manner. First, roll a starting area, then roll to
determine the passages and doors found in
that area. One you have initial passages and
doors, determine the location and nature of
subsequent passages, doors, chambers, stairs, and so
on—each of them generated by rolls on different tables.

Following these instructions can lead to sprawling
complexes that more than fill a single sheet of graph
paper. If you want to constrain the dungeon, establish
limits ahead of time on how far it can grow.

The most obvious limit to a dungeon's size is the
graph paper it's drawn on. If a feature would exceed
the boundaries of the page, curtail it. A corridor might
turn or come to a dead end at the map's edge, or you can
make a chamber smaller to fit the available space.

Alternatively, you can decide that passages leading off
the edge of the map are additional dungeon entrances.
Stairs, shafts, and other features that would normally
lead to levels you don't plan to map can serve a
similar purpose.

STARTING AREA

The Starting Area table produces a chamber or a set of
corridors at the entrance to your dungeon. When rolling
for a random starting area, pick one of the doors or
passages leading into the starting area as the entrance
to the dungeon as a whole.

Once you've selected the entrance, roll on the
appropriate table for each passage or door leading away
from the starting area. Passages each extend 10 feet
beyond the starting area. After that point, check on the
Passage table for each passage to determine what lies
beyond. Use the Beyond a Door table to determine what
lies behind doors and secret doors.

STARTING AREA

d10	Configuration
1	Square, 20 × 20 ft.; passage on each wall
2	Square, 20 × 20 ft.; door on two walls, passage in third wall
3	Square, 40 × 40 ft.; doors on three walls
4	Rectangle, 80 × 20 ft., with row of pillars down the middle; two passages leading from each long wall, doors on each short wall
5	Rectangle, 20 × 40 ft.; passage on each wall
6	Circle, 40 ft. diameter; one passage at each cardinal direction
7	Circle, 40 ft. diameter; one passage in each cardinal direction; well in middle of room (might lead down to lower level)
8	Square, 20 × 20 ft.; door on two walls, passage on third wall, secret door on fourth wall
9	Passage, 10 ft. wide; T intersection
10	Passage, 10 ft. wide; four-way intersection

PASSAGES

When generating passages and corridors, roll on the
Passage table multiple times, extending the length and
branches of any open passage on the map until you
arrive at a door or chamber.

Whenever you create a new passage, roll to determine
its width. If the passage branches from another passage,
roll a d12 on the Passage Width table. If it comes from
a chamber, roll a d20 on that table, but the width of the
passage must be at least 5 feet smaller than the longest
dimension of the chamber.

PASSAGE

d20	Detail
1–2	Continue straight 30 ft., no doors or side passages
3	Continue straight 20 ft., door to the right, then an additional 10 ft. ahead
4	Continue straight 20 ft., door to the left, then an additional 10 ft. ahead
5	Continue straight 20 ft.; passage ends in a door
6–7	Continue straight 20 ft., side passage to the right, then an additional 10 ft. ahead
8–9	Continue straight 20 ft., side passage to the left, then an additional 10 ft. ahead
10	Continue straight 20 ft., comes to a dead end; 10 percent chance of a secret door
11–12	Continue straight 20 ft., then the passage turns left and continues 10 ft.
13–14	Continue straight 20 ft., then the passage turns right and continues 10 ft.
15–19	Chamber (roll on the Chamber table)
20	Stairs* (roll on the Stairs table)

* The existence of stairs presumes a dungeon with more than
one level. If you don't want a multilevel dungeon, reroll this
result, use the stairs as an alternative entrance, or replace them
with another feature of your choice.

PASSAGE WIDTH

d12/d20	Width
1–2	5 ft.
3–12	10 ft.
13–14	20 ft.
15–16	30 ft.
17	40 ft., with row of pillars down the middle
18	40 ft., with double row of pillars
19	40 ft. wide, 20 ft. high
20	40 ft. wide, 20 ft. high, gallery 10 ft. above floor allows access to level above

Doors

Whenever a table roll indicates a door, roll on the Door Type table to determine its nature, then roll on the Beyond a Door table to see what lies on the other side of it. If a door is barred, you decide which side of the door the bar is on. Unlocked doors can also be stuck, at your discretion. See chapter 5, "Adventure Environments," for information on doors and portcullises.

Door Type

d20	Door Type
1–10	Wooden
11–12	Wooden, barred or locked
13	Stone
14	Stone, barred or locked
15	Iron
16	Iron, barred or locked
17	Portcullis
18	Portcullis, locked in place
19	Secret door
20	Secret door, barred or locked

Beyond a Door

d20	Feature
1–2	Passage extending 10 ft., then T intersection extending 10 ft. to the right and left
3–8	Passage 20 ft. straight ahead
9–18	Chamber (roll on the Chamber table)
19	Stairs (roll on the Stairs table)
20	False door with trap

Chambers

Whenever a roll on a table indicates a chamber, use the Chamber table to define its dimensions. Then roll on the Chamber Exits table to determine the number of exits. For each exit, roll on the Exit Location and Exit Type tables to determine the nature and placement of the exit.

Use the tables in the "Stocking a Dungeon" section to determine the contents of a chamber.

Chamber

d20	Chamber
1–2	Square, 20 × 20 ft.[1]
3–4	Square, 30 × 30 ft.[1]
5–6	Square, 40 × 40 ft.[1]
7–9	Rectangle, 20 × 30 ft.[1]
10–12	Rectangle, 30 × 40 ft.[1]
13–14	Rectangle, 40 × 50 ft.[2]
15	Rectangle, 50 × 80 ft.[2]
16	Circle, 30 ft. diameter[1]
17	Circle, 50 ft. diameter[2]
18	Octagon, 40 × 40 ft.[2]
19	Octagon, 60 × 60 ft.[2]
20	Trapezoid, roughly 40 × 60 ft.[2]

[1] Use the Normal Chamber column on the Chamber Exits table.
[2] Use the Large Chamber column on the Chamber Exits table.

Chamber Exits

d20	Normal Chamber	Large Chamber
1–3	0	0
4–5	0	1
6–8	1	1
9–11	1	2
12–13	2	2
14–15	2	3
16–17	3	3
18	3	4
19	4	5
20	4	6

Exit Location

d20	Location
1–7	Wall opposite entrance
8–12	Wall left of entrance
13–17	Wall right of entrance
18–20	Same wall as entrance

Exit Type

d20	Type
1–10	Door (roll on the Door Type table)
11–20	Corridor, 10 ft. long

Stairs

Stairs can include any means of going up and down, including ramps, chimneys, open shafts, elevators, and ladders. If your dungeon has more than one level, the amount of space between levels is up to you. A distance of 30 feet works fine for most dungeons.

Stairs

d20	Stairs
1–4	Down one level to a chamber
5–8	Down one level to a passage 20 ft. long
9	Down two levels to a chamber
10	Down two levels to a passage 20 ft. long
11	Down three levels to a chamber
12	Down three levels to a passage 20 ft. long
13	Up one level to a chamber
14	Up one level to a passage 20 ft. long
15	Up to a dead end
16	Down to a dead end
17	Chimney up one level to a passage 20 ft. long
18	Chimney up two levels to a passage 20 ft. long
19	Shaft (with or without elevator) down one level to a chamber
20	Shaft (with or without elevator) up one level to a chamber and down one level to a chamber

Connecting Areas

When your map is done, consider adding doors between chambers and passages that are next to each other but otherwise not connected. Such doors create more paths through the dungeon and expand players' options.

If your dungeon consists of more than one level, be sure that any stairs, pits, and other vertical passages line up between levels. If you're using graph paper, lay a new page on top of your existing map, mark the locations of stairs and other features shared by the two levels, and begin mapping the new level.

Stocking a Dungeon

Creating a map for your dungeon is only half the fun. Once you have the layout, you need to decide what challenges and rewards are to be found in the dungeon's passages and chambers. Any reasonably large space should be stocked with interesting sights, sounds, objects, and creatures.

You don't need to have every last detail of your dungeon plotted out. You can get by with nothing more than a list of monsters, a list of treasures, and a list of one or two key elements for each dungeon area.

Chamber Purpose

A room's purpose can help determine its furnishings and other contents.

For each chamber on your dungeon map, establish its purpose or use the tables below to generate ideas. Each type of dungeon described in the "Dungeon Purpose"

section of chapter 5, "Adventure Environments," has its own table featuring chambers geared to the dungeon's purpose. For example, if you're building a tomb, use the Dungeon: Tomb table to help you determine the purpose of each chamber. These dungeon-specific tables are followed by the General Dungeon Chambers table, which you can use if your dungeon isn't an exact fit for one of the standard types of dungeon or if you want to mix things up.

Relying on random rolls to stock an entire dungeon can lead to incongruous results. A tiny room might end up being identified as a temple, while the huge chamber next door serves as storage. It can be fun to try to make sense of such strange design ideas, but make changes as you see fit. You can set aside a few key rooms and create specific contents for them.

Dungeon: Death Trap

d20	Purpose
1	Antechamber or waiting room for spectators
2–8	Guardroom fortified against intruders
9–11	Vault for holding important treasures, accessible only by locked or secret door (75 percent chance of being trapped)
12–14	Room containing a puzzle that must be solved to bypass a trap or monster
15–19	Trap designed to kill or capture creatures
20	Observation room, allowing guards or spectators to observe creatures moving through the dungeon

Dungeon: Lair

d20	Purpose
1	Armory stocked with weapons and armor
2	Audience chamber, used to receive guests
3	Banquet room for important celebrations
4	Barracks where the lair's defenders are quartered
5	Bedroom, for use by leaders
6	Chapel where the lair's inhabitants worship
7	Cistern or well for drinking water
8–9	Guardroom for the defense of the lair
10	Kennel for pets or guard beasts
11	Kitchen for food storage and preparation
12	Pen or prison where captives are held
13–14	Storage, mostly nonperishable goods
15	Throne room where the lair's leaders hold court
16	Torture chamber
17	Training and exercise room
18	Trophy room or museum
19	Latrine or bath
20	Workshop for the construction of weapons, armor, tools, and other goods

Dungeon: Maze

d20	Purpose
1	Conjuring room, used to summon creatures that guard the maze
2–5	Guardroom for sentinels that patrol the maze
6–10	Lair for guard beasts that patrol the maze
11	Pen or prison accessible only by secret door, used to hold captives condemned to the maze
12	Shrine dedicated to a god or other entity
13–14	Storage for food, as well as tools used by the maze's guardians to keep the complex in working order
15–18	Trap to confound or kill those sent into the maze
19	Well that provides drinking water
20	Workshop where doors, torch sconces, and other furnishings are repaired and maintained

Dungeon: Mine

d20	Purpose
1–2	Barracks for miners
3	Bedroom for a supervisor or manager
4	Chapel dedicated to a patron deity of miners, earth, or protection
5	Cistern providing drinking water for miners
6–7	Guardroom
8	Kitchen used to feed workers
9	Laboratory used to conduct tests on strange minerals extracted from the mine
10–15	Lode where metal ore is mined (75 percent chance of being depleted)
16	Office used by the mine supervisor
17	Smithy for repairing damaged tools
18–19	Storage for tools and other equipment
20	Strong room or vault used to store ore for transport to the surface

Dungeon: Planar Gate

d100	Purpose
01–03	Decorated foyer or antechamber
04–08	Armory used by the portal's guardians
09–10	Audience chamber for receiving visitors
11–19	Barracks used by the portal's guards
20–23	Bedroom for use by the high-ranking members of the order that guards the portal
24–30	Chapel dedicated to a deity or deities related to the portal and its defenders
31–35	Cistern providing fresh water
36–38	Classroom for use of initiates learning about the portal's secrets
39	Conjuring room for summoning creatures used to investigate or defend the portal
40–41	Crypt where the remains of those that died guarding the portal are kept
42–47	Dining room
48–50	Divination room used to investigate the portal and events tied to it
51–55	Dormitory for visitors and guards
56–57	Entry room or vestibule
58–59	Gallery for displaying trophies and objects related to the portal and those that guard it
60–67	Guardroom to protect or watch over the portal
68–72	Kitchen
73–77	Laboratory for conducting experiments relating to the portal and creatures that emerge from it
78–80	Library holding books about the portal's history
81–85	Pen or prison for holding captives or creatures that emerge from the portal
86–87	Planar junction, where the gate to another plane once stood (25 percent chance of being active)
88–90	Storage
91	Strong room or vault, for guarding valuable treasures connected to the portal or funds used to pay the planar gate's guardians
92–93	Study
94	Torture chamber, for questioning creatures that pass through the portal or that attempt to clandestinely use it
95–98	Latrine or bath
99–00	Workshop for constructing tools and gear needed to study the portal

Dungeon: Stronghold

d100	Purpose
01–02	Antechamber where visitors seeking access to the stronghold wait
03–05	Armory holding high-quality gear, including light siege weapons such as ballistas
06	Audience chamber used by the master of the stronghold to receive visitors
07	Aviary or zoo for keeping exotic creatures
08–11	Banquet room for hosting celebrations and guests
12–15	Barracks used by elite guards
16	Bath outfitted with a marble floor and other luxurious accoutrements
17	Bedroom for use by the stronghold's master or important guests
18	Chapel dedicated to a deity associated with the stronghold's master
19–21	Cistern providing drinking water
22–25	Dining room for intimate gatherings or informal meals
26	Dressing room featuring a number of wardrobes
27–29	Gallery for the display of expensive works of art and trophies
30–32	Game room used to entertain visitors
33–50	Guardroom
51	Kennel where monsters or trained animals that protect the stronghold are kept
52–57	Kitchen designed to prepare exotic foods for large numbers of guests
58–61	Library with an extensive collection of rare books
62	Lounge used to entertain guests
63–70	Pantry, including cellar for wine or spirits
71–74	Sitting room for family and intimate guests
75–78	Stable
79–86	Storage for mundane goods and supplies
87	Strong room or vault for protecting important treasures (75 percent chance of being hidden behind a secret door)
88–92	Study, including a writing desk
93	Throne room, elaborately decorated
94–96	Waiting room where lesser guests are held before receiving an audience
97–98	Latrine or bath
99–00	Crypt belonging to the stronghold's master or someone else of importance

Dungeon: Temple or Shrine

d100	Purpose
01–03	Armory filled with weapons and armor, battle banners, and pennants
04–05	Audience chamber where priests of the temple receive commoners and low-ranking visitors
06–07	Banquet room used for celebrations and holy days
08–10	Barracks for the temple's military arm or its hired guards
11–14	Cells where the faithful can sit in quiet contemplation
15–24	Central temple built to accommodate rituals
25–28	Chapel dedicated to a lesser deity associated with the temple's major deity
29–31	Classroom used to train initiates and priests
32–34	Conjuring room, specially sanctified and used to summon extraplanar creatures
35–40	Crypt for a high priest or similar figure, hidden and heavily guarded by creatures and traps
41–42	Dining room (large) for the temple's servants and lesser priests
43	Dining room (small) for the temple's high priests
44–46	Divination room, inscribed with runes and stocked with soothsaying implements
47–50	Dormitory for lesser priests or students
51–56	Guardroom
57	Kennel for animals or monsters associated with the temple's deity
58–60	Kitchen (might bear a disturbing resemblance to a torture chamber in an evil temple)
61–65	Library, well stocked with religious treatises
66–68	Prison for captured enemies (in good or neutral temples) or those designated as sacrifices (in evil temples)
69–73	Robing room containing ceremonial outfits and items
74	Stable for riding horses and mounts belonging to the temple, or for visiting messengers and caravans
75–79	Storage holding mundane supplies
80	Strong room or vault holding important relics and ceremonial items, heavily trapped
81–82	Torture chamber, used in inquisitions (in good or neutral temples with a lawful bent) or for the sheer joy of causing pain (evil temples)
83–89	Trophy room where art celebrating key figures and events from mythology is displayed
90	Latrine or bath
91–94	Well for drinking water, defendable in the case of attack or siege
95–00	Workshop for repairing or creating weapons, religious items, and tools

Dungeon: Tomb

d20	Purpose
1	Antechamber for those that have come to pay respect to the dead or prepare themselves for burial rituals
2–3	Chapel dedicated to deities that watch over the dead and protect their resting places
4–8	Crypt for less important burials
9	Divination room, used in rituals to contact the dead for guidance
10	False crypt (trapped) to kill or capture thieves
11	Gallery to display the deeds of the deceased through trophies, statues, paintings and so forth
12	Grand crypt for a noble, high priest, or other important individual
13–14	Guardroom, usually guarded by undead, constructs, or other creatures that don't need to eat or sleep
15	Robing room for priests to prepare for burial rituals
16–17	Storage, stocked with tools for maintaining the tomb and preparing the dead for burial
18	Tomb where the wealthiest and most important folk are interred, protected by secret doors and traps
19–20	Workshop for embalming the dead

Dungeon: Treasure Vault

d20	Purpose
1	Antechamber for visiting dignitaries
2	Armory containing mundane and magic gear used by the treasure vault's guards
3–4	Barracks for guards
5	Cistern providing fresh water
6–9	Guardroom to defend against intruders
10	Kennel for trained beasts used to guard the treasure vault
11	Kitchen for feeding guards
12	Watch room that allows guards to observe those who approach the dungeon
13	Prison for holding captured intruders
14–15	Strong room or vault, for guarding the treasure hidden in the dungeon, accessible only by locked or secret door
16	Torture chamber for extracting information from captured intruders
17–20	Trap or other trick designed to kill or capture creatures that enter the dungeon

General Dungeon Chambers

d100	Purpose	d100	Purpose
01	Antechamber	53–54	Laboratory
02–03	Armory	55–57	Library
04	Audience chamber	58–59	Lounge
05	Aviary	60	Meditation chamber
06–07	Banquet room	61	Observatory
08–10	Barracks	62	Office
11	Bath or latrine	63–64	Pantry
12	Bedroom	65–66	Pen or prison
13	Bestiary	67–68	Reception room
14–16	Cell	69–70	Refectory
17	Chantry	71	Robing room
18	Chapel	72	Salon
19–20	Cistern	73–74	Shrine
21	Classroom	75–76	Sitting room
22	Closet	77–78	Smithy
23–24	Conjuring room	79	Stable
25–26	Court	80–81	Storage room
27–29	Crypt	82–83	Strong room or vault
30–31	Dining room	84–85	Study
32–33	Divination room	86–88	Temple
34	Dormitory	89–90	Throne room
35	Dressing room	91	Torture chamber
36	Entry room or vestibule	92–93	Training or exercise room
37–38	Gallery	94–95	Trophy room or museum
39–40	Game room	96	Waiting room
41–43	Guardroom	97	Nursery or schoolroom
44–45	Hall	98	Well
46–47	Hall, great	99–00	Workshop
48–49	Hallway		
50	Kennel		
51–52	Kitchen		

CURRENT CHAMBER STATE

If a dungeon has a tumultuous history, you can roll to determine the current condition of any particular area. Otherwise, if the room is still used for its intended purpose, it remains intact.

CURRENT CHAMBER STATE

d20	Features
1–3	Rubble, ceiling partially collapsed
4–5	Holes, floor partially collapsed
6–7	Ashes, contents mostly burned
8–9	Used as a campsite
10–11	Pool of water; chamber's original contents are water damaged
12–16	Furniture wrecked but still present
17–18	Converted to some other use (roll on the General Dungeon Chambers table)
19	Stripped bare
20	Pristine and in original state

CHAMBER CONTENTS

Once you have a sense of the purpose of the various dungeon chambers, you can think about the contents of those areas. The Dungeon Chamber Contents table allows you to randomly roll contents for a chamber, or you can choose contents for specific areas. If you choose contents, be sure to include an interesting, colorful assortment of things. In addition to the contents shown on this table, refer to "Dungeon Dressing" later in this appendix for additional items and elements to fill rooms.

In the Dungeon Chamber Contents table, a "dominant inhabitant" is a creature that controls an area. Pets and allied creatures are subservient to the dominant inhabitant. "Random creatures" are scavengers or nuisances, usually lone monsters or small groups passing through the area. They include such creatures as carrion crawlers, dire rats, gelatinous cubes, and rust monsters. See chapter 3, "Creating Adventures," for more information on random encounters.

DUNGEON CHAMBER CONTENTS

d100	Contents
01–08	Monster (dominant inhabitant)
09–15	Monster (dominant inhabitant) with treasure
16–27	Monster (pet or allied creature)
28–33	Monster (pet or allied creature) guarding treasure
34–42	Monster (random creature)
43–50	Monster (random creature) with treasure
51–58	Dungeon hazard (see "Random Dungeon Hazards") with incidental treasure
59–63	Obstacle (see "Random Obstacles")
64–73	Trap (see "Random Traps")
74–76	Trap (see "Random Traps") protecting treasure
77–80	Trick (see "Random Tricks")
81–88	Empty room
89–94	Empty room with dungeon hazard (see "Random Dungeon Hazards")
95–00	Empty room with treasure

MONSTERS AND MOTIVATIONS

See chapter 3, "Creating Adventures," for guidance on creating encounters with monsters. To foster variety and suspense, be sure to include encounters of varying difficulty.

A powerful creature encountered early in the dungeon sets an exciting tone and forces the adventurers to rely on their wits. For example, an ancient red dragon might slumber on the first level of a dungeon, a pall of smoke and the sound of its heavy breathing filling the chambers near its lair. Clever characters will do their utmost to avoid the dragon, even as the party's brave thief makes off with a few coins from its hoard.

Not all monsters are automatically hostile. When placing monsters in your dungeon, consider their relationships to nearby creatures and their attitudes toward adventurers. Characters might be able to appease a hungry beast by offering it food, and smarter creatures have complex motivations. The Monster Motivation table lets you use a monster's goals to define its presence in the dungeon.

For large groups of monsters encountered across multiple chambers, motivation could apply to the entire group, or each subgroup could have conflicting goals.

MONSTER MOTIVATION

d20	Goals	d20	Goals
1–2	Find a sanctuary	12–13	Hide from enemies
3–5	Conquer the dungeon	14–15	Recover from a battle
6–8	Seek an item in the dungeon	16–17	Avoid danger
9–11	Slay a rival	18–20	Seek wealth

RANDOM DUNGEON HAZARDS

Hazards are rarely found in inhabited areas, because monsters either clear them away or avoid them.

Shriekers and violet fungi are described in the *Monster Manual*. The other hazards on the table are described in chapter 5, "Adventure Environments."

DUNGEON HAZARDS

d20	Hazard	d20	Hazard
1–3	Brown mold	11–15	Spiderwebs
4–8	Green slime	16–17	Violet fungus
9–10	Shrieker	18–20	Yellow mold

RANDOM OBSTACLES

Obstacles block progress through the dungeon. In some cases, what adventurers consider an obstacle is an easy path for the dungeon's inhabitants. For example, a flooded chamber is a barrier to many characters but easily navigated by water-breathing creatures.

Obstacles can affect more than one room. A chasm might run through several passages and chambers, or send cracks through the stonework in a wider area around it. An area of battering winds that emanates from a magic altar could stir the air less dangerously for hundreds of feet in all directions.

OBSTACLES

d20	Obstacle
1	Antilife aura with a radius of 1d10 × 10 ft.; while in the aura, living creatures can't regain hit points
2	Battering winds reduce speed by half, impose disadvantage on ranged attack rolls
3	*Blade barrier* blocks passage
4–8	Cave-in
9–12	Chasm 1d4 × 10 ft. wide and 2d6 × 10 ft. deep, possibly connected to other levels of the dungeon
13–14	Flooding leaves 2d10 ft. of water in the area; create nearby upward-sloping passages, raised floors, or rising stairs to contain the water
15	Lava flows through the area (50 percent chance of a stone bridge crossing it)
16	Overgrown mushrooms block progress and must be hacked down (25 percent chance of a mold or fungus dungeon hazard hidden among them)
17	Poisonous gas (deals 1d6 poison damage per minute of exposure)
18	*Reverse gravity* effect causes creatures to fall toward the ceiling
19	*Wall of fire* blocks passage
20	*Wall of force* blocks passage

RANDOM TRAPS

If you need a trap quickly or want to drop random traps into a dungeon, use the sample traps presented in chapter 5, "Adventure Environments" or the tables below. If you use the tables, start with the Trap Effects and Trap Trigger tables to decide the type of trap, then use the Trap Damage Severity tables to decide how deadly it should be. For more information on trap damage severity, see chapter 5.

TRAP TRIGGER

d6	Trigger
1	Stepped on (floor, stairs)
2	Moved through (doorway, hallway)
3	Touched (doorknob, statue)
4	Opened (door, treasure chest)
5	Looked at (mural, arcane symbol)
6	Moved (cart, stone block)

TRAP DAMAGE SEVERITY

d6	Damage Severity
1–2	Setback
3–5	Dangerous
6	Deadly

TRAP EFFECTS

d100	Effect
01–04	*Magic missiles* shoot from a statue or object
05–07	Collapsing staircase creates a ramp that deposits characters into a pit at its lower end
08–10	Ceiling block falls, or entire ceiling collapses
11–12	Ceiling lowers slowly in locked room
13–14	Chute opens in floor
15–16	Clanging noise attracts nearby monsters
17–19	Touching an object triggers a *disintegrate* spell
20–23	Door or other object is coated with contact poison
24–27	Fire shoots out from wall, floor, or object
28–30	Touching an object triggers a *flesh to stone* spell
31–33	Floor collapses or is an illusion
34–36	Vent releases gas: blinding, acidic, obscuring, paralyzing, poisonous, or sleep-inducing
37–39	Floor tiles are electrified
40–43	*Glyph of warding*
44–46	Huge wheeled statue rolls down corridor
47–49	*Lightning bolt* shoots from wall or object
50–52	Locked room floods with water or acid
53–56	Darts shoot out of an opened chest
57–59	A weapon, suit of armor, or rug animates and attacks when touched (see "Animated Objects" in the *Monster Manual*)
60–62	Pendulum, either bladed or weighted as a maul, swings across the room or hall
63–67	Hidden pit opens beneath characters (25 percent chance that a black pudding or gelatinous cube fills the bottom of the pit)
68–70	Hidden pit floods with acid or fire
71–73	Locking pit floods with water
74–77	Scything blade emerges from wall or object
78–81	Spears (possibly poisoned) spring out
82–84	Brittle stairs collapse over spikes
85–88	*Thunderwave* knocks characters into a pit or spikes
89–91	Steel or stone jaws restrain a character
92–94	Stone block smashes across hallway
95–97	*Symbol*
98–00	Walls slide together

RANDOM TRICKS

Tricks are quirkier and less deadly than traps. Some are effects left behind by the dungeon's creators, while others might be manifestations of the strange magical energy suffusing the dungeon.

The following tables allow you to generate random tricks. Roll first to determine an object that the trick is placed on, then roll to determine the nature of the trick. Some tricks are permanent effects that can't be dispelled; others are temporary or can be neutralized with a *dispel magic* spell. You decide which is which.

TRICK OBJECTS

d20	Object	d20	Object
1	Book	12	Pool of water
2	Brain preserved in a jar	13	Runes engraved on wall or floor
3	Burning fire	14	Skull
4	Cracked gem	15	Sphere of magical energy
5	Door		
6	Fresco	16	Statue
7	Furniture	17	Stone obelisk
8	Glass sculpture	18	Suit of armor
9	Mushroom field	19	Tapestry or rug
10	Painting	20	Target dummy
11	Plant or tree		

TRICKS

d100	Trick Effect
01–03	Ages the first person to touch the object
04–06	The touched object animates, or it animates other objects nearby
07–10	Asks three skill-testing questions (if all three are answered correctly, a reward appears)
11–13	Bestows resistance or vulnerability
14–16	Changes a character's alignment, personality, size, appearance, or sex when touched
17–19	Changes one substance to another, such as gold to lead or metal to brittle crystal
20–22	Creates a force field
23–26	Creates an illusion
27–29	Suppresses magic items for a time
30–32	Enlarges or reduces characters
33–35	*Magic mouth* speaks a riddle
36–38	*Confusion* (targets all creatures within 10 ft.)
39–41	Gives directions (true or false)
42–44	Grants a wish
45–47	Flies about to avoid being touched
48–50	Casts *geas* on the characters
51–53	Increases, reduces, negates, or reverses gravity
54–56	Induces greed
57–59	Contains an imprisoned creature
60–62	Locks or unlocks exits
63–65	Offers a game of chance, with the promise of a reward or valuable information
66–68	Helps or harms certain types of creatures
69–71	Casts *polymorph* on the characters (lasts 1 hour)
72–75	Presents a puzzle or riddle
76–78	Prevents movement
79–81	Releases coins, false coins, gems, false gems, a magic item, or a map
82–84	Releases, summons, or turns into a monster
85–87	Casts *suggestion* on the characters
88–90	Wails loudly when touched
91–93	Talks (normal speech, nonsense, poetry and rhymes, singing, spellcasting, or screaming)
94–97	Teleports characters to another place
98–00	Swaps two or more characters' minds

RANDOM TREASURES

Use the tables and guidelines in chapter 7, "Treasure" to determine the treasure in each area of your dungeon.

EMPTY ROOMS

An empty room can be a godsend for characters who need a safe place to take a short rest. Characters can also barricade themselves there and take a long rest.

Sometimes such a room isn't as empty as it appears. If the characters search a room carefully, you can reward them with a secret compartment containing a journal belonging to a previous inhabitant, a map leading to another dungeon, or some other discovery.

DUNGEON DRESSING

The tables in this section provide miscellaneous items and points of interest that can be placed in your dungeon. Dungeon dressing can help establish the atmosphere of a dungeon, give clues about its creators and history, provide the basis for tricks and traps, or encourage exploration.

To generate dungeon dressing at random, roll once on each of the following tables: Noises, Air, and Odors. Roll as often as you like on the other tables in this section, or choose appropriate furnishings for the area.

NOISES

d100	Effect	d100	Effect
01–05	Bang or slam	49	Jingling
06	Bellowing	50–53	Knocking
07	Buzzing	54–55	Laughter
08–10	Chanting	56–57	Moaning
11	Chiming	58–60	Murmuring
12	Chirping	61–62	Music
13	Clanking	63	Rattling
14	Clashing	64	Ringing
15	Clicking	65–68	Rustling
16	Coughing	69–72	Scratching or scrabbling
17–18	Creaking		
19	Drumming	73–74	Screaming
20–23	Footsteps ahead	75–77	Scuttling
24–26	Footsteps approaching	78	Shuffling
		79–80	Slithering
27–29	Footsteps behind	81	Snapping
30–31	Footsteps receding	82	Sneezing
		83	Sobbing
32–33	Footsteps to the side	84	Splashing
		85	Splintering
34–35	Giggling (faint)	86–87	Squeaking
36	Gong	88	Squealing
37–39	Grating	89–90	Tapping
40–41	Groaning	91–92	Thud
42	Grunting	93–94	Thumping
43–44	Hissing	95	Tinkling
45	Horn or trumpet sounding	96	Twanging
		97	Whining
46	Howling	98	Whispering
47–48	Humming	99–00	Whistling

AIR

d100	Effect	d100	Effect
01–60	Clear and damp	86–90	Clear and warm
61–70	Clear and drafty	91–93	Hazy and humid
71–80	Clear but cold	94–96	Smoky or steamy
81–83	Foggy or misty and cold	97–98	Clear, with smoke covering ceiling
84–85	Clear, with mist covering floor	99–00	Clear and windy

ODORS

d100	Effect	d100	Effect
01–03	Acrid	66–70	Putrid
04–05	Chlorine	71–75	Rotting vegetation
06–39	Dank or moldy	76–77	Salty and wet
40–49	Earthy	78–82	Smoky
50–57	Manure	83–89	Stale
58–61	Metallic	90–95	Sulfurous
62–65	Ozone	96–00	Urine

GENERAL FEATURES

d100	Item	d100	Item
01	Arrow, broken	62–64	Leaves and twigs
02–04	Ashes	65–68	Mold (common)
05–06	Bones	69	Pick handle
07	Bottle, broken	70	Pole, broken (5 ft. long)
08	Chain, corroded	71	Pottery shards
09	Club, splintered	72–73	Rags
10–19	Cobwebs	74	Rope, rotten
20	Coin, copper	75–76	Rubble and dirt
21–22	Cracks, ceiling	77	Sack, torn
23–24	Cracks, floor	78–80	Slime (harmless)
25–26	Cracks, wall	81	Spike, rusted
27	Dagger hilt	82–83	Sticks
28–29	Damp ceiling	84	Stones, small
30–33	Dampness, wall	85	Straw
34	Dried blood	86	Sword blade, broken
35–41	Dripping blood	87	Teeth or fangs, scattered
42–44	Dung	88	Torch stub
45–49	Dust	89	Wall scratchings
50	Flask, cracked	90–91	Water, large puddle
51	Food scraps	92–93	Water, small puddle
52	Fungi (common)	94–95	Water, trickle
53–55	Guano	96	Wax blob (candle stub)
56	Hair or fur	97	Wax drippings
57	Hammer head, cracked	98–00	Wood pieces, rotting
58	Helmet, badly dented		
59	Iron bar, bent and rusted		
60	Javelin head, blunt		
61	Leather boot		

GENERAL FURNISHINGS AND APPOINTMENTS

d100	Item	d100	Item
01	Altar	50	Hogshead (large cask, 65 gallons)
02	Armchair	51	Idol (large)
03	Armoire	52	Keg (small barrel, 20 gallons)
04	Arras or curtain	53	Loom
05	Bag	54	Mat
06	Barrel (40 gallons)	55	Mattress
07–08	Bed	56	Pail
09	Bench	57	Painting
10	Blanket	58–60	Pallet
11	Box (large)	61	Pedestal
12	Brazier and charcoal	62–64	Pegs
13	Bucket	65	Pillow
14	Buffet cabinet	66	Pipe (large cask, 105 gallons)
15	Bunks	67	Quilt
16	Butt (huge cask, 125 gallons)	68–70	Rug (small or medium)
17	Cabinet	71	Rushes
18	Candelabrum	72	Sack
19	Carpet (large)	73	Sconce
20	Cask (40 gallons)	74	Screen
21	Chandelier	75	Sheet
22	Charcoal	76–77	Shelf
23–24	Chair, plain	78	Shrine
25	Chair, padded	79	Sideboard
26	Chair, padded, or divan	80	Sofa
27	Chest, large	81	Staff, normal
28	Chest, medium	82	Stand
29	Chest of drawers	83	Statue
30	Closet (wardrobe)	84	Stool, high
31	Coal	85	Stool, normal
32–33	Couch	86	Table, large
34	Crate	87	Table, long
35	Cresset	88	Table, low
36	Cupboard	89	Table, round
37	Cushion	90	Table, small
38	Dais	91	Table, trestle
39	Desk	92	Tapestry
40–42	Fireplace and wood	93	Throne
43	Fireplace with mantle	94	Trunk
44	Firkin (small cask, 10 gallons)	95	Tub
45	Fountain	96	Tun (huge cask, 250 gallons)
46	Fresco	97	Urn
47	Grindstone	98	Wall basin and font
48	Hamper	99	Wood billets
49	Hassock	00	Workbench

RELIGIOUS ARTICLES AND FURNISHINGS

d100	Item	d100	Item
01–05	Altar	54	Lectern
06–08	Bells	55	Mosaic
09–11	Brazier	56–58	Offertory container
12	Candelabra		
13–14	Candles	59	Paintings or frescoes
15	Candlesticks		
16	Cassocks	60–61	Pews
17	Chimes	62	Pipes, musical
18–19	Cloth, altar	63	Prayer rug
20–23	Columns or pillars	64	Pulpit
		65	Rail
24	Curtain or tapestry	66–69	Robes
		70–71	Screen
25	Drum	72–76	Shrine
26–27	Font	77	Side chairs
28–29	Gong	78–79	Stand
30–35	Holy or unholy symbol	80–82	Statue
		83	Throne
36–37	Holy or unholy writings	84–85	Thurible
		86–90	Tripod
38–43	Idol	91–97	Vestments
44–48	Incense burner	98–99	Votive light
49	Kneeling bench	00	Whistle
50–53	Lamp		

MAGE FURNISHINGS

d100	Item	d100	Item
01–03	Alembic	54	Magic circle
04–05	Balance and weights	55	Mortar and pestle
		56	Pan
06–09	Beaker	57–58	Parchment
10	Bellows	59	Pentacle
11–14	Book	60	Pentagram
15–16	Bottle	61	Pipe, smoking
17	Bowl	62	Pot
18	Box	63	Prism
19–22	Brazier	64–65	Quill
23	Cage	66–68	Retort
24	Candle	69	Rod, mixing or stirring
25–26	Candlestick		
27–28	Cauldron	70–72	Scroll
29–30	Chalk	73	Sexton
31–32	Crucible	74–75	Skull
33	Crystal ball	76	Spatula
34	Decanter	77	Spoon, measuring
35	Desk	78	Stand
36	Dish	79	Stool
37–40	Flask or jar	80	Stuffed animal
41	Funnel	81	Tank (container)
42	Furnace	82	Tongs
43–44	Herbs	83	Tripod
45	Horn	84	Tube (container)

d100	Item	d100	Item
46–47	Hourglass	85–86	Tube (piping)
48–49	Jug	87	Tweezers
50	Kettle	88–90	Vial
51	Ladle	91	Water clock
52	Lamp or lantern	92	Wire
53	Lens (concave or convex)	93–00	Workbench

UTENSILS AND PERSONAL ITEMS

d100	Item	d100	Item
01	Awl	47–48	Mirror
02	Bandages	49	Needle(s)
03	Basin	50	Oil, cooking
04–05	Basket	51	Oil, fuel
06–07	Book	52	Oil, scented
08–09	Bottle	53	Pan
10	Bowl	54–55	Parchment
11	Box	56	Pipe, musical
12–13	Brush	57	Pipe, smoking
14	Candle	58	Plate, platter, or saucer
15	Candle snuffer		
16	Candlestick	59	Pot
17	Cane or walking stick	60–61	Pouch
		62	Powder puff
18	Case	63	Quill
19	Casket (small)	64	Razor
20–21	Coffer	65	Rope
22	Cologne or perfume	66	Salve or unguent
		67–68	Scroll
23	Comb	69	Shaker
24	Cup	70	Sifter or strainer
25	Decanter	71–72	Soap
26–27	Dish	73	Spigot
28	Ear spoon	74	Spoon
29	Ewer	75	Stopper
30	Flagon, mug, or tankard	76–77	Statuette or figurine
		78–79	Thread
31–32	Flask or jar	80–82	Tinderbox (with flint and steel)
33	Food		
34	Fork	83	Towel
35	Grater	84	Tray
36	Grinder	85	Trivet or tripod
37	Horn, drinking	86	Tureen
38	Hourglass	87–88	Twine
39	Jug or pitcher	90	Vase
40	Kettle	91–92	Vial
41	Key	93	Washcloth
42	Knife	94	Whetstone
43	Knucklebones or dice	95–96	Wig
		97–98	Wool
44	Ladle	99–00	Yarn
45–46	Lamp or lantern		

Container Contents

d100	Item	d100	Item
01–03	Ash	60–61	Lumps, unidentifiable
04–06	Bark	62–64	Oil
07–09	Bodily organs	65–68	Paste
10–14	Bones	69–71	Pellets
15–17	Cinders	72–84	Powder
18–22	Crystals	85–86	Semiliquid suspension
23–26	Dust		
27–28	Fibers	87–88	Skin or hide
29–31	Gelatin	89–90	Spheres (metal, stone, or wood)
32–35	Grains		
36–38	Grease	91–92	Splinters
39–41	Husks	93–94	Stalks
42–46	Leaves	95–97	Strands
47–54	Liquid, thin	98–00	Strips
55–59	Liquid, viscous		

Books, Scrolls, and Tomes

d100	Contents	d100	Contents
01–02	Account records	63–64	Novel
03–04	Alchemist's notebook	65	Painting
		66–67	Poetry
05–06	Almanac	68–69	Prayer book
07–08	Bestiary	70	Property deed
09–11	Biography	71–74	Recipe book or cookbook
12–14	Book of heraldry		
15	Book of myths	75	Record of a criminal trial
16	Book of pressed flowers		
		76	Royal proclamation
17	Calendar		
18–22	Catalog	77–78	Sheet music
23–24	Contract	79	Spellbook
25–27	Diary	80	Text on armor making
28–29	Dictionary		
30–32	Doodles or sketches	81–82	Text on astrology
		83–84	Text on brewing
33	Forged document	85–86	Text on exotic flora or fauna
34	Grammar workbook		
		87–88	Text on herbalism
35–36	Heretical text	89–90	Text on local flora
37–41	Historical text	91–92	Text on mathematics
42–43	Last will and testament		
		93	Text on masonry
44–45	Legal code	94	Text on medicine
46–53	Letter	95	Theological text
54	Lunatic's ravings	96	Tome of forbidden lore
55	Magic tricks (not a spellbook)		
		97–99	Travelogue for an exotic land
56	Magic scroll		
57–59	Map or atlas	00	Travelogue of the planes
60	Memoir		
61–62	Navigational chart or star chart		

APPENDIX B: MONSTER LISTS

MONSTERS BY ENVIRONMENT

The following tables organize monsters by environment and challenge rating. These tables omit monsters that don't customarily inhabit the environments included here, such as angels and demons.

ARCTIC MONSTERS

Monsters	Challenge Rating (XP)
Commoner, owl	0 (10 XP)
Bandit, blood hawk, kobold, tribal warrior	1/8 (25 XP)
Giant owl, winged kobold	1/4 (50 XP)
Ice mephit, orc, scout	1/2 (100 XP)
Brown bear, half-ogre	1 (200 XP)
Bandit captain, berserker, druid, griffon, ogre, orc Eye of Gruumsh, orog, polar bear, saber-toothed tiger	2 (450 XP)
Manticore, veteran, winter wolf, yeti	3 (700 XP)
Revenant, troll, werebear, young remorhaz	5 (1,800 XP)
Mammoth, young white dragon	6 (2,300 XP)
Frost giant	8 (3,900 XP)
Abominable yeti	9 (5,000 XP)
Remorhaz, roc	11 (7,200 XP)
Adult white dragon	13 (10,000 XP)
Ancient white dragon	20 (24,500 XP)

COASTAL MONSTERS

Monsters	Challenge Rating (XP)
Commoner, crab, eagle	0 (10 XP)
Bandit, blood hawk, giant crab, guard, kobold, merfolk, poisonous snake, stirge, tribal warrior	1/8 (25 XP)
Giant lizard, giant wolf spider, pseudodragon, pteranodon, winged kobold	1/4 (50 XP)
Sahuagin, scout	1/2 (100 XP)
Giant eagle, giant toad, harpy	1 (200 XP)
Bandit captain, berserker, druid, griffon, ogre, merrow, plesiosaurus, sahuagin priestess, sea hag	2 (450 XP)
Manticore, veteran	3 (700 XP)
Banshee	4 (1,100 XP)
Sahuagin baron, water elemental	5 (1,800 XP)
Cyclops	6 (2,300 XP)
Young bronze dragon	8 (3,900 XP)
Young blue dragon	9 (5,000 XP)
Djinni, marid, roc	11 (7,200 XP)
Storm giant	13 (10,000 XP)
Adult bronze dragon	15 (13,000 XP)
Adult blue dragon	16 (15,000 XP)
Dragon turtle	17 (18,000 XP)
Ancient bronze dragon	22 (30,000 XP)
Ancient blue dragon	23 (32,500 XP)

DESERT MONSTERS

Monsters	Challenge Rating (XP)
Cat, commoner, hyena, jackal, scorpion, vulture	0 (10 XP)
Bandit, camel, flying snake, guard, kobold, mule, poisonous snake, stirge, tribal warrior	1/8 (25 XP)
Constrictor snake, giant lizard, giant poisonous snake, giant wolf spider, pseudodragon, winged kobold	1/4 (50 XP)
Dust mephit, gnoll, hobgoblin, jackalwere, scout, swarm of insects	1/2 (100 XP)
Death dog, giant hyena, giant spider, giant toad, giant vulture, half-ogre, lion, thri-kreen, yuan-ti pureblood	1 (200 XP)
Bandit captain, berserker, druid, giant constrictor snake, gnoll pack lord, ogre	2 (450 XP)
Giant scorpion, hobgoblin captain, mummy, phase spider, wight, yuan-ti malison	3 (700 XP)
Couatl, gnoll fang of Yeenoghu, lamia, weretiger	4 (1,100 XP)
Air elemental, fire elemental, revenant	5 (1,800 XP)
Cyclops, medusa, young brass dragon	6 (2,300 XP)
Yuan-ti abomination	7 (2,900 XP)
Young blue dragon	9 (5,000 XP)
Guardian naga	10 (5,900 XP)
Efreeti, gynosphinx, roc	11 (7,200 XP)
Adult brass dragon	13 (10,000 XP)
Mummy lord, purple worm	15 (13,000 XP)
Adult blue dragon	16 (15,000 XP)
Adult blue dracolich, androsphinx	17 (18,000 XP)
Ancient brass dragon	20 (24,500 XP)
Ancient blue dragon	23 (32,500 XP)

FOREST MONSTERS

Monsters	Challenge Rating (XP)
Awakened shrub, baboon, badger, cat, commoner, deer, hyena, owl	0 (10 XP)
Bandit, blood hawk, flying snake, giant rat, giant weasel, guard, kobold, mastiff, poisonous snake, stirge, tribal warrior, twig blight	1/8 (25 XP)
Blink dog, boar, constrictor snake, elk, giant badger, giant bat, giant frog, giant lizard, giant owl, giant poisonous snake, giant wolf spider, goblin, kenku, needle blight, panther, pixie, pseudodragon, sprite, swarm of ravens, winged kobold, wolf	1/4 (50 XP)
Ape, black bear, giant wasp, gnoll, hobgoblin, lizardfolk, orc, satyr, scout, swarm of insects, vine blight, worg	1/2 (100 XP)

Monsters	Challenge Rating (XP)
Brown bear, bugbear, dire wolf, dryad, faerie dragon (yellow or younger), giant hyena, giant spider, giant toad, goblin boss, half-ogre, harpy, tiger, yuan-ti pureblood	1 (200 XP)
Ankheg, awakened tree, bandit captain, berserker, centaur, druid, ettercap, faerie dragon (green or older), giant boar, giant constrictor snake, giant elk, gnoll pack lord, grick, lizardfolk shaman, ogre, orc Eye of Gruumsh, orog, pegasus, swarm of poisonous snakes, wererat, will-o'-wisp	2 (450 XP)
Displacer beast, green hag, hobgoblin captain, owlbear, phase spider, veteran, werewolf, yuan-ti malison	3 (700 XP)
Banshee, couatl, gnoll fang of Yeenoghu, wereboar, weretiger	4 (1,100 XP)
Gorgon, revenant, shambling mound, troll, unicorn, werebear	5 (1,800 XP)
Giant ape, grick alpha, oni, yuan-ti abomination	7 (2,900 XP)
Young green dragon	8 (3,900 XP)
Treant	9 (5,000 XP)
Guardian naga, young gold dragon	10 (5,900 XP)
Adult green dragon	15 (13,000 XP)
Adult gold dragon	17 (18,000 XP)
Ancient green dragon	22 (30,000 XP)
Ancient gold dragon	24 (36,500 XP)

GRASSLAND MONSTERS

Monsters	Challenge Rating (XP)
Cat, commoner, deer, eagle, goat, hyena, jackal, vulture	0 (10 XP)
Blood hawk, flying snake, giant weasel, guard, poisonous snake, stirge, tribal warrior	1/8 (25 XP)
Axe beak, boar, elk, giant poisonous snake, giant wolf spider, goblin, panther (leopard), pteranodon, riding horse, wolf	1/4 (50 XP)
Cockatrice, giant goat, giant wasp, gnoll, hobgoblin, jackalwere, orc, scout, swarm of insects, worg	1/2 (100 XP)
Bugbear, giant eagle, giant hyena, giant vulture, goblin boss, hippogriff, lion, scarecrow, thri-kreen, tiger	1 (200 XP)
Allosaurus, ankheg, centaur, druid, giant boar, giant elk, gnoll pack lord, griffon, ogre, orc Eye of Gruumsh, orog, pegasus, rhinoceros	2 (450 XP)
Ankylosaurus, hobgoblin captain, manticore, phase spider, veteran	3 (700 XP)
Couatl, elephant, gnoll fang of Yeenoghu, wereboar, weretiger	4 (1,100 XP)
Bulette, gorgon, triceratops	5 (1,800 XP)
Chimera, cyclops	6 (2,300 XP)
Tyrannosaurus Rex	8 (3,900 XP)
Young gold dragon	10 (5,900 XP)
Adult gold dragon	17 (18,000 XP)
Ancient gold dragon	24 (36,500 XP)

Hill Monsters

Monsters	Challenge Rating (XP)
Baboon, commoner, eagle, goat, hyena, raven, vulture	0 (10 XP)
Bandit, blood hawk, giant weasel, guard, kobold, mastiff, mule, poisonous snake, stirge, tribal warrior	1/8 (25 XP)
Axe beak, boar, elk, giant owl, giant wolf spider, goblin, panther (cougar), pseudodragon, swarm of bats, swarm of ravens, winged kobold, wolf	1/4 (50 XP)
Giant goat, gnoll, hobgoblin, orc, scout, swarm of insects, worg	1/2 (100 XP)
Brown bear, dire wolf, giant eagle, giant hyena, goblin boss, half-ogre, harpy, hippogriff, lion	1 (200 XP)
Bandit captain, berserker, druid, giant boar, giant elk, gnoll pack lord, griffon, ogre, orc Eye of Gruumsh, orog, pegasus, peryton	2 (450 XP)
Green hag, hobgoblin captain, manticore, phase spider, veteran, werewolf	3 (700 XP)
Ettin, gnoll fang of Yeenoghu, wereboar	4 (1,100 XP)
Bulette, gorgon, hill giant, revenant, troll, werebear	5 (1,800 XP)
Chimera, cyclops, galeb duhr, wyvern	6 (2,300 XP)
Stone giant, young copper dragon	7 (2,900 XP)
Young red dragon	10 (5,900 XP)
Roc	11 (7,200 XP)
Adult copper dragon	14 (11,500 XP)
Adult red dragon	17 (18,000 XP)
Ancient copper dragon	21 (27,500 XP)
Ancient red dragon	24 (36,500 XP)

Mountain Monsters

Monsters	Challenge Rating (XP)
Eagle, goat	0 (10 XP)
Blood hawk, guard, kobold, stirge, tribal warrior	1/8 (25 XP)
Aarakocra, pseudodragon, pteranodon, swarm of bats, winged kobold	1/4 (50 XP)
Giant goat, orc, scout	1/2 (100 XP)
Giant eagle, half-ogre, harpy, hippogriff, lion	1 (200 XP)
Berserker, druid, giant elk, griffon, ogre, orc Eye of Gruumsh, orog, peryton, saber-toothed tiger	2 (450 XP)
Basilisk, hell hound, manticore, veteran	3 (700 XP)
Ettin	4 (1,100 XP)
Air elemental, bulette, troll	5 (1,800 XP)
Chimera, cyclops, galeb duhr, wyvern	6 (2,300 XP)
Stone giant	7 (2,900 XP)
Frost giant	8 (3,900 XP)
Cloud giant, fire giant, young silver dragon	9 (5,000 XP)
Young red dragon	10 (5,900 XP)
Roc	11 (7,200 XP)
Adult silver dragon	16 (15,000 XP)
Adult red dragon	17 (18,000 XP)
Ancient silver dragon	23 (32,500 XP)
Ancient red dragon	24 (36,500 XP)

Swamp Monsters

Monsters	Challenge Rating (XP)
Rat, raven	0 (10 XP)
Giant rat, kobold, poisonous snake, stirge, tribal warrior	1/8 (25 XP)
Bullywug, constrictor snake, giant frog, giant lizard, giant poisonous snake, mud mephit, swarm of rats, swarm of ravens, winged kobold	1/4 (50 XP)
Crocodile, lizardfolk, orc, scout, swarm of insects	1/2 (100 XP)
Ghoul, giant spider, giant toad, yuan-ti pureblood	1 (200 XP)
Druid, ghast, giant constrictor snake, lizardfolk shaman, ogre, orc Eye of Gruumsh, swarm of poisonous snakes, will-o'-wisp	2 (450 XP)
Green hag, wight, yuan-ti malison	3 (700 XP)
Giant crocodile, revenant, shambling mound, troll, water elemental	5 (1,800 XP)
Young black dragon, yuan-ti abomination	7 (2,900 XP)
Hydra	8 (3,900 XP)
Adult black dragon	14 (11,500 XP)
Ancient black dragon	21 (27,500 XP)

BULETTE

Underdark Monsters

Monsters	Challenge Rating (XP)
Giant fire beetle, shrieker, myconid sprout	0 (10 XP)
Flumph, giant rat, kobold, stirge, tribal warrior	1/8 (25 XP)
Drow, giant bat, giant centipede, giant lizard, giant poisonous snake, goblin, grimlock, kuo-toa, swarm of bats, troglodyte, violet fungus, winged kobold	1/4 (50 XP)
Darkmantle, deep gnome, gas spore, gray ooze, hobgoblin, magma mephit, myconid adult, orc, piercer, rust monster, scout, shadow, swarm of insects	1/2 (100 XP)
Bugbear, duergar, fire snake, ghoul, giant spider, giant toad, goblin boss, half-ogre, kuo-toa whip, quaggoth spore servant, specter	1 (200 XP)
Carrion crawler, druid, gargoyle, gelatinous cube, ghast, giant constrictor snake, gibbering mouther, grick, intellect devourer, mimic, minotaur skeleton, nothic, ochre jelly, ogre, orc Eye of Gruumsh, orog, polar bear (cave bear), quaggoth	2 (450 XP)
Doppelganger, grell, hobgoblin captain, hell hound, hook horror, kuo-toa monitor, minotaur, quaggoth thonot, phase spider, spectator, veteran, water weird, wight	3 (700 XP)
Black pudding, bone naga, chuul, ettin, flameskull, ghost	4 (1,100 XP)
Beholder zombie, drow elite warrior, earth elemental, otyugh, roper, salamander, troll, umber hulk, vampire spawn, wraith, xorn	5 (1,800 XP)
Chimera, cyclops, drider	6 (2,300 XP)
Drow mage, grick alpha, mind flayer, stone giant	7 (2,900 XP)
Cloaker, fomorian, mind flayer arcanist, spirit naga	8 (3,900 XP)
Fire giant	9 (5,000 XP)
Aboleth	10 (5,900 XP)
Behir, dao	11 (7,200 XP)
Beholder, young red shadow dragon	13 (10,000 XP)
Death tyrant	14 (11,500 XP)
Purple worm	15 (13,000 XP)

Underwater Monsters

Monsters	Challenge Rating (XP)
Quipper	0 (10 XP)
Merfolk	1/8 (25 XP)
Constrictor snake, steam mephit	1/4 (50 XP)
Giant sea horse, reef shark, sahuagin	1/2 (100 XP)
Giant octopus, swarm of quippers	1 (200 XP)
Giant constrictor snake, hunter shark, merrow, plesiosaurus, sahuagin priestess, sea hag	2 (450 XP)
Killer whale	3 (700 XP)
Giant shark, sahuagin baron, water elemental	5 (1,800 XP)
Marid	11 (7,200 XP)
Storm giant	13 (10,000 XP)
Dragon turtle	17 (18,000 XP)
Kraken	23 (50,000 XP)

Urban Monsters

Monsters	Challenge Rating (XP)
Cat, commoner, goat, rat, raven	0 (10 XP)
Bandit, cultist, flying snake, giant rat, guard, kobold, mastiff, mule, noble, pony, stirge	1/8 (25 XP)
Acolyte, draft horse, giant centipede, giant poisonous snake, kenku, pseudodragon, riding horse, skeleton, smoke mephit, swarm of bats, swarm of rats, swarm of ravens, winged kobold, zombie	1/4 (50 XP)
Crocodile, giant wasp, shadow, shadow, swarm of insects, thug, warhorse	1/2 (100 XP)
Ghoul, giant spider, half-ogre, specter, spy, yuan-ti pureblood	1 (200 XP)
Bandit captain, cult fanatic, gargoyle, ghast, mimic, priest, wererat, will-o'-wisp	2 (450 XP)
Doppelganger, knight, phase spider, veteran, water weird, wight	3 (700 XP)
Couatl, ghost, succubus or incubus	4 (1,100 XP)
Cambion, gladiator, revenant, vampire spawn	5 (1,800 XP)
Invisible stalker, mage	6 (2,300 XP)
Oni, shield guardian	7 (2,900 XP)
Assassin	8 (3,900 XP)
Gray slaad, young silver dragon	9 (5,000 XP)
Archmage	12 (8,400 XP)
Rakshasa, vampire	13 (10,000 XP)
Spellcaster or warrior vampire	15 (13,000 XP)
Adult silver dragon	16 (15,000 XP)
Ancient silver dragon	23 (32,500 XP)
Tarrasque	30 (155,000 XP)

PHASE SPIDER

MONSTERS BY CHALLENGE RATING

This index organizes the monsters in the *Monster Manual* by challenge rating.

CHALLENGE 0 (0–10 XP)

Awakened shrub
Baboon
Badger
Bat
Cat
Commoner
Crab
Crawling claw
Deer
Eagle
Frog
Giant fire beetle
Goat
Hawk
Homunculus
Hyena
Jackal
Lemure
Lizard
Myconid sprout
Octopus
Owl

Quipper
Rat
Raven
Scorpion
Sea horse
Shrieker
Spider
Vulture
Weasel

CHALLENGE 1/8 (25 XP)

Blood hawk
Camel
Cultist
Flumph
Flying snake
Giant crab
Giant rat
Giant weasel
Guard
Kobold
Manes
Mastiff

TROGLODYTE

Merfolk
Monodrone
Mule
Noble
Poisonous snake
Pony
Slaad tadpole
Stirge
Tribal warrior
Twig blight

CHALLENGE 1/4 (50 XP)

Aarakocra
Acolyte
Axe beak
Blink dog
Boar
Bullywug
Constrictor snake
Draft horse
Dretch
Drow
Duodrone
Elk
Flying sword
Giant badger
Giant bat
Giant centipede
Giant frog
Giant lizard
Giant owl
Giant poisonous snake
Giant wolf spider
Goblin
Grimlock
Kenku
Kuo-toa
Mud mephit
Needle blight
Panther
Pixie
Pseudodragon
Pteranodon
Riding horse
Skeleton
Smoke mephit
Sprite
Steam mephit
Swarm of bats
Swarm of rats
Swarm of ravens
Troglodyte
Violet fungus
Winged kobold
Wolf
Zombie

CHALLENGE 1/2 (100 XP)

Ape
Black bear
Cockatrice
Crocodile
Darkmantle
Deep gnome
Dust mephit
Gas spore
Giant goat
Giant sea horse
Giant wasp
Gnoll
Gray ooze
Hobgoblin
Ice mephit
Jackalwere
Lizardfolk
Magma mephit
Magmin
Myconid adult
Orc
Piercer
Reef shark
Rust monster
Sahuagin
Satyr
Scout
Shadow
Swarm of insects
Thug
Tridrone
Vine blight
Warhorse
Warhorse skeleton
Worg

CHALLENGE 1 (200 XP)

Animated armor
Brass dragon wyrmling
Brown bear
Bugbear
Copper dragon wyrmling
Death dog
Dire wolf
Dryad
Duergar
Faerie dragon (young)
Fire snake
Ghoul
Giant eagle
Giant hyena
Giant octopus
Giant spider
Giant toad
Giant vulture
Goblin boss

GREEN DRAGON
WYRMLING

Half-ogre
Harpy
Hippogriff
Imp
Kuo-toa whip
Lion
Quadrone
Quaggoth spore servant
Quasit
Scarecrow
Specter
Spy
Swarm of quippers
Thri-kreen
Tiger
Yuan-ti pureblood

CHALLENGE 2 (450 XP)

Allosaurus
Ankheg
Awakened tree
Azer
Bandit captain
Berserker
Black dragon wyrmling
Bronze dragon wyrmling
Carrion crawler
Centaur
Cult fanatic
Druid
Ettercap
Faerie dragon (old)
Gargoyle
Gelatinous cube
Ghast
Giant boar
Giant constrictor snake
Giant elk

Gibbering mouther
Githzerai monk
Gnoll pack lord
Green dragon wyrmling
Grick
Griffon
Hunter shark
Intellect devourer
Lizardfolk shaman
Merrow
Mimic
Minotaur skeleton
Myconid sovereign
Nothic
Ochre jelly
Ogre
Ogre zombie
Orc Eye of Gruumsh
Orog
Pegasus
Pentadrone
Peryton
Plesiosaurus
Polar bear
Poltergeist (specter)
Priest
Quaggoth
Rhinoceros
Rug of smothering
Saber-toothed tiger
Sahuagin priestess
Sea hag
Silver dragon wyrmling
Spined devil
Swarm of poisonous snakes
Wererat
White dragon wyrmling
Will-o'-wisp

CHALLENGE 3 (700 XP)

Ankylosaurus
Basilisk
Bearded devil
Blue dragon wyrmling
Bugbear chief
Displacer beast
Doppelganger
Giant scorpion
Githyanki warrior
Gold dragon wyrmling
Green hag
Grell
Hell hound
Hobgoblin captain
Hook horror
Killer whale
Knight
Kuo-toa monitor
Manticore
Minotaur
Mummy

Nightmare
Owlbear
Phase spider
Quaggoth thonot
Spectator
Veteran
Water weird
Werewolf
Wight
Winter wolf
Yeti
Yuan-ti malison

CHALLENGE 4 (1,100 XP)

Banshee
Black pudding
Bone naga
Chuul
Couatl
Elephant
Ettin
Flameskull
Ghost

COUATL

Gnoll fang of Yeenoghu
Helmed horror
Incubus
Lamia
Lizard king/queen
Orc war chief
Red dragon wyrmling
Sea hag (in coven)
Shadow demon
Succubus
Wereboar
Weretiger

CHALLENGE 5 (1,800 XP)

Air elemental
Barbed devil
Barlgura
Beholder zombie
Bulette
Cambion
Drow elite warrior
Earth elemental
Fire elemental
Flesh golem
Giant crocodile

Giant shark
Gladiator
Gorgon
Green hag (in coven)
Half-red dragon veteran
Hill giant
Mezzoloth
Night hag
Otyugh
Red slaad
Revenant
Roper
Sahuagin baron
Salamander
Shambling mound
Triceratops
Troll
Umber hulk
Unicorn
Vampire spawn
Water elemental
Werebear
Wraith
Xorn
Young remorhaz

SHAMBLING
MOUND

BONE DEVIL

CHALLENGE 6 (2,300 XP)

Chasme
Chimera
Cyclops
Drider
Galeb duhr
Githzerai zerth
Hobgoblin warlord
Invisible stalker
Kuo-toa archpriest
Mage
Mammoth
Medusa
Vrock
Wyvern
Young brass dragon
Young white dragon

CHALLENGE 7 (2,900 XP)

Blue slaad
Drow mage
Giant ape
Grick alpha
Mind flayer
Night hag (in coven)
Oni
Shield guardian
Stone giant
Young black dragon
Young copper dragon
Yuan-ti abomination

CHALLENGE 8 (3,900 XP)

Assassin
Chain devil
Cloaker

Drow priestess of Lolth
Fomorian
Frost giant
Githyanki knight
Green slaad
Hezrou
Hydra
Mind flayer arcanist
Spirit naga
Tyrannosaurus rex
Young bronze dragon
Young green dragon

CHALLENGE 9 (5,000 XP)

Abominable yeti
Bone devil
Clay golem
Cloud giant
Fire giant
Glabrezu
Gray slaad
Nycaloth
Treant
Young blue dragon
Young silver dragon

CHALLENGE 10 (5,900 XP)

Aboleth
Death slaad
Deva
Guardian naga
Stone golem
Yochlol
Young gold dragon
Young red dragon

CHALLENGE 11 (7,200 XP)

Behir
Dao
Djinni
Efreeti
Gynosphinx
Horned devil
Marid
Remorhaz
Roc

CHALLENGE 12 (8,400 XP)

Arcanaloth
Archmage
Erinyes

CHALLENGE 13 (10,000 XP)

Adult brass dragon
Adult white dragon
Beholder (not in lair)
Nalfeshnee
Rakshasa
Storm giant
Ultroloth

Vampire
Young red shadow dragon

CHALLENGE 14 (11,500 XP)

Adult black dragon
Adult copper dragon
Beholder (in lair)
Death tyrant (not in lair)
Ice devil

CHALLENGE 15 (13,000 XP)

Adult bronze dragon
Adult green dragon
Death tyrant (in lair)
Mummy lord (not in lair)
Purple worm
Vampire (spellcaster)
Vampire (warrior)

CHALLENGE 16 (15,000 XP)

Adult blue dragon
Adult silver dragon
Iron golem
Marilith

Mummy lord (in lair)
Planetar

CHALLENGE 17 (18,000 XP)

Adult blue dracolich
Adult gold dragon
Adult red dragon
Androsphinx
Death knight
Dragon turtle
Goristro

CHALLENGE 18 (20,000 XP)

Demilich (not in lair)

CHALLENGE 19 (22,000 XP)

Balor

CHALLENGE 20 (25,000 XP)

Ancient brass dragon
Ancient white dragon
Demilich (in lair)
Pit fiend

CHALLENGE 21 (33,000 XP)

Ancient black dragon
Ancient copper dragon
Lich (not in lair)
Solar

CHALLENGE 22 (41,000 XP)

Ancient bronze dragon
Ancient green dragon
Lich (in lair)

CHALLENGE 23 (50,000 XP)

Ancient blue dragon
Ancient silver dragon
Empyrean
Kraken

CHALLENGE 24 (62,000 XP)

Ancient gold dragon
Ancient red dragon

CHALLENGE 30 (155,000 XP)

Tarrasque

ADULT RED DRAGON

APPENDIX C: MAPS

CREATING A MAP FOR AN ADVENTURE IS A FUN, challenging, and time-consuming endeavor. However, unless you have something specific in mind, you're better off conserving your time and energy by repurposing an existing map. Published adventures and the Internet are terrific sources for maps. A few sample maps are included here as well. Use them as you will!

Ground Floor   Top Floor

One square = 5 feet

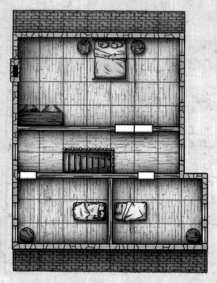

2nd Floor

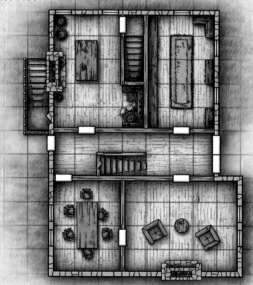

1st Floor

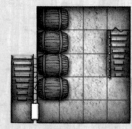

Basement

One square = 5 feet

One square = 10 feet

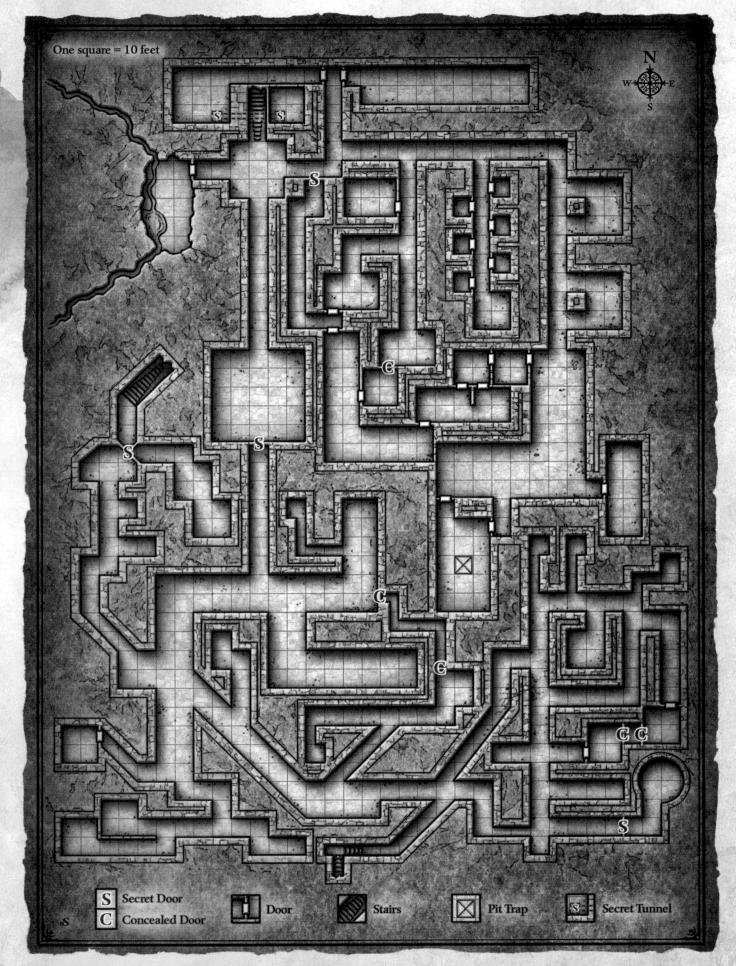

APPENDIX C | MAPS

One square = 5 feet

N
W E
S

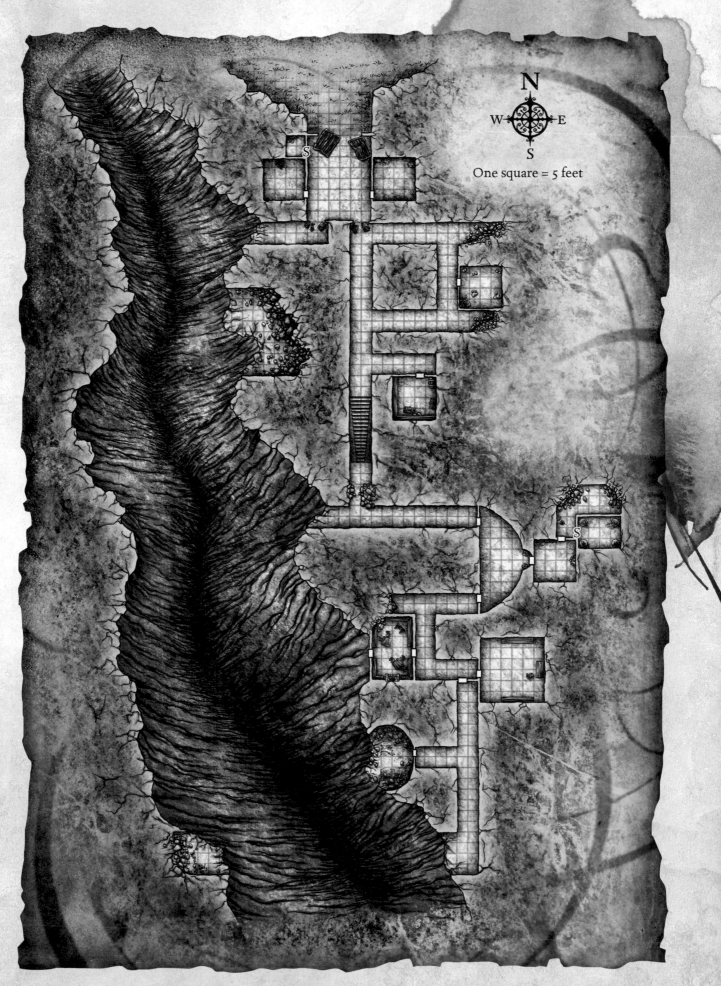

One square = 5 feet

Appendix D: Dungeon Master Inspiration

HERE ARE SEVERAL INSPIRING WORKS THAT CAN help you become a better storyteller, writer, performer, and mapmaker. This is by no means an exhaustive list, but a collection of titles picked out by playtesters and the DUNGEONS & DRAGONS creative team. For more inspirational reading, see appendix E of the *Player's Handbook*.

Atlas Games. *Once Upon a Time: The Storytelling Card Game*.

Bernhardt, William. *Creating Character: Bringing Your Story to Life*.

———. *Perfecting Plot: Charting the Hero's Journey*.

———. *Story Structure: The Key to Successful Fiction*.

Bowers, Malcolm. *Gary Gygax's Extraordinary Book of Names*.

Browning, Joseph & Suzi Yee. *A Magical Medieval Society: Western Europe*.

Burroway, Janet. *Writing Fiction*.

Cleaver, Jerry. *Immediate Fiction*.

Cordingly, David. *Under the Black Flag*.

Egri, Lajos. *The Art of Dramatic Writing*.

Ewalt, David M. *Of Dice and Men*.

Gygax, Gary. *Gary Gygax's Living Fantasy* and the rest of the Gygaxian Fantasy Worlds series.

———. *Master of the Game*.

———. *Role-Playing Mastery*.

Hindmarch, Will. *The Bones: Us and Our Dice*.

Hindmarch, Will & Jeff Tidball. *Things We Think About Games*.

Hirsh, Jr., E.D. *The New Dictionary of Cultural Literacy*.

Ingpen, Robert. *The Encyclopedia of Things That Never Were*.

Kaufmann, J.E. & H.W. Kaufmann. *The Medieval Fortress*.

King, Stephen. *On Writing: A Memoir of the Craft*.

Koster, Raph. *A Theory of Fun for Game Design*.

Laws, Robin D. *Hamlet's Hit Points*.

Lee, Alan & David Day. *Castles*.

Macaulay, David. *Castle*.

Malory, Sir Thomas. *Le Morte d'Arthur*.

McKee, Robert. *Story: Substance, Structure, Style, and the Principles of Screenwriting*.

Mortimer, Ian. *The Time Traveler's Guide to Medieval England*.

O'Connor, Paul Ryan, ed. *Grimtooth's Traps*.

PennyPress. *Variety Puzzles and Games* series.

Peterson, Jon. *Playing at the World*.

Robbins, Ben. *Microscope*.

Schell, Jesse. *Game Design: A Book of Lenses*.

Snyder, Blake. *Save the Cat*.

Swift, Michael and Angus Konstam. *Cities of the Renaissance World*.

Truby, John. *The Anatomy of Story*.

TSR. *Arms and Equipment Guide*.

———. *Campaign Sourcebook/Catacomb Guide*.

———. *The Castle Guide*.

Walmsley, Graham. *Play Unsafe: How Improvisation Can Change the Way You Roleplay*.

Wilford, John Noble. *The Mapmakers*.

Writers Digest. *The Writer's Complete Fantasy Reference*.